Marketing Research

Marketing Research: Management, Method, and Cases

Second Edition

Walter B. Wentz

Harper & Row, Publishers
New York   Hagerstown   Philadelphia   San Francisco   London

Sponsoring Editor: John Woods
Project Editor: Carol Pritchard-Martinez
Production Coordinator: Marian Hartsough
Designer: Majorie Spiegelman
Cover Artist: Nancy Benedict
Compositor: Syntax International
Printer and Binder: Maple Press

MARKETING RESEARCH: MANAGEMENT, METHODS, AND CASES,
Second Edition

Library of Congress Cataloging in Publication Data

Wentz, Walter B
    Marketing research.

    Includes indexes.
    1. Marketing research.   2. Marketing research—
Statistical methods.   3. Marketing research—Case
studies.   I. Title.
HF5415.2.W45   1979   658.8'3'018   79-12652
ISBN 0-06-047006-2

Contents

Part 4
Sampling   203

Part 5
Experimentation   267

Part 6
Applying the Behavioral Sciences   337

Part 7
Multivariate Analysis   425

Part 8
Forecasting   547

Part 9
Simulation   637

Appendixes   693

Glossary   740

Indexes   761

Preface

During the past few decades, marketing research has grown to be a significant element in the marketing mix of many firms. More recently it has emerged as a management tool in many government and other non-commercial organizations. Its growth and proliferation have been motivated by the great increase in the frequency, complexity, risk, and cost-of-error of marketing decisions.

The increased hazard of marketing decisions is largely attributable to the technological revolution of the past thirty years. Fortunately, the same revolution has brought forth some powerful techniques and equipment to aid the researcher. Most notable are the tools of multivariate analysis and the electronic computer.

Objective

As with the original edition, the revision of this text seeks to introduce the reader to the basic tools of marketing research. The emphasis is on application. The book is written for the practitioners—the specialists who must do the research and the line managers who must use it. Implicitly, it is written for students who aspire to either of these roles.

Changes

The original edition was substantially rewritten to make it more digestible and to bring it up-to-date. The changes include discussions of psychographics and qualitative research, an expanded exploration of multivariate analysis, the addition of a set of case studies, and an examination of the limitations, misuse, and abuse of marketing research. Following the dictum that the hope of civilization rests in knowledge and humor, the changes also include a bit of verbal and graphic wit.

Prerequisite Skills

The book's mathematics can be managed by anyone with a glimmer of high school algebra remaining. If there are some terms or symbols that make the reader uncomfortable, a few minutes reading Appendix 1 should relieve the anxiety.

The reader should not be intimidated by a few large equations. To use the equations one must simply insert the data into the formulas as indicated by the symbols. One then performs the arithmetic and gets the answers. An inexpensive pocket calculator will relieve the drudgery of that task.

Portions of the text assume the reader has some familiarity with introductory statistics course. If not, the reader should review Appendix 2. This assignment is appropriate for anyone unfamiliar or uncomfortable with basic statistics.

Acknowledgments

Not since the invention of the printing press, typewriter, and editor has a book been the exclusive work of one individual. Hence, I must thank Professors Masao Nakanishi, Harold Kassarjian, Donald Ratajczak, Roselind Ratajczak, Aaron Tennenbein, William Massy, and Gerald Eyrich. I am especially indebted to Professor Jadish Sheth for his guidance and his contribution in the exploration of multivariate methods. I must thank my past editors Michael Ball, James Campbell, Dorothea Autilio, and Mary Boesch. I must thank my current editors, George Provol, John Woods, Carol Pritchard-Martinez, and Rhoda Blecker. I must give special acknowledgment to Mary Gammons, an able secretary and a good friend whose criticism, patience, wit, and hard work have contributed significantly to seven of my books.

W. B. Wentz
South Pasadena, CA

Marketing Research

Chapter 1
An Introduction to
Marketing Research

Key Concepts

Marketing Research and the Enterprise
MR and the marketing mix

Applications of Marketing Research
The uses of MR in both commercial and social marketing

Misapplications of Marketing Research
The misuse and abuse of MR

The Research Process
The sequence of events from problem definition to the final report

Taxonomy of Marketing Research
The science of classification applied to MR

Key Terms

marketing research
marketing mix
ad hoc study
problem study
continuous study
marketing information system
generic concept of marketing

social marketing
exploratory research
taxonomy
descriptive research
causal research
predictive research
futurology

General Electric has a history of progressive management.
GE was one of the first firms to recognize and practice the
marketing concept. It was among the first companies to include
research in its marketing mix.

One of GE's earliest research projects was to analyze a
new-product idea. The research revealed that the concept was
perceived as noisy, messy, dangerous, and generally undesirable by
most prospective buyers. Clearly, the product would be a disaster
if allowed to reach the marketplace.

Fortunately for both General Electric and the nation's beer
drinkers, management ignored the research and commercialized
the product—the electric refrigerator.

Marketing research is the gathering and analysis of marketing information to assist management in making decisions. These decisions involve the manipulation of the firm's pricing, promotion, distribution and product variables. It is also the study of market phenomena, where the objective is the development of theory and technique.[1]

Adler and Mayer characterize marketing research as "an art form struggling to become a science."[2] Although not yet a science, marketing research has been making progress in techniques and acceptance. Today, marketing research—often called "MR" by its practitioners—is a powerful and widely used management tool in both the commercial and nonprofit sectors. As GE discovered, it is not yet infallible.

Marketing Research and the Enterprise

The Marketing Mix

The combination of resources which make up the firm's marketing program is commonly called the "marketing mix." Management's ability to choose and orchestrate the elements of that mix largely determines the firm's success.

Traditionally marketing has been fragmented into four basic functions: product, promotion, pricing, and distribution. Promotion has then been divided mainly into advertising and personal selling. Each function is found in both the commercial and noncommercial sectors, although emphasis varies considerably.

Lately, marketing research has become so important that it is often considered the fifth element of the marketing mix. MR is unique, however, in that it serves only to support the other four functions. Outside the scholastic

---

[1] The American Marketing Association's Definitions Committee defines marketing research as "the systematic gathering, recording, and analyzing of data about problems relating to the marketing of goods and services." See Ralph S. Alexander, *Marketing Definitions* (Chicago: American Marketing Association, 1971), p. 16.

[2] Lee Adler and Charles S. Mayer, *Managing the Marketing Research Function* (Chicago: American Marketing Association, 1977), p. 1.

community, the research budget is justified only to the extent the research produces better product, promotion, pricing, and distribution decisions.

Recent History

Research became an important marketing function when the technological revolution made marketing a high-stakes, high-risk activity. Since World War II, we've seen the proliferation of new and more complex products and an increase in economies of scale. We've seen new markets emerge, new sources of competition develop, and many businesses become multinational. These changes have been accompanied by huge increases in capital requirements, more business failures, and great penalties for mistakes. Marketing decisions have become more numerous and riskier. A bad mistake in the marketplace can put a firm on the ski slope to oblivion.[3]

Fortunately the technological revolution that magnified the need for good research also provided many new tools. By far the most important is the computer. The computer allows us to manage vast amounts of data and to apply powerful analytical techniques to unscramble them. Without it, the researcher is seriously handicapped. Research activities become limited to qualitative methods and to the generation of only descriptive statistics on the quantitative side. Serious analysis of complex data is virtually impossible.

Applications

Within the academic community, marketing research is the servant of scholarship. MR is used to isolate and explain phenomena observed in the marketplace.[4] It is essential to the development of marketing as a scholarly discipline. In practice—in the field, so to speak—MR is the servant of the decision process.

MR and the Decision Process

In business, marketing research is a staff function. That is, it provides information and advise. Its purpose is to support the decision makers. Hence MR is not a career for the person who wants the glory and excitement of decision-making. These belong to the line managers—the people who make operating decisions and are directly responsible for the success of the firm.

The role of research in the scheme of things is illustrated in Figure 1-1. There we see a research department gathering, reducing, and analyzing data, then providing information and recommendations to line management.

---

[3] For a tour de force of marketing blunders, some aided and abetted by marketing research, see Thomas L. Berg, *Mismarketing* (Garden City, N.Y.: Doubleday (Anchor Books), 1971).

[4] This type of research—dealing with the marketing process—is occasionally labeled "marketing research," while descriptive studies of the marketplace are called "market research." However, this distinction has faded and today the two terms are usually used interchangeably.

Figure 1-1   **The Market Information-Decision-Reaction Cycle**

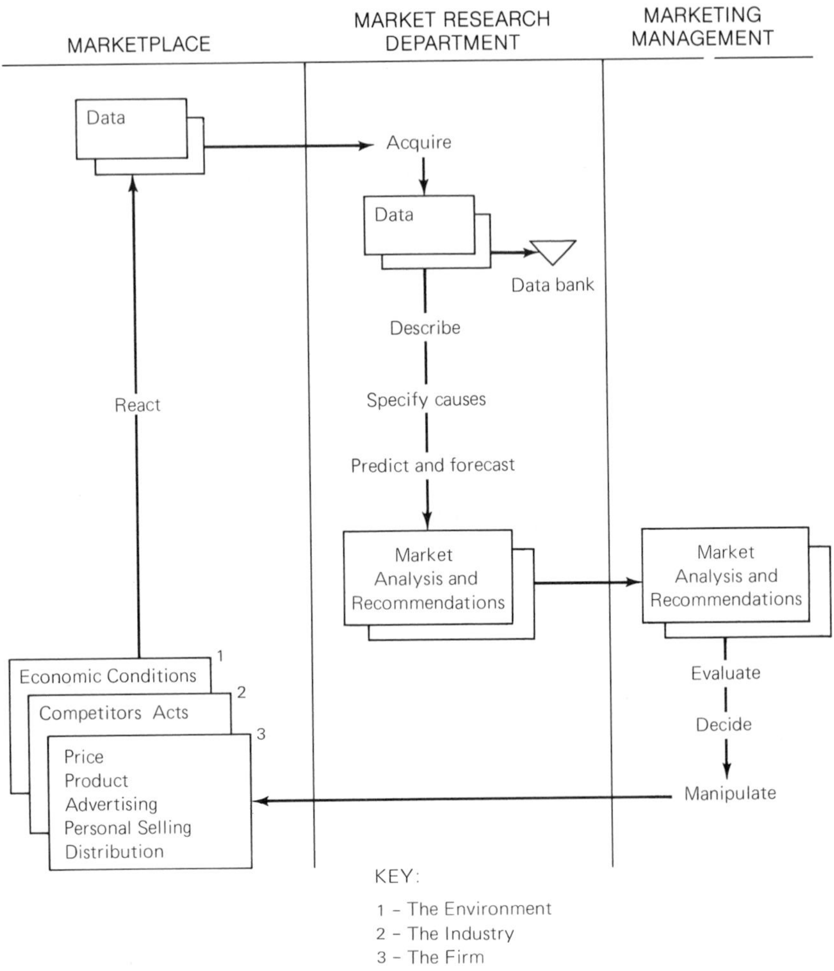

MARKETPLACE   MARKET RESEARCH   MARKETING
                   DEPARTMENT   MANAGEMENT

KEY:
1 – The Environment
2 – The Industry
3 – The Firm

Risk

Research is inserted into the decision process mainly to reduce risk. MR seeks to provide information that will reduce the probability of a wrong decision. It also seeks to expose dangers and opportunities that would otherwise pass unnoticed. The importance of such data is revealed by Table 1-1. There we see the moderate success rate of new products—products that were seldom put into the marketplace without some forethought.

Some product classes—notably processed foods, phonograph records, and books—have a mortality rate of nearly 90 percent: Only one in ten

Table 1-1   **Product Success Rates**

	New Product Ideas	Product Development Projects	New Products Introduced
	Success Percentages		
All Industry Groups	1.7%	14.5%	62.5%
Chemical	2%	18%	59%
Consumer Packaged Goods	2%	11%	63%
Electrical Machinery	1%	13%	63%
Metal Fabricators	3%	11%	71%
Nonelectrical Machinery	2%	21%	59%
Raw Material Processors	5%	14%	59%

Source: Management of New Products (New York: Booz, Allen and Hamilton, 1972), p. 12.

entrants yields a profit. The others are soon withdrawn. The mortality of new-product ideas is even worse.

Marketing research is no guarantor of success. The marketplace is a confluence of forces we don't fully understand. Research yields only partial information, hence only partial solutions. The critical data may be lost in the crazy quilt of information and activity that characterizes many markets.

We don't mean to imply that marketing research focuses only on the product. On the contrary, it is used in support of all the basic marketing functions. The product merely illustrates the risk that research attempts to cope with. Table 1-2 indicates the scope of MR—a sample of research tasks performed in support of the basic marketing functions.

Ad Hoc versus Continuous

Most marketing research projects are ad hoc (one time), dealing with a particular problem at a particular time. The applications in Table 1-2 are mainly of that type.

A specific example of an ad hoc study—or what we might call a "problem study"—is provided by a case from the Airstream company. The Airstream experience also gives us an example of a marketing problem yielding to research.

The firm had long held the dominant position in the luxury travel-trailer market. In fact it held such a majority share of this market that its growth prospects seemed limited. One solution to the problem was to expand its product line downward into the medium-price market. (Note the market segmentation strategy.) Before it did so, the firm needed a lot of information on the products and consumers in that market: How big was the market? What was its geographic distribution? Who was in it? What were the

Table 1-2   **Applications of Marketing Research**

Distribution Decisions	Research Tasks
Select store locations	Identify optimum sites
Select warehouse locations	Identify optimum sites
Specify inventory levels	Determine optimum inventories
Select channels	Identify and evaluate channels
Alter channels	Monitor channel performance
Product Decisions	Research Tasks
Specify product characteristics	Determine consumer preferences
Tailor product to segments	Identify market segments
Develop new product	Conduct focus groups
Select new package	Test market
Set production output	Forecast sales
Reinforce brand loyalty	Measure brand loyalty
Advertising Decisions	Research Tasks
Select media	Evaluate media
Select copy	Test copy
Select advertising theme	Determine buyer attributes
Select among pilot commercials	Test commercials
Change advertising strategy	Measure attitude or sales
Decide if couponing is to be used	Experiment with coupons
Personal Selling Decisions	Research Tasks
Assign salespersons	Define territories
Determine sales strategy	Model buyer behavior
Set sales quotas	Estimate sales potentials
Select incentives	Measure incentive affect
Allocate sales effort	Identify and evaluate prospects
Pricing Decisions	Research Tasks
Set price	Estimate price elasticity
Establish rebate policy	Estimate affect on sales
Segment market by price	Define price segments
Long-Range Planning	Research Tasks
Set sales and profit goals	Prepare economic forecast
Specify diversification objectives	Evaluate new markets

products like? Who were the buyers? What was their purchase behavior? What were their preferences? How did they determine brand choice?

The answers came from an ad hoc study designed and implemented by a research supplier (see Exhibit 3-3). The result was a successful new product line, called "Argosy," supported by a new marketing program. Both were designed to conform to the preferences and behavioral patterns revealed by the study.

Marketing research projects can also be continuous studies. These take the form of ongoing programs for the collection and dissemination of market data. Their objective is to keep management up-to-date on occurrences in the marketplace. Typically they provide data on a week-to-week basis. Such projects are generally called "marketing information systems"[5] and are sufficiently important to warrant further discussion in Chapter 7.

Research in Social Marketing

The generic concept of marketing, formulated by Philip Kotler, rejects the notion that marketing is an intrinsic business technology. The generic concept views marketing as the legitimate tool of every institution with customers or publics.[6] Its use in the noncommercial sector is called "social marketing."

If one embraces the generic concept of marketing, as we shall do, marketing research is useful in all sorts of enterprises. Political parties, police departments, universities, charities, and the Department of Defense are but a few examples.[7] In fact, some of our most powerful techniques have been invented or refined by researchers working outside the commercial sector. Witness the sampling methods developed by the A. C. Nielsen Company and the Gallup Organization in their political opinion polls.

Today marketing researchers are finding many opportunities beyond the boundary of commercial enterprise. Their craft is being applied by all sorts of institutions. The Los Angeles Sheriff's Department is applying it to law enforcement.[8] The National Commission on Consumer Finance and the Federal Reserve Board are using it to evaluate the impact of truth-in-lending legislation on consumer behavior.[9] The U.S. Army uses it to evaluate its recruiting campaigns.

The diffusion of MR in the noncommercial sector suggests its power and usefulness—qualities long recognized by many commercial firms. Properly employed, research is a faithful and productive servant of responsible managers. Unfortunately, it can also be the servant of fools and scoundrels. This is not a pervasive problem, but one that does warrant recognition. Hence, we digress briefly on the misapplication of marketing research. Once that is behind us we can concentrate on MR's positive aspects.

---

[5] Alexander, *Marketing Definitions*, p. 16.

[6] Philip Kotler, "A Generic Concept of Marketing," *Journal of Marketing*, **36**: 1 (April 1972), pp. 46–54.

[7] For some specific illustrations, see Cases 2, 14, 17, and 25 in Walter B. Wentz, ed., *Cases in Marketing Research* (New York: Harper & Row, 1975). [Cases No. 2 is also found at the end of this chapter.]

[8] Harvey M. Adelman and O. J. Kransner, "The Los Angeles County Sheriff's Department: Marketing Research versus 'Deep Throat'," in Wentz, ed., *Cases in Marketing Research*, pp. 103–113. [This case is also found at the end of chapter 9 of this book.]

[9] George S. Day and William K. Brandt, *Consumer Research Contributions to the Evaluation of Public Policy: The Case of Truth in Lending*, Research Paper No. 166 (Stanford, Calif.: Graduate School of Business, Stanford University, July 1973). For further discussion of the role of MR in formulating public policy, see Robert F. Dyer and Terence A. Shimp, "Enhancing the Role of Marketing Research in Public Policy Decision Making," *Journal of Marketing*, **41**:1 (January, 1977), pp. 63–70.

Misapplications

Shortcomings

Marketing research is a sophisticated art and a complex science. As it is practiced in industry, however, MR is occasionally superficial and sloppy. Many practitioners have little or no formal training in the field. MR groups, like many staff functions, are occasionally sumps for former line marketers who failed to succeed in sales, advertising, distribution, or product management. They do not understand the techniques and tools of modern research. At best they are collectors of descriptive statistics and have some mastery of survey techniques. At worst they are charlatans, serving expediency, not management science.[10]

Even the technically competent and sincere sometimes fail.[11] Market researchers, like other technical specialists, sometimes turn inward rather than talk to the marketers about the real problems.

The downfall of many marketing researchers is their enthusiasm for solving problems nobody wants solved. They have an understandable itch to exercise their skills, and often these skills are most applicable to irrelevant problems. Or their attention focuses on the means, the tools and techniques, not the ends. Management is unimpressed. The essence of the issue can be stated poetically:

> While you and I have lips and voices which
>   are kissing and to sing with
> Who cares if some one-eyed son of a bitch
>   invents an instrument to measure Spring with?[12]

Perhaps the real tragedy is when elegant solutions to important problems are reached, but go unheeded. This occurs when the researchers confound line managers with an excursion into petty details or esoteric methods, about which the managers care not at all. This obscures the essence of the findings. Line managers want succinct explanations and explicit recommendations. Bits of detail or method should be introduced only in response to questions.

Another problem, seldom cited yet very real, is the shaky state of the art. There is a considerable amount we don't know. Economic and behavioral

---

[10] The author has seen too much sloppy work from too many sources to moderate this harsh assessment.

[11] The test of staff personnel usually comes with a decline in the firm's earnings. At that time the cost-cutters go to work, eliminating jobs that are perceived as unessential or as making small contributions to the company's welfare. Examples are the recessions of 1968–1971 and 1974–1975. Both were disasters for market researchers.

[12] E. E. Cummings, as quoted by Warren Weaver in "The Imperfections of Science," in S. Rappaport and H. Wright, *Science: Method and Meaning* (New York: Washington Square Press, 1964), p. 16.

facts are elusive. Causes and effects are often unknown or unclear. Theory is deficient. Measuring methods are sometimes inadequate or misleading. Analytical tools are still limited. In short, the scholars dealing in basic (theoretical) research—the ones we occasionally criticize for being esoteric—have a lot of work ahead of them. Their task is no less complicated than that of the biomedical researcher searching for the key to cancer.

Misuse

If we are to believe the textbooks and oratory, the sole purpose of marketing research is to help management make better marketing decisions. Certainly this is the only economic justification for MR. Hopefully, it is also the most prevalent reason for invoking this important element of the marketing mix. However, other incentives often form the motivating force behind the research apparatus. These are mainly political, promotional, psychological, or academic.

Probably the worst abuse of MR is the selective gathering of data to support a position. Searching for—or worse yet, creating—information in harmony with a preconception is not legitimate research.

Marketing research is sometimes an instrument of organizational politics. It is one more way to gain power. It helps ambitious managers to build their empires (more people), improve visibility, and intimidate colleagues. MR is also a handy scapegoat when things go wrong.

Research has also been used to delay or avoid making decisions, and to bury unwanted projects. More than one good idea has been studied to death.

Research is often offered as part of the firm's promotional program. This is especially common in advertising agencies and media. The agencies seek to impress clients with their "scientific" and "modern" approach. The media seek to impress advertisers with their reach and the economic statistics of their trading area. The desire to impress clients and advertisers partially explains jargon-laden research briefings and reports. Esoteric statistical terms and exotic psychological concepts presumably impress prospects, even when they are not understood.

MR also fulfills certain psychological needs. It builds self-esteem, relieves anxieties, and serves as a security blanket for marketing managers, even if they pay little attention to the results. It provides self-fulfillment for technicians by giving them a chance to apply their skills.

The research group often provides a niche for the corporate scholar—the researcher more interested in technique than results. This academic approach to MR—where theory and method are ends in themselves—somewhat explains its fragility. The failure to produce decision-oriented results makes the research function vulnerable to the budget crunch. Marketing research's therapeutic and intellectual values are quickly ignored when the word comes down to cut costs.

Such misuses of marketing research occur only occasionally. Still, the results can be tragic. Managers need all the help they can get. A good

---

Figure 1-2   **The Researcher**

Source: Drawing by Handelsman. *The New Yorker*, November 11, 1974, p. 44. ©1974 by The New Yorker Magazine, Inc.

"Market research is merely what I do. It's not where I am."

research department can be a powerful source of aid. Yet some managers, being unaware of what they are missing, do not clamor for it.[13]

The Research Process

Marketing research is an amalgam of statistics, mathematics, economic and behavioral theory, computer skills, hard work, luck, and common sense. The

---

[13] A good discussion of MR misuse is found in Stewart A. Smith, "Research and Pseudo-research in Marketing," *Harvard Business Review*, **52**:2 (March–April 1974), pp. 73–76.

combination of these elements that will be focused on a specific problem varies with both the researcher and the problem. Few researchers would handle the same problem exactly the same way. Technicians tend to use the methods they know best, and these will vary with the skill, experience, and training of the individual. The basic research process, however, remains much the same. It is summarized in Figure 1-3, which also serves as a guide to our study.

The process starts with problem definition, which again reminds us that MR is decision-oriented. If the research is in the form of a problem study, it usually ends with the dissemination of the findings. Sometimes the findings reveal the need for additional work. Or the study is but one of a series of studies prescribed to solve a problem. Either way the process starts over.

Figure 1-3 **The Marketing Research Process**

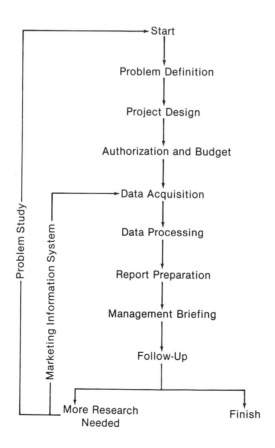

If the research is in the form of a marketing information system, it never exists the loop. Once the system is designed and implemented it continuously returns to data acquisition stage and recycles from there.

Problem Definition

The Marketing Research Committee of the American Marketing Association once stated that "if any one step in a research project can be said to be more important than the others, problem definition is that step."[14] The committee also claimed that "problem definition is the most creative phase of research."[15] Those two assertions are still valid.

Typically, management will bring the problem, loosely defined, to the research group or supplier. It may be very general—e.g., profits are down, market share has declined, or the last election was lost. It may be very specific—e.g., management cannot decide which of three new designs to put into production, the latest ad campaign is not producing sales, or church attendance is down in a Boston parish.

If the problem is stated generally, exploratory research may be needed. An exploratory study seeks to better define the problem and reduce it to manageable dimensions. Usually it is loosely structured, quick, inexpensive, and qualitative. It looks for problems, not solutions. For instance, an exploratory study might reveal that market share is down because consumers are switching to a new brand. Now MR can focus on the question: Why do some buyers prefer the new brand? Once that is answered, management can take appropriate action.

Two things are especially important at the problem definition stage: First, the problem must ultimately be reduced to specific terms. A generally defined problem will yield broad findings and vague recommendations. Second, the problem must be defined so that the study will yield a workable solution. The solution must be decision-oriented, and the decisions must be plausible. It does no good to study pricing if management cannot alter prices.

Project Design

Given the problem, the researcher must devise a scheme to find a solution. The outcome is the project design. It is the plan of action for the study, or for the preparation of the marketing information system.

The project design—often called the "research design"—contains the objective, method, resource requirements, and timetable for the research project. It serves as a road map and foundation for the study. Sloppy work at this juncture assures wasted resources, misleading information, and bad recommendations later. The design stage is extremely important, so much so that we devote all of Chapter 3 to the subject.

---

[14] *Problem Definition*, Marketing Research Techniques series no. 2 (Chicago: American Marketing Association, 1958), p. 5.
[15] Ibid.

Authorization and Budget

Nothing more can happen until the study is authorized and a budget is provided. Authorization may be up to the marketing research manager, or it may require approval of a line manager. (One of the problems in selling research service is in identifying and persuading the person with the authority.) Costs may be charged to an established budget (usually the case with small studies done inside the firm) or special funding may be required. Sometimes the budget must be provided by the unit using the research. Thus the advertising group must pay for an ad study, the sales department must pay for a site-selection study, and so on. As a result, the authorization and budget stage may rest heavily on the researcher's sales ability, not on any technical skills the researcher may have.

Data Acquisition

Data are the fuel of marketing research. Their acquisition is usually the first step in the execution of a project design. Data can be gathered from countless sources by any one of several techniques. We shall discuss these in Part Two.

Data Processing

The data acquisition stage produces a set of raw information which is usually bewildering and often massive. If one is to extract meaning from the data, they must first be processed.

Data processing consist of two tasks: (1) Data reduction and (2) data analysis. Data reduction brings the information down to a manageable and sometimes meaningful size. For example, the Gallup Organization might poll 1500 people on the issue of gun control. Each respondent might be asked three questions, such as: "Do you approve of banning hand guns?" "Should all gun owners be licensed?" "Is present gun legislation adequate?" This would yield 4500 pieces of data (3×1500). The data would make sense only after they had been reduced to six statistics: the percentage of the respondents answering "yes" and the percentage answering "no" to each question.

Frequently descriptive statistics are not enough. There is meaning in the data that can only be unscrambled with rigorous analysis. Thus data analysis often follows, or is made part of, data reduction.

For example, simple data reduction might reveal what portions of the consumers have particular preferences and attitudes. It would probably not indicate how those attitudes determined brand choice. That question would only be answered after rigorous analysis. Fortunately, we have a powerful assortment of analytical tools. We'll introduce them as we progress.

Report Preparation and Management Briefing

The research process culminates in the report. The report conveys to management the findings and recommendations of the study. In form it varies from a telephone call to an elaborate presentation with bound documents, flip charts, colored slides, and a polished lecture. The latter approach is called a "management briefing." Briefings are common, particularly when the work has been done by a research supplier.

Follow up

Line managers are the market researcher's customers. They expect quality, reasonable prices, and service after sales, as do their firm's customers. As the marketing concept claims, they determine the fate and prosperity of the researcher. Follow-up is clearly in order. Its purpose is to:

> Answer new questions
> Aid implementation of the recommendations
> Discover shortcomings in the research design
> Discover and correct errors in data processing
> Compare results against predictions
> Recommend supplemental research, if needed
> Satisfy the political realities of corporate life
> Sell more research

Taxonomy

Taxonomy is the science of classification. The word also means "a system of classification." Taxonomy is in high fashion among scholars, for it helps to define, organize, and understand physical and social phenomena. For example, it has long been used by botonists, who have a complex taxonomy for classifying plants.

Taxonomy is often applied by marketing practitioners, especially in market segmentation. There the object is to group consumers into classes according to some relevant variable such as age, sex, income, shopping pattern, or life style. The marketing mix can then be tailored to one or more specific groups. This allows the enterprise to concentrate its resources where they'll be most productive—to maximize sales, votes, or whatever.

Marketing research is often invoked in marketing taxonomy. We'll examine some of the techniques and results in Part 6. In addition, MR has its own internal taxonomy—a system of classifying its methods and data. These classifications help to organize our study and provide part of the vocabulary we need to communicate with other researchers. Hence, we pause to learn a few words, remembering that insight doesn't necessarily follow vocabulary.

Functional Categories

Marketing research may be classified by function—by what it seeks to do.
    Descriptive research is research that seeks to define or describe a subject.

The subject may be a market, an industry, a distribution channel, a class of advertising media, a marketing problem, or whatever. The objective is to specify what is happening and where. No attempt is made to explain why. For instance, descriptive research might focus on the size, membership, and location of a market. It might describe the reach, cost, and audience of an advertising medium. It might describe in detail a marketing problem that had been previously ill-defined.

Causal research is research that seeks to explain what descriptive research observes. Ideally, it specifies the relationship between variables. That is, it identifies and evaluates those forces that determine consumer behavior and the results in the marketplace. While descriptive research tells us what is happening, causal research tells us why. For instance, descriptive research might reveal that sales are down and buyers are switching to other brands. Causal research would attempt to discover why they were switching and, by implication, what might be done to reverse this behavior.

Causal research draws on both qualitative and quantitative methods. It rests heavily on the analytical skill of researchers and their ability to gather, then unscramble, meaningful data.

Predictive research is research that seeks to predict (forecast) values. These may be current values, such as the potential demand for the firm's product in a new market. Or they may be future values, such as next year's sales.

In predictive research, we look for a statistical relationship between our dependent variable (typically sales) and some measurable or predictable independent variable, such as time. Unlike in causal research, cause and effect are unimportant. A statistical relationship is all we need.

The Kinelogic Company's study of the visual-aids market—what's being sold where and by whom—illustrates descriptive research. The Jurgensen Grocery Company study of store performance—why some stores succeed and others fail—illustrates causal research. Cessna's study of the executive jet market—how many Citations would be sold—illustrates predictive research.[16]

Application

Taxonomies can be useful in organizing objects, such as consumers, or subject matters, such as research methods. They can serve as convenient checklists. For example, in designing a research project one could review Table 3-2 to assure that the alternative methods had all been considered.

Taxonomies can also serve as a straitjacket. They can exclude important, perhaps undiscovered, classifications. They can induce tunnel vision. Since creativity is important, the skilled researcher will often deviate from convention and innovate.

---

[16] The first case can be found in Wentz, ed., *Cases in Marketing Research*. For the others, see the cases at the end of Parts Seven and Eight of this volume.

Futurology

Marketers tend toward short planning horizons. The present is sufficiently dynamic and challenging to absorb their energies. Besides, their rewards are dependent upon current performance, not profits earned ten years from now. This is not to say they wouldn't like a peek at the future. They would, and for this they occasionally turn to futurology, the art of long-range forecasting.

Futurologists draw heavily on the predictive tools of the hard sciences. They take past and existing conditions and extrapolate them into the future. Unfortunately, social and economic forces do not behave as predictably as physical and organic ones. Thus, the projections often miss reality, sometimes by a long way.

Marketing research is mostly confined to the near term, say 12 to 18 months. Occasionally it will venture three years into the future, but seldom further. Management has little incentive to plan much beyond 36 months, because in most industries and institutions three years is sufficient lead time to respond to any change, even a drastic one. Thus futurology, which worries about our world one or more decades hence, is largely irrelevant fun.

There are exceptions. Futurology can suggest areas for concentrated exploration.[17] For instance, the descriptions of energy supplies, life styles, and metropolitan areas of the 1980s suggest that auto makers search for new propulsion devices, colleges consider new curriculums, and city planners look at mass transit alternatives. Many products of the 1970s will fail to satisfy the needs of the 1980s.

Summary

Marketing research serves management by providing information that is used in making marketing decisions. Research became an important part of the marketing mix as marketing became a high-risk, high-stakes activity.

In the academic community, MR is used to isolate and explain phenomena observed in the marketplace. Scholars apply its methods to develop theory and techniques which are often useful to the practitioner.

Marketing research has found application in the non-commercial sector. It is widely used in politics and is frequently applied by government agencies. MR is becoming common in other nonprofit institutions, such as charities, consumer advocate groups, and the military.

Marketing research has not been immune from abuse. Incompetents have done superficial and sloppy research. Skilled technicians have sometimes confused means with ends. Unscrupulous managers have used MR as an instrument of organizational politics. As a result, research departments

---

[17] Perhaps the best-known contemporary futurologists are Dr. Herman Kahn, Director of the Hudson Institute (*The Year 2000* and *The Next 200 Years*), and Alvin Toffler (*Future Shock*). For a guide to the literature and activities of futurology, see *Footnotes to the Future*, published monthly by Futuremics, Inc., Washington, D.C.

sometimes go the way of FORD/DOLE bumper stickers when the firm's budget must be cut.

The research process starts with problem definition. This important step—perhaps the most critical—is followed by project design, authorization and budget, data acquisition, data processing, report preparation, management briefing, and follow-up. Along the way, the researcher chooses from a large variety of tools.

Marketing research has its own taxonomy—a system of classifying information and techniques. These classifications are an important part of the researcher's vocabulary. They'll be introduced throughout the text.

Problems

1 Suggest how the marketing-research operation might be organized and what specific tasks it might perform in each of the following firms: (a) a marketing cooperative for citrus products, (b) a large conglomerate, and (c) a small manufacturer.

2 Suggest an application for marketing research in a specific nonprofit enterprise.

3 Cite one abuse of MR and suggest a way to avoid it.

4 Name the first step in the marketing research process and tell why it is so important.

5 Tell what the project design consists of.

6 Define (a) descriptive research, (b) causal research, and (c) predictive research.

CASE STUDY

Federal Trade Commission: Where Does the Marketing Research Fit?

William L. Wilkie (*William L. Wilkie, Ph.D., is Visiting Research Associate at the Marketing Science Institute and Visiting Lecturer at the Harvard Business School, on leave from the Krannert School, Purdue University.*)

The Federal Trade Commission (FTC) is a government agency, established in 1914, charged with the responsibility of ensuring a fair competitive environment for the U.S. economic system. Its mandate, apart from administering several narrow acts, is surprisingly vague. Section 5 of the original FTC Act declared "unfair methods of competition in commerce" to be illegal and was later amended to include "unfair or deceptive acts or practices" in this category. These statements have historically been interpreted to stress that FTC has authority over both industry structure (competition between marketers) and trade practices (protection of consumers).

Headquarters of the FTC are located at the junction of Pennsylvania and Constitution Avenues in Washington, D.C., while small field offices are located in 11 cities across the country. The commission is governed by five commissioners, each appointed for a seven-year term. No more than three can come from one political party. The commissioners serve both executive and judicial functions: They must determine the policy directions of the agency, approve programs and legal complaints, then hand down judicial findings on the cases and order penalties or other remedies. Commission orders can be appealed in the federal courts.

An abstract of the FTC's organization is given in the figure at the top of the next page. The two areas of particular interest in marketing research are the Office of Policy Planning and Evaluation (OPPE) and the Bureau of Consumer Protection (BCP). The OPPE reports to the commissioners in a staff capacity. Its functions can be likened to those of a corporate planning group in private industry. The Bureau of Consumer Protection is a much larger office, with line responsibilities related to marketing practices as they affect the consumer. Other offices of the FTC deal essentially in legal and trade structure areas.

As we might expect from the vague wording of the FTC Act, there are many programs that could be undertaken by the commission. Most will be unpopular with some percentage of observers, and thus it is not surprising that the FTC has often been

Basic Organization of the Federal Trade Commission

severely criticized. A critical report was issued by Nader's Raiders in 1969. This was followed by a critical report of an American Bar Association committee commissioned by President Nixon to look into Nader's charges. Both groups reported that weaknesses existed at each of the three FTC decision stages: (1) area or case selection, (2) investigation and fact-finding, and (3) remedy generation. Charges included too little activity and too much concern with trivial problems in stage 1, excessive time delays (e.g., four or more years) in stage 2, and weak, ineffective remedies in stage 3.

The agency's response, under the influence of its three newest chairmen, included major changes in organization and staffing, assertion of new powers, and a search for better remedies. Four new programs of particular interest to marketers were instituted: advertising substantiation, corrective advertising, more product information for consumers, and consumer eduction.

The results were mixed. The FTC received much favorable publicity and its budget more than doubled to some $30 million in four years. Many marketers were unhappy, however, and began to ask pointed questions about the actual benefits from the essentially legalistic "activism" of the new FTC.

Problem Setting

Several agency executives, notably Commissioner Mary Gardiner Jones, recognized that the FTC was shifting away from reaction to proaction. Emphasis was turning away from simply rectifying isolated abuses and being directed at broader attempts to improve the consumer environment. This required that the FTC obtain new kinds of information in order to understand the marketplace.

Market research seemed to offer potential for obtaining these insights. Hence, Professor Murray Silverman joined Ms. Jones' staff. His task was to explore the possibilities of applying marketing research to the emerging problems of the FTC. Professor Silverman was instrumental in obtaining two other marketing professors, David Gardner and William Wilkie, to assist in the study. The three planned to submit a report that would explain marketing research, recommend where it should be applied, and propose a program for implementation. They hoped to complete this task between six months and a year after joining the commission.

Late in 1972 they met to put their recommendations in final form. Silverman had gained valuable perspectives on policy considerations in his high-level post. Gardner possessed organizational as well as theoretical insights from his work in the Office of Policy Planning and Evaluation (OPPE). Wilkie had concentrated on line decisions made in the Bureau of Consumer Protection. The three professors were convinced that marketing research would be useful to the FTC. The remaining issues concerned where it should be applied and the best way to organize it as a continuing operation.

Possible Research Areas

There were many areas offering applications for marketing research. These are summarized in the following table.

Program priority research would be aimed at program planning decisions. Consumer environment descriptions refer to measures of an optimal or desired consumer environment. Deviations between it and the observed environment would indicate the extent of program needs.

Models of resource allocation would provide methods for choosing between various programs. In addition to internal dollar costs, research here would attempt to weigh external costs as well as consumer benefits. An example is specification of the value of the consumer benefit derived from removal of a deceptive advertising campaign.

Social cost-benefit measures, in addition to providing inputs to resource allocation models, could serve as performance indicators for the commission. Structural versus trade practice remedy reflects the need to choose between the many alternative programs the FTC could undertake. Alternatives include forced divestitures by large producers, prohibition of certain marketing

Possible Marketing Research Areas
for the Federal Trade Commission

Program Priorities
1. Consumer environment descriptions
2. Models for resource allocation
3. Social cost-benefit measurements
4. Structural versus trade practice remedies

Stimulus Research
1. Advertising effect
2. Personal selling and promotion
3. Pricing
4. Product quality
5. Guarantee and warranty

Response Research
1. Product information
2. Consumer education

Product and Segment Research
1. Special markets
2. Specific products and services

practices, and rules specifying certain marketing procedures. In addition, individual charges could be brought against specific offenses, such as false advertisements. Marketing research might predict the effects of these alternatives, hence be valuable in selecting among them and in allocating FTC budgets.

Stimulus research would provide better understanding of the effects of marketing variables on the consumer. It would involve developing research methods and providing evidence on specific questions.

Advertising effects had received much FTC attention, yet many issues were still unresolved. These included the assessment of deception, the information value of advertising, the effect of emotional copy, the effect of testimonials, advertising influence on prices, and the development of corrective advertising orders.

Personal-selling and promotion research would address such difficult topics as the salesman-buyer relationship and product demand stimulation when consumer defenses are lowered. Examples of these problems include games and sweepstakes, cents-off coupons, negative option selling, "free" trips, spiffing, and door-to-door selling.

Pricing and product quality research would pursue the questions of the relationship between price and quality. *Consumer Reports* ratings have shown low price-quality correlations, yet evidence has indicated that consumers use price to evaluate product quality. In addition, the role of psychic benefits, as opposed to functional performance, needed to be assessed.

Guarantee and warranty research would focus on post-purchase service mechanisms and their role in consumer satisfactions. These include manufacturers' warranties and the dealers' service after sales activities.

Response research would be aimed at new FTC programs to provide consumers with tools for improved decision-making. A program of product information would attempt to make available objective information about brands that consumers could use for better comparisons and choices.

Consumer education would provide better consumer understanding of purchase processes and product characteristics. Marketing research in both cases could address such issues as what consumers need or want to know, how much data to make available, and how to communicate the information.

Product and segment research would pursue special topics of public policy, including the study of special markets. Particular attention would be paid to those groups of consumers who are least able to cope with some aspects of the consumer environment, hence are most susceptible to deceptive trade practices. Examples are children, the poor, the undereducated, and the elderly.

Specific products and services—with high social costs or anticipatory difficulties—would also be examined. Examples include health and safety issues such as nutrition, fire hazards, the effects of over-the-counter drugs, and medical care, as well as purchasing power issues such as credit and buyer insurance. Marketing research in this area would focus on current consumer problems and the means to overcome them.

Implementation Considerations

The three professors realized that the successful introduction of marketing research would have to account for two special characteristics of the FTC. First, a methodological problem could arise from the inability of current marketing research techniques to deal adequately with the issues. Existing research methods reflect an implicit marketing management orientation. While these tools are useful for commercial purposes, they may break down when applied to questions of public policy.

Second, organizational politics indicated that real difficulties could be encountered with FTC personnel. Almost all the professional staff, including all executives, were lawyers. They typically had no training or understanding of marketing or marketing research. They were oriented to winning hearings and court cases. Marketing research could be used to provide supporting evidence for attorneys, yet the professors were not sure whether this was an advantage. It could prove a hindrance to the commission's acceptance of MR and the pursuit of more basic issues.

Other organizational questions needed answers. There was no budget for market research at the FTC. Should a line budget be sought, and if so, at what dollar level? Should a separate MR department be created, or should market research positions be established both in OPPE and BCP? There was also the staffing question: What types of researchers, at what levels of training, should be hired?

Assignment   Prepare a memorandum to the FTC commissioners on how market research should be employed. Two specific recommendations must be made:

1   How research topics should be selected and receive priority, and
2   How the MR function should be organized and budgeted.

In preparing the memo you should consider what research programs you believe the FTC ought to be engaged in.

Part 1
Research
Management
and Design

Introduction

The _____ Manufacturing Co.
_____, Ohio

Dear Professor,

    *I am returning your Marketing Research Questionnaire
unanswered. We do not have a marketing research program of
any kind. We never had and we probably never will in the
foreseeable future.*

    *We have no new product research going on, no strategy
evaluations of any kind, have no idea what our market potential is
and we are a successful company. How and why beats me, just
lucky I guess . . .*

    *I, as an individual, am interested in your findings. If the
company is able to outlive the present Directors, I will be in a
decision-making position and intend to do some modernization . . .*

                          Letter received by a professor of
                          marketing in response to a survey[1]

Managers tend not to clamor for things they do not understand. Hence, managing the firm's research program demands more than technical skills.

In Chapter 2 we examine the strategic problem of fitting research into the firm's marketing mix. We discuss the research manager, looking at his or her tasks, style, image, and success attributes. We look at the issues of project selection. These include priorities, budget, and value analysis. In

---

[1] Lee Adler and Charles S. Mayer, *Managing the Marketing Research Function* (Chicago: American Marketing Association, 1977), p. 4.

conclusion, we look at the problems of controlling and evaluating the overall program as well as individual research projects.

Chapter 3 focuses on research design. We start with problem definition, which is the foundation of good design. We then proceed step by step through the actual process of designing a research project. This includes the technical decisions, such as the selection of method, identification of data sources, selection of data collection technique, and choice of data processing tools. It includes such business decisions as the make-or-buy decision, scheduling, and budgeting. Finally, we examine proposal preparation and an actual research design. Along the way we are well advised to remember H. L. Mencken's caveat: "There's a ready solution for every problem—simple, neat, and wrong."

Chapter 2
Research Management

Key Concepts

Policy Matters
    The role and location of MR in the firm

The Research Manager
    The tasks, style, and attributes of the MR manager

Project Selection: Priorities and Budget
    Assigning priorities and determining the budget for MR projects

Project Selection: Value Analysis
    Estimating the value of Research projects

Control and Evaluation
    Controlling and evaluating projects and the MR program

Key Terms

project manager	Rule of Bayes
rule-of-thumb budgeting	cost-benefit analysis
departmental budgeting	cost-effectiveness analysis
task budgeting	cost-utility analysis
expected value	return on investment (ROI)
net value	flow chart
Bayesian analysis	checklist

Policy Matters

Strategic Issues

Before coming to grips with specific research problems, management must first decide if, when, and how research will be used in the decision process.

Figure 2-1   A Typical Marketing-Research Strategy: Brand-Life Evaluation (A Schematic Diagram of New- and Old- Product Design)

Source: National Family Opinion (Toledo, OH: National Family Opinion, n.d.), p. 5.

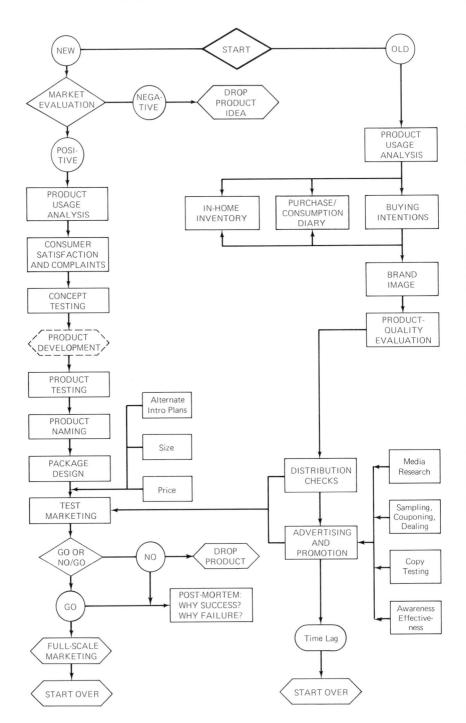

These are strategic issues and involve such questions as:

Does MR belong in our marketing mix? If yes:

Should MR be used to evaluate our advertising?

Where should MR be inserted in product development?

Should MR guide pricing?

Should MR select store sites and guide distribution?

Do we need a continuous flow of data—a marketing information system?

Figure 2-1 illustrates one firm's perception of the strategic role of research. Here we see MR made an integral part of product management. Note how it provides information at key points in the decision process.

Administrative Decisions

If research is made part of the marketing mix, management must then face such administrative questions as:

Where should MR be placed in the organization?

What are the budget requirements?

Should the firm develop its own capability or rely mainly on research suppliers?

The questions are easier to ask than to answer. One can respond with shaky generalities, but these are likely to break down when confronted with a specific situation.

Once the role of research is defined, at least in broad terms, responsibility must be assigned: The research group must be inserted into the firm's organization. Somebody must be designated to manage the function.

Placement

Organizationally, the MR group can rest in a number of places. In a large enterprise, research may be centralized. The MR manager reports directly to the chief executive officer, the VP for marketing, or the director of long-range planning. This is the pattern followed by American Airlines, Chrysler Corp., Anheuser-Busch, and the Federal Trade Commission. Or marketing research may be fragmented and distributed among operating divisions. This is the pattern followed by Rockwell International.

Marketing research may also be placed outside the enterprise. As we'll see in Chapter 4, there are hundreds of firms selling research services. In addition to these research suppliers, most advertising agencies offer marketing research. Some companies, such as Airstream, Bekins, and Toyota, rely almost wholly on outsiders. Others, such as Kawasaki Motors Corporation and the Cessna Aircraft Company, maintain their own research group, yet still draw heavily on suppliers.

Marketing research may be largely ignored. This is the practice at Beatrice Foods. Beatrice Foods is one of the country's largest and most successful firms, which may tell us something about MR we'd rather not hear.

The Research Manager

Tasks

The primary responsibility of the research manager is to produce results—specifically, to provide information required by line management. To this end, the research manager must acquire and direct resources. The resources are aggregated in the form of a budget. The budget is then allocated to get people, equipment, and services.

The acquisition and management of resources typically involves:

Specification of goals	Resolving conflicts
Planning, long-range	Supervising
Planning, short-range	Training
Budgeting	Motivating
Negotiating	Disciplining
Organizing	Cost-controlling
Delegating	Briefing management

In addition to mastering these managerial tasks, the research manager must also be a technician. He or she must be able to perform, or at least understand, the jobs of subordinates and suppliers. The research manager must be able to advise, instruct, and critique on such technical matters as research design, data acquisition and reduction, information analysis, and report writing. The successful managers are also good salespersons and politicians. They can spread the gospel of marketing research and compete for the firm's limited resources.

Style and Image

The style of research managers varies from that of a Paris Island drill instructor to that of a model of participatory management. Their image varies from ivory-tower theorist to Machiavellian pragmatist. Both style and image are important.

Style largely determines the manager's ability to attract good people and get work done. Image largely determines the acceptance of that work by the people it should benefit—the line managers. Unfortunately, image

can contain elements that distract from the job. Operating executives sometimes see researchers and their managers as[1]

technique-oriented rather than problem-oriented

unclear and unimpressive as communicators

unreasonably critical of the intuitions, judgments, and experience of
line executives

passive, rather than active, in identifying areas where research can
contribute

unimaginative, married to clinical data only; fearful of creativity

resistant to controversy on marketing issues

Such perceptions give managers little incentive to support and utilize
marketing research.

Success Attributes

There is probably no prescription that ensures success as a research manager.
There are a number of attitudes and skills that are likely to increase the
probability of success. Most are applicable to project managers and research
analysts as well as to the person in charge. Specifically,[2]

gestalt thinking	the ability to see the whole problem and its effect on the enterprise
executive communication	the ability to communicate with all levels of management, both staff and line[3]
perception	the ability to see and define problems
writing skill	the ability to write proposals and reports that get read and are understood
technical know-how	an awareness, if not a mastery, of the tools of MR
political awareness	an understanding of the informal organization and knowledge of where the power lies

[1] Lee Adler and Charles S. Mayer, *Managing the Marketing Research Function* (Chicago:
American Marketing Association, 1977), p. 21.

[2] These attributes are partially drawn from Emanuel H. Demby, "Success in Marketing
Research? Here Are 15 Key Factors That Will Help Achieve It," *Marketing News*, **10**:7 (January
28, 1977), pp. 4, 5, and 18.

[3] Staff managers provide supporting services to line management. Line managers make
the operational decisions, hence run the enterprise.

| **leadership** | the ability to direct the efforts of others toward a common goal |
| **salesmanship** | the ability to sell ideas and convince others of the validity and usefulness of research findings |

As one ascends the hierarchy of marketing research, one's managerial skills count for more, while one's technical skills count for less. Political savvy and a nose for what is possible may be critical assets. Neither skill is examined in a research text.[4] Hence, the serious student of applied MR is advised to read Niccolo Machiavelli's *The Prince*, Walter Goerlitz's *History of the German General Staff*, and Robert Townsend's *Up the Organization*.

Project Managers

A *project manager* is a person assigned responsibility for the administration and successful completion of a particular project. He or she often leads a team of research analysts and assistants. The job is analogous to that of a brand manager or a product manager. (By job title, the hierarchy of researchers typically runs research manager, project manager, research analyst, research assistant. The assistant is usually the entry-level position.)

The project manager concept is common. If the projects are small, several may be assigned to a single manager. The project manager not only has administrative authority and responsibility, but also controls the resources assigned to the project. Normally he or she reports to the director of marketing research, who in turn reports to the manager (or vice-president) of marketing, or possibly the chief executive officer of the firm. The project manager should work closely with the line manager his or her project is supposed to aid. When marketing research is isolated from line management, it is unlikely to produce practical benefits.

Project Selection: Priorities and Budget

Once the research group is an accepted part of the system, requests for services usually exceed its resources. An ordering of priorities is then necessary. Research requests originate mainly from the group's clientele—the line managers who need information. A competent research manager maintains rapport with these people and helps them identify their information needs. He or she also confronts them with the realities of MR—its power, limitations, and cost. Ultimately, the research manager, some other executive, or a research committee decides what research will or will not be done.

Request Evaluation

A research request involving a significant amount of time or money is often subject to a formal evaluation. The evaluation forces the line manager and

---

[4] The author is aware of one exception: Robert E. D. Woolsey and Huntington S. Swanson, *Operations Research for Immediate Application* (New York: Harper & Row, 1975).

Exhibit 2-1   **Project Request Evaluation Form**

PROJECT REQUEST EVALUATION FORM	TITLE _____1_____ No. 2
	REQUESTED BY ___3___ AREA ___4___ DATE ___5___
	ASSIGNED TO ___6___ SECTION ___7___ DATE ___8___

MARKETING PROBLEM/OPPORTUNITY ____9____

_____

_____

_____

_____

_____

_____

_____

_____

_____

RESEARCH OBJECTIVE _____10_____

_____

_____

_____

_____

_____

_____

_____

_____

RESEARCH PLAN _____11_____

_____

_____

_____

_____

_____

_____

Source: Reprinted from Lee Adler and Charles S. Mayers, *Managing the Marketing Research Function* (1977, pp. 155–156) published by the American Marketing Association.

Exhibit 2-1   **Project Request Evaluation Form (*cont'd.*)**

DATE NEEDED ___12___   CAN DATE BE EXTENDED ___13___   IF SO, UNTIL WHEN ___14___   STATE CIRCUMSTANCES ___15___

ESTIMATED COMPLETION ___16___   PARTIAL RESULTS NEEDED ___17___   STATE CONDITIONS ___18___

NEED:
- ☐ ONLY SIGNIF. INPUT
- ☐ ONE OF FEW SIGNIF. INPUTS
- ☐ ONE OF MANY SIGNIF. INPUTS
- ☐ ONE OF FEW SECONDARY INPUTS
- ☐ ONE OF MANY SECONDARY INPUTS

THIS RESEARCH IS LIKELY TO:

19
- ☐ UNCOVER A PROBLEM/OPPORTUNITY
- ☐ HELP REDUCE EXPENSES
- ☐ HELP SPEND MORE INTELLIGENTLY
- ☐ PROVIDE INSIGHTS INTO A PROBLEM
- ☐ CHANGE/CHALLENGE/CONFIRM EXISTING OPINION
- ☐ HELP IN MAKING A DECISION
- ☐ HELP INCREASE SALES
- ☐ PROVIDE IDEAS FOR COURSE OF ACTION
- ☐ ADD TO GN'L MARKET KNOWLEDGE
- ☐ SUPPLY BACKGROUND INFORMATION

IMPORTANCE:

20

SALES	☐ OVER $10.0 M	☐ OVER $5.0 M TO $10.0 M	☐ OVER $1.0 M TO $5.0 M	☐ OVER $0.5 M TO $1.0 M	☐ UP TO $0.5 M
EXPENSES	☐ OVER $500 M	☐ OVER $250 M TO $500 M	☐ OVER $100 M TO $250 M	☐ OVER $50 M TO $100 M	☐ UP TO $50 M

RESEARCH RESULTS WILL APPLY:

_____ TO ONLY THIS PROBLEM	_____ TO ONE PRODUCT	_____ ONE TIME
_____ TO SIMILAR PROBLEMS	_____ TO SEVERAL PRODUCTS	_____ SHORT TERM
_____ TO NUMEROUS PROBLEMS	_____ BROADLY ACROSS LINE	_____ LONG TERM

FEASIBILITY:

21

SUCCESS	☐ 100%	☐ 95-99%	☐ 80-94%	☐ 65-79%	☐ BELOW 65%
TIMING	☐ 100%	☐ 95-99%	☐ 80-94%	☐ 65-79%	☐ BELOW 65%

COST: TOTAL M & SR COSTS [_____] MAN-HOURS ___ $ ___ PROF. FEES $_____ OTHER M & SR COSTS _____

22

ANY OTHER COSTS _____ SOURCE OF FUNDS _____ ☐ $2 - 5M ☐ $5 - 20M ☐ $20 - 35M ☐ $35 - 50M ☐ OVER $50M

RATING: 23 NEED ☐ 24 IMPORTANCE ☐ 25 FEASIBILITY ☐ 26 COST ☐ P.E. POINTS [27]

DISPOSITION: 28   APPROVALS 30

DO	DON'T DO	APPROXIMATE STARTING DATE	EVALUATORS	REQUESTORS
		29		

the research manager to focus on the need, benefit, feasibility, cost, and risk of the project. Should the request be approved, it lays the groundwork for the project design.

Exhibit 2-1 contains a form for evaluating research requests. Such forms do not assure a perfect ordering of priorities. Yet they help focus the attention of both the researcher and the line manager on the important issues.

Budgeting

No discussion of marketing management is complete without some reference to budgets. The total budget is the most significant constraint on the marketing-research program. Controlling costs may well be the single most important task of research management.

Rule-of-Thumb Budgeting   There are several methods for establishing the research budget. One is to set the total budget by a rule of thumb, using, say, a fixed percentage of the firm's sales. The basis for the percentage value might be the prevailing average for firms of the same size in the same or a similar industry. Often such data are available in published form.[5] For instance, one source indicates that manufacturers of consumer goods spend between .13 and .50 percent of their sales revenues for marketing research, while manufacturers of industrial goods spend between .03 and .30 percent, depending on their size.[6]

Departmental Budgeting   Another method is to have each department or functional area using research resources allocate part of their total budget to marketing research. Individual allocations are based on the user's perceived needs. Collectively, they make up the total budget for the marketing-research program. One advantage of this method is that it encourages the researchers to think in terms of the needs of the other departments.

Task Budgeting   A third alternative is the task method in which budgets are established to support specific tasks, usually on an ad hoc basis. Since this method relates allocations to specific jobs, it makes cost-benefit analysis much simpler. However, it tends to make the total research budget rather volatile. It also makes long-range planning difficult, although a temporary overloading of in-house research facilities can often be relieved by using research suppliers.

Project Selection: Value Analysis

The project selection process is not confined to ordering priorities and preparing a budget. Rational management demands an assessment of the value of the research.

The Need for Value Analysis

There is virtually no limit to the assortment and extravagance of research projects. MR can become a sump for the firm's resources, far out of proportion to its benefits. Hence, value analysis is an important part of

---

[5] For example see Dik Warren Twedt, *Survey of Marketing Research* (Chicago: American Marketing Association, 1978).

[6] Twedt, *A Survey of Marketing Research*, p. 32.

research management. Each time it decides whether to approve a research project, which of several alternative research designs to select, or whether to expand or cut back the firm's research program, management is forced to make a value judgment. It must ask, what is the research worth?

Because the answer to this question is frequently elusive, management is encouraged to make purely intuitive judgments and subject research to less scrutiny than other marketing functions. This is unfortunate for several reasons. For one thing, intuitive judgments tend to produce a less rational allocation of company resources than quantitative analysis. For another, a purely intuitive approach makes the marketing-research group more vulnerable to company politics. When executives lack rigorous decision criteria, they are more easily influenced by personalities, images, and external pressures.

A lack of objective standards for evaluating research also magnifies the sensitivity of the research budget to the economic well-being of the firm. Like other staff functions, marketing research is highly susceptible to decreased budget allocations during economy drives. We have already mentioned that, during periods of declining revenues or falling profits, the research budget is often one of the first victims of the cost-cutter. This is especially true when expenditures are defended solely on the basis of subjective arguments. Budget cuts at this point can be bad for the firm, since a decline in economic fortunes is exactly the sort of problem marketing research may be needed to remedy.

Obviously, then, there is a real need for evaluative criteria and analytical tools that permit a quantitative assessment of the worth of marketing research.

Quantitative Methods of Evaluation

The Ideal Criterion: Expected Value

The single best evaluative criterion for market research is the net increase in the expected value[7] of the management decision(s) attributable to the research. For instance, suppose that management must choose one of several mutually exclusive product variations. If the information provided by marketing research increases the probability of making the correct choice, it will increase the expected value of the decision. This increase in expected value, minus the cost of the research, is the real net value of the research. More precisely, the net value of a market-research project is equal to the expected value of the marketing decision made with the aid of research, less the expected value of the decision without research, less the cost of the research.

This relationship is stated mathematically in the following equation:

$$V_r = (\Pi_{er} - \Pi_e) - C_r \qquad\qquad [2.1]$$

[7] For an explanation of expected value, see Appendix 1.

where

V_r = the net value of market research

Π_{er} = the expected value of the marketing decision when made with the aid of research

Π_e = the expected value of the marketing decision when made without benefit of research

C_r = the cost of the research

In other words, the *net value of the marketing research* is the marginal increase in the expected value of the decision, less the cost of the research. Marketing research should be used whenever this value is positive.

Note that we are dealing with expected values. Research provides more information, but rarely does it tell the firm everything it would like to know about a given phenomenon. Outcomes are seldom certain. At best, research narrows the range of error associated with the probabilities assigned to the possible outcomes of the marketing decision. Thus, the gross value of the research is measured in terms of the reduction in the cost of uncertainty, that reduction being represented by the term $\Pi_{er} - \Pi_e$ in formula 2.1.

Sometimes marketing research does no more than identify one or more possible outcomes associated with the marketing decision. While this information can be extremely useful, it is often difficult to assign a value to it. Although it may result in the rejection of certain decision alternatives whose outcomes are clearly unacceptable, marketing research seldom automates the decision process. People with the responsibility for the results—not the researchers—usually make the line decisions. Generally, research is only one of many inputs—some noneconomic and emotional—that impinge on the decision process. The net-value criterion assumes that the information provided by the research will be used. If it is ignored, the research project has been wasted, and its net value is negative and equal to its cost.

Marketing research can lead to the selection of the wrong alternative. However, research should increase the probability of making the correct selection, and hence increase the average payoff. In other words, marketing research can increase a decision's expected value (by increasing the probability that the best alternative will be identified and chosen), but it does not eliminate possibility of error. Research can lead management to a wrong decision.

Classical Statistical Analysis

The decision to use research must eventually be quantified, for a specific amount of resources must be allocated to the project. The cost of the decision will range from zero (no research) to whatever amount is necessary to design and execute the study. A quantitative evaluation of the net value of the project is the ideal basis for the decision to use or not to use marketing research.

In order to use formula 2.1 to find net value, we must first estimate the expected values of the two alternatives—making the marketing decision with the benefit of research, and making the marketing decision without the benefit of research. This necessitates the identification of each possible outcome—a task that may require some exploratory research—and an estimation of its payoff value. In addition, probabilities must be assigned to each outcome. It is these probabilities that reflect the impact of market research. In fact, one may think of marketing research as an instrument for increasing the chance of making the correct marketing decision by increasing the accuracy of these probabilities.

By expanding formula 2.1, we can develop a more explicit model for evaluating research projects

$$V_r = \left[\sum_{j=1}^{n} \sum_{i=1}^{m} P(D_j|R) \cdot P(x_i|D_j) \cdot x_i \right]_r - \left[\sum_{j=1}^{n} \sum_{i=1}^{m} P(D_j|N) \cdot P(x_i|D_j) \cdot x_i \right]$$
$$- C_r \qquad\qquad\qquad [2.2]$$

where

$P(D_j|R) =$ the probability of decision D_j, given research

$P(D_j|N) =$ the probability of decision D_j, given no research

$P(x_i|D_j) =$ the probability of outcome x_i, given D_j

$x_i =$ the value of outcome x_i

$r =$ with research

V_r and C_r are defined as in formula 2.1

There is a subtle, yet important, point to be made here. The researcher must estimate the probability that management will select a particular course of action when it has the benefit of market research and when it does not. He must also assign probabilities to each possible outcome, given a particular decision. (If these probabilities are based on experience, they are considered "objective." If they are estimated intuitively, they are considered "subjective.")

Presumably, the probability of a favorable outcome, given a particular decision, will be higher when that decision is reached with the benefit of research than without. These probabilities often defy specification. Yet, conceptually, it is this process (this assignment of probabilities) that is invoked whenever the worth of a research project is evaluated. Again we should emphasize that the value of marketing research is the difference in the expected value of the decision with and without research. Of course, this assumes that the information gained by the research will be used by the decision-maker.

For example, assume that management is confronted with the following marketing decision: to commercialize or not to commercialize a new product. These two decision alternatives can be symbolized as D_1 and D_2, respectively.

Assume that the firm's experience shows that with no market research, the probability of D_1 is 0.6; thus, the probability of D_2 is 0.4. Assume further, that since the information provided by research increases the ability of management to discriminate between good and bad products, the probability of commercialization with research drops to 0.5; hence, the probability of D_2 increases to 0.5.

Because the research enables management to identify potentially successful products more often, the probability of success, given commercialization, is improved. Let us assume that experience indicates a successful outcome, x_1, only 40 percent of the time when products are chosen for commercialization without first doing research. Hence failure, outcome x_2, occurs 60 percent of the time. With market research, fewer bad products are selected. Hence, the probability of a successful outcome, x_1, given commercialization, increases, say to 0.7. In both situations—when research is performed and when it is not—the zero-profit outcome, x_3, is certain given the no-commercialization decision, D_2. If outcomes x_1 and x_2 have payoffs of \$500,000 and $-\$200,000$, respectively, and the market research would cost \$30,000, we can compute the net value of the research. We first construct a pair of matrixes, one for the first term in formula 2.2 (Π_{er} in equation 2.1) and one for the second term (Π_e in equation 2.1), as in Tables 2-1 and 2-2. Then we substitute the results in equation 2.1:

$$V_r = (\Pi_{er} - \Pi_e) - C_r \qquad \text{(given as formula 2.1)}$$
$$V_r = (\$145,000 - \$48,000) - \$30,000 \qquad \text{(by substitution)}$$
$$V_r = \$67,000 \qquad \text{(by arithmetic)}$$

Since the net value is positive (\$67,000), marketing research should be employed. Furthermore, since the cost of the research is relatively small ($C_r = \$30,000$) compared to its net value, a moderate error in the probabilities (and hence in the expected values) can be tolerated.

The tree diagram in Figure 2-2 illustrates both the decision options in the example and the general concept of quantitative evaluation of marketing research. Basically, it shows the various paths by which the two alternatives—using and not using research—can lead to each outcome. Each point where a path divides into two or more branches is assigned a distribution of probabilities. (The probabilities at each branching point must sum to unity.) Notice that the probability of branching to an undesirable outcome is lower when marketing research has been done. This is, in essence, the justification of research.

Like the two matrixes, the tree diagram can easily be expanded to accommodate a larger number of marketing decision alternatives and possible outcomes. The principles and the computational procedures would remain unaltered. The decision rule is always the same: *Increase the amount of marketing research until the marginal cost of additional research equals the marginal increase in the expected value of the marketing decision.* In

Table 2-1 A Probability and Value Matrix for a Marketing Decision Using Market Research
(D_1 = commercialize, D_2 = do not commercialize)

Decision Number j	Probability of Decision D_j Given Research, R $P(D_j\|R)$	Outcome Number i	Probability of Outcome x_i Given D_j $P(x_i\|D_j)$	Probability of D_i and x_i $P(D_j\|R) \cdot P(x_i\|D_j)$	Payoff Value of Outcome x_i x_i	Expected Value $P(D_j\|R) \cdot P(x_i\|D_j) \cdot x_i$
1	0.5	1	0.7	.35	$500,000	$175,000
1	0.5	2	0.3	.15	−200,000	−30,000
1	0.5	3	0.0	.00	000	000
2	0.5	1	0.0	.00	500,000	000
2	0.5	2	0.0	.00	−200,000	000
2	0.5	3	1.0	.50	000	000
				1.00		$145,000

$$\Pi_{er} = \sum_{j=1}^{2} \sum_{i=1}^{3} P(D_j|R) \cdot P(x_i|D_j) \cdot x_i = \$145,000$$

Table 2-2 A Probability and Value Matrix for a Marketing Decision Without Using Market Research
(D_1 = commercialize, D_2 = do not commercialize)

Decision Number j	Probability of Decision D_j Given No Research, N $P(D_j\|N)$	Outcome Number i	Probability of Outcome x_i Given D_j $P(x_i\|D_j)$	Probability of D_j and x_i $P(D_j\|N) \cdot P(x_i\|D_j)$	Payoff Value of Outcome x_i x_i	Expected Value $P(D_j\|N) \cdot P(x_i\|D_j) \cdot x_i$
1	0.6	1	0.4	0.24	$500,000	$120,000
1	0.6	2	0.6	0.36	−200,000	−72,000
1	0.6	3	0.0	0.00	000	000
2	0.4	1	0.0	0.00	500,000	000
2	0.4	2	0.0	0.00	−200,000	000
2	0.4	3	0.4	0.40	000	000
			1.0	1.00		$48,000

$$\Pi_e = \sum_{j=1}^{2} \sum_{i=1}^{3} P(D_j|N) \cdot P(x_i|D_j) \cdot x_i = \$48,000$$

Figure 2-2 Tree Diagrams of Marketing Decision With and Without Benefit of Research[a]

RESEARCH ALTERNATIVE (R OR N)	MARKETING DECISION (D_j)	OUTCOME (x_i)	PAY-OFF VALUE	EXPECTED VALUE

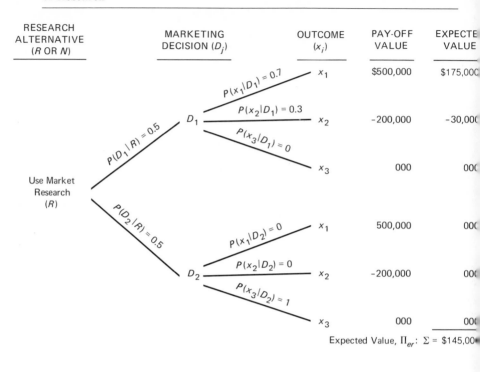

x_1 $500,000 $175,000

$P(x_1|D_1) = 0.7$

$P(x_2|D_1) = 0.3$

D_1 x_2 -200,000 -30,000

$P(x_3|D_1) = 0$

$P(D_1|R) = 0.5$

x_3 000 000

Use Market Research (R)

$P(D_2|R) = 0.5$

$P(x_1|D_2) = 0$ x_1 500,000 000

$P(x_2|D_2) = 0$

D_2 x_2 -200,000 000

$P(x_3|D_2) = 1$

x_3 000 000

Expected Value, Π_{er}: Σ = $145,000

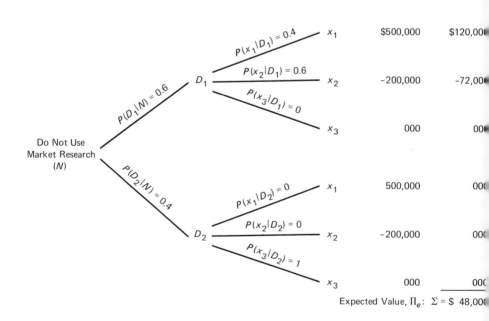

x_1 $500,000 $120,000

$P(x_1|D_1) = 0.4$

$P(x_2|D_1) = 0.6$

D_1 x_2 -200,000 -72,000

$P(x_3|D_1) = 0$

$P(D_1|N) = 0.6$

x_3 000 000

Do Not Use Market Research (N)

$P(D_2|N) = 0.4$

$P(x_1|D_2) = 0$ x_1 500,000 000

$P(x_2|D_2) = 0$

D_2 x_2 -200,000 000

$P(x_3|D_2) = 1$

x_3 000 000

Expected Value, Π_e: Σ = $ 48,000

KEY: D_1 = Commercialize, D_2 = do not commercialize, x_1 = product success
  x_2 = product failure, x_3 = product never reaches market

NOTE: [a]Data is drawn from Tables 2-1 and 2-2.

other words, keep allocating more of the firm's resources to marketing research as long as the results keep increasing the firm's profit. This will produce an optimum level of expenditure for marketing research. Unfortunately, because sufficient information is seldom available for marginal analysis, management must frequently settle for a suboptimum—often subjective—solution to the marketing-research budgeting problem.[8]

Bayesian Analysis[9]

Bayesian techniques can also be employed to evaluate marketing research quantitatively. Bayesian analysis is characterized by the use of subjective probabilities (although not to the exclusion of objective probabilities), the updating of prior probabilities through the introduction of new information, and special rules and postulates.

   This kind of analysis is especially useful when the firm's experience with similar problems is insufficient to yield adequate empirical probabilities. Because it uses subjective probabilities, Bayesian evaluation embraces more information than conventional statistical methods, which are limited to objective probabilities. Scientific orthodoxy holds that the more information there is incorporated into the analysis, the greater is the likelihood of a correct conclusion. If so, the Bayesian approach should lead to a higher frequency of correct decisions, especially when empirical data are scarce.

   There is no algorithm[10] for determining the subjective probabilities needed for a Bayesian analysis. The general procedure is to specify the necessary probabilities by whatever means are appropriate—perhaps by gathering a consensus of knowledgeable managers. Bayes' rule, summed up by the following formula, is then applied to determine the conditional probability of success, given a prediction of success:

$$P(A_i|B) = \frac{P(B|A_i) \cdot P(A_i)}{P(B|A_1) \cdot P(A_1) + P(B|A_2) \cdot P(A_2) + \cdots P(B|A_n) \cdot P(A_n)}$$

(given in Appendix 2 as formula A2.23)

where

   A_i = a particular event from a set of mutually exclusive events
         $A_1, A_2, \ldots A_n$

   B = an outcome that can be reached via (i.e., it is conditional upon)
        event A_i

---

   [8] See W. B. Wentz and G. I. Eyrich, *Marketing: Theory and Application* (New York: Harcourt Brace Jovanovich, 1970), Chs. 6 and 7, for a more detailed discussion of marketing-resources allocation and control.
   [9] Those totally unfamiliar with Bayesian statistics should read the explanation in Appendix 2 before proceeding with this section.
   [10] An *algorithm* is a rigorous mathematical procedure—that is, a series of mathematical operations—for finding an absolute or optimum value.

Once this is determined, we can use the formulas given in the preceding section to specify the expected values of the marketing decision made with and without research and the net value of that research. An example will help to clarify just how Bayesian analysis is used in the evaluation of marketing research.

Suppose a decision must be made as to whether to introduce a new product. The likelihood that the decision will be the correct one will be enhanced by the use of marketing research, but management wonders whether research is justified in view of the fact that it will cost money. An analyst is directed to find the answer.

Let us assume that experience—say, empirical observation—enables the analyst to assign the following conditional probabilities to the predictions of a research project, given two possible states of nature:[11] product success, A_1, and product failure, A_2.

1.   The probability that success will be predicted as a result of the research (a success prediction), B, given a product that will actually be a success, A_1, is 0.8. Or, $P(B|A_1) = 0.8$.

2.   The probability that failure will be predicted as a result of the research (a failure prediction), C, given a product that will actually be a success, A_1, is 0.2. Or, $P(C|A_1) = 0.2$.

3.   The probability of a success prediction, B, given a product that will actually be a failure, A_2, is 0.1. Or, $P(B|A_2) = 0.1$.

4.   The probability of a failure prediction, C, given a product that will actually be a failure, A_2, is 0.9. Or, $P(C|A_2) = 0.9$.

These relationships between predictions and states of nature can be displayed in matrix form, as in Table 2-3, called a *likelihood matrix*. Matrixes are useful in clarifying the problem, especially when there are three or more possible states of nature, and hence three or more probability distributions and sets of predictions. (Note that the conditional probabilities for each given state, such as A_2, must add up to unity $(P(B|A_1) + P(C|A_1) = 1.)$

Table 2-3   A Probability Matrix for a Typical Research Prediction

		State of Nature	
		Product Will Succeed (A_1)	Product Will Fail (A_2)
Research	Success (B)	$P(B\|A_1) = 0.8$	$P(B\|A_2) = 0.1$
Prediction	Failure (C)	$P(C\|A_1) = 0.2$	$P(C\|A_2) = 0.9$

---

[11] The phrase *state of nature* is used in statistics to mean the real or true condition. Of course, the state of nature is usually unknown to the problem-solver, who can only define the possibilities and assign them probabilities.

The likelihood matrix also indicates the degree of uncertainty, hence the quality of the information, associated with the research. If the diagonal cells (going from upper-left to lower-right) each contained a probability of one and the other cells thus contained a probability of zero, the research would be providing perfect information. That is, product success or failure would be correctly predicted in every case. Given this condition of certainty, the marketer could hardly make a bad decision. Unfortunately, marketing research can rarely, if ever, provide perfect information. Usually, there is a real possibility that the research will yield an erroneous prediction, given either state of nature.

Proceeding with our example, we see that the analyst's next step is to draw on the judgment of the firm's marketers. A consensus of qualified executives reveals the following subjective probabilities that the product will be a success, A_1, and a failure, $A_2 : P(A_1) = 0.6$; hence $P(A_2) = 0.4$.

Since we now have two sets of probabilities (the analyst's and management's), we can use Bayesian analysis to determine the probability of success, given a prediction of success, $P(A_1 | B)$. This in turn will allow us to specify the expected values of alternative decisions and thus compute the net value of the marketing research. We proceed by invoking formula A2.23, Bayes' rule

$$P(A_1 | B) = \frac{P(B|A_1) \cdot P(A_1)}{P(B|A_1) \cdot P(A_1) + P(B|A_2) \cdot P(A_2)}$$

(given as formula A2.23)

$$P(A_1 | B) = \frac{0.8(0.6)}{0.8(0.6) + 0.1(0.4)}$$

(by substitution)

$$P(A_1 | B) = 0.923$$

(by arithmetic)

Thus, the probability that the product will prove to be a success if the marketing research predicts success is 0.923. Hence, the probability that the product will fail if research predicts success is $1 - .923$, or 0.077; $P(A_2 | B) = .077$.

The probability that the product will prove to be a failure when the research predicts failure, $P(A_2 | C)$, can be found by again invoking Bayes' rule. (Note "C" has been substituted for "B" to avoid confusing the two outcomes.)

$$P(A_2 | C) = \frac{P(C|A_2) \cdot P(A_2)}{P(C|A_2) \cdot P(A_2) + P(C|A_1) \cdot P(A_1)}$$

(given as formula A2.23)

$$P(A_2 | C) = \frac{0.9(0.4)}{0.9(0.4) + 0.2(0.6)}$$

(by substitution)

$$P(A_2 | C) = 0.75$$

(by arithmetic)

With $P(A_2|C)$ equal to 0.75, the probability that a product will succeed in spite of a prediction of failure, $P(A_1|C)$, must be $0.25(1 - 0.75 = 0.25)$.

If we assume that the payoff for success, x_1, is $3000,000, the penalty for failure, x_2, is $-$200,000$, and the cost of the research project, C_r, is $20,000, we can compute the expected value of the two alternatives (using and not using research) and the net value of the market-research project, V_r. However, we first need to specify the probability that the research will predict success, for only then will the product be introduced (assuming research is used).

The probability that the research will predict success, $P(B)$, is a function of whether the product is truly one that will be successful, A_1, and whether the research will be able to identify potentially successful products, $(B|A_1)$. It is also a function of whether the product is truly one that will fail, A_2, and whether the research will predict success for such a product, $(B|A_2)$. In short, $P(B)$ is the sum of a pair of joint probabilities

$$P(B) = P(B|A_1) \cdot P(A_1) + P(B|A_2) \cdot P(A_2)$$
$$P(B) = 0.8(.6) + 0.1(0.4)$$
$$P(B) = 0.52$$

If $P(B)$ is 0.52, then the probability that the research will predict failure, $P(C)$, must be $1 - 0.52$, or 0.48.

The expected value, Π_{er}, of the marketing decision made with research is simply the sum of the products of the possible outcomes, x_1 and x_2, and their probabilities. The probability of outcome x_1 ($300,000) is equal to the joint probability that the research will predict success, $P(B)$, and the product will be successful given a success prediction, $P(A_1|B)$. The probability of outcome x_2 ($-$200,000) is equal to the joint probability that the research will predict success, $P(B)$, and the product will be a failure given a success prediction, $P(A_2|B)$. We can exclude the results of a failure prediction, C, from our computation since, given a failure prediction, the product would not be introduced. Thus the outcome, x_3, would be zero and can be ignored. Π_{er} is computed as follows

$$\Pi_{er} = P(B) \cdot P(A_1|B) \cdot x_1 + P(B) \cdot P(A_2|B) \, x_2$$
$$\Pi_{er} = 0.52(0.923)($300,000) + 0.52(0.077)(-$200,000)$$

(by substitution)

$$\Pi_{er} = $135,980$$

(by arithmetic)

The expected value, Π_e, of the marketing decision made without research is, again, the sum of the products of the possible outcomes, x_1 and x_2, and their probabilities. Lacking the insight provided by research, we must use the judgmental (subjective) probabilities $P(A_1)$ and $P(A_2)$. Since if the consensus favors success and Π_e proves to be positive, we assume that the product will be introduced, and we can ignore outcome x_3, the result of not introducing the product. Π_e is then

$$\Pi_e = P(A_1) \cdot x_1 + P(A_2) \cdot x_2$$

$$\Pi_e = 0.6\,(\$300{,}000) + 0.4\,(-\$200{,}000) \qquad \text{(by substitution)}$$

$$\Pi_e = \$100{,}000 \qquad \text{(by arithmetic)}$$

We can now solve for V_r, the net value of the marketing research

$$V_r = (\Pi_{er} - \Pi_e) - C_r \qquad \text{(given as formula 2.1)}$$

$$V_r = (\$135{,}980 - \$100{,}000) - \$20{,}000 \qquad \text{(by substitution)}$$

$$V_r = \$15{,}980 \qquad \text{(by arithmetic)}$$

Thus, research increases the expected value of the marketing decision from \$100,000 to \$135,980, while incurring a cost of \$20,000. This yields a net value of \$15,980 for the research project. In arriving at this value, two sets of probabilities—the analyst's, drawn from empirical data, and management's, based on subjective judgments—were explicitly incorporated in the analyses. This is, as we have pointed out, one of the features that distinguishes the Bayesian approach from conventional analysis and—according to the advocates of Bayesian statistics—enhances the quality of the analysis.

Cost-Benefit Analysis

When the value of the marketing decision cannot be expressed in dollars, management can turn to cost-benefit analysis.

Cost-benefit analysis—also called "cost-effectiveness" and "cost-utility" analysis—was originally developed by several federal agencies in response to the need to evaluate alternative projects without the aid of the profit criterion.[12] Basically, it is a system for identifying the decision alternative that will yield the

> maximum benefit
> maximum benefit/cost ratio
> maximum benefit subject to the constraint of a fixed cost, or
> minimum cost, subject to the constraint of a fixed benefit.

The benefit can be expressed in nonmonetary terms, such as the number of respondents interviewed, the number of qualified prospects identified, the number of media evaluated, the number of commercials tested, the statistical

---

[12] Cost-benefit analysis was first used by the U.S. Army Corps of Engineers in the 1930s. It was brought to a high level of sophistication in the 1960s by the Department of Defense, which has used it extensively in choosing between alternative weapon systems.

precision of an estimate, or the obtaining of a specific piece of information. Hence cost-benefit analysis is amenable to situations where profit—the preferred decision criterion—eludes specification.

The hallmark of cost-benefit analysis is not that it consistently yields precise answers (it does not), but that it provides a system for structuring and dealing rigorously with complex problems. Cost-benefit analysis admits problems which defy specification in terms of a dollar-and-cents payoff. While it does not ensure an optimum solution, it helps the decision-maker to think rationally about the problems.

Just as there is no algorithm for determining the subjective probabilities used in Bayesian analysis, so too there is no algorithm for cost-benefit analysis. In fact, a number of different analytical techniques have been gathered under the heading "cost-benefit analysis."[13] Those used to evaluate a particular task will vary from project to project and between institutions. Although there is no unanimity on exactly what constitutes cost-benefit analysis, most practitioners would probably agree that it includes the following steps:

1   The analysis begins with a careful and systematic review and appraisal of the objectives being sought.
2   A criterion or a hierarchy of criteria is established for use in evaluating the alternatives. Since most problems can be considered as suboptimization problems, this will normally require some "higher-level criterion," which is used as the basis for checking solutions to the subproblem for consistency with broader objectives.
3   The relevant alternative courses of action are critically examined with particular reference to the assessment of the economic costs and the benefits or gains associated with each of the alternative methods of achieving the stipulated objectives.
4   Variations in the time patterns of benefits among alternatives are explicitly treated.
5   Uncertainty is recognized as an important aspect of any planning problem and is explicitly treated.
6   A model of a more or less formal nature is constructed in order to make explicit the assumptions and relations being utilized. The consistency, sensitivity, and validity of the model are carefully evaluated.[14]

[13] For an in-depth introduction to cost-benefit analysis, see Charles J. Hitch and Ronald N. McKean, *Economics of Defense in the Nuclear Age* (Cambridge: Harvard University Press, 1963); Ronald N. McKean, *Efficiency in Government through Systems Analysis* (New York: Wiley, 1958); and David Novick, ed., *Program Budgeting* (Washington, D.C.: U.S. Government Printing Office, 1964).

[14] Ralph L. Day, "Optimizing Marketing Research through Cost-Benefit Analysis," *Business Horizons*, **9**:3 (Fall 1966), pp. 45–54.

In using this method to evaluate marketing research, step number one is to review the marketing objective of the decision-maker. Examples are increased sales or market share, the penetration of a new market, the broadening of the product line, the optimization of price, the selection of a new package design, or the optimization of the media mix. Next, the objective(s) of the research must be defined, within the context of the marketing objective. The objective of the research should serve the end the decision-maker has in mind. For instance, if the decision-maker's objective is to optimize price, the objective of the research might be to estimate the product's price elasticity.

Step two involves defining the benefits to be used as evaluative criteria. The benefits must be relevant to the objective. They must be quantifiable, unless what is wanted is a single and explicit piece of information, such as an estimate of price elasticity, and the objective is to minimize cost.

Also at this point, multiple benefits must be arrayed in order of their importance and minimum benefit levels specified. In addition, the person doing the evaluation must decide if the ultimate purpose of the analysis is to maximize benefits, maximize the benefit/cost ratio, minimize cost, or whatever.

Step three involves the specification of the research alternatives, including the no-research option, and an estimation of their respective benefits and costs. For instance, given a need for consumer-preference data, one might specify the following three alternatives:

a telephone survey
a mail survey
no research

Of course, with the exception of the no-research option, only those alternatives yielding at least the specified minimum benefits are admissible.

Step four is appropriate when (1) the benefits occur over time and (2) time is a significant factor. For instance, a high level of benefits achievable ten months hence may be nowhere near as useful as a lower level achievable in three months, and should be discounted accordingly. Time is also a common constraint. Often the decision-maker must commit to a course of action by a certain date; thus, any information provided after the deadline is useless.

When the research benefits can be expressed in monetary terms, the future streams of benefits and costs can be discounted to obtain the present value of each research alternative.[15] When benefits are nonmonetary, a subjective adjustment in benefit values is necessary in order to include the time variable in the analysis.

---

[15] See Wentz and Eyrich, *Marketing: Theory and Application*, pp. 108–110, for an explanation of the technique of discounting future streams of income (benefits) and costs to determine their present value.

Step five provides for the explicit inclusion of risk into the analysis. Risk is in the form of probabilities assigned to the possible outcomes (expressed as payoff benefits) of each research alternative. Since the outcome of research is seldom certain, the benefits associated with each research alternative are weighted by the probability that they will be achieved. The result is an expected value for the benefits of each research option.[16]

Step six calls for the preparation of a formal model that will yield numerical values for the benefits and costs of the research alternatives. These values are in the dimension defined in step two and reflect the time and risk variables specified in steps four and five.

Although a digression on decision models is outside the scope of this text, a simple example will help to illustrate step six and the conclusion of a cost-benefit analysis. Assume that four research alternatives, R_i, have been specified, including no-research, R_4. Associated with each alternative is a set of outcomes representing the level of benefits (the payoffs) that could occur. For instance, research alternative R_1 might yield 200, 300, or 400 usable survey responses (or qualified prospects, interviews, etc.), depending on the state of nature at the time. (These benefits would be expressed in terms of their discounted present value if time was a significant factor.) Probabilities

Table 2-4   **Cost-Benefit Analysis Model**

		Pay-off (Benefit) Matrix[a]			Decision Values		
		Contingencies (Possible States of Nature)			Expected Value of Benefit	Cost	Benefit/ Cost Ratio
		C_1	C_2	C_3			
	R_1	200 (.1)	300 (.6)	400 (.3)	320	$8,000	.040:1
	R_2	300 (.1)	400 (.6)	500 (.3)	420	10,000	.042:1
Research Alternatives	R_3	400 (.3)	500 (.5)	600 (.2)	490	20,000	.025:1
	R_4	0 (1.0)	400 (0)	500 (0)	000	000	...

[a] Benefits and probabilities appear in the cells.

[16] The expected value of an alternative is the sum of the products of each possible outcome and its probability of occurrence. See Appendix 1 for a detailed explanation.

are assigned—probably subjectively—to each of the outcomes, and expected values are computed. Costs are also estimated, and the benefit/cost ratios specified. This completes the analysis. The next step is up to the decision-maker. He or she must apply the appropriate decision criterion (the maximum benefit, the minimum cost, etc.) to select between research alternatives. The necessary decision values are shown in the model seen in Table 2-4.

Return on Investment

Some companies may find return on investment (ROI) a suitable criterion for evaluating marketing research. This approach to value analysis is a departure from the previously discussed methods on two counts. First, the primary objective is the evaluation of the total research program, not simply individual projects. Second, the analysis is made after the research is done, not before.

ROI value analysis, as applied by one major corporation, Oscar Mayer and Company, starts with a review of each research project executed during the fiscal year. Projects are reviewed with the individuals who originally requested them. During the review the user is asked to estimate the worth of the findings. If he did not use the information, the project is considered to have been worth nothing and given a rating of zero. If the information is judged redundant or simply an elaboration of what was already obvious to the user, the project is also given a zero rating.

Next, the worth of the individual projects is aggregated to obtain the gross value of the research program. Then, on the assumption that management would usually make the correct decision even without benefit of marketing research, the worth of the program is discounted 60 percent. The ratio between this adjusted value and the total research budget yields the return on investment for the marketing-research program. The following formula applies.[17]

$$\text{ROI} = \frac{0.40 \text{ (worth of findings)}}{\text{annual marketing-research budget}} \qquad [2.3]$$

Given the ROI, some useful judgments may be made about the quality and quantity of the firm's market research. The research ROI can be compared to those of other departments, the firm as a whole, or current investment opportunities. (ROI is a common index of performance.) If the comparison is favorable, perhaps more of the firm's resources should be allocated to marketing research. If the comparison is unfavorable, a reduction in the marketing research program, or at least an audit to determine why performance is so poor, may be in order.

Of course it is important to remember that the research ROI is an estimated value. Since both the worth of the findings and the discount are

---

[17] Dik W. Twedt, "What Is the 'Return on Investment' in Marketing Research?" *Journal of Marketing*, **30**:1 (January 1966), p. 62.

determined subjectively, it lacks the precision associated with ROI figures for other business endeavors. Oscar Mayer's experience indicates that the value may tend to be inflated; one year's ROI was 351 percent.[18] However, if it is rigorously applied, this method should be superior to a purely judgmental evaluation of the firm's research program.

Qualitative Methods of Evaluation

A meaningful quantitative evaluation of marketing research is often impossible, even using subjective probabilities and Bayesian statistics. It may also be unnecessary. Qualitative evaluation may make the need for market research obvious. Management may know that exploratory research is essential to the adequate definition of a marketing problem, or for the identification and clarification of the firm's options. For example, if the company is extending its operations into another geographic market, research may be necessary to determine the alternative distribution channels. If the firm wants to expand its product mix through acquisitions, research may be required to locate and evaluate candidates. If the advertising director wants to consider television commercials as a promotional option, research may be needed to determine the alternatives in terms of programs, times, and costs, as well as the commercials' effectiveness. The need for such projects may be obvious, even if their net value is elusive.

Sometimes research is justified as a precautionary measure. For instance, continuous monitoring of the market serves as an early-warning system to alert management to any changes in sales, market shares, or competitors' strategies. Corrective or exploitative measures are usually more effective, and less expensive, if initiated early. Research can serve this end.

When common sense dictates the use of marketing research, it is foolish to spend the time or the resources attempting to make a rigorous value analysis of the project. Of course, such an analysis may be necessary to pacify the detractors or, later, to appraise the benefit of the marketing research function. However, it should not delay or interfere with the project itself when good judgment suggests the need is obvious. When a critical marketing decision can clearly benefit from research, management should immediately authorize the design and execution of a research project without delaying for an excursion into value analysis.

Project Control and Evaluation

Project Control

Controlling a marketing-research project involves the same skills and techniques associated with the management of resources in other marketing

---

[18] Twedt, "What Is the 'Return on Investment' in Marketing Research?" p. 63. (This value, although high, is not ridiculously so. Market research can easily yield returns equal to several times its cost.)

departments, or, for that matter, in the firm as a whole. Since an in-depth coverage of this topic may be found in most marketing-management texts,[19] we shall attempt only a brief review of the subject here.

Project management entails setting performance standards, monitoring the project, and controlling its human and material resources. The performance standards consist of a schedule (timetable) of events and criteria for the tasks that are to be performed. (Examples are the number of respondents to be interviewed, the type of information to be gathered, the kind of reports needed, and, of course, costs.) A budget is essential, except for the most trivial projects.

Monitoring requires an information-feedback system that provides regular reports on the project's progress. This information is compared to the performance standards in order to identify problems that warrant corrective—or, in some cases, exploitative—action by the project manager.

Control must be exercised over the resources assigned to the project. People may have to be reassigned, additional data gathered, more questionnaires sent out, more computer time authorized, and funds reallocated. Sometimes it is necessary to redefine the project's objectives or alter the performance standards in light of new information or changes in the needs of line management. Flexibility is important. Blind adherence to an original plan of action can lead to disaster.

Research management may seem complicated, and frequently it is. The handling of large research projects involving dozens of participants, tens of thousands of dollars, and a large amount of the firm's resources can be a complex task. The use of flow charts, loading charts, PERT networks, computers, or other tools of scientific management is occasionally necessary.

Marketing-research managers must not become so absorbed in the control of individual projects that they neglect the management of the research as a whole. If they do, direction of the marketing-research program will go by default to the individual or department making the loudest demands for the services of the researchers. Often a formal system is needed to help the director establish priorities for various projects and ration resources between competing users of market research.

Flow Charts

A venerable tool of business management applicable to the design and control of marketing-research projects, is the flow chart. A *flow chart* is a schematic diagram of a sequence of events from beginning to end of a project. Generally it includes the alternative paths through which the project may flow and between which the designer must choose. The chart also serves as a reminder of the tasks that may have to be performed at various points and forces the designer to order the various elements of the

---

[19] Philip Kotler, *Marketing Management: Analysis, Planning, and Control,* third ed., (Englewood Cliffs, N.J.: Prentice-Hall, 1977) is a good example.

Figure 2-3   A Typical Logical-Flow Chart for a Research Project

Source: Adapted from James H. Myers and Coskun Samli, "Management Control of Marketing Research," *Journal of Marketing Research*, **6**:3 (August 1969), p. 272.

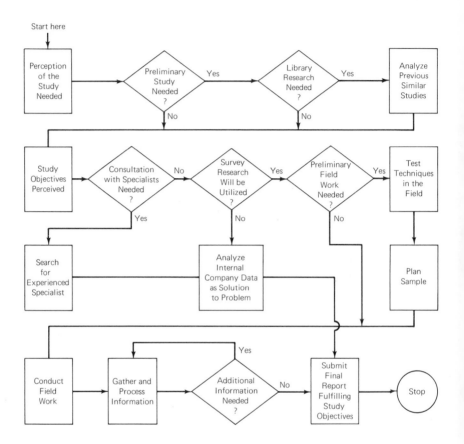

project with respect to both sequence and time. An example of logical-flow analysis as it might be applied to marketing-research design and control is shown in Figure 2-3.

Project Evaluation

Both the researcher who prepares it and the manager who uses it should know how to evaluate the outcome of marketing research. By mastering the art of criticism, the producer is better able to design and execute research projects. By being able to critique the research, the user can better apply it. Decisions based on misunderstood or improperly evaluated information can be bad ones.

Errors

No research apparatus will consistently yield perfect results in the social sciences. Economics and business are no exception. There is just too much

Table 2-5   **Summary of Common Research Errors**

Data Collection: Inquiry	*Data Collection: Secondary Data*
Statistical errors	Nonrepresentative data
Questionnaire errors	Unreliable data
Interviewer errors	
Respondent errors	
Data Collection: Observation	*Data Reduction*
Instrumentation error	Coding mistakes
Operational error	Transcription errors
Nonrepresentative subjects	Editing oversights
	Nonmetric data confused with metric data
Data Analysis	*Report Preparation*
Wrong tools	Typographical errors
Nonmetric data confused with metric data	Misplaced emphasis
Erroneous assumptions	Bad choice of words
Programming errors	Omissions
Mathematical errors	

going on out there that we haven't yet isolated or don't yet understand. Even if this weren't so, we would still be handicapped by imperfect tools. We cannot always measure with accuracy. Our analytical methods often prove inadequate. Budget and time constraints frequently prevent us from doing what needs to be done.

When we study what goes on in the marketplace, we face the hazard of many errors. Some are unavoidable. Random error (the luck of the draw), associated with sample data, is illustrative. The trick is to avoid error where possible and to recognize, minimize, and estimate it when it cannot be precluded. Recognition comes from technical competence and experience. Minimization comes from imaginative design, careful execution, and large samples. Estimation comes from inferential statistics, when applicable, and judgment.

Table 2-5 summarizes research errors. The table is included not to intimidate the potential user nor to engage in jargon-mongering, but to illustrate the problem and to alert the reader. The errors that are listed will be explored in detail as we progress through the book.

Checklists

The checklist in Exhibit 2-2 provides a guide to research evaluation. It is useful in criticizing the finished product or the design before the actual research has started. The list can also be applied as the project unfolds, and errors can often be detected and eliminated during the research process.

Another example of the use of checklists was shown in the second half of Exhibit 2-1. Although that document was designed mainly for evaluating research requests, it can also serve as a bench mark for judging the completed project.

Exhibit 2-2   **A Guide to Research Evaluation**

Characteristic	Completely Incompetent (1)	Poor (2)	Mediocre (3)	Good (4)	Excellent (5)
1. Problem is clearly stated					
2. Hypotheses are clearly stated					
3. Problem is significant					
4. Assumptions are clearly stated					
5. Limitations of the study are stated					
6. Important terms are defined					
7. Relationship of the problem to previous research is made clear					
8. Research design is described fully					
9. Research design is appropriate for the solution of the problem					
10. Research design is free of specific weaknesses					
11. Population and sample are described					
12. Method of sampling is appropriate					
13. Data-gathering methods or procedures are described					
14. Data-gathering methods or procedures are appropriate to the solution of the problem					
15. Data-gathering methods or procedures are utilized correctly					
16. Validity and reliability of the evidence gathered are established					
17. Appropriate methods are selected to analyzed the data					
18. Methods utilized in analyzing the data are applied correctly					
19. Results of the analysis are presented clearly					
20. Conclusions are clearly stated					
21. Conclusions are substantiated by the evidence presented					
22. Generalizations are confined to the population from which the sample was drawn					
23. Report is clearly written					
24. Report is logically organized					
25. Tone of the report displays an unbiased, impartial scientific attitude					

Source: Stephen Isaac and William B. Michael, *Handbook in Research and Evaluation* (San Diego: Robert R. Knapp, 1971), p. 156.

Program Evaluation

Again, one must not let the trees obstruct the view of the forest. The research program as a whole should be evaluated by the research manager. He or she may do it alone or invoke the aid of a committee.

Advisory Committees   The market-research program should be periodically reviewed to ensure that the projects being undertaken are those most relevant to the objectives of the firm. Meyers and Samli argue that a marketing-research advisory committee is the best instrument for this purpose.

Such a committee would, ideally, be composed of representatives of all the departments that use market research (for example, advertising, sales, product-planning, brand-management, and distribution personnel). Its task would be to identify the problem areas of greatest importance to the company as a whole, to direct the research department's attention to the information needs in these areas, and to assign priorities to these needs.[20] The advisory committee need not attempt to evaluate individual research projects or be concerned with method or research designs. Its purpose is simply to provide overall direction for the research program.

Audits   A periodic audit is a useful substitute for, or supplement to, the research advisory committee. The purpose of the audit is to evaluate the efficiency of the marketing-research program and, again, its relevance to the objectives of the firm. A typical audit asks such questions as:

> Does the research program serve the objectives of the firm?
>
> Are research resources being used where they will do the most good?
>
> Is the information provided by the research being used by the line managers?
>
> Are schedules being met?
>
> Are costs being controlled?
>
> Is the research budget inadequate or excessive?
>
> What is the return on investment?
>
> Are the researchers using appropriate and modern techniques?

Obviously, the auditor must be independent of the research group and should report directly to a senior executive. Ideally, he should be from outside the marketing department, and preferably from outside the firm. A formal audit report should be prepared that includes both findings and recommendations. After a reasonable amount of time—say, six months—has elapsed, a check should be made to determine if the research program has been modified in accordance with the recommendations, and, if not, why not.

Problems

1   Would marketing research be relevant to (a) the Pepsi Cola Company, (b) the U.S. Department of Commerce, (c) an industralized farm? If not, explain why not.

---

[20] James H. Myers and A. Coskun Samli, "Management Control of Marketing Research," *Journal of Marketing Research*, **6**:3 (August 1969), p. 275.

2   Where would you insert the MR function in a chain of department stores, such as Macy's or the Broadway?

3   When Ferdinand Hauslein, Jr., became the director of marketing for Neiman-Marcus, the Dallas-based specialty store chain, his first goal was the establishment of a strong research function. List the tasks he should have attended to at once.

4   Prepare a set of criteria for evaluating research requests at the Buick Division, General Motors Corp.

5   Firm A, which is planning to introduce a new product, must choose between several mutually exclusive product variations. Management has identified various alternatives, estimated the possible outcomes for each, and assigned probabilities to them. The best expected value for the new product is a profit of $985,000. However, management feels it could make a better decision if it had certain information that could be obtained by marketing research. In fact, it estimates that this information would increase the expected value of the new product to $1,200,000 and would virtually preclude the possibility of a disastrous error in judgment. What is the maximum amount management should authorize for the research project, and why?

6   How might you judge the value of each of the following: (a) a proposed study of price elasticity for the Kinney Shoe Company and (b) the marketing-research program at Mattel (a toy manufacturer). Specify what methods you would use and explain why they would be appropriate.

7   What sort of data would you need to carry out the value analyses asked for in problem 6? How might it be obtained?

8   How might the Columbia Yacht Corporation use cost-benefit analysis to select among three alternative designs for a survey of boat-owners? Assume that the objective of the survey is to determine the demographic, economic, and selected behavioral characteristics of boat-buyers.

9   A proposed research project will cost $35,000. The marketing decision the project will facilitate involves the use of a new promotional strategy. If it is successful, it is expected to increase profits by $180,000. If it is unsuccessful, profits will drop by $200,000. A management consensus gives the promotional change a 70 percent chance of success. The experience of the market-research department indicates that research will correctly identify a superior promotional strategy 80 percent of the time, and an inferior strategy will be correctly identified 90 percent of the time. Estimate the net value of the research.

10   Cite some errors that might emerge in the Columbia Yacht study, described in problem 8.

Chapter 3
Research Design

Key Concepts

Design Process
> The steps that lead from problem definition to the final research report

Problem Definition
> The pre-design task of diagnosing and specifying the research problem

Research Method
> One taxonomy of alternative research methods

Data Requirements
> Finding and processing the fuel of marketing research

Business Decision
> The make-or-buy, schedule, and budget decisions

Key Terms

exploratory research	causal method
hypothesis	comparative method
null hypothesis	ex post facto method
historical method	true experimental method
descriptive method	quasi experimental method
developmental method	action method
case and field method	make-or-buy decision
correlational method	

Anatomy of Research Design

Design Process

The anatomy of research design is shown in Figure 3-1. The actual design process, which is preceded by problem definition, tends to follow these

Figure 3-1   **Anatomy of Research Design**

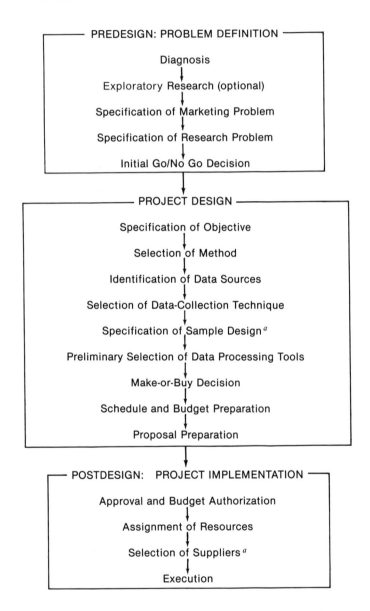

PREDESIGN: PROBLEM DEFINITION

Diagnosis

Exploratory Research (optional)

Specification of Marketing Problem

Specification of Research Problem

Initial Go/No Go Decision

PROJECT DESIGN

Specification of Objective

Selection of Method

Identification of Data Sources

Selection of Data-Collection Technique

Specification of Sample Design [a]

Preliminary Selection of Data Processing Tools

Make-or-Buy Decision

Schedule and Budget Preparation

Proposal Preparation

POSTDESIGN: PROJECT IMPLEMENTATION

Approval and Budget Authorization

Assignment of Resources

Selection of Suppliers [a]

Execution

[a] when applicable

steps. However, a creative researcher often deviates from the script. For instance, he or she might jump ahead and estimate the budget to see if the project is feasible. An elegant research design is of little value if the resources are unavailable to support it.

Certain elements of the design are often considered back in the problem-definition stage. Time and budget requirements or technical feasibility (method) may make the problem unmanageable from a research viewpoint. The alternatives are then narrowed: The use of MR can be rejected; the problem can be redefined to more manageable limits; or management can accept a lower level of performance, meaningless information, or less reliable data.

Design Variations   Designing marketing-research projects is largely an art. The design may specify the use of some very rigorous scientific tools. However, the preparation of a research project depends heavily on the imagination, ingenuity, and resources of the designer, as well as his or her knowledge of research technology. Seldom would two analysts propose exactly the same design to achieve a given research objective.

The same information can often be obtained by any of the several research techniques, although the quality and cost of the results and the speed with which they are gotten may vary considerably. For instance, a study of consumer preferences might be made using historical data, a survey, or experimentation—alone or in combination. The survey could use a random or nonrandom sample, or it could use objective or projective questions, which could be asked by mail, by telephone, or by personal interviews. The analysis could be confined to descriptive statistics, or multivariate analysis could be employed.

Each technique, singularly and together, has special virtues and deficiencies. No method is optimum under all circumstances. What is effective and economical one time may be useless or far too costly another time. Only when the needs of the decision-maker and the availability of the resources are known, can the analyst properly design a research project.

Line Management

Outside the academic community where research is the servant of scholarship, MR usually begins and ends the same place—with line management. Line management is the key to problem definition, which is the first step in good research. Line management is the recipient and final judge of the end results—the information produced by the study. Hence the designer is advised to remember the iron law of marketing research:

People would rather live with a problem they cannot solve, than accept a solution they cannot understand.

Line management should be part of the design process. Managers should not be burdened with the details, but they should understand the essence of the research plan. They should know what they will and won't get out of the project.

Predesign: Problem Definition

The researcher can be confronted with a clear-cut problem. This is especially so with research suppliers, such as Market Facts and the Gallup Organization, who typically receive orders for a precisely defined set of data.

Conversely, the researcher often faces an undefined, or poorly defined, problem: The line manager does not know what he wants. Or worse yet, he thinks he knows, but doesn't.

Neiman-Marcus provides an illustration. When the specialty store chain first established a serious research function, its manager was deluged with research requests. Store executives wanted image studies, psychographics, multivariate analysis, segmentation studies, and so forth. They'd acquired just enough research vocabulary to make specific requests. Unfortunately, vocabulary does not ensure insight. Means—the tools of the trade—were confused with ends. Fortunately, the research manager was sufficiently persuasive to convince the executives that their job was to help him define their marketing problems, while his job was to select the research tools.

Diagnosis

The first task is diagnosis. Researchers are analogous to medical doctors. They must first find out where the patient hurts.

The researcher should be familiar with the firm's market and its marketing program. (If not, some education is in order.) Familiarity allows the researcher to ask probing questions and provoke fruitful discussion with the client. The astute researcher will often identify a marketing problem before it is noticed by a line manager.

There is no standard procedure. On the contrary, the initial diagnosis is usually informal and unstructured. A request form, such as we saw in Exhibit 2-1, may be useful. However, forms and checklists can become straitjackets if not used with care.

Although the original inquiry should seldom be constrained, the problem should ultimately be defined in rather narrow terms. A broadly defined problem can be difficult to manage and yield findings that are too vague to translate into action; it can generate unreasonable expectations; it can also develop a ferocious appetite for resources.

Typically, the diagnosis will follow a pattern similar to the one seen in Exhibit 2-1. The diagnosis may be concluded several ways: Research may be rejected because the problem is too trivial, MR is inappropriate, the cost is too high, or the solution has suddenly been revealed by other means. Or research may clearly be in order. In this case, the problem definition stage moves to completion. Or the diagnosis may reveal only vague images. Exploratory research is then in order.

Exploratory Research

Occasionally the problem is so vague as to require exploratory research. The objective of the exploratory study is to bring the problem into focus and produce a rigorous definition.

An illustration of an explorative study would be the questioning of a small sample of consumers on their attitudes toward a particular brand or product class. The method used would probably be nondirective, using open-ended interviews or questionnaires. The goal might be to obtain insight into why the firm's product was not selling well. Although such a study would be unlikely to produce fully reliable results, it might give the researchers ideas that could be restated as hypotheses for further testing. For instance, research might show the respondents indicating a dislike for certain product features, the availability of substitutes at lower prices, or an inadequacy in distribution. This might suggest more extensive descriptive research—perhaps as an extension of the exploratory study—to determine if a significant portion of the market population was dissatisfied with a product characteristic, was sensitive to price, or was inadequately served by the firm's distribution system.

The exploratory study may allow the general problem, the decline in sales, to be redefined in a form that lends itself to more rigorous analysis and provides a basis for management action. The real point at issue may be, "What product characteristics are preferred by consumers?" "What is the product's price elasticity and optimum price?" or "How many retail outlets are needed to offer service comparable with that offered by competitors?" These are manageable questions, which can often be answered with precision.

Specification of the Marketing Problem

Diagnosis or exploratory research should lead to a clear statement of the marketing problem. This statement should be in line-management terms. For instance: Switch buyers from brands A and B to the firm's brand. Assign missionary salespersons to the five largest markets. Or optimize prices. (More examples are found in Table 3-1.)

The formulation of the marketing problem should be shared with the client—the fellow employee or customer the researcher is attempting to serve. Without the client's participation, there is little assurance that the research will be focused on the right problem. One can easily define problems that are intellectually exciting and technically challenging, but which are of no interest to management. Besides, getting line managers involved tends to get them committed. They are more likely to support the project and carefully consider its outcome if involved early in the process.

Specification of the Research Problem

In essence, the research problem is a restatement of the marketing problem in research terms. For instance, if the marketing problem is to optimize

Table 3-1 **The Problem Definition Process: Examples**

General Situation	→ Diagnosis →	→ Marketing Problem →	→ Research Problem
Market share is declining.	Customers are switching to brand A.	Reinforce brand loyalty.	Find out why brand A is preferred.
Sales are down.	Store traffic is down.	Build store traffic.	Find out why fewer people are visiting store.
Profit declined.	Big advertising compaign failed.	Design new ad campaign.	Evaluate alternative ads and media.
Product line is growing obsolete.	New product is needed.	Select new product for commercialization.	Evaluate alternative product designs.
Distribution is weak.	More stores are needed.	Insert new stores.	Evaluate prospective store locations.
A new product line is being introduced.	Promotional resources must be allocated to geographical markets.	Assign sales force and distribute local-advertising budget.	Identify and array high-sales-potential markets.
Personal-selling costs are high.	Salespersons spend a lot of time and money on travel.	Route salespersons more efficiently.	This is not a MR problem: It is a network problem and should be assigned to the operations research group.

price, the research problem would be to estimate the price elasticity of the product. (Other examples are found in Table 3-1.)

The nature of the design, the success of the project, the implementation of the findings, and sometimes the survival of the researcher hinge on this step. The research problem becomes the project objective. It must be manageable, obtainable, consistent with the marketing problem, and clearly understood by the client. If these criteria cannot be met, the project should probably be abandoned before it enters the design phase.

Research Objective and Method

Objective

The first step in the actual design process is to state the research objective. The research objective is simply the research problem which was specified during the problem definition stage.

The objective is both a challenge and a promise: It is the goal of the project and the researcher's commitment to the client. Should the objective not be achieved, the researcher stands to lose his credibility or possibly his job or customer.

The statement of objective is especially important when suppliers are involved. It tells the supplier what to produce. It tells the buyer what to expect for the money.

Often the research objective is framed as a hypothesis (H) for testing. A hypothesis is a tentative assumption made for argument or for testing. Examples:

> **H:**   The product's price is inelastic.[1]
> **H:**   Store A is preferred because of its high fashion image.
> **H:**   There is no difference in buyer preference between package X and package Y.
>
> **H:**   There is no difference in self-image between Toyota Celica and Datsun 280Z buyers.

The last two examples illustrate the null hypothesis, sometimes symbolized as "H_0." The *null hypothesis* assumes there is no difference between objects: Any differences observed between their respective data sets is a result of chance.

The advantage of the null hypothesis is that it lends itself to a number of testing techniques. These analytical tools, such as the chi square test, lead to the acceptance or rejection of the hypothesis. Hence, we can determine if one package is preferred to another, if the self-image of one brand's buyers are significantly different from another brand's buyers, etc.

---

[1] A large price increase would induce a small drop in sales. See any microeconomic text for discussion.

Method

Seldom will two research designers reach the same objective via identical routes. Usually, the need for information will yield to several techniques. The designer will usually choose the one he or she knows best.

Choice of method is dictated primarily by the information requirements and the availability of data. Secondarily, choice is governed by experience, skill, and the availability of time and resources.

The more common methods are shown in Table 3-2. The list should not be considered exhaustive. There are many variations and combinations of these techniques. New ones are being developed. In fact, Table 3-2 is but one taxonomy. There are others. This one introduces the reader to the basic methods, but like many such lists can induce tunnel vision. The trick in good research design is not to force the project into an established method, but to adapt old methods and new ideas to the problem at hand.

Data Requirements

Sources and Collection

Research feeds on data (though a cynic might argue that it feeds on money). The identification of sources and selection of the collection method are important steps in research design. The quality of the data that goes into a study largely determines the quality of information that comes out.

Data acquisition—the locating and collecting of information—is so important that the next few chapters are allocated to the subject. For now, just a few observations are in order.

First, the research designer should be familiar with the data sources. If this is not the case, some investigation is in order. The availability of raw (unprocessed) information, or the ability to generate it, will significantly determine the practicality, cost, and time of the project. For instance, if demographic data are required, they may be available at the local library. Acquisition would be relatively quick and cheap. If consumer attitudes must be measured, a survey of selected buyers may be required. This process could be complex, expensive, and time-consuming.

Second, the research method will largely determine where and how data are collected. If the preferred method demands information that is too hard to find or too costly to collect, an alternative will have to be used.

Third, management must often tell, or be told, how accurate the findings will be. The standards for accuracy can significantly influence this portion of the design. High accuracy requirements may demand that fresh data be collected, where moderate accuracy might permit the use of available information. Demographic data based on the 1970 census of population is illustrative. It's old, somewhat inaccurate, but readily available and cheap.

Sample Design

If a survey is in order, sample design will largely control accuracy. Large samples tend to give more reliable results than do small ones, but large samples cost more and take longer to collect and process.

The type of sample—probability, judgment, stratified, etc.—will influence accuracy, cost, and time. It will also determine one's ability to estimate the range of error which is always assumed to be present in sample data. Hence, sample design, when relevant, is an important element of research design.

Data Processing Tools

Raw data are generally confusing to the researcher and useless to the line manager. Hence, the research design usually calls for their reduction and analysis. Reduction (the summarizing of data) is typically done by computer. The preparation of the data for the computer and its subsequent processing should be cited in the design, and covered by the budget.

The excitement in research is largely in the analysis. Finding patterns and extracting meaning from a crazy quilt of data taxes the skills and imagination even of brilliant researchers. Analytical techniques have proliferated in recent years, thanks mainly to the diffusion of the electronic computer. There is a large and growing assortment from which to choose. This is not to say there is a solution for every analytical problem. Nor can we claim to have tools that are independent of data. On the contrary, most tools have a great appetite for the stuff.

The dependence of analytical tools on data is the main reason they should be considered during the design stage. The type of analysis one wants to do will largely determine the type and quantity of data which must be collected.

The assortment of analytical tools is suggested by the partial listing in Table 3-3. The choice of method is limited by the skill and imagination of the researcher, the extravagance of the data, and the state of the art.

The choice of analytical tools also impinges on the budget. Data costs money and more data are usually better than less. Most of the analytical tools require a computer, some consuming considerable computer time. Fortunately, the programs (instructions) telling the computer how to analyze the data need not be prepared by the researcher. Libraries of analytical programs are available for ready installation. Two examples are the Statistical Package for the Social Sciences (SPSS) and the BioMed Package (BMD).[2] Your college computer lab probably has one of these installed.

We develop the concepts and applications of these tools later. However, one point should be made before we move on: If the researcher is to prescribe an analytical method in the design, it may have to be defended.

---

[2] SPSS is available through the National Opinion Research Center at the University of Chicago. BMD is available through the Health Sciences Computing Facility at the University of California at Los Angeles.

Table 3-2 Nine Basic Methods of Research

Method	Purpose
Historical	To reconstruct the past objectively and accurately, often in relation to the tenability of an hypothesis.
Descriptive	To describe systematically a situation or area of interest factually and accurately.
Developmental	To investigate patterns and sequences of growth and/or change as a function of time.
Case and Field	To study intensively the background, current status, and environmental interactions of a given social unit: an individual group, institution, or community.
Correlational	To investigate the extent to which variations in one factor correspond with variation in one or more other factors based on correlation coefficients.
Causal-Comparative or Ex Post Facto	To investigate possible cause-and effect relationships by observing some existing consequence and searching back through the data for plausible causal factors.
True Experimental	To investigate possible cause-and-effect relationships by exposing one or more experimental groups to one or more treatment conditions and comparing the results to one or more groups not receiving the treatment (random assignment being essential).
Quasi-Experimental	To approximate the conditions of the true experiment in a setting that does not allow the control and/or manipulation of all relevant variables. The researcher must clearly understand what compromises exist in the internal and external validity of his design and proceed within these limitations.
Action	To develop new skills or new approaches and to solve problems with direct application to the applied, e.g., the marketplace.

Table 3-2 **Nine Basic Methods of Research** (*cont'd.*)

Method	Example
Historical	Berg's postmortem of the Rheingold defeat in the West Coast beer market. *Objective:* Learn what mistakes were made.
Descriptive	Kinelogic's study of the structure of the industry and market for sound-filmstrip equipment. *Objective:* Evaluate the opportunities, segments, and competition.
Developmental	Cessna's study of the demand for a small executive jet—the pattern and growth of sales over time. *Objective:* Build a model to estimate future sales.
Case and Field	The Sorensen Group's study of the Cleveland electorate. *Objective:* Discover how to reelect Mayor Stokes.
Correlational	Jurgensen Grocery Company's study of the relationship between store sales and external factors, e.g., population and income. *Objective:* Build a model to evaluate prospective sites.
Causal-Comparative or Ex Post Facto	Gallup and Robinson's study of the decline of Westinghouse's loss of market share. *Objective:* Determine cause.
True Experimental	AT&T's experiment with alternative survey questionnaires using truly random samples of respondents. *Objective:* Choose most efficient survey method.
Quasi-Experimental	Pacific Telephone and Telegraph Company's experiment with advertising as a means of demarketing directory assistance calls. (Test market was not randomly chosen.) *Objective:* Develop a new technique for product evaluation.
Action	The Ajax Advertising Agency's development of a product evaluation model. *Objective:* Develop a new technique for product evaluation.

Source: A portion of this table is drawn from Stephen Isaac and William B. Michael, *Handbook in Research and Evaluation* (San Diego: Edits/Robert R. Knapp, 1971), p. 14 and is reproduced with permission. All rights reserved. The Berg case is found in Thomas L. Berg, *Mismarketing* (Garden City, NY: Doubleday (Anchor Books), 1971). All other examples are in Walter B. Wentz (Ed.), *Cases in Marketing Research* (New York: Harper & Row, 1975) or in this volume.

Table 3-3 Common Analytical Tools

Tools	Purpose	Examples	Typical Applications
Descriptive Statistics	Summarize data.	Mean, median, mode, range, standard deviation.	Compute the average age of a store's customers.
Inferential Statistics	Generalize findings, based on sample data, to a population and estimate error.	Sample mean, median. . . . Standard error of the mean, confidence interval.	Estimate market shares from a sample of consumer purchase diaries.
Tests of Difference	Determine if two or more sets of objects are significantly different with respect to some characteristic. Also, hypothesis testing.	Chi-square test, U-test, analysis of variance, Spearman test, t-test, F-test.	Determine if married sales-persons perform better than single ones.
Measures of Dependence	Measure statistical dependence between variables.	Correlation analysis, regression analysis, discriminant analysis, canonical analysis.	Estimate advertising's effect on sales.
Measures of Association	Measure statistical association between variables or between objects. Group variables or group objects into sets.	Factor analysis, cluster analysis, multidimensional scaling, nonmetric scaling, latent structure analysis.	Group customers according to life styles.
Qualitative Analysis	Reveal attitudes, beliefs, and behavior. Frame hypothesis for qualitative analysis.	Common sense, economic and behavioral theory.	Determine possible reasons for the rejection of a male cosmetic.

Line managers, like most of us, tend to be uncomfortable with things they don't understand. Few of them are familiar with the more exotic tools of data analysis.

Business Decisions

Several business issues must be confronted in research design, even when the designer works in the noncommercial sector. These are the make-or-buy decision, the schedule, and the budget.

Make-or-Buy

All or part of a given marketing study can be performed by a vendor. Numerous firms sell computer time, market data, and the services of interviewers, statisticians, and analysts. Research consultants—outsiders who participate in the design and management of the project—are also available from both college faculties and commercial houses such as Arthur D. Little, Inc.; A. C. Nielsen; and Booz, Allen, and Hamilton. These institutions often serve as full service suppliers, taking responsibility for both the design and execution of the project.

Economies of scale and specialization may allow the outsider to perform tasks for less than it would cost the sponsor to do the work. This is especially true for small and medium-size companies that cannot maintain large research departments. Another advantage is that when services or entire studies are purchased from a vendor, the work is often done for a fixed price or a time-and-materials charge with a specified maximum. This allows the user to predict the total research cost with greater precision than would have been possible had the work been done within the firm. Also, the vendor's charges terminate with the completion of the project.

Another argument in favor of outsiders, especially consultants, is their objectivity. Objectivity is not so much a matter of expertise as it is one of detachment. The outsider is usually divorced from the personal loyalties and conflicts that develop within the firm. He also has nothing to gain from political maneuvering. At the same time he usually has a fresher—or at least different—perspective on the problem; his experience tends to be broader and he is less likely to be affected by industry folklore. Of course if the consultant has a vested interest in the outcome of the research—as, for example, when an advertising agency does a study of a client's advertising program—one can hardly expect a high degree of objectivity.

If the decision is made to buy all or a portion of the work from a supplier, a set of specifications is usually prepared. The specifications indicate what is to be provided, often how the task is to be done, and a schedule. The specifications are then sent to qualified suppliers along with an invitation to bid on the job.

The qualification of vendors rests on the buyer's judgment and experience, and on the reputation of the supplier. Sometimes an evaluation form, such as is shown in Exhibit 3-1, is used.

Exhibit 3-1   **Supplier Evaluation Form**

Project Control Number _____
SUPPLIER EVALUATION FORM—Surveys
Supplier: Date:
Project Description: Project:
                                        Project #

(Evaluate each item below and mark with "X". See Implement. Sect. as needed.)	*Distinguished Himself*	*Okay*	*Source of Concern*	*Doesn't Apply*
1. Marketing Insight				
2. Fundamental Design				
3. Questionnaire Construction				
4. Field Supervision				
5. Tab Design				
6. Analysis				
7. Report Organization				
8. Quality of Report Writing				
9. Quality of Presentation Materials				
10. Personal Presentation				
11. Delivery Time				
12. Cost Estimate				

Explain items checked as "Distinguished Himself" and "Source of Concern" (use reference numbers).

                          Signature: _____

                               Title: _____

Source: From "Use of Marketing Research Contractors," *by Lawrence D. Gibson.* In Handbook of Marketing Research *by R. Ferber* (ed.). Used with permission of the McGraw Hill Book Company. (New York: McGraw-Hill, 1974).

Before departing from the subject of research suppliers, we should issue a warning. In the words of one of the past decade's most successful marketers:

> The effective ones [consultants] are the one-man shows. The institutional ones are disastrous. They waste time, cost money, demoralize and distract your best people, and don't solve problems. They are people who borrow your watch to tell you what time it is and then walk off with it.

Exhibit 3-2   **Research Project Schedule**

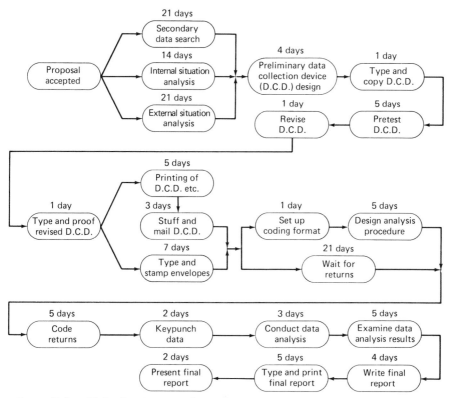

Source: Robert W. Joselyn, *Designing the Marketing Research Project* (New York: Petrocelli/ Charter, 1977), p. 142.

Don't use them under any circumstances. Not even to keep your stockholders and directors quiet. It isn't worth it.[3]

This assessment may be as biased as it is harsh. Many of the large suppliers are capable of doing a good job. However, it brings us to an important point: The quality of a supplier's work is ultimately determined by the quality of the people assigned to the job. This is especially true for the project manager, who will guide the work to successful completion or disaster.

Schedule

When a researcher asks a client when the information is needed, the answer is often, "Yesterday." Line managers sometimes invoke MR in desperation. Time can be very precious and MR can fall victim to the tyranny of urgency. Even when the research request is not submitted in panic, a due date is still appropriate.

[3] Robert Townsend, *Up the Organisation* (Greenwich, CT: Fawcett, 1970), p. 86.

Some sort of a schedule is required for three reasons: first, to determine the time needed to execute the project; second, to assure the project is completed in time to be of use to the client; and third, to manage the flow of activities.

Schedules vary from an informal assignment of dates and activities to elaborate PERT[4] networks. An example was shown in Exhibit 3-2.

Budget

A researcher with an unlimited budget and license to meddle in all of the firm's affairs would be as happy as God in France. Unfortunately, such jobs do not exist. The budget constraint is a fact of organizational life.

The cost of the research must be debited to some person, department, or customer. Hence, the cost should be estimated and included in the proposal as a budget.

The cost of marketing research can usually be predicted with a fair amount of precision. In general, total project costs can be consistently estimated within ± 10 percent; the error in these estimates is usually less than 5 percent.

Research costs include expenditures for labor, material, and services. Labor costs include the salaries of the project manager, the analysts, statisticians, interviewers, mathematicians, psychologists, computer programmers, secretaries, and other in-house personnel whose time is charged directly to the project. Material costs include expenditures for travel, forms (such as questionnaires), IBM cards or magnetic tape, postage, telephone service, and so on. They usually account for less than one-third of the total cost. The cost of services includes charges for computer time and consumer-panel data, as well as fees for interviewers and consultants who are not part of the firm's regular staff. Such services are often used when the firm cannot justify full-time employment of the special equipment or personnel needed for a project.

An overhead charge—or "burden"—is often assigned to cover costs which cannot be traced to, and do not vary directly with, individual marketing studies. Overhead costs can be distributed among the research projects in a number of ways. One method is to add an overhead charge for each hour of direct labor charged to the project. A typical rate is $4 to $10 per hour, depending on the size of the overhead accounts. Another popular method is to charge to each project an amount equal to a fixed percentage (typically 20 to 50 percent) times the total direct expenses—the labor, material, and service costs—traceable to the project.[5]

---

[4] Planning Evaluation and Review Technique. This sophisticated method of project scheduling and control is described in several marketing texts. For example, see E. Jerome McCarthy, *Basic Marketing*, fifth ed. (Homewood, IL: Irwin, 1975), pp. 544–546.

[5] For a further discussion of the computation of marketing costs and their allocation, see Wentz and Eyrich, *Marketing: Theory and Application*, ch. 4.

Proposal

The research design usually emerges as a proposal. The proposal states the objective, method, schedule, and cost of the project. The proposal is then submitted to the client for approval and budget authorization. The client may be a line manager within the firm, a research committee, or a customer.

Illustration

A specific example will help bring the problem of research design into focus. Exhibit 3-3 describes a research project designed to help the management of a travel-trailer company make certain marketing decisions with respect to its planned entry into the medium-priced trailer market. The material in this exhibit represents a plan of action for the study. It is the end product of the cycle of design tasks discussed earlier.

Before submitting the plan, the researchers held several meetings with the client's marketing executives in order to define the problem precisely and to learn what kind of information the company needed. Exploratory research proved unnecessary, since the executives already knew what kind of decisions had to be made. The basic problem—how to successfully penetrate the medium-priced trailer market—had in effect been defined by an earlier management decision.

The client, which held a dominant position in the luxury travel-trailer market, had elected to enter the medium-price market in order to expand its total sales and make better use of its technological, manufacturing, and marketing capabilities. Certain economies of scale, especially on the marketing side, indicated that this type of diversification would be highly profitable.

Having made the commitment to enter this new market, management had to make decisions on product characteristics (such as the trailer lengths), prices (keeping it within the $2,500 to $4,000 range), and promotion. As the retailers dealt primarily with a local clientele—trailer buyers tend to confine their shopping to dealers within 30 miles of their homes—the client needed information on the strength of the local markets in order to determine how to distribute its resources over the national market. In addition, the firm's advertising agency needed a profile of medium-priced trailer buyers to aid it in preparing copy and selecting media. The necessary information was specified in Part I of the research proposal, "Objectives."

The next task was to identify and evaluate the available data sources and specify the method. Since trailer-owner registration lists, as well as lists of trailer manufacturers, were both available and inexpensive, it seemed probable that the needed data could best be gathered by means of a mail survey of medium-price trailer owners and written inquiries to manufacturers. A visit to the publishers of several trade journals also seemed in order; not only were such people a good data source, but they had a good perspective on the market. The nature of the data available from surveys and inquiries made a statistical evaluation, using techniques such as sampling

Exhibit 3-3   **A Research Proposal**

(714) 624-1481

Claremont Research Associates

POST OFFICE BOX 266   CLAREMONT, CALIFORNIA 91711, U.S.A.

Proposal for a Study of the Medium-Price Travel-Trailer Market

I. Objectives

1. Describe the $2,500–$4,000 travel-trailer market in the United States.
   a. Determine its size—the number of units sold and the total dollar volume.
   b. Determine the geographical distribution of unit sales.
   c. Determine product features and their distribution by retail trailer price.
   d. Determine the distribution of prices.
   e. Determine the portion of new trailer sales involving trade-ins.

2. Determine a personal profile of buyers; include the following characteristics:
   a. Age
   b. Family status (i.e., married, etc.)
   c. Occupation
   d. Income
   e. Family size
   f. Brand of automobile
   g. Hobbies
   h. Use of trailer (i.e., fishing trips, etc.)

3. Determine the distribution of the following factors involved in sales:
   a. The number of dealers visited before a purchase is made
   b. The time between the first visit and the purchase
   c. Rental or dealer demonstrations during the shopping period

4. Determine the order of motivating influences affecting the choice of a brand.

II. Method

1. Obtain the following information from the client:
   a. Vehicle (trailer) registration lists for states, where available
   b. A list of trailer brands to be included in the study
   c. A list of trailer manufacturers
   d. A list of its own dealers

2. Visit publishers of travel-trailer trade journals.

3. Execute a randomized (by registered owner) and stratified (by state) sample survey of trailer owners.
   a. Use the client's list of registered owners as the population universe.
   b. Use a mail questionnaire to collect raw data.
      1. Review the questionnaire with the client before mailing.
      2. Include an inducement, to be furnished by the client, with half the question-naires.
   c. Mail 200 questionnaires to evaluate the questionnaire and survey design before executing the bulk of the survey.
   d. Mail 2,000 questionnaires, plus as many additional questionnaires as required to produce a minimum of 200 statistically useful replies.

4. Analyze the survey data and summarize it in tabular or graphical form.

Exhibit 3-3 A Research Proposal (*cont'd.*)

5. Correlate the survey data with economic and demographic data for the regional markets, using linear regression analysis.

6. Collect literature from manufacturers and summarize the data.

7. Prepare a formal written report and give the client a personal briefing.

III. Schedule and Price
1. The study will be completed within 120 days of receipt of the client's purchase order.

2. The price is $X plus direct expenses. Expenses will not exceed $X and will be fully documented.

Submitted by W. B. Wentz and G. I. Eyrich

Source: A proposal for a study of the medium-priced travel-trailer market submitted by Claremont Research Associates to a major recreational vehicle manufacturer.

and regression analysis, feasible. The data sources and techniques to be used were described in Part II of the proposal, "Method."

At this point the resources needed for the study—in this case, the two consultants themselves, a research assistant, a secretary, and some computer time—could be specified. The approximate cost of the work and the length of time needed to produce results were included in the "Schedule and Price" section of the proposal. The research project's design was then complete. The final plan of action was submitted to the client and approved by its vice-president of marketing. Work was then begun.

Problems

1 List the sequence of events that typically precedes the project design process.

2 List the sequence of events that is typically included in the research design process.

3 Discuss briefly the role of the line manager in research design.

4 Explain the function of exploratory research.

5 State each of the following assumptions in the form of a null hypothesis: (a) Sears's customers are like J. C. Penney's customers with respect to income. (b) Raising the price of Chevrolets by $100 will not significantly reduce sales.

6 Specify the data requirements for testing the two hypotheses (problem 5).

7 Specify the data processing tools for testing the two hypotheses (problems 5 and 6).

8 Prepare a brief research proposal for determining student recreational-reading preferences on your campus. (Such a project would aid the bookstore in stocking trade books and magazines.)

Part 1
Summary

The first job of research management is to decide if and where MR fits into the system. If research is made part of the marketing mix, management must then insert it somewhere in the organization, assign responsibility for its direction, and provide a budget.

Because research can be a drain on the firm's resources, an ordering of priorities is necessary. A request-evaluation procedure is needed to identify and rank those projects that warrant attention. However, ultimate authorization usually rests on value analysis.

Value analysis is a critical step in project selection. There are several criteria. The ideal one is expected value, which can be estimated with either classical or Bayesian statistics.

Cost-benefit analysis can be invoked when the value of the marketing decision cannot be expressed in dollars. It admits the dollar-cost of the research but substitutes nonmonetary values for the benefit.

Project selection is followed by control and evaluation. Control requires standards be set, performance be monitored, and resources be reallocated as needed. A timetable and budget are both important.

Both the researcher and the line manager must evaluate results. Criticism makes the researcher better able to design and execute projects, and it allows the manager to better use the information. Marketing research is seldom error-free, but the extent of error should be minimized so far as time, technique, and resources permit, and estimated so management's confidence in, and use of, the information is consistent with its quality.

Problem definition is the foundation of good research design. The first step in problem definition is diagnosis. The marketing situation which precipitated the research request must be diagnosed and then specified as a manageable problem. This task may require exploratory research, which serves to focus the problem and produce questions or hypotheses for further study.

The final step in problem definition is the stipulation of the research problem. This tells us what information is needed and then becomes the objective of the research design. The design process starts with the statement of objective, followed by the identification of data sources, selection of data collection method, specification of sample design (when applicable), and the preliminary selection of data processing tools. These steps are followed by the business decisions: the make-or-buy decision, scheduling, and budget preparation. Finally, the design is assembled in the form of a research proposal.

The proposal, containing the objective, method, schedule, and cost of the project, is submitted to the client for approval and budget authorization. If approved and funded, work begins.

CASE STUDY 1

Kawasaki Motors Corporation: A Media Evaluation Study

Walter B. Wentz

Kawasaki Motors Corporation is a typical Japanese trading company. The firm, which is a wholly owned subsidiary of Kawasaki Heavy Industries of Japan, is responsible for the marketing of Kawasaki motorcycles and related products in the United States.[1] An example of a Kawasaki product is shown in the photograph on the following page.

As we know it today, the American motorcycle market is a creation of the Japanese. Before their arrival in the early 1960s, the U.S. market was small, offered a limited selection of models, and was dominated by Harley-Davidson. Off-road riding, formal competition, and respectability were virtually unknown. Customers wore police uniforms or dirty leather jackets. Image and sales were less than outstanding.

Mr. Honda changed all this. His story, in both Japan and the United States, is a classic of entrepreneurship. He is a giant in the class of Ford (United States) and Krupp (Germany). Today his firm sells more than half the motorcycles used in America, Honda is a household word, and a police record is no longer prerequisite to membership in a motorcycle club. Harley-Davidson, which now has less than 5 percent of the market, is selling more units than it did before the Japanese entry.

Kawasaki appeared to be in a perennial battle for third place with Suzuki, both holding about a 10 percent share of the market. Yamaha ranked number two. Kawasaki Motors' president, Mr. Yoji Hamawaki, wanted to be number two, especially if he could get there by selling more large street-cycles. The big street-cycles, like the one in the photograph, yield significantly more profit than the small off-road and enduro bikes, or the small (below 400 cc) street-cycles.

To this end, Alan Masek, general manager, and Dale Stevenson, director of marketing, began looking at alternative advertising media. Direct-mail advertising appeared attractive. So did the possibility of offering a customer incentive to induce prospects to visit a Kawasaki dealer. Neither was being used by competitors, and innovation was in order if Yamaha and Suzuki were to be displaced.

---

[1] Kawasaki built a factory in Lincoln, Nebraska, in 1977, but still imports many of its motorcycles from Japan.

A Kawasaki Street Bike

Source: Courtesy of Kawasaki Motors Corporation, USA.

Marketing Decision

1   Accept or reject direct-mail advertising.
2   Accept or reject the use of a buyer incentive, such as a free gift for test-riding a new Kawasaki or a premium tied in with the purchase of a new motorcycle.

Information Needs

1   The cost-benefit ratio of direct-mail advertising.
2   The cost-benefit ratio of the incentives.

A study of the large-motorcycle buyer, made by Claremont Research Associates, had shown the small motorcycle to be the entry vehicle. Large cycles were invariably trade-up purchases.

Dealers are not known for their cooperation or business acumen.

Kawasaki acquires data on each of its customers from its warranty cards.

R. L. Polk and Company, Detroit, collects motorcycle registrations and compiles market statistics. It sells name lists for two to seven cents per name, depending on quantities and amount of discrimination. Names can be selected by Zip code, city, state, and region, as well as by brand and model of motorcycle purchased.

Assignment   Design a research project that will yield the information needed by management.

Part 2
Data Acquisition

Introduction

> *Be careful of reading the writing on the wall, it may be a forgery.*
>
> —N. Kahn[1]

Data acquisition is usually the first step in the execution of a research design. Generally, more is better than less. Data which are available quickly and economically are best of all, assuming they meet the tests of relevance and reliability.

As research is fueled with data, a knowledge of data sources is the keystone to a researcher's success. Sources vary from field to field. However, we can prescribe some guidelines to their location and their use. We can also specify some sources and search procedures that are useful to almost all marketing-research people.

An important institution in the research business is the research supplier, and the quest for data often starts there. Hence, Chapter 4 is devoted to both sources and suppliers.

If data are not readily available, the researcher must generate his or her own information, usually with a survey. Surveys are common in both commercial and social marketing research. Selecting a survey method, designing a questionnaire, recognizing and minimizing errors, and administering the survey are critical skills. They are the subject of Chapter 5, which concludes our introduction to data acquisition.

---

[1] As quoted in Lee Adler and Charles S. Mayer, *Managing the Marketing Research Function* (Chicago: American Marketing Association, 1977), p. 121.

Chapter 4
Sources and
Suppliers

Key Concepts

Taxonomy of Data
The common method of classifying data

Data Quality
The variation in the quality of data, some of which is not highly reliable

Data Sources
Where to find prerecorded information

Consumer Panels
Using a group of people as a source of information on purchase behavior, media response, or product usage

Research Suppliers
The role of outside specialists in market research

Key Terms

primary data
secondary data
prerecorded data
original data
GIGO
mother-in-law research
net change
gross change
consumer-purchase panel
store-audit panel
media-measurement panel
audiometer
product-testing panel

tracking study
laboratory panel
galvanic skin response (GSR)
tachtistoscope
pupilometer
brain wave analysis
voice pitch analysis (VOPAN)
preview houses
field houses
survey supervisor
technology dissemination
    centers
syndication

The Data

Taxonomy

Data can be classified according to who collected them and why they were collected:

Primary data:	data collected by, or expressly for, the firm
Secondary data:	data collected by an outsider, not expressly for the firm
Prerecorded data:	data collected for some other purpose, before the study; such data are also called "historical data," and can be primary or secondary
Original data:	data collected expressly for the study at hand.

Prerecorded data are usually the cheapest and most readily available, especially if they are within the firm. The federal government is by far the richest source of prerecorded data. Virtually every federal agency gathers, records, and disseminates information. These secondary data are readily available. Unfortunately, prerecorded data are often inadequate, outdated, or not properly aggregated for the job at hand, making original data a necessity.

Quality

The results of any research depend heavily on the quality of the data. In the jargon of computer programmers, "garbage in, garbage out" (GIGO). Once truly bad data are in, no amount of wit, wisdom, memory, or inspiration can salvage the study. The findings must be scrapped, and the research begun again, or the project terminated.

Seldom will data have the purity of a Gregorian chant. We usually accept some error, or at least recognize its likelihood. In fact, good research will specify the range of error associated with its findings. This is legitimate, honest, and a sign of technical competence. When we collect the data ourselves, we should recognize the possibilities of error, and minimize it through careful research design and well-supervised data collection.

When we use data collected by somebody else, we are dependent upon the skill and integrity of our source, so here we are most vulnerable. A statement of quality seldom accompanies the information provided by others. This does not say the data are unreliable and useless, only that they should be applied with caution.

The assumption that the original data contained no errors is implicit in the results of many research projects. Even the confidence intervals frequently included in statistical analyses seldom allow for errors in the original data, save for the random errors of statistical sampling.

If observations of GNP, population, retail sales, and so on are presented without qualifications, they are generally accepted at face value. There is, unfortunately, a naive tendency to accept printed numbers without question.

The respectability of the source is not sufficient reason to blindly accept data. For instance, federal agencies report population, income, consumer spending, and price levels to a fraction of a percent, which is patently ridiculous. Such variables cannot be consistently estimated within several percentage points of their true values. (Some agencies, such as the Bureau of the Census, provide rules for calculating the confidence intervals of their data.) Kuznet's study of national-income accounts concluded that the government's estimates of the gross product of the construction, water-transportation, real-estate, and direct-service industries were in error by at least 30 percent.[1] Yet authors, scholars, researchers, and other users of government statistics continue to accept them at face value.

In estimating short-run changes, such as the monthly change in retail sales or the purchasing power of the dollar, government satisticians are on particularly shaky ground, yet they are enthralled by a meaningless pursuit of pinpoint accuracy. Published data are full of illustrations: Retail sales are recorded to the nearest dollar; population values are given to the nearest one-millionth of a percent.[2] Such numbers imply extreme precision, when in fact they are often crude estimates.

A number of popular assumptions are not supported, in any consistent fashion, by empirical findings. One is the belief that errors in observation cancel one another out. This assumption is safe only under restricted conditions—such as randomization—and only for certain data. Frequently, such errors are cumulative instead of self-cancelling.

Another misconception is that the most recent data are always the most accurate. Generally this is true, but the exceptions are too common to ignore. Changes in personnel, increases in the complexity of the observed phenomenon, and shifts in respondents' attitudes can decrease the quality of information. Still another fallacy is the idea that the integrity of government statisticians is unimpeachable. This is not so. They are just as capable of lies or shoddy work as members of other groups. Outright fraud or the representation of crude guesswork as precise estimation is often practiced in the name of the national interest. One has only to look as far as the military's claims of victory in Vietnam, the Department of Defense's cost figures on the F-111 and C5-A, or the economic growth rates published by the Soviet Union and the People's Republic of China to see examples of "creative statistics."[3]

---

[1] Oskar Morgenstern, "Qui Numerare Incipit Errare Incipit," *Fortune*, **68**:4 (October 1963), p. 173.

[2] Morgenstern, "Qui Numerare Incipit Errare Incipit," p. 172.

[3] For one exposition of this phenomenon, see William J. Proxmire, *Report from Wasteland: The American Military-Industrial Complex* (New York: Praeger, 1970). Also see David Wise, *The Politics of Lying* (New York: Random House, 1973).

The private sector is perhaps even less pure. "Creative accounting" long ago reached the level of an art form. The allocation of revenues and costs—the criteria for which are still a subject of professional debate—can lead to profit-and-loss statements that are very misleading. This is especially true in companies where costs not traceable to specific operations—such as supervision and institutional advertising—must be allocated to a number of product lines.

Sales information, particularly plans and projections, is frequently distorted. Few managers want competitors, creditors, suppliers, or tax collectors to be privy to marketing data. When pressed for information—as they often are by trade associations, chambers of commerce, and government statisticians—they may oblige with inaccurate data.

Not only are some figures outright lies, but correct information is often "edited." Those numbers reflecting favorably on the firm, industry, or political subdivision involved are published, while unfavorable data are conveniently ignored.

This criticism of published data is not a condemnation of its use. On the contrary, the bulk of it is acceptably accurate, since there is usually little incentive to distort data and the sources are generally honest. Besides, the researcher may have nowhere else to go; firsthand investigation may be too time-consuming or too expensive. Analysts must be aware of the problem, critical of their sources, and willing to qualify their own findings to reflect the possible inaccuracy of their inputs. Skepticism is a virtue in marketing research.

Assuring the reliability of the raw data solves only the first in a series of quality control problems. Failure to recognize the type of numbers one has, sloppy data reduction, and the improper use of analytical tools are all potential pitfalls. They will be discussed in detail later, for each can change good raw-data into a bundle of misinformation.

Sources: Prerecorded Data

The capability of a research group is largely determined by the number and quality of its data sources. A competent researcher knows how to find information relevant to his or her field of interest. Some common sources are cited in Table 4-1.

Internal Sources

Most research groups build libraries and files. These typically contain general-interest publications, such as the *Statistical Abstract of the United States* and *Survey of Current Business*. They usually include special-interest publications, such as trade journals, as well as special reports, clipping, and past studies.

Most firms, especially large ones, amass a great amount of data applicable to marketing research. The requirements of the Internal Revenue

Table 4-1   **Common Data Sources**

Prerecorded Data	
Internal Sources	External Sources
Company library	Public and university libraries
Research file	Government agencies
Sales Department	Trade associations
Accounting Department	Newspapers
Engineering Department	Banks
Manufacturing Department	Trade publications
Advertising Department	Suppliers, customers

Original Data				
Surveys	Panels[a]	Trips to Delphi	Experimentation	Simulation

[a] Overlaps with surveys.

Service, the Securities and Exchange Commission, regulatory agencies, and the firm's own credit department force it to gather and record a wealth of information. Within the marketing department itself, people such as the sales manager, product or brand managers, the advertising manager, and the distribution manager, are likely to be collectors of market data. One of the first tasks of the marketing researcher should be to audit the prospective data sources both inside and outside the firm. Often a little cooperation from other departments will produce a good deal of useful information. If the firm uses an electronic data processing system to manage accounting, inventory, sales, or distribution records, the internal data relevant to marketing research can quickly be retrieved. All that may be needed is some additional coding and the preparation of some relatively simple computer programs.

External Sources

The firm's suppliers and customers may have useful data accessible to the researcher. Talks with the company's own sales force or its dealers can provide useful data and insights. However, the researcher should beware of paying too much heed to industry folklore, much of which is invented and perpetuated by salespersons. Reports of firsthand experiences can be valuable, but only if superficial opinions and sloppy judgments are ignored.

Many institutions are good sources of secondary data. Public agencies are by far the most prolific, but private organizations can also be useful. These include banks, newspapers, chambers of commerce, trade associations, and special-interest publishers. Such institutions as the Bank of America, the *Los Angeles Times*, the Motorcycle Industry Council, and *Flying* magazine have research staffs that provide reams of data. Some of their information

Exhibit 4-1

HAWAII

HAWAII
S&MM ESTIMATES

POPULATION—12/31/77 / RETAIL SALES BY STORE GROUP 1977

METRO AREA County City	Total Population (Thousands)	% Of U.S.	Median Age of Pop.	% of Population by Age Group				Households (Thousands)	Total Retail Sales ($000)	Food ($000)	Eating & Drinking Places ($000)	General Mdse. ($000)	Furniture/ Furnish./ Appliance ($000)	Automotive ($000)	Drug ($000)
				18-24 Years	25-34 Years	35-49 Years	50 & Over								
HONOLULU	731.2	.3358	26.2	17.3	16.6	16.9	18.5	208.5	2,477,173	474,382	388,939	484,846	115,802	333,753	158,200
Honolulu	731.2	.3358	26.2	17.3	16.6	16.9	18.5	208.5	2,477,173	474,382	388,939	484,846	115,802	333,753	158,200
•Honolulu	372.7	.1711	29.6	16.2	16.4	17.1	24.0	121.5	1,992,991	318,698	336,931	412,778	102,157	263,756	116,997
SUBURBAN TOTAL	358.5	.1647	23.6	18.5	16.7	16.6	12.8	87.0	484,182	155,684	52,008	72,068	13,645	69,997	41,203
OTHER COUNTIES															
Hawaii	78.4	.0360	31.2	10.4	11.8	16.7	28.9	23.7	266,629	76,450	38,040	28,150	16,555	42,103	15,040
Kauai	34.4	.0157	31.9	8.9	13.3	16.1	29.7	10.8	124,331	34,926	19,660	17,042	7,729	20,735	313
Maui	60.0	.0276	31.6	10.2	12.4	16.3	29.4	18.5	194,270	48,466	32,823	23,996	13,323	17,969	12,633
TOTAL METRO COUNTIES	731.2	.3358	26.2	17.3	16.6	16.9	18.5	208.5	2,477,173	474,382	388,939	484,846	115,802	333,753	158,200
TOTAL STATE	904.0	.4151	27.0	15.9	15.7	16.8	20.6	261.5	3,062,403	634,224	479,462	554,034	153,409	414,560	186,186

HAWAII
S&MM ESTIMATES

EFFECTIVE BUYING INCOME 1977

METRO AREA County City	Total EBI ($000)	Median Hsld. EBI	% of Hslds. by EBI Group: (A) $8,000-$9,999 (B) $10,000-$14,999 (C) $15,000-$24,999 (D) $25,000 & Over				Buying Power Index
			A	B	C	D	
HONOLULU	4,587,916	18,893	5.5	16.2	30.7	31.8	.3457
Honolulu	4,587,916	18,893	5.5	16.2	30.7	31.8	.3457
•Honolulu	2,689,274	18,995	5.5	15.4	28.6	33.5	.2200
SUBURBAN TOTAL	1,898,642	18,776	5.5	17.3	33.7	29.5	.1257

EFFECTIVE BUYING INCOME 1977
S&MM ESTIMATES

METRO AREA County City	Total EBI ($000)	Median Hsld. EBI	% of Hslds. by EBI Group: (A) $8,000-$9,999 (B) $10,000-$14,999 (C) $15,000-$24,999 (D) $25,000 & Over				Buying Power Index
			A	B	C	D	
OTHER COUNTIES							
Hawaii	420,330	15,047	7.6	20.7	29.9	20.3	.0344
Kauai	206,906	17,297	5.8	18.7	34.1	23.8	.0163
Maui	319,547	14,795	7.6	20.3	30.4	18.7	.0258
TOTAL METRO COUNTIES	4,587,916	18,893	5.5	16.2	30.7	31.8	.3457
TOTAL STATE	5,534,699	18,136	5.9	16.9	30.7	29.5	.4222

Source: From Sales and Marketing Management. Annual Survey of Buying Power (1978). © 1978 S&MM Survey of Buying Power.

is culled from government publications or from studies made or sponsored by themselves. Some is collected from their members, customers, or own files. Often the data are available free or for a nominal charge.

When it comes to external data sources, there are too many possibilities to be covered by words. One of the great problems of a twentieth-century human being is how to manage all the data being collected and recorded. The stuff is everywhere. A few of the sources commonly useful to marketers are the *Statistical Abstract of the United States, Survey of Current Business, Federal Reserve Bulletin, Census of Population, Census of Business, Annual Survey of Manufacturers, County Business Patterns, Sales and Yearbook of International Trade Statistics,* the *Fortune Directory,* and the *Rand McNally Commercial Atlas and Marketing Guide.*

One popular source of secondary market information is *Sales and Marketing Management Annual Survey of Buying Power.* An example of the information found there is seen in Exhibit 4-1. (Additional sources of external secondary data are cited in Appendix 3.)

Source Finders

Possibly the best source finder is the local librarian. Virtually all university and metropolitan libraries have well-trained research librarians, some of whom have an uncanny knack for finding secondary data.

Good libraries also have a set of source finders called "guides," "directories," "indexes," and "bibliographies." Examples are McGraw-Hill's *How and Where to Look It Up*, Bowker's *Ulrich's Periodicals Directory*, Wilson's *Business Periodicals Index*, and the American Marketing Association's *Basic Bibliography on Marketing Research.*

A number of research suppliers serve as source finders. The Information Source, Inc., has over a half-million documents on file. For an hourly fee, it turns loose a clerk who locates items relevant to the client's problem.

The Library Search

The quest for prerecorded data from external sources often starts at the library. Federal depository libraries (most major libraries are designated as such) can prove especially fruitful. Federal depository libraries are libraries designated to receive publications distributed by the U.S. Government Printing Office. This distribution covers most of the Department of Labor and Department of Commerce publications, including the Bureau of the Census documents so important to marketing.

The library search process is outlined in Figure 4-1.

Evaluating Secondary Data

Most marketing research is fueled with secondary data. Cost, speed, and availability motivate its use, yet there is danger in succumbing to economy and convenience. Evaluation is in order before one scoops up secondhand

Figure 4-1   The Library Search Process

Source : Adapted from C. William Emery, *Business Research Methods* (Homewood, IL : Richard D. Irwin, 1976) p. 183. © 1976 by Richard D. Irwin, Inc.

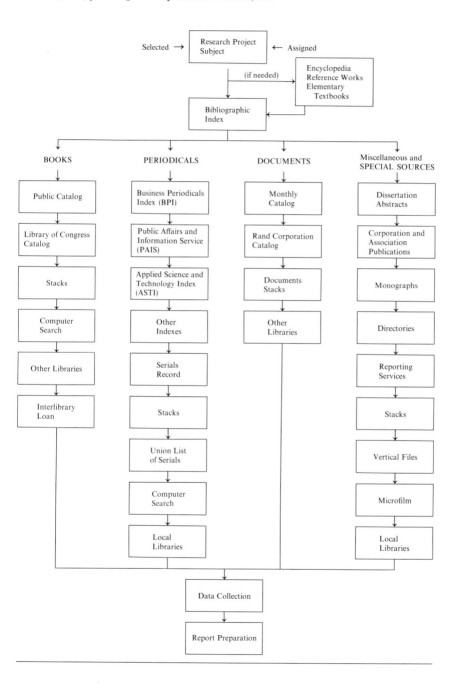

information. A procedure for evaluation is found in Figure 4-2, revealing the issues one should face before opting for secondary data.

Some suppliers have computerized this process. Predicast, for one, has catalogued annotated bibliographies on a computer. The client can lease a terminal and access this information directly, getting within minutes a list of specific sources of the needed data.

In evaluating secondary information, one should not focus exclusively on the data, but should also consider the source itself. Again, skepticism is in order.

Newspaper and magazine publishers are unlikely to include data derogatory to their media or the market they serve. In addition, information

***Figure 4-2*   Evaluating Secondary Data**

Source: Robert W. Joselyn, *Designing the Marketing Research Project* (New York: Petrocelli/ Charter, 1977), p. 54.

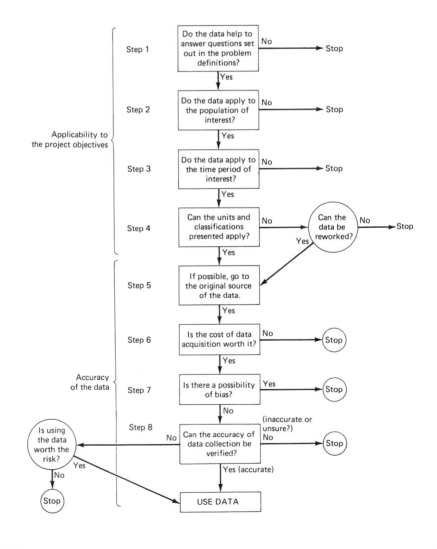

may be presented visually in a way that distorts relationships—this is especially easy when graphs or bar charts are used.[4] However, the data are usually free, and a competent analyst will not ordinarily be fooled by such subterfuges.

Whenever historical information is used, the validity of the source should be considered. If the source is questionable, the information should be checked or discarded, or the resulting analysis qualified. Sometimes data can be checked by comparing them with similar information from an independent source. Often it is wise to trace the data back to their original source, even if the immediate source seems unimpeachable. If a spot check of randomly selected bits of data fails to reveal any discrepancies, the balance of the information can usually be accepted at face value.

Sometimes the data source may provide accurate figures but omit information that would lead to undesirable conclusions. In addition, the data are often accompanied by an analysis whose sole purpose is to serve the interests of the sponsor. Again, competent researchers will ignore this kind of data, either doing their own analysis or checking carefully on the pedigree of their source.

Using External Data Sources: A Case Study

The use of historical and secondary data is illustrated by a fibre-box manufacturer. The firm wanted to determine the total market potential for corrugated and fibre boxes in the Phoenix standard metropolitan statistical area (SMSA). Using the national data contained in *Fibre Box Industry Statistics*, an annual publication of the Fibre Box Association, it was able to determine the consumption of fibre boxes as a function of SIC (Standard Industrial Classification) major group codes (shown in column 1 of Exhibit 4-2). A Bureau of the Census document, *County Business Patterns*, told the firm the number of employees in each major SIC-code industry (column 2). By dividing the fibre box consumption by the employee population, it was able to compute the average consumption of fibre boxes per employee in each major SIC-code industry (column 3). It could then estimate the market in the Phoenix area by multiplying the average consumption of fibre boxes per employee times the number of employees in each of the major SIC-code industries in the Phoenix area. The latter data were available from the *County Business Patterns*.

The study described above represents an imaginative use of historical data. First, the problem was defined in terms of a management need—namely, the estimation of the demand for fibre boxes in the Phoenix SMSA. Next, likely—and readily accessible—government sources were checked for relevant data. Then the industry's trade association was queried. Finally, a method was devised to estimate the size of the Phoenix market, using the available data. The result was an answer—a figure for the estimated

---

[4] See Darrell Huff, *How to Lie with Statistics* (New York: Norton, 1954) for an exposition of the common methods of data distortion without the use of fraud.

consumption of fibre boxes in the Phoenix SMSA—that was extremely useful to management in allocating marketing resources to that area.

Sources: Original Data

When the sources of prerecorded data prove unfruitful, the researcher must abandon the project or gather original data.

Surveys, Experimentation, and Simulation

The most common source of original data is the survey. As Figure 4-3 illustrates, one enters the marketplace and observes or asks what is going on.

Sometimes one must make things happen in order to generate the necessary data. In this case an experiment is performed, in the laboratory or in the field, and the results are recorded. The trial of a new product, TV commercial, or sales promotion in a test market—say, Denver or San Diego—is illustrative.

Figure 4-3   **Supermarket Survey**

Source: Reprinted by permission of the publisher from *Management Review*, July 1970. © 1970 by the American Management Association, Inc. All rights reserved.

"Do you mind if Mr. Rose rides along?
He's checking consumer attitudes."

SIC Major Group Code	Using Industry	Value of Box Shipments By End Use ($000)[a] 1	Employment By Industry Groups[b] 2	Consumption Per Employee By Industry Groups (1 ÷ 2) (Dollars) 3	Maricopa County (Phoenix SMSA) Employment By Industry Groups[b] 4	Maricopa County (Phoenix SMSA) Estimated Share of the Market (3 × 4) ($000) 5
20	Food and kindred products	586,164	1,578,305	371	4,973	1,845
21	Tobacco	17,432	74,557	233	...	...
22	Textile-mill products	91,520	874,677	104	...	...
23	Apparel	34,865	1,252,443	27	1,974	53
24	Lumber and products (except furniture)	19,611	526,443	37	690	26
25	Furniture and fixtures	89,341	364,166	245	616	151
26	Paper and allied products	211,368	587,882	359	190	68
27	Printing, publishing, and allied industries	32,686	904,208	36	2,876	104
28	Chemicals and allied products	128,564	772,169	166	488	81
29	Petroleum refining and related industries	28,328	161,367	175	...	...
30	Rubber and miscellaneous plastic products	67,551	387,997	174	190	33
31	Leather and leather products	8,716	352,919	24	...	...
32	Stone, clay, and glass products	226,621	548,058	413	1,612	666
33	Primary metal industries	19,611	1,168,110	16	2,889	46
34	Fabricated metal products	130,743	1,062,096	123	2,422	298
35	Machinery, except electrical	58,834	1,445,558	40	5,568	223
36	Electrical machinery, equipment, and supplies	119,848	1,405,382	391	6,502	553
37	Transportation equipment	82,804	1,541,618	53	5,005	265
38	Professional, scientific instruments, etc.	13,074	341,796	38	...	...
39	Miscellaneous manufacturing industries	200,473	369,071	543	376	204
90	Government	10,895	...	...	...	...
	Total	2,179,049[c]	...	...	...	4,616

Source: U.S. Department of Commerce, Measuring Markets: A Guide to the Use of Federal and State Statistical Data (Washington, D.C.: U.S. Government Printing Office, 1966), p. 51.

[a] Based on data reported in Fibre Box Industry Statistics 1963.

[b] U.S. Bureau of the Census, County Business Patterns, First Quarter 1962, Pts. 1 and 9.

[c] U.S. Bureau of the Census, 1962 Annual Survey of Manufacturers: General Statistics for Industry Groups and Industries (M62(AS)-1 revised), Table 1—General Statistics for Industry Groups and Industries: 1962, 1961, and 1958, p. 10.

Occasionally one can simulate a marketing situation and generate artificial data. For instance, you may have played a marketing game on a computer, then observed the changes in sales and market shares as you made changes in the marketing mix.

Each of these sources—survey, experimentation, and simulation—are sufficiently complex and important to warrant lengthy discussion. Hence, they are deferred for exploration later.

Consultation Methods

Often information is gathered by consulting experts. Purchasing agents are canvassed about their future buying plans; airline executives are queried on the characteristics they want in the next generation of jet transports; advertising agencies' creative staffs are canvassed for their ideas on new promotional campaigns. These information-gathering excursions are called "trips to Delphi," a tribute to the home of the great oracles (experts) of Greek mythology. (The Delphi method is discussed more fully in Chapter 22.)

Mother-in-law research (again we encounter jargon) is similar. The researcher, or often the line manager, simply consults with family or friends. They're consumers and their opinions and ideas can be valuable. For instance, when Edwin H. Land asked his family what they wanted in a camera, the response was "instant pictures." The result of this bit of mother-in-law research was one of the most successful products of our time, the Polaroid camera.

If the oracles and mothers-in-law cannot illuminate the problem, the researcher might turn to a panel.

Sources: Panels[5]

A *consumer panel* is a group of people (members of a market population) who are used to provide information on purchase behavior, media habits, or product usage. The panels usually function continuously, with the individual participants being retained for an extended time period. Occasionally ad hoc panels will be formed, particularly for product-testing.

Data are collected from panel members via personal interviews, telephone interviews, or mail questionnaires. The questionnaires include consumer diaries, which are probably the most common vehicles for recording panel data. The *diary* is a running account of the panelist's purchases or—in the case of media studies—his listening, viewing, or reading choices during a specified period. Because the task tends to be rather long and detailed, an incentive is often provided. Exhibit 4-3 shows a typical diary—

---

[5] This section draws on the work of Professors Harper W. Boyd, Jr., and Ralph L. Westfall, *An Evaluation of Continuous Consumer Panels as a Source of Marketing Information* (Chicago: American Marketing Association, 1960). In addition, considerable information was provided by executives of Pulse, Inc.; Market Facts, Inc.; Market Research Corp. of America; Booz, Allen, and Hamilton, Inc.; Arthur D. Little, Inc.; National Family Opinion, Inc.; and Perceptual Research Services, Inc.

(9-8989)-20

CONSUMER MAIL PANELS 100 SOUTH WACKER DRIVE - CHICAGO, ILLINOIS 60606

PURCHASE DIARY FOR FOUR-WEEK PERIOD OF

SUNDAY, OCTOBER 26, THROUGH SATURDAY, NOVEMBER 22

Dear Panel Member,

Here's your Purchase Diary for the four-week period of:

SUNDAY, OCTOBER 26, THROUGH SATURDAY, NOVEMBER 22

As you know, it is important that I know whether or not you have purchased each category in the diary during this four-week period. Please be sure for each category in which there have not been any purchases that you have "X'd" the box at the top of the category to tell me so. When it is time to mail this diary back to me, just refold it so my return address shows on the outside. Then, staple or tape it closed and drop it in the mail.

A few things to remember. . .

1. Please review all categories each day to be sure you do not overlook any purchase activity by you or other members of your household. The product category listing on the back page will help you to easily find each category.

2. Enter the information asked for each purchase on the same day it occurs, so as to be sure not to overlook reporting it. A good time to do this for most of the categories would be soon after a shopping trip.

3. Make a separate entry for each purchase occasion.

4. Purchase activity by all members of your household—not just yourself—is to be reported. Below is a calendar of the current four-week period. At the end of each day, please check with the other members of your household to see if any purchases of the diary categories were made.

   Please indicate for each day whether or not you or any members of your household made any purchases of the categories in your diary.

Exhibit 4-3   **An Example of a Consumer Purchase Diary** *(cont'd.)*

5. If you make more purchases than I have provided room for in any of the categories, please write the information required on a separate piece of paper and enclose it when you mail your diary back to me.

6. When making your purchase entries, look at the label of the item, so as to be sure all the information you record is correct.

7. Please be sure you fill in all the information I ask about each purchase. Try not to leave anything blank. Looking at the label on the package, can, jar or bottle will make it easier for you to fill in everything completely—and accurately.

8. The most important thing is that you accurately record only the purchases you make during this diary period.

9. At the conclusion of the current four-week period, I will send you your diary for the next four-week period. Please do not return this present diary to me until

SUNDAY, NOVEMBER 23

Thank you very much for your continued help.

Cordially,

Marie

I have improved the plan for the number of S&H Green Stamps you can earn for the prompt return of your diaries. Let me explain it to you . . .

1. For your prompt completion and return of this diary at the end of the current four-week period, I will credit your account with . . .

   100 S&H GREEN STAMPS

2. In addition, if this diary is a consecutive return with the diary for the immediate previous four-week period, I will also credit your account with a BONUS of . . .

   50 ADDITIONAL S&H GREEN STAMPS

3. In addition, for each diary you return, your name will be entered in the "Bonus Pool". The more diaries you return, the more times your name is entered. Prizes in the "Bonus Pool" are:

   ONE 1st Award of 250,000 S&H GREEN STAMPS
   ONE 2nd Award of 100,000 S&H GREEN STAMPS
   ONE 3rd Award of 50,000 S&H GREEN STAMPS
   TWENTY-TWO 4th Awards of 20,000 S&H GREEN STAMPS EACH

DAILY PURCHASE RECORD

For each of the categories in my diary, I've checked with the other members of my household, and there were:
("X" ONE BOX FOR EACH DAY ON THAT DAY)

Date:	One or More Purchases Made and Entered In My Diary	No Purchases Made		Date:	One or More Purchases Made and Entered In My Diary	No Purchases Made
October 26	☐	☐		November 9	☐	☐
October 27	☐	☐		November 10	☐	☐
October 28	☐	☐		November 11	☐	☐
October 29	☐	☐		November 12	☐	☐
October 30	☐	☐		November 13	☐	☐
October 31	☐	☐		November 14	☐	☐
November 1	☐	☐		November 15	☐	☐
November 2	☐	☐		November 16	☐	☐
November 3	☐	☐		November 17	☐	☐
November 4	☐	☐		November 18	☐	☐
November 5	☐	☐		November 19	☐	☐
November 6	☐	☐		November 20	☐	☐
November 7	☐	☐		November 21	☐	☐
November 8	☐	☐		November 22	☐	☐

(9889-9)

USE A SEPARATE LINE FOR EACH DIFFERENT PURCHASE

OVEN CLEANERS

(Enter information for each purchase on day purchased.)
"X" here → ☐ if NO purchases were made in this category during these 4 weeks.

Date of Purchase:	Brand (Write In):	Number of Ounces (Write In):	Type ("X" Whether):			Number of Containers (Write In):	Price Per Container (Write In):
			Aerosol (Metal Can)	Paste (Glass Jar)	Other (please specify):		
			☐	☐			
			☐	☐			
			☐	☐			

SPECIAL PURPOSE BATHROOM CLEANERS   *(Only those products called "Bathroom Cleaner" on the label)*

(Enter information for each purchase on day purchased.)
"X" here → ☐ if NO purchases were made in this category during these 4 weeks.

Date of Purchase:	Brand (Write In):	Number of Ounces (Write In):	Type ("X" Whether):			Number of Containers (Write In):	Price Per Container (Write In):
			Aerosol (Metal Can)	Plastic Squeeze Bottle	Other (Please Specify):		
			☐	☐			
			☐	☐			
			☐	☐			

ALL-PURPOSE SPRAY CLEANERS

(Enter information for each purchase on day purchased.)
"X" here → ☐ if NO purchases were made in this category during these 4 weeks.

Date of Purchase:	Brand (Write In):	Number of Ounces (Write In):	Type ("X" Whether):				Number of Containers (Write In):	Price Per Container (Write In):
			Aerosol (Metal Can)	Pump Spray (Plastic Bottle)	Refill (plastic bottle — no pump)	Other (Please Specify):		
			☐	☐	☐			
			☐	☐	☐			
			☐	☐	☐			

Exhibit 4-3   **An Example of a Consumer Purchase Diary** *(cont'd.)*

AEROSOL AIR FRESHENERS AND AEROSOL SPRAY DISINFECTANTS

(Enter information for each purchase on day purchased.)
"X" here → ☐ if NO purchases were made in this category during these 4 weeks.

Date of Purchase:	Brand (Write In):	Number of Ounces (Write In):	Type ("X" Whether) Aerosol Air Freshener	Aerosol Spray Disinfectant	Number of Containers (Write In):	Price Per Containers (Write In):
			☐	☐		
			☐	☐		
			☐	☐		

TOILET BOWL CLEANERS

(Enter information for each purchase on day purchased.)
"X" here → ☐ if NO purchases were made in this category during these 4 weeks.

Date of Purchase:	Brand (Write In):	Number of Ounces (Write In):	Aerosol (Metal Can)	Liquid (Plastic Bottle)	Type ("X" Whether): Tablet	Packet	Powder or Granule	Other (Please Specify):	Number of Containers (Write In):	Price Per Container (Write In):
			☐	☐	☐	☐	☐	☐		
			☐	☐	☐	☐	☐	☐		
			☐	☐	☐	☐	☐	☐		

SUNBURN AND TANNING PREPARATIONS
(Include all products used either for the prevention or relief of sunburn; and products for either indoor or outdoor tanning.)

(Enter information for each purchase on day purchased.)
"X" here → ☐ if NO purchases were made during these 4 weeks.

Date of Purchase:	Brand (Write In):	Number of Ounces (Write In):	Type ("X" Whether): Tube	Plastic Squeeze Bottle	Jar	Spray	Other	Number of Containers (Write In):	Price Per Container (Write In):	Purchased Primarily for Use of: ("X" ONE) Entire Family	Adult Males (20 years & over)	Adult Females (20 years & over)	Teenage Males (13-19 years)	Teenage Females (13-19 years)	Children (12 years & under)
			☐	☐	☐	☐	☐			☐	☐	☐	☐	☐	☐
			☐	☐	☐	☐	☐			☐	☐	☐	☐	☐	☐
			☐	☐	☐	☐	☐			☐	☐	☐	☐	☐	☐

(9-8989)

USE A SEPARATE COLUMN FOR EACH DIFFERENT PURCHASE

FIRST AID BANDAGES AND DRESSINGS (NOT TAPE ROLLS)

(Enter information for each purchase on day purchased.)
"X" here → ☐ if NO purchases were made in this category during these 4 weeks.

Date of Purchase: _____ (9-11)

Brand and Package Size: ("X" ONE) (12-15)

CURAD				
Plain Pad (9 bandages)	☐ 1--	☐ 1--	☐ 1--	☐ 1--
Plain Pad (24 bandages)	☐ 2--	☐ 2--	☐ 2--	☐ 2--
Plain Pad (31 bandages)	☐ 3--	☐ 3--	☐ 3--	☐ 3--
Plain Pad (37 bandages)	☐ 4--	☐ 4--	☐ 4--	☐ 4--
Plain Pad (47 bandages)	☐ 5--	☐ 5--	☐ 5--	☐ 5--
Plain Pad (48 bandages)	☐ 6--	☐ 6--	☐ 6--	☐ 6--
Plain Pad (75 bandages)	☐ 7--	☐ 7--	☐ 7--	☐ 7--
Plain Pad (79 bandages)	☐ 8--	☐ 8--	☐ 8--	☐ 8--
Plain Pad (other number)	☐ 9--	☐ 9--	☐ 9--	☐ 9--
Telfa Pad (any number)	☐ 0--	☐ 0--	☐ 0--	☐ 0--
Transparent Pad (any number)	☐ X--	☐ X--	☐ X--	☐ X--
Extra-Wide Pad (any number)	☐ R--	☐ R--	☐ R--	☐ R--
Medicated Pad (any number)	☐ -1-	☐ -1-	☐ -1-	☐ -1-
"Other" Curad Package Type	☐ -2-	☐ -2-	☐ -2-	☐ -2-

JOHNSON & JOHNSON BAND-AIDS				
Plastic Strips (12 bandages)	☐ -3-	☐ -3-	☐ -3-	☐ -3-
Plastic Strips (31 bandages)	☐ -4-	☐ -4-	☐ -4-	☐ -4-
Plastic Strips (32 bandages)	☐ -5-	☐ -5-	☐ -5-	☐ -5-
Plastic Strips (34 bandages)	☐ -6-	☐ -6-	☐ -6-	☐ -6-
Plastic Strips (36 bandages)	☐ -7-	☐ -7-	☐ -7-	☐ -7-
Plastic Strips (45 bandages)	☐ -8-	☐ -8-	☐ -8-	☐ -8-
Plastic Strips (70 bandages)	☐ -9-	☐ -9-	☐ -9-	☐ -9-
Plastic Strips (79 bandages)	☐ -0-	☐ -0-	☐ -0-	☐ -0-
Plastic Strips (100 bandages)	☐ -X-	☐ -X-	☐ -X-	☐ -X-

FIRST AID TAPE (NOT BANDAGES OR DRESSINGS)

(Enter information for each purchase on day purchased.)
"X" here → ☐ if NO purchases were made in this category during these 4 weeks.

Date of Purchase: _____ (9-11)

Brand Bought: ("X" ONE) (12-13)

BAUER & BLACK				
Plastic Flesh Tone	☐ 1-	☐ 1-	☐ 1-	☐ 1-
Plastic Transparent	☐ 2-	☐ 2-	☐ 2-	☐ 2-
Regular	☐ 3-	☐ 3-	☐ 3-	☐ 3-
Wet-Pruf	☐ 4-	☐ 4-	☐ 4-	☐ 4-

JOHNSON & JOHNSON				
Clear Tape	☐ 5-	☐ 5-	☐ 5-	☐ 5-
Dermicel	☐ 6-	☐ 6-	☐ 6-	☐ 6-
Plastic Tape	☐ 7-	☐ 7-	☐ 7-	☐ 7-
Red Cross	☐ 8-	☐ 8-	☐ 8-	☐ 8-
Waterproof Tape	☐ 9-	☐ 9-	☐ 9-	☐ 9-
ZO Tape	☐ 0-	☐ 0-	☐ 0-	☐ 0-

PARKE-DAVIS				
Bayconony	☐ X-	☐ X-	☐ X-	☐ X-
Bayhesive	☐ R-	☐ R-	☐ R-	☐ R-
Standard Tape	☐ -1	☐ -1	☐ -1	☐ -1
Waterproof Tape	☐ -2	☐ -2	☐ -2	☐ -2

3M COMPANY				
Blenderm	☐ -3	☐ -3	☐ -3	☐ -3
Micropore	☐ -4	☐ -4	☐ -4	☐ -4

Exhibit 4-3   **An Example of a Consumer Purchase Diary (cont'd.)**

REXALL

Regular Tape	□ -5	□ -5	□ -5
Waterproof Tape	□ -6	□ -6	□ -6
OTHER BRAND	□ -7	□ -7	□ -7

Length of Roll: ("X" ONE)   (14)

5 Yards	□ 1	□ 1	□ 1
10 Yards	□ 2	□ 2	□ 2
Other Length	□ 3	□ 3	□ 3

Number of Rolls Purchased: (15-16)

Where Purchased: ("X" ONE)   (17)

Grocery or Food Store	□ 1	□ 1	□ 1
Drug Store	□ 2	□ 2	□ 2
Department Store	□ 3	□ 3	□ 3
Discount Store	□ 4	□ 4	□ 4
Other Store	□ 0	□ 0	□ 0

(79-80)   1 2   1 2   1 2

Plastic Strips (other numbers)

Plastic Strips (other numbers)	□ -R-	□ -R-	□ -R-	□ -R-
Sheer Strips (12 bandages)	-1	-1	-1	-1
Sheer Strips (31 bandages)	-2	-2	-2	-2
Sheer Strips (32 bandages)	-3	-3	-3	-3
Sheer Strips (34 bandages)	-4	-4	-4	-4
Sheer Strips (36 bandages)	-5	-5	-5	-5
Sheer Strips (45 bandages)	-6	-6	-6	-6
Sheer Strips (70 bandages)	-7	-7	-7	-7
Sheer Strips (79 bandages)	-8	-8	-8	-8
Sheer Strips (100 bandages)	-9	-9	-9	-9
Sheer Strips (other numbers)	□ -0	□ -0	□ -0	□ -0
Cotton Pads (any number)	□ --X	□ --X	□ --X	□ --X
OTHER BRAND	□ --R	□ --R	□ --R	□ --R

With Mercurochrome? ("X" ONE)   (16)

Yes	□ 1	□ 1	□ 1	□ 1
No	□ 2	□ 2	□ 2	□ 2

Number of Packages Purchased (Write In):   (17-18)

Where Purchased: ("X" ONE)   (19)

Grocery or Food Store	□ 1	□ 1	□ 1	□ 1
Drug Store	□ 2	□ 2	□ 2	□ 2
Department Store	□ 3	□ 3	□ 3	□ 3
Discount Store	□ 4	□ 4	□ 4	□ 4
Other Store	□ 0	□ 0	□ 0	□ 0

How Purchased: ("X" ONE)   (20)

At the regular price	□ 1	□ 1	□ 1	□ 1
At a reduced price or cents-off	□ 2	□ 2	□ 2	□ 2

(79-80)   1 1   1 1   1 1   1 1

1   2   3   4   5   6   7   8

one used to record purchases of various types of cleaners, suntan preparations, and band-aids.

Economies of Scale

There are large economies of scale in the establishment and operation of a consumer panel. Few firms can justify the total cost of such a panel, especially when a continuous purchase record is needed. As a result, specialization and cost-sharing are common. Commercial firms, government agencies, and colleges operate consumer panels and offer the data to various users.

The Marketing Research Corporation of America; the American Research Bureau; the A. C. Nielsen Company; National Family Opinion, Inc.; J. Walter Thompson, Inc.; and the *Chicago Tribune* are major commercial suppliers. Except for the latter two—an advertising agency and a newspaper—they specialize solely in marketing research, primarily in the gathering of market data for client firms. The U.S. Department of Agriculture, the Bureau of Labor Statistics, Michigan State University, and the University of Georgia are among the public institutions operating consumer panels.

Advantages and Limitations of Panel Data

The chief advantages of the consumer panel are its availability, its continuity, and its sensitivity. The major services are available to anyone prepared to pay the fee or, in the case of public institutions, willing to take the time and incur the nominal cost of procurement. Commercial suppliers offer very current data, often tailoring them to meet the client's needs. Public institutions generally offer the data as is and provide few, if any, special services. The panels themselves operate continuously, and immediately reflect even slight changes in consumer behavior.

The continuous record of consumer behavior provided by the panel allows aggregate changes in sales to be analyzed. It also permits direct comparisons of behavior at different points in time. Boyd and Westfall suggest that the greatest asset of such panels may be their ability to measure both net and gross changes in consumer purchases.[6] The *net change* is the difference in total sales or customers between two time periods. The *gross change* is the sum of all changes that occur—the turnover in units or customers.

For example, assume that 500 members of a panel purchased a particular product during one period and 475 members purchased the product during a subsequent period. This would be a net change of -25. Assume, further, that 125 of those who purchased the good during the second period had not purchased it during the first period. The gross change would be -150. Although sales have declined only 5 percent, 30 percent of the original customers have been lost. Where brand loyalty is a significant

---

[6] Boyd and Westfall, *An Evaluation of Continuous Consumer Panels as a Source of Marketing Information*, p. 7.

factor in sustaining sales, this would be alarming information, warranting immediate action by the firm's researchers and other marketing personnel. This ability to distinguish between new and repeat purchasers is one of the advantages of consumer panels. (Such information is essential to the operation of a number of stochastic models of consumer behavior.)

The great sensitivity of the panel gives the firm data on the effects of short-run changes in marketing variables. Company records are usually inadequate for such purposes unless a company operates its own retail outlets. A change in demand will affect retailers' inventories immediately. If it persists, it will eventually be reflected in wholesalers' inventories as well, and ultimately in the number of orders received by the producer. However, by that time, it may be too late to take full advantage of an increase, or to counteract a decrease, in demand. In addition, the variations in retail sales would be cushioned by partial absorption by wholesale and retail inventories. The consumer panel allows retail-purchase information to flow directly from the consumer to the researcher. This responsiveness is especially important in market experimentation, when one or more variables are manipulated over a short period of time (usually one to four weeks) to determine their effect on sales.

Of course panel data also have limitations. The highly structured format of the questionnaires makes panels useless for exploratory research. Their flexibility is also limited, since they are generally operated by research suppliers who are attempting to maximize the aggregate benefit to a group of subscribers. Data requirements unique to one client can sometimes be accommodated, but only if the client is willing to absorb the costs of preparing a special diary (or questionnaire) and, possibly, forming a new panel from the supplier's reserve of candidates.

Types of Panels

Consumer panels can be classified in several ways as a pedagogic convenience. For example, they can be classified as continuous or ad hoc. Depending on the level at which the data are recorded, they can be categorized as consumer panels (also serving as an inclusive term for panels in general) or store-audit panels. Depending on their function, they can be classified as purchase panels, media-measurement panels, or product-testing panels. They can be field or laboratory panels, depending on whether data are recorded in the marketplace (including the respondent's home) or in the artificial environment of a laboratory (usually a theater, an office, or a motel suite).

Continuous Consumer-Purchase Panels   The continuous consumer-purchase panel is perhaps the type most widely used. The members maintain purchase diaries in which they report the quantity of purchases they make and the brands they buy during the reporting period. An alternative to the diary is to interview the panel members. This technique is less common, however, since it is more expensive and introduces the problems of recall and interviewer bias.

The recall error may be significant. There is evidence that consumers tend to understate their purchases, especially when a significant period of time is involved and many of the purchases are minor. When interview data were compared to panel-diary data, the interviews revealed significantly smaller purchases for the same market population. Although it is too soon to draw conclusions about the overall statistical superiority of either method, the diary may be more valid for certain purposes.[7]

Recall errors can be a problem even when diaries are used, especially when the participant procrastinates until the end of the reporting period before entering purchases. This problem can be moderated, although not eliminated, by using weekly diaries, by instructing the participants properly, and by spot-checking the results.

Continuous Store-Audit Panels   The continuous store audit panel provides information not only on retail purchases but on institutional and industrial purchases as well. (The latter groups are usually insignificant, constituting no more than 5 percent of total sales.) It is commonly used in estimating market shares and absolute sales. Because it distinguishes between types of retailers, it is useful for market-channel decisions. However, since it ignores the purchase behavior of individual consumers, it is useless in studies of brand loyalty.

Media-Measurement Panels   The media-measurement panel is designed to measure the size and composition of the audiences of radio programs, television shows, and periodicals, although it is used most often in studies of live media. It provides the same data as telephone surveys and readership audits, but the data transmission vehicle is either an audiometer or a diary. The *audiometer* is an electronic device that attaches to a radio or television set. It records the time the unit is on and what station it is tuned to. The A. C. Nielsen Company has approximately 1,500 audiometers installed in 1,100 homes. It gathers data on audience composition and viewing habits as well as audience size. Participants remain on the panel for a year or more.

The American Research Bureau maintains television panels, but relies on diaries for data. A panel member's diary is maintained for one month, at which time it is returned and the participant drops out of the panel. Members are recruited by mail. They receive the diary, accompanied by an invitation to participate in the survey and instructions telling them to record what time the set is on, what program is on, and who in the family is watching. Two weeks later a follow-up letter is sent encouraging the recipient to maintain the diary and return it promptly at the end of the observation period. Those who do participate are paid a small fee.

---

[7] *Response Variation Encountered with Different Questionnaire Forms*, Marketing Research Report no. 163 (Washington: U.S. Department of Agriculture, April 1957), as cited in Boyd and Westfall, *An Evaluation of Continuous Consumer Panels as a Method of Market Evaluation*, p. 17.

Product-Testing Panels Product-testing panels are set up on an ad hoc basis to field-test new products or significantly modified models of established products. The product is provided—usually free—to the participants, who keep a record of when they use it and comment on its virtues and deficiencies. Product-testing panels are usually small, and random selection of the participants is not as critical as it is in the case of other panels. Thus, they are frequently organized by the producer's own research department.

Types and Characteristics of Panel Data

Both continuous consumer-purchase panels and continuous store-audit panels are capable of providing the following major types of data:

1 information on total consumer purchases, by national, regional, state, and local markets

2 information on total consumer sales, by brand, product class, or product-class subsets (e.g., types of coffee, such as instant, drip, percolator, or regular)

3 information on market shares, by brand, product class, or product-class subsets

4 information on sales trends and seasonal variations

Continuous consumer-purchase panels can also provide information on brand switching and the results of changes in consumer demographics or life styles. Brand-switching information is one of the most important forms of data in marketing research. For instance, once a new high-velocity good[8] is introduced to a market—usually with the aid of an incentive, such as a tie-in offer, a coupon, or a special discount—repeat purchases are needed to sustain sales. If a large number of those who tried the product go back to buying other brands, the product is in trouble. Immediate steps must be taken to identify and correct the problem.

Changes in purchasing habits induced by shifts in consumer demographics or life style have an important implication for long-range forecasting as well as product and channel decisions. As Boyd and Westfall point out, consumer panels have not generally been used to collect this kind of information in the past, but the potential for such applications is there. Panels can provide relatively complete data on such dynamic features of the economy as changes in buying habits induced by a move to the suburbs, the arrival of a couple's first child, or an increased emphasis on leisure-time activities.[9]

Panel Membership

The quantity and quality of consumer-panel data depends largely on the size and composition of the panel. Any number of people can be used. There

---

[8] A *high-velocity good* is a product with a high turnover, such as cake mixes or cigarettes. Sales of such items depend heavily on repeat purchases.

[9] Boyd and Westfall, *An Evaluation of Continuous Consumer Panels as a Method of Evaluating Market Research*, p. 11.

are many stories, some presumably true, of marketing executives basing major decisions on information provided by panels of one—their wives. However, anything from a dozen to 1,500 people would not be considered unusual. Chrysler used an ad hoc panel of 12 to evaluate its turbine-powered automobile. Nielsen uses a continuous panel of 1,100 families to estimate the size of radio and television audiences. Michigan State University employed nearly 1,000 households for four years to gather information on various phenomena.

Ideally, the consumer panel should be a representative sample of the market population. The ideal is never really met, but it is approached with sufficient closeness to justify the assumption of representativeness. This is a pragmatic accommodation, but apparently a workable one, judging by the millions of dollars spent annually by client firms for panel data.

Invalidity in panel data stems from the same errors that are associated with other forms of survey information discussed in the coming chapter. In addition, the continuous nature of most panels makes attrition— dropouts—an important source of trouble. Attrition not only reduces panel size, it introduces a particular bias into the data. Stable members tend to remain in the panel, while unstable and mobile members fall by the wayside. This tends to bias the panel in favor of the stable members, generally the more conservative and wealthier households or more mature and successful stores, whose purchasing habits may be markedly different from those of the other participants. These units, taken as a group, are not representative of their universe, although they may mirror a substantial portion of it.

Theoretically, a randomly selected panel is ideal if large-scale projections based on the sample data are to be made. This is not always easy to come by. Some years ago, for example, the Market Research Corporation of America attempted to create a nationwide consumer panel using a probability sample. Of those selected, 37.3 percent refused to participate, 10.5 percent dropped out during the training period, and 5.6 percent of those who remained failed to return one or more of their diaries during the three-month reporting period.[10] The residual participants probably did not have the same distribution of characteristics as the original, randomly chosen households, but there was little the firm could do about it at that point.

Other panel operators have had similar experiences. National Family Opinion, Inc. (NFO) reports that only about 10 percent of the families invited to participate in its mail panel agree to do so.[11] However, the company claims that its panel, which consists of 55 segments of 1,000 members each, is representative of the market population, since it is balanced against current census projections of certain demographic and social characteristics, such

---

[10] *Establishing a National Consumer Panel from a Probability Sample*, Marketing Research Report no. 40 (Washington, D.C.: U.S. Department of Agriculture, June 1953), p. 19, as cited in Boyd and Westfall, *Continuous Consumer Panels as a Method of Evaluating Market Research*, p. 13.

[11] National Family Opinion, Inc., "The Validity of Mail Panel Research," *NFO Digest* **12**, no 2 (September 1969), p. 1.

as age, income, and location. Apparently NFO does not use all its recruits, but selects an appropriate number from each of its demographic-social classifications to form panel segments whose properties are distributed in the same proportion as the populations they represent. Obviously the panel cannot be a random sample, since those who refuse to cooperate must be excluded. However, it may be quite satisfactory as a judgment sample, providing it is as representative as NFO suggests.

The distribution of panel members' demographic and social characteristics is especially important when intuitive judgments, rather than randomization, are used to ensure representativeness. It is also significant when researchers are attempting to determine the relationship between consumer behavior and one or more of these characteristics. Most consumer-panel data are gathered by mail, with participants recruited through the same medium. The kind of data gathered on participants is indicated in the first part of Exhibit 4-3.

Maintaining the representativeness of a consumer panel becomes more difficult over time, as its composition and the composition of the universe it purports to represent change. Members must be replaced, but not on such a sweeping scale that the panel's continuity is disrupted. One of the important advantages of consumer panels is the unique ability they give the researcher to observe changes in buying habits within the same households or stores. Nevertheless, new recruits must be found: (1) when a member of the original group dies or drops out or, in the case of stores, goes out of business; (2) when a shift in the distribution of social and demographic characteristics among panel members makes it different from the distribution found in the market population; and (3) when the members' behavior begins to be affected by their participation in the panel for too long a period. There is little evidence to date as to the extent of the error presumably introduced by these problems. However, logic suggests that the errors can be significant, and appropriate steps should be taken by panel sponsors to prevent, or at least moderate, them.

Uses of Panel Data

Panel data are used much like market data from other sources. However, their special advantages make them particularly valuable for experimentation. For instance, their continuity allows the researcher to observe sales, manipulate a marketing variable, observe the new level of sales, again change the marketing variable, and again observe the change in sales. By employing statistical techniques such as analyses of variance or regression analysis, the researcher can then estimate the effect of the marketing variable on sales.

Subscribing to a consumer-panel service allows the firm to quickly detect shifts in the distribution of market shares and identify a competitor whose performance warrants study. In effect, the panel provides a running audit of the marketplace.

Consumer panels are especially useful for tracking studies. *A tracking study is* the monitoring of a product's acceptance over time. Consumer awareness, trial, and usage information is collected. These data tell the seller how well advertising is getting through, how many people are trying the product, and what portion of the buyers is making repeat purchases.

Repeat purchases mean life or death for foods and convenience goods such as cereals, frozen juices, soaps, and cigarettes. Given the repeat purchase data, one can invoke such analytical tools as the Markov chain, to predict future sales and market shares. The results of the tracking studies often lead directly to changes in production orders, promotional strategy, or the scrapping of a product.

A number of suppliers offer consumer survey programs designed especially for tracking. An example is Walker Research's BRANDTRAK, a standardized approach to the collection of product-tracking data.

Panel data are also useful for studies of market segmentation. They will reveal whether a particular channel, market area, or consumer group accounts for a disproportionate share of the product or brand's sales. For instance, Pulse, Inc.'s syndicated survey "Brand/Metrics" once showed that local market shares for a national brand of beer ranged from a low of 2 percent in Cincinnati, Ohio, to a high of 58.8 percent in Charlotte, West Virginia.[12] These data, along with the market-share information for each of the other 33 locales in the survey, were extremely useful to the firm's marketing department. Such information is very important for channel and promotional decisions. It is especially useful if coupled with audience-profile data provided by media-measurement panels. Consumer panels can provide considerable data that are unavailable from other sources—at least not on such a continuous basis, in such detail, and so soon after a phenomenon occurs.

Laboratory Panels

Laboratory panels are a special kind of consumer panel, used primarily to evaluate advertising. They are most often used by behavioral scientists attempting to explain human reactions to selected stimuli. Psychologists, especially those belonging to the Gestalt or Freudian schools, argue that biological and physiological traits are so universal that random selection of panel members is not important. In addition, they claim, a large panel is unnecessary. (These assertions have been the subject of considerable dispute.) Hence, they emphasize the identification and measurement of stimulus response, not the method of selecting panel members, nor sample size.

Data-Collection Techniques   The normal procedure with laboratory panels is to expose the panelists to stimuli, usually advertising messages, and observe their reaction. Several techniques are used to collect data. Some are active, requiring the members' overt participation. For instance, the panelists may be asked to push buttons or pull levers to indicate their

---

[12] Pulse, Inc., *The Pulse Beat* (July 21, 1969), p. 1.

preference for particular stimuli such as a picture or an advertising layout. Or they may be tested to determine which stimuli they remember best. Other techniques require the participants cooperate only to the extent of allowing themselves to be subjected to the stimuli. Occasionally, harmless recording instruments may be affixed to a part of their bodies.

When a person reacts to stimuli, physiological changes occur. These changes can be recorded—using a camera, electrodes, or a thermocouple— and their frequency and amplitude used as an index of the stimuli's effectiveness. For example, the panel may be shown a series of television commercials or magazine advertisements—sometimes without the written copy— and the response data used to identify the most provocative ad.

Galvanic skin response (GSR), a measure of skin conductivity, and pupilary dilation are commonly used variables. Both these measurements correlate with measurements of interest, pleasure, and information absorption. Thus, if skin conductivity increases or pupils dilate more in response to one stimulus, that stimulus is considered a superior attention-getter and presumably a superior promotional device.

A special instrument, called a *tachtistoscope*, is used to test the relative impact of words and symbols. The tachtistoscope is a projector that flashes a still picture onto a screen for a very short, metered period—usually a fraction of a second. The panel members are confronted with a series of such pictures, each containing an alternative word, phrase, symbol, or arrangement of words and symbols. They are then tested to determine which alternatives they remember. The one that is remembered most often or most vividly is assumed to have had the most impact.

Laboratory subjects are also used for tracking eye movement, a clue to several behavioral phenomena. Eye movement reveals the importance of shelf position, buyer search patterns, the connection between brand preference and visual impact, and the attention-getting power of alternative package designs. Along with pupil dilation, it indicates visual impact, viewer involvement, and aesthetic appeal. The raw data are gathered with an eye-movement recorder and pupilometer system like the one shown in Figure 4-4.

A recent innovation in measuring response to stimuli is brain-wave analysis. The level of brain activity in the left hemisphere is compared with that of the right hemisphere, because each side is the seat of different emotional and motor responses. The comparison supposedly reveals whether the respondent reacted favorably or unfavorably to a stimulus, such as a TV commercial.

Perhaps the newest technique (fad?), is voice pitch analysis, called "VOPAN" by its chief practitioner, Consumer Response Corporation. A respondent is exposed to a stimulus, such as an advertisement or a new product. Questions are then asked and the answers are recorded on tape. Later, the voice-pitch characteristics are analyzed to evaluate the truthfulness and intensity of the answers. Presumably, the greater the change in voice pitch, the greater the commitment to the answer.

Some of the gadgets and gimmicks of data collection may make one wonder if their purpose is not mainly to impress clients. Even if we assume

Figure 4-4   The PRS Eye Movement Recorder System

Source: Perceptual Research Services, Inc.

the devices are legitimate, laboratory panels still have some serious shortcomings.

Deficiencies   One problem with laboratory panels is in generalizing findings to the population. Are the panel respondents truly representative of the universe from which they were drawn? When dealing with the volunteers who are used for GSR, eye tracking, brain-wave analysis, and VOPAN, one usually has a small, thus statistically shaky, sample. Even if the sample is large, are the people who participate somehow different?

The laboratory panel's chief deficiency is its failure to measure the most significant marketing variable—sales. In fact, the panel-response data are far down in the hierarchy of advertising effects, since they measure only the attention-getting quality of the material and only under very artificial conditions. Physiological data alone are seldom sufficient, since the promotional tactic or product variation evoking the greatest physical response also could conceivably alienate prospective buyers rather than win them over.

The laboratory panel can separate the obviously drab material from that which is more interesting, but that task can probably be performed just as easily, and more economically, by any competent advertising specialist. The method's ability to make distinctions that can be generalized to the market population is open to question. The laboratory panel is not continuous. Often there is little information on the membership's economic or demographic characteristics. The experimental environment is a poor replica of the world in which the promotional message will ultimately be delivered. Also, the participants are probably paying closer attention to the medium than they would under normal conditions. Furthermore, the participants are not randomly selected and may not be a good cross-section of the market population.

On the other hand, the laboratory-panel data may sharpen the researcher's ability to discriminate between adequate and slightly superior material. If this increases the efficiency of a major promotional campaign by just a few percentage points, the cost of the panel may be well justified. (Value analysis should be used in deciding whether to use a panel.) There is tremendous competition for the attention of the consumer, and even a slight increase in the impact of an advertisement or the desirability of a product feature can be a significant advantage in the marketplace.

Audience Studies, Inc.[13]   The best illustration of how this method works is provided by its largest practitioner, Audience Studies, Inc. (ASI), which tests nearly 1500 commercials per year using laboratory panels. ASI operates primarily through a worldwide network of *preview houses*—theaters in which selected audiences are subjected to various audio-visual stimuli. The breadth of ASI's investigations is suggested by the demographic range of its panels. Even preschoolers are used as panelists. (This is one aspect of market research that perhaps should not be overlooked by those concerned with the social implications of modern marketing.)

The use of the "in-theater" technique (a phrase coined by ASI) as a basic vehicle for collecting data is defended on the following grounds: First, it provides a controllable and clean environment ("clean" meaning free from exogenous disturbances). Second, it permits a number of diversified measurements to be taken at a reasonable cost. Third, it is an effective means of pretesting promotional campaigns and new shows. And fourth, it makes the replication of basic samples feasible and allows the efficient recruitment of target-group augmentations to these samples.[14]

ASI's panel members are recruited at shopping centers or other areas where there is heavy pedestrian traffic and by telephone, using reverse directories.[15] The candidates are subjected to a brief personal interview, and panelists are selected on the basis of quotas designed to ensure a representative audience. The sole incentive for participation is the promise of a private showing of new television material, yet ASI claims that acceptance of its invitations can run as high as 40 percent. (An invitation is seen in Exhibit 4-4.)

---

[13] I am indebted to Mark E.B. Pinney, Director of Research Administration for Audience Studies, Inc., for his assistance in preparing this material.

[14] *A Synopsis of Advertising Testing Services and Procedures* (Los Angeles: Audience Studies, Inc., n.d.), p. 1.

[15] For an explanation of reverse directories see the glossary or Chapter 9.

***Exhibit 4-4*   An Invitation to a Preview House**

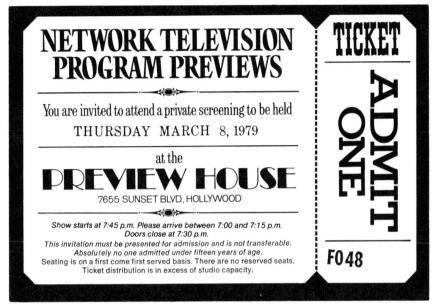

NETWORK TELEVISION PROGRAM PREVIEWS

You are invited to attend a private screening to be held

THURSDAY   MARCH   8, 1979

at the

PREVIEW HOUSE

7655 SUNSET BLVD., HOLLYWOOD

Show starts at 7:45 p.m. Please arrive between 7:00 and 7:15 p.m.
Doors close at 7:30 p.m.
This invitation must be presented for admission and is not transferable.
Absolutely no one admitted under fifteen years of age.
Seating is on a first come first served basis. There are no reserved seats.
Ticket distribution is in excess of studio capacity.

TICKET

ADMIT ONE

F048

Source: Audience Studios, Inc.

Upon reaching the theater, panel members are instructed in the laboratory procedure and then exposed to an assortment of screened commercials and TV pilots lasting about two hours. Some of this is the test material; the rest is control material used to compare the audience's reactions with those of preceding groups. The control material, such as a "Mr. Magoo" cartoon, allows ASI to judge the representativeness of the panel. It also serves to acquaint the members with their role in the study, as it usually precedes the test material. The control material provides a datum against which the responses to the test material can be measured.

Data are collected by "interest recorders" operated by the respondents (using rheostat dials mounted on the arms of their seats), finger sensors, questionnaires, and—in the case of children—cameras. This information is then correlated with the stimuli in the audio-visual material.

An interesting ruse—common in laboratory-panel work—is used to measure the effect of commercials on brand preferences. Upon their arrival, respondents are asked to fill in a questionnaire that, among other things, asks them to indicate which of a list of branded products to be given as door prizes they would like to receive. After their exposure to the test commercials, the respondents are again asked to indicate their preferences, under the guise that not everybody received the initial prize list and some members of the group were therefore left out of the prize pool. The shift in brand preferences is, of course, indicative of the commercials' power.

After the data have been recorded and reduced, a variety of statistical techniques are used to evaluate the persuasiveness of the test commercials or potential popularity of the television pilots. The quality of this evaluation is substantially enhanced by the control data, which can be compared with a massive amount of normative data collected from thousands of other panels.

ASI claims that it has been 90 percent accurate in predicting Nielsen ratings for television shows and actual box-office receipts for motion pictures (which may also be tested using ASI's in-theater technique). Although it has no comparable bench mark for judging the accuracy of its evaluation of television commercials, the company believes firmly that its approach is a valid one. Certainly the reactions of an audience not preconditioned by previous exposure to the commercials will often illuminate qualities in the material that its creators may have missed.

Research Suppliers

Time, limited personnel, and technology often drive the researcher to a supplier for his or her data needs.

Commercial Services

There are hundreds of firms in the United States that do various kinds of work associated with marketing research. These firms are generally called *research suppliers*. Their services range from project design through data acquisition, processing, and analysis. Some, like the Market Research Corporation of America, offer a whole spectrum of research services. Others, like Datab, Inc., offer only special services. Examples are seen in Figure 4-5.

The success of research suppliers stems from economies of scale and job specialization. They offer staffs of trained, experienced personnel, as well as access to special equipment that cannot be duplicated by the marketing-research departments of most companies. Even those firms that could muster the personnel and equipment needed for a major project—say, a nationwide consumer survey using personal interviews—would probably not need this capability on a continuous basis. It is faster and cheaper to use a research supplier.

Research suppliers offer their services on both an ad hoc and a continuous basis. For instance, consumer-behavior studies and store audits are often one-time projects and may be sold accordingly. Conversely, consumer panels usually operate continuously and the resultant flow of data is sold to many firms on a subscription basis.

Data Collectors

There are a number of research suppliers, called *field houses*, specializing in the collection of survey data. Examples are Monitor Surveys, Inc.; West Coast Community Surveys, Inc.; and the Drossler Research Corporation.

Some data collectors specialize in gathering information on advertising media. Pulse, Inc.; Daniel Starch and Staff, Inc.; and the A. C. Nielsen Company are especially prominent in this field.

Figure 4-5 **Examples of Outside Research Services**

Source: Reprinted from John G. Keane, "Some Observations on Marketing Research in Top Management Decision Making," *Journal of Marketing* (October 1969, p. 11), published by the American Marketing Association.

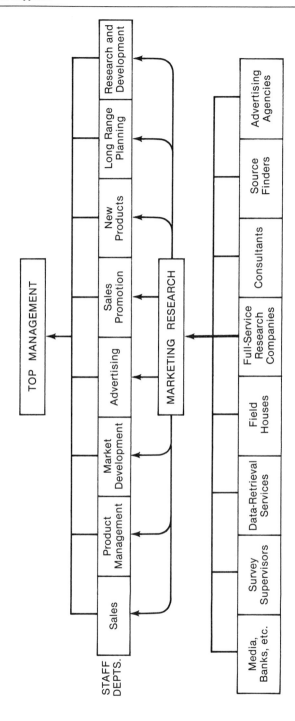

Pulse uses personal interviews to determine the demographic and product-use characteristics of the audiences of different radio stations. Starch uses personal interviews to rate the effectiveness of periodical advertising. Nielsen uses electronic devices to measure television and radio audiences. Their survey data are used by firms all over the country, especially in evaluating their advertising. Other media-research firms use telephone interviews or mail questionnaires to accomplish the same thing.

Pulse also offers market-share information based on personal interviews conducted thrice yearly in consumers' homes. This service—called "Brand/Metrics"—is offered for 35 local markets, such as Columbus, Jacksonville, Cincinnati, and Los Angeles. It is typical of the continuous information service that has become important to researchers in the convenience-goods fields. Brand-share data are offered by local market for 30 product classes, including gasoline, beer, deodorant, soap, dog food, toothpaste, soft drinks, and sliced white bread. Similar information is available on a weekly basis from firms such as Speedata, Inc., which conducts continuous audits of warehouses and retail stores in selected market areas.

Survey Supervisors

One of the unique features of the institutional arrangement of marketing research is the *survey supervisor*, a small independent operator who maintains a staff of interviewers to conduct surveys in a local area. The interviewers are usually housewives who do part-time work on call. The survey supervisor (usually a former interviewer) works as an independent contractor for a field house or directly for a research user. Surveys are generally bid for and executed on an ad hoc basis, with the survey supervisor working for a number of different firms over time. In most cases, clients pay unit prices—so many dollars per completed interview.

Survey supervisors neither participate in survey design nor perform analysis of survey data; they simply use questionnaires and follow instructions provided by their clients. They make contact with field houses or user firms by word of mouth and through the Marketing Research Association. Because of their quick-response capability (often they can provide the needed data within 48 hours of receiving the questionnaires), they are popular with many firms whose research departments maintain a current list of survey supervisors.

Data Retrieval Services

Data retrieval services have recently been developed to use computerized data banks and programed retrieval systems. Two types of services are available to subscribers. Since they are complementary, they are often sold together. The first is the *literature survey*. As new articles, books, or special information is reviewed, catalogued, annotated, and recorded in the data bank, it is compared to profiles of the subscribers. These profiles describe the subjects of interest to a client and his or her information needs. When a new piece of information that conforms to part of the client's profile is acquired, the title of the book or report is listed, along with a brief description, and sent to the subscriber. If the subscriber feels it is of value, he or she requests a copy of the document. The usefulness of such services depends on the quantity and quality of the documents reviewed, the accuracy and completeness of the cataloguing, and the precision and detail of the profiling. The catalogue and profiles are stored in a computer, which performs the matching operation.

The second service offered by these organizations is the *data search*. In this case, a client must take the initiative. He advises the data retrieval service of his problem or his need for specific information. A specialist reduces this request for help to a form digestible by the computer, which searches its data bank for information that conforms to the specifications. For instance, the client may need information on the petroleum-transportation industry in the southeastern United States. The resultant printout lists all the items in the services library containing or likely to contain information on this topic, together with a brief description of each item. The client selects those which seem most applicable, and copies are given or loaned to him. Often the service's library is contained on microfilm.

Sometimes a remote computer terminal is placed in the client's office, thus providing instantaneous access to the computer data bank. One example is Control Data Corporation's CYBERNET, a commercial data storage and retrieval service specializing in census information. The system consists of a centralized data bank and remote terminals that can be located anywhere in the country. Users can get immediate printouts of census information and related statistics simply by keyboarding their requests in the proper format.

The most grandiose information-retrieval programs have been sponsored by the federal government. For example, there are nine *technology-dissemination centers*, operating in conjunction with the National Aeronautics and Space Administration (NASA), offering this service.[16] Although they were primarily established as storage and retrieval centers for scientific and technical information, they also provide marketing data. They gather information from NASA and other government agencies, review the literature (including specialized marketing periodicals such as the *Journal of Marketing*), and acquire data from participating private sources. Although the reaction to the program thus far has been disappointing, the implications

---

[16] The dissemination centers are: Aerospace Research Applications Center (ARAC), Indiana University, Bloomington, Indiana; Center for Application of the Sciences and Technology (CAST), Wayne State University, Detroit, Michigan; Knowledge Availability Systems Center, University of Pittsburgh, Pittsburgh, Pennsylvania; Midwest Research Institute (Project ASTRA), 50th and Cherry Streets, Kansas City, Kansas; Office of Industrial Application, University of Maryland, College Park, Maryland; Science and Technology Research Center, North Carolina Board of Science and Technology, Durham, North Carolina; Technology Use Studies Center, Southeastern State College, Durant, Oklahoma; Technology Application Center, University of New Mexico, Albuquerque, New Mexico; Western Research Applications Center, University of Southern California, Los Angeles, California.

of the method are exciting. Some of its advocates envision the eventual construction of a gigantic data bank containing the bulk of human knowledge. The key to this intellectual treasure chest would be a properly coded punch card specifying the client's needs.

IBM has experimented with an in-house information storage and retrieval system similar to that sponsored by NASA. It too performs the literature survey and the data search and retrieval functions described above. However, its clientele are the employees of the firm, primarily engineers and managers. The system may eventually be placed on the market, where it would probably find customers among large firms or syndicates of small companies.

If a computerized service is unavailable, the market researcher will have to rely on manual methods. A competent research librarian can be a valuable asset if the research department is large enough to support one. If nothing else, researchers should at least learn their way around the local library.

The computerized retrieval services—as well as the more mundane manual systems of data storage, search, and retrieval—are part of the emerging science of information management. Marketing information systems—"MIS" in the vernacular—are becoming increasingly computerized and integrated. Ideally, they should combine a variety of data storage and manipulative functions, providing management with ready access to current market statistics, predictions, and forecasts. Although in its infancy, the MIS concept is rapidly diffusing among the major manufacturing corporations. We shall examine its theoretical potential later, both as a tool and as a philosophy of marketing management.

Free Data and Services   As we mentioned earlier, local market data are sometimes available free of charge from companies seeking to promote their nonresearch services or to attract business into their market area. The *Chicago Tribune*, the *Phoenix Gazette*, and the Bank of America are examples. The same thing is sometimes done on the national level by periodicals such as *The New Yorker* and *Newsweek*. However, these data are usually economic or demographic and rarely contain brand information.

Some firms, such as the *Los Angeles Times*, offer free or below-cost research services to big customers. The *Times*, for instance, has conducted surveys and consumer panels, tailored to the specifications of big advertisers, such as the Broadway department stores and Sears.

Cost-Sharing

The economies of scale associated with research suppliers are often the result of joint sponsorship of a project by several clients. Joint sponsorship is called "syndication." Usually the co-sponsors are not competitors. Hence, they lose nothing by sharing the information. They can gain considerably by splitting the cost. For example, a mail survey entailing, say 450,000 questionnaires, executed by National Family Opinion, Inc., might cost as much as a half-million dollars or more. So large a sum could not be justified by a single client, but the project could easily be afforded by a group of firms. The same principle of cost diffusion applies to the continuous information-gathering services. Here again, syndication is common.

Special Services

Research suppliers not only collect data, they will also design research projects, process the data, and perform analyses. However, not all suppliers offer the same range of services. Thus, the company best equipped to gather the data may not be equipped to assist the client in the matter of project design or to interpret findings. The latter functions are often separated from the data collection function. Some major research firms, such as Booz, Allen, and Hamilton, and Arthur D. Little, Inc., specialize in project design and data analysis, generally leaving the task of data collection to another firm. Other companies, such as Market Facts, Inc., offer a complete range of services, although their data-gathering capability may be limited to a few special areas and methods.

Hundreds of companies now offer data reduction and analysis services. These firms offer time-sharing arrangements, programming assistance, and program libraries, and give small research departments access to highly sophisticated computers at a cost they can afford. A small research department can now have a computer capability—for as little as $500 per month— comparable to that of a major corporation or university.

Problems

1   What raw data would probably be needed for a study of (a) the automobile market, (b) the aluminum market, and (c) the prescription-drug market? What historical sources might provide this information?

2   Cite a specific source that might provide each of the following kinds of information: (a) a method for determining profile of Chevrolet buyers, (b) the consumer price index, and (c) the sales of a major competitor.

3   Using the *Statistical Abstract of the United States* or the *Economic Almanac*, answer the following questions:

    a   What was the total demand for color television sets in 1976? Has the demand been increasing?

    b   If the Brunswick Corporation chose to sell exclusively to bowling alleys, how many potential customers would it have in the United States?

    c   If school children consume an average of $32.40 worth of new textbooks annually, what is the worth of the aggregate market for such textbooks in the New England states?

4   Comment on the reliability of the data provided in answer to problem 3.

5   Suggest some advantages (if any) and possible drawbacks, for each of the following firms, of subscribing to the consumer-panel services of the Market Research Corporation of America: (a) General Mills, (b) IBM, and (c) Safeway Stores.

6   In its promotional literature, National Family Opinion stresses the loyalty of its panel members. NFO argues that this loyalty results in a very high rate of return of consumer diaries and "reinforces reliability."[17] Do you agree, and why or why not*o*

7   The recruitment and maintenance of panel members are the most difficult problems in consumer-panel operation. The root of the trouble is the requirement that the panel be representative of the market population from which it is drawn. Suggest some methods of ensuring the representativeness of a panel at its inception and during its lifespan.

8   Suggest some research problems that could benefit from the use of (a) continuous consumer-panel data, (b) store-audit panel data, and (c) laboratory-panel data. Be specific, and explain how the data would be used.

9   List the advantages and disadvantages of contracting work to research suppliers.

10   Is there anything about Exhibit 4-4 that bothers you? If so, what is it?

---

[17] *National Family Opinion, Inc.* (Toledo, Ohio: National Family Opinion, n.d.), p. 8.

Chapter 5
Surveys

Key Concepts

Survey Methods
Alternate ways of collecting survey data—their virtues and vices

Errors in Survey Data
Sampling error, respondent errors, and interviewer (or observer) errors

Survey Design
The procedure for preparing a survey

Key Terms

descriptive data
explanatory data
observation
inquiry
telephone interviews
mail questionnaires
personal interviews
group interviews

sampling error
respondent error
interviewer error
observer error
interviewer bias
nonsampling error
self-concept
pretest

Purpose

Often, when the well of prerecorded data runs dry, the researcher must enter the marketplace and gather data firsthand. A survey is in order.[1]

---

[1] The serious student of surveys should review the *Journal of Marketing Research*, **14**:3 (August 1977), which is a special issue on survey research.

Applications

Surveys are so pervasive that the reader has likely been a respondent. They are very common in commercial marketing. Surveys are used to describe markets, measure attitudes, preferences, and opinions, and track consumer behavior. They are often part of experiments and consumer panel designs.

Surveys also illustrate the use of the marketing arts outside the commercial sector. Hardly a newscast goes by without reporting the results of a recent survey, typically involving voter preferences or public opinion on some current issue. Most are conducted by MR suppliers, such as the Gallup Organization and the A. C. Nielsen Company.

Surveys are also finding their way into the court-room, where they serve as evidence of public attitudes and opinions. For instance, the Los Angeles County Sheriff's Department authorized a survey of California adults to determine attitudes toward obscenity. The objective was to define "community standards." The Supreme Court had ruled that such standards, if specified, could be used in the arrest and prosecution of pornographers.[2]

Other examples of surveys in the courtroom are a survey of consumer beliefs in a deceptive advertising case, a survey of food store customers in a trading area case, and a survey of consumer perceptions in a trademark infringement case. Each of these surveys was conducted by a marketing research supplier. In each case a member of the research firm was required to testify as an expert witness.

Surveys are now common in administrative hearings conducted by the regulatory agencies.[3] These studies may be made just for the hearings. Or, they may have been conducted for more conventional uses, but subpoened by the agency. One supplier, Burke Marketing Research, specializes in such surveys. The "Burke Claim Support Studies" are surveys designed just for regulatory agencies.

Descriptive vs. Explanatory Data

At the very least, marketing research should be able to describe a significant (to the firm) market phenomenon. What is happening? When and where is it happening? For example, have sales changed? By how much? When, and in what regions? Is there a new competitor in the market? If so, what are the characteristics and price of its product, and what is its market share? Such information is called *descriptive data*.

The information gathered must include data on the variable most relevant to the marketing problem, usually sales. If the objective of the research is to explain the cause of either the magnitude or the changes in the relevant variable, then data must also be gathered for each of the possible

---

[2] The details of this survey are found in Case Study 4 at the end of Part 4 in this book.

[3] An excellent summary of the use of surveys in legal and quasi-legal proceedings is found in E. Dean Howard, "Marketing Research Gains Acceptance in Legal and Quasi-legal Proceeding," *Marketing News*, **9**:17 (March 12, 1976), pp. 1, 4, and 5. Also see the Case Study at the end of Chapter 1.

explanatory variables. Such information is called *explanatory data* and is associated with the independent variables of causal research. Typical explanatory—or "independent"—variables are price, advertising, consumer preferences, and actions by competitors.

Basic Survey Methods

Survey data can be gathered by observation or inquiry. *Observation* involves a direct examination of the variable(s)—watching consumer behavior, counting dealer inventories, or comparing prices. *Inquiry* involves the questioning of respondents who are sometimes middlemen but more often consumers.

Observational data are more reliable than data obtained by inquiry, but generally less useful. The basic *modus operandi* of observation is simple: One or more members of the research team goes into the field to observe buyer behavior, sometimes using electronic devices. There is no direct contact with the buyers themselves. Alternatively, the researchers may inspect inventories or shelf displays to see how quickly the product is moving and whether sales have been affected by a market experiment. Sometimes consumer reaction to a point-of-purchase display is observed, using cameras or one-way mirrors. Traffic studies (important to store-location decisions) are often made. Head counts and vehicle information are acquired by observation. For example, one way to determine a store's market area is to observe the license numbers of the cars in its parking lot. Owners' addresses can be found by checking with the state's department of motor vehicles. Then the geographic distribution of the store's customers can be determined.

If measures are taken to ensure random sampling, and the field workers are properly instructed and supervised, data produced by observation should be reliable. However, these kinds of surveys are moderately expensive and time-consuming. Also, most observational techniques are limited to some form of counting, restricting their application.

Forms of Inquiry

Inquiry data can be obtained in three ways: (1) by personal interviews, (2) by telephone and (3) by mail questionnaires. We shall examine each of these three methods in turn.

Personal Interviews   Personal interviews are obtained by having one or more members of the research team go into the field to question either middlemen or consumers face to face. The interview may take place in the respondent's home or office. It may be held on the street, in a store, or, as shown in Exhibit 5-1, in a shopping mall.

The personal interview is the most flexible survey method. It is also the most expensive, the most time-consuming, and the most vulnerable to error. Its chief virtue is its ability to accommodate unstructured questions. This is extremely useful in exploratory research, where the usual objective is to define

Exhibit 5-1   **A Personal Interview**

Source: Courtesy of Burke Marketing Research, Cincinnati, OH.

the problem more clearly. The interviewer, often using a tape recorder, simply directs the conversation toward the right subject and encourages the person to keep talking. Hopefully, the subject will reveal attitudes or behavioral patterns, bring up problems, or contribute ideas that had previously eluded the the researchers.

The personal interview also works well with structured questions. Individual items can be more complicated, and the questionnaires themselves longer, than with a phone or mail survey. The nonresponse error also can be minimized by using skilled field workers, since it is much easier to hang up the telephone or ignore a mail questionnaire than it is to turn away a personable and determined interviewer. Even if the field worker uses a structured questionnaire, the personal interview may still uncover supplemental data about aspects of the problem that did not occur to the researchers in preparing the questionnaire.

An illustration of how a personal interview works is provided by Exhibit 5-2, which contains excerpts from a major brewery's study of its relationship with the franchised wholesalers of its beer. These independent middlemen played an important role in both the distribution and the promotion of the brewery's product, and a good relationship between the two was critical. As is typical in such cases, the data were collected by a research supplier, Westat Research, Inc.

The topics covered by the interview included the effect of a recent strike, the performance of the brewery's district sales managers and other members of its marketing staff, the franchise agreement, and the marketing programs of competing breweries. Since the entire questionnaire ran for 17 pages and involved a number of open-ended questions, it would have been virtually impossible to administer by telephone or mail.

Like other survey methods, the personal interview has its special disadvantages. One problem is the bias introduced into the data by the interaction between the interviewer and the respondent. Another drawback is the time required to recruit and train interviewers and the management problems associated with the maintenance and supervision of field personnel. Of course, these latter problems can be alleviated by using a research supplier, many of whom specialized in personal interviews.

The personal interview is also the costliest method of collecting survey data. The cost per interview will vary considerably, depending on the length and complexity of the questionnaire, the level of skill required of the interviewer, the geographic distribution and availability of respondents, and the minimum level of nonresponse specified. For instance, a cost of $10 per respondent is typical for a 25-minute interview gotten through door-to-door canvassing with the sample membership distributed two to the block, no callbacks required, and a moderately long but well-structured questionnaire used. The cost might be considerably lower—say, $2 per respondent—if the interviews were very short, if a simple and highly structured questionnaire was used, and if the respondents were customers at a shopping center. On the other hand, the cost might be very high—say, $100 per respondent—if the interview were to run for several hours, using sophisticated projective techniques.

One method of economizing is to use *group interviews*. This technique brings together a number of respondents, usually six to twelve, who participate in group discussion. The discussion is led by an interviewer who keeps the conversation on the right subject, encourages reluctant members to participate, and records the dialogue. The format is usually unstructured, to give the subjects more latitude in responding. Unfortunately the method is very susceptible to bias since the group members are often not truly representative of the population from which they are drawn and there is a pronounced interaction between respondents.

Exhibit 5-2   **Wholesaler Study Using Personal Interviews**

INSTRUCTIONS TO THE INTERVIEWER

1. Turn on your tape recorder before beginning each interview.
2. Indicate the fact that every wholesaler's anonymity will be completely protected and that we even prefer them not to discuss the survey with other wholesalers, company personnel, or other persons.
3. Emphasize the importance of obtaining as objective a report as possible on all aspects of the survey.

*   *   *   *

II. This section deals with [the Company's] management, starting with the district manager's level. First, consider the field marketing group, including your district manager, your division manager, and the regional manager.

   12. On the average, would you say you see your district manager

(a)	once a week or more	☐
(b)	2–3 times a month	☐
(c)	once a month	☐
(d)	once every 2–3 months	☐
(e)	less than once every three months	☐

   13. On a typical visit here, what kind of activities does your district manager normally engage in? (*PROBE FOR SPECIFIC ACTIVITIES.*)

_____

_____

_____

_____

Now, think about the general relationship you have with your district manager from the viewpoint of (a) your personal relationship, (b) communications between you or your salesmen and him, and (c) his ability to help supervise the work of your sales representatives.

   14. Would you rate
     (a) your personal relationships with your district manager as

(a)	excellent	☐
(b)	good	☐
(c)	fair	☐
(d)	poor	☐

     (b) communications between yourself or your salesmen and your district manager as

(a)	excellent	☐
(b)	good	☐
(c)	fair	☐
(d)	poor	☐

*   *   *   *

III. This section pertains to the whole history of your equity agreement with [the Company]. As you may recall, the original equity agreement was presented to the wholesalers in January 1967. Then, in January 1969, a revised agreement was presented to the wholesalers. This was followed by a further revised agreement in May 1969.

First, please think about any effect the original 1967 equity agreement had on your operations.

Exhibit 5-2   **Wholesaler Study Using Personal Interviews (*cont'd.*)**

23. (a) Did this original equity agreement have any effect on your operations?

        Yes   ☐
        No   ☐   *(SKIP TO Q.24.)*

    (b) In what ways?   *(CHECK AS MANY AS APPLY)*

        Additional warehouse space was built   ☐
        Trucks or other equipment was purchased   ☐
        Office help was added   ☐
        New operating efficiencies were obtained   ☐
        More emphasis was given to other brands   ☐
        Additional promotional or advertising expenditures were made   ☐
        The number or quality of the sales staff was increased   ☐

        Other (specify) _____
        _____
        _____

24. Could you give me a rough estimate of approximately how many additional
     capital expenditures you would say were made as a direct result of this original
     equity agreement?

                          $ _____

                    *   *   *   *

Source: Adapted from a 1967 retailer study conducted by Westat Research Inc., Bethesda, Md.
Reprinted by permission.

Group interviewing is popular in exploratory research. It has proven
especially useful, as well as economic, in generating and testing product and
promotional ideas.

Telephone Interviews   The telephone interview is similar to the personal
interview, but the format is less flexible and the quantity of data that can be
gathered from an individual respondent is more limited. However, it does
have certain advantages. Given a specific amount of time and money, telephone interviews can reach a greater number of respondents, distributed over
a larger geographic area, than can personal interviews. The telephone interview is a much faster method of obtaining data than the mail questionnaire,
and the number of nonrespondents is relatively low if callbacks are used. The
cost per respondent is also low; $7.50 for a 15-minute interview is typical.
Finally, the interviewing can be done on very short notice—sometimes less
than 24 hours—thanks to the numerous research suppliers who provide this
kind of service. For these reasons, the telephone interview is probably the
most common method of collecting survey data.

Exhibit 5-3 shows the format for a telephone interview used in a study
of the citrus market, sponsored by the Florida Department of Citrus. Ironi-
cally, the research supplier was located in California, but the firm conducted telephone surveys nationwide. The objective of the survey was to
gather data on consumer awareness of, attitudes toward, and behavior in

Exhibit 5-3   **National Consumer Survey Using Telephone Interviews**

Hello, may I speak to the lady of the house? My name is _____
and I'm calling for Drossler Research Corporation, a national consumer research company. We are taking a survey on meal planning and I would like to
ask you a few questions.

1. When you think of things to drink for breakfast, what beverages do you
   think of? (CIRCLE BEVERAGE MENTIONED FIRST UNDER "1ST
   MENTION"–CIRCLE ALL OTHERS MENTIONED UNDER "OTHERS
   MENTIONED.") What other beverages come to mind?

2. When you think of things to drink for people watching their weight, which
   beverages come to mind? What others come to mind?

	Q. 1		Q. 2	
	Breakfast		Weight Watching	
	1st MENTION 15	OTHERS MENTIONED 16	1st MENTION 17	OTHERS MENTIONED 18
DO NOT READ LIST				
Coffee	1 . . .	1	1 . . .	1
Milk	2 . . .	2	2 . . .	2
Tea	3 . . .	3	3 . . .	3
Orange Juice	4 . . .	4	4 . . .	4
Grapefruit Juice	5 . . .	5	5 . . .	5
Other Fruit Juices . .	6 . . .	6	6 . . .	6
Fruit Drinks, Punches, Ades, Kool-Aid, etc.	7 . . .	7	7 . . .	7
Soft Drinks	8 . . .	8	8 . . .	8
Other _____ (SPECIFY)	X . . .	X	X . . .	X
None	Y . . .	Y	Y . . .	Y

*   *   *   *

regard to the purchase of citrus products, especially orange juice. The sponsor
is deliberately not identified, and the study camouflaged as "a survey on meal
planning" in order to avoid prejudicing the responses. If the respondents
knew the real purpose of the interview, they might tend to give answers
favorable to the product rather than revealing their true feelings. (Notice how
the interviewer's instructions are incorporated into the questionnaire.)

Unfortunately telephone-interview data are biased in favor of households with listed telephones. Since the lack of a telephone or an unlisted telephone is frequently associated with a special social or demographic
characteristic, this tends to make the survey not representative of the entire
market population. For instance, prominent and wealthy people often have

Exhibit 5-3   **National Consumer Survey Using Telephone Interviews (*cont'd.*)**

4. Do you recall seeing or hearing any advertising or commercials recently for orange juice?

25

Yes   1

No   2

SKIP TO QUESTION 5

4a. In your own words, would you please describe the advertising?
(PROBE)

_____ 26

_____ 27

_____

4b. What did the advertising say about orange juice? What else did it say?   (PROBE)

_____ 28

_____ 29

_____

4c. Whose orange juice was being advertised?

_____ 30

_____

IF FLORIDA MENTIONED ABOVE, SKIP Q. 5 AND READ INSTRUCTIONS AT THE BOTTOM OF THIS PAGE.

IF FLORIDA NOT MENTIONED IN QUESTIONS 4a, 4b OR 4c, ASK Q. 5.

unlisted numbers (considered a status symbol in some circles) in order to avoid sales personnel and other unwanted callers. Very poor people sometimes have no telephone or do not list their phones to avoid being harassed by bill collectors. The exclusion of these two groups, in whole or in part, may, of course, be irrelevant if the very wealthy are an insignificant segment of the market and the very poor cannot afford the product. When unlisted phones are a problem, random dialing may be the solution.[4]

---

[4] For ways to deal with the unlisted telephone problem, see E. Laird Landon, Jr., and Sharon K. Banks, "Relative Efficiency and Bias of Plus-One Telephone Sampling"; and Clyde L. Rich, "Is Random Digit Dialing Really Necessary?"; both in *Journal of Marketing Research*, **14**:3 (August 1977), pp. 294–299 and 300–305. Another useful article is Mathew Hauck and Micheal Cox, "Locating a Sample by Random Digit Dialing," *Public Opinion Quarterly*, **38**:3 (Summer 1974), pp. 253-260.

5. Do you recall seeing or hearing any advertising or commercials recently for Florida orange juice?

<u>31</u>

Yes . . . . | 1

No . . . . | 2

Don't Know . . . . | Y

SKIP TO QUESTION 6a

5a. In your own words, would you please describe the Florida orange juice advertising?   (PROBE)

_____   <u>32</u>

_____

_____   <u>33</u>

_____

5b. What did the advertising say about the orange juice? What else did it say?   (PROBE)

_____   <u>34</u>

_____

_____   <u>35</u>

_____

INTERVIEWER:

A. IF GIRL SINGING ABOUT ORANGE JUICE <u>NOT</u> MENTIONED IN QUESTIONS 4a/4b OR QUESTIONS 5a/5b, ASK QUESTION 6a.

B. IF GIRL SINGING ABOUT ORANGE JUICE MENTIONED, BUT ANITA BRYANT <u>NOT</u> MENTIONED IN QUESTIONS 4a/4b OR 5a/5b, SKIP TO QUESTION 6b.

C. IF ANITA BRYANT SINGING ABOUT ORANGE JUICE MENTIONED IN QUESTIONS 4a/4b OR 5a/5b, SKIP TO QUESTION 6f.

6a. Do you recall seeing or hearing any advertising recently featuring a girl who sings about orange juice?

<u>36</u>

Yes . . . . | 1 ASK Q. 6b

No . . . . | 2 SKIP TO Q. 6c

6b. What was the name of the girl in the advertising who sings about the orange juice?

<u>37</u>

Anita Bryant . . . . | 1 SKIP TO Q. 6d

Other _____ | X
(SPECIFY) | ASK Q. 6c

Don't Know . . . . | Y

6c. Do you recall seeing or hearing any advertisements recently featuring Anita Bryant, who sings about orange juice?

<u>38</u>

Yes. | 1 ASK Q. 6d |

No 2

Don't Know . . . . Y

```
INTERVIEWER:

IF GIRL SINGING NOT RECALLED ("No" IN Q. 6a AND
"No/Don't Know" IN Q. 6c), SKIP TO Q. 7.

IF ANY RECALL OF GIRL SINGING IN QUESTIONS 4a, b, c/5a,
b/6a, b, c, ASK QUESTIONS 6d, e, f, AND g.
```

6d. Would you please describe this advertising?   (PROBE)

_____ <u>39</u>

_____

_____ <u>40</u>

_____

6e. What (else) did the advertising say about orange juice? What else did it say?   (PROBE)

_____ <u>41</u>

_____

_____ <u>42</u>

_____.

6f. How would you say you liked (Anita Bryant) (the girl) in the advertising you saw or heard—would you say you liked her very much, quite a bit, slightly, or not at all?

<u>43</u>

Very Much 1
Quite a Bit 2
Slightly 3
Not at All. 4
Don't Know . . . . Y

6g. Where did you see or hear this advertising? (DO NOT READ LIST)

<u>44</u>

Radio 1
Magazine 2
Newspaper 3
TV 4
Billboard 5

Other _____ X
           (SPECIFY)
Don't Know . . . . Y

*   *   *   *

Source: Adapted from a Survey conducted by Drossler Research Corp., San Francisco, Cal., for Florida Department of Citrus, September 1970. Reproduced by permission.

Exhibit 5-4   National Consumer Survey Using a Mail Questionnaire

---

Clip and mail only the answer portion of each page. ——→

FAMILY MONEY MANAGEMENT
QUESTIONNAIRE

DON'T MISS THIS CHANCE TO BE HEARD!

These are the Official Rules for Better Homes and Gardens $25,000 Money Management Sweepstakes

1. Fully complete the Family Money Management Questionnaire.

2. Be sure to print your full name and address in the appropriate spot. Put the answer portions of the questionnaire into an envelope and mail it to: Money Management Questions, 1716 Locust, Des Moines, Iowa 50303.

3. In order to qualify for the prize money, you should try to fill out the questionnaire as completely as possible. There are no right or wrong answers. We want you to express your own honest preferences, ideas, and opinions.

4. The 50 winners will each receive $500. They will be selected on or about January 1, 1968, from a random drawing of all questionnaires submitted. Winners will be notified on or about January 15.

5. You are encouraged to submit a questionnaire from both the October and November issues. These questionnaires are different—thus, you are eligible to win $500 for each month's entry—total $1,000. Each entry must be mailed separately; they must be postmarked not later than December 4, 1967, and received no later than December 15.

6. All questionnaires, contents, and ideas therein become the property of Meredith Publishing Company, and may be used for whatever purposes the company deems appropriate. However, your name will be held in complete confidence—unless, of course, you are chosen as a winner.

7. A list of winners will be published in the May 1968 issue of Better Homes and Gardens. Sorry, but we cannot answer individual inquiries about the Sweepstakes or the winners.

8. Any resident of the United States may enter—except in states where sweepstakes are prohibited. Employees of Meredith Publishing Company, its subsidiary and affiliated companies, their advertising agencies, and their families are ineligible.

9. This Sweepstakes is subject to all federal and state regulations. Any liability for federal, state, or other taxes or duties imposed on a prize received will be the sole responsibility of the prize winner and not of Meredith Publishing Company.

Want your opinions to count? Then spend a few minutes on this Better Homes and Gardens Money Management Questionnaire. You could be $500 richer, too, since 50 of our respondents will receive a $500 sweepstakes bonus. Because the survey spans several financial areas, from insurance to food-buying, you'll want this to be as much of a family project as you can. Then you will be giving us information vital to a sound editorial program —and by the time you finish, chances are you'll be looking at your own family money planning in a new light.

Your reply will be kept in strict confidence by our editors. No one will put your name on any list, or try to sell you something as a result of your reply. Be as frank as you wish, too. Winners are drawn at random, so your answers can't possibly influence your chances.

When you finish, you may have additional comments. Feel free to send them along on a separate sheet.

Questions   Answers

Please circle number next to the answer that comes closest to your opinion. Circle only one number unless question asks for several.

1. How do you feel about the availability of credit today— through credit cards, charge accounts, installment buying, and the like?

1. 1 Too easy for people to buy on credit
   2 Still not easy enough for people to buy on credit
   3 Credit availability is about right

2. How successful do you think American business has been in regulating itself through voluntary codes of ethics?

2. 1 Very successful   2 Fairly successful
   3 Not too successful   4 Not at all successful

3. How desirable do you feel it would be to have the federal government test and grade a wider range of consumer products?

3. 1 Very desirable   2 Somewhat desirable   3 Not desirable

4. The cost of living has risen in the past two years. Do you feel that prices of any of the following have risen far out of line from the others? Circle as many as apply.

4. 1 Clothing 2 Cosmetics 3 Furniture 4 Housing
   5 Taxes 6 Food products 7 Public transportation
   8 Medical expenses 9 Repair services 10 None of these

5. How do you feel advertising affects the price of most of the products you buy?

5. 1 Generally raises price   2 Generally lowers price
   3 Makes no difference in price

6. As the cost of community services rises (for schools, street improvements, sanitation facilities, welfare services, etc.), what action would you *most prefer? Least prefer?*

6.

	Most Prefer	Least Prefer
New or higher sales taxes	1	2
New or higher income taxes	3	4
Increased corporation taxes	5	6
More federal aid for schools, urban projects	7	8
Further increases in property taxes	9	10
Reduce the community services	11	12

7. Do you feel that the cost of sending a youngster to college should be deductible from the parent's federal income tax?

7. 1 Yes   2 No   3 No opinion

8. Would you be willing to pay additional Social Security taxes to extend Medicare benefits to persons younger than 65?

8. 1 Yes   2 No   3 No opinion

BETTER HOMES AND GARDENS, OCTOBER, 1967

Another drawback of telephone interviews is that they are necessarily restricted to verbal questions administered orally. Pictures, such as those used in thematic-apperception tests (TAT), cannot be employed. The interview period is usually limited to 20 minutes, and the questions must be specific; an unstructured format is not feasible.

Exhibit 5-4   **National Consumer Survey Using a Mail Questionnaire (*cont'd.*)**

Mail in this portion.

Questions

Answers

26. Do you think you can get a better deal on a new car by shopping a number of dealers selling the same make?

26. 1 Yes   2 No

27. Do you figure you'll get about the same trade-in price for your present car whether it's in good condition or not?

27. 1 Yes   2 No   3 Don't own a car

28. Which do you feel usually charges you the lowest interest on the purchase of a new car?

28. 1 The auto dealer   2 A finance company   3 A bank   4 A credit union   5 All about the same   6 Don't know

29. How do you feel about new auto safety features beyond those presently required?

29. 1 Should be standard equipment with all buyers paying for them   2 Should be optional features at extra cost

30. National averages put the annual costs for owning a new medium-sized car at around $1,000 per year during the first three years. In your opinion, which of the following makes up the *largest* part of the $1,000 cost? The *smallest*?

30.
	Largest	*Smallest*
Depreciation and financing	1	2
Insurance, taxes, licensing	1	2
Gasoline, maintenance, repairs	1	2
Don't know	1	2

31. About how much would you estimate you pay for gas and oil to operate the car you drive?

31. 1 One-two cents per mile   2 Three-four cents   3 Five-six cents   4 Seven-eight cents   5 Nine-ten cents   6 Eleven-twelve cents   7 Don't know   8 Don't drive a car

32. Certain drivers with accident or violation records must pay higher premiums for their auto insurance. In writing these policies, the insurance companies:

32. 1 Perform a valuable and necessary service   2 Keep many dangerous drivers behind the wheel   3 Make large profits from the higher rates

33. How often do you shop at more than one grocery store to take advantage of "specials"?

33. 1 About every week   2 At least once a month   3 Almost never   4 Never

34. How do you feel nationally advertised brands usually compare in *price* to local brands or grocery chain brands? In *quality?*

34.
	Price	*Quality*
National brands higher	1	2
National brands lower	3	4
About equal	5	6

35. Many food and household products are sold in "fractional" quantities (such as 1 pound 13¾ ounces or 1 pint 6 ounces). What do you think is the main reason manufacturers do this?

35. 1 To serve customers with a wider choice of sizes   2 To make it hard to compare prices of different size packages   3 To permit use of standard-size containers   4 To allow for recipes which call for odd quantities

36. How do you usually choose among brands of canned, bottled, or packaged foods?

36. 1 Compare weights and volumes   2 Compare price   3 Compare labels   4 Normally stay with brands I know

37. Which of these characteristics of convenience foods (such as cake mixes, prepared complete dinners, instant mashed potatoes) is most important to you?

37. 1 Time saving   2 Work saving   3 Fewer ingredients to buy and stock   4 Decreases waste
Your comment: _____

38. Has the *percentage of your total income* spent for food changed during the past two years?

38. 1 Has increased greatly   4 Has decreased slightly   2 Has increased slightly   5 Hasn't changed   3 Has decreased greatly

39. Which would be more likely to influence your decision to buy a major appliance?

39. 1 The manufacturer's reputation and warranty   2 The local dealer's reputation for service

40. Which would be likely to have more influence on your decision to buy a major appliance?

40. 1 The place where I can get the lowest price   2 Reputation of manufacturer or dealer

41. How would you rate the durability of the majority of *small* appliances you have bought during recent years?

41. 1 Well-built, trouble-free   2 Fairly well-built, require occasional service   3 Poorly built, too often need repair   4 Haven't purchased any small appliances in recent years

42. You are about to make a credit purchase. Assuming the sales price is acceptable, which of these considerations would be most important to you?

42. 1 Total interest   2 Amount of down-payment or trade-in   3 Size of your monthly payments   4 Never buy on credit
Your comment: _____

BETTER HOMES AND GARDENS, OCTOBER, 1967

Mail Questionnaires   The mail questionnaire, usually accompanied by an explanatory letter and return envelope, is a popular method of reaching mass markets. It is the easiest and cheapest survey device and requires no field workforce. The cost per response is low—usually less than 90 cents—and the study can cover a wide geographic area. The errors induced by interviewer-

Exhibit 5-4   National Consumer Survey Using a Mail Questionnaire (*cont'd.*)

Mail in this portion. **Answers**	**Questions**
43. 1 A percentage rate 2 Total dollars of interest	**43.** In installment buying, is it more helpful to you to have the finance charge expressed as:
44. 1 A law requiring the same wording of finance charges on all credit contracts 2 Let each company decide on wording of finance charges that best suits the nature of its business	**44.** Which would you favor regarding interest and finance charges on credit contracts?
45. 1 None 5 $50,000 2 $5,000 6 $75,000 3 $10,000 7 $100,000 4 $25,000 8 Don't know	**45.** How much life insurance would you recommend for a typical 35-year-old father of two with income of $10,000 a year?
46. 1 Most life insurance coverage should be on the breadwinner 2 Term insurance is always the best buy in life insurance 3 Employer's group insurance is sufficient for most families 4 Life insurance doesn't keep pace with inflation 5 By shopping around, you usually can get a better buy	**46.** Following are six statements about life insurance. Circle the number of each statement you feel is *true*.
47. 1 Annually 2 When have increase in family income 3 When have increase in family 4 Let agent set up review 5 Don't have life insurance 6 Never	**47.** How frequently do you feel you should review your life insurance program with an agent?
48. 1 Much too high 2 High but justified by research costs 3 Not out of line with other medical expenses 4 Considering the benefits, price is reasonable Your comment: _____	**48.** How do you feel about the price of prescription drugs today?
49. 1 Almost always 3 Occasionally 2 Whenever possible 4 Never	**49.** When you purchase drugs prescribed by your physician, do you shop around for the best buy?
Now please answer these questions about you and your family.	
50. Ages:	**50.** Ages of children under 18:
51. ☐ Under 25 ☐ 25-34 ☐ 35-44 ☐ 45-54 ☐ 55-64 ☐ Over 65	**51.** Age of household head:
52. ☐ Man ☐ Woman	**52.** Household head is:
53. ☐ Grade school ☐ Some high school ☐ High school grad ☐ Some college ☐ College graduate ☐ Graduate work	**53.** Education of household head:
54. ☐ Full-time ☐ Part-time ☐ Not at all ☐ No wife in household	**54.** Is the wife employed outside the home:
55. ☐ Central city (50,000 or larger) ☐ Suburb of a large city ☐ Small city or town (less than 50,000) ☐ Rural	**55.** Where do you live?
56. ☐ Own ☐ Rent	**56.** Do you own or rent your home?
57. _____	**57.** What make(s), year(s) of car do you own?
58. ☐ Husband ☐ Wife ☐ Both ☐ Other member	**58.** Which member of the family filled out this questionnaire?
NAME.................................... ADDRESS................................. CITY............STATE......ZIP CODE......	REMEMBER, if you have comments on any questions, please feel free to send them along on a separate sheet of paper. BETTER HOMES AND GARDENS, OCTOBER, 1967

respondent interaction are avoided, and the respondent can remain anonymous. (This can be important when sensitive information, such as a person's age or income, is being solicited). Rural areas are easily reached, and respondents can fill out the questionnaire at their leisure.

Exhibit 5-4   National Consumer Survey Using a Mail Questionnaire (*cont'd.*)

Mail in this portion.

Answers

Questions

---

9. 1 Always   2 Usually   3 Seldom   4 Never

9. Do you follow a consistent program of saving *before* bills are paid and other obligations or desires are met?

---

10. 1 Husband   2 Wife   3 Both husband and wife   4 Am single

10. In your household, who usually pays the bills?

---

11. 1 Increase cost   2 Decrease cost   3 Make no difference

11. How do you feel trading stamps affect the cost of food?

12.

	Husband	Wife	Both
New refrigerator	1	2	3
New carpet	1	2	3
New sofa	1	2	3
New wall paneling	1	2	3
	4 I do, because I'm single		

Your comment:_____

12. In deciding what specific brand to buy, who in your household makes the decisions when picking:

---

13. 1 Yes   2 No

13. Are you satisfied with the amount you are saving?

---

14. 1 Budget food only   2 Budget certain family expenses, but not all   3 Budget total family expenses   4 Have no budget of any kind

14. Do you have a spending plan or budget in which you allot a specified amount of money to food, household needs, clothing, car expenses, entertainment, etc.?

---

15. 1 Money is dribbled away in small amounts by careless, day-to-day spending   2 The family makes expensive purchases impulsively whether they need them or not   3 Just don't have enough income for their needs

15. Of the statements at left, which one is the most common reason families develop serious financial problems?

---

16. 1 Charge accounts lead to financial irresponsibility   2 Charge accounts teach financial responsibility

16. Which comes closest to your views on charge accounts for teen-agers?

---

17. 1 Fall behind the national trend in cost of living   2 Stay comparatively even   3 Move ahead of living costs

17. Do you expect your income in the next five years to:

---

18. 1 Better than ten years ago   2 About the same   3 Not as good as ten years ago

18. What do you think of the workmanship in today's new houses?

---

19. 1 Condition and appearance of the house itself   2 Quality of the neighborhood   3 Quality of schools

19. Which of the following would you rate as most important in establishing the sales price of an existing house?

---

20. 1 More expensive than buying on installment credit   2 Less expensive than buying on installment credit   3 Cost runs about the same for installment or package method

20. Would you say that financing major appliances by making them part of a new-house mortgage package is:

---

21. 1 Very difficult   2 Fairly difficult   3 Not too difficult

Your comment:_____

21. Do you find it difficult to learn about new building products?

---

22. 1 Too low   2 Too high   3 About right

22. Many mortgage lenders use the formula of 2½ times annual income to determine how much house the average family can afford. Do you feel this is:

---

23. 1 Yes   2 No   3 Am now renting

23. Comparing your present annual income and the approximate market value of your home today, are you living in *less* house than the 2½-times formula allows?

---

24. 1 Already invest in common stocks   2 Not interested   3 Risk too great   4 Not familiar enough with stock market   5 Too much investment required   6 Too much time required   7 Still building up basic savings and life insurance   8 Don't believe in any speculative investment   9 Don't have money to invest

24. If you do not now invest in common stocks, what are your major reasons? Circle as many as apply

---

25. _____   _____
          (make)   (year)
Your comment:_____

25. In your opinion, what was the best car you ever owned?

BETTER HOMES AND GARDENS, OCTOBER, 1967

The disadvantages of this method are its slowness—it generally takes up to a month to get the majority of replies back—and the likelihood of mistakes and omissions. As a rule, the response is relatively poor. A 40-percent or better return is exceptional, except when the subject of the inquiry is an ego-involved product. A 5- to 10-percent return is common.[5] The data may be biased in favor of people with a special interest in the subject, who are more likely to respond. Also, the method excludes illiterates and those who do not read the language used in the questionnaire. Unstructured, long, or complicated questions are impractical, since they tend to be ignored or misinterpreted.

Exhibit 5-4 shows the first part of a mail questionnaire that appeared in *Better Homes and Gardens*, a well-known national special-interest magazine. The purpose of this particular survey was to gather data on respondent attitudes and behavior with respect to household money mangement. Notice the readability and attractiveness of the questionnaire, which is enhanced by the use of cartoons and several styles of type. Note also the incentive of $25,000 in prize money, designed to encourage participation.

Errors in Survey Data

Three types of errors are associated with survey data: (1) sampling error, (2) respondent error, and (3) interviewer (or observer) error. They are often present and should be understood by the researcher, who must attempt to minimize and measure them. They should also be understood by the line marketer, who should understand the credibility of the data upon which she or he may base important decisions.

Sampling Error

Sampling error is error in data induced by chance. It occurs because every element (member) of the population is not included in the sample. We can never be certain of the distribution of a population characteristic unless we have accurate data on every element in that population. This is seldom possible. However, sampling—or "statistical"—errors can be precisely estimated if the sample is drawn randomly from the population as a whole. Randomness is thus a highly desirable property. Whenever possible, it should be specified in the survey design.

The larger the sample is, the smaller the sampling error. A large sample is a statistical virtue. Unfortunately, as the size of the sample increases, so too does the cost of the survey. Furthermore, with more respondents, the study will take longer to complete.

---

[5] For a study of mail-survey response, including the use of incentives, see Michael S. Goodstadt, et al., "Mail Survey Response Rates: Their Manipulation and Impact," *Journal of Marketing Research*, **14**:3 (August 1977), pp. 391–395.

Statistical error is unavoidable with sample data, but it can at least be calculated if the data have been randomly obtained. The analyst can only guess at the possible error if the data are nonrandom. With random data the range of error (confidence interval) can be stipulated, at any chosen confidence level, for each statistical parameter. Thus, averages, dispersions, and other statistical measurements of the market can be qualified so that the survey information can be used intelligently by management.

Respondent Errors

Respondent errors result from the failure of some elements in the sample to give accurate information. Respondent errors are caused by nonresponse, self-selection, misunderstanding, conscious or unconscious misrepresentation, ignorance, and poor predictions. These problems are often induced or aggravated by poor questionnaire design.

Nonresponse   Nonresponse, defined as the failure of one or more selected population elements to reply to the inquiry, can seriously bias survey data.[6] The problem of nonresponse may be especially acute among particular classes of elements within the population, and hence bias the data by preventing proportional representation of those classes. For example, households that are empty during the day—when personal or telephone interviews are commonly attempted—differ in various ways from those where one or more members are usually at home. The empty home would be unlikely to contain small children or elderly persons, but might very well house working adults, and possibly school-age children. Such families would have different social, demographic, and behavioral characteristics than those with stay-at-home members. If these nonresponders are ignored, a substantial and unmeasurable error may be introduced into the survey data.

Nonresponse can be minimized by a good follow-up program, during which a second attempt is made to contact the nonresponders. This second attempt is usually made at a different time or with a different medium than that used for the original inquiry. For instance, if during the first phase of the program personal or telephone calls were attempted during normal working hours, the follow-up calls would be made at night or on the weekend. If nonresponse is a problem with a mail survey, personal or telephone interviews might be tried with those who failed to return the original questionnaire. Or the original medium may be tried again. Sometimes a duplicate of the original questionnaire, accompanied by a courteous reminder, will draw a response.

---

[6] A method of estimating this error is found in J. Scott Armstrong and Terry S. Overton, "Estimating Nonresponse Bias in Mail Surveys," *Journal of Marketing Research*, **14**:3 (August 1977), pp. 396–402.

A partial solution to the nonresponse problem, at least with mail surveys, is to offer an incentive. Frequently money or a premium is enclosed with the questionnaire or is sent upon its completion and return.[7] The researcher can seldom reduce the nonresponse to zero, although he can lower it to a level (say, less than 5 percent) that can be safely ignored. In some cases, especially with mail surveys, there may be little he can do about a large nonresponse. However, the results may still be valid if the number of responses equals or exceeds the minimum required sample size *and* if the nonresponders can be assumed to have the same set of relevant characteristics as the responders. In other words, the responders must be representative of the population from which they were drawn, including the nonresponders. This assumption can be tested by taking a sample of the nonresponders—if necessary, by an aggressive follow-up program—and comparing it with the original responders. If the two sets, the responders and the nonresponders, are the same with respect to all relevant population characteristics, the sample data are considered free of nonresponse errors.

Self-selection   Self-selection is related to the problem of nonresponse. Particularly in the case of mail questionnaires, people who feel very strongly about the survey subject are more likely to respond than those who know little about it or are indifferent. Such partisanship biases the responses in favor of extreme positions. If the survey includes personal questions, the self-selection phenomenon will tend to exclude poor performers. People whose personal failures would be exposed by questions about their job, income, or other status-related subjects frequently refuse to cooperate, especially in personal interviews.

Misunderstanding   Misunderstanding results from poor communication. Take, for example, the children's game "Whisper," in which a number of youngsters sit in a circle and a message given to one individual is relayed orally from person to person. By the time the message gets back to the originator, it usually bears little resemblance to what she said. The question in the mind of the analyst is subject to the same distortion as it moves outward to the respondent. Likewise, the answer given by the respondent may be misunderstood by the analyst, who frequently has a couple of intermediaries between himself and the respondent.

Communication often fails at the respondent's end because he does not listen to or read the question carefully or because the question is ambiguously worded. Repetition and simplicity are the best insurance against respondent carelessness. Care in preparing the questionnaire, pretesting, and the use of personal interviews are ways to avoid ambiguity. A question that appears

---

[7] Consensus holds that incentives increase response rate. However, there has been some concern about incentives inducing a bias. Although the research in this area has been sparse, it tends to conclude that response bias is negligible. See William J. Whitmore, "Mail Survey Premiums and Response Bias," *Journal of Marketing Research*, **13**:1 (February 1976), pp. 398–400.

extremely obvious to the analyst may have a different meaning for a respondent. A researcher who asks, "What make of automobile do you own?" may expect to elicit a brand name and get instead the name of the manufacturer or a model.

Conscious Misrepresentation   Conscious misrepresentation is encouraged by several factors. Perhaps the most common is the respondent's eagerness to impress the interviewer by portraying himself in the best possible light, even if this involves some "minor" alteration of the facts. People tend for example, to understate their ages or overstate their incomes if they believe these misstatements will be to their advantage, or will enhance their self-image. Sometimes an apparently innocent question proves to be psychologically loaded. An illustration was uncovered by Mason Haire:[8]

> A brewery made two kinds of beer. To guide their merchandising techniques they wanted to know what kind of people drank each kind, and particularly, what kind of differences there were between the two groups of consumers. A survey was conducted which led up to the questions "Do you drink the *Light* or *Regular*?" (These were the two trade names under which the company marketed.) After identifying the consumers of each product it was possible to find out about the characteristics of each group so that appropriate appeals could be used, media chosen, etc.
>   An interesting anomaly appeared in the survey, however. The interviewing showed (on a reliable sample) that consumers drank *Light* over *Regular* in the ratio of 3 to 1. The company had been producing and selling *Regular* over *Light* for some time in a ratio of 9 to 1.

Haire attributes the failure of the question to elicit a true response to its implied meaning as perceived by the respondent. Presumably, many people interpreted it "Do you drink the regular, run-of-the-mill product, or do you drink the one that is more refined and shows more discrimination and taste?"[9] This would explain the preponderance of "Light" answers.

Respondents perceive the answers to many questions not only as indexes of their social status and level of personal achievement, but as reflecting their personality. They frequently give answers that reinforce their self-concept, no matter how unrealistic this may be. (*Self-concept* is one's idealized view of oneself and may have little to do with reality.)

The self-concept—sometimes called "self-image"—problem is especially acute when the interview is held in a public place. The presence of friends, associates, or even strangers can motivate misrepresentation. Other

---

[8] Mason Haire, "Projective Techniques in Marketing Research," *Journal of Marketing*, **14**:5 (April 1950), p. 649. This is a classic article in the literature of MR.

[9] Haire, "Projective Techniques in Marketing Research," p. 650.

people are often in hearing range during personal interviews, especially when public areas are used.

Respondents are often eager to please the interviewer and give answers that they think he or she wants to hear. For example, if a sample of housewives are asked what brand of detergent they prefer, and the interviewers identify themselves with a particular brand, the data very probably will be biased in favor of the interviewers' brand.

Unconscious Misrepresentation   Unconscious misrepresentation is a complex psychological phenomenon. Very often a respondent will rationalize a purchase decision in terms of social norms or desired self-image when in fact the decision was primarily motivated by a less-than-admirable psychogenic drive. For instance, a man may tell himself that he needs an expensive automobile because of its superior functional qualities–the roominess, comfort, and additional safely associated with a heavy car. He may even feel that he is, to an extent, acting out of a noble desire to protect his family. Yet his true motive may be quite different, and he himself may not clearly understand it. Many motives are buried in the subconscious mind. The decision may be a direct result of a desire for status, prestige, identity with a particular social or professional group—of which the respondent may or may not be a member— or aggressiveness. According to some psychologists, it may even be related to a desire for sexual gratification.

We know that instances of unconscious misrepresentation occur, but they are not easy to identify or measure. On the contrary, the whole area of consumer psychology is fraught with disagreement, contradictions, and uncertainty. There are tools for dealing with the problem as it pertains to data acquisition. However, there is no simple or reliable method for identifying and evaluating this source of respondent error in market studies. Sometimes all the analyst can do is recognize the possibility of this type of error and try to use survey methods that will minimize its effects. This may mean avoiding psychologically sensitive questions, using anonymous questionnaires, or employing projective techniques—devices that also help minimize the problem of conscious misrepresentation.

Ignorance   Ignorance on the part of the respondent can produce respondent error, especially when it is coupled with laziness, the desire to please the interviewer, or the hope of an inducement. The respondent may not know the answer or be uncertain about it, yet give what appears to be a truthful, accurate response. The correct information may be unavailable, or the respondent may simple be too lazy to find it. If anxious to reply to the question, the respondent may make up an answer, or guess, rather than not respond, admit ignorance, or find the correct information. Questions such as "What brand of motor oil are you using?" "What television shows did you watch last week?" or "How many times did you dine out last month?" are particularly likely to elicit guesswork or outright lies.

Poor Predictions   Poor predictions made by respondents as to their own behavior can introduce errors into data, or, more precisely, lead the analyst to erroneous conclusions. If respondents are truthful about their intentions, then the data are not erroneous, for in this case the data are a measurement of intentions, not behavior. If intentions are equated to behavior, however, the error may be substantial. A study of consumer behavior as related to expressed intentions indicates that a six-month projection of purchase plans can vary as much as 100 percent from the actual purchases made during that period, at least with respect to consumer durables. The correspondence between actual and projected purchases was moderately good for utilitarian items (refrigerators and washing machines), but very poor for luxury items (television sets and air-conditioners, which at the time were not taken for granted as part of the average household).[10]

Interviewer Errors

Interviewer errors are analogous in many ways to respondent errors. They can be avoided entirely only by eliminating the interviewer, which means using a mail survey and opening the door to yet other errors. *Interviewer errors*—often called *interviewer bias*—can result from the interaction

Figure 5-1 **Personal Information Is Often Difficult to Obtain**

"Can I have a different question?"

[10] "Quarterly Survey of Buying Intentions," *Federal Reserve Bulletin* (November 1962), p. 1423.

between the interview and the respondent, mistakes in interpretation and transcription, or fraud. Like respondent errors, interviewer errors are encouraged by sloppy questionnaire design.

Errors from Interaction   Ideally, the interviewer should be perfectly neutral with respect to the interview questions. No gesture, word, or expression should imply approval or disapproval or in any way encourage a particular answer. Maintaining a completely neutral facade often demands considerable skill, especially when psychologically loaded questions are involved. Figure 5-1 is illustrative.

One advantage of using a research supplier to gather data is that it allows interviewers to appear detached from the sponsor. They are thus more likely to be given a true picture of the situation. Often the identity of the sponsor can be completely hidden, as in the case of the citrus survey. Also, an interviewer who identifies with the supplier is less apt to encourage favorable responses.

The interviewer's style of dress, way of introducing himself, mannerisms, attitude, age, and sex, all affect—often subtly—the success of the interview. No interviewer is without a personality, and respondents, like anyone else, react to personality. Training can minimize, but seldom eliminates, this kind of bias.[11]

Errors in Interpretation and Transcription   This kind of error is possible only when the interviewer listens to and then transcribes the respondent's answers. Thus, the problem can be avoided by using a written questionnaire and having the interviewee fill in the answers. An alternative is to equip the interviewer with a tape recorder. Unfortunately, in some cases a written questionnaire may make the interview too structured, while recording everything the respondent says may make the problem of data reduction too cumbersome. A third alternative is to thoroughly train the interviewers, but this is both time-consuming and expensive. Close supervision may also help, but it too is expensive.

Fraud   The possibility of interviewer cheating, or fraud, cannot be ignored. Interviewers fake responses for various reasons. Sometimes no effort is even made to interview the respondents. In other cases, the interviewer is simply too embarrassed to ask a particular question. Or the interviewee may be unable to answer a question and the interviewer may decide to help out, putting down whatever seems to fit the situation or, in some instances, anything that comes to mind.

Some research specialists claim to have developed trick questions that can be included in a questionnaire or interview form to reveal cheating. (They

---

[11] For case studies of interviewer error, see J. R. McKenzie, "An Investigation into Interviewer Effects in Market Research," and Barbara Bailer, Leroy Bailey, and Joyce Stevens, "Measures of Interviewer Bias and Variance," both in *Journal of Marketing Research*, **14**:3 (August 1977), pp. 330–336 and 337–343.

are naturally reluctant to state the exact nature of the questions, since this would destroy their effectiveness.) The most common methods of preventing interviewer fraud are audits (usually in the form of spot checks on reported respondents), good supervision, and cross-checks. Often the mere announcement that an audit will be made is sufficient to discourage cheating. The same remedies apply when the survey data are obtained by observation rather than by inquiry.

Uncovering Interviewer Error   Interviewer errors can often be detected by a statistical cross-check, comparing the data recorded by each interviewer with that obtained by all the others. If one or more statistics are further apart than they should be, taking into account the normal discrepancies attributable to random error, then either the respondents assigned to that interviewer are different from the population as a whole *or* interviewer error is distorting the data. In either case, the situation should be examined.

One approach is to resample that segment of the population assigned to the original interviewer, using a different interviewer. If the new sample conforms statistically to the total sample, exclusive of the portion in question, the original was probably biased and should be discarded. Furthermore, remedial action should be taken to ensure that the problem does not recur. If the new sample is not significantly different from the original interviewer's sample, the answer may be that this segment of the population is truly different from the rest.

Minimizing Nonsampling Errors   *Nonsampling errors* are survey errors introduced by the respondents and interviewers (or observers). They are the errors we've just discussed. Lipstein offers some broad guidelines for minimizing them:[12]

1   Keep the sample survey as easy to execute as possible.
2   Use the smallest sample consistent with the study objectives.
3   Restrict the questionnaire to data essential to the main issue.
4   Pretest the questionnaire. Regularly undergo the interview yourself to determine your ability to answer and find how much fatigue is involved in answering the questionnaire.
5   Make efforts to minimize fatigue for participants.
6   Whenever possible, for future guidance, rotate key questions to discover when respondent fatigue begins.
7   Establish procedures for keeping both respondent and interviewer involved in the study.
8   Don't ask consumers questions they can't really answer.
9   Don't ask the interviewer to do the impossible. Such requests encourage sloppy work and cheating.

[12] Benjamin Lipstein, "Here Are 9 Rules for Minimizing Non-sampling Errors in Surveys," *Marketing News* (January 17, 1975), p. 8.

Survey Design

Design Process

The survey design process typically follows this track:[13]

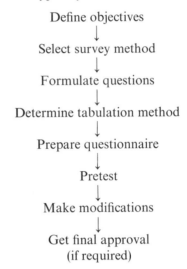

Define objectives
↓
Select survey method
↓
Formulate questions
↓
Determine tabulation method
↓
Prepare questionnaire
↓
Pretest
↓
Make modifications
↓
Get final approval
(if required)

The objectives (raw data needs) usually fall out of the problem definition, contained in the basic research design. Hence, the first major task is usually to select the survey method.

Selecting the Survey Method[14]   The method-selection process is outlined in Figure 5-2. Its success rests largely on a knowledge of the respondents and an understanding of the information to be gathered. Success also depends on an awareness of the virtues and vices of the alternative survey methods.

Questionnaire Preparation   The key here is question formulation. A bundle of behavioral and scaling problems, which we meet in Chapter 14, may have to be considered. Even a simple question, demanding either a "yes" or "no" answer, can yield misleading results. We saw an example earlier.

Questions are prompted by the information needs. They are constrained by the intelligence, vocabulary, and willingness of the respondents and by the survey method. For instance, children, who are now receiving

---

[13] This outline is based partially on William R. Wynd, "Six-step Basic Program Can Help Volunteers Solve Research Probelms," *Marketing News*, **11**:5 (September 9, 1977), p. 12.

[14] For an expanded discussion of survey design, with special attention to the changing views and problems of alternative methods of inquiry, see Martin R. Frankel and Lester R. Frankel, "Some Recent Developments in Sample Survey Design," *Journal of Marketing Research*, **14**:3 (August 1977), pp. 280–293.

Figure 5-2   **Survey Technique Selection Process**

Source: Robert W. Joselyn, *Designing The Marketing Research Project*, New York: Petrocelli/Charter, 1977, p. 93.

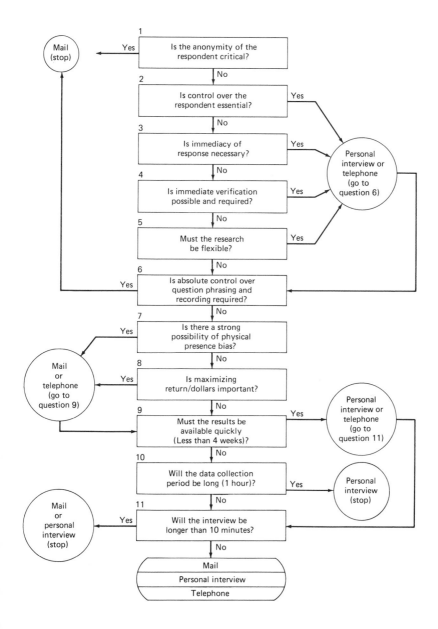

considerable attention as consumer trainees, are weak in verbal skills. Mail surveys are no place for complex or long questions.

Generally, the questionnaire preparation process starts with the information needs. It ends with consideration of the form of data the questionnaire will produce. Examples are seen in Exhibit 5-5.

Exhibit 5-5 **The Questionnaire Preparation Process: Examples**

Information Needed	Intended Use	Questions	Table
Do people want a strong centralized business district or should the development of neighborhood shopping centers be encouraged?	Make provision in the comprehensive plan for the outcome preferred and zone accordingly.	Which of the following statements best describes your attitude toward business development in our town? a. Businesses should be concentrated in a well-defined central business district. b. Business should be allowed to locate in small neighborhood shopping centers. c. I don't care one way or the other.	Attitudes toward business development: Attitude Number Percent Concentrate ——— ——— Disperse ——— ——— Don't care ——— ——— Total ——— 100
How many people own bicycles and how do they feel toward the development of well defined bicycle paths? What are the attitudes of people who don't own bicycles toward the development of bicycle paths?	If enough bicycle owners and non-owners are in favor of developing well defined paths, then a "bicycle committee" should be appointed to make recommendations on routes and signing. What constitutes "enough owners" will be determined by the city council based upon the results of the questionnaire.	Do you own a bicycle? ☐ yes ☐ no How do you feel about the following statement: A well defined system of bicycle paths should be developed in out city.	Bicycle owner and non-owner attitudes toward the following statement: A well defined system of bicycle paths should be developed in our city. Owners Nonowners Attitude No. % No. % Strongly agree —— —— ——

What characteristics of our town should be preserved? Is there something that people look for when they locate here that we would want to keep?

☐ Strongly agree
☐ Partially agree
☐ Can't say
☐ Partially disagree
☐ Strongly disagree

If we can identify the good characteristics people see in our town, we should try to preserve them. Results of the survey may identify specific factors for the planning commission or city council.

Please indicate the one thing you like most about our town and want to see preserved.

Partially agree	—	—
Can't say	—	—
Partially disagree	—	—
Strongly disagree	—	—
Total	100	100

This is an open-ended question. All responses must be read and tabulated.

Things Liked Most	Frequency of Mention	
	Number	Percent
	—	—
	—	—
	—	—
Total		100

(Responses will tend to cluster around several characteristics.)

Source: Reprinted from William R. Wynd, "Six-step Basic Program Can Help Volunteers Solve Research Problems," *Marketing News*, **11**:5 (Sept. 9, 1977), p. 12, published by The American Marketing Association.

The questionnaire—called esoterically "the survey instrument"—will be less vulnerable to bias if a few rules-of-thumb can be followed:

Keep it short—no unnecessary questions
Don't ask questions the respondents may not be able to answer
Rotate check-off answers if order is likely to favor one response[15]
Don't depend on interviewers to untangle tricky questions
Pretest

Pretest   A *pretest* is a small survey conducted in order to test the questionnaire. The pretest should be used, even if the respondents must be fellow employees. The purpose is to identify awkward, confusing, or easily misunderstood questions. Modifications can then be made and the final questionnaire can be submitted for approval (if required).

Sample Design   If the market population is small, or if only a sample of the population is to be surveyed, sample design will be important. For instance, a small population may require a respondent incentive to assure adequate response.

Usually the sample size and distribution are specified in the basic research design. If not, the sample design will be part of the survey preparation. These issues will be faced in Chapter 8. First we'll look at data processing.

Problems

1   Surveys are necessary to collect the following data: (a) the quantity of Tide detergent sold in the Denver SMSA during a week-long period, (b) the size of the national audience of a network TV show, and (c) the reason for a sudden shift in consumer preferences in the automobile market. Which data gathering technique is appropriate in each case, and why?

2   What types of errors would you expect in each of the surveys recommended in answer to problem 1?

3   What might be done to eliminate or minimize these errors?

4   Would you use a pretest in any of the surveys cited in the first problem? Why?

5   What type of errors would you suspect in the data derived from the surveys in Exhibits 5-2, 5-3, and 5-4?

6   Specify an information need, such as a requirement for student food preferences. Select a survey method to gather these data. Defend your choice.

7   Prepare a questionnaire for collecting the data (previous problem).

---

[15] For example, if respondents are asked to check their favorite brand, the same brand should not appear first on every questionnaire.

Part 2
Summary

Research feeds on data which may be classified by their sources as primary or secondary information. Data may also be classified as prerecorded or original information, depending on whether or not they were expressly collected for the study at hand. Prerecorded data are usually the most convenient and cheapest form of information, but are not always reliable, useful, or even available.

Internal sources of prerecorded data typically include the researcher's own library and the sales, accounting, and credit records. External sources are numerous. They include banks, newspapers, trade associations, and the public libraries. Government agencies are the most prolific.

Original data are gathered through surveys, experimentation, and simulation. Consumer panels are often used to provide an ongoing source of market data and are especially useful in tracking studies.

Panels are often maintained by research suppliers. Suppliers are an important part of the research system, providing everything from data collection to a full line of research services.

Surveys are the most pervasive method of collecting original data, being common in both commercial and social marketing research. They are conducted through observation or inquiry. Inquiry is done by personal interview, telephone interview, or mail questionnaire. Each method has its own set of advantages and shortcomings. The latter may include sampling error, respondent error, or interviewer error.

The survey design process focuses mainly on the selection of the survey method and questionnaire design. As with most data acquisition jobs, it significantly influences the ultimate quality of the research project.

CASE STUDY 2

Leslie's Clothing Store: A Store Image Problem

Richard J. Lutz (*Richard J. Lutz is Associate Professor of Marketing, Graduate School of Management, University of California at Los Angeles.*)

Leslie's Clothing Store, founded in 1970, specializes in women's fashions, located in a downstate Illinois town of approximately 100,000 people. Before 1970 Leslie's was a medium-sized, full-line department store which, under different management, had served the community for nearly 40 years. Then in 1970, new owners decided to change the store drastically. They immediately changed its name and gradually liquidated inventories in all departments not related to women's fahions.

Concurrent with inventory liquidation, Leslie's shrank from the four floors it had previously occupied to one floor of approximately 10,000 square feet. This single floor was redecorated at a cost of $100,000. In addition to carrying women's sportswear and fashion apparel, Leslie's featured several related lines of goods: shoes, cosmetics, purses, lingerie, and accessories. It also had a linen department, which was a holdover from the old department store days.

By 1973 Leslie's was experiencing a severe sales drought. Sales volume and customer traffic through the store had been steadily dropping during the three years since the store's reorganization. The problem had finally reached crisis proportions. Customer acceptance of Leslie's Clothing Store was apparently quite low.

Marketing Decision

The immediate reaction of Leslie's management was to engage in an extensive advertising campaign to draw customers back into the store. An aggressive local advertising agency was granted a $25,000 one-year contract to accomplish this task. However, the account executive assigned to Leslie's analyzed the problem from a marketing perspective and reach the following conclusion: Extensive advertising might be able to pull customers into Leslie's, but advertising alone would not solve Leslie's problems.

While advertising is an important element of the marketing mix, it is only one element. Attention must be paid to other areas as well—the product or service being offered, price, distribution, and customer segments.

Upon a critical examination of Leslie's store layout and inventory and several discussions with store management, the account executive became convinced that Leslie's problems stemmed from two interrelated shortcomings in the current marketing program:

1   Leslie's management believed that the fashion-oriented woman was most likely to be fortyish. This appeared to be a mistaken assessment of the target market.

2   Probably as a result of the expectation that the prospective customer was more or less middle-aged, Leslie's was a "frumpy" store, with conservative clothing and a generally outmoded merchandising strategy.

The account executive realized that if his assessment was correct, increased advertising would be fruitless. Customers could be drawn to the store once. They would quickly disappear, however, unless the store was changed to meet their expectations.

Information Needs

The account executive reported all this to the management of Leslie's, which promptly rejected his assessment as naive and reflective of his inexperience in the women's fashion market. After he had countered by pointing out that no experience was sometimes better than an experience of failure, a compromise was reached. An independent consultant would conduct a survey of women in the community to determine the following:

1   The image of Leslie's as a women's fashion store.
2   The age group of the fashion-conscious women making up the target market.
3   Current patronage habits of the target market buyers.
4   Criteria utilized by the target market buyers in selecting a clothing store.

Based on the results of this survey, a decision would be made as to whether Leslie's would have to make substantial changes in product lines and service procedures. Then the agency could intelligently prepare the advertising campaign.

Special Requirements

Leslie's management was not prepared to spend more than $2,000 for the survey. It wanted to obtain the information as cheaply as possible.

Several local consultants were invited to submit proposals. The consultants were given approximately the same information presented here. The survey was to determine the four pieces of market data previously listed.

Assignment   Write a proposal to conduct the needed survey. Your proposal should include the following items:

1   Sample size and selection procedure. Justify it fully—representativeness is important.

2   Type of survey (e.g., personal interview, phone interview, etc.). Justify.

3   Questionnaire showing all questions necessary to obtain the needed information. The questions should flow logically and be worded in suitable fashion. Rough draft questions will not suffice. A note should be made as to how each question relates to the purposes of the survey.

4   Method of analysis. How will the data be analyzed to answer the research questions? What statistical procedures, if any, would be used? Present sample tables if that will help clarify the form of the results.

5   A complete cost estimate. What will be your total bill to Leslie's? How will the total be broken down? Itemize all expenses. (Do not forget your consulting fee.)

6   A time estimate. How long will it be from the initiation of the project to the presentation of results to Leslie's management? Time is of the essence. Justify your time estimate in terms of the activities that will be occurring (e.g., interviewer training, report typing, etc.).

Part 3
Data Processing

Introduction

In its search for a site for a new Porsche-Audi store in the Los Angeles/Long Beach SMSA,[1] the American Research Institute gathered 11,137 pieces of data. For its study of consumer behavior in the Tucson SMSA, the Broadway Department Store MR group gathered 108,869 pieces of information. To analyze the Houston market, Neiman-Marcus's research people, aided by a supplier, gathered 91,980 pieces of data. Making sense out of these data in their raw form was virtually impossible.

One typically exits the data acquisition stage with a confusing mass of information. The mismanagement of such data can put the research process on a ski slope to oblivion.

Data processing is the conversion of raw data to useful information. The procedure is outlined in Figure 6-1, early in the next chapter. Chapter 6 focuses mainly on the reduction and preliminary analysis of data. Data must be reduced to make them manageable. They usually must be analyzed to extract their meaning.

The challenge and excitement of marketing research rests largely in data analysis. After introducing its basic methods in Chapter 6, we shall introduce more techniques, throughout the balance of the book. The analysis of data has become high art and sophisticated science, thanks to the diffusion of the computer and the proliferation of new analytical methods during the past twenty years. These tools allow us to find meaning in a crazy-quilt of data. Without them, the probability of discovery is often as remote as the chance of finding a Picasso in your attic.

---

[1] Standard Metropolitan Statistical Area.

The marketing information system is a continuous and integrated approach to data processing. The acceptance of the system concept has been motivated by the information explosion and management's need to keep abreast of the marketplace. Marketing information systems are becoming common in both the commercial and social sectors. They can be an important part of the research apparatus. We examine them in Chapter 7.

Chapter 6
Data Reduction and Analysis

Key Concepts

The Nature of Data
Error, the mathematical properties of numbers, and ceteris paribus

The Reduction Process
Raw data's conversion to useful information

Data Analysis
Some basic techniques of analyzing information

Significance Tests
Ways of assessing the apparent relationship between variables

Simple Correlation Analysis
Specifying the statistical relationship between two variables

Key Terms

metric data
nonmetric data
parametric data
nonparametric data
ceteris paribus
data reduction
coding
precoding
postcoding
code book
editing
tabulating

posting
rostering
frequency distribution
scatter diagram
contingency table
cross break
cross tabulation
chi square
significance level
simple correlation analysis
Pearson r

The Nature of Data

Both the quality and essence of numbers vary dramatically. So do the assumptions under which data are collected. These realities should be kept in mind throughout the research process and when the findings are being studied by line management.

Error

Data is subject to error from the time the first piece of information is collected until the final report has been typed. Unfortunately, errors are cumulative. Rarely does one mistake offset another.

These errors were summarized back in Table 2-4. We deal with them as we explore the various stages and techniques of marketing research. Those that are relevant to the data reduction process include coding mistakes, transcription errors, editing oversights, and the confusion of nonmetric with metric data.

Data error should be minimized and estimated, never ignored. Research in business and the social sciences is seldom done in a pristine environment. It is done in an extremely complex and noisy one and with imperfect tools. Error is virtually inevitable.

Error is minimized by careful research design and supervision. Error is estimated with certain statistical tools, when applicable, or subjective judgment. Research data and the ultimate findings should be qualified with an estimate of the error. Without such a qualification, the users cannot rationally decide how much confidence they should have in the information.

Metric versus Nonmetric Data

There is nothing to prevent us from taking two or more numbers and subjecting them to mathematical manipulation. We can add, subtract, multiply, and divide all we want. We can do it by hand, by pocket calculator, or by computer. However, the results may be pure nonsense.

For example, we could take the team roster of the New York Jets and and manipulate the numbers assigned to the players. We could add them, compute their mean and variance, and perform other sorts of arithematic operations. Clearly, we would produce meaningless values. The original data are nominally scaled: The numbers serve only to identify, not to count or measure. The data are nonmetric.

We could make similar calculations with research data which are nonmetric, but our mistake might not be so obvious. For instance, we might be working with attitude or preference data which appear metric, but which are really nonmetric.

Metric data are data for which the units of measurement are interchangeable. Weights, lengths, temperatures, and revenues are illustrative. Ratio and interval scales are metric. The property of *interchangeability* allows metric data to be directly subjected to most kinds of mathematical

Table 6-1 Metric versus Nonmetric Numbers

Type	Criteria	Use	Permissable Mathematical Operations	Examples
Metric[a]				
Ratio scale	Intervals are equal Zero is absolute	To indicate relative size and interval	$\times, \div, +, -$	Population, income, age
Interval scale	Intervals are equal Zero is arbitrary	To indicate interval	$+, -$	Temperature centigrade or Fahrenheit
Nonmetric[b]				
Ordinal scale[c]	Intervals are unequal Only order is significant	To indicate order (rank)	None	Class standing, an order of preference, e.g., 1st, 2d, and so on
Nominal scale	Values are only names with no mathematical significance	To identify	None	The number on a football jersey, a respondent identification number, a number representing a color

[a] Also called "parametric."
[b] Also called "nonparametric."
[c] Also called "rank ordered."

and statistical manipulation. Metric data thus lend themselves to rigorous quantitative analysis. They are generally the preferred form of information.

Data that are metric can be used in conjunction with all the statistical techniques discussed in this book. They can also be used in conjunction with most of the techniques for handling nonmetric data. In these cases, the nonmetric methods often serve as short cuts. They yield less precise results than conventional techniques, but because they usually involve less mathematics, they tend to be faster. Nonmetric methods are useful in handling metric data when quick answers are needed and high precision is not essential.

Nonmetric data are data for which the units of measurement are not interchangeable. Value judgments, attitudes, and preference ratings are illustrative. Nominal and ordinal scales are nonmetric.

Nonmetric data lend themselves to mathematical and statistical manipulation only to a limited extent. However, there are some special statistical tools designed primarily for the analysis of such data.

As the mathematical character of numbers varies dramatically, we must know what kind of data we're working with. Table 6-1 shows the standard taxonomy for classifying numbers according to their mathematical properties. Unfortunately, there is not always a clear line between classifications. Often we assign numbers to a higher classification than they truly warrant. For instance, we may treat interval-scale data as ratio-scale data although they may not conform perfectly to the ratio-scale criteria. Perhaps this is why economists tend to use the terms "parametric" and "nonparametric."[1]

The issue of metricity should be faced during the design stage. Scales should be chosen which will be compatible with the planned analysis. It should also be considered during the data reduction and analysis stages, to assure that proper tools are selected.

As we'll see shortly, nonmetric data can yield to statistical analysis. However, we must invoke special tools.[2] We do not have the flexibility we enjoy with metric numbers.

Ceteris Paribus

We must not forget that great qualifier, *ceteris paribus*, meaning "all things remaining equal." Theoreticians can make that assumption. Practitioners often cannot, unless they are willing to risk an outcome significantly different from the one predicted. For example:

We hear of a museum in a certain Eastern city that was proud of its amazing attendance record. Recently a little stone building

---

[1] The prefix "para" means "similar to" or "like."

[2] For a vigorous guide to these techniques, see Myles Hollander and Douglas A. Wolfe, *Nonparametric Statistical Methods* (New York: Wiley, 1973). For a less rigorous but comprehensive guide, see Sidney Siegel, *Nonparametric Statistics for the Behavioral Sciences* (New York: McGraw-Hill, 1956).

was erected nearby. Next year attendance at the museum mysteriously fell off by 100,000. What was the little stone building? A comfort station.[3]

Ceteris paribus is a common qualifier in economics. Perhaps that is why economists have been accused of sometimes assuming away the problem and solving the residual.[4] *Ceteris paribus* is often appropriate in marketing where we are frequently interested in isolating a particular phenomenon. For example, to properly manipulate price we need to know the price elasticity of our product. That is, we need to know what will happen to sales if we change price, *ceteris paribus*.

Unfortunately, all things may not remain equal. Advertising, the competitors' products, buyer population, weather, etc., may all change. These should not influence the pricing decision, however, unless they disrupt the sales-price relationship.

When *ceteris paribus* breaks down, data can be very confusing. The firm may lower price, only to see sales go down. That doesn't mean the company has made economic history. The demand curve has not suddenly turned upward.[5] It simply means that other forces have overridden the effect of the price change. What the firm observes in the marketplace is the net effect of all the forces, only one being its price. Management must defer to the marketing research group to unscramble the data and isolate the sales-price relationship.

The Reduction Process

A mass of raw data is usually useless to the line manager and confusing even to the expert researcher. One cannot comprehend hundreds—in many cases, thousands—of pieces of information. To bring order out of the chaos, the data must be reduced and analyzed.

Data reduction is the summarizing of information. It starts with the raw data—the stack of completed questionnaires, sales records, or whatever—and ends with some numbers. In the case of purely qualitative research, it starts with notes, transcriptions, or tape recordings and ends with a few pages of description. In the process of condensation, some information is lost and some understanding is gained. The groundwork is laid for serious analysis.

The data reduction process is summarized in Figure 6-1. It starts with coding.

[3] W. Allan Kallis and Harry V. Roberts, *The Nature of Statistics* (New York: Free Press, 1962), p. 160.

[4] An economist was once stranded on a desert island with several other people. They had lots of canned goods, but no tools. Each survivor was asked to suggest a way to open the cans. The economist replied by saying, "Now assuming we had a can opener. . . ."

[5] A basic tenet of economic theory is that the demand curve is negative. It always slopes downward: The higher the price, the lower is the demand. The lower the price, the higher is the demand, *ceteris paribus*.

Figure 6-1   **The Data Processing Procedure**

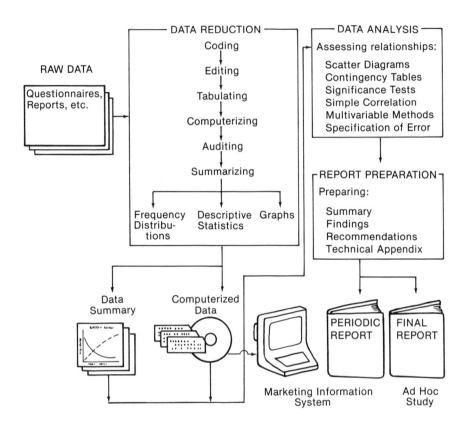

Coding

Coding is the categorizing of respondent answers (or other information) by assigning labels (usually numerical) to them. The method to be used should be decided in the design stage of the survey, since it will determine, to a large extent, the format of the questionnaire. A good coding technique will result in a well-organized and more understandable questionnaire, reduce survey errors, and facilitate editing and tabulating of the raw data. No one system will work for all research projects, but common sense and a few guidelines should suffice in most cases.

The questionnaire designer should clearly understand the objectives of the research project, so that he can prepare questions which will elicit relevant answers. These answers must be classifiable into exhaustive and mutually exclusive categories. For instance, if the objective is to prepare a life-style and demographic profile of Buick-owners, the questions must relate to the consumer—not the car—and yield answers that will fit the appropriate life-style and demographic categories.

This is not always easy. Unstructured and open-ended questions do not lend themselves to rigorous coding, for the designer can seldom anticipate every possible response. Depending on the study's objective, however, rigorous coding may be unnecessary. In exploratory research, the objective is to get ideas or insights, not material that will stand up under quantitative analyses. Under these conditions, small nonrandom samples are typical, and precise data tabulation—hence, precise coding—is not required.

The actual assignment of labels to answers can be done before or after the survey is executed. If it is done before, the process is called *precoding*. For instance, consumer-profile studies often seek information about the respondent's occupation. Assuming that a two-digit code is acceptable in the tabulation phase of the study, the following system could be used by the survey designer:

Code	Occupational Category[6]
01	Professional or technician
02	Farmer or farm manager
03	Manager, proprietor, or official
04	Clerical worker
05	Salesman
06	Craftsman or shop foreman
07	Operative[7]
08	Private-household worker
09	Service worker
10	Farm laborer or foreman
11	Laborer (nonagricultural)
12	Retiree
13	Military person

These 13 categories could be offered as alternative responses to the question, "What is your occupation?" or to the instruction, "Check your occupation in the following list." A box or line ($\square$ or ____) would be placed adjacent to each option, with the code number printed lightly under or alongside it if precoding was desired. (For examples of actual precoding, see Exhibits 5-3 and 5-4.)

Since 13 answer-options would consume a lot of space on the questionnaire, a sentence-completion format, such as, "Your occupation is _____" might be used instead of a multiple-choice arrangement. It would then be up to the interviewer or the editor to postcode the answer by selecting the appropriate job category and recording the code number in the designated space.

---

[6] The first 11 of these categories represent actual U.S. Department of Labor classifications. (No sexism is intended. These are USDL labels.)

[7] Semiskilled workers.

Postcoding lends itself to shorter questionnaires. This can be important, especially in mail surveys, where a lengthy format can discourage respondents and sharply reduce the number of questionnaires returned. Postcoding may also be useful in avoiding confusion, particularly with mail surveys. For example, the term "operative" in the preceding list of occupations would not be correctly interpreted by the majority of respondents, although it is a standard U.S. Department of Labor job category. An experienced interviewer or editor, on the other hand, would know immediately that maintenance personnel, an electrical assembler, a gardener, or any other semiskilled worker should be coded "07." Of course, the more precise and clearer the precoding is, the less skilled the interviewer or editor need be, and the less time the data processing will take.

Postcoding requires the preparation of a code book. A *code book* is a guide assigning labels (usually numbers) to answers, e.g., 1 = YES, 2 = NO, 0 = NO RESPONSE. It is used in the editing process and is usually only a page or two long.

Editing

Editing refers to cleaning up, and sometimes postcoding, of the raw data. Often, it is necessitated by improperly executed questionnaires, due either to respondent carelessness or interviewer sloppiness. The researcher has little control over the former, although the incidence of respondent errors can be reduced by clear and concise questions and simple instructions. Bad work by interviewers is another matter; it can be controlled by better recruiting, training, and supervision.

Good editing can never compensate entirely for respondent and interviewer errors or sloppiness in completing questionnaires. The only real solution is to prevent the problem from arising, through careful survey design and good research management.

Editing involves, basically, reviewing each questionnaire to check for (1) adherence to survey instructions, (2) legible, complete, consistent, and intelligible answers, and (3) correct coding.[8]

Errors (when detected) and omissions can be handled in three ways: First, the entire questionnaire can be discarded, thus reducing the sample size and possibly biasing the data. (For example, the less literate members of the market population are more prone to do sloppy work. Discarding many of their questionnaires would mean that they would be inadequately represented in the sample.) Second, the errors and omissions can be tallied separately under such headings as "incorrect responses" or "no response." Sometimes what is left out can be revealing. It might, for example, indicate a repulsion toward or a disinterest in a particular aspect of the survey.

[8] For a detailed discussion of these points, see Harper W. Boyd, Jr., and Ralph Westfall, *Marketing Research: Text and Cases*, rev. ed. (Homewood, IL: Irwin, 1964), pp. 516–517; or Chester R. Wasson, *The Strategy of Marketing Research* (New York: Appleton-Century Crofts, 1964), p. 315.

Third, the "correct" answers can be entered by the editor. This kind of guesswork should be avoided, since it can easily bias the data. Unfortunately, it may be necessary if enough questionnaires are to be salvaged to provide a large enough sample. However, it is indicative of either a very poor questionnaire design or bad survey management.

Tabulating

Tabulating is the posting—or "rostering"—of the data onto work sheets, punch cards, or other collection media. If the raw data have been properly coded, this part of the task is easy, requiring only time and patience. Normally the questionnaires are first checked and coded (if precoding was not used) by an editor, who eliminates or corrects unacceptable responses. A clerk then posts the data into a table, usually in matrix form. Or, if computers are to be used in the analysis, a key-punch operator will prepare a punch-card deck or magnetic disk. This task is often performed outside the firm by a service bureau specializing in data processing. The cost runs about 10 cents per card, with each card carrying up to 80 columns of data. If the cards are to be verified (checked for transcription mistakes), the cost increases by about 6 cents per card. (Verification will reduce transcription errors from about 3 percent to about 0.5 percent of the cards.)

Generally, if more than a hundred questionnaires are involved, each has over ten questions, and data analysis is not to be limited to simple descriptive statistics, the coded answers should be transcribed onto cards or a disk. One card will be required for each questionnaire—more if the coded responses require over 80 columns (one digit or Arabic letter is allowed in each column).[9] Once the data are computerized, they can be manipulated with a speed, ease, and accuracy that cannot be matched by manual methods.

The traditional key-punch system is gradually being replaced by a cardless system, which is faster, cheaper, and more convenient. The cardless system puts the data directly onto disk or magnetic tape. This method is more consistent with the criteria of a good rostering system—high speed, high accuracy, and low cost.

Like the other steps in the data reduction process, tabulating[10] should be considered during survey design. It is especially relevant to the preparation of the questionnaire. For example, if the questionnaire provides for direct coding, as it does back in Exhibit 5-3, posting onto work sheets is unnecessary. The key-punch operator can work directly from the source document, saving time and money, as well as reducing transcription error.

Computerizing (Optional)

Computerizing starts during the tabulating. If the data are to be computerized, they must be tabulated in a form the computer can digest. Usually,

---

[9] IBM's System/3 uses a square punch card that accepts up to 120 columns of data.
[10] An excellent guide to tabulating (rostering) and coding is found in Bruce W. Tuckman, *Conducting Educational Research* (New York: Harcourt Brace Jovanovich, 1972), pp. 254–264.

they must be punched on cards or paper tape, or imprinted on magnetic tape or magnetic disk. Next they must be entered into the computer via card or paper-tape reader, magnetic tape drive, or disk drive. Once in the computer, they can be manipulated with speed, ease, accuracy, and economy. A rule-of-thumb: If there are more than a few hundred pieces of information, or if sophisticated analytical tools are to be applied, computerize the data.

Auditing

Several randomly chosen cases should be pulled from the rostered data and checked against the original documents. This is especially important with computerized data, which should be checked both before and after they have been entered into the computer. This is easy to do, particularly with data processing packages like SPSS.

Summarizing

Data are summarized by reducing them to a few numbers representing the essence of the original (raw) information. This is the heart of the reduction process.

Metric data can be summarized with either frequency distributions or descriptive statistics. Nonmetric data are limited to frequency distributions.

A *frequency distribution* is simply a table showing a set of characteristics in one column and the number of objects having each characteristic in an adjoining column. In marketing research, the characteristics are typically ages, incomes, sales, brand preferences, attitudes, or test scores. The objects are typically consumers, stores, trading areas, or salespersons. Exhibit 6-1 illustrates.

Exhibit 6-1   **Data Reduction and Descriptive Statistics: An Illustration**

Raw Data (Xs) 20, 38, 15, 31, 32 . . . 18, 31, 40, 33, 44

Frequency Distribution

Score Interval	Tally	Frequency (f)	Cumulative f	Cumulative f %
42–44	|||	3	120	100
39–41	||| |||		11	117	98
36–38	||| |||	8	106	88
33–35	||| ||| ||| ||| |||	23	98	82
30–32	||| ||| ||| ||| ||| ||| |||	35	75	63
27–29	||| ||| ||||	14	40	33
24–26	||| |||	10	26	22
21–23	||| ||||	9	16	13
18–20	|||		6	7	6
15–17			1	1	1
	Total (N) = 120			

***Exhibit 6-1   Data Reduction and Descriptive Statistics:
An Illustration (*cont'd.*)***

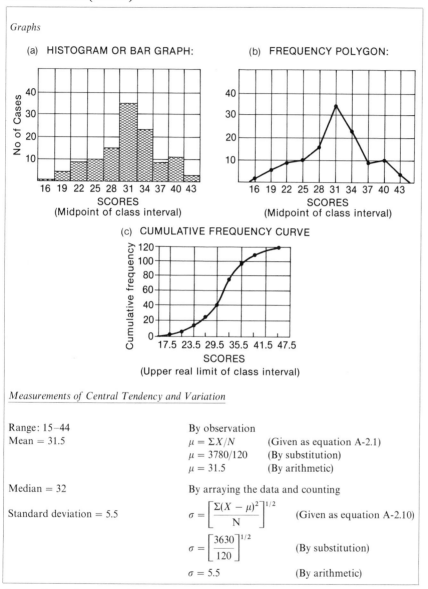

Graphs

(a) HISTOGRAM OR BAR GRAPH:

(b) FREQUENCY POLYGON:

SCORES
(Midpoint of class interval)

SCORES
(Midpoint of class interval)

(c) CUMULATIVE FREQUENCY CURVE

SCORES
(Upper real limit of class interval)

Measurements of Central Tendency and Variation

Range: 15–44	By observation	
Mean = 31.5	$\mu = \Sigma X/N$	(Given as equation A-2.1)
	$\mu = 3780/120$	(By substitution)
	$\mu = 31.5$	(By arithmetic)
Median = 32	By arraying the data and counting	
Standard deviation = 5.5	$\sigma = \left[\dfrac{\Sigma(X - \mu)^2}{N}\right]^{1/2}$	(Given as equation A-2.10)
	$\sigma = \left[\dfrac{3630}{120}\right]^{1/2}$	(By substitution)
	$\sigma = 5.5$	(By arithmetic)

Source: Drawn from example in Stephen Isaac and William B. Michael, *Handbook in Research and Evaluation* (San Diego: EdITS Robert R. Knapp, 1971), pp. 118–119.

Frequency distributions are often presented on graphs. Bar graphs are useful with both metric and nonmetric data. Frequency polygons and cumulative frequency curves are limited to metric data. These too are illustrated in Exhibit 6-1.

Table 6-2 Selecting Measures of Central Tendency and Dispersions

Central Tendency—When to Use the Three Averages:
1. Compute the arithmetic *mean* when:

 a. The greatest reliability is wanted. It usually varies less from sample to sample drawn from the same population.
 b. Other computations, as finding measures of variability, are to follow.
 c. The distribution is symmetrical about the center, and especially when it is approximately normal.
 d. We wish to know the "center of gravity" of a sample.

2. Compute the *median* when:

 a. There is not sufficient time to compute the mean.
 b. Distributions are markedly skewed. This includes the case in which one or more extreme measurements are at one side of the distribution.
 c. We are interested in whether cases fall within the upper or lower halves of the distribution and not particularly in how far from the central point.
 d. An incomplete distribution is given.

3. Compute the *mode* when:

 a. The quickest estimate of central value is wanted.
 b. A rough estimate of central value will do.
 c. We wish to know what is the most typical case.

Dispersion—When to Use the Three Measures of Dispersion:
1. Use the *range* when:

 a. The quickest possible index of dispersion is wanted.
 $$\frac{\text{Range}}{6} \cong \text{one standard deviation when } N \geqslant 100$$
 b. Information is wanted concerning extreme scores.

2. Use the quartile deviation (semi interquartile range) when:

 a. The median is the only statistic of central value reported.
 b. The distribution is truncated or incomplete at either end.
 c. There are a few very extreme scores or there is an extreme skewing.
 d. We want to know the actual score limits of the middle 50 percent of the cases.

3. Use the *standard deviation* when:

 a. Greatest dependability of the value is wanted.
 b. Further computations that depend upon it are likely to be needed.
 c. Interpretations related to the normal distribution curve are desired.

 (*Note:* The standard deviation has a number of useful relationships to the normal curve and to other statistical concepts.)

Source: From *Fundamental Statistics in Psychology and Education,* J. P. Guilford. Copyright © by the McGraw-Hill Book Company, 1965. By permission of McGraw-Hill Book Company.

Descriptive statistics can include many different parameters or statistics summarizing the data. The initial data reduction typically includes averages and measurements of dispersion. For instance, we might summarize a set of age data as having a mean (average) of 34, a range of 18 to 59, and a standard deviation of 8.

A guide to the selection of the appropriate average and measurement of dispersion is found in Table 6-2. Average and dispersion are usually the first things we want to know about our data. They measure the central tendency and variability of our objects—important information.

Example

Assume we've been asked to reduce a data set of 120 observations. These data are the sales made by the firm's salespersons. Management needs a meaningful summary of the information so it can judge the performance of the employees.

First we construct a frequency distribution. From it we draw three graphs. We also compute the mean, median, range, and standard deviation. Our work is shown in Exhibit 6-1. Now management has a simple, yet comprehensive picture of the productivity of its sales force.

Output

The output of the data reduction process is typically a summary of the information and a set of computerized data. The data summary includes frequency distributions, descriptive statistics, and graphs, as applicable. These may be all that management needs or wants to see. If so, the research process terminates.

The computerized data include all the usable information in the original raw data. The difference is the data have been coded, put in a form a computer can read, and presumably audited. The data are usually punched on cards or paper tape, or imprinted on magnetic tape or disk. The information is now ready for serious analysis.

Data Analysis

The tools of data analysis are numerous and varied. Many are quite complex. Few researchers are competent and comfortable with them all. When a problem may yield to different tools, we tend to try the one we know best.

The methods to be applied should be tentatively selected during the design stage of the research process. The type of data collected will limit the type of analytical tools that can be used. For instance, regression analysis would not work if one had collected only nonmetric information.

Ideally we should have flexibility when we reach the data analysis stage. There we might find it necessary to apply two or more analytical tools to unscramble the meaning of the data. For this reason, we'd like most—preferably all—of our information to be expressed in ratio-scale values.

Table 6-3 Choosing a Statistical Test

Type and Number of Independent Variables (columns) / **Type and Number of Dependent Variables** (rows)

Dependent type	Dependent #	Interval: 1	Interval: More than 1	Ordinal: 1	Ordinal: More than 1	Nominal: 1	Nominal: More than 1
Interval (Row 1)	0		Factor analysis				
	1	Correlation (Pearson's r)	Multiple correlation	Transform ordinal variable into nominal and use C-1, or transform the interval variable into ordinal and use B-2, or transform both variables into nominal and use C-3		Analysis of variance (or t-test)	Analysis of variance
	More than 1		Multiple correlation				
Ordinal (Row 2)	0				Coefficient of concordance (W)		
	1	Transform ordinal variable into nominal and use C-1, or transform the interval variable into ordinal and use B-2, or transform the interval variable into nominal and use C-2		Spearman correlation, Kendall's tau (τ)		Sign test, median test, U-Test, Kruskal-Wallis	Friedman's two-way analysis of variance
	More than 1						
Nominal (Row 3)	0						
	1	Analysis of variance (see C-1)		Sign test, median test, U-test. Kruskal-Wallis (see C-2)		Phi Coeff. (ϕ), Fisher exact test, chi-square	Chi-square
	More than 1	Analysis of variance (see C-1)		Friedman's two-way analysis of variance (see C-2)			

Column A = Interval · Column B = Ordinal · Column C = Nominal

Source: From Conducting Educational Research by Bruce W. Tuckman (New York: Harcourt Brace and Jovanovich, 1972), p. 229, c 1972 by

Data analysis typically starts with the frequency distributions and descriptive statistics. Often they reveal sufficient insight, and further analysis is unnecessary. Of course, we'd like an assessment of the error, especially if we've sampled a small portion of the population. There are ways to do this. We'll introduce them later.

Common Sense

Throughout the research process we invoke one tool more than others— common sense. It is the most powerful analytical tool in our inventory. Other methods only supplement it. Unfortunately, they are sometimes allowed to obscure it.

When the data set is small (under 30 observations) common sense can sometimes be applied directly to the raw information. Usually the data must first be reduced. The products of the reduction process, the frequency distributions and the descriptive statistics, will often provide sufficient information for the astute analyst. If not, other techniques must be invoked, especially in the search for relationships between variables. None, however, should be allowed to take precedence over common sense.

Relationships Between Variables

Marketing research tends to focus on the relationship between variables. The sale/price relationship, the brand-preference/taste relationship, and the consumer-attitude/advertising relationship are illustrative. Here we must go beyond our initial statistics. To draw meaning from the data we must apply one or more analytical tools. These range from simple scatter diagrams and contingency tables to exotic multivariate techniques.

For now, we'll confine ourselves to the problem of analyzing the relationship between just two variables, such as sales and advertising. Often we must cope with multiple relationships occurring simultaneously. Sales, for instance, may be fluctuating because of changes in advertising, price, distribution, weather, competition, consumer preferences, income, population, and so forth—all changing at the same time. The techniques of multivariate analysis, however, will be deferred to Chapter 16. One must learn to walk before learning to run.

Once the data are collected, there are a number of methods that can be applied to assess the relationship, if any, between two variables. The more common techniques are summarized in Table 6-3. Some determine if a statistically significant relationship exists. Others estimate the strength of the relationship. Choosing a technique depends on one's objective, willingness to exercise equations, and the nature of the data.

Scatter Diagrams

A *scatter diagram* is simply a two-variable data set plotted in a two-dimensional space. One variable is scaled on the vertical axis, the other variable on

Figure 6-2   **Scatter Diagrams: Sales versus Advertising**

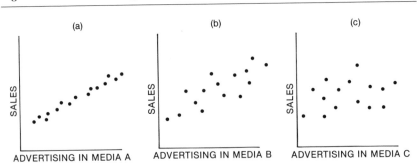

the horizontal one. Scatter diagrams are used to reveal correlation between two metric variables.

For instance, assume a firm advertised in three regional markets using a different medium for each. Sales were then plotted against the level of advertising. In Figure 6-2, we see the results: Sales are highly correlated with medium A advertising. They're moderately correlated with medium B advertising. They seem wholly unrelated to medium C advertising. Medium C should likely be dropped, for increasing or decreasing advertising in it does not change sales.

Contingency Tables

A *contingency table* is a cross tabulation of data on two variables: It is a set of rows and columns showing how respondents are jointly distributed between two variables.

Contingency tables are also called "two-way classification tables," "cross breaks," "cross tabulations," or simply "cross tabs." In effect, they are the combination of two frequency distributions—one laid upright and one laid sideways.

Cross tabs are used to reveal an association between variables. They are especially useful with nonmetric variables. However, they are also compatible with metric data.[11]

Frequently, a cross tabulation will throw a relationship into bold relief. We see an example in Table 6-4(A), which compares motorcycle ownership with sex. There is a pronounced relationship: Women don't buy motorcycles. Unless a firm has solved a problem that has thus far eluded Honda, Kawasaki, et al., it is wasting its resources trying to sell motorcycles to women.

Often the relationship between variables is foggy and we must move beyond the contingency table. Table 6-4(B) illustrates this point. There

[11] Usually, one must first assign the metric values to intervals, as is done in frequency distributions.

Table 6-4   **Contingency Tables**

A.   Sex Versus Motorcycle Ownership (sample size = 2,470)

	Males	Females
Owners	341	9
Nonowners	820	1300

B.   Sales Performance Versus Marital Status (sample size = 60)

	Married	Single
High sales	3	1
Medium sales	14	12
Low sales	10	13
No sales	3	4

seems to be some correlation between marital status and sales performance, but it may not be significant. If so, management should not favor married people in the hiring of salespersons. To confirm the relationship, we must perform a significance test.

Significance Tests

Sometimes a relationship between variables is apparent, but not real. This is often true when we are dealing with small samples (less than 30 observations), a lot of variables, or a low-intensity relationship. In short, what we first see as a statistical relationship may be nothing more than chance variation in the data—statistical error.

To assess the significance of the relationship, we apply a test of statistical significance. The most common is the chi square.

Chi Square Test   The chi square test tells us if there is a statistically significant difference between frequency distributions. Hence, it is especially useful with contingency tables.

The chi square test starts with the hypothesis that there is no significant difference between frequency distributions. This is appropriately called the "null hypothesis." ("Null" means none.) Presumably any observed difference is a result of chance. For instance, we know a perfectly balanced coin should yield five heads out of ten flips. Yet we would not be surprised if we got six heads. We would attribute the difference between the two distributions—the theoretical and the actual—to chance. However, if we got nine heads out of ten flips, we'd reject the hypothesis that there is no significant difference. We would assume our coin was different from an honestly balanced one.

As with many statistical test, we compute a statistic based on our data and compare it with a statistic drawn from a table. If the computed value is greater, we reject the hypothesis and assume that a significant difference does exist. The computed chi square value (χ^2) and the degrees of freedom (d.f.) for entering the table are found as follows.

$$\chi^2 = \sum \frac{(f_1 - f_2)^2}{f_2} \qquad [6.1]$$

where

χ^2 = computed chi square

f_1 = frequency in a cell in the first frequency distribution

f_2 = frequency in the adjoining cell in the second distribution

d.f. = $(r - 1)(k - 1)$ [6.2]

r = number of rows

k = number of columns

The table value of chi square is found by entering a chi square table with the degrees of freedom and the significance level. Degrees of freedom is calculated with equation 6.2. Significance level, which indicates the risk of a mistake, is chosen by judgement. The researcher must decide how much risk is acceptable. The table then yields the critical (table) value of chi square.

The *significance level* indicates the probability of being wrong. In the chi square test, the significance level (s.l.) is the probability that identical underlying distributions have yielded observed distributions that produce a computed chi square value greater than the table value. If our computed chi square is greater than our table chi square, then we know our exposure to error is no greater than the significance level. That is, there is a fixed-percentage chance that we will reject a hypothesis that should have been accepted.[12]

For example, if we entered the table (found in Appendix 4-4), with d.f. = 3 and a significance level of .05, we'd get a critical value of 7.82. We could then say that the chance of getting a computed chi square of greater than 7.82, even if our hypothesis is correct, is only 5 percent. If our computed chi square exceeded 7.82, we'd be comfortable rejecting the hypothesis. There would be little chance we'd be wrong.

---

[12] This is called a "Type I" or "alpha (α)" error. See Appendix 2, "Testing Hypotheses."

Exhibit 6-2   **Applying the Chi Square Test**

Null Nypothesis	H_0: There is no statistically significant difference between the performance of married salespersons (f_1) and unmarried sales persons (f_2).
Solution	$\chi^2 = \Sigma(f_1 - f_2)^2/f_2$ (Given as equation 6.1)

Contingency Table

		Marital Status				
		Married	Single	$(f_1 - f_2)$	$(f_1 - f_2)^2$	$(f_1 - f_2)^2/f_2$
		(f_1)	(f_2)			
	High sales	3	1	2	4	4.00
Sales	Medium sales	14	12	2	4	.33
Performance	Low sales	10	13	-3	9	.69
	No sales	3	4	-1	1	.25

$$\Sigma(f_1 - f_2)^2/f_2 = \overline{5.27}$$
Computed $\chi^2 = 5.27$ (by arithmetic)

d.f. $= (r - 1)(k - 1)$ (Given as equation 6.2)
d.f. $= (4 - 1)(2 - 1)$ (By substitution)
d.f. $= 3$ (By arithmetic)
Significance level (s.1.) $= .05$ (By judgment)
Table $\chi^2 = 7.82$ (From table)
Computed $\chi^2 <$ Table χ^2 @ .05 significance level

Decision	Do not reject the null hypothesis. That is, until more conclusive data are found, assume that marital status has nothing to do with sales performance.

Exhibit 6-2 illustrates the chi square test. Here we analyze the data in Table 6-4(B). Our objective is to decide if there is a statistically significant relationship between two variables—sales performance and marital status. If our data fail the test of statistical significance, we have not proven the hypothesis correct. We have only failed to prove it incorrect. Lacking more conclusive evidence, we have little choice but to accept it. However, there is always a chance we're wrong. More data might result in a different conclusion. Or, it might reinforce our original conclusion, making us more confident of our decision. As usual, more data are better than less data.

As chi square is concerned with frequency distributions, it is congenial with nominal data. In fact, chi square will work with any type of data as long as we first assign the data to frequency distributions. This breadth of application and the test's simplicity are why chi square is so popular.

Other Tests   If our data are ordinal, interval, or a combination of types, we have other tests to choose from. The more common ones are cited in Table

6-3. Choice depends mainly on the nature of the data and the number of variables involved. We shall examine several of these methods later in the book.

If we have ratio data, we can apply virtually any analytical technique consistent with the number of variables we're working with. We may have to transform the data. For instance, with chi square we'll have to put it into frequency distribution. However, that is seldom much trouble.

Once we're assured of a statistically significant relationship, we'll likely want to know the magnitude and direction of the relationship. For that information we must turn to other tools, such as correlation analysis.

Simple Correlation Analysis

Simple correlation analysis measures the statistical relationship between two variables. There are many ways of performing this analysis. Most yield a correlation coefficient which tells us two things: (1) the statistical relationship's magnitude and (2) its direction.

A correlation coefficient generally runs from $+1$ to -1. A value of one, plus or minus, indicates a perfect correlation. A value of zero indicates no correlation. The sign $(+$ or $-)$ indicates direction. Thus, $+.95$ would indicate a high correlation between two variables that moved together in the same direction. Figure 6-2(A) is illustrative. A correlation of $-.80$ would indicate a strong correlation between two variables that moved in opposite directions. Sales and price are examples. A near zero correlation coefficient would indicate that the two variables were unrelated, as in Figure 6-2(C).

Correlation is sometimes spurious. That is, the observed relationship is induced by chance variation. The variables are not statistically related. This is especially common in very small samples (less than 10 observations). Hence, a test of statistical significance, such as chi square, is often made along with the correlation analysis. If the test is failed, the results of the correlation analysis are ignored.

Pearson r   Probably the most common measurement of simple correlation is the Pearson product moment correlation coefficient, called simply the "Pearson r." The Pearson r produces a correlation coefficient between 0 and ± 1. One of several computational methods can be applied.[13] Perhaps the easiest is:

$$r = \frac{\Sigma xy}{\sqrt{(\Sigma x^2)(\Sigma y^2)}} \qquad\qquad [6.3]$$

[13] For example, see N. M. Downie and R. W. Heath, *Basic Statistical Methods*, fourth ed. (New York: Harper & Row, 1974), ch. 7. This chapter also provides an excellent discussion of the Pearson r and its applications.

where

r = correlation coefficient (Pearson r)

x = deviation of $X(x = X - \bar{X})$ (see footnote 14)

y = deviation of $Y(y = Y - \bar{Y})$ (see footnote 14)

To illustrate, take the analysis of seven weeks of car sales at a successful Ford agency. On the assumption that there was a strong relationship between total car sales (new and used) and the number of salespersons employed, a correlation analysis was made. The process, which is limited to metric data, is illustrated in Exhibit 6-3. It reveals a strong correlation ($r = .78$) between sales and sales-force size.

The analysis is slightly shaky because of the small sample. Before management accepts the findings, a test of statistical significance is in order.[15] Had the sample been large (over 30 observations), the high correlation coefficient alone would have been evidence enough to reject the null hypothesis.

Exhibit 6-3   **Computation of Pearson r**

	Evaluation of a Sales (Y)/Sales-Force-Size (X) Relationship						
Obs.	Y	X	y	y^2	x	x^2	xy
1	30	17	5	25	6	74	30
2	25	10	0	0	-1	1	0
3	28	13	3	9	2	4	6
4	17	9	-8	64	-2	4	16
5	32	13	7	49	2	4	14
6	23	7	-2	4	-4	16	8
7	20	8	-5	25	-3	9	15
	$\Sigma Y = 175$	77		$\Sigma y^2 = 176$		$\Sigma x^2 = 74$	$\Sigma xy = 89$
	$\bar{Y} = 25$	$\bar{X} = 11$					

$$r = \frac{\Sigma xy}{\sqrt{(\Sigma x^2)(\Sigma y^2)}} \quad \text{(Given as equation 6.3)}$$

$$r = \frac{89}{\sqrt{(74)(176)}} \quad \text{(By substitution)}$$

$$r = .78 \quad \text{(By arithmetic)}$$

Note: $y = Y - \bar{Y}$ $x = X - \bar{X}$

---

[14] The deviation is simply the difference between an observed value of a variable, say Y, and its mean, $\bar{Y}$.

[15] If the chi square test is used, the two frequency distributions (the Y values and X values) will have to be converted to percentages. Otherwise the two scales will not be compatible.

Table 6-5   **Some Common Methods for Analyzing Relationships Between Variables**

Method	Statistical Tools
Simple tabulation	Tally, frequency distribution, bar graph
Descriptive statistics	Mean, median, mode, range, standard deviation
Cross tabulation	t and z tests Chi square test Analysis of variance Discriminant analysis
Response configuration analysis (cause and effect)	Simple correlation analysis Regression analysis Factor analysis Clustering techniques
Respondent configuration analysis	Factor analysis Clustering techniques Canonical techniques Automatic Interaction Detector
Salience analysis (Determinant attitudes)	Simple correlation analysis Simple covariance analysis
Stimulus positioning analysis (Product positioning)	Factor analysis Nonmetric scaling Discriminant analysis

Source: Based partially on material provided by James Meyers.

Other Methods   There are numerous methods of dealing with correlation or, more broadly, the relationship between variables. The more common ones are shown in Table 6-5. We'll meet many as we progress through the book.

Selection is determined mainly by the nature of the data (metric vs. nonmetric) and the number of variables. So far we've confronted only the two-variable case. Often the data are confounded by the simultaneous effect of three or more variables. Analysis of these variables one pair at a time may reveal little of what is going on. If so, we must turn to multivariable methods. We'll sample the delights of these techniques later, especially in Part 6 where we explore multivariate analysis.

A Note of Encouragement

The process of data reduction and analysis may seem time-consuming and tedious. The equations may be intimidating—the next worst thing to corporeal punishment.

Not so! Today's researcher seldom tackles data manually. He or she does the reduction and analysis with a computer, or, has it done by a local service bureau, which uses a computer. The computer is preprogrammed. That is, it has one of the common statistical packages that allow the data to be reduced and analyzed without having to write programs. These packages, such as SPSS and BMD, are readily available. They provide a broad range of data processing techniques, including the tools of multivariate analysis encountered later. One simply enters the data and specifies the statistics to be computed, such as the mean, standard deviation, chi square, etc. A simple statement to the computer will also produce frequency distributions, bar charts, and so forth. However, users must understand what these things are if they are to specify the appropriate procedures and interpret the resulting statistics. Such understanding is the central purpose of this book.

A Word of Caution

As we progress through the text, we'll be adding more and more techniques to our toolbox. We'll also run the danger of becoming so enthralled with the means that we lose sight of the ends. Students must remember that this is not a course in statistics. Practitioners must remember the danger of turning inward and not talking to the marketers with the real problems. Both should focus on the disease, not the cure. To this end, we should keep in mind Walkup's first five laws of statistics, cited in Table 6-6.

Table 6-6   **Walkup's First Five Laws of Statistics**

Law No. 1
Everything correlates with everything, especially when the same individual defines the variables to be correlated.

Law No. 2
It won't help very much to find a good correlation between the variable you are interested in and some other variable that you don't understand any better.

Law No. 3
Unless you can think of a logical reason why two variables should be connected as cause and effect, it doesn't help much to find a correlation between them. In Columbus, Ohio, the mean monthly rainfall correlates very nicely with the number of letters in the names of the months!

Law No. 4
If you need a lot of statistical analysis to find out what your experiments mean, drop the whole thing and go back and refine your variables and your experiments to eliminate "noise" and extraneous effects.
    The need for complex statistics suggests that (1) variables have not been isolated in the design of the experiments or (2) "noise" has gotten into the system. In either case, experiments should be redesigned. Otherwise the results cannot be trusted very far.

Law No. 5
The most legitimate use of statistics is to help us discover natural laws and principles that will eliminate the need for statistics!

Source: Lewis Walkup's "First Five Laws of Statistics," *The Bent* (Summer 1974), publication of The Tau Beta Pi Association, National Engineering Honor Society. University of Missouri Alumni Magazine.

Report Preparation

After the data have been processed, the results must be interpreted. The salient findings must be conveyed to management, and recommendations must be made. A report must be prepared. Although the report may take the form of a casual telephone call, more likely it will be written.

Style

Research reports are sometimes rich in technical jargon. Such language is confusing and seldom necessary. It is occasionally used to hide the absence of any reasonable thought. A good report can be easily understood by a line manager unskilled in the craft of marketing research. It should be written with this person in mind.

Format

The format of the report will vary between authors, subjects, and clients. Typically it includes three parts, in this order:

> Summary
> Findings and Recommendations
> Technical Appendix.

The summary is a brief condensation of the findings and recommendations. It recognizes that few managers have the time and inclination to read details. Frequently, separate copies of the summary are reproduced and distributed to managers with only a passive interest in the study.

The findings and recommendations section covers the details. The details are there for the manager who needs all of the information and for the manager who wants the specifics on a finding or recommendation noted in the summary.

The technical appendix is for an explanation of the design and techniques of the research project. This section also serves as a depository for all the esoterica dear to the researcher. It is useful as a technical reference, should the study be replicated or adapted to a similar problem in the future.

The format of an MR report is illustrated in Exhibit 6-4. This is presented, not as a standard, but as one design out of many that seems to work.

Pitfall

Sometimes the report finds it way into the files without touching the decision process. This is tragic. Marketing research is usually too expensive and important to be ignored. Good research can significantly improve the probability of a correct decision by line management. It should not be allowed to founder on the shoals of poor communications.

This pitfall can usually be avoided by following a few simple rules: First, keep management advised and involved throughout the research process. Second, write the report from the user's point of view and in language

Exhibit 6-4   **A Research Report Format**

Source: Outline of a product study made for Mitsubishi Aircraft International by the American Research Institute.

he or she understands. Third, conduct a skillful management briefing—one that is short, to the point, and not esoteric. And, fourth, follow up. If the report is being ignored, learn why.

Problems

1   Which of the following are metric data? (a) A set of numerical codes representing brand preference, (b) the population counts for each census tract in the Boston SMSA, or (c) the rank order a respondent's cola preferences derived during a taste test of 5 formulations.

2   Define *ceteris paribus* and cite an example not found in the text.

3   List the steps typical of a data reduction process.

4   How would you code the responses to a multiple choice question involving preference for the colors red, green, and blue?

5   Thirty respondents were asked to state which of three colors (red, green, or blue) they preferred for Macy's standard Christmas gift

box. Two failed to answer and three were indifferent. The remaining responded R,R,G,B,B,R,G,R,B,B,R,G,B,R,G,G,B,G,R,R,G,B,B,G,R.
Prepare a frequency distribution of the responses.

6   Of the respondents reporting family incomes of $35,000 or over, 70
    shopped at Bullock's, 30 at the May Company, and 50 at Robinson's.
    Of those reporting family incomes between $25,000 and $34,999,
    60 shopped at Bullock's, 35 at May Company, and 55 at Robinson's.
    Prepare a contingency table of these data.

7   In the previous problem, does family income influence choice be-
    tween the three department stores, once income exceeds $34,999.
    Defend your answer.

8   Given these data, estimate the relationship (if any), between sales and
    advertising insertions in the local newspaper.

Week	Sales	Advertising
1	30 cases	1 insertion
2	42	2
3	22	1
4	35	2
5	60	2
6	21	0
7	32	2
8	40	2
9	45	3
10	52	3

Chapter 7
Marketing Information Systems

Key Concepts

Information management
The problems and techniques of data management

System installation
Benefits versus cost, problems and parameters, and the design procedure of marketing information systems

MIS as a management philosophy
Philosophical issues that accompany the installation of a marketing information system

Key Terms

marketing information system	system authority
management access time	data bank
information recency	microdata
information aggregates	macrodata

Information Management

The information explosion is possibly the most pervasive phenomenon of the past few decades. Certainly the management and exploitation of this information, for the betterment or abuse of humanity, is one of the important issues of our time. Corporate managements in particular have become painfully aware of the flood of statistical data and new technology that must be dealt with, segments of which can be vital to the prosperity—and in some cases, the survival—of the firm. The result has been the emergence in many quarters of formal management information systems. A few, such as NASA's Technology Information System, described earlier, are general-purpose systems available to anyone willing to subscribe. Most, however, are tailored to particular firms, are proprietary, and deal with special fields.

Information management consists of gathering, cataloguing, storing, and retrieving data. These functions are common to all information systems, although they are sometimes called by different names. More sophisticated systems also perform analytical functions, varying from simple arithmetic operations, such as aggregating sales data, to forecasts using complex analytical or simulation models.

The management of large quantities of information has been made practical by the advent of the high-speed digital computer. Once the data have been gathered, catalogued (classified), and prepared in a form that is digestible by a computer—such as punch cards or magnetic tape—their storage and retrieval is an inexpensive and extremely fast process. A firm with on-line computer service can retrieve data in a matter of seconds. Once the necessary computer programs have been prepared, analytical functions can be performed with comparable speed. We see an illustration in Exhibit 7-1.

The management of marketing information differs from the management of other forms of information mainly in that it deals with marketing data. Often the marketing system is combined with other information systems designed to handle financial, manufacturing, purchasing, engineering, and credit data. The information requirements of other departments in the firm are usually compatible with those of the marketing department. In fact, these departments will draw on much of the same data.

***Exhibit 7-1*   An MIS Terminal.**

Source: Courtesy of Intelligent Systems Corporation.

Marketing information systems—sometimes called "MIS"[1]—are on-going programs for the collection and dissemination of market data. They might be thought of as market monitors. They provide management with a regular series of reports, which are typically issued weekly or monthly. They give management current data on such things as sales and market shares, usually for both the company's and for competing brands. Figure 7-1 is illustrative.

Formal marketing information systems are apparently used by the majority of the nation's 500 largest industrial firms, although most of them tend to be secretive about the details. In one study, 58 percent of these firms refused to answer requests for information—a surprisingly large lack of cooperation for an MIS survey.[2]

Figure 7-1   A Marketing Information System

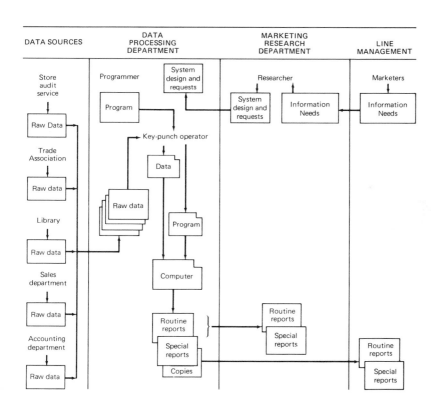

[1] "MIS" is also a common abbreviation for management information systems, of which marketing information systems are a special case. Again, the words and abbreviations are not always used consistently.

[2] Arnold E. Amstutz, "Marketing Oriented Management Systems: The Current Status," *Journal of Marketing Research*, **6**:4 (November 1969), p. 484.

The data from those firms which did respond suggest that there is a "dramatic difference between the theoretical capabilities of management systems described in the literature and those actually used or planned by operating companies."[3] A vast majority of the companies were concerned only with the more elementary functions of an information management system, to the exclusion of the analytical function. Even more disturbing is the fact that the vast majority of the respondents seemed unaware of, or unconcerned with, decision structures designed to help management assimilate and use information. This attitude may change as more rigorously trained graduates of business schools advance into the upper echelon of command and demand a broader application of the tools of scientific management.

System Installation[4]

Value Analysis

In making the decision whether to establish and maintain a formal MIS, management is again confronted with a problem of value analysis. In short, it must determine the benefits of the proposed system and compare them to the costs.

In general, the benefits of MIS are

—a reduction in the opportunity cost of wrong decisions

—a reduction in the opportunity cost of delayed decisions

—a smaller information loss

—less distortion of the data

—increased speed and efficiency in analyzing problems and making decisions.

Of course, these benefits are based on the assumption that management will use the system once it is installed. To be useful, the MIS must be included in the firm's strategic planning and accepted by its line managers as part of their philosophy of marketing management.

To "buy" the benefits, the firm incurs the continuing cost of collecting, processing, storing, retrieving, and disseminating the data, as well as the initial cost of designing and installing the system. MIS can be very expensive, depending on its sophistication and the ability of the system's sponsor to find other users willing to share the costs.

Conceivably, one could design an optimum MIS, given the marketing decision structure of the firm. Or one could optimize the decision structure, given a particular MIS. The ideal solution, the simultaneous optimization of

---

[3] Amstutz, "Marketing Oriented Management Systems: The Current Status," p. 496.
[4] I am especially indebted to Professor Masao Nakanishi for his assistance on this section.

both the decision structure and the MIS, is probably an unobtainable goal. Thus management may have to settle, initially, for suboptimum conditions.

Possibly the best practical approach to getting a workable MIS is to install and evaluate it incrementally. The more obvious information requirements can be identified first, and an MIS designed to satisfy them. Once the system is operational, it can then be integrated into the marketing decision structure. If the initial scale of operation is kept small, the system will be more manageable and less disruptive than a large and inclusive MIS would be.

Up to this point, cost-benefit analysis will have to be fairly subjective. However, once experience is accumulated, management can use more rigorous methods. If the system has been accepted and proven efficient on a small scale, it can be expanded—again, incrementally—to provide more information to more decision-makers. As the MIS grows, it will probably exhibit increasing returns to scale; that is, it will become more efficient as it increases in size. This should also be taken into account in evaluating the system.

In spite of its great benefits, at least in theory, the MIS has hardly been contagious. A number of factors work for and against installation, including:[5]

For	Against
The data explosion	Fear—the giant system syndrome
Computer hardware development	Communications gap between MR
Lowering computer costs	people and line managers
Improved computer software	Lack of computer availability
Better market models	Lack of trained personnel
Increasing population of	Failure to design a balanced system
computer-oriented managers	Poorly specified benefits
Greater stress on planning	
Accumulating evidence of benefits	

System Design Problems

The design of an MIS—like the design of a general management information system—should take into consideration the needs of the firm, the availability of resources, and the problems of implementation. The first condition may

---

[5] Both lists are drawn mainly from David B. Montgomery, *Marketing Information and Decision Systems*, Research Paper No. 150, Research Paper Series (Stanford, CA: Graduate School of Business, Stanford University, April 1973), pp. 2 and 16.

be considered objectively, in terms of the important decisions that confront the marketers. The second condition must be considered in terms of the existing resources and the ability of the system's champions to compete for them. The third condition is largely organizational and may involve some political maneuvering.

The design parameters, or objectives, of an MIS may be defined in terms of five dimensions of system evaluation:

—management access time
—information recency
—information aggregation
—analytic sophistication
—system authority.[6]

Amstutz suggests two other dimensions, namely, cost and compatibility. However, cost could be classified as a constraint rather than a parameter. And zealous proponents of scientific management might argue that it is the firm's organizational and decision structures that should be changed to accommodate the MIS, and not vice versa.

Management access time can vary from seconds to months. If the system is designed to include a fully computerized data bank, if management is authorized to have direct access to the stored data and programs, if there are an adequate number of remote computer terminals and management is trained in their use, then marketing information can be provided in seconds, as long as the necessary raw data have been stored in the system. At the other extreme, if the data are insufficient and must be manually stored and manipulated, it may take months to get all the information needed for a decision.

Information recency can also vary from seconds to months. If the system is a real-time system designed to record events as they occur, anybody with access to the computer (usually via a remote terminal) can get the information immediately. Changes in inventory, work in process, sales, and purchases are often recorded in this manner. However, if the data bank is dependent on inputs from daily, weekly, or monthly tabulations, or quarterly and annual reports, the information will be correspondingly old.

Information aggregates vary from line items—such as orders for individual parts, or data on specific transactions—to industry totals. Between these extremes, the data can be aggregated by invoice, brand, product, salesman, sales region, division, or company. The ability of the system to aggregate items depends on the level of detail of the raw data and the extent to which they are identified with different levels of aggregation. For instance, if all the sources of raw data would cooperate, General Motors could design an MIS that would aggregate Chevrolet sales at every level. However, one

    [6] Amstutz, "Marketing Oriented Management Information Systems: The Current Status," p. 495.

could hardly expect GM's competitors to provide information that would let GM disaggregate their total sales to the levels specified.

The *analytical sophistication* of these systems varies from the very elementary to the very complex. The more advanced MIS uses simulation, regression, Bayesian decision theory, and other analytical tools to forecast sales and to predict the outcomes of alternative marketing mixes. Their analytical power comes from the inclusion of analytical and simulation models in their design. These models, which normally take the form of computer programs that use the information stored in the data bank, are the product of marketing research. Since marketing research depends heavily on the data provided by MIS and, at the same time, provides raw data and models for the system, the two functions—research and the MIS—feed on each other. For this reason, the MIS is generally the responsibility of the firm's marketing-research staff.

System authority refers to the importance of the MIS in the decision process. This too is highly variable. The system can be ignored, in which case its authority is zero; it can be used with discretion; or it can be relied upon blindly. The usefulness of a given system in the marketing decision process depends largely on its accessibility, its analytical sophistication, and its acceptance by line management. This last factor can hardly be overemphasized. If the system is capable and confidence in it runs high, an MIS can relieve management of a lot of bothersome chores, such as routine pricing decisions in a multiproduct firm (e.g., a department store). It can also facilitate major decisions if senior executives encourage their subordinates to support important recommendations with analyses provided by the firm's MIS.

Design Procedure

There is no standard routine for designing and installing marketing information systems, nor can existing systems be easily adapted to different firms. Designers must usually start at the beginning, although they can adapt existing systems components, such as computer hardware and programs, as they progress.

The designer generally performs the following tasks, operating within the constraints imposed by the firm's resources and politics:

—determines what decisions must be made by marketing management

—determines what information is needed to make these decisions.

—determines where this information can be found and which sources can be tied directly into the data bank.

—selects analytical tools for generating information that cannot be gotten from available sources.

—determines the form in which information is needed by management.

—determines how important the accessibility and recency of the information is.

—prepares the procedures and selects the tools for the collection, reduction, storage, manipulation, and dissemination of the information.

—prepares a plan for the installation, maintenance, and upgrading of the system and the instruction of line management in its use.

Although the last task above may appear to be outside the realm of MIS design, it is a vital step. Without it, the system may never be accepted by management, but will remain an interesting and possibly expensive exercise in systems design. For the full potential of an MIS to be realized, it must be understood and endorsed by management, and its information must be assimilated by those making the marketing decisions.

The Data Bank

The *data bank* is the storage center of the system. It contains all the raw data fed into the system from outside, as well as data generated by the models within the system. It is the heart of the MIS.

The data bank is the most important feature of the system design because the ways in which the data can be manipulated depends on how they are stored. If information is not appropriately disaggregated, classified, and recorded, it may be impossible to use certain analytical tools. If sales are recorded by geographic regions and advertising expenditures are not, it may be impossible to determine the precise relationship between them. If sales are aggregated by brand and selling expenses are recorded by district, it will be impossible to specify the sensitivity of sales to personal selling, except in a general and crude way.

The physical form in which data are stored is also extremely important. If they are put on punch cards or magnetic tape, they are usually amenable to manipulation. If they are stored in some form of mechanical file—such as Addressograph plates—manipulation may be difficult or even impossible, unless the system designer had the foresight to anticipate every analytical requirement or the data bank is limited to a few thousand bits of information. For instance, in one study of a direct-mail advertising program, certain very useful information was buried in the data. Had it been stored on punch cards or tape, it could have been retrieved in under an hour by a computer. Stored as it was on 700,000 Addressograph plates, retrieval would have taken 13 man-years.

Flexibility is the dominant criterion in the design of a data bank. It is achieved by disaggregating the data and then storing it in a form that can easily be digested by a computer. Data should be disaggregated to the finest level of detail commensurate with the system budget and the probable information needs of the firm. They can always be aggregated. For instance, weekly figures can always be totaled to obtain a figure for monthly, quarterly, or yearly sales. However, they cannot be disaggregated to obtain precise data on daily sales, although an average-daily-sales figure could be calculated.

Unfortunately, very detailed "microdata" are more difficult and expensive to collect and store, than are aggregated "macrodata." The additional cost must be balanced against the anticipated need for the information. The designer must take into account the fact that the initial design of the data bank will set critical limits on the future modification and expansion of the MIS, especially with respect to its analytical capabilities.

Commercial Services

The advent of computer time-sharing[7] has encouraged several research suppliers to offer their clients a shared marketing information system. One system—called "MARKINF"—is a product of the A. C. Nielsen Co., which specializes in the collection of sales and media data. Since MARKINF illustrates shared marketing information systems, it is worth examining.

MARKINF is available to a variety of subscribers, some of whom are competitors. It is not an inclusive system designed to serve all the needs of the marketing department. To this extent, it might be considered a limited-application, or special-use, system. For one thing, it does not provide for the collection and storage of company-generated data. A purist might argue that it is therefore not truly an MIS. However, MARKINF is a formal, fairly sophisticated system for the management of a certain set of market data.

The Nielsen system uses no unique techniques or equipment; only the application is innovative. Remote terminals, on-line (continuous) service, direct access, and time-sharing are common in computer technology. In fact, much of MARKINF is similar to the sole-user information systems developed by such firms as IBM and Pillsbury. For these reasons, it is a good illustration of MIS.

MARKINF consists of two parts, or elements. The first is the data bank, called "DATA BASE." The second is the data retrieval and manipulation language. The data base is a collection of survey data gathered by Nielsen on selected products and brands. It consists primarily of information on sales and market shares over time, classified according to brands, product classes, and geographic markets.

Subscribers to MARKINF are provided with remote on-line terminals which they can use to get information from DATA BASE and to request selected types of analyses. This is done by entering on the terminal (which is essentially a teletypewriter, with a keyboard and a printing device) an appropriate command in the prescribed computer language. For example, a client might want to know the average sales for product "102" during time

---

[7] Computer time-sharing refers to the collective use of a single computer by two or more organizations who jointly bear the expense of the operation. The computer itself occupies a single location, but it is operated from remote terminals in dozens of different locations. Advances in computer technology have made such a system practical. The heart of a computer system is its central processing unit (CPU), which performs the arithmetical and logical operations. The CPU is an extremely complex and expensive piece of machinery, but because it performs complicated tasks in a matter of seconds and can handle several problems simultaneously, it can serve many users without overloading.

periods "11" through "14," in dollars, in the Houston and St. Louis markets. He would type the following instruction—or "command"—on his terminal:

```
?RET MKT (HOU;STL) ;PROD (102) ;PER (11-14) ;FCT ($VOL)
?AVE
```

Within seconds, the computer would respond by printing the desired information on the client's terminal.

The operation of the system can be mastered by a subscriber in a few hours. The terminal is similar in appearance to an electric typewriter. The language consists of a few dozen code words, most of which are obvious contractions of their everyday counterparts. The system's data bank and its analytical models are described in an accompanying manual. They require no mathematical or statistical skills to use, other than those needed to understand the meaning of the answers, which are sometimes expressed in statistical terms. Since he had direct access to the disaggregated data, the user can also apply his own analytical tools or aggregate the data to conform to his (or her) needs.[8]

There are other commercial services that could be classified as information systems, such as NASA's Technology Transfer Program, described earlier. Predicasts offers a large data base of economic and business information. It also offers an on-line retrieval service that can be installed, via remote terminal, in the client's office.

MIS as a Management Philosophy

The implications of MIS extend far beyond marketing research. This is true even when the system is designed solely for the benefit of the marketing department, rather than as part of the management information system of the firm as a whole. Even a relatively simple marketing information system requires the cooperation of numerous persons outside the department. Sales personnel, accountants, product managers, advertising executives, and credit managers are but a few of the people whose continuous cooperation may be vital to the maintenance of the MIS. A more sophisticated MIS may require a major alteration of the firm's accounting and logistics systems before it can be put into operation.

If a marketing information system is to be fully exploited, a reorganization of the marketing department also may be in order. The economics of computer operation force the centralization of data processing and the elimination of many clerical functions. Hence, certain administrative and clerical jobs become superfluous, and some supervisory positions can be dropped or consolidated. If the information system picks up the raw data at the acquisition point—say, from purchase orders or invoices—and then transmits them directly to the computer, middle-management reports be-

---

[8] *"MARKINF"—An On-line Timesharing System To Retrieve and Manipulate A. C. Nielsen Marketing Information,* unpublished draft of "a description and preliminary reference manual," provided by William F. Massy, Stanford University.

come obsolete. Instead of being prepared at different levels of command, then sent upward, the reports are prepared by the data processing center and disseminated downward. This denies intermediaries the opportunity to alter the data or bias reports as they (the reports) move upward—a very common problem in management communications.

MIS provides a direct link between the data acquisition point and the data processing center. It also provides for computerization of the manipulation and storage of the data. Thus, the higher echelons of management have much faster and more direct access to marketing information. This encourages centralization of control, since all the ramifications of a decision can be considered by anyone with access to the system. Related problems can be considered together and a solution chosen that will more nearly optimize the allocation of the firm's resources. For instance, linear programming might be used to determine the optimum distribution of the total advertising budget among several brands in a multiple-product firm or several market segments. Management decision techniques such as the rule of proportionality or marginal analysis can be invoked to maximize total company profit rather than the profit or revenue from a particular item.[9] In short, an MIS moves the firm from suboptimization methods toward optimization techniques, by permitting more variables to be explicitly considered in a given decision situation.

Obviously, the hierarchy of command (the decision system) must be consistent with the information system, if the latter is to be fully exploited. Thus the installation of an MIS can be very disruptive even when the MIS is tailored to conform with the present chain of command. Many decisions that were formerly made independently by junior managers will now be made in concert, at a higher level in the organization. Often, entire echelons of management are eliminated. Junior managers become vulnerable to closer scrutiny and are relieved of certain prerogatives. The entire organization becomes more amenable to observation, and hence to control.

On the other hand, managers may be glad to be relieved of many routine administrative chores. Then, too, an MIS can provide sales personnel with a wealth of current market information and forecasts that are impractical under conventional reporting systems. These make their job easier. Thus, an MIS means greater freedom from administrative burdens plus quicker and better market intelligence for many line managers. The penalty may be a lessening of their authority and greater accountability for performance. Surprisingly enough, in some cases it may mean more authority for line managers. In those areas where decisions can be made without materially influencing the outcomes of other people's decisions, delegation of authority may be appropriate. The MIS gives senior managers current information on the performance of their subordinates, and wrong decisions are likely to surface quickly. Thus, management by exception becomes a

---

[9] For a detailed discussion of management decision techniques as they pertain to the allocation of marketing resources, see W. B. Wentz and G. I. Eyrich, *Marketing: Theory and Application* (New York: Harcourt Brace Jovanovich, 1970), Part III.

viable alternative in the supervision of subordinates and will work even when those subordinates are far removed from the home office.

A byproduct of MIS is the tendency of marketing-research personnel to become more involved with line managers. On the whole, this is considered a good thing. Market research is valuable only insofar as it facilitates line decisions. However, it does pose problems of supervision. Control becomes more difficult as loyalties become divided and as individual analysts become more identified with the clientele they serve.

MIS can frequently be extended to serve the needs of other departments, such as engineering and production control. The marginal cost of such a move is often nominal, and the benefits may be substantial. Marketing information, especially on consumer tastes, is useful in product design; good market forecasts are essential to production planning. Of course, as the scope of the services it performs grows, the MIS tends to evolve into a general management information system for executives throughout the company.

An MIS, in its most sophisticated form, represents a radically new approach to the management of enterprises. It entails a philosophy of management that stresses inquiry and analysis, places considerable reliance on formalized decision-making. It values computerization, efficiency, and cost reduction over the retention of unnecessary managerial and clerical personnel. If it is installed too abruptly, it can cause a painful confrontation between those who see it as a help and those who view it as a threat. Very often it is best to introduce such a system gradually, and let it evolve from within.

A gradual expansion of the firm's MIS is sensible from several viewpoints. For one thing, there are no ready-made and inclusive systems that can be quickly adapted to the needs of a particular firm. Many system components—computers, terminals, data storage devices, and some programs—are simply purchased. However, the marketing information system itself must be designed for the individual firm. (The exception, perhaps, is a limited-application system such as MARKINF.) The information and management systems must complement—hence, be adapted to—each other. Old procedures and organizational structures must be replaced. Problems in new systems must be identified and corrected. All this takes time.

An Example: Pillsbury's MIS[10]

The Pillsbury Co.—a major producer of baking products—began a systematic approach to information management in 1956. Initially, the objective was to streamline the flow of paperwork and substitute electronic data processing (EDP) for clerical procedures whenever a cost savings was

---

[10] For a detailed discussion of the Pillsbury experience, see Terrance Hanold, "Management by Perception," *Information Systems Review*, 1:1 (1966), pp. 6–7; and Robert D. Buzzell, Donald F. Cox, and Rex V. Brown, *Marketing Research and Information Systems: Text and Cases* (New York: McGraw-Hill, 1969), pp. 745–779.

demonstrable. Later, an effort was made to consolidate identical functions and centralize operations. Thirty-three branch accounting offices were consolidated into four, eventually into one, as manual procedures were replaced with automatic ones—a process made possible by the installation and continued upgrading of an electronic digital computer.

As the computerization and consolidation process continued, it brought in its train a growing data bank and greater analytical capabilities. As the information system grew, the company adapted its organization to it. The number of clerical jobs was reduced. Branch sales managers were relieved of many administrative functions, as well as the task of preparing reports for the divisional offices. The administrative workload of the plant managers was also reduced by transferring all inventory, payroll, costing, and scheduling functions to corporate headquarters in Minneapolis. As a result, they were able to concentrate more on engineering and production problems. Several echelons in the chain of command were eliminated, and executives found themselves much nearer the field.[11]

After a decade of growth, the emphasis shifted from the problems of data acquisition and processing to data analysis and the use of the MIS in decision-making. The system's advocates again moved with prudence and wisdom. Seminars were conducted to acquaint line managers with its availability and use. A chart room was established, mainly for the benefit of senior executives. The charts were updated daily and gave detailed information on the company's operations and sales, as well as statistics on relevant environmental factors such as commodity prices.[12] Remote computer terminals were installed, and analysts were assigned to aid managers in using the system. Special computer programs to provide data analysis were added to the system.

The impact of the MIS on Pillsbury's management has been significant. Terrance Hanold, the firm's executive vice-president, credits it with shifting the company from "management by intuition" to "management by perception."[13] If Pillsbury's experience is any indication, good marketing information systems cannot be designed and operated in isolation. They must be an integrated part of the firm's organization and its system of resource control. Hence, they must be part of the firm's management philosophy.

Problems

1   Cite and briefly discuss problems that you would expect to encounter in the management of a large quantity of market information. How might you deal with these problems?

---

[11] Hanold, "Management by Perception," p. 7.
[12] Buzzell, Cox, and Brown, *Marketing Research and Information Systems: Text and Cases*, p. 753.
[13] Hanold, "Management by Perception" p. 8.

2   Suggest methods of routinely gathering, cataloguing, storing, and retrieving market data for one of the following: (a) a shoe manufacturer, (b) a large department store, or (c) a farm cooperative.

3   Prepare a schematic diagram of the market information system you have prescribed in response to the previous question.

4   Discuss how you would install the preceding MIS and cite specific benefits that line management would derive from the system.

Part 3
Summary

Data, in their raw form, are generally useless for making marketing decisions. They must be processed into useful information.

In processing data, one must first recognize the nature of the information—the likely presence of errors and the metric (or nonmetric) quality of the numbers. One must also remember the great qualifier, *ceteris paribus*.

Data processing usually fragments into two stages—reduction and analysis. The reduction process consists generally of coding, editing, tabulating, computerizing, auditing, and summarizing the raw data. The summaries typically take the form of frequency distributions, descriptive statistics, or graphs.

Many tools can be invoked during the data analysis stage. The most powerful is common sense. Others include scatter diagrams, contingency tables, significance tests, and simple correlation analysis.

Data processing usually concludes with a formal report. This typically includes a summary, a section on findings and recommendations, and a technical appendix. Sometimes the information becomes part of a marketing information system.

The management of marketing information has become a formidable task in recent years. The wealth and complexity of data available has given birth to the marketing information system (MIS), which is a formal system for gathering, cataloguing, storing, retrieving, and analyzing market data. Essentially an adaptation of the relatively new and fast growing science of information management to the field of marketing, the more sophisticated MIS provides management with ready access to current statistics, predictions, and forecasts. The number of MIS's in use is growing rapidly, and although most of the present systems have as yet failed to realize their full potential as tools of modern marketing management, they are nevertheless increasing in sophistication and power. Computerized and integrated marketing-information systems may well prove to be the most exciting and powerful marketing tool of the 1980s.

CASE STUDY 3

Zanadu Oil Company: Analyzing the F-310 Experience

Jack Healey and Harold H. Kassarjian (*Jack Healey is a doctoral candidate and Harold H. Kassarjian is Professor of Marketing at the Graduate School of Management, University of California at Los Angeles.*)

During the 1960s, the oil industry was characterized by a high degree of competition, especially in the retail gasoline market. With a homogeneous product generating only limited brand loyalty, the major oil companies resorted to a broad range of marketing tactics in an effort to increase their share of the gasoline market. Many of these approaches, however, resulted in only short-range benefits—and sometimes long-range losses.

One frequently implemented strategy was to increase the number of retail outlets. A car's fuel tank can hold only so many gallons of gasoline, and the driver will have to stop and have it filled when it becomes empty. Hence, the oil firms assumed that an increased number (and therefore accessibility) of a company's service stations would generate a proportionate increase in its sales. By the late 1960s, however, many of the major companies found that they had built too many service stations and that many were not operating profitably.

Another effective, but short-range tactic used by gasoline marketers in the 1960s involved regional price wars. The price-war approach had one goal—to encourage consumers to switch brands. It was hoped that a certain proportion of the switchers would become loyal to the new brand. The two major drawbacks of the price war were that it reduced the unit profit on the gasoline and, as competitors retaliated by dropping their prices, the new customers soon returned to their old brands.

It was the task of oil company marketing executives in the 1960s, therefore to develop means by which their companies could differentiate their products while avoiding price competition.

In February 1970, Seymour Profit, president of Zanadu Oil Company, called a meeting of the company's executives to evaluate their marketing strategy for 1970–1971. Attending the meeting with Mr. Profit were the following officers: (1) Willard Kracmorgas, vice-president of refinery operations, (2) Frank

Sellitt, vice-president of marketing, (3) William Balance, vice-president of finance, and (4) Zeke N. Searchit, vice-president of research and development.[1] At the meeting, Mr. Profit had Mr. Searchit report on the technical research his division had been conducting over the past year on a new gasoline product. This new product contained an additive, "S-103," designed to reduce the amount of air pollution produced by an automobile. The new additive was, Mr. Searchit stated, a similar but improved version of F-310, an additive introduced in a test market in January 1970 by Standard Oil Company of California.

After considerable discussion and evaluation of the opportunities and risks inherent in marketing this new product, the group decided in favor of introducing it, contingent on the outcome of an MR study. Frank Sellitt was authorized to immediately conduct a study to analyze consumer response to Standard Oil's recently introduced F-310 product.

Research Plan

Six weeks after F-310 was introduced by Standard Oil of California in the Los Angeles marketing area, with a heavy advertising and promotional campaign, Michael Sharpe, a marketing research consultant, was commissioned by Frank Sellitt to conduct the marketing-research study for Zanadu. The study objective was to determine the awareness of F-310 in the minds of consumers and to measure consumer attitudes toward F-310 and air pollution.

Because Frank Sellitt had already done some thinking about the marketing strategy for Zanadu's new additive, S-103, he worked with Michael Sharpe to develop hypotheses for the research. First, they hypothesized that individuals showing greater concern for air pollution would be more aware and receptive to F-310 advertisements. They would be able to identify both brand and additive names. It was also hypothesized that they would claim to be more willing to pay a slightly higher price for a pollutant-free gasoline than their less-concerned counterparts.

On the assumption that car owners would have a greater opportunity to see, smell, and experience smog on the highways and freeways, they also hypothesized that this group would show greater concern for air pollution than nonowners of automobiles.

---

[1] Names have been changed to protect the innocent, not to mention the authors and the publisher. However, there is nothing fictitious about the products or the data.

Further, they hypothesized that heavy users of gasoline and large-car owners would be more concerned than light users and small-car owners.

Since individuals who are better educated and in higher socio-economic categories were thought to be more aware of social issues, they hypothesized that these persons would exhibit a higher level of concern about air pollution. Finally, the apparently intense concerns of the younger generation about war and peace, minority relations, political issues, and the general quality of life in society led to the hypothesis that respondents under 30 years of age would be more concerned about pollution than would those over 30.

Because of the time and budget constraints, Santa Monica, California, was chosen for data collection from among numerous similar small cities within the Los Angeles—Orange County area. Santa Monica is an incorporated city contiguous to Los Angeles. The approximately 100,000 residents represent a wide range of income, occupation, home value, age, education, and ethnic groups.

The sample of homes was selected on a probability basis by listing the blocks from the 1960 U.S. Census of Housing along with the total number of occupied dwelling units. The dwelling units were then totaled and, starting at a random point, the block in which every nth dwelling unit was located was chosen for study.

Measurement of Attitudes Toward Pollution   Three separate approaches were used to measure concern about air pollution. On the assumption that the most salient problem might emerge from an unstructured, open-ended approach, the following question was initially asked: "In the coming years this country faces many serious problems. What in your opinion is the single most important problem facing us?"

The second measure was made by presenting the respondents with a card listing a number of social issues—crime, population, inflation, pollution, and minority relations—then asking: "Of the following list of problems, what in your opinion is the most important? ... Now, which of these do you feel is the least serious?"

The third measure of attitudes towards air pollution was an attempt to gauge the intensity of feelings. Respondents were presented with a drawing of a centigrade thermometer and asked: "Some people are very upset about air pollution and others couldn't care less. On this thermometer, if 100 represents people who are extremely worried about air pollution and 0 represents people who just don't care. Where would you place yourself?" Because results of these three measures were highly intercor-

Table C3-1   **Most Serious Problem Facing Society Today (Open-Ended Responses)**

Air pollution	31.4%
Victnam war	11.6
Minority problems (blacks)	9.9
Inflation	8.7
Population	7.0
Crime	6.6
International affairs	1.7
Taxes	1.7
Others/unclear/no opinion	21.4
	100.0
Size of sample	(242)

related, results of the first question only are presented (see Table C3-1).

Brand Awareness and Purchase Hypotheses and Findings   To test for awareness of the names F-310 and Standard Oil Company, respondents were asked: "In the last couple of months, one of the gasoline companies has been advertising that it has a new gasoline that supposedly reduces dirty exhaust and air pollution. What is the name of the new gasoline? ... Which company is it?" (see Table C3-2).

All respondents in a family unit owning a car were asked if they would be willing to pay two cents per gallon more for a pollution free gasoline (see Table C3-3).

Respondents were also asked: "What brand of gasoline do you most often purchase?" (see Table C3-4).

Table C3-2   **Product Awareness and Concern About Pollution**

	Most Important Issue		
	Pollution	Other	Total
Name of Company			
Standard/Chevron	71.0%	59.0%	62.8%
Other	11.9	11.5	11.6
Don't Know	17.1	29.5%	25.6
	100.0%	100.0%	100.0%
Name of Product			
F-310	48.7⎱ 67.1	35.5⎱ 49.4	39.7⎱ 55
Approximate name	18.4⎰	13.9⎰	15.3⎰
Other name	1.3	1.8	1.6
Don't know	31.6	48.8	43.4
	100.0%	100.0%	100.0%
Size of sample	(76)	(166)	(242)

Table C3-3   Pay More for Pollution-Free Gasoline and Concern About Pollution

	Highly Concerned	Less Concerned
Willing to pay more	88%	87%
Not willing to pay more	12	13
	100%	100%
Size of sample	(72)	(147)

Table C3-4   Most Often Purchased Brand

	Most Important Issue		
Brand	Pollution	Other	Total
Standard/Chevron	20.8	25.2	23.7
Shell	26.4	21.8	23.3
Other major brands	44.4	35.4	38.4
Minor brands	2.8	6.1	5.0
Don't know	5.6	11.5	9.6
	100.0%	100.0%	100.0%
Size of sample	(72)	(147)	(219)

Usage Hypotheses and Findings   On the assumption that heavy users of gasoline would have a greater exposure to smog, the second set of hypotheses stated that heavy users of gasoline would express greater concern for air pollution. Heavy users were defined as consumers who purchased more than 15 gallons per week. This group consisted of approximately the top quartile of the sample (25.6 percent). There were no significant differences, however, between the heavy and light users in their concern about air pollution.

Related to rate of usage, it was hypothesized that automobile owners would be more concerned about air pollution than respondents from families without an automobile. Further, it was hypothesized that small-car owners (families owning a car with an engine of less than 200 horsepower or 200 cubic inch displacement) would be less concerned than large-car owners (families owning at least one car exceeding the above specifications). No significant differences existed between car ownership and pollution concerns or between these concerns and the size of car owned.

Demographic Hypotheses and Findings   The third set of hypotheses involved demographic data Young people seem to be most concerned with the destruction of the environment and most intense in their feelings about social issues. Therefore, it was hypothesized that respondents under 30 would have greater representation in the high-concern group than in the low-concern group. The data indicate no significant differences between the two groups.

Analysis of other demographic data—such as education, self-identified social class membership, estimated home value, occupation, sex, marital status, and political party preference—yielded similarly nonsignificant results.

Discussion

After looking over the results of this study, Michael Sharpe gave the findings back to his analyst, Hy Detale, and asked him to apply the appropriate statistical tests to any data not already examined and to write up a brief report interpreting the results from the viewpoint of the Zanadu Oil Company and their new product. Sharpe also told Detale that Zanadu Oil would be interested in any recommendations concerning further research the company should undertake.

Assignment

1   Assume you are Hy Detale and carry out the work assignment requested by Michael Sharpe. Be very specific in all the recommendations you make in your brief report.

2   In December 1970, Frank Sellitt asked Michael Sharpe to prepare a research proposal for a follow-up study. He explained that just as Zanadu was about to introduce its new product, S-103, the market environment for such a product changed. The effectiveness of Standard's F-310 in reducing the number of air pollutants had been strongly challenged by the California State Air Resources Board and several consumer groups. The Federal Trade Commission had filed a complaint against Standard Oil of California to cease and desist misleading advertising of F-310. Mr. Sellitt was concerned that this negative publicity could have a destructive effect on Zanadu's forthcoming introduction of S-103. He wanted a consumer research study to be conducted to measure consumers' awareness of the negative publicity and their attitudes toward F-310 and toward gasoline with pollution-reducing additives generally.

Assume you are Hy Detale and write a proposal for the new research. The proposal should include (1) sample composition, (2) questionnaire, (3) statistical techniques for the analyses, and (4) time and cost estimates.

Part 4
Sampling

Introduction

The Los Angeles County Sheriff's Department (LASD) is charged with enforcing anti-obscenity laws. Within its jurisdiction are many theaters, bookstores, and individuals dealing in material some people consider pornographic and illegal.

Pornography cases have been difficult to prosecute because of the vagueness of the law as interpreted by the courts. Today there are three judicial criteria for judging pornographic material. Such material is deemed unlawful if it (1) appeals primarily to prurience, (2) has no redeeming social or scientific value, and (3) is substantially beyond community standards.

The third criterion seemed to offer an unambiguous standard with which to judge the legality of obscene material, if it could be specified. Such a standard would be quite useful to law enforcement agencies, prosecuting attorneys, judges, and juries.

In an effort to establish community standards, as they apply to pornography, LASD sponsored a sample survey. The sampling was designed and supervised by two college professors skilled in marketing research. The techniques they used influenced the outcome of several pornography trials in California.[1]

The use of MR was not surprising, for many public agencies have recently been turning to it for solutions to many of their problems. Police officers and other public officials even study the methods of marketing

---

[1] For details of the LASD experience, see Harvey M. Adelman and O. J. Krasner, "Los Angeles County Sheriff's Department: Marketing Research versus 'Deep Throat,'" at the end of Part 4. For other applications of MR outside the commercial sector, see Cases Nos. 2, 7, 13, 17, and 25 of Walter B. Wentz, ed., *Cases in Marketing Research* (New York: Harper & Row, 1975). [Case No. 2 is also found at the end of Chapter 1 of this book.]

research under federal grants provided by the Law Enforcement Assistance Administration.

In Part 2 we explored surveys, a popular method of data acquisition. We discussed their objectives, types, methods of physically collecting data, and the kinds of errors associated with them. We also noted that surveys could be categorized statistically as either population or sample surveys. Of the two, the sample survey is by far the most important.

Sampling is a valuable tool for market researchers, since it relieves them of the usually costly (and frequently impossible) task of designing and executing a population survey. Now in Part 4, we examine sampling in depth.

Chapter 8 focuses on sampling design and sampling error. We begin with a look at sampling procedures and the steps in sampling design. Next we examine random and nonrandom samples and the ways in which random error, which is always present in sample data, can be evaluated. We shall then examine some methods of specifying sample size, which is the most important factor in controlling random error and the cost of the survey. We shall also discuss statistical efficiency, which plays an important role in the selection of sampling methods.

Chapter 9 is allocated to sampling methods. We start with a discussion of sample selection and its attendant problems. We then look at the alternative methods of sampling. Each offers a different mix of complexity, error, and cost.

Some applications of Bayesian statistics are included. Bayesian techniques have become a popular and controversial topic in applied research. They are especially attractive to market researchers, since they permit the formal incorporation of subjective information into the analytical process and are particularly useful when there is a shortage of empirical data.

In our excursion through sampling, we encounter considerable technical material, especially in Chapter 9. Care must be taken not to fall victim of the pettiness of detail. This technology simply adds to the set of tools we're collecting to give us flexibility and power in dealing with practical research problems.

Chapter 8
Sampling Design and Sampling Error

Key Concepts

The Design Process
The steps in sampling design, census versus sample—the benefits and problems of including every member of the population

Judgment Versus Random Samples
Alternate types of samples—their virtues and vices

Evaluating Random Error
Estimating the error induced by sampling

Controlling Random Error
The effect of sample size and the matter of statistical efficiency

Key Terms

census
population
universe
element
parameter
statistic
population survey
judgment sample
random sample
simple random sample
probability sample
nonrandom sample
nonprobability sample

random error
statistical error
statistical bias
confidence level
confidence interval
sequential survey
standard error of the sample
   mean
magnitude of possible random
   error
standard error of the sample
   proportion
statistical efficiency

The Design Process

Census and sampling procedures tend to follow the tracks shown in Figure 8-1. *A census*—also called a "population survey"—is a survey which draws data on every member of the population. From the design standpoint, a census is usually simple. Sampling can be rather complex.

The sampling design procedure typically involves six steps:

First, the market population must be defined. The researcher must know "who" or "what" is to be studied.

Figure 8-1   **Census and Sampling Procedures**

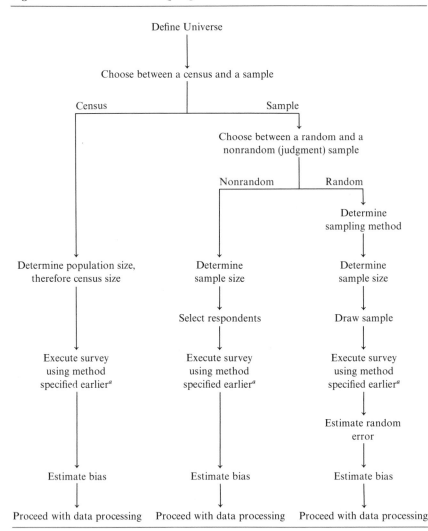

[a] Observation or inquiry. If inquiry, use mail survey, personal interview, or telephone interview.

Second, he or she must decide between a census and a sample survey. A census makes analysis of the data easy and certain. Unfortunately, this kind of survey is usually either impossible or very impractical because of the population's size. This leaves the sample survey, which gathers data on only a portion of the population. Sampling inevitably introduces some degree of uncertainty into the data.

Third, if a census is rejected, a choice must be made between a random and a nonrandom sample. From an analytical viewpoint, a random sample is preferable since it allows the estimation of random error. However, a nonrandom sample is often more practical and sometimes produces acceptable results.

Fourth, the researcher must determine the sampling method—the subject of the next chapter. Here he or she is confronted with a variety of techniques, each with a different set of virtues and vices.

Fifth, if sampling is to be used, the size of the sample—the number of members of the population to be included—must be specified. Generally, sample size is governed by the confidence level and the range of possible error management is willing to accept.

Sixth, the sample must be drawn. Selecting the members of the population who are to be queried or observed is often a difficult task. If the sample is to have the extremely desirable property of randomness, it is theoretically necessary to identify every member of the population and to use a selection process that will give each person a known probability of being chosen. This is often impossible, although an acceptable compromise can usually be devised.

After execution of the survey, during the data processing stage, one usually specifies random error and estimates bias. The problem of error is mentioned because it is intimately tied to the decisions made in steps two through five of the design procedure. Coping with error and making correct design decisions requires an understanding of market populations and the alternative forms of sampling.

Census versus Sample

Market Populations

A population—sometimes called a "universe"—is any complete set of elements having a given characteristic (or characteristics) in common. For instance, the adult population of Pasadena might be defined as every person over 17 living in that city. Any individual meeting the age and residence requirements would be an *element*, or "member," of that population. The universe (population) will include all of the elements having the specified property or properties. Typical market populations are teenagers, the steel industry, retail grocery stores in the Boston SMSA, and large government entities such as the Department of Defense. Population sizes range from millions of elements (typical of markets for consumer goods) to just one. There are only a few

Figure 8-2

Source: © King Features Syndicate, Inc., 1975.

"YOU'D BETTER TALK TO MY HUSBAND, HE CONSUMES MORE THAN ANYONE I KNOW."

one-element market populations, but those are important. The U.S. Department of Defense is the world's largest market for certain produce classes; its total annual purchases exceed $100 billion. Yet it is a single-element population. NASA is another. American manufacturers do not sell spacecraft to anyone else.

An accurate description of the population, including its size and the whereabouts of its members, is essential for a census. It is important to sampling, if the data are to be statistically significant. Significance demands assurance that the sample is representative of its universe. Such assurance comes from a design based on a clear understanding of the population from which the sample is to be drawn. There should be no confusion, as there is in Figure 8-2, as to who belongs in the sample.

Census

Market data are occasionally drawn from every member of the population—a population survey or "census." More frequently, however, they are drawn from a selected sample of the population—a sample survey. When sampling is used, the population data—called the population "parameters"—are inferred from the sample data, called sample "statistics."[1] Parameters are never truly known, but only estimated when sample data are used.

In describing the characteristics of a market population, the ideal situation is to have accurate data on every element. However, this is seldom possible, rarely practical, and usually unnecessary. There are a few exceptions, notably markets for military goods and certain industrial products, such as jet-transport planes. Nevertheless, markets for most industrial goods, and practically all consumer goods, are far too large to allow for a census.

Sampling

The only alternative to a census—assuming that historical data are unavailable—is sampling. If the sample is truly representative of the population from which it is drawn, it should have the same distribution of relevant characteristics. (*A relevant characteristic* is one that is important with respect to the subject being studied.)

A representative sample will yield data that can be generalized to the population by statistical inference. Some degree of error is inevitable, since the sample is virtually never perfectly representative of the population. Even if it were a perfect representation, the researcher would not know it, since without a population survey she would have no basis for exact comparisons. If a population survey was practical, she would not be wasting time with sample data.

Since physical and financial constraints usually preclude a population survey, the market researcher must rely in most cases on sampling. The skillful use of good sampling techniques will provide representative data. The proper use of inferential statistics will allow those data to be generalized to the market population. Furthermore, it will reveal the range of possible error, the amount of confidence the firm may have in the results.

---

[1] The terms "parameter" and "statistic" can be confusing. For instance, "parameter" is used in statistics slightly differently than it is used in mathematics. See Appendixes 1 and 2 for a complete explanation of the two terms.

Judgment versus Random Samples

The are two kinds of samples, judgment samples and random samples. A *judgment sample*, also called a "nonrandom" or "nonprobability" sample, is one in which every element of the population does not have a known probability of being selected. A *random*, or "probability," *sample* is one in which every element has a known probability of being selected.

The distinction between a judgment and a random sample may seem like a technicality, but it is not. Unless the selection probabilities are known, the tools of inferential statistics are useless, and the researcher has no reliable way of specifying random error.

Random Error

Random error, also called "statistical random error,"[2] was defined earlier as the error in sample data resulting from the fact that the sample is not truly representative of the population from which it was drawn. It is induced by chance—the "luck of the draw" in gamblers' parlance. As random error tends to decrease with sample size, researchers favor large samples.

Random error is present in all sample data, except in fortuitous cases when a sample is drawn that just happens to be a perfect representation of the population in question. Not only is this an extremely rare event, but, as we have already pointed out, when it does occur there is no way of detecting the fact. Although random error cannot be measured exactly, it can be estimated, provided the data are obtained from a random sample. Without such an estimate, the researcher cannot rigorously evaluate the statistics derived from the sample. Hence, he cannot be sure how reliable they really are.

Statistical Bias and Nonsampling Errors

Researchers tend to focus on random error, for it is the most manageable. Yet there are two other types of errors common in sample surveys—statistical bias and nonsampling errors.

Statistical bias is the unintentional favoring of one group of elements over another. It is induced by improper sampling techniques and small samples. For example, a sample of women would be biased in favor of non-working women if the sample was drawn through telephone interviews made during working hours. Statistical bias tends to diminish with increasing sample size, but not always. An important segment of the population may be excluded, regardless of sample size. Of course, the problem is eliminated with a census.

Nonsampling errors are errors unrelated to the sampling process. They include a large assortment of evils. Sloppy posting of data, respondent error, interviewer bias, computational mistakes, and typographical errors are but a few examples. Enlargement of the sample size, even the use of a census,

---

[2] This term is somewhat incorrect for it includes both random error and statistical bias.

is no help. On the contrary, such errors tend to increase as the sample gets larger.

Some Uses of Judgment Samples

Sometimes it is not necessary for the sample to be truly representative; hence, randomization is not important and a judgment sample will suffice. Researchers simply select subjects at will, relying on their own judgment as to who should be included. Judgment samples are often used during the exploratory phase of a study, when the researcher is looking for ideas, attempting to discover problems, or simply wants to pretest questionnaires for clarity. At this point he or she is not trying to get complete answers or data that can be put in precise statistical form and generalized to the market population. Thus, a high degree of representativeness is unimportant.

Occasionally it is possible to select, using judgment alone, a sample that is truly representative of the market population. For instance, the city of Denver is often used as a representative sample of the United States. The social and demographic characteristics of Denver are roughly the same as those of the nation as a whole. Thus, it is a popular test market for national advertisers and producers of nationally distributed goods. Of course, it is not an appropriate test market for products whose sales are sensitive to weather or elevation, at least not when the data are to be generalized to the whole country.

Sometimes several nonrandom samples are used and the combined findings generalized to the national market. For example, Gillette uses data from a number of "barometer" cities as the basis for its analysis of the entire U.S. market. These cities are deemed representative of the various regions of the country with respect to sales of razor blades. It is much easier and cheaper to gather data from a few cities than from the entire nation, even assuming that the sample would be the same size in either event. This is especially true when, as in the case of Gillette, repeated studies are made.

Frequently, judgment and randomization are combined. A segment of the market population, such as the residents of Denver, may be selected using just judgment, and the actual sample drawn randomly from that segment. Of course, inferential statistics may be used only in generalizing the data to the segment (Denver), not in generalizing it to the entire market population. That must be done using other means, perhaps by developing a system of weights, based on past observations of both the local and the national markets.

The size of a nonrandom sample is usually determined intuitively or by the research budget. Yet another way is to draw more and more elements until a clear pattern of observations or responses has emerged.

Limitations and Hazards of Judgment Samples

A population is described in the same statistical dimensions when the data are from a judgment sample as it is when the data are from a random sample or from the entire population. Means, medians, modes, variances, standard deviations, proportions, frequency distributions, and so on have the same meaning. However, when a judgment sample has been used, nothing definite can be said about the variability of these statistics. The researcher cannot legitimately use the formulas for confidence intervals and statistical tests of significance with nonrandom sample data; hence, quantitative statements cannot be made with respect to statistical errors.

The hazard inherent in a judgment sample was dramatically demonstrated in 1936 when *Literary Digest*, a magazine similar in format and political persuasion to today's *Reader's Digest*, conducted a sample survey to determine the probable winner of that year's presidential election. The *Digest* used a sample of 2,350,176 respondents. This enormous sample (much smaller numbers are used in modern political polls) was supposedly representative of the voting population. In reality, it was not. It was a judgment sample drawn from the magazine's subscribers (mostly Republicans), automobile-registration lists, telephone directories, and voter-registration lists. The survey designer erred in thinking that these sources would provide a representative sample of the voting public. On the contrary, the sample was clearly biased in favor of the more affluent members of the population, who tended to vote Republican. The year 1936 was the middle of the Great Depression; only the affluent could afford automobiles and private telephones at that time.

Even had a random sample been drawn from those sources, it would have been representative only of certain segments of population. As it was, the respondents could not possibly be considered a random sample with respect to the voting population. Thus, the *Literary Digest* could not, if it wanted to, develop a meaningful estimate of the range of possible error. The sample's size was actually seductive. The magazine's judgment sample could not converge with a random sample of the voting population due to the restrictive nature of the sources.

The results of the survey indicated that the Republican candidate, Alfred Landon, would defeat the Democratic candidate, Franklin Roosevelt; 56 percent of the respondents favored Landon, and only 41 percent favored Roosevelt, with the remainder undecided. As it turned out, 60 percent of the voters, half again as many as the survey indicated, favored Roosevelt. The error in the judgment sample was so gross that it brought the previously respectable *Literary Digest* into disrepute, and the magazine eventually went out of business.

Judgment samples are not always unreliable. On the contrary, the Gallup poll experience demonstrates that expertly selected judgment samples can be truly representative. However, without a sound basis for choosing a judgment sample, generalizations from the survey data may be highly unrealistic. Worse yet, the decision-maker may place too much confidence in the survey findings, since the range of error is undefined.

There are situations where a judgment sample is used intentionally, to ensure that the data will be biased in favor of a particular member or members of a market population. This is likely when one or a few members of the population are more important than the others. For example, it would be extremely unwise for a researcher sampling the steel industry to exclude U.S. Steel, even if the company was not one of the elements drawn in a random selection. Because U.S. Steel produces over one-third of our domestic output of steel, *any* sample that excluded it from the market population would be nonrepresentative.

Some Uses of Random Samples

A short time ago, we defined a random sample as one in which each element had a known probability of being selected. This is the technically correct definition. In practice, random sampling usually means that every element has an *equal* probability of being selected, a situation that is simply a special case of the known-probability condition. (Such a sample is called a "simple random sample.")

Equal probability of selection is a convenient and practical criterion of randomness. It is seldom met completely, but it can frequently be approximated with sufficient closeness to allow the analyst to proceed. Randomizing the sample in this way does not make the data error-free, but it does enable the researcher to stipulate the possible range of the error. This is very important in decision-making.

When a random sample is drawn, there is always the possibility that certain segments of the population will be disproportionately represented, thus introducing a serious statistical error into the data. For example, suppose we have a market population of a million households, 20 percent of which buy Brand X. A random sample of 100 households would be unlikely to turn up exactly 20 purchasers of Brand X, making it a perfect representation of the population as far as brand choice is concerned. In fact, the probability is 0.21 that the number of Brand-X buyers in the sample will be less than 15 or more than 25. However, the chance that there will be fewer than 10 or more than 30 Brand-X buyers is only 0.012. Theoretically, the distortion could be even worse, with less than 5 or more than 35 households in the sample being Brand-X buyers. However, the chance that the sample will be that gross a distortion of reality is less than 1 in 10,000.[3]

The statistical error can be reduced by increasing the size of the sample. It can be eliminated only by enlarging the sample to include every element in the population, in which case it would no longer be a sample, but a population survey.

Evaluating Random Error

Before discussing the question of sample size, it is necessary to delve further into the matter of sampling. We have seen in earlier chapters that errors can be introduced into survey data from several sources. Poor sampling techniques can bias the sample in favor of one or more segments of the population.

---

[3] The reader may confirm these probabilities by employing the formula for the Z-statistic for a binomial distribution (formula A2.15) and the table of Z-values in Appendix 4.

A badly worded questionnaire or an unskilled interviewer can encourage respondents to favor particular answers. Respondents themselves can intentionally or unconsciously distort the truth.

Sloppy work in posting data, in arithmetic, in computer programming, and in the choice and application of mathematical and statistical tools can also affect the validity of a survey. This kind of thing usually comes under the heading of mathematical errors. We shall not deal with such errors in this text, except in a general way, since they are essentially personnel problems. Good training, good supervision, and pride of workmanship, combined with frequent checking of numbers and methods, are the usual remedies.

Chance, or luck, almost always results in some kind of error in sample data. Chance mishaps can even affect population-survey data, unless the measuring instruments used are themselves error-free.

Chance causes random error. That is, it causes variations—hence, non-representativeness—in the kind of sample elements drawn from a population and in the measurement of those elements.[4] (The term "reliability" is sometimes used in referring to the quality of a sample survey with respect to its random error. The term "validity," on the other hand, is used more often in referring to its freedom from mathematical and other error.) Because it is the result of chance, random error is subject to the laws of probability, and its distribution about the true value of the statistic can be described.[5] Its range can be specified *provided* the data are from a randomly drawn sample.

A population parameter or a sample statistic (such as a mean, a standard deviation, or an *F*-ratio) may be a point value such as 2.5, 45, or 3,468, or a proportion, such as 0.135, 40 percent, or 2/3. The concepts behind the determination of the magnitude of random error and the range of error associated with estimates of parameters are the same for both point values and proportions. However, the methods of computation are slightly different.

Specifying Random Errors in Point Values

Point values such as total sales, average household consumption of a product, and audience size are the most common type of parameter estimated from sample data. The standard error of the sample mean, $\sigma_{\bar{x}}$, is used in specifying the random error of point-value statistics. By multiplying the appropriate *Z*-statistic by $\sigma_{\bar{x}}$, we can get a value for the magnitude of possible random error, *E*. The *Z*-statistic is determined by the confidence level and can easily

---

[4] An example from the physical sciences should clarify this point. If we have a barrel full of nails of several lengths, a random selection of some nails will yield a representative sample, subject only to random error. Thus, we may, by chance, draw a disproportionate number of nails of a particular size. In addition, if each sample nail is measured to the nearest ten-thousandth of an inch, the measurements themselves will vary by chance, for all rulers and most micrometers are not consistently accurate to the fourth decimal place.

[5] This distribution varies with the type of statistic. For example, the random error associated with the mean is normally distributed (the classical bell-shaped curve), whereas the distribution of random error of the *F*-ratio is skewed.

be found by referring to a normal distribution table such as that given in Appendix 4.

If the size of the sample, *n*, used to estimate the population parameter is below 30 ($n < 30$), a *t*-statistic should be substituted for the *Z*-statistic. Because the *t*-distribution is wider than the normal distribution, it is more appropriate to a small sample.[6] (Small samples tend to have larger errors.) Like the *Z*-statistic, the *t*-statistic can be found most simply by referring to the appropriate table.

The range of possible random error, called a *confidence interval*, is simply the estimated value of the population parameter plus and minus *E*. Hence, if random-sample data yield an estimate of the demand for Brand A of 3,500 units and *E* equals 400 units at a particular confidence level, say, 95 percent, the probability is 0.95 that the true demand for the brand is between 3,100 and 3,900 units (3,500 − 400 and 3,500 + 400).

The preceding discussion summarizes the procedure for the estimation of random error prescribe in Appendix 2. This procedure is commonly used in marketing research. The following illustration, drawn from a basic marketing textbook, shows how it works in practice.

A dairy company needed to know the daily consumption of milk in a market consisting of 2,000 households. A population survey was rejected as too expensive, but sampling seemed a practical alternative. Fifty households were randomly selected for the sample. Follow-up calls were made to ensure that each member of the sample responded, thus eliminating one source of possible bias. The daily milk consumption of each household was tabulated and an average, $\bar{X}$, for the sample calculated, using a standard statistical formula. These data are shown in Table 8-1.

Table 8-1   **Estimating the Random Error in Milk-Consumption Statistics**

Household (*i*)	Daily Milk Consumption (X_i)	Sample Deviations ($X_i - \bar{X}$)	Squares of the Sample Deviations ($X_i - \bar{X})^2$
1	3.0	0.5	0.25
2	0.0	−2.5	6.25
3	2.9	0.4	0.16
⋮	⋮	⋮	⋮
50	3.2	0.7	0.49
$n = 50$	$\Sigma X_i = 125.0$		$\Sigma(X_i - \bar{X})^2 = 39.7$
	$X = \Sigma X_i/n$		(formula for mean)
	$\bar{X} = 125.0/50$		(by substitution)
	$\bar{X} = 2.5$		(by arithmetic)

Source: From *Marketing: Theory and Application,* by W. B. Wentz and G. I. Eyrich, copyright © 1970 by Harcourt Brace Jovanovich, Inc. and reproduced with their permission.

---

[6] See Appendix 2 for a comparison and discussion of the two distributions.

The sample mean, $\bar{X}$, is 2.5. Hence, the average daily consumption of milk is 2.5 quarts per household. Thus, the sample statistic, $\bar{X}$, serves as an estimate of the population parameter μ, the true average. Assuming that the sample is representative of the population from which it was drawn, we can infer that the total consumption by this market is 5,000 quarts per day $(2.5 \times 2,000 = 5,000)$.

This is only a sample estimate of the true value of daily milk consumption; hence, it is subject to random error. The dairy firm's management needed to know the possible range of that error. It first used the data in Table 8-1 to calculate the standard deviation of the sample, s, with the aid of the following formula. (Note that the symbol "$\hat{\sigma}$" can be substituted for "s" for the sample statistic "s" is an estimate ($\hat{\ }$) of population parameter σ.)

$$s = \left[\frac{\Sigma(X - \bar{X})^2}{n - 1} \right]^{1/2} \qquad \text{(given as formula A2.11)}$$

$$s = \left[\frac{39.7}{50 - 1} \right]^{1/2} \qquad \text{(by substitution)}$$

$$s = 0.9 \qquad \text{(by arithmetic)}$$

The standard error of the sample mean, $\hat{\sigma}_{\bar{X}}$, is then estimated again using a standard statistical formula

$$\hat{\sigma}_{\bar{X}} = \frac{s}{\sqrt{n}} \qquad \text{(given as formula A2.16)}$$

$$\hat{\sigma}_{\bar{X}} = \frac{0.9}{\sqrt{50}} \qquad \text{(by substitution)}$$

$$\hat{\sigma}_{\bar{X}} = 0.127 \qquad \text{(by arithmetic)}$$

The next step was to find the appropriate Z-value, which is drawn from a normal distribution table (Appendix 4) for the desired confidence level ($c.l$), in this case, 95 percent. Since an area on both sides of the mean was involved and normal distribution tables are calibrated for only one side, .95 was divided by 2 and the table entered with the value 0.4750. This reveals a Z-statistic of 1.96.

The magnitude of possible random error, E, was then computed as follows

$$E = Z_{c.l}\hat{\sigma}_{\bar{X}} \qquad \text{(given as formula A2.17)}$$

$$E = 1.96(.127) \qquad \text{(by substitution)}$$

$$E = 0.25 \qquad \text{(by arithmetic)}$$

Finally, the confidence interval (the range of possible random error) was specified.

$$\bar{X} - E < \mu < \bar{X} + E \qquad \text{(given as formula A2.19)}$$

$$2.5 - 0.25 < \mu < 2.5 + 0.25 \qquad \text{(by substitution)}$$

$$2.25 < \mu < 2.75 \qquad \text{(by arithmetic)}$$

Thus, the true value, μ, of the average household consumption of milk was between 2.25 and 2.75 quarts per day; the probability was 0.95 that μ would be within this range.

The total daily consumption, K, of the market population is simply the product of the population size, N, and the mean average consumption, μ, of the elements ($K = N \cdot \mu$). Thus, the confidence interval for total daily consumption was quickly computed by multiplying the confidence interval of the average household consumption by 2,000. This yielded a range of 4,500 to 5,500 quarts per day, at the 95 percent confidence level. The firm thus obtained an estimate of a population parameter (milk consumption), along with an explicit statement of the range of random error, found with a relatively small and inexpensive sample, simply by using randomization and the tools of inferential statistics.

Had the firm's management specified a higher level of confidence, the confidence interval would have been larger. They would have used the same analytical procedure, but a different Z-value. For instance, at the 99 percent confidence level, Z equals 2.58. Hence, $2.17 < \mu < 2.83$. Or, for the total population, $4,340 < K < 5,660$ at $c.l. = 0.99$. If the firm's experience in similar markets indicated that it would capture 30 percent of the new market, then management could be 99 percent confident that it would sell between 1,302 and 1,698 quarts per day.

Specifying Random Errors in Proportions

Instead of estimating a point-value statistic, the researcher often estimates a proportional statistic, using data from a random sample. Proportions are appropriate when an attribute is being studied.

An attribute is a characteristic of one or more elements of a population, such as a consumer attitude or behavior. An attribute may be qualitative, such as brand preference, or quantitative, such as age or income. Such characteristics are often measured or estimated in terms of the proportion of the market population possessing them. Proportional estimates can be evaluated in the same way as point estimates, using slightly different formulas.

For example, the random error of the estimate of a proportion is specified much the same way as the random error of a point estimate. The mathematics are also similar, the only difference being the use of the standard error of the proportion, s_π, rather than the standard error of the mean, $\hat{\sigma}_{\bar{X}}$.

To illustrate, assume that the milk-consumption survey just described included a question on a population attribute such as the type of milk preferred. Say that the firm wanted to determine what proportions of the market population preferred whole, low-fat, and nonfat milk in order to rationally manipulate the product variable. If 20 of the 50 respondents indicated a preference for low-fat milk, the proportion, Π, of the population preferring low-fat milk would be estimated at 40 percent: $\pi = (n_i/n) = (20/50) = .40$. The standard error, s_π, of this estimate would be found as follows

$$s_\pi = \left[\frac{\pi(1 - \pi)}{n}\right]^{1/2}$$ (given as formula A2.13)[7]

$$s_\pi = \left[\frac{0.40(1 - 0.40)}{50}\right]^{1/2}$$ (by substitution)

$$s_\pi = 0.069$$ (by arithmetic)

The random error at the 95 percent confidence level is

$E_\Pi = Z_{c.l}s_\pi$ (given as formula A2.18)

$E_\Pi = 1.96(0.069)$ (by substitution, with the Z-value selected for the 95% confidence level)

$E_\Pi = 0.135$ (by arithmetic)

The range of error is

$\pi - E_\Pi < \Pi < \pi + E_\Pi$ (given as formula A2.20)

$0.40 - 0.135 < \Pi < .40 + 0.135$ (by substitution)

$0.265 < \Pi < 0.535$ (by arithmetic)

Thus, the probability is 0.95 that the true value of the proportion (the population parameter), Π, will be between 26.5 percent and 53.5 percent.

If management insisted on a particular confidence level but refused to accept the resulting confidence interval, the problem could be corrected by increasing the sample size, n. In the extreme case, the width of the confidence interval could be reduced to zero by increasing the sample size until it equaled the size of the population ($n = N$). This would then be a population survey which would be entirely free of random error ($E = 0$) unless some was introduced by the measuring device. Normally, however, the confidence interval can be brought within reasonable limits by using a manageable sample.

---

[7] The second term in formula A2.13 has been ignored because the sample size, n, is less than 10 percent of the population size. This term, the finite multiplier, could have been included, but it would have complicated the calculations and have made no significant difference in the outcome. See Appendix 2 for discussion.

Figure 8-3   **The Distribution of Sample Means for Sample Sizes of 3, 10, and 150**

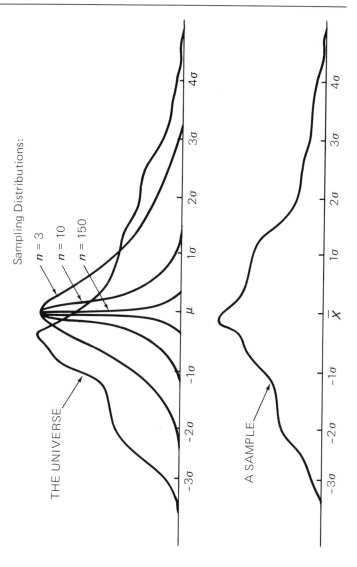

Sample Size and Efficiency

Controlling Random Error

The size of the sample controls random error. More precisely, the sample size controls the width of the confidence interval at the specified confidence level. This is illustrated in Figure 8-3, which shows how the sample means, the $\bar{X}$'s, cluster more closely about the true population mean, μ, as the sample size, n, increases.

Sample size also influences survey costs. An increase in sample size reduces random error but increases the costs of gathering—and, to a minor extent, processing—the survey data. Thus, survey designers must choose between greater precision and lower costs. They cannot arbitrarily specify a large sample size without risking the waste of company resources.

The marginal effect of sample size diminishes as the sample grows larger. In other words, adding several elements to a small sample would have a much greater effect on the confidence interval than adding the same number of elements to a large sample. This is apparent in Figure 8-3, where an increase in the sample's size from 3 to 10 reduces the magnitude of possible error, E, by nearly two standard deviations, σ, while an increase from 10 to 150 reduces E by only 1σ (approximately). In addition, the random error is not decreased in proportion to the increase in sample size. An examination of formulas A2.13 and A2.16 will reveal that sample size, n, must be increased four times to decrease the magnitude of error, E, by one-half.

Specifying Sample Size

The first step in the specification of sample size is to select the confidence level and the width of the confidence interval. These are properly management decisions, dictated by the executives' willingness to assume risk, the cost of reducing risk, and the cost of a mistake. Risk (or uncertainty) is inherent in most business decisions, and the willingness to assume it varies greatly. Theoretically, expected value[8] should determine the selection of decision options. However, expected value seldom makes an allowance for the psychological cost of risk.[9] The ability of decision-makers to bear the psychological cost varies greatly. A decision option that is attractive to one manager may be flatly rejected by another who finds its probability of failure unacceptable.

The cost of reducing risk is usually the cost of marketing research; it is generally the only form of insurance available against losses from bad marketing decisions. The cost of a mistake—that is, the cost of a bad deci-

---

[8] See Appendix 1 for an explanation of expected value.

[9] By substituting utility values for monetary values, we can build a risk model that incorporates the psychological factor. However, the problem of quantifying utility is very difficult, and the results are never precise. For a detailed exploration of risk (and uncertainty) models, see Wentz and Eyrich, *Marketing: Theory and Application*, (New York: Harcourt Brace Jovanovich, 1970) ch. 6.

sion based on erroneous survey data—is the most important determinant of the confidence level and the width of the confidence interval. Technically, the sample size should be increased until the marginal cost of the sample equals the marginal savings caused by the increase in the expected value of the decision. However, such precise marginal analysis is done infrequently.[10] Usually, a crude intuitive judgment is made. If the marketing decision involves a good deal of risk and failure will be expensive, management will probably specify a high confidence level and be willing to sustain the cost of a sample large enough to bring the range of possible error within narrow limits. Of course, in opting for a large sample, management is reducing only the probable random error. It is not buying protection against respondent and interviewer bias or computational mistakes.

A confidence level of 95 percent is common. That leaves a 5 percent risk of being wrong, or—more specifically—of the true population statistic being outside the range of possible error specified by the confidence interval. A 5 percent risk appears acceptable in the case of most marketing decisions.

The confidence interval is usually specified in terms of the magnitude of error, *E*. The value selected for *E* depends largely on the sensitivity of the decision outcome to the value of the population parameter. For instance, if the profit (or loss) associated with the decision alternative is quite sensitive to sales—as is usually the case in ventures with high fixed costs—a large value for *E* will be unacceptable. If a moderate error in the data would not affect the outcome significantly, or if the decision could not result in a substantial loss—typical if the research is only exploratory and the fixed cost of the venture is low—a relatively large *E* might be acceptable. Or, it might be preferable to an expensive large sample.

One difficulty in selecting the magnitude of possible error, *E*, is the lack of information about the population parameter itself. Of couse, the gathering of such information is the purpose of the survey. If management belives that the parameter will be well beyond the critical value, a narrow confidence interval is not necessary. For instance, the break-even point of jet aircraft sales is about 100 units. If predicted demand is close to this critical value, an error of 20 units could mean the difference between financial disaster and a respectable profit. (This is due to the high fixed cost associated with aircraft manufacturing.) If the predicted demand far exceeded the break-even quantity—if it was say, 300 units—an error of 20 units would not be serious.

One way of getting around this dilemma is to use a *sequential survey*. Here the population parameters are estimated first from a small sample, then again from a larger sample if the first estimate is near the critical value. The second estimate will probably be close to the first one. However, the confidence interval will be narrower, due to the increase in sample size. The process can be repeated until the confidence interval is within the desired limits.

[10] For a detailed explanation of marginal analysis in decision making, see Wentz and Eyrich, *Marketing: Theory and Application*, (New York: Harcourt Brace Jovanovich, 1970) ch. 3.

Sample Size for Point Values

Sample size for estimating point values (such as a mean) is specified with the following formula:

$$n = \left(\frac{Z_{c.l.}\hat{\sigma}}{E}\right)^2 \qquad \qquad [8.1]$$

where

n = the sample size for estimating a point value

Z = the Z–statistic corresponding to the desired confidence level (c.l.)

$\hat{\sigma}$ = the estimated value of the standard deviation of the population parameter

E = the maximum acceptable magnitude of error

The values for Z and E are predetermined by the confidence level and the acceptable magnitude of possible error specified by management. The value for $\hat{\sigma}$ is obtained from previous statistical studies of similar markets or similar products in the same market. If historical data are unavailable, a satisfactory value for $\hat{\sigma}$ can usually be determined by a rule of thumb. A conservative estimate of the standard deviation of the population parameter is usually one-sixth of the expected range. For instance, in the dairy example, the range of daily milk consumption might be estimated as between zero and six quarts per household. Using the one-sixth rule, the estimated standard deviation of the parameter would be one ($\hat{\sigma} = 1$). Since 99.7 percent of all normally distributed values will fall within ± 3 standard deviations of their mean average, $\hat{\sigma} = 1$ should be sufficiently large.

Frequently, pilot surveys, using a small sample of the population, are conducted to pretest questionnaires. These surveys sometimes produce enough data to estimate σ.

We can explore the specification of sample size by expanding our dairy firm example. Suppose that management wants to be 99 percent confident ($c.l. = .99$) that the true value of the population parameter—in this case the true mean, μ—will be within 0.1 quart ($E = .1$) of the sample mean, $\bar{X}$. This would mean that the estimate of the total daily milk consumption, K, for the market population would be in error by no more than 200 quarts. A normal distribution table reveals that $Z = 2.58$ at a confidence level of .99. E has been specified by management as .1. If surveys in similar markets indicate that .8 is a realistic estimate of the standard deviation of the population parameter, then

$$n = \left(\frac{Z_{.99}\hat{\sigma}}{E}\right)^2 \qquad \qquad \text{(given as equation 8.1)}$$

$$n = \left(\frac{2.58(0.8)}{0.1}\right)^2 \qquad \qquad \text{(by substitution)}$$

$$n = 426 \qquad \qquad \text{(by arithmetic)}$$

Hence, a sample containing 426 elements must be drawn at random from the market population if the survey is to perform within the limits set by management. However, if management were to agree to a possible error of ± 0.2 quarts—putting the estimate for the total market within ± 400 quarts of the true daily consumption—the sample could be reduced to 106 households. This would reduce the sampling cost considerably, especially if the data were to be gathered using personal interviews.

Another alternative that would reduce the time and cost of the survey would be to retain a confidence interval of 0.2 quarts ($E = 0.1$), but lower the confidence level to 0.95, a more conventional value. This would reduce the necessary sample size from 426 households to 250.

Sample Size for Proportions

Sample size for estimating proportions is found by applying this formula:

$$n = \left(\frac{Z_{c.l.}}{E_\Pi}\right)^2 \pi(1 - \pi) \qquad [8.2]$$

where

n = sample size for estimating a proportion

Z = the Z-statistic corresponding to the desired confidence level (*c.l.*)

π = the approximate value of the proportion

E_Π = the maximum acceptable magnitude of error of the proportion

To illuminate the problem, assume management wants to know what portion of its market population likes to shop on Saturday. It wants the estimate of this value accurate within $\pm 5\%$ ($E = .05$). The researcher, to whom job security is important, wants to be 99 percent sure the estimate is within the specified range. (At a confidence level of .99, $Z = 2.58$.) The approximate value of the proportion to be estimated through the survey is thought to be 70 percent ($\pi = .70$). Thus

$$n = \left(\frac{Z_{.99}}{E_\Pi}\right)^2 \pi(1 - \pi) \qquad \text{(given as equation 8.2)}$$

$$n = \left(\frac{2.58}{.05}\right)^2 (.70)(1 - .70) \qquad \text{(by substitution)}$$

$$n = (51.6)^2(.70)(.30) \qquad \text{(by arithmetic)}$$

$$n = 559 \qquad \text{(by arithmetic)}$$

Unfortunately, the sample size (*n*) required to stay within the prescribed range of error (*E*) is very sensitive to the value of the proportion. And the proportion is the thing we are trying to estimate through our survey! The safest way to confront this dilemma is to assume the worst case—the situation demanding the largest sample size—which is a proportion of 50 percent (π = .50). In our example, this would produce a sample size of 666. If our survey produced a different proportion—say the 70 percent originally predicted—then our error would be even smaller than the one management specified as the maximum acceptable.

Another solution is the sequential survey mentioned earlier. One simply draws a moderate-sized sample, then computes the proportion and the confidence interval at the desired confidence level. If the interval is too wide, another sample is drawn and pooled with the first. The process is repeated until the total sample yields an acceptable confidence interval. If time or resources expire before this point is reached, management will have to accept a wider confidence interval or a lower confidence level as well as the notion that MR is less than perfect.

The effect of sample size on error is summarized in Figure 8-4.

Figure 8-4   Effect of Sample Size on Error

Source: Based in part on Robert W. Joselyn, *Designing the Marketing Research Project* (New York: Petrocelli/Charter, 1977), p. 106.

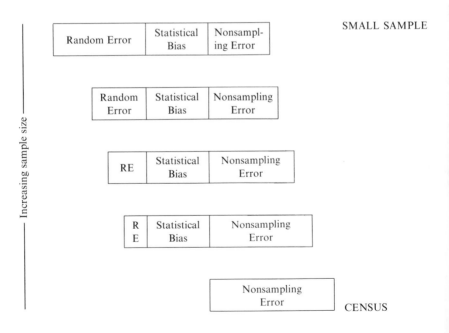

Note: Statistical bias may not reduce as sample size increases, except that it will disappear in a census. Although the number of nonsampling errors tends to increase with sample size, it tends to remain proportionate to the sample.

Statistical Efficiency

The statistical efficiency of alternative methods of random sampling is a function of their relative precision. A sampling technique is considered more efficient than an alternative method if it yields estimates that are more precise (have a smaller standard error), given the same size sample. Conversely, the more efficient method will yield results that are equally as precise as those produced alternatively but with a smaller sample.

Efficiency is relative. Hence, a measurement of efficiency entails a comparison. Generally, *statistical efficiency* is expressed as a percentage based on the ratio of the standard error produced by an unrestricted single-stage sample[11] to the standard error produced by the method under consideration. Which standard error is used depends upon which statistic is of interest. If, for instance, the mean were most relevant, the standard error of the mean would be employed. Specifically

$$E_A = \frac{\hat{\sigma}_u}{\hat{\sigma}_A} \cdot 100 \qquad\qquad [8.3]$$

where

E_A = the statistical efficiency of sampling method A, expressed as a percentage

$\hat{\sigma}_u$ = the standard error of the appropriate statistic, e.g. mean, produced by an unrestricted single-stage sample of size n

$\hat{\sigma}_A$ = the standard error of the appropriate statistic, produced by sampling method A of size n.

If the survey design specifies the degree of precision required, regardless of the sampling method, then efficiency may be defined by the relative size of the sample required. Given the desired standard error, the sample size is computed for each method, including unrestricted single-stage sampling. The following formula is used to compute efficiency

$$E_A = \frac{n_u}{n_A} \cdot 100 \qquad\qquad [8.4]$$

where

E_A = the efficiency of sampling method A, based on relative sample size and expressed as a percentage

n_A = the size of the sample gathered by method A

n_u = the size of the sample gathered by the unrestricted single-stage method

---

[11] *Single-stage* samples contain a single set of observations; *multistage* samples, on the other hand, involve subsets of data.

Sampling costs are roughly proportional to sample size. Thus, an increase in statistical efficiency often means lower costs. Of course, other factors than size affect the costs of the survey, and these may offset the savings from reducing the sample size.

Stratified random sampling,[12] for example, is the most statistically efficient sampling technique. Yet it may not be the least expensive way of collecting a sample that will yield sufficiently precise results. On the contrary, if personal interviewing is being used and the market population is spread over a large geographic area, cluster sampling may be cheaper, even though the size of the sample needed to obtain an equal amount of precision is greater.

Problems

1   Cite the advantages and disadvantages of using a population survey, a sample survey, a judgment sample, and a random sample in (a) a study of future material requirements in the automobile industry; (b) a study of consumer reactions, using taste tests of artificial flavors for a new brand of toothpaste; and (c) a study to determine the size audience reached by a network television show.

2   A market-research firm conducts a random survey of 80 households to determine the number of preschool children living in a particular area. The sample mean is 1, the squares of the sample deviations sum to 1.2, and there are 30,000 households in the area. Estimate the population of preschool children, and specify the confidence interval associated with your estimate at the 95 percent confidence level.

3   A brewery subscribes to a consumer-panel service to get current retail-sales information on the Denver SMSA, which it uses as a test market to evaluate promotional programs. During the period that an experimental point-of-purchase advertising campaign was in force, 25 of the 440 Denver beer buyers on the panel indicated they switched to the firm's brand, while 5 switched from the firm's brand to another brand. Estimate the increase in the fims's market share, and specify the confidence interval, at the 95 percent confidence level, associated with your estimate. How much of this increase should be attributed to the experimental advertising?

4   If the client sponsoring the sample survey in problem 2 demanded that the magnitude of error not exceed 500 children at the 98 percent confidence level, what would be the appropriate sample size?

5   A market-research firm has discovered that three random-sampling methods, A, B, and C, yield the same variance for sample sizes of 75, 100, and 80, respectively. Method C is a single-stage, unrestricted

---

[12] The various methods of sampling are explained in Chapter 9.

sample. What is the statistical efficiency of methods A and B? If the fixed costs are the same for both methods, how much more must a method A response cost (compared to a method B response) before method B becomes more economical?

Chapter 9
Sampling Methods

Key Concepts

Problems in Sampling
Gathering the sample, assuring representativeness, and obtaining population lists

Unrestricted Random Sampling
Methods for drawing sample elements from the population as a whole

Restricted Random Sampling
Methods for increasing precision or lowering cost

Bayesian Statistics
Combining Bayesian analysis with classical statistics to better understand the sample data

Key Terms

unrestricted random sample	cluster sampling
restricted random sample	area sampling
clusters	sequential sampling
strata	quota sampling
reverse directory	stratified sampling
list brokers	proportional stratification
list houses	cross-stratification
systematic sampling	proportional sampling
equal-interval method	optimal sampling
random-number sampling	disproportionate sampling
multiple-stage sampling	expected values

General Problems in Sampling

Sample Gathering

The process of gathering a sample is usually difficult if the sample must be representative and the population is large. First, every element in the population can seldom be identified or counted. Unlisted telephones, outdated tract maps, residence-sharing, incomplete membership lists, erroneous and incomplete registration lists, the turnover of businesses and personnel, and many other things hinder identification and counting.

Second, seldom does every element in the population have a known probability of being selected—an essential condition of a truly random sample. Frequently, samples are drawn from a population on the assumption that each member has an equal opportunity of being chosen, whereas the method of data acquisition excludes certain portions of the population. For instance, a telephone-interview survey would exclude households without a telephone or with an unlisted number. A door-to-door survey conducted during the daytime would exclude working people. Such exclusions would bias the sample.

Third, only rarely will every element selected for the sample respond to an inquiry, and the probabilities of the different classes of elements responding will be unknown. This is especially true in the case of mail questionnaires, for which the response rate is typically below 50 percent and often much lower. Furthermore, the nonresponders may not be normally distributed over the sample. Certain types of people may be less likely to respond than others, and hence be underrepresented. For instance, illiterates, working women, and very busy people are less likely to respond to mail questionnaires than literate persons, housewives, and retired people. Households with only working-adult members are less likely to respond to a telephone call or a knock at the door than those with elderly or young members. Thus, a sample that is representative with respect to the selection of its elements may not produce representative responses, and again the data will be biased.

These three problems—identification, selection probability, and response probability—are usually present in all surveys. Although they cannot be eliminated, they can often be reduced by a careful listing of members of the market population, random selection procedures, and follow-up inquiries designed to corner nonresponders. The data will seldom be pure, nevertheless, they should be sufficiently unbiased to permit a valid analysis. Of course, even a very valid sample survey will contain random error.

Representativeness

It is necessary that the sample be representative of the population only with respect to those characteristics that are relevant to the study. For example, if a soft-drink manufacturer was conducting a taste test, the panel of tasters would have to be representative only insofar as their reactions to taste were concerned. If the distribution of income, family status, or shopping habits of those in the sample differed from that of the population, it would be of no consequence. The sample data, which would consist of the respondents' preferences for the various flavor options, would still be unbiased. However, if brand preferences, recreational expenditures, or reading habits were being studied, then the sample could not be considered representative if income and other variables were not distributed the same way in both the sample and in the population.

When the relevant respondent characteristics are evenly distributed throughout the population, sample selection is easy. Most biological traits and basic psychological drives are so distributed. Taste, vision, hearing, smell, hunger, and thirst are common to all humans and will not vary appreciably between large ($n > 30$) samples. Thus, reactions to flavors, colors, sounds, smells, and other sensory stimuli can be generalized to the population even when the sample is selected arbitrarily. Many firms even use their own employees in studies of such stimuli, a procedure that would in most other cases produce extremely biased data.

When the relevant respondent characteristics are economic or demographic, sample selection is more difficult. For instance, suppose an advertiser wanted a survey of the television-viewing habits of the population served by the Los Angeles stations. Twelve telephone books contain listings for this geographic area. The researcher could easily select people at random from these books, drawing as many names as needed to meet the requirement of sample size. However, the group chosen would be representative only of the Los Angeles area households with listed telephones, not of the area's population. Households with very low incomes and those with very high incomes would tend to be excluded, for reasons given previously. The sample, hence the data and the statistical inferences drawn from them, would clearly be biased.

One way to deal with this problem is to use telephone interviews and select respondents by random-number dialing. The random numbers are created by combining the prefix of the local numbers with four or five digits produced by a random number generator. A simple variation of random-number dialing is the plus-one method: Telephone numbers are compiled by adding one to each number drawn at random from the directory.[1]

Occasionally bias is acceptable and can be tolerated as an alternative to the expense of gathering a truly representative sample. If high-income households are a minor portion of the advertiser's market and poor people cannot afford the products, this kind of bias is not really a problem. In fact, if the aggregate population value, N, could be reduced to reflect the sample's exclusion of poor people, the analysis might be even more relevant to the needs of the advertiser. When this kind of bias is unacceptable, the researcher may have to use a sampling technique that ensures a representative sample despite the uneven distribution of population characteristics. Such techniques, called "stratified sampling methods," will be discussed shortly.

Obtaining Population Lists

The first task in sampling is to put together an acceptable list of the members of the population from which the sample will be drawn. The techniques for

---

[1] For discussion, see E. Laird Landon, Jr., and Sharon K. Banks, "Relative Efficiency and Bias of Plus-One Telephone Sampling," *Journal of Marketing Research* **14**, no. 3 (August 1977), pp. 294–299. Another useful article is Mathew Hauck and Michael Cox, "Locating a Sample by Random Digit Dialing," *Public Opinion Quarterly* **38**, no. 3 (Summer 1974), pp. 253–260.

doing this vary. It may be the most difficult part of the research project. Occasionally this step can be neglected, as in the case of certain kinds of taste testing. Often it can be made more manageable by area sampling, which we will discuss shortly.

Ideally, the list should include the name, address, and telephone number of each element in the population, together with any other relevant data. Sometimes getting a complete list is easy. For example, if researchers want to survey automobile owners in a given state, they have only to go to the state department of motor vehicles for a complete list. Or they can go to a commercial list broker, such as R. L. Polk and Company. Registration lists do not include telephone numbers, but they do include the brand, model, and year of the car. The Federal Aviation Agency sells comparable lists (on magnetic tape if desired) of licensed pilots and registered aircraft owners. The United States Coast Guard publishes a directory of large boats (5 net tons and over), with owner names and addresses.

Some lists, such as those made from tract maps, contain only the addresses, not the names, of the residents in a given area. They are used in drawing samples for door-to-door canvassing. Tract maps and reverse directories are often used to ensure a geographically representative sample when a telephone-interview survey is to be used. *A reverse directory* indexes telephone subscribers by city and street, not by name, as is normal. By specifying a sample that is geographically representative, the researchers can usually be sure of a moderately representative sample with respect to economic, demographic, and ethnic characteristics. If they are especially interested in particular economic, demographic, or ethnic groups, the same devices—tract maps and reverse directories—are useful in locating them.

Specialized lists are frequently available from list brokers, trade associations, professional organizations, and chambers of commerce, as well as from federal, state, and local government agencies. Lists are often available from the firm's own accounting or credit department. In addition, published directories and catalogues provide lists of professionals in some fields. These specialized lists are often partial and biased, but they may be sufficiently representative so that random sampling of them will produce reasonably reliable results. They should, however, be used with discretion, since samples drawn from them are never truly random with respect to the whole population.

If the list of prospective respondents is incomplete and nonrepresentative, a researcher can replace it, supplement it, or use it for a nonrepresentative judgment sample. Or if segments of the list are complete, he or she may do area sampling. The only other alternative is to discard the survey and look for another method of obtaining the data.

Of course, even if the list is partial and not representative, the survey sample drawn from it may still be randomized. However, technically, the results of the survey may be statistically generalized only to the names on the list, not to the population from which the list is drawn. The same is true of the random error. It can be specified only with respect to the list, not the population. Statistically speaking, the list becomes a population. Of course, the list population may be substantially different from the population of interest to the researcher.

Information about the greater population from which the list is drawn may be inferred from the findings of the survey if something is known about the differences between that population and the list. Often, aggregate data are available on the population that allow adjustments to be made in the survey findings so that they can be generalized to the population. For instance, an analysis of the survey data might reveal a precise correlation between the respondents' income and their consumption of a particular item. If the distribution of income for the population was known, the total consumption of the item could be estimated for that population.

Drawing the Sample

Once the researcher has put together an acceptable list of the population, the next task is to draw the sample, keeping in mind restrictions placed on its size by the sample design. If a judgment sample is wanted, the respondents are selected in accordance with judgmental criteria. For instance, the survey design might stipulate a sample consisting of firms with more than 500 employees, stores with annual sales in excess of $1 million, or households within a given geographic area.

The design may stipulate a criterion, such as respondent income, that is not specified on the list but can be gotten from questionnaires. In this case, the sample would be drawn at random, but would be larger than the specified size to allow for respondents outside the stipulated income range. Data from such respondents would be discarded.

Several selection methods may be employed to yield a random sample of the size specified by the survey design. Since under certain conditions some methods are less expensive or provide a more representative sample than others, we shall examine each in detail.

Rather than do the sample selection himself, the market researcher frequently buys it from a commercial service. These firms—called "list houses" or "list brokers"—will draw a sample from a master list in accordance with the buyer's instructions. For instance, the buyer may order a random drawing of a given number of elements from each subset—or stratum—of the master list. The subsets may be geographic or may pertain to some other property of the list members, such as model year or brand of automobile, airplane, or boat.

The master list is a population list or presumably a large representative sample of a population. The population is typically all aircraft owners, Honda motocycle owners, doctors, college students, professors teaching marketing, Catholics, Republicans, senior citizens, and so on. List brokers tend to specialize in certain kinds of populations and sell lists at rates that normally are in the range of 20 cents to one dollar per name. List brokers are found in *Standard Rate and Data* and in a monthly magazine, *Direct Marketing*. They are frequently the quickest and cheapest source of a sample, particularly one drawn from a nationwide population.

Unrestricted Random Sampling

Unrestricted versus Restricted Sampling

In an *unrestricted random sample* each element is drawn from the population as a whole. Each undrawn element in the population has a chance of being selected. This tends to produce a sample with the same distribution of characteristics as the population. Thus, if 4 percent of the population sampled has an annual family income in excess of $35,000, 4 percent of the sample will tend to have family incomes of over $35,000 also. However, chance variations may cause a segment of the population to be misrepresented. This misrepresentation may be significant, especially when either the segment or the sample is small. A random sample of 25 could easily miss families with this high an income completely. Or, it could include two such households, thus overstating their importance by 100 percent. (They would form 8 percent of the sample, versus 4 percent of the population.) Such errors can be specified, thanks to the randomness of the sample, in the same manner we used in the preceding chapter. However, the range of possible error—that is, the confidence interval—may be substantial, even at low confidence levels.

Unrestricted sampling also tends to produce a sample whose geographic distribution is similar to that of the population. If a market population is distributed over several states, the sample will tend to be distributed over the same states. This can present some practical problems in data collection, especially when personal interviews are used.

In a *restricted random sample*, the elements are drawn from selected segments of the population. Thus, there are two or more stages in the selection processes. The population is divided into segments, or "subsets," on the basis of an appropriate criterion such as income, size, industry, or geographic area. A decision is then made as to which segments to include in the pool from which the sample elements will be drawn. The drawing itself is the next step. Sometimes the chosen segments will be subdivided into still smaller subsets and a number of them used as the source of the sample elements.

If the objective is to reduce the time and cost of data collection, a geographic division is appropriate. A small number (usually six to ten) of the subsets—called "clusters" in this case—is randomly selected, and the sample elements drawn from it.

If the objective is to increase statistical efficiency—that is, reduce the confidence interval for a given sample size—the population will be divided according to income, size, or some other relevant variable. Each of these subsets—called "strata"—is used to produce the sample. Elements are drawn from the strata in proportion to their distribution in the population. If a particular stratum is representative of 4 percent of the population, then 4 percent of the sample is drawn from it. The representativeness of the sample is thus assured.

Sometimes restricted and unrestricted methods are combined. For example, unrestricted sampling may be used in the second or third stage of a restricted-sample design, when it is time to draw the actual elements from the selected clusters or strata.

Arbitrary-Selection Sampling

A researcher using arbitrary selection assumes that the elements are randomly distributed on the population list as far as any relevant variables are concerned. Respondents are selected by any means that is convenient. If a sample size of 100 has been specified, the researcher may simply choose the first 100 names on the list. This is considered an unrestricted technique because, in effect, the sample elements are drawn from the population as a whole.

Systematic Sampling

Systematic sampling is the selection of every i^{th} member of a population after starting with a randomly chosen member. In systematic sampling, the researcher recognizes that the elements on the population list may be nonrandomly distributed with respect to one or more relevant variables. For instance, they may be arrayed by income, purchases, size, or geographic area. Even an alphabetical listing may be nonrandom, because certain names are associated with particular ethnic groups. A sample drawn from such a list by an arbitrary method—say, by choosing the first 200 elements— would not be representative.

Systematic sampling—also called the "equal interval method"—selects every i^{th} element on the list, starting with an element between 1 and *i*. The first element is selected randomly, usually with the aid of a table of random numbers.[2] The interval is determined by the following formula

$$i = \frac{N}{n} \qquad\qquad [9.1]$$

where

    i = interval length

    N = the number of elements on list (ideally, N will equal the number of elements in the population)

    n = the sample size

For example, assume that a population list contains 2,463 elements, *N*, and a sample of 200 is needed. *i* would then equal 12.31, which would be rounded off to the nearest integer, 12. A number between 1 and 12, inclusive, is randomly selected by any convenient method. If, say, 8 is the number cho-

---

[2] A *table of random numbers* is simply a collection of digits, selected by a random process, from the numbers zero to nine, inclusive. They are usually arrayed in groups of four or five and posted in the order they are generated. The reader can generate a set of random numbers by tossing a ten-sided die, spinning a pointer on a ten-position dial, or using any other mechanical or electronic device that gives each digit an equal probability of being selected on each trial. Today, most random-number tables are prepared using a computer. Most marketing researchers consult published tables (such as those in Appendix 4) or use a computer.

sen, the sample will consist of the 8th, 20th, 32nd, . . . 2,456th elements, a total of 204 (which is preferable to the 188 elements, 12 below the specified sample size, that would have resulted had the interval been rounded to 13). The quality of randomness is preserved, since each element in the list has an equal probability of being selected.

Random Number Sampling

The *random-number method* uses a table of random numbers to select the sample from the respondent list. First, the list must be numbered. This is usually done by assigning a series of numbers, starting with one, to the elements on the list. The method of assigning numbers is of little consequence, as long as no two elements have the same number. The simplest and most convenient approach, however, is to assign numbers sequentially.

Next, the researcher arbitrarily selects a position in the table (say, the first row, second column, first page) and reads the number. If an element's number matches the first number drawn from the table, that element is included in the sample. (In drawing a number from the table, the researcher must always use enough digits so that the highest number on the list has a possibility of being drawn. Thus, if the list runs from 1 to 5,429, four-digit numbers can be read from the table.) The next number in the table is then read, and if it matches the number of an element on the list, that element joins the sample. This process is continued until enough elements have been selected.

In reading numbers from the table, the researcher can proceed in any systematic way. Most people read down the columns, working their way across the page as successive columns are completed. Every digit—or only the first one, two, three, or four digits, as needed—can be read from the four- or five-digit groups. When a number duplicates a previously selected number or does not match one of the elements, it is discarded.

For example, assume that a population list has been numbered sequentially from 1 to 398 and that a random sample of 30 is required. Using the table of random numbers in Appendix 4, starting with the sixth row, the second column, and proceeding down the columns, we would get 080, 051, 080, 420, 162, and so on. The value 420 would be discarded since it is outside the range of assigned numbers and the second 080 would be ignored for it is redundant. If we wanted to economize by not wasting any digits, we would use the last digit in every group. Then our series of random numbers would be 080, 605, 130, 806, and so on. Conservation of digits is a bit awkward, but it is occasionally necessitated by a small table and the need for many large random numbers.

There are several variations of the basic random-number technique. One is a multiple-stage system. Here the population list is divided into equal parts, several of which are selected by the random-number method. These parts are then used as the source of sample elements, which are, again, selected by the random-number method.

This method is often employed when a telephone directory is used for the population list. Page numbers are selected using a table of random numbers. An equal quantity of names is drawn from each chosen page—using the random-number technique—to make up the sample. This is far easier than using the single-stage method just described, since the researcher would then have had to number—or at least count—each name in the directory.

Restricted Random Sampling

Cluster Sampling

Another approach to random sampling is to divide the population into small groups, called "clusters." (If the clusters are geographic, the method is also called "area sampling." A random sample of clusters is drawn, and from this is taken either a population or a random sample of elements. The single advantage of cluster sampling is its relative cheapness, and this is significant only when data are collected by personal interview.

This form of multiple-stage sampling is economical and when the population being surveyed is spread out over a large geographic area, for it substantially reduces interviewer travel and time. If rural households in Ohio are being surveyed and 100 elements are needed for the sample, clustering may be the most practical method. If 5 counties are drawn at random and 20 households are randomly chosen from each one, the sample will still be random.[3] However, collecting the data will be much less costly than it would have been had a single-stage random method been used. Had the sample elements been drawn directly from the state as a whole, the sample would have been spread out over most of the state's 88 counties (chance would probably exclude some counties). The cluster method concentrates the sample in 5 counties. Thus, the interviewing task is simplified, and the researcher need identify the rural households in only 5 counties, not in 88.

Cluster sampling is commonly used in selecting random samples from urban populations, too. The city is divided into blocks, a number of blocks is randomly chosen, and a population or random survey is then made of the households in each chosen block. In randomizing the selection of elements within the blocks, each block is treated as a separate population.

Cluster sampling is not as statistically efficient as unrestricted single-stage sampling. That is, it will not produce estimates of the population parameter which are as precise (have as small an error) as those yielded by the alternative methods, assuming the sample size is the same. However, the reduction in costs may justify the loss in precision. Even if the sample size is increased to ensure a desired degree of precision, the net cost savings may still be significant.

The total variance—hence, the standard error—of the sample mean, in any kind of multiple-stage sampling, is equal to all the variance accumu-

---

[3] Each household will have a known chance (although not an equal chance) of being selected. Thus, the analyst may choose to weight the data on the basis of the respondents, selection probabilities. For instance, more weight might be given the sample drawn from a heavily populated county than from a lightly populated one.

lated during each stage of the sampling. In the case of cluster sampling, there is variance in the sample statistic between, as well as within, clusters. Thus, random error will be introduced in selecting the sample clusters as well as in selecting the sample elements within the chosen clusters. Of course, the latter source of error can be reduced to zero by executing a population survey within the clusters.

The standard error of the sample mean is used in specifying the random error of a point-value statistic. (The sample mean, $\bar{X}$, is our estimate of the population mean, μ, which is the parameter we are trying to evaluate. When cluster sampling has been used to derive that mean, the following equation will give us the standard error:

$$s_{\bar{\bar{X}}} = \left[\frac{M - m}{(M - 1)m\bar{N}^2} \cdot \frac{\sum\limits_{i=1}^{m} (N_i \bar{X}_i - \bar{X}_N)^2}{m - 1} \right.$$

$$\left. + \frac{1}{mM\bar{N}^2} \cdot \sum\limits_{i=1}^{m} \frac{N_i{}^2(N_i - n_i)}{N_i - 1} \cdot \frac{s_{2,i}^2}{n_i} \right]^{1/2} \qquad [9.2]$$

where

$s_{\bar{\bar{X}}}$ = the standard error of the sample mean for the entire sample

$\left(\text{Note: } \bar{\bar{X}} \text{ is the estimate of the population mean, } \mu; \bar{\bar{X}} = \dfrac{\Sigma N \bar{X}_i}{m\bar{N}} \right)$

M = the number of clusters in the population

m = the number of clusters in the sample

$X_{i,j}$ = the observed value of the statistic for an element, j, in a cluster, i

i = a cluster

j = an element within a cluster

N_i = the size of cluster i

$\bar{N}$ = the mean size of the clusters

n_i = the size of the sample drawn from cluster i

$\bar{X}_i$ = the mean of cluster i $\left[\bar{X}_i = \left(\sum\limits_{j=1}^{n_i} X_{i,j} \right) \middle/ n_i \right]$

$\bar{X}_N$ = the estimated mean of the cluster totals $\left(\bar{X}_N = \dfrac{\Sigma N_i \bar{X}_i}{m} \right)$

$s_{2,i}^2$ = the variance within cluster i $\left(s_{2,i}^2 = \dfrac{\sum\limits_{i=1}^{m} \sum\limits_{j=1}^{n_i} (X_{i,j} - \bar{X}_i)^2}{\sum\limits_{i=1}^{m} n_i - m} \right)$

Equation 9.2 will yield an unbiased value even when clusters of unequal size are used. (The cluster samples, n_i, may or may not be all the same size.) However, if all the clusters are equal size and their samples are all equal size, this rather awkward equation can be replaced with formula 9.3, which is a bit more manageable—a fact that should be taken into account in the design of the sample.[4]

$$s_{\bar{X}} = \left(\frac{M-m}{M-1} \cdot \frac{s_b^2}{m} + \frac{N-n}{N-1} \cdot \frac{s_w^2}{nM} \right)^{1/2} \tag{9.3}$$

where

$$s_b^2 = \text{the variance between clusters} \left(s_b^2 = \frac{\sum\limits_{i=1}^{m} (\bar{X}_i - \bar{\bar{X}})^2}{m-1} \right)$$

$$s_w^2 = \text{the variance within a cluster} \left(s_w^2 = \frac{\sum\limits_{i=1}^{m} \sum\limits_{j=1}^{n} (X_{i,j} - \bar{X}_i)^2}{m(n-1)} \right)$$

$\bar{\bar{X}} = $ the sample mean (the entire sample), which is the estimate of

the population mean, $\mu \left(\bar{\bar{X}} = \dfrac{\Sigma \bar{X}_i}{m} \right)$

$N = $ the number of elements in a cluster (the same for all clusters)

$s_{\bar{X}}$, m, etc. are defined as before

If the population parameter to be estimated is a proportion, Π, not a point value, the following equation can be used to obtain the standard error of the sample proportion:

$$s_{\hat{\Pi}} = \left[\frac{M-m}{(M-1)m\bar{N}^2} \cdot \frac{\sum\limits_{i=1}^{m} (N_i\hat{\Pi}_i - \hat{\Pi}_N)^2}{m-1} + \frac{1}{mM(\bar{N})^2} \right.$$

$$\left. \cdot \sum\limits_{i=1}^{m} \frac{N_i^2(N_i - n_i)}{N_i - 1} \cdot \frac{s_{2,i}^2}{n_i} \right]^{1/2} \tag{9.4}$$

---

[4] There are a number of equations for computing $s_{\bar{X}}$, each designed to accommodate different sets of assumptions—for example, equal or unequal clusters. If in doubt as to which equation best fits the situation, the researcher should consult a good sampling textbook. One is William G. Cochran's *Sampling Techniques*, 2nd ed. (New   : Wiley, 1963).

where

$s_{\hat{\Pi}}$ = the standard error of the estimate, $\hat{\Pi}$ $\left(\text{Note: } \hat{\Pi} \text{ is the estimate}\right.$

of the population proportion, Π, $\hat{\Pi} = \dfrac{\Sigma N_i \hat{\Pi}_i}{m\bar{N}}\right)$

$\hat{\Pi}_i$ = the estimated proportion in cluster i

$\hat{\Pi}_N$ = the estimated average number of units belonging to the category

of interest within a cluster $\left(\hat{\Pi}_N = \dfrac{\displaystyle\sum_{i=1}^{m} N_i \hat{\Pi}_i}{m}\right)$

$s_{2,i}^2$ = the variance of the proportion in cluster i

$$s_{2,i}^2 = \left(\frac{\displaystyle\sum_{i=1}^{m} n_i \hat{\Pi}_i (1 - \hat{\Pi}_i)}{\displaystyle\sum_{i=1}^{m} n_i - m}\right)$$

M, m, etc. are defined as before

Equation 9.4 will yield an unbaised value even when the clusters, or the samples, are unequal. However, if the clusters are of equal size and their samples are of equal size, the following, less cumbersome, equation can be used.[5]

$$s_{\hat{\Pi}} = \left[\frac{M - m}{M - 1} \cdot \frac{\Sigma(\hat{\Pi}_i - \hat{\Pi})^2}{m(m - 1)} + \frac{N - n}{N - 1} \cdot \frac{1}{Mm(n - 1)} \cdot \sum_{i=1}^{n} \hat{\Pi}_i(1 - \hat{\Pi}_i)\right]^{1/2}$$

$$[9.5]$$

where

$s_{\hat{\Pi}}$, M, etc. are defined as before. However the computation of $\hat{\Pi}$ is also a bit easier when clusters are equal and samples are equal: $\hat{\Pi} = \Sigma\hat{\Pi}_i/m$.

If there is homogeneity between clusters, cluster sampling offers a collateral benefit. By comparing the means and variances of the sample clusters, the researcher can evaluate the reliability of the survey method. If statistically meaningful differences exist, but the individual clusters are

[5] Again the researcher is advised to consult a sampling textbook if in doubt whether a standard-error equation conforms to the assumptions of the sampling design.

believed to be essentially the same with respect to the relevant variables, then the researcher should be suspicious of the methods or interviewers used in the survey. (See p. 171 for an explanation of the ways of testing for significant differences between clusters.)

Sequential Sampling

In *sequential sampling*, a series of samples are drawn until one or more pre-determined criteria are met. The sequential samples may be drawn from the universe as a whole (unrestricted sampling) or from particular clusters or strata (restricted sampling). A minimum significance level, minimum cluster sizes, or a minimum confidence interval are typical predetermined criteria.

The objective of sequential sampling is to use the smallest possible sample and still meet the survey design criteria, even when the standard deviations of the estimated population parameters are unknown. If researchers are unable to estimate these standard deviations, they cannot specify the size sample needed to produce the desired confidence intervals. They can specify an excessively large (thus excessively expensive) sample to make sure that the confidence intervals will fall within the desired ranges, or they can do sequential sampling.

In sequential sampling a series of samples, $n_1, n_2, n_3, \ldots n_n$ are drawn at random from the population. The entire first sample, n_1, is surveyed, and the desired statistics are computed and evaluated. If the confidence intervals (or other criteria specified in the survey design) are not met, the entire second sample, n_2, is surveyed. The data from n_2 are added to the original data, and the desired statistics are recomputed and reevaluated. Since the sample is now larger (it is equal to the combined total of n_1 and n_2), the confidence intervals will be shorter. Other conditions that depend on sample size, such as the number of elements in a given stratum, will also improve. The process of adding additional samples to those already surveyed is continued until the specified criteria are met.

If the essential condition of randomness is to be preserved, each sample, $n_1, n_2, \ldots n_n$, must be drawn at random from the population and *used in its entirety*. Samples of equal size are unnecessary. The first sample is usually the largest, the second somewhat smaller, and so on. In fact, the additional samples may be very small in size and large in number so that the total sample can be enlarged gradually.

The main virtue of sequential sampling is that it enables the researcher to hold down costs by keeping down the sample size. It is especially economical when the unit cost is high. A high unit cost is common when personal interviews and complex techniques are used. However, if the unit cost is low, the time and effort needed to draw a series of random samples may offset the savings from using the method and result in a higher total cost.

Sequential sampling is often appropriate when a marketing decision involves two mutually exclusive alternatives, especially when the decision is based on the statistical evaluation of a market attribute. For instance, a firm may have to choose between two variations of a product and undertake a sequential survey to determine consumer preference. Data could be collected and analyzed on an ongoing basis until it became clear which of the two variations the majority of the market population liked. If the market strongly favored one variation, this would probably become clear before too long, and the survey could be discontinued.

Nonrandom sequential sampling is sometimes used in exploratory research. The researcher keeps increasing the sample size until enough information is obtained to define the problem properly. He or she can then form hypotheses to be tested by a more careful survey. As is usually the case with sequential sampling, the chief benefit is the cost savings.

Stratified Random Sampling

Stratified random sampling methods divide the population into groups—called "strata"—that are internally homogeneous and externally heterogeneous. In other words, the elements within a particular group are the same with respect to the relevant population parameters. However, they differ from the elements in the other groups with respect to those characteristics. For instance, a study of leisure-time activities might divide a market population into three strata: households with incomes below $10,000; households with incomes between $10,000 and $18,000; and households with incomes over $18,000. Thus, income would be the parameter used to assign sample elements to their appropriate stratum. The elements (households) within each stratum would be homogeneous with respect to income class, but the strata themselves would be heterogeneous with respect to this variable.

This homogeneity within groups and heterogeneity between groups is one of the essential differences between strata and clusters. Division into clusters is based on a characteristic—usually geographic area—that make sampling easier. Ideal clusters are internally heterogeneous and externally homogeneous—the reverse of the strata.

Once the strata to be used in the survey are designated, a predetermined number of elements is chosen from each one. This is the other essential difference between stratified sampling and cluster sampling. In stratified sampling, the sample is drawn from every group, not just from a few randomly selected clusters. In most other respects, the mechanics of stratified sampling and cluster sampling are the same. Both methods are variants of multiple-stage sampling.

The objective of stratified sampling is to ensure the desired representativeness by ensuring proper representation of each segment of the population, and to provide greater precision (smaller standard errors) than one might get using other sampling methods with the same size sample. It is especially effective when important segments comprise only small portions of the population.

For example, high-income families might constitute only 2 percent of a market population. Chance variation in the selection of the sample could easily exclude or include a disproportionate number of elements from this group. Stratified sampling prevents this by first dividing the population into income groups (strata) and then drawing a proportionate number of sample elements from each group. Thus, high-income families, which constitute 2 percent of the population, would constitute 2 percent of the sample also.

The preceding example illustrates the proportional stratified sample. *Proportional stratification* assures that the elements are distributed among the sample in the same proportions as they are distributed in the population, with respect to the stratifying parameter. Sometimes nonproportional samples are desired. This is the case when a particular stratum is significantly more (or less) important than indicated by its size, or when optimum sample selection (discussed shortly) is desired. Either way, stratified sampling assures the desired representativeness.

In selecting the stratifying parameter, the researcher should pick a statistic that is relevant to the variable being evaluated. That is, he should select a population parameter that correlates closely with the one being evaluated. For instance, if the purpose of the study is to analyze savings habits, income is a logical choice for the stratifying parameter. Other common stratifying parameters are family size, age, ethnic group, occupation, industry, and geographic location. When two or more parameters are used to stratify the population, say, income and family size, it is called *cross-stratification.*

Stratification is done by (1) deciding what variables should be used to define the strata, (2) deciding the number of strata to be used, and (3) allocating the population elements among the strata. Once the population has been stratified, the sample may be drawn proportionately from each stratum (thus ensuring each group exact representation), or it may be drawn optimally (in such a way as to minimize the standard error of the estimate). Either technique serves only to determine the *number* of elements to be drawn from each stratum, given a specified total sample size. The randomness of the sample is preserved as long as the elements drawn from each stratum are randomly selected.

Proportional Sampling

Proportional stratification is produced by proportional sampling. *Proportional sampling* allocates the sample elements among the sample strata in proportion to the relative size of the corresponding population strata. Thus, a stratum that represented 28 percent of the population would get 28 percent of the sample. The number of elements, n, drawn from a particular stratum, i, is expressed by the following equation

$$n_i = \frac{N_i}{N} \cdot n \qquad [9.6]$$

where

n_i = the number of sample elements from stratum i

N_i = the total number of elements in stratum i

N = the total number of elements in the population

n = the total sample size

(Note: N_i/N is sometimes abbreviated "W_i.")

Formula 9.6 will ensure a representative sample with respect to the variables used to stratify the population. However, it will not provide the smallest standard deviation (hence, the smallest random error) possible with stratified sampling. To do this, more elements must be drawn from the stratum with the largest standard deviation. This is done by dispropor-tionate sample selection.

Optimal Sampling

Optimal (disproportionate) sampling minimizes the random error for a given total sample size by allocating the total sample among the strata according to the following formula. Note that there is no caret ($\hat{\ }$) over σ. This implies that the population parameter σ is actually known, not esti-mated. (A statistic calculated from sample data could be substituted if the actual parameter were not known. The symbol "$\hat{\sigma}$" or "s" would then replace "σ.")

$$n_i = \frac{W_i \sigma_i}{\Sigma(W_i \sigma_i)} \cdot n \qquad [9.7]$$

where

n_i = the number of sample elements from stratum i

W_i = the proportion of the population represented by stratum i ($W_i = N_i/N$, where N_i and N are defined as in equation 9.6),

σ_i = the standard deviation within stratum i, and

n = the total sample size

The total sample size, n, required for an optimally allocated stratified sample is

$$n = \frac{(\Sigma W_i \sigma_i)^2 \cdot (Z)^2}{\sigma^2} \qquad [9.8]$$

Table 9-1   **Alternative Sample-Allocation Methods for Stratified Sampling**

(i)	Income Stratum	W_i	Basic Data			Proportional Allocation	Disproportionate (Optimal) Allocation, Costs Excluded			Disproportionate (Optimal) Allocation, Costs Included		
			σ_i	C_i	$\sqrt{C_i}$	$(2)(N)$	$W_i\sigma_i$	$\dfrac{W_i\sigma_i}{\Sigma(W_i\sigma_i)}$	$(8)(N)$	$W_i\sigma_i/\sqrt{C_i}$	$\dfrac{W_i\sigma_i/\sqrt{C_i}}{\Sigma(W_i\sigma_i/\sqrt{C_i})}$	$(11)(N)$
(1)	(1)	(2)	(3)	(4)	(5)	(6)	(7)	(8)	(9)	(10)	(11)	(12)
1	Under $2,000	18%	$100	$2.50	1.6	72	1,800	4.1%	16	1,125	3.8%	15
2	$2,000–3,999	31	250	2.00	1.4	124	7,750	17.5	70	5,536	18.9	76
3	4,000–5,999	24	400	2.00	1.4	96	9,600	21.6	86	6,857	23.4	94
4	6,000–7,999	14	700	2.00	1.4	56	9,800	22.1	89	7,000	23.8	95
5	8,000–9,999	7	1,000	2.50	1.6	28	7,000	15.8	63	4,375	14.9	60
6	10,000–14,999	4	1,200	3.20	1.8	16	4,800	10.8	43	2,667	9.1	36
7	15,000 and over	2	1,800	4.00	2.0	8	3,600	8.1	33	1,800	6.1	24
		100%				400	44,350	100.0%	400	29,360	100.0%	400

Source: Reprinted with permission of The Macmillan Company from *Research Methods in Economics and Business* by Robert Ferber and P. J. Verdoorn. © by The Macmillan Company, 1962.

where

n = the total sample size

Z = the Z statistic for the desired confidence level

σ^2 = the variance of the total sample (specified as desired)

W_i is defined as before

Ferber and Verdoorn have suggested that formula 9.7 be modified to include a cost factor, when the information is available and when data collection costs are significant and vary between strata:[6]

$$n_i = \frac{W_i \sigma_i/(C_i)^{1/2}}{\Sigma[W_i \sigma_i/(C_i)^{1/2}]} \cdot n \qquad [9.9]$$

where

C_i = the cost of gathering data on a single member of stratum i

n_i, W_i, σ_i, and n are defined as before

Three methods of allocating sample elements among strata—proportionally, optimally when cost is a factor, and optimally when cost is not a factor—are illustrated in Table 9-1. This specified sample size is 400 elements ($n = 400$), and the population distribution (shown in column 2) for seven income strata (column 1) is known.

Determining Population Distribution

Stratified sampling requires a knowledge of the distribution of the population with respect to the stratification criteria. An examination of the three preceding formulas (9.7, 9.8, and 9.9) will show that W_i—the ratio of N_i to N—must be known in order to solve the sample-allocation problem. In addition, it is desirable to be able to allocate every element on the population list to its appropriate stratum prior to selecting the sample.

Distribution of the population among strata is often impossible, since the necessary stratification data are unavailable by element except through the survey itself. This is typically true when income is used to define strata. In this case, published aggregate data are usually available. They will provide a frequency distribution showing the number of elements, N_i, for a set of income classes, i. Thus, the necessary W_i can be computed, although there may be no way to distribute the individual elements (usually identified by a different source) between the income strata. This dilemma is accommodated by a technique called quota sampling.

---

[6] Robert Ferber and P. V. Verdoorn, *Research Methods in Economics and Business* (New York: Macmillan, 1962), p. 245.

Quota Sampling

Quota sampling is a special case of stratified sampling. The mechanics are nearly the same, but the sample is drawn from the population as a whole and the responses are stratified. Quota sampling is an application of sequential sampling to stratified sampling. Sequential sampling is used until each stratum has the right number of sample elements.

The number, or "quota," of observations (responses) required for each stratum is determined by the appropriate equation—usually formula 9.8 or 9.9. The survey is begun, and the responses are distributed among the strata on the basis of the stratification criteria and the data on the questionnaires. When a stratum quota is filled, any additional questionnaires falling into that class are discarded. The survey is continued (and the sample expanded) until the last quota is filled.

If researchers elect to make an optimal sample selection, they will need an estimate of the variance, σ_i, of the population statistic, X, within each stratum, i. (See formulas 9.8 and 9.9.) An optimal sample will mean a significantly smaller standard error in the total sample when there is a wide difference in the variances of the different strata.

Specifying the value for each σ_i may pose a problem. The two methods suggested earlier are useful. However, if neither of them is appropriate, the researcher may have to settle for a proportional sample, at least until sufficient data are gathered to allow each σ_i to be estimated.

Computing the Standard Error

The standard error of a sample mean, $\bar{X}$, when that mean is derived from a stratified sample, is computed by one of the following formulas, depending on which method of sample allocation was used. (Readers with a statistical background will recall that standard error is simply another term for the standard deviation and is used when the standard deviation is being used as a measure of the error introduced by random variations in sample data.) If proportional sampling was used, the following equation applies:

$$\sigma_{\bar{X}} = \left[\Sigma W_i^2 \left(\frac{N_i - n_i}{N_i - 1} \right) \frac{\sigma_i^2}{n_i} \right]^{1/2} \qquad [9.10]$$

where

$\sigma_{\bar{X}}$ = the standard error of the sample mean

$W_i = N_i/N$

N_i = the size of stratum i

N = the size of the population

n_i = the size of sample drawn from stratum i

σ_i^2 = the true variance of stratum i

If the sample sizes, n_i, are small relative to the size of their respective strata, N_i—say $n_i \leq 0.1 \ N_i$—then the preceding formula can be compressed as follows

$$\sigma_{\bar{X}} = \left[\Sigma W_i^2 \frac{\sigma_i^2}{n_i} \right]^{1/2} \qquad [9.11]$$

When an optimal sampling method was used, the following equation is appropriate:

$$\sigma_{\bar{X}} = \left[\frac{(\Sigma W_i \sigma_i)^2}{n} - \frac{\Sigma W_i \sigma_i^2}{N} \right]^{1/2} \qquad [9.12]$$

where

σ_i = the true standard deviation of stratum i

n = total sample size

$\sigma_{\bar{X}}, W_i$, etc. are defined as before

This equation too can be compressed if $n_i \leq 0.1 N_i$, for all i:

$$\sigma_X = \frac{\Sigma W_i \sigma_i}{\sqrt{n}} \qquad [9.13]$$

If the true variance, σ_i^2, hence the true standard deviation, σ_i, of each stratum is unknown, the estimated variance, s_i^2, and estimated standard deviation, s_i, derived from the sample data (see Appendix 2), can be substituted. The result will be $s_{\bar{X}}$, the estimated value of the true standard error of the mean, $\sigma_{\bar{X}}$. Also, it is not necessary for the strata to be equal in any of the preceding four equations, 9.10–9.13.

If the sample is small ($n < 30$), the term ($n - 1$) should be substituted for n in formula 9.13.

Confidence Intervals

Once the standard error has been computed, confidence intervals for the population statistics can be calculated for the desired confidence level. If the sample is small (less than 30), the *t*-distribution should be used to compute the confidence interval. Otherwise, the normal distribution *Z*-statistic should be used.

An illustration will help to clarify the computation and use of the standard error and computation of confidence intervals in stratified sampling. Assume that a proportional distribution was made of the 400-element

Table 9-2 Computing the Standard Error of the Estimate When Stratified Sampling Is Used

i	Income Stratum	$W_i(\%)$	W_i^2	σ_i	σ_i^2	n_i	$W_i^2(\sigma_i^2/n_i)$
1	Under $2,000	18	0.032	100	10,000	72	4.4
2	$2,000–3,999	31	0.096	250	62,500	124	49.2
3	4,000–5,999	24	0.058	400	160,000	96	96.6
4	6,000–7,999	14	0.020	700	490,000	56	175.0
5	8,000–9,999	7	0.005	1,000	1,000,000	28	178.5
6	10,000–14,999	4	0.002	1,200	1,440,000	16	180.0
7	15,000 and over	2	0.0004	1,800	3,240,000	8	162.0
		100				$n = 400$	$\Sigma W_i^2 \dfrac{\sigma_i^2}{n_i} = 845.7$

$$\sigma_{\bar{X}} = \left[\Sigma W_i^2 \frac{\sigma_i^2}{n_i} \right]^{1/2} \quad \text{(given as equation 9.11)}$$

$$\sigma_{\bar{X}} = (845.7)^{1/2} \quad \text{(by substitution and arithmetic)}$$

$$\sigma_{\bar{X}} = 29.1 \quad \text{(by arithmetic)}$$

sample ($n = 400$) described in Table 9-1 and that the sample mean, $\bar{X}$, of the population parameter, family debt, was $1,210. By using selected data from Table 9-1, making the computations shown in Table 9-2, and applying formula 9.11, we can find the standard error of the sample mean $\sigma_{\bar{X}}$, which is $29. Note that the sample sizes are small relative to the sizes of their strata populations, hence formula 9.11 vice 9.10 was invoked.

Once we know the sample mean, $\bar{X}$, of the population parameter and its standard error, σ_X, we can use formulas A2.0 and A2.0 to find the magnitude of error, E, and the confidence interval, *c.i.* (A confidence level of 95 percent is assumed.)

$E = Z_{c.l.}\hat{\sigma}_{\bar{X}}$	(given as equation A2.17)
$E = 1.96(29.0)$	(by substitution, $Z_{.95} = 1.96$)
$E = 57$	(by arithmetic)
$\bar{X} - E < \mu < \bar{X} + E$	(given as equation A2.19)
$1,210 - 57 < \mu < 1,210 + 57$	(by substitution)
$1,153 < \mu < 1,267$	(by arithmetic)

Thus, the true (universal) mean, μ, of the population is within the range $1,153–$1,267 at the 95 percent confidence level. In other words, we are 95 percent certain that the interval $1,153 to $1,267 contains the true average family debt for the population from which the sample was drawn.

The reader will note that the standard error, σ_X (standard deviation), of the total sample mean is much less than the standard deviation, σ_i, of the individual strata. This shows the power of sample size to reduce the standard deviation, and hence the range of possible error. $\sigma_{\bar{X}}$ is based on a sample of 400 elements, whereas σ_i is based on samples with as few as 8 elements.

If the population parameter being estimated is a proportion instead of a point value, a slightly different formula must be used to compute its standard error.

$$\sigma_{\bar{\Pi}} = \left[\Sigma \frac{W_i^2 \Pi_i(1 - \Pi_i)}{n_i} \left(\frac{N_i - n_i}{N_i - 1} \right) \right]^{1/2} \qquad [9.14]$$

where

$\sigma_{\bar{\Pi}}$ = standard error of the proportion for the entire sample (Note: the proportion for the entire sample, $\bar{\Pi}$, is the weighted average of the proportions of the individual strata, $\hat{\Pi}_i$. $\bar{\Pi} = \Sigma W_i \Pi_i$.)

Π_i = proportion of stratum i

W_i, N_i, and n_i are defined as before

If the size of each stratum, n_i, is 10 percent or less of the stratum population, N_i—that is, $n_i \leq 0.1N_i$ for each i—then a less cumbersome formula can be invoked:

$$\sigma_{\overline{\Pi}} = \left[\sum \frac{W_i^2\Pi_i(1 - \Pi_i)}{n_i} \right]^{1/2}$$ [9.15]

A Digression on Bayesian Statistics in Marketing Research

Classical Analysis

The methods of statistical analysis used in this book are primarily those of classical statistics. Frequency distributions, objective probabilities, correlation techniques, analyses of variance, and regression analysis are just a few of the tools of classical statistics. Judgment plays a role in the selection of those tools, and in the way they are used. It dictates, for instance, the choice of a confidence level, the formulation of a null hypothesis, and the selection of a significance test. However, judgment is never explicitly incorporated into the derivation of a statistical value.

Bayesian Statistics

Our exploration of sampling would be incomplete if the subject of Bayesian statistics was ignored. Bayesian statistics is associated primarily with the analysis, rather than the collection, of information. However, it is relevant to a discussion of sampling design and conventional sampling methods. The balance of the book is devoted mainly to data analysis within the traditional—that is, non-Bayesian—framework. So, this is a convenient point to digress on Bayesian methods, particularly the complementary use of conventional sampling methods and Bayesian techniques.

The basic tools of Bayesian statistics are described in Appendix 2. Bayesian methods offer an opportunity to explicitly incorporate subjective probabilities, hence management judgment, and the benefit function into the analysis. This is particularly important when there is not enough empirical data to permit the computation of objective probabilities at an acceptable level of confidence.

Over the years, Bayesian analysis has been expanded to include a large assortment of techniques involving subjective probabilities, in addition to those propounded in Bayes' eighteenth-century essay. An elementary application of Bayesian methods would be to poll managers, salespersons, or staff specialists on the probability of success of a particular product, the proportion of a market population that would buy it at a specific price, or the likelihood that a proposed promotional strategy would capture a specified minimum of the market. These would be subjective probabilities.

A more sophisticated application of Bayesian statistics would be to sample the market population—using conventional methods—and use these data to modify the subjective probabilities. (Thus, the sampling design must provide for the collection of both subjective and objective information.) The resultant posterior probabilities would—according to the advocates of Bayesian statistics—be superior to both the subjective probabilities garnered by polling management and the objective probabilities provided by the market survey.

Using Sample Data   Bayesian analysis uses sample data to estimate the *probability* of a particular value of a population statistic. This is in contrast to the point estimate, qualified by a confidence interval, associated with orthodox methods. For example, Bayesian analysis might produce an answer such as, "The probability is 0.87 that 25 percent of the market population prefers Brand A." Classical statistics would tell the researcher, "25 percent of the population prefers Brand A; the confidence interval is 22–28 percent at the 95 percent confidence level." In other words, Bayesian analysis treats the population statistic as a variable, having a distribution.

Because it uses judgment probabilities, the Bayesian method incorporates more information into the analysis. This is, in a sense, an accommodation, and the researcher forfeits the ability to specify the range of possible error associated with an estimate. According to its advocates, this disadvantage is more than offset by the ability to use all of the available knowledge. The use of more complete information is clearly a virtue. Whether the price paid for it—the loss of the ability to specify the range of possible error—is justified is a judgment that must be made by management, or by the researcher.

For example, assume that management is faced with the decision whether to commercialize a new product. Assume, further, that cost-revenue analysis shows that the item will have to capture 20 percent of the potential market if the firm is to break even. Its market analysts have postulated three possible events, or "states of nature," that seem reasonable in light of the company's experience with similar products in comparable markets. The first possible event, A_1, is the capture of only 10 percent of the market (product failure). The second possible event, A_2, is the capture of 20 percent of the market (break even). The third possible event, A_3, is the capture of 30 percent of the market (product success).

Talks with the firm's marketing personnel have produced the following judgment probabilities: $P(A_1) = 0.3$, $P(A_2) = 0.2$, and $P(A_3) = 0.5$.

Not wanting to base its recommendations solely on these subjective probabilities, the marketing research department has obtained permission to survey a small random sample of the market population. The survey is conducted, and 4 respondents out of a sample of 20 indicate that they would buy the product. This outcome—4 successes out of 20 trials—is defined as Outcome B.

Given B, the firm's analysts are now prepared to determine the posterior probability that event A_3 (product success) is the true state of nature and will occur. The Bayesian theorem requires that the subjective prior probabilities be specified first. This was done by polling the firm's experienced marketers. (However, had the marketers been totally ignorant of the product's potential, Bayes' Postulate could have been used to obtain the probabilities.)

Bayes' Theorem also requires that the conditional probabilities for Outcome B, given each possible event, A_1, A_2, and A_3, be determined. In this case, they can be computed using the binomial theorem and the sample data. For each possible event, the possibility of outcome B (4 successes, x, out of 20 trials, n) can be computed with formula A1.2, the equation of the binomial distribution. However, with this large a sample size ($n = 20$), the formula is cumbersome, and a binomial-distribution table can be consulted instead.[7]

The table is entered with the number of successes, x, and the number of trials, n—data which were provided by the survey—and the probability, p, that success will result from a given trial. The probability of a success is provided by the definition of the event. Thus, p = 0.10 for event A_1, a market share of 10 percent. That is, if A_1 is the event, there is a 10 percent chance that any given respondent will be a purchaser of the new product. The binomial-distribution table simply tells us the probability that Outcome B (4 purchasers out of 20 respondents) will occur, given event A_i. As it turns out, $P(B|A_1) = 0.0898$, $P(B|A_2) = 0.2182$, and $P(B|A_3) = 0.1304$. Having obtained this information from the table, the analyst can proceed with Bayes' formula. Since the management decision to commercialize the new product will be based primarily on the probability that the product will succeed, it is most important to solve the equation for event A_3

$$P(A_3|B) = \frac{P(B|A_3) \cdot P(A_3)}{P(B|A_1) \cdot P(A_1) + P(B|A_2) \cdot P(A_2) + P(B|A_3) \cdot P(A_3)}$$

(given as formula A2.23)

$$P(A_3|B) = \frac{0.1304(0.5)}{0.0898(0.3) + 0.2182(0.2) + 0.1304(0.5)}$$ (by substitution)

$$P(A_3|B) = 0.48$$ (by arithmetic)

$P(A_1|B)$ and $P(A_2|B)$, together with the judgment and conditional probabilities used in their computation, are shown in Table 9-3.

Thus, subjective probabilities (provided by the marketers) have been combined with objective probabilities (provided by the survey) to yield a posterior probability. Having taken all the available information into consideration, the marketing-research department is now prepared to advise

---

[7] A third alternative, when $n > 100$, is to compute the Z-values and use a normal distribution table. When the sample is large and the probability of success in a single trial is between 0.10 and 0.50, the binomial distribution is approximated by a normal distribution.

Table 9-3   **Data Used in Computing Bayesian Posterior Probabilities**

i	Possible Event (A_i)	Judgment or Prior Probability $[P(A_i)]$	Most Likely Event, Based on Survey Data Only $(x = 4, n = 20)$	Conditional Probability $[P(B\mid A_i)]$	Bayesian Posterior Probability $[P(A_i\mid B)]$
1	Market share = 10%	0.30			0.199
2	Market share = 20%	0.20	*	0.0898	0.321
3	Market share = 30%	0.50		0.2182	0.480
		1.00		0.1304	1.000

Table 9-4   **An Expected-Value Matrix Using Bayesian Statistics**

Decision Alternative	Event (A_i)	Outcome (X_i)	Posterior Probability $[P(A_i\mid B)]$	Product of Outcome × Probability $[P(A_i\mid B)\cdot X_i]$
1. Commercialize	(1) Mkt. share = 10%	−$40,000	0.199	−$7,960
	(2) Mkt. share = 20%	zero	0.321	000
	(3) Mkt. share = 30%	90,000	0.480	43,200
			Total expected value of alternative 1 :	$35,240
2. Do not commercialize	(1) Mkt. share = 10%	zero[a]	0.199	000
	(2) Mkt. share = 20%	zero[a]	0.321	000
	(3) Mkt. share = 30%	zero[a]	0.480	000
			Total expected value of alternative 2:	000

[a] There can be no payoff if the product is not commercialized.

the decision-maker that there is a 48 percent chance that the new product will be successful. This estimate incorporates both the subjective probabilities provided by the marketing personnel and the objective probabilities based on the survey.

Expected Values   Perhaps the most significant advantage of Bayesian statistics is the ability it gives the researcher to compute the expected values of the decision alternatives. The benefit (or loss) to be obtained by following a certain course of action can be explicitly incorporated into the statistical analysis because of the probabilities assigned to each possible outcome. In the preceding example, management had two decision alternatives: (1) Commercialize or (2) do not commercialize the new product. The expected value of each alternative is the sum of the products of each possible outcome times the outcome's probability.

To illustrate, assume that cost-revenue analysis reveals the following outcomes for events A_1, A_2, and A_3, respectively: (1) a gross profit of $-\$40,000$; hence, a loss of \$40,000; (2) a gross profit of zero; and (3) a gross profit of \$90,000. By multiplying these payoffs by the posterior probabilities assigned to each event, the product for each outcome can be calculated. The sum of these products is the expected value for the first decision alternative. The expected value for the second decision alternative is zero, since the firm can neither lose nor make money on a product it does not commercialize. (These computations are summarized in Table 9-4.) Alternative 1 (commercialize) is the best of the two options, since its expected value is a profit of \$35,240. Of course, we are assuming that there are no opportunity costs and that the cost of capital and all other relevant expenses have been included in the computation of the outcomes.

The Bayesian method has also given the decision-makers other useful information. If they elect to commercialize the new product, the probability of failure is 0.199. The probability of just breaking even is 0.321. The probability of reaching *or* passing the break-even point is 0.801 (0.321 + 0.480). Although there is slightly less than an even chance (0.480) that the new product will succeed, the probability of actually losing money is relatively low (0.199).

The firm's analysts could have estimated the expected value of the alternatives using only the judgment probabilities, but this would have meant excluding the empirical information provided by the survey. (The survey data and classical statistical analysis alone would not have provided expected values.) By using the Bayesian approach, they were able to exploit both judgmental and empirical sources of information. The prior probabilities (provided by the marketers) were altered by the empirical data (provided by the sample survey), revealing posterior probabilities that were substantially different—0.199, 0.321, and 0.480 versus 0.3, 0.2, and 0.5.

Alternative Approaches   In the example just concluded, point values were selected for the three events, A_1, A_2, and A_3, which allowed point values to be computed for the expected values of each outcome. Point estimates make for easier computations, but proportions too could have been used. Also, three possible events hardly exhaust the real-world possibilities. On the contrary, the firm's actual market share—if the product were commercialized—could be anywhere from zero to 100 percent.

From the decision-maker's viewpoint, a small number of explicit possibilities is often adequate, as long as they are realistic. In this case, there were only two decision alternatives—commercialize and do not commercialize. Any market share over 20 percent would have justified an affirmative decision. Similarly, any market share under 20 percent would have made alternative 1 a bad choice. The analyst can make the analytical model a bit more realistic by increasing the number of events. For instance, in the preceding problem, he or she might have specified seven possible events—$A_1, A_2, \ldots A_7$—representing market shares of 5 percent, 10 percent, 15 percent, 20 percent, 25 percent, 30 percent, and 35 percent, respectively. The analytical procedure would be the same as before. Only the number of calculations would increase. The complexity of the decision model, like the approach used to obtain a prediction, is up to the researcher and depends on his or her perception of the firm's needs and resources.

Problems

1   What kind of sample would you select, and how would you select it, for each of the following projects: (a) a study of the purchasing habits of aluminum buyers; (b) a study of brand loyalty in the soft-drink market; and (c) an estimate of the distribution, by income class, of household expenditures for recreational goods and services. Defend your choice.

2   How would you draw a random sample of 500 automobile owners from a complete vehicle registration list? (Assume that 1,782,420 vehicles are registered, 85 percent of which are automobiles.) What statistical bias might be introduced into the sample?

3   If the objective of the survey in question 2 is to gather ownership data by income class (income would be one of the survey questions) and if the distribution of population by income class is available, how can a representative sample be ensured?

4   Using the data in the table below, distribute a sample of 200 elements among the five strata so as to minimize random error. If the sample mean is 18, what is the confidence interval at the 95 percent confidence level?

Stratum	Population	Standard Deviation of the Population Parameter
A	2,500	4
B	1,500	1
C	4,500	4
D	500	3
E	5,000	2

5   A market analyst perceives that a new fibre his firm is examining may capture 5, 10, or 20 percent of the synthetic-fibre market, depending on which of the present materials it can displace. His intuitive estimate of the probability of each event (a market share of 5, 10, or 20 percent) is 0.3, 0.3 and 0.4, respectively. The accounting department estimates that if the first event occurs, the firm will lose $400,000. If the second event occurs, it will just break even on the product. If the third event occurs, it will make a profit of $600,000. Since the outcome is so uncertain, management asks for market research. A survey is conducted in which 5 out of 20 industrial buyers state that they would switch to the new material. (a) Using both the judgmental and empirical information available to the firm, estimate the probability that the new fibre will capture each of the three possible market shares. (b) Estimate the expected value of the decision to commercialize the product, first using prior probabilities only and then the posterior probabilities yielded by Bayesian analysis. (c) Estimate the gross value of the market research.

Part 4
Summary

Sampling is the statistical art (or science) that produces the sample survey, one of the most important methods of data acquisition. Sampling relies heavily on inferential statistics, a body of techniques by which data gathered on a portion of a population can be generalized to the population as a whole. Inferential statistics also provides a means of specifying the magnitude of the statistical error associated with the generalization.

Designing a sample involves defining the market population, selecting between a population and a sample survey, choosing between a judgment and a random sample, specifying the size of the sample, selecting the sample, and specifying the method of observation or inquiry to be used. The survey is then executed, and the resultant data tallied and analyzed.

Although a nonrandom, or judgment, sample is often representative of the population, only a random sample allows the analyst to use inferential statistics, hence specify the statistical (random) error. For point estimates, the magnitude of possible random error is the product of the standard error of the mean and the Z-statistic. The value of the Z-statistic is determined by the level of confidence specified by management. (When the sample is small, the t-statistic is substituted for the Z-statistic.) The confidence interval is then specified by adding the error value to, and subtracting it from, the sample statistic. The resultant values are the limits of the range of random error associated with the point estimate at the specified confidence level. The range of random error is specified in a similar manner when the estimate is a proportion, but the standard error of the proportion is used in lieu of the standard error of the mean. In either case, the probability of error decreases as the size of the sample increases, approaching zero as the sample approaches the size of the population.

The statistical efficiency of a sampling method is a function of the ratio of the precision of that method to the precision of an unrestricted single-stage sample of equal size. It is useful in selecting the most appropriate sampling technique, especially when combined with cost information on the alternatives.

Certain sampling problems—identifying the population involved, determining the selection and response probabilities—can seldom be eliminated. However, they can be made manageable by the proper choice of a sampling method. The appropriateness of a given method depends on the nature of the population being sampled and the resources of the researcher.

Arbitrary selection is the easiest and cheapest sampling method when population lists are available that are randomized with respect to the critical characteristics of the population. Systematic sampling is preferable when the lists are not randomized with respect to these characteristics. Cluster sampling is a way of reducing survey costs while maintaining the randomness of the sample. Sequential sampling keeps survey costs at a minimum while producing data that meet a desired criterion such as a minimum range of error or a minimum number of respondents with a particular characteristic. Except for cluster sampling, these are all unrestricted random sampling techniques.

Stratified random sampling is a restricted random sampling technique that divides the population into strata and then draws a specified number of respondents from each stratum. This ensures a greater degree of representativeness in the sample, especially when one or more strata comprise only a small portion of the population.

In proportional sampling, the number of elements drawn from each stratum depends on the percentage of the population the stratum contains. Optimal sample selection distributes sample elements disproportionately among strata, but minimizes the random error for a given sample size. Quota sampling—a special case of stratified sampling—draws elements from the population as a whole, then distributes them among the strata. The total sample size is increased until each stratum's quota of respondents has been reached.

Bayesian analysis combines subjective and objective probabilities to predict the probable outcome of alternative decisions. The subjective probabilities are provided by company personnel with experience relevant to the problem at hand. The objective probabilities are provided by historical or survey data. Thus, survey data can be complemented with management judgment.

CASE STUDY 4

Los Angeles County Sheriff's Department: Marketing Research versus "Deep Throat"

Harvey M. Adelman and O. J. Krasner (*Harvey M. Adelman, Ph.D., is Professor of Quantitative Methods and O. J. Krasner, D.B.A., is Professor of Management, School of Business and Management, Pepperdine University.*)

The Los Angeles County Sheriff's Department (LASD) is responsible for policing the unincorporated area of Los Angeles County and, under contract, a number of incorporated communities within that county. Like other California law enforcement agencies, it must enforce the state's antiobscenity laws. Its jurisdiction contains many theaters, bookstores, and individuals dealing in material that some people would consider pornographic and illegal.

To aid the department in establishing operational criteria to judge seemingly obscene material, the LASD engaged the services of two consultants. Both were trained psychologists and skilled in the techniques of marketing research. The tools of MR appeared useful in defining working criteria that would conform to the rather vague requirements of the law.

The consultants accepted the study, subject to certain conditions. First, the raw data—if you'll excuse the pun—would be collected and coded by them. The deputies would not have physical access to the completed questionnaires. Members of the department, however, would be used to distribute the questionnaires as directed by the consultants. Second, the LASD would accept the findings as presented. No effort would be made to modify the consultants' report, should it contain findings in conflict with the notions of the department.

Law Enforcement Problem

The prosecution of pornography cases has been difficult because of the vagueness of the law as well as the interpretations of the law handed down by the courts. Currently there are three legal criteria for judging obscene material, including live exhibitions:

1   Primary appeal to prurience.
2   No redeeming social or scientific value.
3   Substantially beyond community standards.

In cases involving the first two criteria, behavioral scientists have testified for both the prosecution and the defense. The result has been ambiguity in interpretation and a failure of these two criteria to distinguish between pornography and nonpornography as far as the juries have been concerned. The third criterion seemed to offer the possibility of an unambiguous measure upon which juries could base a decision.

Previous community-standards studies had flaws that prevented unambiguous interpretations. Some of these were:

1   Limited study. Some studies assumed the preexistence of a community standard. Study questions dealt with opinions about that standard. The responses were difficult to apply to a specific event, such as a particular movie, book, or magazine.

2   Biased samples. "Community" is defined in California statutes as all Californians of majority age. Many previous studies drew their samples in theater lobbies or supermarkets. The results were not congruent with statutory requirements.

3   Interviewer effect. Previous studies used face-to-face interviewing. In an attitudinally sensitive area like pornography, the results could have been biased by interaction with the interviewer.

4   Limited media. Many studies did not investigate all types of media, such as live entertainment, picture, and movies. Their applicability was therefore limited.

The research problem was to measure community attitudes towards pornography. These attitudes must relate to the entire state, apply to most media, be relatively free of bias, and yet be acceptable criteria for law officers, attorneys, and jurors.

Decisions

Law enforcement officers, and subsequently district attorneys and jurors, must decide if material is obscene under the law. To make such an assessment, one needs criteria more specific than those offered by the law. The measurement of community attitudes towards pornography seemed to offer the best opportunity to define such criteria. However, if the criteria are to be invoked by the decision-makers to the satisfaction of the courts, they must: (1) apply throughout the state, (2) apply to most media, and (3) be relatively free of bias.

Research Design and Data

The objective of the study was to measure citizens' attitudes toward pornography and from these establish obscenity criteria

Exhibit C4-1   Survey of Representative Adults in the State of California

Purpose
To ascertain the average adult's level of tolerance (limits of candor) regarding sexually oriented matter and conduct. (Persons 18 years of age or older.)

Methodology
A random-stratified probability sampling

Date of Survey
May 1973

Instrument Designers and Methodological Advisers
Dr. Harvey M. Adelman
  Professor of Quantitative Methods (School of Business)
Dr. O. J. Krasner
  Professor of Management (School of Business)
  Pepperdine University
  1121 West 79th Street
  Los Angeles, California 90044

Interviewers
Sergeant Jack C. Greenlees
Sergeant Harold H. Hippler
Deputy Raphael Kenealy
  Los Angeles County Sheriff's Department, Vice Bureau

Approach
Before the initiation of the survey, four in-depth advisory training sessions were held with interviewers by Doctors Adelman and Krasner. A survey instrument—a mail questionnaire—was designed to elicit the respondents' opinions. A test sample was acquired and necessary adjustments made to assure instrument quality.
  Interviewers were counseled and trained in method, approach techniques, objectivity, and problems of liaison supervision.

Data
1. 5,200 survey questionnaires were distributed.
2. 1,444 questionnaires were returned and analyzed.

Survey Location Selection
1. Each of the 58 California counties were included.
2. Geographical distribution was 65 percent urban, 35 percent rural.
3. Questionnaires were allocated to each county, based on that county's proportion of population to the total state population and utilizing a figure of 5,000 survey instruments.
4. A preselection of the city with the largest population was made in each county. Other cities in each county were obtained by random selection.
5. A grid system, for selecting respondents and stratifying the sample, was used for the counties and cities. This was built by using the Rand Corporation's random number generator, *A Million Random Digits With* 100,000 *Normal Deviates.*
6. Contact was made at every third cross in the grids.
7. At least two personal surveys were made in each county.
8. All other survey instruments were mailed back to a prearranged post office box. Mail was picked-up only by Doctors Adelman and Krasner.
9. Survey data were tallied by Doctors Adelman and Krasner and analyzed with a computer.

Exhibit C4-1 Survey of Representative Adults in the State of California (*cont'd.*)

Interviewer Dress and Introduction
Business suits were worn and the following introduction was used: "Good morning, Sir (Ms.). I represent the Behavioral Research Institute. The institute is conducting a survey throughout the state. There is no obligation and responses are totally anonymous. Would you please take a few minutes of your time to fill out the questionnaire. Here is a self-addressed, postage prepaid envelope for your convenience. Thank you."

Relevant Points
The title Behavioral Research Institute was chosen so as to remove any bias of officialdom or "police taint."
   Identification cards were worn on the interviewers' lapels. Each card bore a photograph of the interviewer and the wording, "Authorized Member—Behavioral Research Institute. Individual whose signature and photograph appear hereon is an official Behavioral Research Institute team member."

meeting the specified standards. The research design and resulting data are shown in Exhibits C4-1 and C4-2. (Respondents are profiled in Exhibit C4-3.) These were submitted to the court in the case of California versus the Pussy Cat Theater. They accompanied the testimony of the two consultants who served as expert witnesses on behalf of the prosecution.

The case involved the movie *Deep Throat*, which allegedly violated the pornography laws of the state of California. All jurors were shown the movie at the start of testimony. Later, because of intrinsic interest, they were shown the movie a second time. The remainder of the case was devoted to testimony for the prosecution and the defense in the three areas of interest to the law.

For prurience, the defense provided behavioral scientists who maintained that such movies were entertaining and offered the figures on attendance in support. The prosecution contended that such movies were actually harmful and reported, in some instances, that attendees were picked up for masturbation. For redeeming social or scientific value, the defense argued that movies of this type could be used to cure sexual psychoses. The prosecution countered that this type of explicit material was psychologically dangerous.

The remainder of the case rested on the issue of community standards, with the defense presenting two community surveys taken in the lobby of the Pussy Cat Theater. Most of the people polled there said that movies like *Deep Throat* are "good" and "entertaining." The prosecution countered with the survey presented here.

Exhibit C4-2 Sample Questionnaire with Responses Tallied

BEHAVIORAL RESEARCH INSTITUTE COMMUNITY REACTION SURVEY

INSTRUCTIONS: A study is being conducted of a cross section of citizens as to how they feel about picture, movies or live entertainment which involves sexual exposure or activity. PLEASE DO NOT PUT YOUR NAME ON THIS QUESTIONNAIRE. IT IS MOST IMPORTANT THAT YOU COMPLETE THE QUESTIONNAIRE AS TRUTHFULLY AS YOU CAN. GIVE YOUR PERSONAL REACTION—NOT YOUR GUESS AS TO HOW OTHERS FEEL. Thank you for your cooperation.

Male 49.4%   Female 50.2%   Age 39.5   Racial or Ethnic Group: White 84.7%, Black 7.3%, Brown 6.5% and Other 1.5%   Married 66.9%   Single 18.3%   Divorced 8.2% Widowed 4.9%

Occupation ___

Education (check highest level reached): 6th Grade or less .4%   7–11 Grade 8.7%
High School Grad. 36.8%   Two years College 30.5%   Four years college or more

Ages of Children ___

Total Family Income: $4,000 or less 7.6% $4–7,000 13.2% $7–13,000
19.3% $13–19,000 21.0% $19–25,000 9.1%   Over $25,000 8.2%
32.4%

PLEASE PUT AN 'X' IN THE COLUMN THAT BEST REFLECTS HOW YOU FEEL ABOUT EACH STATEMENT THAT IS PRESENTED BELOW.		Strongly Agree	Agree	Neither Agree nor Disagree	Disagree	Strongly Disagree
	Total %					
1. In live entertainment offered in public places, it is OK to expose male and female sex organs. (5)		149 10.3	276 19.1	99 6.9	241 16.7	658 45.6
2. In films offered in public places, it is OK to expose male and female sex organs. (5)		169 11.7	319 22.1	90 6.2	237 16.4	624 43.2
3. In still photographs offered for display or purchase in public places, it is OK to expose male and female sex organs. (5)		154 10.7	282 195.	108 7.5	297 20.6	597 41.4
4. In still photographs contained in magazines offered for purchase in public places, it is OK to expose male and female sex organs. (5)		170 11.8	326 22.6	143 9.9	225 15.6	566 39.2
5. Bars and theaters that show performers nude should not be allowed to open in this community. (1)		481 33.3	252 17.5	110 7.8	259 17.9	334 23.1
6. Bars and theaters that show humans in actual or pretended sexual intercourse should not be allowed to open in this community. (1)		607 42.1	243 16.8	85 5.9	202 14.0	301 20.9

Question	(1)	(2)	(3)	(4)	(5)
7. Bars and theaters that show films of sex organs in actual or pretended intercourse should not be allowed to open in this community. (1)	593 / 41.1	218 / 15.1	81 / 5.6	238 / 16.5	312 / 21.6
8. Bars and theaters showing live or film presentations of a person manipulating one's own genitals should be allowed to open in this community. (5)	121 / 8.4	194 / 13.4	113 / 7.8	241 / 16.7	963 / 52.9
9. Bars and theaters showing live or film presentations of a person's sex organs in contact with the body parts of another person should be allowed to open in this community. (5)	124 / 8.6	224 / 15.5	108 / 7.5	231 / 16.0	750 / 52.0
10. Viewing in a bar or theater of motion or still pictures of sexual intercourse does not have an unwholesome appeal to the viewer. (5)	131 / 9.1	227 / 15.7	216 / 15.0	291 / 20.2	556 / 38.5
11. Viewing of live sexual intercourse being performed in a bar or theater does not have an unwholesome appeal to the viewer. (5)	120 / 8.3	198 / 13.7	207 / 14.3	297 / 20.6	594 / 41.2
12. Viewing of motion or still pictures of sex organs of one person being manipulated by parts of the body of another person does not have an unwholesome appeal to the viewer. (5)	122 / 8.5	220 / 15.2	196 / 13.6	291 / 20.2	585 / 40.5
13. An adult person has the right to see any kind of sexual act depicted in pictures or live displays he wants to. (5)	405 / 28.1	379 / 26.3	179 / 12.4	188 / 13.0	269 / 18.6
14. If our current laws do not prohibit public displays of live nude human bodies, they should so prohibit. (1)	451 / 31.3	348 / 24.1	127 / 8.8	223 / 15.5	277 / 19.2

15. If our current laws do not prohibit live or filmed public displays of human sex organs in activity, they should so prohibit. (1)

507	358	111	196	254
35.1	24.8	7.7	13.6	17.6

16. Our current laws about sex acts in public should be enforced. (1)

591	377	169	124	140
41.0	26.1	11.7	8.6	9.7

17. Pictures and live displays depicting human sexual intercourse or other sex organ manipulations do not have an unwholesome appeal to the viewer. (5)

137	223	194	308	528
9.5	15.5	13.4	21.3	36.6

18. It is OK to present male and female nudity, live or in pictures, in a place open to the public. (5)

172	305	103	289	538
11.9	21.1	7.1	20.0	37.3

19. It is OK to present real or pretended human sexual acts, live or in pictures, in a place open to the public. (5)

151	242	88	295	631
10.5	16.8	6.1	20.4	43.7

PLEASE PUT A CIRCLE AROUND THE WORD THAT BEST DESCRIBES HOW YOU FEEL ABOUT VIEWING REAL OR PRETENDED SEX ACTS IN MOVIES (WHEN ORGANS ARE EXPOSED):

None of these (Please write your own expression: _____
512–35.5%

Entertaining	*Shameful*	*Enlightening*	*Dull*	*Relaxing*
121–8.4%	186–12.9%	29–2.0%	116–8.0%	6–0.4%
Interesting	*Unhealthy*	*Arousing*	*Morbid*	*Comic*
102–7.1%	94–6.5%	109–7.5%	93–6.4%	25–1.7%

TO UNDERSTAND YOUR RESPONSES ON THE PRECEDING QUESTIONNAIRE, WE MUST UNDERSTAND WHETHER YOU FOUND THE QUESTIONS DIFFICULT TO INTERPRET. SO PLEASE TAKE ONE MORE MOMENT TO ANSWER THE FOLLOWING:

1. Were the questions clear and understandable to you?
   Yes, all of them 61.5% Almost all of them 22.0% Most of them 9.6% Few or none of them 2.2%

2. If there were any particular *words or phrases* that you had difficulty understanding, please list them here (explain briefly what you understood them to mean):
   12.5% listed something

3. If there were any particular *questions* which you had difficulty understanding, please indicate the question number here (and explain the nature of your difficulty):
   15.3% listed something

Exhibit C4-3   California 1973 Statewide Community-
Standard Survey

Demographic and Statistical Data utilized in the submitting of 5,000 survey instruments, to the representative proportion of the adult citizenry of the State of California.

The statistical information was obtained from the 1970 Bureau of Census reports, the 1970 *New York Times Encyclopedia Almanac*, and the Los Angeles County Sheriff Department's Research and Development Bureau.

Total State Population: 19,953,134

Females	10,136,449	50.7%
Males	9,816,685	49.3%
White	15,561,032	78.0%
Mexican-American	2,200,000	10.0%
Negro	1,400,143	7.0%
Other	791,959	5.0%

Research Issues

The defense cross-examination revealed several critical issues with respect to the LASD survey. These were:

1   The wording of the term "public places" allowed for an interpretation of supermarkets, billboards, and the like. Obviously, the community would not allow such activity in these locations.

2   Approximately two-thirds of the people polled did not respond. It was contended that these were probably the most liberal or those most sanguine about public displays of explicit sexual matter.

3   The questions were too ambiguous to allow for a unilateral interpretation.

4   The anonymity of the questionnaire did not allow for checking the respondents. The possibility that the deputies had filled them in was also raised.

Assignment   Consider yourself another expert witness, serving the court. Prepare a critique of the obscenity criteria. Specifically argue that the study did (or did not) yield a measurement of community standards that meets the three requirements cited in the "Decisions" section. If you judge the study inadequate or erronneous, recommend a design that would yield data meeting the specified standards.

Part 5
Experimentation

Introduction

> *Aerosol sprays once accounted for 75 percent of the $500 million deodorant market. Then scientists discovered that the aerosol propellants could deteriorate the ozone in the earth's atmosphere. The deodorant manufacturers scrambled to develop new roll-on and pump-spray substitutes. Market shares and large profits hung on management's ability to select the right product.*
>
> *A flood of new deodorants came off the pilot production lines, destined for a select group of cities. These communities were test markets. Here experiments were conducted to identify the nonaerosol deodorants that could make the most noise at the cash register. The winners are now seen on your drugstore and supermarket shelves.*

Market experimentation is the manipulation of one or more independent variables (price, advertising, etc.) to determine their effect on one or more dependent variables (usually sales). Normally the manipulation is done in the marketplace, although a laboratory is occasionally used. When experimentation is conducted in the field, it is often called *test marketing*—a phrase that is commonly used to denote the experimental introduction of a new product.

If all other variables could be held constant while each of the selected variables was manipulated, the changes in the dependent variables would be entirely attributable to the manipulation. Market experimentation would be no more difficult than a simple laboratory experiment in chemistry or physics. Unfortunately, this is seldom the case. Competitors alter their prices and promotional strategies, the weather changes, consumer income rises, buyer preferences shift, retailers fail, and numerous other uncontrolled variables change—thus distorting the results of the experiment.

Counteracting such disturbances—actual or threatened—in the experimental environment calls for a variety of design alternatives and techniques of analysis. The research objectives, the number of controlled variables to be manipulated, and the constraints imposed by time, cost, security, and the product also influence the design of market experiments and the choice of analytical tools.

Chapter 10 starts our exploration of experimentation with an introduction to its vocabulary, applications, virtues, and limitations. Here we again examine hypothesis-testing, a key concept in experimentation.

In Chapter 11, we focus on experimental designs. These range from simple, naive experiments to exotic factorial designs. They offer a set of solutions applicable to a number of sticky research problems.

Chapter 12 is allocated to the analysis of experimental data. Here we acquire the tools needed to unscramble the meaning of often confusing information.

Chapter 10
Anatomy of
Experimentation

Key Concepts

Basic Ideas
Uses, definitions, test markets, and objectives

Virtues and Limitations
The advantages and disadvantages of experimentation

Experiment Validity
Problems and solutions in assuring both external and internal validity

Key Terms

experimental treatment	Type II error
test units	external validity
control units	interaction
test market	internal validity
observation	maturation
replication	order effect
extraneous forces	double switchover
experimental error	instrumentation
systematic error	regression
significance level	differential selection
Type I error	mortality

Introduction to Experimentation

Common Uses

Market experimentation is most frequently associated with consumer products, especially food and convenience goods. However, it is not limited to these product classes or to the product variable alone. It is, in fact, very useful in the evaluation of promotional strategies, especially advertising alternatives, as well as in the testing of pricing and, to a lesser extent, distribution tactics. Experimentation is most valuable when the market instrument being evaluated is divisible—that is, when the alternatives are clearly distinguishable—and when a change in marketing strategy will not precipitate an unacceptable response from competitors. (Competitors will often alter their own strategies in order to confuse the results of an experiment.) Its usefulness also depends on the ability of the researcher to isolate the effects of manipulations, which in turn depends on the experimental design chosen, the analytical tools applied, and the skill with which the test runs.

Some of the most common market experiments are tests of price elasticity, the effectiveness of a new package, consumer color preferences, and the acceptance of a new product. Television commercials and magazine advertisements are often tested in this way to determine which of several alternatives has the greatest effect on sales or gets the best response from the audience (sales effects cannot always be measured directly).

Definitions

The following technical terms are widely used in the literature of experimental research. We shall take a moment to review their definitions.

The *experimental treatment* is the manipulation of the independent variable(s) being tested. Examples are a price change, a new package, a new distribution channel, and a change in advertising media.

Test units are the individuals, firms, or markets whose response to the experimental treatment is being studied or who are simply observed during the test period. (The former are called "experimental" and the latter "control" units.) Examples are consumers, stores, distributors, and geographic markets.

Test markets are a special case of test units. They are the geographic areas, usually cities or SMSA's, that are subjected to the experimental treatments.

The *observation*—also called the "outcome"—is the value of the dependent variable (usually sales) as a result of a given treatment in a particular test unit. For example, sales might equal 1,100 units as a result of the ith treatment at the jth store.

Replication is the repetition of an experiment, duplicating the original conditions exactly or as nearly as possible. Several replications may be made usually to increase the precision of the estimate of experimental error.

Extraneous forces are any variables, exclusive of the experimental treatment variables, that influence the dependent variable (i.e., the response of the test units). There are two types: (1) differences between test units such as in location or size, and (2) uncontrollable exogenous variables, such as weather, local business conditions, or acts by competitors. Differences in test units are normally determined by the experimental design; hence, the e usually known and subject to some control. Uncontrollable variables e exogenous to the test but can influence the data. Their effect can frequently ⊢ minimized by using a random selection of test units.

The *experimental error*—also called the "residual," "residual variation," hance variation," and "residual error"—is the variation in the dependent riable not accounted for by the experimental treatment or by extraneous rces whose total effect has been identified and measured. This unexplained riation in the response of the test units is caused by the inherent variability tween even "perfectly matched" test units, the effects of unidentified ogenous forces, and nonconstant errors in measurement. (A constant ror in measurement, e.g., the persistent overstatement of income or an terviewer's preference for upper-class neighborhoods, is a form of statistical as, sometimes called *systematic error*.)

Experimental error is inevitable. A realistic goal for researchers is to sign and execute an experiment that will have an acceptable experimental ror and sufficient random properties so that the techniques of statistical ference can be used to specify that error.

est Markets

ccasionally, an experiment is conducted throughout the firm's entire arket. More frequently, it is conducted in a test market. Table 10-1 lists me common ones.

Test markets have several advantages. First, it is easier to isolate and easure the variables, both the endogenous variables controlled by the re- archer and the exogenous variables outside control.

Second, local test markets are necessary if control groups, which are an sential part of certain experimental designs, are to be used.

Third, experimentation at the local level is far less expensive than at e national level.

Fourth, withdrawal is easier if the new strategy proves a failure.

The Coca-Cola Company's experiment with king-size bottles is a well- own example of the intelligent use of local test markets. Because it was a nificant departure from the traditional 6-1/2-ounce bottle, the larger size s field-tested in several test markets before it was added to the product e on a national scale. The experiment provided the data needed to make a cise estimate of the national demand. The cost was not prohibitive since e firm had only to purchase enough bottles, new bottling equipment, and troductory advertising to serve the test markets. Had the king-size bottles oven a failure, the project could have been scrapped before a major estment was made.

Television commercials are frequently tested in a similar manner. Two three pilot commercials are prepared and each is shown in a separate test arket. Changes in sales are observed, recorded, adjusted for differences in ogenous variables between markets, and then compared. The most ective commercial is the one selected for network showing.

Table 10-1   Frequently Used Test Markets

STANDARD MARKETS[a]	CONTROL MARKETS[a]
Albany-Schenectady-Iroy	**Burgoyne, Inc.**
Atlanta	*Mini Markets*
Boston	Binghamton NY
Buffalo	Charleston SC
Cincinnati	Omaha
Cleveland	Providence RI
Columbus OH	Tuscon
Dallas-Fort Worth	*Micro Markets*
Dayton	Bangor ME
Denver	Eureka CA
Des Moines	Gainesville FL
Fort Wayne IN	Lima OH
Fresno CA	Odessa TX
Grand Rapids-Kalamazoo	**Marketest,** division of Market Facts
Houston	*Binghamton NY
Indianapolis	Columbus OH
Jacksonville	*Dayton
Kansas City	*Erie PA
Madison WI	*Fort Wayne IN
Minneapolis-St. Paul	*Fresno CA
New Orleans	Grand Rapids
Oklahoma City	Nashville
Omaha	*Orlando
Orlando	Springfield, Mass.
Peoria IL	*Wichita
Phoenix	**Nielsen Data Markets**
Portland ME	*Boise ID
Portland OR	*Green Bay WI
Providence RI	*Portland ME
Quad Cities: Rock Island and	*Savannah GA
Moline IL; Davenport and	*Tucson
Bettendorf IA	
Rochester NY	
Rockford IL	
Sacramento CA	
St. Louis	
Salt Lake City	
San Diego	
Seattle	
South Bend IN	
Spokane	
Syracuse	
Tampa-St. Petersburg	
Tuscon	

Source: Reprinted by permission from *Sales & Marketing Management* magazine. Copyrig 1978.
* Indicates cities in which the company maintains permanent distribution, merchandising, a auditing services.
[a] Control markets differ from standard markets in that they are continuously monitored by t suppliers indicated.

Objectives

A market experiment can serve two objectives: (1) It can test a hypothesis, and (2) it can specify the relationships between variables. The first objective is present, at least by implication, in every type of market experiment.

Testing Hypotheses[1]   The usual goal of market experimentation is to test whether there is a significant difference in outcomes as a result of changes in an experimental variable. For instance, the marketing manager might ask if there is a significant difference in sales because of a change in package design. The null hypothesis, H_0, usually states that there is no significant difference between between sales at the test units (stores) subjected to one treatment (the old package) and sales at the test units subjected to the other treatment (the new package). Statistical analysis is then used to test this presumption at the desired significance level (usually 0.05 or 0.01).

The *significance level* indicates the probability that the difference in outcomes did not occur by chance. Thus, if the hypothesis is tested at the 0.05 significance level, there is an alpha risk of 0.05. In other words, the chance of a Type I error (rejecting H_0 when H_0 is true) is 5 percent. However, this does not tell us anything about the beta risk—the probability of making a Type II error (accepting H_0 when H_0 is false).

The acceptance of the hypothesis at a particular significance level does not guarantee that it is correct. It simply means that the statistical evidence is not adequate to force its rejection. Hence, the possibility of a Type II error exists. It is always possible that H_0 is false and the alternative hypothesis (i.e., that there is a significant difference between observations) is correct.

A Z-distribution, a t-distribution, an X^2-distribution, or an F-ratio distribution—whichever is appropriate—is used to test the null hypothesis, H_0. If the test reveals that the probability that H_0 is true is below the pre-determined significance level, H_0 is rejected. Rejection exposes the analyst and the decision-maker to the possibility of a Type I error, the probability of the error being equal to the significance level. Conversely, if the test reveals that the probability of H_0 being true is equal to or greater than the significance level, H_0 is accepted, and the analyst and decision-maker are exposed to the possibility of a Type II error, whose probability is unknown. However, as the probability of a Type I error decreases, the probability of a Type II error increases.

Both in framing the hypothesis and in selecting the confidence level, the analyst must take into account the firm's sensitivity to error. For instance, if a Type I error would be disastrous, a very high level of significance—say, 0.01 or 0.005—is appropriate. This low alpha risk is achieved at the cost of a higher beta risk. Hence, the implications of a Type II error must also be considered.

---

[1] Readers unfamiliar with the basic techniques of testing hypotheses, particularly such terms as "null hypothesis" and "Type I error," should take a few minutes to read the section on this topic in Appendix 2.

This dilemma can be avoided only by increasing the number of observations, n, in the experiment. This will increase the degrees of freedom, d.f.; and the critical test statistic (the Z-value, t-value, χ^2-value, or F-value, whichever is appropriate) will become smaller for each level of significance.[2] If the test results force the rejection of the null hypothesis, the alpha risk will be lower, without the beta risk increasing. Unfortunately, getting more observations may be too costly or physically impossible.

If the firm is very sensitive to a Type II error, but not so sensitive to a Type I error, the null hypothesis should be tested at a low significance level—say, between 0.10 and 0.25. This will increase the probability of a Type I error, but significantly decrease the probability of a Type II error.

To illustrate, assume that test marketing has indicated that a particular product variation, such as a new model, will increase sales. This is inferred from the fact that the sales of the test units offering the new model were higher than the sales of the test units offering the old model. However, there is always the possibility that the difference in observations is due to chance, not the change in the product. Thus, the analyst must test the hypothesis that there is no significant difference between the sales of the first model, Y_1, and the sales of the second model, Y_2. In other words, the demand for one model is the same as the other. This is the null hypothesis, H_0, which can be stated mathematically as $H_0: Y_1 = Y_2$, or $H_0: Y_1 - Y_2 = 0$.

As usual in hypothesis testing, there are four possibilities:

1   the hypothesis is true and will be accepted
2   the hypothesis is true and will be rejected (a Type I error)
3   the hypothesis is false and will be accepted (a Type II error)
4   the hypothesis is false and will be rejected.

If (1) or (4) occurs, the analysis was correct and management's decision, if based on the research, will be correct also. However, if (2) or (3) occurs, the analysis was in error and the management decision based on it will be wrong. Unless the market analyst can provide management with perfect information—a rarely obtainable goal—some kind of error is always possible. A good research design can seldom prevent this situation entirely. Marketing research only reduces uncertainty; it does not eliminate it. In reducing the possibility of one type of error, the analyst increases the risk of another type of error, *unless* the scope of the experiment can be expanded by additional observations.

If management must select one of the two models tested, and if there is no significant difference in their costs, a Type I error would be harmless. If management selected one model, thinking it was superior to the other model, whereas in fact it made no difference which one they chose, no real harm would ensue. Thus, a high alpha risk is perfectly acceptable and is an insignificant penalty to pay for the reduction in the beta risk.

---

[2] Degrees of freedom and critical test statistics are explained in Appendix 2.

On the other hand, a Type II error could have a significant opportunity cost. If H_0 was accepted, when it was really false, management, assuming that there was no significant difference in the sales potential of the two models, might choose the wrong one. Unless circumstances—such as a personal preference or significant cost considerations—bias the decision-maker, the chance of selecting the superior model, given a Type II error, is only 50 percent. Thus the expected value of the opportunity cost of the Type II error under these circumstances is 0.5 times the potential profit lost by selecting the inferior model. If the expected value of the opportunity cost is high, then the chances of a Type II error should be minimized. The beta risk is reduced by increasing the alpha risk—that is, by lowering the level of significance used in testing the hypothesis.

Frequently, a formal test of a hypothesis is unnecessary; intuition, prior knowledge, or a visual inspection of the data will provide a sufficient basis for accepting or rejecting it. Yet, irrespective of the method used, some kind of analysis is implied in the execution of a market experiment. For instance, the analyst might be confident that there is a significant relationship between sales and price, and hence reject H_0 without a statistical evaluation. However, a market experiment might still be in order to achieve the second objective of experimentation, namely the specification of the relationship between the two variables.

Specifying Relationships

The ultimate goal of marketing research is the specification of the relationships between marketing variables—ideally, the relationships between sales and each of the marketing instruments (price, promotion, distribution, and the product), or between sales and time or the exogenous variables that also influence demand. The sales-time relationship, as well as the relationship between sales and the exogenous determinants of demand, does not lend itself to specification by experimentation. However, the relationships between sales and the marketing instruments are often very amenable to specification through experimentation. This is because the essence of experimentation is controlled changes in independent variables. The researcher cannot manipulate time or exogenous variables, but can often control the firm's marketing instruments.

Experimentation helps the researcher to specify relationships by generating empirical data. The data are then subjected to analysis to produce an equation. For instance, price might be manipulated to generate a series of sales and price values. Regression analysis could then be used to derive an explicit sales-price equation. Given this information (which could easily be expressed in terms of price elasticity), the marketer would have little trouble selecting the optimum price and hence maximizing profit with respect to the price variable.

The analytical techniques used to specify real-world relationships require empirical data. When the data do not exist, experimentation is often the only practical way to generate them. Sometimes the data can be produced synthetically by market simulation, but even then some empirical information is needed to construct the simulation model.

Virtues and Limitations of Experimentation

Virtues

Market experiments are excellent tools for causation studies. If properly designed and executed, they will reveal, with a good deal of accuracy, the effect of a change in a marketing variable on another critical variable. Not only is the effect stated quantitatively, the maximum range of error of the estimate is specified at the desired confidence level. It is even possible to test two or more independent variables simultaneously.

Risk is minimized, since the variables can usually be manipulated on a small scale. Effects can be measured before the decision is made to generalize the changes to the firm's entire market. Since experimentation is normally done in the marketplace, the experimental environment is both real and current. While gathering the data needed to specify causal relationships, the experimenter is also obtaining information that may prove vital to the construction of a predictive model.

Limitations

Practical constraints often preclude experimentation or make its results considerably less reliable than the decision-maker would like them to be. The researcher must take into consideration the compatibility, contamination, management, and mortality of test units, as well as time, realism, product divisibility, security, and cost.

Compatibility   The experimenter needs either one or more pairs of perfectly matched units (to ensure equal pressures from extraneous forces) or a large number of dissimilar units (to average out the effect of the extraneous forces). However, choice may be limited to a small number of dissimilar units.

Contamination   One unit, usually the control unit, can be contaminated by another, usually an experimental unit. For instance, the experimental treatment may be a price cut. If the customers of the control units (where the price is held constant) get word of the lower price at the experimental units, they may shift their patronage to the latter. This would exaggerate the effect of the experimental treatment. The obvious solution is to isolate the control units from the experimental units, but this can be extremely difficult, especially when the variable being manipulated is price or promotion.

Management   The management of the test units may prove troublesome. If the experimenter has no authority over the units, the experimental treatments may be distorted. Lack of cooperation, rigidity of behavior, and undesirable responses from test-unit personnel are typical problems. Where participation is voluntary, as when the test units are retail stores not belonging to the sponsor of the experiment, these difficulties can be severe. Their resolution often depends on the persuasiveness and ingenuity of the experimenter. Sales personnel may fail to cooperate, or they may go to the other extreme and give an unusual amount of attention to the subject of the experiment. Sales personnel may be slow in adapting to the experimental treatment if it requires a disruption of their usual routine. A store manager may choose to exploit an experimental price by advertising it. Test units may inaccurately record sales data. Even the simple act of giving special attention to a group or its activities often leads to a change in normal behavioral patterns.

Mortality   Test-unit mortality is especially troublesome when the researcher is dependent on consumers for time-series data and the experiment must be run for a long time. Take, for example, a shoe manufacturer who test markets a new material and then purchases consumer-panel data to measure its acceptance. The shoes may be worn for a year or two before the buyers demonstrate their satisfaction (or dissatisfaction) by repeating their purchase (or shifting to a brand using the old material). In the meantime, a number of the original buyers may die, leave the market area, or simply drop out of the panel.

Time   Time can be a handicap. First, the design and execution of a market experiment may take many weeks. Decisions cannot always wait that long. Second, the duration of the experimental treatment is usually relatively short, and the full effect may not be apparent until later. Thus, the results of the experiment may understate the true effect of the manipulated variable. Conversely, any kind of change is a novelty, and with time its effects may wear off. Especially in the case of convenience goods, such as breakfast cereals, newness alone is often enough to induce sales.

Realism   Achieving sufficient realism can be a problem. The simple fact that variables are being experimentally manipulated can result in unrealistic conditions. For instance, when Coca-Cola introduced king-size Coke into a local market, sales were not the same in *that* market as they would have been had the firm introduced the product nationally. Many transients—who would have been exposed to the new product's promotion in their home towns had the change been general—were unaware of the item. Local residents whose viewing and reading activities were confined primarily to national media were much less sensitive to the company's promotional effort during the experiment, since the advertising was confined to local media.

Divisibility   Often the technical properties of a product preclude the production of a small amount for test purposes. A commercial airliner is one example. The fixed cost is so high that the total cost of the few units required for test marketing is prohibitive. Divisibility can also be a problem with respect to the promotional variable. Advertising in national media cannot always be purchased on a local basis. This increases both the cost of the test and the possibility of contaminating the control units. However, recent technological advances have made the use of national media for local campaigns considerably more practical. *Time, Life, The Wall Street Journal,* and many other newspapers and magazines now have regional or local editions that accept advertising directed at specific areas. Local TV stations can use "cut-ins" to insert local commercials into network programs. Thus, the problem is not as severe as it once was.

Security   Fear of revealing new product variations or other marketing strategies to competitors, who might copy them or prepare retaliatory measures, can severely constrain market experimentation. Tradeoffs must often be made between the need for tight security and the need for realism. Premature publicity may ruin the effect of the change when it is introduced nationally.

Cost   Cost is always a limiting factor. Experimentation can be expensive and financially risky—although much less risky than a nationwide or permanent change in a marketing variable. The experimenter must compete with other members of the marketing department, or for that matter, with other members of the firm as a whole, for the company's limited resources.

There are countless methods for circumventing, eliminating, or minimizing the effects of many these problems. The empirical literature abounds with suggestions. Although most of the solutions are designed to meet the needs of a particular experiment, they can often be adapted to the research at hand.[3]

Experiment Validity

Experiments attempt to replicate real-world phenomena and provide information that can be generalized to the universe they are used to study. Marketing experiments, although they provide much useful information, seldom achieve these goals completely. The marketplace is too complex to duplicate in miniature, either in the field or in the laboratory. Even in the rare case where it is practical to involve the firm's entire market in an experiment, the results cannot be generalized with absolute confidence. The numerous forces at work in that market will change over time; the same tactics used in the experiment may evoke a different response at a later date.

Validity is an issue, however well-designed and executed an experiment is. Both the research technician and the decision-maker should be aware of

---

[3] The *Journal of Marketing Research* is probably the best single source of information on marketing-research techniques, including experimentation.

the causes of invalidity. They should also appreciate the fact that few if any experiments are perfectly valid. As a pedagogical convenience, we shall distinguish two kinds of validity: (1) external validity and (2) internal validity. The problems that beset the researcher in either case are similar to those encountered in sample surveys.

External Validity

External validity refers to the representativeness of the test units. Are they, as a group, a true, if tiny, replica of the universe under study? Or is the test group in some way different, thus introducing a systematic bias into the experimental data? (The term "systematic" is used here to distinguish this form of bias from random error.) Just as the external validity of survey results is limited by a less-than-representative sample, so too the external validity of experimental results is impaired by errors in the selection of test units. The remedy is to make a random selection of test units. Unfortunately, this is not always possible. When randomization is impractical, the analyst will find it hard to generalize the experiment's results to the entire market. Also, the decision-maker will not have the benefit of a rigorous statistical evaluation of the findings.

Interaction between the test units and the experimenter, or between various phases of the experiment, can also compromise the external validity of the findings. Even if the test units are perfectly representative of their universe when they are selected, differences may develop by the time they are subjected to the experimental treatments. These differences may be induced by conditioning caused by one of the earlier steps in the experiment.

For example, a preliminary experiment might be designed to detect and measure differences between the experimental and control groups before the experimental treatment is applied. Such pretests are especially useful when only two test units are available and dissimilarities are suspected. Unfortunately, the pretest may sensitize the experimental group to the experimental treatment and cause it to overreact. This interaction between the pretest and the treatment could bias the results, making generalizations based on them faulty.

Replication of an experiment also introduces the interaction problem, unless the new test units have been isolated from the original ones. In fact, the process of selection itself makes the test units somewhat different from the other units in the universe. This was clearly demonstrated in the now-famous Westinghouse studies, which used employees as test units. People selected for the experiments felt "special." As a result, their attitudes changed, and they developed a test-unit *esprit de corps* that distinguished them from other Westinghouse employees.[4]

External validity is hard to measure because the factors that degrade it are not always obvious and their effects can be obscure. Nevertheless, the

---

[4] Fritz J. Roethlisberger and W. J. Dickson, *Management and the Worker* (Cambridge: Harvard University Press, 1939).

problem should at least be recognized, and compensatory ad hoc adjustments made in the research design and the data whenever possible.

Internal Validity

Internal validity refers to the correctness of the apparent relationship between the experimental treatment and the dependent variable. Are the differences in observed values attributable to the differences in treatment or are they influenced by other factors? Fortunately, inferential statistics provides tools for the detection and estimation of error in the measurement of treatment effects. Also, there are means of reducing this error—that is, constraining the loss of internal validity—although some of them entail a reduction in external validity.

Campbell and Stanley have identified eight causes of decreased internal validity:

history
maturation
testing
instrumentation
regression
differential selection
mortality
interaction[5]

History   History refers to the change of extraneous forces overtime. Time lowers internal validity by allowing extraneous forces to change. Thus, their effect on the test units at the time one set of observations is made is different from their effect at the time of a subsequent set of observations. This difference will be reflected in the observation values and included in the effect attributed to the experimental treatments unless preventative steps are taken or the data are adjusted.

The longer the interval between observations, the more sensitive the experiment is to history. The way to eliminate this disturbance is to reduce this interval to zero by using cross-sectional data, which are gathered from each test unit simultaneously. Unfortunately, this is not always practical.

An alternative remedy is to measure the historical disturbance by dividing the test group into experimental and control units and adjusting the data accordingly. Of course, the analyst must then accept the assumption that history will affect the experimental and control groups equally.

Maturation   Maturation refers to the change in test units over time. Participants grow older, their attitudes change, they become more or less

[5] D. T. Campbell and J. C. Stanley, "Experimental and Quasi-Experimental Designs for Research on Teaching," in N. L. Gage, ed., *Handbook of Research on Teaching* (Chicago: Rand McNally, 1963), pp. 171–246.

sensitive to stimuli, they become bored or tired, and their interests shift. Maturation invalidates experimental data in the same way the passage of time does. The remedies for errors caused by maturation are the same as those for errors caused by history.

Testing   Testing induces a loss of internal validity when there is interaction between consecutive tests or treatments. This interaction compromises internal validity in much the same way as it compromises external validity—by altering the characteristics of the test units. For instance, if a test unit is subjected to a series of tests or treatments, the attitudes or the sensitivity to the treatments may change. Taste testing is an example. If a participant is asked to comment on the flavor of a number of unidentified beverages, her reaction to each one will be conditioned by the previous drink. If the first drink was especially dry, the second drink will tend to taste sweet, even though it too may be on the dry side. This is called an *order effect* and is obviously undesirable.

Testing also lessens internal validity by inducing learning. A classical example is the IQ test. Testees tend to score higher on a second test—even though the questions are different—because the first test has taught them something about IQ examinations. They will be more familiar with the style and format, have a better feel for the time they can allot to each question, be able to read and comprehend the questions quicker, and be more comfortable with the examination during the second testing. As a result, they will do better. The improvement, however, in no way indicates a change in IQ, which, according to psychiatrists, remains constant.

Housewives, sales personnel, and store managers also learn from tests and treatments, and this learning may alter their attitudes or make them more or less responsive to stimuli. For instance, the test units may be subjected to a series of advertisements for a brand of soap. If the experimenter used the Starch method,[6] the ads might be buried in copies of popular magazines or journals. The participants would then be queried as to which ads, and how much of each one, they read. However, one advertisement can condition the respondent to be more sensitive to a following ad. The second ad may be noticed more frequently than it would have been had the test unit not been exposed to the previous treatment (i.e., the earlier advertisement) and thus receive a higher score. Promotional instruments tend to have a cumulative effect, and the one that pushes the consumer across the purchase threshold would pro ably not have succeeded without the help of the preceding promotional effort. Obviously this kind of interaction must be avoided, or its effects taken into account, if the tactic or instrument under study is to be correctly evaluated.

There are several methods—preventative and remedial—for dealing with testing problems. Ideally, these safeguards should be incorporated into

---

[6] For a description of the Starch method of readership evaluation, see *A Brief Outline of the Scope, Method, and Technique of the Starch Magazine Advertising Readership Service* (Mamaroneck, N.Y.: Daniel Starch and Staff, 1955).

the original research design, not treated as an afterthought. Market-research problems are usually more manageable when they are anticipated.

One solution is to avoid testing problems completely by subjecting each experimental unit to a single treatment and only one test. Of course, this may be impossible, especially when there is a shortage of test units or before and after tests are required.

Another solution is to develop data on test units exposed to several treatments or market tests as well as on units subjected to single treatments and single tests. These data can then be used to estimate the extent of the testing disturbance and obtain an adjustment factor.

Another remedy—called the *double switchover*—is to use multiple-test units and rearrange the order of treatments assigned to each unit. The scores for the respective treatments are then averaged. For instance, if three beverage flavors, A, B, and C, were being tested, the participants could be randomly distributed among six test groups. The first group would taste A, B, and C in that order. The second group would taste A first, then C, and then B. The third group would taste B first, then A, and C. Groups 4, 5, and 6 would taste B, C, and A; C, A, and B; and C, B, and A, respectively. The final score for each flavor would be the average of the scores assigned that flavor by the participants. Since every possible order of experimental treatments was tried, averaging the scores should cancel out the testing disturbance and neutralize the order effect.

There are times when none of these methods is practical. Often, the analyst and decision-maker will simply have to recognize the imperfections in the experiment and bear in mind the possibility that the findings may not be entirely valid.

Instrumentation   Instrumentation problems result from variations in the instruments of data collection. In marketing research, they are usually associated with the human element. A group of human observers is never perfectly homogeneous. One observer may measure a variable or respond to participants' answers in a different way from another. Or, his or her personality may cause the respondents to react differently. In addition, individual observers change with time and experience. Hence, they may interpret the results of an experiment differently from one time to the next.

A mechanical failure may cause an instrumentation error, and hence bias the data, when mechanical devices are used to make observations. In some research designs, very complex instruments such as television cameras, psychogalvanometers, eye cameras, pulse counters, or audiometers are used. Malfunctions in this equipment can result in the loss of important observations or the recording of erroneous data.

Instrumentation problems can be minimized by simplified research designs; more highly structured and objective questionnaires; careful selection, training, and supervision of observers; and good quality control and monitoring systems. If personnel and equipment are randomly assigned to the test units, discrepancies due to instrumentation can be treated as experimental error.

Regression   Experience shows that people with extreme characteristics tend to become more normal over time. A poor salesman will tend to improve as he learns to deal with clients. A star athlete will decline in prowess over time. This phenomenon is known as "regression." (The term should not be confused with regression analysis, which we will study later.) If a test group has a disproportionate number of participants who hold extreme views, regression will induce a shift in the opposite direction and toward the norm. This will bias the data in the direction of the shift.

Regression is similar to maturation in that it disturbs—and hence lessens the validity of—experimental data through changes in the test units over time. In fact, it may be viewed as a special case of maturation, where the change in the test units is a result of their reverting to previous characteristics or becoming more normal. For instance, suppose that an experiment has been designed to determine the effectiveness of an incentive program for the firm's distributors. An experimental group is to be compared to a control group, but the experimental group has been assigned a disproportionate number of distributors who performed very poorly at the time the original set of observations was made. Because of the regression phenomenon, these units will tend to perform better during the test period, regardless of whether they receive the experimental treatment (i.e., the incentive).

The remedy for regression error is to eliminate participants with extreme positions or to distribute them evenly between test units. However, the first solution might reduce external validity, since the test units would no longer be truly representative of the universe from which they were drawn. The second solution is probably best when both an experimental and a control unit are used, or when there are as many high as there are low extremes. In the latter case, participants with extreme positions should be divided into a high and a low set distributed evenly and randomly between the test units.

Differential Selection   Differential selection is the selection of a different type of respondents for one group than another. It introduces internal or external invalidity by making the experimental group different from the control group (or vice versa) or by making the test units as a whole different from the universe they supposedly represent. The problem stems from poor selection, which in turn results from a poor research design or self-selection. The latter is occasionally unavoidable, since the participants are often volunteers. People who volunteer for such experiments are likely to differ in attitudes, personality, or life styles from those who do not volunteer. They may be more extroverted, have more leisure time, or be particularly interested in the subject of the experiment. In any event, they are unlikely to be a perfect mirror of the universe from which they are drawn.

Self-selection may also affect the success of the experimental treatment. For instance, if a test market must be sampled to determine the effect of the treatment, and the units selected for the sample contain uncooperative people, the resultant nonresponse can bias the experimental data just as it does conventional survey data.

If participants are allowed to decide which group they will be in, the experimental or the control group, the researcher may wind up with two very different groups. This will complicate the analysis, since differences in behavior caused by the differences between the two groups may be erroneously attributed to the experimental treatment.

The best preventative for differential selection is random selection of the test units. When this is not practical, the analyst can attempt to identify characteristics that distinguish test units from the norm and estimate their effect. This information can then be used to adjust the data and, hopefully, eliminate the bias. Unfortunately, since the procedure does not lend itself to statistical evaluation, the analyst cannot be sure of the extent to which adjustments may be in error.

Mortality   Mortality is the attrition of test units over time. It compromises internal validity by changing the mix of test units during the course of the experiment. Test-unit attrition, as we mentioned earlier, is caused by store closures, deaths, moves away from the test area, and participant disinterest or alienation. That these losses will increase with time is to be expected. The dropouts differ from the participants who remain (otherwise they would not have dropped out); hence, when they leave, the mix automatically changes.

Mortality is a problem because of the analyst's inability to determine whether the dropouts share a unique characteristic that will influence the outcome of the experiment. For example, if the experiment runs for a long time, mortality will eliminate a disproportionate number of senior citizens and highly mobile households. Thus, the group tested at the end of the experiment would be different from the group tested at the start. However, whether this difference will affect the outcomes, and if so, how and to what extent, is a question that cannot be answered with a high degree of confidence, nor can a range of error for the estimate be defined.

The remedy for mortality is to stratify the test units on the basis of their expected mortality. A sufficient number of extra units can then be selected for the strata with a high predicted mortality so that a representative group will remain at the end of the experiment. If some of the reserve units are not needed, their performance can simply be disregarded. It is important, however, that the original units and the reserve units be selected randomly, whenever possible, and that the discarding of extra units also be handled randomly. Only in the stratification process should the researcher discriminate between units.

Another remedy for mortality is to shorten the experiment and pursue an aggressive follow-up program to discourage dropouts. This, however, may be impractical, or may lead to other problems less acceptable than mortality.

Interaction   Interaction is the effect induced by interaction between experimental and control groups. For instance, a sale made at an experimental-group store might induce a sale at a control-group store (the "keeping-up-with-the-Joneses" phenomena, or simply a purchase by one housewife being observed with approval by a neighbor). The solution is to isolate the two groups—often a difficult task.

Problems

1   Suggest a market experiment that would provide useful data on price, promotion, distribution, or product characteristics for each of the following firms: (a) Knudsen Dairy Products Company, (b) Gruen Watch Company, and (c) IBM.

2   Select and describe a market you would use to test television commercials for a nationally marketed product. Defend your choice. (Suggestion: Consult the *Economic Almanac* for data.)

3   Assume that a series of television commercials is to be tested in the market you have just picked. What are some of the practical problems that might arise during the research? What kinds of errors might there be in the data, and what could be done to minimize them?

4   Assume that consumer-panel data are purchased for the period immediately before, during, and after the showing of each television commercial in the test market you have described. Sales could then be correlated with the experimental treatments to evaluate the promotional power of each commercial. What reasons, if any, might you have to question the validity of the findings?

Chapter 11
Experimental Designs

Key Concepts

Naive Experiments
   The easiest, but most hazardous, approach to experimentation

Accounting for Extraneous Forces
   Designs for isolating and measuring the net effect of outside variables

Factorial Experiments
   Designs for revealing the simultaneous effects of multiple variables

Key Terms

criterion variable	level
determinant variable	treatment
naive experiment	response
control unit	factor effect
experimental unit	main effect
experimental error	Latin square
factorial experiments	Greco-Latin square
factor	

Experimental designs vary from the simple and naive to the complex and sophisticated. As the researcher moves from the first extreme to the second, the quality of the data improves, as does the precision and accuracy of the information and forecasts produced by the analysis. Unfortunately, the time needed to perform the research and the costs increase accordingly. In selecting a particular design and adapting it to the problem at hand, the experimenter must decide what kind of trade-offs can be made between experimental results and costs. As in other types of research, often the only way to obtain better results is to devote more resources to the project.

The basic experimental designs are simple, yet they are the foundation of most of the more elaborate and powerful methods. They involve a simple mathematical statement of the relationship between a dependent variable, such as sales, and a single independent variable, such as price. (The dependent variable is often called the "criterion variable," for it is used to judge the effect of the experimental treatment. The independent variable is often called the "determinant" or "determinant variable," for it determines the value of the dependent variable.) This simplicity is both a virtue and a vice. It makes the study easy to prepare and execute and keeps the costs down. However, too simple a design may mean ignoring factors that substantially influence the outcome of the experiment. Also, it limits the researcher to the manipulation of a single determinant (independent) variable.

Whether a basic experimental design will prove to be sufficient depends largely on the consistency of the exogenous variables and whether the experimenter is content to be able to manipulate a single controlled variable. If the exogenous variables are themselves changing, or if the researcher wants to manipulate two or more endogenous variables simultaneously, a more complex design will be necessary. With sophistication comes power as well as complexity and generally higher costs.

Naive Experiments

Naive experiments are those based on the assumption that the net effect of the extraneous forces will remain unchanged during the experimental treatment. Any change in the dependent variable is attributed entirely to the treatment. Stated in notational form

$$E + U = Y_2 - Y_1 \quad \text{and} \quad U = 0 \text{ (for naive experiments only)} \quad [11.1]$$

where

E = the effect of the experimental treatment

U = the net effect of changes in the extraneous forces

Y_1 = the value of the dependent variable before the treatment

Y_2 = the value of the dependent variable after the treatment

To illustrate, assume that the manufacturer of a convenience good wants to test the effect, E, of a new package design on the sales, Y, of its product. If he or she were using a naive design, the market analyst would select a test unit (say, the Denver SMSA), measure the dependent variable (sales), introduce the new package, and again measure the dependent variable. If there were any difference in sales, it would be attributed entirely to the new package.

For example, suppose sales of 1,000 units per week, Y_1, were recorded immediately before the introduction of the new package and sales of 960 units per week, Y_2, afterwards. The effect of the new package would presumably be to reduce sales by 40 units per week ($E = -40$), or 4 percent. The experimenter would have to conclude that the new package was inferior to the old one.[1] This is a reasonable conclusion *if* one accepts the assumption that $U = 0$. That is, there was no change in the extraneous forces between the observation of Y_1 and Y_2, or if there were changes, their effects cancelled each other out.

Accounting for Extraneous Forces

Adjusting for Known Changes in Extraneous Forces

A naive experiment can be upgraded by taking into account the effect of extraneous forces. Since U is now unequal to zero, it is convenient to rearrange equation 11.1 slightly, giving us

$$E = (Y_2 - Y_1) - U \quad \text{and} \quad U \neq 0 \qquad\qquad [11.2]$$

where E, U, Y_2, and Y_1 are defined as before

Assume that the product in the previous illustration has a cross elasticity, with respect to the price of competing goods, of 0.6. Knowing this, the experimenter decides to observe competitors' prices (an extraneous force) during the course of the experimental treatment. Sure enough, one sees the firm's competitors cut their prices by 10 percent immediately after the new package is introduced. The researcher calculates that this change in extraneous forces will decrease sales of the firm's product by 60 units per week ($U = -60$). The effect on the decision variable, E, is significant.

$E = (Y_2 - Y_1) - U$	(given as equation 11.2)
$E = (960 - 1,000) - (-60)$	(by substitution)
$E = 20$	(by arithmetic)

We can see now that the effect of the experimental treatment is clearly positive. Sales are up 2 percent over what they would have been without the new package. The researcher can now recommend its adoption, assuming that the concomitant increase in cost, if any, is justified by the increase in revenues.

The quality of the experiment has obviously been improved by including the effect of extraneous forces. However, the method still ignores the possibility of experimental error. Also, we have not yet arrived at a general method for measuring the effect of extraneous forces.

---

[1] If the new package were significantly cheaper than the old one, adopting it might increase the firm's profit, despite the drop in sales.

Control and Experimental Units

It is often useful to divide test units into control and experimental subsets. A *control unit*—also called a "test-control unit"—is a test unit that is not subjected to the experimental treatment. Any variation in the value of the dependent variable associated with the control unit is assumed *not* to be a result of the treatment. Hence, the control unit can be used to isolate the effect of changes in the extraneous forces, *U*. Of course, if these assumptions are to stand, the control unit must be isolated from the experimental treatment.

An *experimental unit*, the type of test unit we have been discussing up to now, is a test unit subjected to the experimental treatment. By pairing the proper experimental and control units, we can automatically adjust the experiment's findings for the effect of the extraneous forces. We begin with a pair of simultaneous equations, one of which expresses the change in the dependent variable associated with the control unit and one of which expresses the change associated with the experimental unit. As formula 11.2 indicates, the change in the experimental unit's dependent variable, *Y*, is the sum of *E* (the effect of the experimental treatment) and *U* (the effect of the extraneous forces). However, since the control unit is not subjected to the experimental treatment, any change in its dependent variable, *Y'*, must be attributed to *U*. By making these statements concurrently and solving the resultant equations simultaneously, we can obtain equation 11.3, which is very useful for marketing research.

$$E + U = Y_2 - Y_1 \qquad \text{(given as equation 11.2)}$$

$$U = Y'_2 - Y'_1 \qquad \text{(by definition)}$$

$$E = (Y_2 - Y_1) - (Y'_2 - Y'_1) \qquad \text{(by linear algebra}^2) \; [11.3]$$

where

$Y_1 = $ the value of the dependent variable associated with the experimental unit at the start of the experiment

$Y_2 = $ the value of the dependent variable associated with the experimental unit at the end of the experiment

$Y'_1 = $ the value of the dependent variable associated with the control unit at the start of the experiment

$Y'_2 = $ the value of the dependent variable associated with the control unit at the end of the experiment

E and U are as defined before

---

[2] In this case, the second equation was substituted for U in formula 11.2, thus eliminating U. For other methods of solving simple simultaneous equations, the reader should consult an algebra textbook.

If the researcher has properly matched the two test units, equation 11.3 will yield an estimate of the effect of the experimental treatment, E, that is undistorted by the effects of the extraneous forces, U. He or she need not even identify and measure the effects of each of these forces, since they are automatically aggregated and eliminated by the inclusion of the control group in the experimental design.

Suppose we return, once again, to the package-testing problem described earlier. This time, however, the experimenter, assuming that other exogenous variables besides competitors' prices may change and thus influence the results of the experiment, decides to employ a control unit. Two test units are selected—say, two supermarkets which are nearly alike in terms of the extraneous forces that affect them. Each is equally accessible physically, has the same number of competitors, and attracts the same type of customers. Furthermore, each does about the same volume of business and has similar management policies. The two stores are far enough apart so that the sales of one do not significantly influence the sales of the other. One is designated as the experimental unit and the other as the control unit.

Observations of the dependent variable, Y, are made at both supermarkets, the experimental and the control unit, immediately prior to the experimental treatment and designated Y_1 and Y'_1, respectively. The treatment is then administered (to the experimental unit only) and a second set of observations, Y_2 and Y'_2, is made. Daily sales at the control and experimental units are 105 and 90 units, respectively, at the start of the test and 99 and 93 units, respectively, after the new package is introduced at the experimental unit. Using formula 11.3, the researcher calculates that the effect, E, of the new package on the dependent variable (sales) was an increase of 9 units.

$$E = (Y_2 - Y_1) - (Y'_2 - Y'_1) \qquad \text{(given as equation 11.3)}$$

$$E = (93 - 90) - (99 - 105) \qquad \text{(by substitution)}$$

$$E = 9 \qquad \text{(by arithmetic)}$$

Judging from the experience of the control unit, which did not have the benefit of the new package, the effect, U, of the extraneous forces was to reduce sales of the researcher's brand. To make the right packaging decision, it is not necessary to know what those forces were, only what their aggregate effect was.

A difference in the sales volume at the test and control units can distort the results of the experiment. This distortion is slight in the example, but it could be important if the difference in original volumes was significant, as is often the case. The problem can be avoided by comparing relative, rather than absolute, values. Formula 11.3 then becomes:

$$E_\% = \left[\left(\frac{Y_2 - Y_1}{Y_1} \right) - \left(\frac{Y'_2 - Y'_1}{Y'_1} \right) \right] \cdot 100 \qquad [11.4]$$

where

$E_\%$ = the effect of the experimental treatment expressed as a percentage

Y_1, Y_2, Y'_1, and Y'_2 are defined as before

Substituting the values used in the preceding example in equation 11.4 gives us

$$E_\% = \left[\left(\frac{Y_2 - Y_1}{Y_1} \right) - \left(\frac{Y'_2 - Y'_1}{Y'_1} \right) \right] \cdot 100 \qquad \text{(given as equation 11.4)}$$

$$E_\% = \left[\left(\frac{93 - 90}{90} \right) - \left(\frac{99 - 105}{105} \right) \right] \cdot 100 \qquad \text{(by substitution)}$$

$$E_\% = \left[\left(\frac{3}{90} \right) - \left(\frac{-6}{105} \right) \right] \cdot 100 \qquad \text{(by arithmetic)}$$

$$E_\% = 9.05\% \qquad \text{(by arithmetic)}$$

This value is practically the same as one would get by calculating the percentage of pretest sales at the experimental unit represented by E ($9/90 = 10.00\%$). However, had the test units not been so evenly matched, the results might have been very different.

If the experimental unit had a pretreatment sales volume of 180 units and a posttreatment sales volume of 186 units (only double the previous figures), we would estimate the effect of the treatment as an increase in sales of 6.67 percent, using formula 11.3

$$E = (Y_2 - Y_1) - (Y'_2 - Y'_1) \qquad \text{(given as equation 11.3)}$$

$$E = (186 - 180) - (99 - 105) \qquad \text{(by substitution)}$$

$$E = 6 - (-6) = 12 \qquad \text{(by arithmetic)}$$

$$\text{Change} = \frac{12}{180} = 6.67\% \qquad \text{(by arithmetic)}$$

The real change, however, was 9.05 percent, as the previous calculations show. This result can be verified by again using formula 11.4.

$$E_\% = \left[\left(\frac{Y_2 - Y_1}{Y_1}\right) - \left(\frac{Y'_2 - Y'_1}{Y'_1}\right)\right] \cdot 100 \qquad \text{(given as equation 11.4)}$$

$$E_\% = \left[\left(\frac{186 - 180}{180}\right) - \left(\frac{99 - 105}{105}\right)\right] \cdot 100 \qquad \text{(by substitution)}$$

$$E_\% = \left[\left(\frac{6}{180}\right) - \left(\frac{-6}{105}\right)\right] \cdot 100 \qquad \text{(by arithmetic)}$$

$$E_\% = 9.05\% \qquad \text{(by arithmetic)}$$

When it is impractical to pair test units with approximately even volumes, equation 11.4 should be used. The experimenter will probably want the effect of the experimental treatment expressed as a percentage anyway, so that the test market experience can be generalized to the firm's total market.

Experimental Error

By introducing the control unit into the experiment, the researcher has presumably isolated the effect of the experimental treatment from the effect of the extraneous forces. However, the results can still contain experimental errors. Chance can distort the data.

This problem can be dealt with by using a larger number of test units that are selected at random from the universe of possible test units. For example, if the firm's product was sold in 90 stores, 20 could be selected at random, 10 to be used as control units and 10 as experimental units. The distribution of units between the control and experimental groups should also be randomized.

The experimental error is indicated by the confidence interval of the experimental effect. The technique for estimating it is essentially the same as the technique used earlier to estimate the confidence intervals associated with statistics derived from random data.

When there are several multiple test units, the experimental effect can be viewed as the difference between two averages. The first average, or mean, is the average change in sales for the experimental units, $\bar{X}_E$. The second mean is the average change in sales for the control units and is symbolized as $\bar{X}_C$. Thus,

$$\bar{E} = \bar{X}_E - \bar{X}_C \qquad [11.5]$$

where

$\bar{E}$ = the mean experimental effect

$\bar{X}_E$ = the mean change in the dependent variable for the experimental units

$\bar{X}_C$ = the mean change in the dependent variable for the control units

Since the stores will probably vary in size, the change in sales is expressed as a percentage instead of an absolute value to make the data on each of the 20 units compatible. The change in sales $(Y_2 - Y_1)$ can be readily made a percentage simply by dividing it by the pretreatment value, Y_1, and multiplying by 100. This is done for every test unit. The results are then totaled for both the experimental and the control units, giving us ΣX_E and ΣX_C, respectively. By dividing each sum by the number of test units it represents, we can compute the two means $\bar{X}_E$ and $\bar{X}_C$.

Table 11-1 shows the percentage change in sales for the 20 stores selected at random from the population of 90 stores. The average change, $\bar{X}_E$, at the 10 stores subjected to the experimental treatment was 11.11

Table 11-1 The Percentage Change in Sales During an Experimental Treatment

Experimental Units		Control Units	
Store (i)	% Change	Store (j)	% Change
1	+13.7	1	+2.4
2	+7.0	2	+4.8
3	+9.8	3	−1.2
4	+14.6	4	+3.6
5	+6.2	5	+4.1
6	+13.8	6	+2.1
7	+5.4	7	+0.9
8	+18.6	8	−0.7
9	+15.3	9	+4.6
10	+6.7	10	+1.7
$\sum\limits_{i=1}^{10} X_{E_i} = 111.1$		$\sum\limits_{j=1}^{10} X_{C_j} = 22.3$	

$$\bar{X}_E = \frac{\sum\limits_{i=1}^{10} X_{E_i}}{10} = \frac{111.1}{10} = 11.11 \qquad \begin{array}{l} \bar{E} = \bar{X}_E - \bar{X}_C \\ \bar{E} = 11.11 - 2.23 \\ \bar{E} = 8.88 \end{array} \qquad \bar{X}_C = \frac{\sum\limits_{j=1}^{10} X_{C_j}}{10} = \frac{22.3}{10} = 2.23$$

percent. The average change at the 10 stores used as control units was 2.23 percent. Thus, the effect of the experiment was to increase sales by 8.88 percent (11.11% − 2.23%). However, this value presumably includes an experimental error, which should be specified before the decision-maker uses the information.

We are now interested in establishing a confidence interval for the estimated change of 8.88 percent. The standard deviation, or standard error, of $\bar{E}$ is[3]

$$s_E = \left[\frac{\sum\limits_{i=1}^{n_E} (X_{E_i} - \bar{X}_E)^2 + \sum\limits_{j=1}^{n_C} (X_{C_j} - \bar{X}_C)^2}{n_E + n_C - 2} \right]^{1/2} \cdot \left[\frac{1}{n_E} + \frac{1}{n_C} \right]^{1/2} \qquad [11.6]$$

where

s_E = the standard error of the mean experimental effect

n_E = the number of experimental units

n_C = the number of control units

X_{E_i} = the percentage change in sales for experimental unit i

X_{C_j} = the percentage change in sales for control unit j

$\bar{X}_E$ = the average percentage change in sales for the experimental units

$\bar{X}_C$ = the average percentage change in sales for the control units

The calculations for $\Sigma_{i=1}^{n_E} (X_{E_i} - \bar{X}_E)^2$ and $\Sigma_{j=1}^{n_C} (X_{C_j} - \bar{X}_C)^2$ are presented in Table 11-2.

Using the method described in Appendix 2, we can now proceed with the computation of the confidence interval, at an arbitrarily selected con-

---

[3] The standard deviation for the difference between means is a pooled estimate of the two individual standard deviations. Since the simple standard deviation is

$$s = \left[\frac{\Sigma(\bar{X}_i - \bar{X})^2}{n - 1} \right]^{1/2}$$

then a pooled estimate is

$$s = \left[\frac{\Sigma(X_i - \bar{X})^2 + \Sigma(Y_i - \bar{Y})^2}{(n_X - 1) + (n_Y - 1)} \right]^{1/2}$$

Readers who are uncomfortable with these terms and equations are again advised to read Appendix 2.

Table 11-2   **The Calculation of** $\sum\limits_{i=1}^{n_E} (X_{E_j} - \bar{X}_E)^2$ **and** $\sum\limits_{i=1}^{n_E} (X_{C_j} - \bar{X}_C)^2$

i	X_{E_i}	$X_{E_i} - \bar{X}_E$	$(X_{E_i} - \bar{X}_E)^2$	j	X_{C_j}	$X_{C_j} - \bar{X}_C$	$(X_{C_j} - \bar{X}_C)^2$
1	+13.7	+2.59	6.7081	1	+2.4	+0.17	0.0289
2	+7.0	−4.11	16.8921	2	+4.8	+2.57	6.6049
3	+9.8	−1.31	1.7161	3	−1.2	−3.43	11.7649
4	+14.6	+3.49	12.1801	4	+3.6	+1.37	1.8769
5	+6.2	−4.91	24.1081	5	+4.1	+1.87	3.4969
6	+13.8	+2.69	7.2361	6	+2.1	−0.13	0.0169
7	+5.4	−5.71	32.6041	7	+0.9	−1.33	1.7689
8	+18.6	+7.49	56.1001	8	−0.7	−2.93	8.5844
9	+15.3	+4.19	17.5561	9	+4.6	+2.37	5.6169
10	+6.7	−4.41	19.4481	10	+1.7	−0.53	0.2809

$$\sum_{i=1}^{10} (X_{E_i} - \bar{X}_E)^2 = 194.5490 \qquad\qquad \sum_{j=1}^{10} (X_{C_j} - \bar{X}_C)^2 = 40.0410$$

The standard deviation of $\bar{E}$ is thus

$$s_{\bar{E}} = \left[\frac{194.549 + 40.041}{10 + 10 - 2}\right]^{1/2} \cdot \left[\frac{1}{10} + \frac{1}{10}\right]^{1/2} \qquad \text{(by substitution into equation 11.6)}$$

$$s_{\bar{E}} = \left[\frac{234.59}{18}\right]^{1/2} \cdot \left[\frac{1}{5}\right]^{1/2} \qquad \text{(by arithmetic)}$$

$$s_{\bar{E}} = 1.61 \qquad \text{(by arithmetic)}$$

Source: From *Marketing: Theory and Application,* by W. B. Wentz and G. I. Eyrich, copyright © 1970 by Harcourt Brace Jovanovich, Inc., and reproduced with their permission.

fidence level of 95 percent, for our estimate of the experimental effect

$$\bar{X} - E < \mu < \bar{X} + E$$

(given as equation A2.19 Note: Do not confuse the symbol E here [random error] with the E in equation 11.5. Also, μ now represents the true value of the experimental effect.)

$$\bar{E} - z_{.025}s_E < \mu < \bar{E} + z_{.025}s_E \qquad \text{(by substitution)}$$

$$8.88 - 1.96(1.61) < \mu < 8.88 + 1.96(1.61) \qquad \text{(by substitution)}$$

$$5.72 < \mu < 12.04 \qquad \text{(by arithmetic[4])}$$

Thus, we can be 95 percent sure that the true value of the experimental effect, E, is between 5.72 and 12.04. Hence, the range of possible error is

---

[4] Statistically inclined readers will note that the confidence multiplier for large samples, the Z-statistic, has been used. A more conservative approach would have been to use the confidence multiplier for small samples, the t-statistic. This would have yielded a confidence interval of $1.30 < \mu < 16.46$.

large. This is not unusual in real-world experiments. However, it may be very discouraging to experimenters. It may even cause them to reevaluate their research design and consider using a more sophisticated approach. It may also be disturbing to decision-makers, causing them to put little trust in the findings and perhaps insist on further research.

However, if all the firm really needs to know is whether the experimental treatment truly has a positive effect on sales, a large confidence interval may not be disturbing. Obviously, there is a statistically significant relationship between sales and the experimental treatment in the example. (The null hypothesis, $H_0: E = 0$, must be rejected at the 97.5 percent confidence level—the 0.025 level of significance.) This information alone may enable the marketer to make the right decision.

Factorial Experiments

Factorial experiments are experiments designed to reveal the simultaneous effects or two or more variables. For this reason, and because they also give the researcher the opportunity to detect interaction between two independent variables, they are more efficient than naive designs.[5] Before we begin our exploration of factorial designs, we must define several terms whose meaning in this context differs from their ordinary, or popular, meaning.

A *factor* is an independent variable manipulated or observed during an experiment. Examples are the price or color of products and the distribution channels used by firms.

A *level* is a value at which a factor is examined. It may be quantitative—say, $5, $6, or $7 if the factor is price—or it may be qualitative—say, red, gold, or white if the factor is color.

A *treatment*, or "treatment combination," is a set of levels (one for each factor) used in a particular trial. Examples are a $5 price and a gold package or a $6 price and a red package.

A *response* is the numerical result of a particular treatment. For instance, sales of 340 units might be the response to the $5-price/red-package treatment.

The *factor effect* is the change in response produced by a change in level of the factor. For example, the color factor is held constant while the price factor is set at levels of $5 (one treatment) and $6 (another treatment). If the two trials produce sales responses of 340 and 310 units, respectively, the effect of the price factor is a drop in sales of 30 units. If there are three or more treatment levels, the effect of the factor will have to be measured a bit differently, perhaps by finding the average of the difference in responses at each treatment level.

The *main effect* is the average effect of a factor after all the treatments have been tried. If every change in the level of a factor produces the same re-

---

[5] One of the most lucid discussions of this topic for readers in any field is found in Owen L. Davis, ed., *The Design and Analysis of Industrial Experiments* (New York: Hafner, 1956), ch. 7. Much of this section is based on Davis's work.

sponse, regardless of the variation in the levels of the other factors, then that factor is independent of the other factors and its main effect is attributable to changes in it alone. If this is not the case, then there is interaction between this factor and one or more other factors in the experiment.

Interaction is the influence of one factor on the effect of another, and of course was defined earlier. For example, the effect of an increase in the size (level) of a soft-drink advertisement (factor) may be to increase sales (response) by 4,000 units when the temperature (second factor) is 90° (level) but by only 1,500 units when the temperature is 70°.

Uses of Factorial Designs

Application   The virtues of factorial designs can best be illustrated by an example. Assume that an experimenter wants to test the effect on sales of two factors, price and package color. The simplest experiment would evaluate the effect of price at two levels, P_0 and P_1, and the effect of color at two levels, C_0 and C_1. Three treatments must be applied. The first is the original price/color combination, P_0, C_0. The response to this treatment we shall call $R(P_0, C_0)$. The second treatment P_1, C_0 is a new price, P_1, and the original package color, C_0. The response to this treatment, which will be used to estimate the effect of price, we shall call $R(P_1, C_0)$. The third and final treatment is P_0, C_1; the response, which will be used to estimate the effect of color, we shall call $R(P_0, C_1)$. The effect of each factor, price and color, is computed by subtracting the response to the first treatment from the response to the treatment in which its level was changed

$$\text{Effect of price} = R(P_1, C_0) - R(P_0, C_0)$$

$$\text{Effect of color} = R(P_0, C_1) - R(P_0, C_0)$$

Note that three treatments—P_0, C_0; P_1, C_0; and P_0, C_1—are required to get estimates of two experimental effects. Even this does not yield enough data to permit an estimate of experimental error. This requires a measure of the variability of the experiment, gotten by replication. To see how much, if any, variability existed, the researcher would have to repeat each treatment at least twice. Thus, at least six experiments would be necessary, although half would use duplicate treatments.

We can get the same information with fewer experiments by adding another treatment. Thus, in the example, four experiments will do the work of six. The additional treatment, which allows variability to be measured without replication, is P_1, C_1; the response is $R(P_1, C_1)$. We can now obtain two estimates for both the price and color factors

$$\text{Effect of color} = R(P_1, C_1) - R(P_1, C_0)$$

and

$$R(P_0, C_1) - R(P_0, C_0)$$

$$\text{Effect of price} = R(P_1, C_0) - R(P_0, C_0)$$

and

$$R(P_1, C_1) - R(P_0, C_1)$$

Assuming that there is no interaction between the variables, the difference in the two estimates of the effect of a factor is attributable to experimental error. This variation can be used to estimate the confidence interval associated with the estimate of experimental effect. If several observations of variation are needed (if the degrees of freedom are to be increased), then replication will again be required. However, fewer experiments will be required if the fourth treatment is used. With the four-treatment factorial design, 4, 8, and 12 experiments would yield the same quantity of information as 6, 12, and 18 experiments would yield using the basic design.

Matrices

Matrices are useful in describing factorial designs. For instance, the preceding experimental design (in its basic form) and the responses to each treatment could be depicted as in Table 11-3.

The effect of the color factor is revealed by comparing response $R(5, G)$ with response $R(5, B)$. A change from gold to blue reduced sales by 60 units. The effect of the price factor can be found by comparing response $R(5, G)$ with $R(6, G)$. An increase in price from \$5 to \$6 reduced sales by 30 units.

Assuming that there is no interaction between the two factors, the differences in responses between pairs of observations will be the effect of experimental error (or exogenous forces if they are at work). For example, the difference between $R(6, G) - R(5, G)$ and $R(6, B) - R(5, B)$ in the illustration is the experimental error in the observation of price. In this case the difference is zero $[(370 - 400) - (310 - 340) = 0]$, and we must assume that there is no experimental error and no net effect from exogenous forces. The experimental error in the observations of color is also zero $[(340 - 400) - (310 - 370) = 0]$, which also suggests an absence of experimental error and exogenous forces.

If the fourth treatment produces a different response from those obtained before, it may be due to either experimental error or interaction between the two factors. This latter possibility would never be revealed by altering only one factor at a time. For example, suppose that the previous experiment had revealed the data in Table 11-4.

A change in price now yields a different change in sales for each level of the color factor $[R(6, G) - R(5, G) = -30$ and $R(6, B) - R(5, B) = -40]$. The effect of color is also different at each level of price $[R(5, B) - R(5, G) = -60$ and $R(6, B) - R(6, G) = -70]$. If the experimenter is certain that the price and color factors do not interact, then the discrepancy in the observations must be due to experimental error.

Error, exogenous disturbances, and interaction can be evaluated by techniques discussed in the following chapter. For now, we need only recognize their existence and the fact that their presence may be detected in factorial experiments.

Table 11-3 **A Simple 2 × 2 Factorial Design**

		Package Gold (G)	Package Blue (B)
Price	$5	$R(5, G) = 400$	$R(5, B) = 340$
	$6	$R(6, G) = 370$	$R(6, B) = 310$

Table 11-4 **A Factorial Experiment Revealing Experimental Error or Interaction**

		Package Gold (G)	Package Blue (B)
Price	$5	$R(5, G) = 400$	$R(5, B) = 340$
	$6	$R(6, G) = 370$	$R(6, B) = 300$

Treatment Requirements

Factorial designs can have any number of factors or levels. However, for each additional level, the total number of treatments must be doubled. The total number of treatments, T, hence the total number of cells in a representative matrix, may be expressed as

$$T = \prod_{i=1}^{n} L_i \qquad [11.7]$$

where

T = the minimum number of treatments

Π = an operational symbol indicating that the following variables should be multiplied[6]

L_i = the number of levels of each factor, 1 through n

For instance, if the analyst wanted to measure the effect of color at 3 levels ($L_1 = 3$) and price at 4 levels ($L_2 = 4$), 12 treatments would be required.

[6] For example, $\prod_{i=1}^{4} x_i$ is equivalent to $x_1 \cdot x_2 \cdot x_3 \cdot x_4$. If $x_1 = 1$, $x_2 = 3$, $x_3 = 5$, and $x_4 = 6$, then $\prod_{i=1}^{4} x_i = (1) \cdot (3) \cdot (5) \cdot (6)$, or 90.

In the previous example, $L_1 = 2$ and $L_2 = 2$; hence only 4 treatments ($T = 2 \cdot 2 = 4$) would be needed. If 3 factors—say, color, price, and size—were to be evaluated at 3, 4, and 2 levels, respectively, then 24 treatments would be necessary. Thus, the minimum number of treatments increases rapidly with an increase in the number of factor levels. This makes the cost—and in some cases the impracticality—of an experiment increase sharply with increases in either the number of factors or the number of levels. Nevertheless, the simultaneous manipulation or observation[7] of variables made possible by a factorial design still makes the experiment much more efficient than an experiment that gathers data on each variable separately.

The effect of each factor can be estimated by measuring the difference between the responses (shown in the matrix cells) at different factor levels. If more than 2 levels are used and their differences are not equal, the average difference may be used. For instance, if price has 3 treatment levels (L_1, L_2, and L_3), the price factor's effect may be considered the average of $R(L_3) - R(L_2)$ and $R(L_2) - R(L_1)$. This would be appropriate if L_1, L_2, and L_3 were equal distances apart; if, say, there were a $1 difference between each level.

If the price treatment levels are equal distances apart, and the differences in responses are not equal, three possibilities exist: First, the relationship between the dependent variable and the factor is nonlinear. Second, there is interaction between factors. Third, there is experimental error. Thus, if the analyst measures the gross effect[8] of a factor at several treatment levels and finds little or no variation, he or she can assume that the differences in responses are primarily attributable to the changes in the factor. The gross effect is thus equal to the true main effect of the factor. If this is not the case, then the researcher must turn to an analysis of variance to explain the discrepancies in the observations.

An Example

For example, assume that the analyst has designed and executed an experiment to determine the effect of two factors, price and advertising, at three and two treatment levels, respectively. (The treatments and the responses are indicated in Table 11-5.)

We can now compute the gross effect of the two levels of advertising, Plans A and B, for each price level

Gross effect at $P_1 = \$10$: $R(10, B) - R(10, A) = 280 - 300 = -20$

Gross effect at $P_2 = \$12$: $R(12, B) - R(12, A) = 240 - 260 = -20$

Gross effect at $P_3 = \$14$: $R(14, B) - R(14, A) = 180 - 200 = -20$

---

[7] The factors being evaluated (e.g., the weather, the price of a competitor's goods, or a competitor's advertising) may not be amenable to manipulation by the experimenter.

[8] The gross effect includes the effect of the factor plus interaction effects and experimental errors.

Table 11-5   **A 3 × 2 Factorial Experiment**

		Advertising	
		Plan A	Plan B
Price	$10	R(10, A) = 300	R(10, B) = 280
	$12	R(12, A) = 260	R(12, B) = 240
	$14	R(14, A) = 200	R(14, B) = 180

Since each observed effect is equal, there is no point in computing the average effect (revealed by totaling the gross effects and dividing by 3). The equality of factor effect at each price level suggests that there is no interaction. That is, the effect of advertising is not influenced by price—there is no experimental error, and there are no unidentified exogenous variables influencing the observations. Advertising Plan A simply produces sales of 20 more units than Plan B, at least when the price of the good is in the $10 to $14 range.

An examination of the responses to price reveals that a $2 price increase from $10 to $12 reduces sales by 40 units; $R(12, A) - R(10, A) = -40$ and $R(12, B) - R(10, B) = -40$. However, a $2 increase that raises the price from $12 to $14 reduces sales by 60 units; $R(14, A) - R(12, A) = -60$ and $R(14, B) - R(12, B) = -60$. This difference in responses could be due to a nonlinear demand function for the good, experimental error, or the influence of an exogenous variable. The assumption of interaction between price and advertising is rejected since the price-factor effect is the same between $10 and $12 at each level of advertising. The price-factor effect also holds constant between the $12 and $14 level when the advertising level is changed.

Latin Squares

If researchers are quite confident that there is no interaction between factors, they can drastically reduce the cost of a factorial experiment by using a Latin square. A *Latin square* is a special case of factorial design which is always square and which assumes no interaction between factors.

The assumption of no interaction is not as untenable as it might appear. Economic and business literature abounds with successful single-equation linear models based on just such a presumption. This is not to say that one should always assume there is no interaction between factors. However, empirical studies have indicated that interaction often does not occur and that even when it does its effects are often so slight that they can be ignored.

In a conventional 3-factor, 3-level factorial design, 27 different treatments would be required. To simplify matters, we shall assume that the 3 factors are A, B, and C and have levels A_1, A_2, A_3, B_1, B_2, B_3, C_1, C_2, and C_3. These 27 treatments would then be

$A_1B_1C_1$	$A_1B_1C_2$	$A_1B_1C_3$
$A_1B_2C_1$	$A_1B_2C_2$	$A_1B_2C_3$
$A_1B_3C_1$	$A_1B_3C_2$	$A_1B_3C_3$
$A_2B_1C_1$	$A_2B_1C_2$	$A_2B_1C_3$
$A_2B_2C_1$	$A_2B_2C_2$	$A_2B_2C_3$
$A_2B_3C_1$	$A_2B_3C_2$	$A_2B_3C_3$
$A_3B_1C_1$	$A_3B_1C_2$	$A_3B_1C_3$
$A_3B_2C_1$	$A_3B_2C_2$	$A_3B_2C_3$
$A_3B_3C_1$	$A_3B_3C_2$	$A_3B_3C_3$

In a Latin-square design, only 9 treatments would be used

$A_1B_1C_1$	$A_2B_1C_2$	$A_3B_1C_3$
$A_1B_2C_2$	$A_2B_2C_3$	$A_3B_2C_1$
$A_1B_3C_3$	$A_2B_3C_1$	$A_3B_3C_2$

Inspection reveals that the Latin-square design repeats each individual treatment (A_1, A_2, A_3, B_1, B_2, B_3, C_1, C_2, and C_3) 3 times but does not repeat joint treatments such as A_1B_1 or A_1B_2. In contrast, the conventional 3-factorial design repeats both the individual and the joint treatments 3 times. Not repeating the joint treatments has no disadvantages *if* there is no interaction between factors. Hence, the Latin-square design is as statistically satisfactory and considerably more economical for evaluating the effects of variations in A, B, and C.

By definition, a Latin square—sometimes called a "Greco-Latin square"—is square: That is, it is a n × n, or a n × n × n, etc., design. Each factor is thus tried at the same number of levels. This restriction can sometimes be relieved, and the result (n × m, etc.) will still be more efficient than the conventional factorial design.[9]

Table 11-6   **A Latin-Square Design**

		Advertising Plan		
		A_1	A_2	A_3
	$3	$R(3, A_1, C_1)$ 750	$R(3, A_2, C_2)$ 875	$R(3, A_3, C_3)$ 900
Price	$4	$R(4, A_1, C_2)$ 820	$R(4, A_2, C_3)$ 800	$R(4, A_3, C_1)$ 700
	$5	$R(5, A_1, C_3)$ 850	$R(5, A_2, C_1)$ 650	$R(5, A_3, C_2)$ 810

Package Color
C_1 = Red
C_2 = Gold
C_3 = White

[9] For discussion, see William G. Cochran, *Sampling Techniques* (New York: Wiley 1963), p. 229.

To see the uses of the Latin-square design, assume that the analyst wants to test 3 factors—price, advertising, and package color—each at 3 levels. The analyst assumes that the factors do not interact, or that the interaction is so small that it can be ignored. This critical assumption allows a reduction in the number of treatments from 27 to 9 (the Latin square). (However, if the researcher is wrong, if two or more factors do interact substantially, the data will be distorted and he or she will not know it. What seems to be a difference in responses due to experimental error may be largely the result of the unperceived interaction.)

The experiment uses the treatments indicated in Table 11-6. The responses (unit sales) are shown in each cell. The effect of the factors can now be evaluated by aggregating and comparing the responses for each level of each factor. For instance, for Advertising Plan A_1, the aggregate sales were

$$\Sigma A_1 = R(3, A_1, C_1) + R(4, A_1, C_2) + R(5, A_1, C_3)$$

$$\Sigma A_1 = \quad 750 \quad + \quad 820 \quad + \quad 850$$

$$\Sigma A_1 = 2{,}420$$

Sales for all levels and factors were

Advertising	Price	Color
$\Sigma A_1 = 2{,}420$	$\Sigma \$3 = 2{,}525$	$\Sigma C_1 = 2{,}100$
$\Sigma A_2 = 2{,}325$	$\Sigma \$4 = 2{,}320$	$\Sigma C_2 = 2{,}505$
$\Sigma A_3 = 2{,}410$	$\Sigma \$5 = 2{,}310$	$\Sigma C_3 = 2{,}550$

If maximization of sales is the objective (cost data are not provided in this particular problem), then Advertising Plan A_1, a price of $3, and the color gold, are the best choices and 3, A_1, C_2 is the best treatment. However, the Latin-square design has two very important properties that may have eluded the reader. First, it does not reveal the response to the best combination of factor levels if, by chance, the researcher fails to include that combination in the experimental design. In Table 11-6, the best response (900) was obtained from the combination 3, A_3, C_3. However, the aggregates of the factor levels reveal that 3, A_1, C_2 is actually the best combination. Unfortunately, since it was not included in the square, we have no value for its response.

This is a common problem with Latin squares, since the researcher has no way of knowing in advance which combination of factor levels will be the best. Happily, there is often a remedy. When the researcher discovers that she has not included the best treatment in her original design, she simply does another experiment. Of course, this means an additional treatment. However, the total number of treatments will still be far below that required by a conventional factorial design.

A second drawback of Latin squares is that they fail to specify the relationship between the dependent variable (sales, in the example) and each of the independent variables. It is evident that Advertising Plan A_1 will produce more sales than A_2 or A_3, but it is not apparent how many more sales it alone will produce. To find this out, the researcher would have to know the contribution of the other factors, so that their effects could be removed from A's response values.

The problem is evident when one considers the price variable. An increase in price will reduce sales *if* everything else remains equal. This assumption is intuitively acceptable, logically defensible, and borne out by experience when the real price levels are aggregated and compared. However, everything else does not remain equal in a Latin-square design. One cannot measure the factor effect by computing the differences between cells as one would in a conventional factorial experiment.

For example, suppose we were to try to measure the difference between any cell in the $3 row and the adjoining cell in the $4 row. Even where the effect of one factor can be nullified by staying within a given column—say, A_1—the effect of the changes in the levels of the other factor—in this case, color—will prevent us from isolating the effect of the row factor, price. For instance, when the price was raised from $4 to $5 and Advertising Plan A_1 was used, sales increased 30 units. How much of that increase was a result of the change in color from white to gold we cannot know. There are mathematical techniques for specifying each factor's effect on the dependent variable, as well as the size and distribution of the experimental error, given the right data. The fact that the Latin square does not produce data amenable to this kind of analysis is the design's greatest shortcoming.

Problems

1   Consumer-panel data revealed that a firm was selling 12,000 cases per month of its instant coffee in the Boston SMSA. After the introduction of a premium—a free measuring spoon with each jar—sales increased to 12,200 cases per month. During the period when the premium was given, a major competitor cut its price 10 percent in an apparent effort to disrupt the experiment. However, a recent price study showed the firm's price cross elasticity, with respect to the competitor's brand, to be 0.8. (Thus, the competitor's 10 percent price decrease should have induced a decrease of 8 percent in the firm's sales.) What was the effect of the premium on sales?

2   In order to evaluate the usefulness of detail sales personnel, a large food processor decided to experiment. Three detail salespersons were hired, trained, and assigned to a major SMSA, where they were directed to call on 112 specific stores, selected at random from the 224 retailers carrying the firm's product. (The retailers bought the product from independent wholesalers.) A store audit revealed that the total sales of the stores not visited increased from 900 to 980 units during the test period, whereas the sales of the stores visited by the

detail people increased from 890 to 1,142. What was the effect of the detail salespersons on sales?

3   An experiment is designed to test, simultaneously, the effect on sales of a change in a product's package and its size. A series of experimental treatments are applied in a test market in the following order and with the indicated results: (a) with the old package and the old size, sales equal 680; (b) with the old package and the new size, sales equal 780; (c) with the new package and the old size, sales equal 650; and (d) with the new package and the new size, sales equal 760. Evaluate the sales effect of the new package and the new size. Is there any indication of experimental error or interaction between factors? How might the experimental design be improved?

4   If researchers want to test the effect of two colors, three prices, and a promotional deal simultaneously in the New York SMSA, how many experimental treatments will they need? Design the experiment.

5   Can a Latin-square design be used in the preceding problem? If not, what change would be necessary to allow the use of a Latin square? What assumption would be necessary?

Chapter 12
Analysis of Experimental Data

Key Concepts

Chi Square Test
Using a common test of statistical significance to evaluate the effect of an experimental treatment

Analysis of Variance
A method of comparing means to determine if there is a statistically significant difference between outcomes

Bayesian Statistics
Using experimental data to produce more reliable probabilities

Key Terms

variation
variance
deviation
analysis of variance

Diagnosing Differences

The analysis of experimental data focuses mainly on differences: Are the outcomes of the various treatments or treatment levels different? If so, are the differences statistically significant? Or, is it likely that the observed differences are due to chance variations in the data?

Often these questions yield to simple observation and common sense. Other times the noise that is so common in the marketplace obscures the answer. Strong analytical tools must be invoked.

Chi Square Test

Often one can construct a tableau of the experimental data and apply the chi square test. (The technique was explained in Chapter 6.) For instance,

Exhibit 12-1   Tableau of Experimental Data

	Sales			
Pair	Experimental Units		Control Units	
A	Store 1;	80 cases	Store 2;	64 cases
B	Store 3;	100 cases	Store 4;	98 cases
C	Store 5;	72 cases	Store 6;	81 cases
D	Store 7;	120 cases	Store 8;	118 cases
E	Store 9;	48 cases	Store 10;	44 cases
F	Store 11;	30 cases	Store 12;	30 cases

one might experiment with a new point-of-purchase display in six test units (stores). Each test unit could be matched with a control unit of similar characteristics. The two frequency distributions—the test-unit observations and the control-unit observations—could be compared as shown in Exhibit 12-1. The chi square test would then be applied to determine whether there was a statistically significant difference between the two distributions.[1] If not, management would be foolish to allocate more funds to the new point-of-purchase display.

Means and Variation

Variation is the dispersion of observations about their mean. A common measurement of variation is *variance*, the average (mean) of the deviations squared. A *deviation* is simply the difference between an observation and the mean of the observations.[2]

In experimentation, our interest often rests on means and their differences. Variance is sometimes analyzed to determine if those differences are significant.

If the difference in the mean response to two treatments is very small, it is probably due to random error and should not be considered evidence of the superiority of one treatment. If the difference in mean response is very large, it probably is due to the superior effectiveness of one treatment. For example, if an average of 10 items per store were sold in the test market during the period before a test commercial was shown and an average of 10.1 items were sold during the test period, one could hardly argue that the commercial had a significant effect. Conversely, if an average of 10 items were being sold before the commercial was shown and an average of 20 items were sold during the test period, one could hardly doubt the ad's ability to stimulate demand.

---

[1] SPSS and many other statistical packages make this test extremely easy. One simply specifies the chi-square option when running the usual cross tabulations.

[2] For further explanation, see Appendix 2.

As the analyst's experience grows, his or her intuition will improve and he or she should be able to make reliable judgments even when the difference in means is not so extreme as it is in the example. However, even a skillful analyst cannot rely entirely on subjective evaluations. There are many instances when it is hard to know whether a difference is a meaningful one. This is true even when only a single factor is involved. When more than one factor is being manipulated or observed, their effects cannot be disentangled, much less evaluated, without applying analysis of variance or other multi-variate analytical techniques.

Analysis of Variance: Basic Concepts

Definition

Analysis of variance is a tool from inferential statistics used to determine if the difference(s) between means of two or more samples is small enough to be attributable to chance or large enough to be attributed, at least in part, to the factors under study. It is used in market experiments and in other types of marketing research to determine the significance of the out-comes and to separate the effects of different variables. In essence, analysis of variance compares the mean responses of different subsets of test units.

Variance is analyzed in determining the significance in the difference between means, for the dispersion of observed values about their mean indicates the amount of chance variation present in the data. Analysis of variance determines if this chance variation is sufficient to account for the difference between means. If there is no statistically significant difference between means, we assume the samples are the same with respect to the characteristic under study.

Assumptions and Preconditions

Like other analytical methods, variance analysis demands certain assumptions and imposes certain preconditions. This is true whether we are dealing with single- or multiple-factor experiments or any other method of gathering and comparing data on different segments of a population.

The first assumption required is that the data are generated by test units that were randomly selected from normally distributed populations. The results of an experiment are of little use if they cannot be generalized to the universe the researcher wants to evaluate. The generalizations emerging from an analysis of variance will be invalid if the test units are not a represen-tative sample of the universe or if the probability of their deviating from the norm cannot be estimated. Random selection is the only way to ensure this. Thus, in order to use variance analysis, the researcher must be able to properly define the universe (usually a market population), identify its members, and obtain a random selection of experimental units. This is not always possible, at least not entirely. Nevertheless, the assumption of random selection is implicit in both the selection of test units and the assignment of treatments (cells in the matrix). If the constraints of the real world preclude perfect randomization of the test units, the researcher will have to make whatever accommodations reality and conscience will allow.

The second assumption required is that the data are *homoscedastic*— that they have a constant standard deviation (hence, constant variation and variance). In analyses of variance, it is assumed that the data sets—the columns, rows, and cells—used to compute the variance due to chance (experimental error) are equally vulnerable to random variation.

The third assumption required is that the observations used to estimate the variance due to chance are independent with respect to random variation. In other words, the chance variation in one observation is not influenced by the chance variation in another observation.

The fourth assumption required is that the effects of the various sources of variation—the factor treatments, interaction, and experimental error—are additive, not multiplicative. Without this assumption, the technique prescribed for the separation of the total variation into its components is inappropriate and the results are invalid.

The most important precondition is that the data be discrete and not continuous. The factor levels must have discrete values. This is usually an attainable goal since most marketing variables are discrete, although they are frequently treated as continuous to simplify computations. When the data are continuous, or include a large number of different discrete values, they can be transformed by grouping the observations into convenient classes, such as a series of price intervals. Usually this is unnecessary, since the essence of experimentation is manipulation of endogenous variables by the researcher, who has the option of selecting discrete values.

One precondition common to most quantitative analyses, but *not* required for an analysis of variance, is the quantification of the factors. This is one of the method's great virtues as far as marketing research is concerned. Various combinations of purely qualitative factors such as colors, advertising copy, distribution channels, and package designs can be tested without having to assign arbitrary numerical values to the treatments. If management needs to evaluate, say, alternative package designs, experimentation combined with an analysis of variance is an excellent solution. Analysis of variance is among the market researcher's most valuable analytical tools.

Analysis of Variance: Single-Factor Experiments

The single-factor experiment, because it is the simplest, serves as a convenient stepping-stone to a more detailed exploration of variance analysis. For example, assume that management is considering a new promotional tactic.

Table 12-1 Analysis of Variance Computations for a Single-Factor Experiment Testing the Relative Effectiveness of Two Promotional Instruments (Stage 1: Preliminary Calculations)

	Experimental Treatments (A)				
	Treatment Set 1 (Contest)		Treatment Set 2 (Premium)		
Test Unit (i)	Sales with A_1 $(Y_{j=1})$	Test Unit (i)	Sales with A_2 $(Y_{j=2})$	Total (ΣY)
1	50	6	53	103
2	46	7	54	100
3	45	8	47	92
4	51	9	49	100
5	48	10	57	105
Totals	$\Sigma Y_1 = 240$		$\Sigma Y_2 = 260$	$\Sigma\Sigma Y = 500$
No. of observations	$n_1 = 5$		$n_2 = 5$	$\Sigma n = 10$
Means	$\bar{Y}_1 = 48$		$\bar{Y}_2 = 52$	$\bar{\bar{Y}} = 50$

Summations of squared deviations:
$\Sigma y_1^2 = (50 - 48)^2 + (46 - 48)^2 + (45 - 48)^2 + (51 - 48)^2 + (48 - 48)^2 = 26$
$\Sigma y_2^2 = (53 - 52)^2 + (54 - 52)^2 + (47 - 52)^2 + (49 - 52)^2 + (57 - 52)^2 = 64$
$\Sigma\Sigma y^2 = 26 + 64 = 90$
$\Sigma \bar{y}^2 = n_1(\bar{Y}_1 - \bar{\bar{Y}})^2 + n_2(\bar{Y}_2 - \bar{\bar{Y}})^2 = 5(48 - 50)^2 + 5(52 - 50)^2 = 40$

Preliminary evaluation has narrowed the choice to two alternatives: a contest, A_1, and a premium, A_2. The final selection is to be based on a market experiment. Ten SMSAs have been selected as test units and randomly distributed between two groups, or treatment sets, which are assumed to be homogeneous. Group 1 is subjected to treatment A_1, and Group 2 is given treatment A_2. The results are shown in Table 12-1.

On first inspection, it appears that alternative A_2, the premium, is the more effective promotional device. Group 2 sold 260 units during the test period, while Group 1 sold only 240. The average test unit in Group 2 sold 52 units, and the average test unit in Group 1 sold only 48. However, a closer examination of the outcomes reveals an inconsistency: *Some* Group 1 test units outsold *some* Group 2 units. There is considerable variation among test-unit responses that cannot be explained by the difference in treatments. This variation is found within the columns. For instance, the sales of Group 1 units varied from a low of 45 to a high of 51, even though the group was supposedly homogeneous and the test units all received the same experimental treatment. The variation in Group 2 is even worse, ranging from 47 to 57 units. This suggests that there are random disturbances present in the data *which may also account for the difference between the test-group totals and means.* Further analysis is needed before the researchers can assume that there is a significant difference between the two groups with respect to sales, hence that treatment A_2 is truly more effective than treatment A_1.

Testing the Null Hypothesis

Statistically speaking, an analysis of variance tests the hypothesis that the true means of the test-unit sets are equal. The null hypothesis, H_0, is that $\mu_1 = \mu_2$. (If several factors—say, three prices or five advertisements—are involved, the null hypothesis is $\mu_1 = \mu_2 = \ldots \mu_n$.) If the null hypothesis is correct, then the test-unit sets are from the same universe with respect to the dependent variable (usually sales), and the treatments under evaluation have the same effect on each set. Thus, there is no difference in their ability to influence sales.

If the null hypothesis fails the test, we must conclude that the means are truly different, $\mu_1 \neq \mu_2$. That is, we cannot attribute the difference in observed means to chance variation in the observations. The treatments under study then do have different effects.

The following algorithm gives us the procedure for the analysis of variance for a single-factor experiment involving two or more treatments. For convenience, it is broken into two stages totalling 11 steps.

Stage 1: Preliminary Calculations

1   Assign each observation, Y_i, to its respective treatment set, j. (j identifies the set of elements receiving a particular treatment, t.)

2   Sum the observations for each treatment set, ΣY_j, and for the total experiment, $\Sigma\Sigma Y$.

3   Compute the mean for each set, $\bar{Y}_j$, and for the total experiment, $\bar{\bar{Y}}$.

4   Compute the square of the deviation for each observation, $(Y_{ij} - \bar{Y}_j)^2$. This is the deviation of Y_{ij} from the treatment-set mean, $\bar{Y}_j$.

5   Sum the squared deviations for each set (Σy_j^2). This is the internal variation for that set, j.

6   Add up the sums of the squared deviations of all the sets to get the total variation, $\Sigma\Sigma y^2$. Also sum the squared deviations of the set means $(\Sigma\bar{y}^2 = \Sigma n_j(\bar{Y} - \bar{\bar{Y}})^2)$.

Stage 2: Computation of Critical Statistics

7   Calculate the degrees of freedom, *d.f.*, for each source of variation (the experimental treatment, t, and experimental, or random error, R). The degrees of freedom equals the number of observations used in calculating the variation minus the number of statistics estimated in calculating the variation.

8   Compute the variance, s^2, for each source of variation (the experimental treatment, t, and experimental, or random, error, R) by dividing the source's variation by its degrees of freedom: $s_t^2 = \Sigma\bar{y}^2/d.f._{\cdot t}$ and $s_R^2 = \Sigma\Sigma y^2/d.f._{\cdot R}$.

9   Compute the F-ratio, F_C. $F_C = s_t^2/s_R^2$.

10   Find the critical F-ratio, F_T, at the desired level of significance, *s.l.*, using a table of F-values.

11   Compare the computed F-value, F_C, with the table F-value, F_T, to test the null hypothesis that there is no significant difference between the effects of the experimental treatments ($\mu_1 = \mu_2$). If $F_C > F_T$, it must be rejected.

The Method in Practice: An Application

Let us now return to the experiment whose results are given in Tables 12-1 and 12-2 to see how this procedure might be followed in practice.

First, we assign the observations involved in treatment A_1, the contest, to set 1 and those involved in treatment A_2, the premium, to set 2 (Step 1). We then add up the responses for each set and for the entire experiment and compute the means (Steps 2 and 3). Next, we compute the square of the deviations and sum these values for each set (Steps 4 and 5). Then we take the sum of the summed squares of the deviations of sets and means (Step 6).

Next, we calculate the degrees of freedom for each source of variation. (Step 7). The variation between treatment sets is presumably due to the difference in treatments applied to Groups 1 and 2. Two observational values are used in calculating this variation. These are the means of the two columns, $\bar{Y}_1$ and $\bar{Y}_2$. One statistic, the experimental mean, $\bar{\bar{Y}}$, is also used. Hence, the variation attributable to treatment effects has one degree of freedom ($d.f. = 2 - 1 = 1$).

The variation within treatment sets, on the other hand, is presumably due to experimental (random) error. Ten observational values ($i = 1, 2, \ldots 10$) are used in computing the sum of the sum of the variation within the treatment sets, and two statistics, $\bar{Y}_1$ and $\bar{Y}_2$. Hence, the variation attributable to experimental error has eight degrees of freedom ($d.f. = 10 - 2 = 8$).

Next, we calculate the variance, s^2, for each source of variation (Step 8). At this point we are ready to use the F-test to determine the likelihood that the two treatment sets are part of the same universe, as far as sales are con-

Table 12-2   **Analysis-of-Variance Computations for a Single-Factor Experiment Testing the Relative Effectiveness of Two Promotional Instruments (Stage 2: Computation of Critical Statistics)**

Sources of Variation	Amount of Variation	Degrees of Freedom	Variance	Computed F-Ratio	Table F-Ratio
Experimental treatment, t (variation between treatment sets)	$\Sigma \bar{y}^2 = 40$	$d.f._{\cdot t} = 1$	$s_t^2 = 40$	$F_C = 3.54$	$F_T = 5.32^a$
Experimental (random) error, R (variation within sets)	$\Sigma \Sigma y^2 = 90$	$d.f._{\cdot R} = 8$	$s_R^2 = 11.3$		

[a] The requirement of a .05 level of significance is assumed.

cerned. If so, there is obviously no difference in the effect on sales of the two promotional treatments. The null hypothesis will stand.

The calculated F-ratio, F_C, is 3.54 (Step 9), and the table F-ratio, F_T, is 5.32 at the 0.05 significance level (Step 10). To use the table of F-values, we need to know the degrees of freedom for the numerator and denominator of the F-ratio equation. These were calculated (Step 7) as 1 and 8, respectively.

F_C is obviously less than F_T (3.54 < 5.32); hence, the null hypothesis cannot be rejected. There is insufficient statistical evidence to support the contention that there is a difference in sales effect between the contest and the premium. Another selection criterion is needed. Cost is the obvious choice. If costs are equal, then the start-up time needed, the anticipated reaction of competitors, distribution problems, or some other alternative criterion can be used to choose between the two alternatives.

If researchers still believe there is a difference in the effectiveness (with respect to sales) of the two strategies, they have two options. First they can obtain additional observations, if they are willing to spend still more time and money on the project, by expanding the experiment to include more test units or replicating the original experiment. This would increase the degrees of freedom, ideally without increasing the variation significantly. The net result would be the rejection of the null hypothesis or its acceptance at a higher level of significance—say, 0.01. The failure of the experimental results to support the rejection of the null hypothesis, in spite of the difference in treatment means, may be due to an inadequate number of observations. In this case, more observations would remedy the problem. Either way, the decision-maker would have more confidence in the decision.

The researchers' second option is to use the original data and computations, evaluating them at a lower level of significance. For instance, if the *s.l.* were reduced to 0.10, F_T would drop to 3.46, which is less than F_C, and the null hypothesis could be rejected. However, by rejecting the null hypothesis the analysts open the door to a Type I error (rejecting a true statement). Going from *s.l.* = 0.05 to *s.l.* = 0.10 doubles the probability of a Type I error (it is now 10 percent). However, Type I error will not really matter in the example, since management must choose between the contest and the premium anyway. If the experiment favors the premium when in fact there is no difference between the two alternatives, no harm is done. [Note that the sum of the treatment outcomes (ΣY_1 and ΣY_2)—hence, their means ($\bar{Y}_1$ and $\bar{Y}_2$)—favor the premium, not the contest. However, this information is useless unless the analysis of variance demonstrates that there is a significant difference between the two.]

On the other hand, increasing the probability of a Type I error reduces the probability of a Type II error (by an undetermined amount). In the example, this would benefit the firm, since a Type II error (accepting a false statement) could be harmful. If the premium is truly a more effective promotional instrument and the null hypothesis is not rejected, then management could easily select the inferior alternative. In fact, the prudent approach under these circumstances would be to test the hypothesis at the 0.25 significance level. This would mean a 25 percent chance of making a Type I error, but, given the situation, that is of no consequence. The probability of making a Type II error would be greatly reduced, and that is very important in this particular example.

Selection of a significance level—a judgmental, not a statistical, decision—is extremely important from the viewpoint of the decision-maker. The relative hazards of a Type I and Type II error should always be considered in the experimental design. If a Type I error will be more painful to the firm than a Type II error, a high significance level—*s.l.* = 0.05 or 0.10—should be used. If the convers is true (as it was in the example), a low level of significance—*s.l.* = 0.25—should be used.

Analysis of Variance: Multiple-Factor Experiments

As we have already explained, there is frequently an advantage to manipulating more than one controllable independent variable or observing the effects of one or more uncontrollable variables. For instance, the researcher may want to manipulate both price and advertising, while also observing the effect of the size of the store on the sale of a product. Thus, the effects of the three variables must be separated and evaluated in analyzing the results of the experiment. The basic procedure of variance analysis is the same as in single-factor experiments, but the researcher needs much more data and the manipulations are more complicated. In fact, when more than three factors are involved it is best to forego an analysis of variance in favor of regression analysis, using dummy variables for nonquantitative factors.

Steps in Multiple-Factor Analysis

The first step in a multiple-factor analysis is to prepare a treatment-set matrix and assign the test units to cells. If the experiment involves two factors, A and B, each cell will contain a different combination of those factors. Several observations will be needed for each combination order to estimate the experimental error. These can be obtained by assigning several test units to each cell, or, if test units are in short supply, the experiment can be replicated over time—using only a few test units in each cell. One test unit per cell will suffice if the researcher is willing to subject it to the same experimental treatment several times.

After the experiment is executed and the outcomes are posted in the matrix, the columns and the rows are totaled and their means calculated. The entire matrix is also totaled, and an overall average, $\bar{\bar{Y}}$, is computed.

At this point, the analyst may be tempted to make some intuitive judgments about the experimental treatments' effects on the dependent variable. This is not necessarily a bad idea, for the sensitivity of sales to one or both of the factors may be obvious, especially to a skilled analyst. However, the variations in the observed data can be due to either factor, to chance (experimental error), or to interaction between the factors. The total variation should be broken down into its respective components before any particular source of variation is credited with having a significant effect on the dependent variable. A mere visual inspection of the raw data, the summations, or the means can be very misleading.

Total variation is analyzed by first computing the total variation between the columns, which represent the different levels of factor A. Next, the total variation between rows, representing the different levels of factor B, is computed. Then the total variation within the cells is calculated. This variation must be due to experimental error, since all the observations within a given cell are subjected to the same experimental treatment.

When the variations between the columns and rows and within the cells are aggregated, they may not equal the total variation, because of interaction between the factors. Interaction is not uncommon. For instance, sales may be much more sensitive to personal selling when advertising expenditures are large than when advertising outlays are meager. Or sales may vary significantly when price is manipulated in a discount store, but be fairly insensitive to price in the more prestigious specialty shops. In the multiple-factor model, interaction is represented by the difference, if any, between the total variation and the sum of the column, row, and cell variations.

Rather than computing interaction variation directly, we shall first compute the total variation and then subtract the sum of the column, row, and cell variations. The total variation is found by simply aggregating the variation of each observation in the experiment, using $\bar{\bar{Y}}$ as the mean.

The dimension initially used in measuring variation in the analysis of variance process is the squared deviation. The deviation is simply the difference between an observation and a mean. It can also be the difference between the mean of a subset of experimental observations and the overall mean. The squared deviation is a convenient measure of variation because of its unique mathematical and statistical properties, not the least of which is the elimination of the minus signs by the squaring process. In addition, the squared deviations can be easily converted to variances by correcting them for degrees of freedom. Variance is the common statistic in the formal measurement of variation, and its computation admits the use of a powerful set of statistical tools.

The variance is computed for each source of variation by simply dividing the variation by the appropriate number of degrees of freedom. The formulas for the different components of variation and for the degrees of freedom used in the analysis of a two-factor experiment are shown in Tables 12-3 and 12-4.

After the variations are converted to variances, the F-ratios are computed by applying the same formula used in single-factor analysis, $F_C = s_c^2/s_R^2$. The analyst simply divides the variance attributed to the factors under examination by the variance attributed to experimental error. If this value, F_C, equals or exceeds the F-ratio from the table, F_T, the null hypothesis that there is no significant relationship between the dependent variable and the factor under examination is rejected. A statistical relationship does exist between the two variables.

Table 12-3   **Formulas for Computing the Components of Total Variation in a Two-Factor Experiment**

Variation between columns (attributable to treatment A), V_A

$$V_A = \sum_{j=1}^{a} [n_j(\bar{Y}_j - \bar{\bar{Y}})^2] \qquad [12.1]$$

Variation between rows (attributable to treatment B), V_B

$$V_B = \sum_{i=1}^{b} [n_i(\bar{Y}_i - \bar{\bar{Y}})^2] \qquad [12.2]$$

Variation within cells (attributable to chance, i.e., experimental error), V_C

$$V_C = \sum_{\substack{i=1 \\ j=1}}^{\substack{b \\ a}} \sum_{r}^{n_r} (Y_{r_{ij}} - \bar{Y}_{ij})^2 \qquad [12.3]$$

Total variation, V_T

$$V_T = \sum_{\substack{i=1 \\ j=1}}^{\substack{b \\ a}} \sum_{r=1}^{n} (Y_{r_{ij}} - \bar{\bar{Y}})^2 \qquad [12.4]$$

Variation due to interaction, V_I

$$V_I = V_T - (V_A + V_B + V_C) \qquad [12.5]$$

Variance, s^2, from a given source, X

$$s^2 = \frac{V_X}{d.f._X} \qquad [12.6]$$

where Y = dependent variable (observed value of the outcome)
$\bar{Y}$ = dependent variable (observed value of the outcome)
$\bar{Y}$ = mean of a set of observations
$\bar{\bar{Y}}$ = mean of all the observations
j = level of factor A (column number)
a = total number of factor-A levels (total number of columns)
i = level of factor B
b = total number of factor-B levels
n = total number of observations in a column, row, or cell
N = total number of observations in the experiment
r = number of a particular replication of a treatment (number of an observation in a particular cell)
$d.f.$ = degrees of freedom
V = variation
s^2 = variance

The Method in Practice: An Application

The use of variance analysis in a multiple-factor experiment can be illustrated most easily using a two-factor design. Suppose, for example, that the researcher wants to manipulate a product's price and distribution channel. Three levels of price, $6, $7, and $8, and two distribution channels, discount stores and specialty shops, are being considered. The product could be anything from perfume to a household appliance.

Table 12-4   **Formulas for Computing Degrees of Freedom Needed in a Two-Factor Experiment**[a]

For computing the variance induced by factor A, $d.f._A$

$$d.f._A = a - 1 \qquad\qquad [12.7]$$

For computing the variance induced by factor B, $d.f._B$

$$d.f._B = b - 1 \qquad\qquad [12.8]$$

For computing the variance induced by experimental error (chance variation), $d.f._C$

$$d.f._C = N - (ab) \qquad\qquad [12.9]$$

For computing the variance induced by interaction, $d.f._I$

$$d.f._I = (a - 1)(b - 1) \qquad\qquad [12.10]$$

For computing the variance induced by all the sources of variation, $d.f._T$

$$d.f._T = N - 1, \text{ or} \qquad\qquad [12.11]$$

$$d.f._T = d.f._A + d.f._B + d.f._C + d.f._I \qquad\qquad [12.12]$$

[a] Variables are defined as in Table 12-3.

Table 12-5   **A Multi-Factor Experimental Design Testing Price at Three Levels and Channels at Two Levels**

		Price (A)		
		$6 (1)	$7 (2)	$8 (3)
Channel (B)	Discount stores (1)	Treatments A$_1$ and B$_1$. Five replications using five test units.	Treatments A$_2$ and B$_1$. Five replications using five test units.	Treatments A$_3$ and B$_1$. Five replications using five test units.
	Specialty shops (2)	Treatments A$_1$ and B$_2$. Five replications using five test units.	Treatments A$_2$ and B$_2$. Five replications using five test units.	Treatments A$_3$ and B$_2$. Five replications using five test units.

The experimental design is shown in matrix form in Table 12-5. The price treatments have been arbitrarily assigned to columns and the channel treatments to rows. This creates six cells ($3 \cdot 2 = 6$). Each cell contains a different treatment, and the six cells together contain every possible combination of prices and channels. The subsequent analysis of variance will require a measurement of the variation of the dependent variable, sales, within the cells. Thus, there must be enough test units to replicate each treatment at least several times.

The researchers can repeat the experiment several times using the same set of test units, thereby generating time-series data, or they can use a different set of test units each time, thereby generating cross-sectional data. The first option is usually the easiest and cheapest, but it has the usual disadvantages associated with time-series data. The researchers will have to adjust the data to compensate for the effect of carry-over from previous treatments and seasonal variation. The second option has the usual disadvantages of cross-sectional data. The researchers will have to adjust the data to allow for differences in the test units. For example, a product's sales in New York City could not be compared with its sales in Boston until an adjustment had been made for differences in population, income, buying power, and other significant exogenous variables.

Since we are interested here mainly in the method of variance analysis, not test-unit selection, we shall assume that a representative portion of the firm's total market has been subdivided into 30 territories. The territories are distributed randomly among the six cells, permitting five replications of each treatment. The Y values (sales) are adjusted for differences in exogenous variables between territories. The results are posted in Table 12-6, along with the first set of computed values—the total and mean sales for each treatment and the experiment as a whole.

An examination of the experimental data reveals that sales vary from 34 to 66, averaging 50 per test unit. Sales are clearly sensitive to one or more variables associated with the experiment. The analysts' job is to separate this total variation into its components—each associated with one of the independent variables in the experiment—and evaluate them. The sources of variation are the price and channel used, experimental error, and interaction (between the price and the channel).

The variation introduced by manipulations in price is indicated by the variation between columns (in the example). The variation introduced by a change in channels is indicated by the variation between rows. The variation introduced by experimental error is represented by the variation within the cells. The variation introduced by interaction is represented by the difference between the total variation and the sum of the variations introduced by the changes in prices and channels and by chance (experimental error).

The variation between columns is computed using equation 12.1.

$$V_A = \sum_{j=1}^{a} [n_j(\bar{Y}_j - \bar{\bar{Y}})^2] \qquad \text{(given as equation 12.1)}$$

$$V_A = 10(58.5 - 50)^2 + 10(50.5 - 50)^2 + 10(41.0 - 50)^2$$

(by substitution)

$$V_A = 10(72.25) + 10(0.25) + 10(8.10)$$

(by arithmetic)

$$V_A = 1,535$$

(by arithmetic)

Table 12-6　Data Matrices for an Analysis of Variance in a Multiple-Factor Experiment Raw Data[a]

Channels (i)	Replication (r)	Prices (j) $6 (1)	$7 (2)	$8 (3)	All Prices (Totals)
Discount stores (1)	1	66	48	36	150
	2	60	59	40	159
	3	67	52	35	154
	4	58	51	40	149
	5	59	50	34	143
Specialty shops (2)	1	53	52	45	150
	2	58	45	46	149
	3	51	49	39	139
	4	57	48	46	151
	5	56	51	49	156
All channels (totals)		585	505	410	1,500

Summations and Means

Discount stores (1)	$\sum Y_{11} = 310$ $\bar{Y}_{11} = 62$	$\sum Y_{12} = 260$ $\bar{Y}_{12} = 52$	$\sum Y_{13} = 185$ $\bar{Y}_{13} = 37$	$\sum Y_{1j} = 755$ $\bar{Y}_{1j} = 50.3$
Specialty shops (2)	$\sum Y_{21} = 275$ $\bar{Y}_{21} = 55$	$\sum Y_{22} = 245$ $\bar{Y}_{22} = 49$	$\sum Y_{23} = 225$ $\bar{Y}_{23} = 45$	$\sum Y_{2j} = 745$ $\bar{Y}_{2j} = 49.7$
All channels	$\sum Y_{i1} = 585$ $\bar{Y}_{i1} = 58.5$	$\sum Y_{i2} = 505$ $\bar{Y}_{i2} = 50.5$	$\sum Y_{i3} = 410$ $\bar{Y}_{i3} = 41.0$	$\sum Y = 1,500$ $\bar{Y} = 50$

[a] Cells contain sales figures.

The variation between rows is computed using equation 12.2.

$$V_B = \sum_{i=1}^{b} [n_i(\bar{Y}_i - \bar{\bar{Y}})^2]$$ (given as equation 12.2)

$$V_B = 15(50.3 - 50)^2 + 15(49.7 - 50)^2$$ (by substitution)

$$V_B = 15(0.09) + 15(0.09)$$ (by arithmetic)

$$V_B = 2.7$$ (by arithmetic)

The variation within the cells is computed using equation 12.3.

$$V_C = \sum_{\substack{i=1 \\ j=1}}^{b \; a} \sum_{r}^{n_r} (Y_{r_{ij}} - \bar{Y}_{ij})^2$$ (given as equation 12.3)

$$\sum_{r=1}^{5} (Y_{r_{11}} - \bar{Y}_{11})^2 = (66 - 62)^2 + (60 - 62)^2 + (67 - 62)^2 + (58 - 62)^2$$
$$+ (59 - 62)^2 = 70$$

$$\sum_{r=1}^{5} (Y_{r_{12}} - \bar{Y}_{12})^2 = (48 - 52)^2 + (59 - 52)^2 + (52 - 52)^2 + (51 - 52)^2$$
$$+ (50 - 52)^2 = 70$$

$$\sum_{r=1}^{5} (Y_{r_{13}} - \bar{Y}_{13})^2 = (36 - 37)^2 + (40 - 37)^2 + (35 - 37)^2 + (40 - 37)^2$$
$$+ (34 - 37)^2 = 32$$

$$\sum_{r=1}^{5} (Y_{r_{21}} - \bar{Y}_{21})^2 = (53 - 55)^2 + (58 - 55)^2 + (51 - 55)^2 + (57 - 55)^2$$
$$+ (56 - 55)^2 = 34$$

$$\sum_{r=1}^{5} (Y_{r_{22}} - \bar{Y}_{22})^2 = (52 - 49)^2 + (45 - 49)^2 + (49 - 49)^2 + (48 - 49)^2$$
$$+ (51 - 49)^2 = 30$$

$$\sum_{r=1}^{5} (Y_{r_{23}} - \bar{Y}_{23})^2 = (45 - 45)^2 + (46 - 45)^2 + (39 - 45)^2 + (46 - 45)^2$$
$$+ (49 - 45)^2 = 54$$

$$V_C = 70 + 70 + 32 + 34 + 30 + 54$$

$$V_C = 290$$

The total variation is computed by summing the squared differences between the observations and the overall mean of each observed value, as indicated by equation 12.4.

$$V_T = \sum_{\substack{i=1 \\ j=1}}^{\substack{b \\ a}} \sum_{r=1}^{n} (Y_{r_{ij}} - \bar{\bar{Y}})^2 \qquad \text{(given as equation 12.4)}$$

$$V_T = (66 - 50)^2 + (48 - 50)^2 + (36 - 50)^2 + \cdots (49 - 50)^2$$

$$\text{(by substitution)}$$

$$V_T = 2,130 \qquad \text{(by arithmetic)}$$

The variation introduced by the interaction between experimental treatments is found simply by summing all the other components of total variation and subtracting that sum from the total variation. Equation 12.5 applies:

$$V_I = V_T - (V_A + V_B + V_C) \qquad \text{(given as equation 12.5)}$$

$$V_I = 2,130 - (1,535 + 2.7 + 290) \qquad \text{(by substitution)}$$

$$V_I = 302.3 \qquad \text{(by arithmetic)}$$

The next task is to compute the degrees of freedom for each source of variation, using equations 12.7 through 12.12, so that the variation can be converted to variance. The results are posted in Table 12-7, along with the other critical statistics.

The variance is computed simply by dividing each type of variation by the appropriate number of degrees of freedom, using equation 12.6. Again, the results are posted in Table 12-7.

Table 12-7 **Critical Statistical Values for an Analysis of Variance in a Multiple-Factor Experiment**

Sources of Variation	Amount of Variation (V)	Degrees of Freedom (d.f.)	Variance (s²)	Computed F-Ratio (F_C)	Table F-Ratio[a] (F_T)
Price	1,535.0	2	727.5	60.12	5.61
Channel	2.7	1	2.7	.22	7.82
Experimental Error	290.0	24	12.1	—	—
Interaction	302.3	2	151.2	12.49	5.61
Total	2,130.0	29			

[a] *s.l.* = .01

The final step, the calculation of the F-ratios, is accomplished simply by dividing the variance from each source by the variance attributed to experimental error, s_R^2. The results are shown in Table 12-7, along with the table values of the F-ratios (from Appendix 4). To find the table F-ratio, we need only to know the degrees of freedom associated with each numerator (each kind of variance other than s_R^2) and the degrees of freedom associated with the denominator (the variance due to experimental error), which have already been calculated. In the example, the denominator *d.f.* is 24.

By comparing the computed F-ratio, F_C, with the table F-ratio, F_T, we can test the null hypothesis for each source of variation at the desired level of significance (*s.l.* = 0.01 in the example). If F_C is equal to or greater than F_T, the hypothesis is rejected. In other words, we can test the proposition that there is no significant relationship between the dependent variable, sales, and each of the factors being manipulated. In addition, we can test the proposition that there is no significant interrelationship between factors, as far as their effect on sales is concerned.

Obviously there is a significant relationship between sales and price in the example. Even at the 0.01 significance level (a confidence level of 0.99), the computed F-ratio far exceeds the table F-ratio and the null hypothesis must be rejected. Surprisingly, the distribution channel has virtually no effect on sales. Even if the significance level were reduced to 0.25, the null hypothesis would still stand (F_C = 0.22 and F_T = 1.39 at *s.l.* = 0.25).

There is a significant interaction between experimental factors (the price and the channel). Even at the 0.01 significance level, the null hypothesis must be rejected. This fact has important marketing implications. Sales are significantly less sensitive to price in the specialty shops than in the discount stores. Price is clearly elastic when discount stores are used, but slightly inelastic when specialty stores are used.[3] Revenue can be maximized by making the price $8 and selling through the specialty shops. Of course, the ultimate objective of the firm is to maximize profit, not revenue, and the final decision would have to take into account the total-cost function also.

Bayesian Techniques and Regression Analysis

Bayesian Statistics

Sometimes an experiment is run in order to upgrade subjective probabilities provided by marketing executives or analysts. These prior probabilities—so

---

[3] Price is *elastic* when a percentage increase in price produces a greater percentage decrease in sales. Price is *inelastic* when a percentage increase in price produces a smaller percentage decrease in sales. For a discussion of price elasticity, see Walter B. Wentz *Marketing* (St Paul, MN: West Publishing Co., 1979), pp. 361–367.

named because they are estimated before any empirical data are gathered—are really statements of the marketers' intuitive appraisals of the success potential of a given alternative. They can be incorporated into the analysis using Bayesian statistics.

For example, suppose a firm is confronted with a new-product decision. It must decide whether to introduce a new product in its national market. The consensus among the executives—including the product-line manager, the director of marketing research, and others—is that the probability of success is 0.70.

A successful product, designated outcome A_1, is defined as one that will produce a million or more dollars in sales annually nationwide. Conversely, an unsuccessful product, designated outcome A_2, is defined as one that will produce less than a million dollars in sales annually. Since $P(A_1) = 0.70$, $P(A_2) = 0.30$. Of course, these are subjective (judgment) probabilities.

The firm has done considerable test marketing in the past, and experience shows that sales of products destined for success in the national market exceed 5,000 units in the test market 90 percent of the time. This outcome, test-market sales greater than 5,000, is designated B. Thus, $P(B|A_1) = 0.90$. Experience also shows that test-market sales can exceed 5,000 units when a product will be unsuccessful in the national market. This has happened in 20 percent of the cases involving products unsuccessful nationally. Thus, $P(B|A_2) = 0.20$. These are objective probabilities, for they are based on empirical data.

If a test-market experiment is conducted and the outcome is B (test market sales exceed 5,000), Bayes' Rule can be used to upgrade the prior probability of success to a presumably more reliable posterior probability that also reflects the empirical findings—in other words, to find the probability of A_1 given the reality of B. What is $P(A_1|B)$? The answer is found as follows

$$P(A_1|B) = \frac{P(B|A_1) \cdot P(A_1)}{P(B|A_1) \cdot P(A_1) + P(B|A_2) \cdot P(A_2)}$$

(given as equation A2.23)

$$P(A_1|B) = \frac{0.90(0.70)}{0.90(0.70) + 0.20(0.30)} \qquad \text{(by substitution)}$$

$$P(A_1|B) = 0.91 \qquad \text{(by arithmetic)}$$

The posterior probability of the new product's success is 0.91, which is far more likely to encourage a favorable decision than the prior probability of 0.70. Furthermore, the new value reflects the information provided by the market experiment. The intuition of the marketing experts has been combined with the empirical findings of the researcher. The Bayesian method has combined the subjective information with the objective data to produce a conditional probability. This is presumably a better index of success than could be provided by classical statistical techniques, because it takes into consideration a greater amount of information.

We should point out, once again, that care must be taken in translating academic arguments into practical applications. A case has just been made for the use of market experimentation to complement management judgment, thus increasing the quality of information upon which an important marketing decision is to be based. But market experimentation should *not* be authorized until a value analysis has been made. In the preceding example, management should have asked whether the additional information and posterior probabilities obtainable were truly worth the direct expense, plus the opportunity costs, of the experiment. The latter include the losses that can result from tipping off the competition about the product and delaying its introduction in the national market. In short, the cure can be worse than the disease.

Regression Analysis

Frequently regression analysis—a rigorous statistical method for estimating the relationships between variables—is more appropriate for processing experimental data than variance analysis. This is especially true when the data are continuous and the analyst is anxious to specify relationships between variables as well as test for significance. If three or more factors are being evaluated simultaneously, regression analysis is often the most appropriate analytical tool. In fact, experiments are often designed especially to generate data for this method.

Regression analysis requires two assumptions: (1) that the dependent variable is a continuous function and (2) that all the variables are metric. However, practical accommodations are usually possible. To be truly continuous, a variable must have an infinite number of points over its domain. (Were it plotted, there would be no breaks in the curve.) This is seldom true of marketing variables. For instance, there is no such thing as automobile sales of 1,238,602.35679 units. However, continuity can usually be assumed for purposes of computation and the answers rounded off to realistic values. The problem of quantification can sometimes be accommodated by using dummy variables. Interaction is referred to as "joint correlation" or "multi-collinearity" in regression analysis. It can be dealt with using several techniques that are discussed later in the book.

The process of designing and executing an experiment is essentially the same regardless of the method used to process the data. Test units are selected, treatments are assigned, and raw data are generated by the same means for a regression analysis as for an analysis of variance. Even certain analytical tools, such as the F-distribution used in the determination of significance, are common to both methods. (Regression analysis is explored in detail in Part 7.)

Problems

1   Apply the chi-square test to the data in Exhibit 12-1 to determine if the experimental treatment made a statistically significant difference in sales.

2   A homogeneous set of ten test units (stores) are selected to evaluate a point-of-purchase promotional program. Five stores are used as experimental, and five as control, units. During the course of the experiment, the experimental units sell, respectively, 8, 9, 7, 8, and 10 cases of the firm's product. The control units sell 9, 6, 6, 7, and 8 cases, respectively. Evaluate the promotional program, using variance analysis.

3   A multiple-factor experiment is designed to evaluate two advertising strategies, 1 and 2, and three package designs, A, B, and C. Thirty-six stores are selected as test units. Their sales (adjusted for differences in exogenous variables) are as follows

Treatment Set	Sales
(1, A)	90, 95, 93, 100, 92, 95
(1, B)	90, 94, 96, 88, 82, 90
(1, C)	69, 80, 85, 83, 78, 75
(2, A)	70, 62, 90, 77, 81, 90
(2, B)	75, 80, 79, 75, 76, 75
(2, C)	76, 58, 75, 70, 71, 70

Evaluate the different advertising strategies and package designs, using variance analysis.

4   Discuss the assumptions and preconditions implicit in the experiment described in question 3, and suggest some possible conditions (in the marketplace) that might compromise them.

5   A consultant is engaged to evaluate the marketability of a new product. He estimates the chance of success to be only 0.5. Given this less-than-optimistic appraisal, but still feeling enthusiastic about the product, management elects to supplement its consultant's opinion with an experiment. A pilot production run is made and the new product is introduced into a test market where it is successful. Past experience indicates a product that will be successful nationally is successful in the test market 80 percent of the time. A truly unsuccessful product (nationally) will succeed in the test market 30 percent of the time. Using the available information, estimate the success probability of the new product.

Part 5
Summary

Market experimentation entails the manipulation of one or more independent marketing variables to determine their effect on a dependent variable, usually sales. It is frequently used in consumer-goods industries to evaluate promotion, price, and product alternatives. Test markets are usually used for this purpose.

Market experimentation can have one or two objectives. The first is the testing of a hypothesis. This objective is always present, at least by implication. The second is the specification of relationships between variables.

Although it is a very useful tool for causation studies, market experimentation has several limitations. The researcher must take into consideration the compatibility, contamination, and mortality of test units, as well as time, realism, product divisibility, security, and cost.

The validity of market experiments is vulnerable to compromise. External validity—the representativeness of the test units—can be lessened by systematic error induced by improper selection techniques. Interaction also lessens external validity. Internal validity—the correctness of the apparent relationship between variables—can be compromised by time, test-unit maturation, the testing itself, the instruments used, regression, differential selection, mortality, and interaction.

Experimental designs vary in complexity, sophistication, power, and cost. Often a basic design will suffice, especially if the researcher is satisfied with manipulating a single variable and can adjust the data for known changes in extraneous forces. Such adjustments usually require the use of both control and experimental units.

Experimental error is almost always present in experimental data and can seldom be removed. However, if test units are randomly selected, it can be estimated and expressed as a confidence interval about the estimated value of the population parameter.

Factorial designs allow the concurrent manipulation of two or more variables. This makes the experiment more powerful, and often more efficient, than basic designs (which allow only one variable to be changed). The most efficient factorial design is the Latin square. However, it is valid only when there is no interaction between variables.

The tools of data analysis—especially analysis of variance—are used to confirm the existence of a significant relationship between marketing variables. Such relationships may be implied by experimental data, when in fact they do not actually exist. Without such an analysis, the results of an experiment can be very misleading.

Analysis of variance provides the researcher with a means of testing hypotheses, using experimental data. It focuses on the means of samples or of the subsets of test units.

The chi-square test is also applicable. For instance, the chi-square test might be applied to determine if the distribution of responses in a group of test units is significantly different from those observed in a group of corresponding control units.

Bayesian statistics can also be used, allowing the researcher to explicitly include judgment probabilities in the analysis. Regression analysis, which we study later, is often applicable to experimental data. It allows the researcher to rigorously estimate relationships between variables.

CASE STUDY 5

Pacific Telephone and Telegraph Company: An Advertising Experiment

John G. Myers (*John G. Myers, Ph.D., is Associate Professor of Marketing, School of Business Administration, University of California at Berkeley. Professor Myers acknowledges the assistance and cooperation of the Pacific Telephone and Telegraph Company in the preparation of this case. He gives special thanks to Mr. Clyde Rich, Supervising Statistician, for providing source material*)

The Pacific Telephone and Telegraph Company is the largest supplier of residential and industrial telephones and related services in the western United States. It is also affiliated with one of the nation's biggest corporations, the American Telephone and Telegraph Company. One service Pacific provides is known as "DA," or "Directory Assistance." By dialing a three-digit number, a caller can request, from a service representative or operator, the phone number of any other party with a listed telephone. DA is a logical extension of the services generally offered to any residential or industrial customer.

The volume of DA calls for the total Pacific Telephone system was large and still growing in 1971. In one average-sized California city, for example, the volume of DA calls had increased from 47,000 calls per day in 1969 to a projected 59,000 calls per day in 1972. These figures were based on the month (September) that tended to be the highest-usage month of the year. Generally, the summer months and the fall and Christmas period were high-usage months, although there was a marked and regular decline in November. DA service was a significant cost item. The labor and equipment involved in maintaining the service in the early 1970s was costing the company in the neighborhood of $40–$50 million per year. Demarketing was clearly in order.

Before 1971, the company had made several attempts to reduce the incidence of DA dialing. Operators had been trained to suggest politely that callers could find numbers in their telephone directories. Other educational programs, internal control programs, and some limited consumer advertising had also been tried. None of these alternatives appeared to have a significant impact on the steadily rising data of DA calls. One executive proposed that the only reasonable solution was a charge for such calls. This proposal was under serious consideration by a marketing planning group in the spring of 1971.

Exhibit C5-1   **Pacific Telephone Company Demarketing Ad**

THE $55,000,000 PHONE CALL AND HOW TO PUT A STOP TO IT.

It takes $55,000,000 a year to pay the Operator expense on calls to Directory Assistance...for numbers that are <u>already listed in the local directory</u>.

Who pays this cost?

In an immediate sense, the phone company does. But as a public utility, our operating costs ultimately affect the rates that you are charged. In the long run it's you, the customer, who pays.

So, if you care about the cost of your service, do something about it.

The most important thing is to keep the book near your phone. And use it, whenever you can.

Make a list of the numbers you use most often, or that you may need in a hurry. If you're not sure about how to look up certain types of numbers, here are a few suggestions:

Use the INDEX.
The Index at the front of the book tells you where to find things.

For EMERGENCY NUMBERS:
You'll find them on the inside of the front cover.

For GOVERNMENT LISTINGS:
Yellow Pages—See GOVERN—MENT OFFICES.
White Pages—as follows: State offices—See California state of
City offices—See (name of city) City of
County offices—See (name of county) County of
Federal offices—See United States Government

For LETTERS USED AS NAMES:
Find the beginning of the listings of that letter. Example: R. L. Institute—See beginning of the R's. It will be listed alphabetically.

For NUMBERS USED AS NAMES:
Find the number as it is spelled. Example: 299 Corner Cafe—See Two Nine Nine Corner Cafe.

IF YOU CARE ABOUT COST,   USE THE BOO

Courtesy of the Pacific Telephone Company.

Project Design

Before proceeding with the DA service charge, management decided to experiment with a new advertising campaign designed to discourage customers from making DA calls. An MR budget was established to see if it could be shown that advertising could reduce the incidence rate in one test-market city. The overall plan included: (1) pretesting of television commercials to determine their effectiveness and to see if they produced any negative reactions, (2) conducting an eight-week campaign in one test-market city, and (3) setting up internal and external procedures to measure the effects of the campaign on DA volume and customer attitudes.

Measures of attitudinal and behavioral response were to be obtained before and after the eight-week advertising campaign. The results were to be compared with a forecast of what DA rates would have been without the advertising. In addition, the test market DA rate was to be compared with the company's overall DA rates across the system.

Fresno, California, was chosen as the test city. An eight-week advertising program was prepared using two TV spots and several radio spots, newspaper advertisements, and bill inserts. [An example is seen in Exhibit C5-1.] The principal themes of the advertisements were "Dial it yourself" and "The $55 million phone call." The campaign cost $14,000. Pretesting of the advertisements was done by a Los Angeles testing firm, Audience Studies, in a theater called "Preview House." In this type of test, viewers record their reactions on a hand-held device, according to various degrees of interest in or liking for the program and commercials. These responses are recorded on computer tape for interpretation later.

The results of the pretest of the two television spots seemed satisfactory. Both spots attracted interest and attention without creating measurable negative reactions in the viewing audience.

A summary of the essential procedures and phases of the study is given below:

Phase I, Pre-ad Campaign   An attitude survey was done of Fresno residents during May and June 1972 to determine attitudes and opinions about the company's cost of providing directory assistance service and about possible charges for DA service. A total of 337 Fresno customers were interviewed by telephone.

Phase II, Ad Campaign   The campaign was run for two months, July and August 1972, and involved television and radio spots, newspaper ads, and a special bill insert. Advertising emphasized the cost of providing the service, the number of calls made for numbers in the directory, and themes like: "If you're concerned about the cost of your telephone service, please look up numbers in the phone book whenever you can."

Phase III, Post-ad Campaign   This phase consisted of two additional studies: (1) an advertising awareness survey done in September to determine coverage of the advertising among heavy residential DA users, and (2) a post-ad campaign attitude survey also done in September. The awareness survey involved 604 heavy-usage customers stratified by two usage levels. One-half of the sample was randomly drawn from heavy users making 21–60 calls and one-half from very heavy users making 61 or more calls during May and June. The post-ad attitude survey was a telephone interview study of 333 residential customers following the same procedures used in the pre-ad phase.

In all phases, detailed call tracking was established in four Fresno prefixes. Two of these prefixes had predominantly residential customers, and the other two had predominantly business customers. These data provided the primary information by which the company attempted to trace the effects of the advertising campaign on the actual behavior of customers with respect to DA rates.

Data

Figure C5-1 shows monthly DA call volume in Fresno from January 1969 to November 1972. There is a marked regularity of the seasonal pattern from year to year. On this basis, the company had forecast a projected volume without advertising, as shown. In September 1972, for example, the peak month, the projection was about 59,000. The figure shows that actual volume following the July–August campaign was only about 53,000, and the long-term growth pattern appeared to have been broken. The company calculated that the average volume decrease for the five months, July–November, was 9 percent.

Figure C5-2 shows that the trend in Fresno did not occur on a company-wide basis during the period. The company overall was experiencing a growth rate during the period of about 7 percent over 1971, while Fresno, starting in August, showed a decrease to below 1971 volume. Some other highlights from the awareness and attitude phases of the study were:

1   Among heavy users, ad recall was very high—about 75 percent. Four out of ten heavy users who had seen or heard advertising said that they used the directory more often than they did before seeing the ads. They acknowledged that exposure to the advertising was what motivated them to make fewer DA calls.

Figure C5-1   **Average Business-Day Volume for Fresno Directory Assistance**

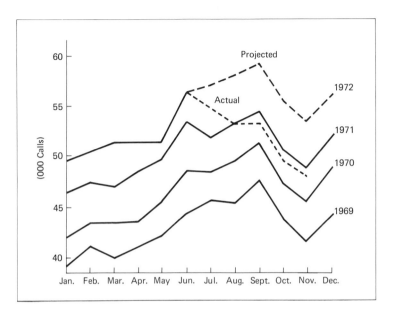

Figure C5-2   **Increase in Average Business-Day Assistance Volume: Comparison of PT & T and Fresno (Percent Change from 1971 to 1972)**

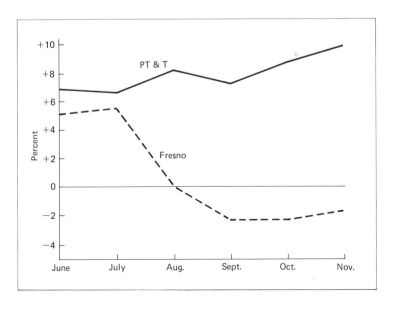

2   Some favorable shifts in attitudes and opinions about
the cost of providing DA service and about possible DA
charges were revealed in the attitude surveys. After the
advertising, more people (26 percent versus 38 percent)
said that DA service "costs a lot" for the company to
provide. In the post-ad campaign survey, more people (48
percent versus 60 percent) said they would look up local
numbers in the directory. This shift occurred almost
entirely among respondents who said they had seen or
heard the test advertising. And finally, fewer respondents
in the post-ad campaign survey felt that the idea of a DA
charge was "completely unreasonable" (43 percent versus
34 percent). These studies also provided valuable information on some of the demographic and life-style characteristics of heavy DA users compared with the general
population. Heavy users, for example, tended to be
younger, self-employed, and in professional and managerial positions.

The results of the Fresno test were encouraging to company
executives. It appeared that in Fresno the advertising campaign
had had a significant and dramatic effect on call volume. An
analysis was made of the cost savings resulting from the campaign
in Fresno and it was determined that, excluding overhead and
equipment expenses, the company had saved $44,000 in wage and
salary benefits over a five-month period as a result of the decreased volume. If the 9 percent call rate reduction could be
maintained for one year, the savings would be $106,000. The
production and media costs of the campaign were calculated to
be $14,000.

Marketing Decisions

In the spring of 1972, the marketing planning group was attempting to determine what action should be taken for the coming
year. A proposal vigorously put forward by one executive was
that the company impose a minimal charge for DA assistance,
which would be added to a customer's regular monthly bill.
Another executive suggested that a system-wide campaign be
developed along the lines of the Fresno campaign and be launched
in the fall of 1972. It was estimated that throughout the system
there were about a million DA calls daily and that annual expense
for operators and equipment handling these calls was about
$55 million.

Although nobody knew precisely what a system-wide
campaign would cost, the company's advertising agency had
suggested that it would be about $500,000. The head of the mar-
keting research group suggested a third alternative. He proposed

that the company set aside additional funds for continued research on advertising effects on DA call volume and, in effect, repeat the Fresno experiment in other test markets before proceeding with a system-wide campaign or imposing a charge for the service. These executives were aware of the increasing amount of publicity being generated at the time by citizen groups against advertising by utility companies. Many of these groups were arguing that because of the environmental and energy crisis, public utilities should be restricted from advertising. They claimed funds should be used to reduce customer telephone charges rather than be wasted on activities like advertising.

Assignment   Answer each of the following questions:

1   Based on the figures given in the case, what is the economic value to the company of the advertising expenditures invested in the Fresno test market?

2   All other considerations aside, and assuming that a decision is made to launch a system-wide advertising campaign, how much money should the company invest in such a campaign?

3   In your own words, describe the Fresno test market experiment.

4   What features of a true experimental design are included? What features are not included?

5   Discuss the assumption that the savings in Fresno could be projected to cover the full year.

6   What action should the marketing planning group have taken in the spring of 1972?

Part 6
Applying the
Behavioral Sciences

Introduction

> "We put a premium on ideas. And there is an awareness of
> social responsibility and a concern for practical efficiency. The
> advanced technical skills of the staff cover a rich diversity of
> disciplines, including economics, business, mathematics and data
> processing; philosophy, sociology, communications, and the fine
> arts; chemistry, physics, and engineering."
>
> From a Predicasts, Inc., brochure

Predicasts is one of the world's largest marketing research suppliers.
The description of its staff is illustrative of the breadth of disciplines that
contribute to marketing research. Early in its development, modern MR
rested on a narrow foundation of economics. Today it rests on a broad
foundation of disciplines, the most prominent being the behavioral sciences.

The behavioral sciences, especially psychology and sociology, are
invoked in an attempt to explain why phenomena occur in the marketplace.
By explaining consumer behavior, some of which appears irrational, psychology and sociology have contributed significantly to the theory and
practice of marketing. They provide marking research with some of its most
powerful tools.

In Chapter 13, we focus on the relationship between the behavioral
sciences and marketing research. We examine some of the fads and fashions
that have characterized the application of the behavioral sciences in MR.
We also review a bit of psychology and the factors that influence human
behavior in the marketplace.

Chapter 14 looks first at the collection of behavioral data. Here we
encounter a wide assortment of techniques. Behavioral data seldom yield
to the simple methods that work well with conventional demographic and
business information.

Chapter 14 concludes with an introduction to qualitative research. Qualitative research embraces several techniques that are currently in high fashion in marketing research circles. Of these, the focus group is probably the most pervasive.

In Chapter 15, we face the often messy problems of scaling and data analysis. In applying the behavioral sciences, especially psychology, we tend to produce data that are much less manageable than the types of information we've discussed thus far.

Caution and a critical attitude should prevail through Part 6. We are exploring an area rich in conflict as well as promise. There has recently been a great proliferation of theories and methods in the field of consumer research. Not all are valid.[1]

[1] For a critical appraisal see Jacob Jacoby, "Consumer Research: A State of the Art Review," *Journal of Marketing*, **42**:2 (April 1978), pp. 87–95.

Chapter 13
Marketing Research and the Behavioral Sciences

Key Concepts

Objective and Limitations
What the behavioral sciences can and cannot do in MR

Models of Consumer Behavior
Ways of describing the purchase process

Explanations of Consumer Behavior
Alternative explanations of our behavior in the marketplace

Attitudes and Hidden Cues
The role of attitude and hidden cues in determining consumer behavior

Psychographics
The latest fashion in consumer research

Key Terms

consumer-behavior model
psychological needs
psychogenic needs
biological needs
id
ego
superego
motivation research
motivation analysis
sociobiology

sociometry
sociogram
sociometric diagram
attitude
cognition
cues
cognitive dissonance
psychographics
life style
stochastic element

Objective and Limitations

Objective

The objective of the behavioral sciences in marketing research is to explain the *why* of consumer behavior. Other disciplines deal mainly with *what* happens in the marketplace, attempting to answer such questions as, "What effect does advertising have on sales?" "What is the most efficient distribution channel?" "What is the relationship between unit sales and price?" "What is the most productive advertising medium?" The behavioral sciences attempt to answer such questions as, "Why are sales sensitive to advertising?" "Why is a particular distribution channel more efficient?" "Why is a product price inelastic?" "Why does a particular advertising medium produce the most sales?"

Knowing *what* the situation is can be extremely useful information. Often it is all the marketer needs. For instance, say economic analysis has revealed that the relationship between unit sales, Y, and advertising expenditures, X, is $Y = 10,500 + 0.2X$. Within limits, the marketing manager can now optimize the outlay for advertising. He or she knows that sales will rise by 0.2 units for every dollar spent on advertising. Five dollars of advertising will be needed to sell each additional unit.

Although this is important information for the immediate allocation of promotional resources, it provides no insight into how the sales–advertising relationship might be altered. If the reasons behind this relationship were understood, the firm might be able to increase the impact of its advertising. Perhaps the parameter 0.2 could be increased to 0.3, a 50 percent improvement in productivity. If so, sales could be increased considerably without a penny more being spent on advertising. Or the present level of sales could be sustained with an appreciably lower advertising budget.

Whereas other forms of marketing research attempt to specify parameters, only the behavioral sciences offer insights into how best to change them. They seek to reveal the intellectual and emotional processes that underlie a purchase decision, and which are the primary determinants of demand. The marketer who understands the root causes of buyer behavior can employ his or her marketing instruments much more productively.

Limitations

The use of the behavioral sciences in marketing research is limited by a number of factors: One is that the behavioral scientists do not fully understand human behavior, and there is considerable controversy and many unexplained phenomena. Another problem is time and cost. Many of the techniques are expensive and time-consuming. Yet another limitation is the number, power, and reliability of the mathematical and statistical tools applicable to behavioral data. Behavioral information is not always congenial with our quantitative skills. As a result, behavioral studies often lack depth in analysis, specificity, or generality. Unhappily, as we relieve one of these problems, we often aggravate another.

The depth of an inquiry or analysis depends on the ability of the researcher to get resources and on the research method he or she selects. Objective techniques are more limited than projective methods and cannot probe as deeply. However, as the depth of inquiry and analysis increases, specificity and generality often decline. (Psychology leans heavily on projective techniques which we'll explain in the next chapter.)

The specificity obtainable decreases as one moves from purely parametric data toward nonparametric data. The applicability of statistical specifications—such as averages, deviations, error intervals, and significance levels—declines rapidly as researchers probe deeper into the mind of the respondent. The further they delve into consumer psychology, the more subjective the inquiry becomes. Subjective data do not lend themselves to mathematical manipulation, although a few techniques are available. Thus, findings based on data obtained with projective techniques cannot be specified as precisely or evaluated as rigorously as the quantitative (and usually parametric) data associated with objective methods.

The extent to which findings can be generalized also decreases as one moves into the more subjective areas of behavioral analysis. When samples are large and data are quantitative, research findings can be safely generalized to the market population. High costs and the limited number of trained specialists available make large samples impractical in the more complex and time-consuming psychological studies, especially those using Freudian techniques. In addition, statistical tools become less useful. The ability to generalize statistical findings declines as one moves away from objective techniques. [A zealous practitioner of Freudian psychology would argue against this statement, taking the position that human qualities are sufficiently universal for the information taken from a very small sample ($n < 10$) to be generalized to a population. However, this claim is not supported by statistics, although it may seem logical to many people.]

These limitations are significant, but do not justify the outright rejection of the behavioral sciences, or even some of the more subjective techniques. All have their place in the study of market phenomena, for they offer the only means of uncovering the psychological and sociological determinants of demand. Some techniques are best suited to exploratory research. However, the findings of the exploratory studies can then be restated in the form of hypotheses that can be tested by more conventional methods of research.

Models of Consumer Behavior

The behavioral sciences can be used in many ways in marketing research. One application is to discover the pattern of the purchase process, that is, to investigate the sequence of events leading to the eventual acceptance or rejection of a product. A symbolic or diagrammatic description of this pattern is called a *consumer-behavior model.* One of these models is shown

Figure 13-1 A General Consumer-Behavior Model

Source: Adapted from W. B. Wentz and G. I. Eyrich, *Marketing: Theory and Application* (New York: Harcourt Brace Jovanovich, 1970) and reproduced with their permission.

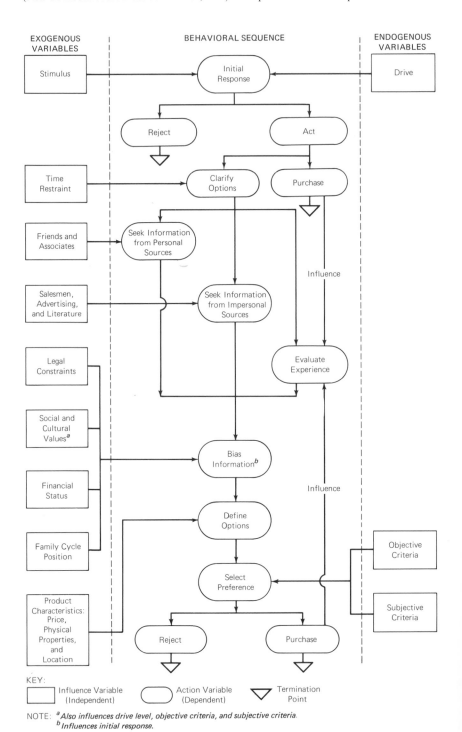

KEY:

☐ Influence Variable (Independent)   ⬭ Action Variable (Dependent)   ▽ Termination Point

NOTE: [a] *Also influences drive level, objective criteria, and subjective criteria.*
[b] *Influences initial response.*

in Figure 13-1, which serves as an introduction to the behavioral aspect of marketing.

Applications

Behavioral models can be used to study the psychological needs that may play a role in the behavioral process associated with a particular product or brand. They can be used to search out attitudes that encourage or prevent the purchase of particular products or brands, or that encourage or prevent the acceptance of particular promotional messages. Models can be used to look for consumer needs that are not satisfied by present products. And they can be used to group consumers into market segments.

The behavioral model may be the end product of the research project. Such models are very useful in showing the line managers, particularly the advertising manager and the sales manager, the points at which they can affect the consumer decision process. For example, if impersonal sources of information are ignored by most buyers, advertising via mass media probably should be minimized or revised to be more productive. If personal contacts play a vital role in the behavioral process, every effort should be made to influence the people who influence the buyers. Buyers of differentiated industrial products often turn to company engineers for advice in selecting both products and brands. The engineers may be sensitive to advertising—particularly that which reaches them through specialized technical journals—while the buyers may be virtually immune to it, relying solely on the judgment of the technical personnel.

The behavioral model may also be a means to the end product of a research project. It may serve to identify the areas that need a careful examination. For instance, the model may reveal that a strong perceptual bias is blocking the consumer's assimilation of the firm's promotional messages. An attitude survey may be needed to determine the reason for this bias. Once buyers' attitudes toward the product are known, the firm can alter its promotional message or its selection of media to accommodate them. If they cannot be circumvented, they may have to be changed—forcing the firm to revamp its entire promotional strategy. Failing this, it may even be necessary to withdraw the product from certain markets. Behavioral analysis can be used to determine the practicality of changing the prevalent prohibitory attitudes.

Constructing a Behavioral Model

A model of consumer behavior can take several forms. One of the most common is a schematic diagram such as Figure 13-1. Occasionally the schematic diagram is transformed into a computerized model, using a more mathematical format and a computer language. A schematic, or a graphic, model is usually a prerequisite to a computerized model. It also has the advantages of being easily understood and not requiring a mathematical specification of the relationships between the variables.

A general model, such as Figure 13-1, can often be adapted to a particular product. Or the researcher may prefer to start with no preconceptions about the behavioral pattern of the consumer, allowing it to emerge during the course of the investigation. General behavioral patterns frequently come to light during the exploratory phase of a market study.

After the preliminary design has been completed, the model can be refined by testing hypotheses. This testing is often done by surveys, preferably performed using random sampling techniques. For instance, exploratory interviews may indicate that most buyers rely heavily on information received from sales personnel. (This is usually the case when the product is an industrial good.) Since the respondents interviewed during the exploratory phase of the project may not be representative of the market population, a randomized sample survey may be required to test the hypothesis that buyers of the product under study depend on sales personnel for information. As an economy measure, the same survey can be used to gather information necessary to test other hypotheses about the model.

Alternative Models

Consumer-behavior models abound in the literature. Most are drawn from psychology, although some are based on sociological, economic, or political theory.

The best-known model is probably the one developed by Professors J. A. Howard and J. N. Sheth.[1] This is a rich but complex analog. It describes the process of buyer behavior and the influence of the forces shaping that behavior.

Other models are also important. The *Freudian psychoanalytic model* describes the consumer as a creature controlled solely by subconscious, sex-oriented, drives. The *Pavlovian learning model*—or "stimulus-response model"—depicts consumers as being conditioned by repetitive stimuli associated with need-satisfying rewards. The *Veblian model* shows the consumer as a child of the environment, with the society dictating behavior and consumption patterns. The *Marshallian model* has the consumer in the role of a purely rational and economic person, set on utility maximization. The *Hobbesian model*, especially relevant to the industrial buyer, describes the consumer as a political creature, concerned primarily with his or her own welfare but willing to make concessions to others for fear of a "war of every man against every man."[2]

Social psychology offers models adaptable to consumer behavior. These include the *McClelland model*, which stresses achievement motivation; the *Goffman model*, which conceives the buyer as a role player; the *Festinger model*, which is built on cognitive dissonance theory, and the *Reisman model*, which stereotypes buyers as tradition—directed, inner-directed, or outer-

---

[1] See John A. Howard and Jagdish N. Sheth, *The Theory of Buyer Behavior* (New York: Wiley, 1969). The model appears in numerous other books and articles.

[2] For a concise description of these models, see Philip Kotler, "Behavioral Models for Analysis Buyers," *Journal of Marketing* **29**, no. 4 (October 1965), pp. 37–45.

directed.[3] In each case, of course, the behavioral pattern is determined primarily by social forces.

The Goffman model warrants brief separate discussion, for it explains some of what we see in distribution, product, and promotion. Goffman draws from the vernacular of the theater to describe human behavior. Life is a stage. People are actors performing roles prescribed by reference groups or conforming to an idealized self. Our idealized self is the role we aspire to and may be far removed from our real one.[4]

Advertising and personal selling often make blatant appeals to the idealized self by identifying the prospect with a romantic or heroic role in a glamorous enviornment. Cadillac owners are shown arriving with attractive companions at posh country clubs; Marlboro smokers are hairy-chested he-men.

Goffman sees products as props which the actors (consumers) use to convey an image to an audience. Symbolic properties of goods are dominant—a view consistent with the motivation research interpretation of consumer behavior.

Explanations of Consumer Behavior

Psychological Needs

The history of the behavioral sciences in MR is largely that of psychology. Psychology deals mainly with psychological needs. *Psychological needs* are learned needs that an individual acquires early in life by observation and interaction with the environment. Examples are the needs for recognition, aggression, and affiliation. These needs exist in addition to the basic human drives—called "biological needs"—of hunger, thirst, pain-avoidance, and sex.[5]

Although there is general agreement among behavioral scientists with respect to the existence of psychological needs, there is no universally accepted definition or list of what they are. However, most lists conform reasonably to that in Exhibit 13.1. This reflects the Gestalt view which sees behavior as an essentially rational response to psychological forces. Little attention is given to the irrational drives associated with Freudian psychology, although the need for "exhibition" and "abasement" do have Freudian implications.

---

[3] For an introduction to these models and a bibliography, see Charles D. Schewe, "Selected Social Psychological Models for Analyzing Buyers," *Journal of Marketing* **37**:3 (July 1973), pp. 31–39.

[4] The definitive work here is Erving Goffman, *The Presentation of Self in Everyday Life* (Garden City: Doubleday Anchor, 1959). For a more contemporary development, see Gardner Lindzey and Elliot Aronson, *The Handbook of Social Psychology*, 2nd ed. (Reading, MA: Addison-Wesley, 1968).

[5] Freudian psychologists would argue that psychoglogical drives stem from the sex drive. However, most psychologists today do not believe this. Many psychiatrists go so far as to claim that sex is not a drive at all, but an "appetite," since it is not essential to the individual's survival.

Exhibit 13-1   **Psychological Needs**

A.   *Needs Associated Chiefly with Inanimate Objects*
  1.   Acquisition: the need to gain possessions and property.
  2.   Conservation: the need to collect, repair, clean, and preserve things.
  3.   Orderliness: the need to arrange, organize, put away objects; to be tidy and clean; to be precise.
  4.   Retention: the need to retain possession of things; to hoard; to be frugal, economical, and miserly.
  5.   Construction: the need to organize and build.

B.   *Needs Expressing Ambition, Will Power, A Desire for Accomplishment and Prestige*
  6.   Superiority: the need to excel, a composite of achievement and recognition.
  7.   Achievement: the need to overcome obstacles, to exercise power, to strive to do something difficult as well and as quickly as possible.
  8.   Recognition: the need to excite praise and commendation, to demand respect.
  9.   Exhibition: the need for self-dramatization; to incite, amuse, stir, shock, or thrill others.
  10. Inviolacy: the need to remain inviolate, to prevent a depreciation of self-respect, to preserve one's "good name."
  11. Avoidance of inferiority: the need to avoid failure, shame, humiliation, ridicule.
  12. Defensiveness: the need to defend oneself against blame or belittlement, to justify one's actions.
  13. Counteraction: the need to overcome defeat by restriving and retaliating.

C.   *Needs Having to Do with Human Power Exerted, Resisted, or Yielded To*
  14. Dominance: the need to influence or control others.
  15. Deference: the need to admire and willingly follow a superior, to serve gladly.
  16. Similance: the need to imitate or emulate others, to agree and believe.
  17. Autonomy: the need to resist influence, to strive for independence.
  18. Contrariness: the need to act differently from others, to be unique, to take the opposite side.

D.   *Needs Having to Do with Injuring others or Oneself*
  19. Aggression: the need to assault or injure another; to belittle, harm, or maliciously ridicule a person.
  20. Abasement: the need to comply and accept punishment, self-depreciation.
  21. Avoidance of blame: the need to avoid blame, ostracism, or punishment by inhibiting unconventional impulses; to be well behaved and obey the law.

E.   *Needs Having to do with Affection Between People*
  22. Affiliation: the need to form friendships and associations.
  23. Rejection: the need to be discriminating; to snub, ignore, or exclude another.
  24. Nurturance: the need to nourish, aid, or protect another.
  25. Succorance: the need to seek aid, protection, or sympathy; to be dependent.

F.   *Additional Socially Relevant Needs*
  26. Play: the need to relax, amuse oneself, seek diversion and entertainment.
  27. Cognizance: the need to explore, to ask questions, to satisfy curiosity.
  28. Exposition: the need to point and demonstrate; to give information, explain, interpret, lecture.

Source: From *Introduction to Psychology*, 4th Edition, by Ernest R. Hilgard and Richard C. Atkinson, copyright © 1953, 1957, 1962, and 1967, by Harcourt Brace Jovanovich, Inc. and reproduced with their permission.

If one or more psychological needs plays an important role in the consumer's selection of alternative brands or products, it behooves the marketer to be aware of them. In the case of some products, such as raw materials and energy, they are probably unimportant. In the case of others, primarily consumer goods, they can be significant. Only psychological needs—or their irrational Freudian counterparts—can explain the demand for mink coats, diamond jewelry, Cadillacs, and costly medals. Certainly, much less expensive substitutes have the same functional properties.

Unfortunately, identifying psychological needs—also called "psychogenic needs" is often difficult. How do you measure the need for recognition? How can you know how many sales are attributable to exhibition? How can you test the importance of avoidance of blame in creating a barrier between an advertising message and a prospective buyer? Consumer-behavior analysis cannot answer these questions with precision. However, it does offer tools that will often identify psychological factors significant in the marketing of a particular good. It also offers techniques for arraying these factors, in order of their importance, with respect to the acceptance of a particular brand or product.

The Freudian Viewpoint

Another interpretation of human behavior that occasionally forms the basis for marketing research is provided by Freudian psychology. According to Freud's now-famous theories, every individual has an id, an ego, and a superego. The *id* is a bundle of instinctive needs, of which the desire for sexual gratification is by far the most dominant. The *superego* is a collection of social values—that is, ethics and morals—acquired from society and in conflict with the id. The *ego* is the mediating device that balances the conflict between the socially unacceptable needs of the id and the constraints of the superego.

Consumer-behavior analysis, when based on Freudian psychology, attempts to identify the exact instinct—oral, anal, phallic, or Oedipal—and psychological constraints involved in the behavioral process associated with a particular product. Data collection and analysis lean heavily on the techniques of psychoanalysis, which are expensive and time-consuming. They also lack statistical reliability.

Other Viewpoints

Different viewpoints and techniques have come in and out of fashion since the behavioral sciences first impacted on MR. Many have left legacies that are with us today.

One of the most important movements in marketing research was motivation research. *Motivation research* is the application of clinical psychology to the study of consumer behavior. It seeks to explain market phenomena by revealing the psychological reasons, particularly those buried deep in the subconscious mind, for people's behavior. Its theories and techniques are based largely on Freudian psychology.

The apostles of motivation research—also called "motivation analysis"—perceived image as superior to substance and symbolic properties as superior to functional ones. This applied to everything from soap to politicians.[6]

Motivation research, popular in the 1950s, did not live up to its promises. The motivation researcher was pushed aside by the experimental psychologist and the marketing scientist. Psychoanalysis yielded to experimental psychology and mathematical modeling.[7] Consumers, who had been seen as a bundle of suppressed desires, disappeared into the computer. They emerged as a collection of regression coefficients, summation signs, and eigen values. Descriptions of consumer behavior became sets of numbers and Greek symbols.

The search for the motivating forces which shape our behavior in the marketplace has recently led to psychographic analysis, which we will discuss shortly.

A Stochastic Element?

The fundamental premise of psychological theory has been that all behavior is caused. That is, there are one or more biological, psychological, or external forces, alone or in combination, which determine any given behavior. The trick is to identify it or them.

This determinist philosophy prevails in economics and the behavioral sciences, although not in the hard sciences. For instance, in the study of electron behavior, an element of chance has long been recognized. An event or process that contains an element of chance, such as the flipping of a coin, is called "stochastic." Were it not for stochastic phenomena, insurance companies and Las Vegas casinos would be out of business.

If there is a stochastic element in the brain influencing our actions, then it is not possible, even in principle, to fully explain or predict individual behavior. Even if all behavior is caused, but by a multitude of variables of unpredictable frequency, then behavior remains, in practice, stochastic.

The stochastic theory has recently emerged in the marketing literature. It offers some persuasive arguments, supported with data, suggesting that the acts of consumers are significantly determined by chance.[8]

---

[6] The most famous (or infamous) introduction to motivation research is Vance Packard's exposé, *The Hidden Persuaders* (New York: Mentor, 1954).

[7] For a contemporary excursion into marketing science and its application to consumer behavior, see Leonard J. Parsons and Randall L. Schultz, *Marketing Models and Econometric Research* (New York: Elsevier North-Holland, 1976). Examples of these applications are found in *Econometrica, Psychometrica, Management Science, Journal of Operations Research, Journal of Marketing,* and especially the *Journal of Consumer Research* and the *Journal of Marketing Research.*

[8] For instance, see Frank M. Bass, "The Theory of Stochastic Preference and Brand Switching," *Journal of Marketing Research* 11: 1 (February 1974), pp. 1–20. This discussion draws liberally from that article.

Sociobiology[9]

A new and controversial discipline has appeared on the frontier of the behavioral sciences. It may raise havoc with many of our cherished theories and techniques. The discipline is *sociobiology* which attempts to explain behavior biologically. Its major tenet is that behavior is determined genetically. The key to behavior is DNA, the coded molecule that determines the nature of all organisms.

If the sociobiologists are correct, past explanations of consumer behavior make little sense: Our genes, not our psychological needs, govern our behavior in the marketplace. (The nature of our genes is determined by DNA.) What we do rests mainly on heredity, not conditioning.

Sociobiology has not yet appeared in marketing research, nor in the literature of marketing. Should it arrive, it will assault the conventional wisdom and may lay waste to much of the theory and many of the tools of contemporary research. Of course, the theories of sociobiology are still unfolding and may ultimately prove of little substance.

Sociological Factors

Another interpretation of human behavior is based on sociology and social psychology. Here the consumer is perceived as the product of the environment, primarily of contact with other people. Psychological needs such as ambition, will power, the desire for accomplishment and prestige, and all needs having to do with affection between people, are considered by social psychologists to be largely the result of social interaction.

Gratification of these desires—as well as the needs having to do with human power exerted, resisted, or yielded to—is seen as a function of personal performance measured by standards set by society. Thus, peer groups, social influences, social classes, reference groups, and culture play important roles in shaping behavioral patterns. Although it is generally the individual, and not a group, who makes a purchase decision, group values and mores must usually be taken into account in preparing a marketing strategy.

Sociometry

Sociometry is a subset of sociology that deals with the relationships among members of a group. It is a special area of behavioral research that is sometimes applicable to market studies. Sociometry's unique tool is the *sociometric diagram*. Commonly called a *sociogram*, it shows the leader-follower-colleague relationships and the flow of information among group members. It is especially useful in identifying influential members and defining the group's communications network. Sociometry and the sociogram have

---

[9] For a lay introduction to sociobiology, see "Why We Do What We Do," *Reader's Digest* 111: 668 (December 1977), pp. 183–190. For a tour de force, see Edward Wilson, *Sociobiology: The New Synthesis* (Cambridge, Mass.: Harvard University Press (Belknap Press), 1975).

many applications in the study of innovation diffusion—how new ideas, technology, styles, and products spread within a society. This subject is extremely important to marketers responsible for the successful introduction of new brands or products.

The sociogram is simple in principle, although it can become cumbersome in application, particularly when a large population is involved. A suitable number of population members are interviewed and asked to identify the members to whom they turn for advice, whom they exchange information with, and to whom they give counsel. In order to simplify the diagram, the respondents are sometimes asked to name the single most important member in each category. (Nonresponse is a critical factor in studies using sociograms and cannot be tolerated.) The votes are then tallied, usually in a matrix, and then plotted. The plot—which is the sociometric diagram—shows respondents as boxes or dots. Their relationships—if any—with the other respondents are indicated by lines from one box or dot to another. A box with a large number of connecting lines is identified as a leader and an important terminal in the communications network. From the marketer's viewpoint, this element should be a focal point for promotion, especially during a product's introductory phase.

A typical sociometric diagram is shown in Figure 13-2. This particular sociogram depicts the interactions between members of a small neighborhood group. It shows the flow and intensity of communications between members and clearly identifies the key individuals (and presumably the leader) in the exchange of information. "The numbers represent the total reported interactions by telephone or in person per week. The solid-line boxes represent [the] specified group. The dashed-line boxes represent subsidiary friendships mention[ed]."[10]

This plot, along with similar sociograms for each of 19 other neighborhood groups, was prepared in the course of an innovation-diffusion study designed to evaluate the impact of small neighborhood groups on their members' behavior. The groups were identified by randomly selecting a woman within a particular area and then asking her to name the women within her neighborhood whom she saw most often and with whom she was most friendly. Each woman mentioned, as well as the original woman, was personally interviewed to determine the direction and intensity of the communication links within the group, as well as other information relevant to the study.

A classic example of the application of sociometry to marketing research is provided by a study of the diffusion of a new drug in the medical community by Coleman, Katz, and Menzel.[11] Coleman et al. interviewed 228 doctors, 125 of whom were used in the analysis. Each respondent was

[10] Thomas S. Robertson, "The Effect of the Informal Group Upon Member Innovative Behavior," in Robert L. King, ed., *Marketing and the New Science of Planning* (Chicago: American Marketing Association, 1968), pp. 334–340.

[11] James Coleman, Elihu Katz, and Herbert Menzel, "The Diffusion of an Innovation Among Physicians," *Sociometry* 20 (December 1957), p. 254.

Figure 13-2 **An Example of a Sociogram**

Source: Reprinted from Thomas S. Robertson, "The Effect of the Informal Group Upon Member Innovative Behavior," in Robert L. King, ed., *Marketing and the New Science of Planning*, p. 336, published by the American Marketing Association.

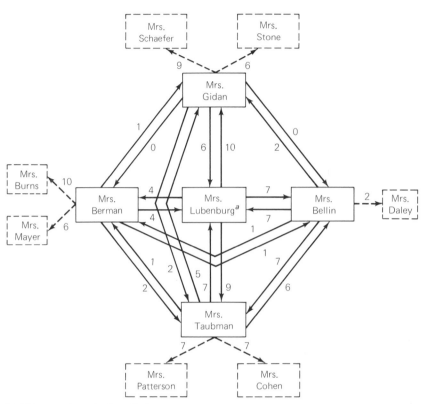

a Initial respondent who identified group.

asked the following questions: To whom did he most often turn for advice and information? With whom did he most often discuss his cases in the course of an ordinary week? Who were the friends, among his colleagues, whom he saw most often socially? Each time, he was asked to name names. The answers indicated the links by which he was connected to other members of the local medical population. Other information, such as the length of time it took the respondent to adopt the new drug (this was the dependent variable in the study) and various attributes of the respondent, was also included.

The results of the study showed the influence of personal attributes— such as age, journal readership, institutional affiliation, and selected attitudes—and professional and social relationships on the speed and extent of the diffusion of the new drug. In addition, the innovators, early adopters, late adopters, and laggards were identified and stereotyped. This information, revealed by sociometric techniques, was obviously of value only to marketers of pharmaceuticals. The methods used to obtain and analyze it, however, have application in many markets.

Unfortunately, sociometry is not practical for identifying specific leaders in large groups. At best it can be used to identify a representative sample of leaders in a large market population. The sample leaders—if they will cooperate—can then be surveyed to identify any useful traits that could be generalized to the rest of the leaders in the population. For instance, the researcher might discover that a particular trade journal, magazine, television program, or professional association was favored by the leader set. If so, promotional efforts could be concentrated in that medium.

Sociometry can also be used in the preparation of consumer-behavior models to identify the personal sources, if any, to whom the buyer turns in the quest for information. It helps, too, in determining the degree of influence personal information sources have in the buyer's decision process.

Attitudes and Hidden Cues

Consumer Attitudes

Rather than dealing directly with psychological needs, the marketer may often settle for an analysis of consumer attitudes. A considerable amount of marketing resources—especially in the area of promotion—are expended every year in an effort to change or establish consumer attitudes.

Attitude may be defined as a predisposition to act in a certain way in certain situations or toward certain people or things. A consumer's attitude may have no basis in reality, yet may still determine behavior. Hence, it is a logical subject for investigation.

Attitude is often described as having four components: (1) cognition, (2) a value system, (3) evaluation, and (4) intensity. Behavioral analysis offers techniques for describing—and in some instances, measuring—each with respect to a particular brand or product.

Cognition refers to the individual's state of awareness with respect to a given subject. It varies from ignorance to casual awareness, to detailed knowledge and can include both real and imagined information. Cognition is affected by the individual's value system, which serves as an information filter and introduces a perceptual bias into the store of knowledge.

The individual's value system is a higher order of personal preferences. According to social psychologists, it is the result of psychological needs and social constraints. According to Freudian psychologists, it is the outcome of the battle between the id and the superego. Value systems vary between individuals but are sufficiently similar within a given social, economic, or ethnic class to allow some generalizations. The literature of social psychology provides enough descriptions of the value systems prevalent in various social, economic, and ethnic classes to satisfy most marketing-research needs.

An evaluation is the result of applying the value system to knowledge. It is the component of attitude most frequently measured. From it are deduced the underlying psychogenic needs involved in a given behavioral process.

Intensity refers to the strength and rigidity of an attitude. If an evaluation is favorable and intensity is high, purchase behavior will probably follow—assuming of course that the product is available and the consumer can afford to buy it. If the good is one that is bought repeatedly, brand loyalty may develop. If an evaluation is negative and intensity is high, the seller will be confronted with a severe, perhaps impenetrable, barrier. If intensity is low, the attitude will be susceptible to change, and hence vulnerable to manipulation by the seller.

Attitudes and Expressed Intentions versus Behavior

Evidence suggests that expressed attitudes, as well as intentions, and actual purchase behavior frequently conflict. Consumers do not always do what they say they will do, nor does their performance always reflect their apparent attitudes. Tables 13-1 and 13-2 illustrate.

The literature is rich with examples. For instance, a study of soft drink buyers showed that only 55 percent purchased the brand they claimed to prefer and only 41 percent chose the brand that evoked the most favorable attitude.[12]

There are a number of explanations for this inconsistency. First, the respondent may misinterpret the interviewer's question. Second, the the respondent may not be sure of personal intentions or attitudes, but be anxious to satisfy the interviewer. Third, circumstances may change between the time of the survey and the time of the final purchase decision. Fourth, the respondent may be somewhat unstable; that is, his or her psychogenic needs may change sharply and often. Or the respondent may act irrationally, in ways that conflict with actual attitudes. Fifth, there may be a stochastic process at work. And last, as indicated earlier, there is a lot about human behavior we don't yet know.

The first two sources of inconsistency can generally be attributed to a poor survey design or incompetent interviewers. The third possibility is simply another case of the uncertainty that typifies life in general. The fourth source of inconsistency is not common, and if the sample is large enough, the unanticipated buy decisions will equal the unanticipated decisions not to buy. In other words, they will tend to be normally distributed and will cancel each other out.

Despite the inconsistencies, it seems reasonable to assume that there is a positive correlation between consumer attitudes and intentions and behavior. If the researcher has succeeded in discovering the respondent's true attitude or intention, it may indeed be indicative of subsequent behavior.

---

[12] Frank M. Bass, Edgar A. Pessemier, and Donald R. Lehmann, "An Experimental Study of Relationships Between Attitudes, Brand Preference, and Choice," *Behavioral Science* 17: 4 (November 1972), p. 535.

Table 13-1   **Relationship Between Concurrent Attitudes and Usage for Selected Brands of Consumer Products (According to Percent Using)**

Brand Rating	Cigarette Brand	Deodorant Brand	Gasoline Brand	Laxative Brand
Excellent	68%	44%	57%	65%
Very Good	23	30	36	27
Good	7	24	11	14
Fair to Poor	2	2	8	3

Source: Reprinted from Alvin A. Achenbaum, "Knowledge Is a Thing Called Measurement" in Lee Adler and Irving Crespi, ed., *Attitude Research at Sea*, 1966, published by the American Marketing Association.

Table 13-2   **Comparison of Appliance Buying Intentions and Behavior (for Three National Brands)**

Brands	Proportion of Intenders Actually Buying the Appliance as Planned	Percent of Buyers Who Purchased Brand as Intended
A	44%	68%
B	42	24
C	30	57

Source: Reprinted from Robert W. Pratt, Jr., "Understanding the Decision Process for Consumer Goods: An Example of the Application of Longitudinal Analysis," in Peter D. Bennett, ed., *Marketing and Economic Development*, 1965, published by the American Marketing Association.

Of course, one of the purposes of discovering consumer attitudes and intentions is to alter them so that they will be favorable to the firm's product. If an attitude or intention is correctly defined and is not so intense as to preclude any alternation, a skillfull use of promotional instruments may be all that is needed to induce a desired response. Follow-up surveys are often conducted to determine if a promotional campaign has perceptibly altered consumer attitudes or intentions.

Hidden Cues

Specific bits of information—such as a price, color, or brand—that serve as stimuli in the consumer decision process are called *cues*. Many, like price, are obvious to both the consumer and the marketer. Some, like the manufacturer's reputation, are not always obvious to the seller, but can be determined by objective or projective inquiry techniques. Other cues are entirely hidden. They affect purchase behavior but go unrecognized by the consumer who is either totally oblivious of them or unaware of their effect. These hidden cues can be the cause of misleading behavioral acts if they go undetected by the researcher.

Even when a consumer's behavior is consistent with her apparent attitude—that is, when her purchases conform with her expressed preferences—the information she gives may be misleading. The attitudes expressed or the behavioral pattern described, although consistent with the actual purchases, may have had little to do with these purchases. Attitudes are often altered to conform with behavior in order to reduce *cognitive dissonance*, the psychological term for the perceived incongruity between an attitude and behavior. If it is sufficiently intense, cognitive dissonance can induce a serious emotional disturbance.

Responses are often chosen to conform to social norms or the respondent's perception of the interviewer's desires. Sometimes psychological forces supress the real reason for behavior. Fortunately, the behavioral sciences provide the market researcher with some tools, primarily projective techniques, that may help to deal with these problems.

Consumer behavior is sometimes affected by external factors of which the respondent is virtually oblivious.[13] Hidden cues can exist in the environment, be integral to the product, or be intentionally provided by the seller. Although they have never been popular as regular promotional instruments, they have been used experimentally for many years. Cox cites examples dating as far back as 1932.[14]

In one experiment, a sample of 250 housewives were confronted with four pairs of silk stockings that were identical except for their scent. The scents were so faint that only six of the 250 respondents noticed them. One pair was judged best by 50 percent of the housewives—statistically, a highly significant portion. The basis for the selection was given as quality of texture, weave, feel, wearing qualities, lack of sheen, and weight. Yet, all four options were identical in these respects. The favored choice had a "narcissus" scent, while the pair of stockings chosen least often (it received only 8 percent of the vote) had the usual natural (factory)scent.[15]

In a similar experiment, two piles of nylon stockings were placed on a store counter. One pile was scented with an "orange" aroma. In all other respects, the piles were identical. Yet 90 percent of the buyers selected stockings from the scented pile. When asked why, many replied that their choice

---

[13] A classic example is the radical increase in the sale of soft drinks that occurred in motion-picture theaters where beverage commercials were flashed on the screen during the movie. The messages were so brief that they were unnoticed by the conscious mind. However, they made an impression on the subconscious mind that was sufficient to induce overt behavior. See J. J. Bachrach, "The Ethnics of Tachistoscopy," *Bulletin of Atomic Scientists* 15 (1959), pp. 212–215.

[14] Donald F. Cox, "The Measurement of Information Value: A Study in Consumer Decision Making," *Emerging Concepts in Marketing* (Chicago: American Marketing Association, 1962), pp. 413–421.

[15] Donald A. Lair, "How the Consumer Estimates Quality by Subconscious Sensory Impressions," *Journal of Applied Psychology* (June 1932), p. 241

appeared to be of better quality and would probably last longer and wear better than the stockings in the other pile.[16]

To cite yet another instance, a dairy discovered that cream-colored ice cream was considered by consumers to be richer than white ice cream, even though the white ice cream contained the most butterfat (the objective measurement of richness). Similarly, detergent manufacturers discovered that color influenced housewives' opinions about the cleaning power of a product.[17]

These hidden stimuli are not explicitly revealed in surveys of consumer attitudes. The researcher must look for hints of their existence in observed behavior or in the narratives gathered in personal interviews. (Unstructured data collection techniques, such as story completion and picture frustration, are sometimes fruitful.) The observations or narratives may suggest a cue hypothesis that can be tested by experimentation and accepted or rejected at a desired level of significance.

The silk-stocking study is illustrative. Here we have the argument that consumers will subconsciously respond to perfume, which serves as a behavior-inducing cue in the selection of stockings. We could frame a null hypothesis, H_0, in the form $H_0:p_A = 0.25$. In other words, the probability of selecting Stocking A when the choice is random, is 0.25. One would expect a random choice if the perfume had no effect, because the four pairs of stockings are identical in all other respects. Thus, the hypothesis $H_0:p_A = 0.25$, is equivalent to saying that the perfume is not an effective cue.

The null hypothesis can be tested using the formula for the Z-statistic of a binomial distribution and a normal distribution table such as that in Appendix 4. Since the number of successful outcomes (X) is 125 (50 percent of the 250 respondents selected A), the number of observations (n) is 250, and the probability of a successful outcome (p_0) is 0.25 (if the null hypothesis is correct), the Z-statistic is 9.1:

$$Z = \frac{X - np_0}{\sqrt{np_0(1 - p_0)}} \qquad \text{(given as formula A2.15)}$$

$$Z = \frac{125 - 250(0.25)}{\sqrt{250(0.25)(1 - 0.25)}} \qquad \text{(by substitution)}$$

$$Z = \frac{62.5}{\sqrt{46.875}} \qquad \text{(by arithmetic)}$$

$$Z = 9.14 \qquad \text{(by arithmetic)}$$

A normal distribution table will show that even at the .001 level of significance, the critical Z-value is only 3.09. There is only an infinitesimal

---

[16] *Women's Wear Daily* (January 1961), p. 5.
[17] Cox, "The Measurement of Information Value," pp. 413–421.

probability (far less than .001) that as many as 125 buyers could have selected A by pure chance. Hence, that hypothesis must be rejected. The hidden cue almost certainly affected their behavior.

Of course, the difficult task is the detection of the hidden stimuli. The hidden-cue phenomenon has been recognized for over 40 years, and its existence has been conclusively demonstrated. The role of cues in the consumer-behavior process has also been thoroughly described.[18] Methods of quantitative analysis have been found applicable to their evaluation, once they are identified.

Although very few methods have been developed for the detection of specific hidden cues, many analytical tools will reveal the existence of hidden stimuli. The researcher should be alert for signs of them in an examination of behavioral data. For instance, when a coefficient of correlation (a statistic used in regression analysis) indicates that a substantial portion of the variation in the dependent variable is unexplained, the researcher may suspect the presence of hidden cues in the behavioral process.

Sometimes it is helpful to construct a matrix in which all conceivable cues are represented by columns and the behavioral—and presumably dependent—variables (such as sales, brand preferences, or attitude) are represented by rows. The analyst then looks for factors whose pattern of variation appears similar to that of the behavioral variable. When such a cue is found, it can be subjected to an appropriate test of significance. Or, if the data are insufficient, further research can be done.

Psychographics[19]

In an effort to hang flesh and blood on the consumer, instead of dull statistics, William D. Wells and other scholars developed psychographics.

"Psychographics" is a neologism not in wide currency in psychology, but recently popular in the marketing literature. *Psychographics* are the elements of a person's life style which relate to his or her behavior as a consumer. They are his or her activities, interest, and opinions, shown in Table 13-3. These basic dimensions—called "AIO"—have recently been expanded to include personality, ownership, and occupational adequacy.[20]

With psychographics, we find market segments, target audiences, and other groups of people described as "young swingers," "middle American," "homebodies," or as "fashion-conscious," "child-oriented," "nervous," and so forth. (Each stereotype represents a particular mix of psychographic traits.)

---

[18] See John A. Howard, *Marketing Management: Analysis and Planning*, rev. ed. (Homewood, IL: Irwin, 1963), chs. 3 and 4; and Engle et al. *Consumer Behavior*, chs. 3–6.

[19] This section draws heavily on the work of William D. Wells and James Myers. The author is indebted to both of them for their assistance in the preparation of this material.

[20] Other definitions—Wells has tallied 18 so far—include such components as attitudes, values, needs, perceptions, and self-image.

Table 13-3   **Life-Style Dimension**

Activities	Interests	Opinions
Work	Family	Themselves
Hobbies	Home	Social issues
Social Events	Job	Politics
Vacation	Community	Business
Entertainment	Recreation	Economics
Club Membership	Fashion	Education
Community	Food	Products
Shopping	Media	Future
Sports	Achievements	Culture

Source: Adapted from Joseph T. Plummer, "The Concept and Application of Life Style Segmentation," (*Journal of Marketing* 38:1, (January 1974), p. 33) published by the American Marketing Association.

By describing the consumer in psychographic terms—called collectively "life style"[21]—we confront the marketer with information that is presumably more useful than sterile demographic data. For instance, if the heavy users of a product are generally family-oriented, active in community affairs, conservative in dress, and strong believers in thrift and the Republican Party, this may be far more important than their income, age, and employment. The psychographic qualities have meaningful implications for product and package design, for copywriting, and for media selection. The conventional demographic profile is often useless.

An illustration of psychographics in action is an analysis of the eye makeup market. The heavy users—hence, the target market—of eye makeup were discovered to share a number of psychographic traits. Taken together, these qualities separate them from the occasional users and nonusers. The heavy users tend to be interested in fashion, appearance, and attractiveness to men. They like parties and socializing, but not housework and grocery shopping. They are more style-conscious than utilitarian, more contemporary than traditional. Movies and the "Tonight Show" are popular TV fare for them, while panel shows and westerns are not. In short, the heavy user emerged as a bit of a "swinger."[22]

Media audiences may also be described in psychographic terms. Thus, the *Reader's Digest* buyers emerge as the soul of conservative middle-class values, *Time* readers are more liberal than the *Newsweek* readers,

---

[21] "Life style" and "psychographics" tend to be used interchangably. However, Wells feels there is a difference worth preserving. Namely, life style focuses on cultural attributes, while psychographs stresses psychological ones. See William D. Wells, *Life Style and Psychographics* (Chicago: American Marketing Association, 1979), pp. 319–320.

[22] William D. Wells and Douglas J. Tigert, "Activities, Interests, and Opinions," *Journal of Advertising Research* 11, no. 4 (August 1971), pp. 28–29. For a discussion of the data and techniques used to arrive at such conclusions, see Chapter 17 of the book you are now reading.

etc.[23] Given a psychographic portrait of the target market and each of the likely media audiences, the marketer is started on the way to optimum medium selection.

The trick in applying psychographics is to correlate life style with purchase behavior. If we divide a market into clusters of people sharing sets of psychographic characteristics, we must know which clusters buy which products or prefer which brands.[24]

Psychographic analysis is a complex and expensive process which can lead up blind alleys. For instance, we may get neat life-style clusters whose members prefer a conflicting mix of products or a cross section of competing brands. Or we might group people by product or brand preference, only to discover that the groups share much the same mix of psychographic traits.

Psychographics confronts us with other problems. These include the use of subjective judgment and the difficulty in correlating with the census data and other easily accessible market information. The subject is rich in technical problems, hence limitations. These largely explain why psychographics has "failed to deliver on promises that never should have been made in the first place."[25] These limitations also prompt the continuing search for better tools of analysis. They keep open the door for the admission of other behavioral disciplines.

Problems

1   What information might consumer-behavior analysis supply, not available from the traditional types of market research, which would be useful to the following people: (a) an advertising account executive for Volkswagen, (b) a regional sales manager for Gillette, and (c) a director of new-product development for General Foods.

2   Drawing on your own observations and personal experience, construct a behavioral model of one of the following phenomena: (a) the purchase of a new automobile, (b) the purchase of a nonprescription cold remedy, or (c) the purchase of a numerically controlled milling machine.

[23] Douglas J. Tigert, *A Psychographic Profile of Magazine Audiences: An Investigation of a Media's Climate* (an unpublished paper presented at the American Marketing Association Consumer Behavior Workshop, Ohio State University, 1969).

[24] For other examples of applied psychographic research see Suzan P. Douglas and Christine D. Urban, "Life-Style Analysis to Profile Women in International Markets," *Journal of Marketing* 41: 3 (July 1977), pp. 46–54; and Elizabeth A. Richards and Stephen S. Sturman, "Life-Style Segmentation in Apparel Marketing," *Journal of Marketing* 41: 4 (October, 1977), pp. 89–91.

[25] Richard J. Reiser, *Psychographics: Marketing Tool or Research Toy?* (White Plains, NY: Behavioral Analysis, 1972), p. 1. This is a concise, nontechnical introduction to the subject.

3   What psychological and sociological factors might affect the behavior described in your answer to the previous question?

4   What techniques would you recommend for identifying and evaluating each of the factors listed in the answer to question 3? Defend your choice.

5   What psychographic qualities would you think are applicable to consumers of (a) CB radios, and (b) large motorcycles?

Chapter 14
Data Collection and
Qualitative Research

Key Concepts

Objective versus Projective Techniques
Alternative ways to get the truth

Structured Tests
Ways to gather data using questions with constrained answers

Unstructured Tests
Ways to gather data using questions with unconstrained answers

Qualitative Research
Focus groups and other alternatives to quantitative methods

Selecting a Method
Criteria for judging alternative ways of gathering-behavioral data

Key Terms

objective techniques
projective techniques
structured test
unstructured test
open-end test
attitude-scaling test
monadic test
paired comparison test
triangular comparison test
error-choice test
semantic-differential test
word association test

sentence completion test
story completion test
picture-frustration test
thematic-apperception test
role playing
psychodrama
qualitative research
focus group
validity
cross validation
reliability
split-half analysis
homographic free association test

Objective versus Projective Techniques

The collection of behavioral data burdens us with problems we seldom encounter in gathering demographic and economic information. Isolating and evaluating the psychological and sociological forces that determine consumer behavior can require any of numerous techniques, some of which are very complex. Just knowing what to look for can be a challenge.

Objective Techniques

Objective techniques confront the respondent with direct questions about the respondent. They are based on the assumption that the respondent is both able and willing to reveal a behavioral pattern and to give the reasons for actions. The researcher simply asks direct questions and accepts the answers at face value. The United States Census, for example, is conducted in this way.

Objective techniques work well when the research deals with subjects that do not involve the respondent's self-image or have a high emotional content. They can be useful in defining wholly rational behavioral patterns and in identifying functional reasons for the respondent's actions. If the respondent can remain anonymous, objective techniques can also be used in research on more sensitive matters, such as personal income and sex. However, in order to guarantee anonymity, researchers may have to forego using telephone and personal interviews unless the interviewers are very skillful. They are thus limited to using mail questionnaires with a fairly structured format.

Objective techniques work well in gathering factual information. They have proven useful in collecting demographic, social, and economic data, as well as information on purchase behavior. Answers to questions about family size, domicile, a person's occupation, and brand preferences are usually accurate, but questions that require a good memory for details or that conflict with self-image or attitudes are less likely to produce accurate replies. Accuracy decays with both time and the decline in the regularity or importance of purchases. Respondents may remember what television shows they saw last night, but not all those they saw a week ago. They may remember without error the brands of the last two cars they purchased, but not the brands of the last two sets of spark plugs they bought.

If a respondent's self-image is involved in the answers, accuracy can deteriorate drastically. For example, surveys on purchases of alcoholic beverages invariably understate the quantities bought, simply because the large buyers do not like to portray themselves or their households as heavy drinkers. Statements about personal income and magazine preferences also tend to conform more with the respondent's self-image than with his or her actual behavior.

Objective methods may be appropriate when matters of opinion are involved, as long as the range of possible answers does not include opinions that do violence to established social norms or the respondent's conception of what the interviewer feels is acceptable. If the questions do not meet these criteria, then the answers are vulnerable to distortion. When psychological barriers confront the researcher, objective methods must be discarded and projective techniques invoked instead.

An illustration of how objective techniques occasionally break down is provided by the beer-preference survey mentioned earlier. The survey was made to guide a brewery in the merchandising of its light and dark brews. It was designed to reveal what kind of people drank each kind of beer and, in particular, what differences existed between the two categories of customers. By identifying the buyers of each of the two product variations (light and dark) and then determining their significant characteristics, appropriate promotional appeals and advertising media could be selected.

The questionnaire contained the following objective questions, among others: "Do you drink _____ beer?" "Do you drink the *Light* or *Regular*?" (The words "Light" and "Regular" were used in the trade names of each type of beer.) The answers showed that the firm's customers preferred the "Light" to the "Regular" (dark) beer by a ratio of three to one. However, the company had been selling nine times as much "Regular" as "Light." Hence, the objective questions resulted in data that were in violent contradiction to actual consumer behavior. Obviously, something was distorting the respondent's answers, making an objective approach useless.[1]

Projective Techniques

J. Pierpont Morgan said, "A man generally has two reasons for doing a thing; one that sounds good and a real one." Projective techniques seek to unveil the real one.

Projective techniques are based on the assumption that the respondents are either unable or unwilling to reveal their behavioral pattern and give the reasons for their actions. There are many cases, as the beer-preference survey demonstrates, in which buyers will say they did one thing, whereas in fact they did something else.

Projective techniques confront the respondents with third-person questions, which allow them to transfer, or "project," their attitudes onto a third party or an inanimate object. For example, instead of asking a person whether he or she thought flying was safe (the objective approach), the interviewer might ask if the respondent thought other people believed flying to be safe. This kind of question gives respondents the opportunity to attribute their own feelings to the "other people" and hence avoid damaging their own self-image. A respondent might be fearful of flying, but unwilling to admit this fear because it create feelings of inferiority as a person. Hopefully, the projective question would tell the researcher whether the drive

---

[1] Mason Haire, "Projective Techniques in Marketing Research," *Journal of Marketing*, **14**:5 (April 1950), p. 649.

for self-preservation was an important psychological factor in the purchase of airline tickets or private aircraft.

A classic example of the failure of respondents to reply accurately to objective questions is provided by Mason Haire's Nescafé study.[2] Sales of Nescafé, a major brand of instant coffee, were disappointing, and an attitude survey was undertaken to determine why. A simple objective questionnaire asking, "Do you use instant coffee?" and (if the answer was no), "What do you dislike about it?" was used. The prevailing answer to the second question was, "I don't like the flavor." The simplicity and cliché-like quality of this reply made the researchers suspicious of its validity. Consequently, another survey was executed in an effort to uncover the truth. The new survey used a projective approach.

This time, a pair of shopping lists, identical except for the type of coffee specified, was used (see Exhibit 14-1). The first list called for Nescafé instant coffee. The second list called for a popular brand of conventional drip-grind coffee. Personal interviews were used to collect the data. Fifty housewives were shown the first list and another 50 were shown the second list. Each was asked to describe the type of woman that would have prepared the list she saw.

The two sets of responses revealed distinctly different profiles of the hypothetical shopper. Forty-eight percent of the respondents shown the Nescafé list described the woman who made it up as lazy, while a statistically insignificant 2 percent of the respondents with the regular-coffee list described their shopper as lazy. A significant number of the Nescafé respondents described the shopper as not a good wife; none of the regular-coffee respondents suggested this. The pattern was the same for the traits of thriftiness and good planning. Unlike the regular-coffee buyer, the instant-coffee buyer was seen as a lazy, disorganized, thriftless woman who was a poor wife as well—a rather unflattering image.

The purchase of Nescafé clearly did violence to the accepted role of the housewife. As Professor Haire suggests, making coffee was a serious and

Exhibit 14-1   **Shopping Lists Used in a Nescafé Study**

Shopping Lists I	*Shopping Lists II*
Pound and a half of hamburger	Pound and a half of hamburger
2 loaves Wonder bread	2 loaves Wonder bread
bunch of carrots	bunch of carrots
I can Rumford's Baking Power	I can Rumford's Baking Powder
Nescafé instant coffee	1 lb. Maxwell House Coffee (Drip Ground)
2 cans Del Monte peaches	2 cans Del Monte peaches
5 lb. potatoes	5 lb. potatoes

Source: Mason Haire, "Projective Techniques in Marketing Research," *Journal of Marketing* (April 1950), p. 651.

[2] Haire, "Projective Techniques in Marketing Research," p. 653.

ymbolic act for the homemaker. Her rejection of instant coffee had little to do with its flavor but was caused by the dimunition she felt in her self-image. The convenience and simplicity of instant coffee detracted from the idealized stereotype of the housewife and conflicted with the psychological needs of orderliness, retention, recognition, inviolacy, and nurturance.

An additional group of 50 respondents—whose relevant characteristics appeared to match those of the first group—was selected and given the same projective test. After each respondent completed her description of the hypothetical shopper, the interviewer asked to see her pantry, on the pretext that he wanted to look at her stock of food items. This allowed him to determine if the respondent had any instant coffee. Those who had no instant coffee tended to describe the Nescafé shopper in the usual unflattering terms. Those who had instant coffee saw the Nescafé shopper in a much more favorable light.[3] This third study reinforced Haire's original interpretation of the projective data. It also revealed a high statistical correlation between attitude and behavior. In this case at least, psychological factors clearly affected consumption.[4]

If these studies are any indication, the market researcher must accept the fact that objective techniques can result in misleading data. This does not mean that objective methods are always unreliable. On the contrary, they can be powerful research tools. However, the researcher must understand their inadequacies in dealing with certain behavioral situations, particularly those involving intense psychogenic needs and information about which the respondent is sensitive. In these cases—and they are often hard to recognize—projective techniques, designed to penetrate the psychological barrier between interviewer and respondent, may be the only answer. Sometimes this barrier can be removed by using mail questionnaires and guaranteeing the respondent anonymity of reply. This opens the door for the use of objective techniques, but imposes some serious restrictions on the researcher, particularly with regard to the length and complexity of the questions and the need for a structured format.

Structured Tests

Structured versus Unstructured Tests

A *test* is a set of one or more questions. Tests are designed to reveal the respondent's true behavior, belief, attitude, motive, psychological need or other attribute relative to the study. There are a number of basic formats for such tests.

---

[3] Haire, "Projective Techniques in Marketing Research," p. 655.

[4] The validity of the Nescafé study has been questioned. See Conrad R. Hill, "Haire's Classic Instant Coffee Study—18 Years Later," *Journalism Quarterly* **45** (August 1968), pp. 466–472. For an affirmation of Haire's findings, see Frederick E. Webster, Jr., and Frederick von Peckman, "A Replication of the Shopping List Study," *Journal of Marketing* **34**:2 (April 1970), pp. 61–63; or Jagdish N. Sheth, "Projective Attitudes Toward Instant Coffee in Late Sixties," *Markeds Kommunikasion* **2**:3 (June 1971), pp. 18–24.

In addition to being categorized as objective or projective, the test may be classed as structured or unstructured. The *structured tests* ask for brief, specific answers; often the respondent is limited to a list of specified replies. For instance, a structured test might ask such questions as, "What brand of coffee has the best flavor?" "Do most people fear flying?" or "Which of the following traits should a good neighborhood have?" Structured tests are easier to administer than unstructured tests. Less-skilled interviewers are needed and the data are easier to tabulate and compare.

Unstructured tests offer the respondent wide latitude in framing answers. There is usually no limit to the answers' length, although there may be a limit on the time the respondent can spend on them. No effort is made to elicit a prespecified reply. Some unstructured tests are designed solely to get the respondent talking about the subject.

Unstructured tests are especially suited to projective techniques, although they are sometimes used with objective methods, particularly for exploratory research. Since they are susceptible to both respondent and interviewer bias, skilled interviewers are required. The resultant data are less manageable than those provided by structured tests, primarily because of the difficulty of categorizing and aggregating the answers.

Following are the more common structured tests.

Specific-Direct-Question Tests

The specific-direct-question test is the simplest of the objective techniques. This structured test is generally limited to inquiries about matters that do not have a high emotional content, except in cases where the respondent remains anonymous. As stated previously, in order to preserve respondent anonymity, however, the researcher must generally forego telephone or personal interviews.

Specific-direct-question tests are generally highly structured, containing primarily fill-in or multiple-choice questions such as:

I buy an average of _____ gallons of gas each week.

My suits cost (a) under $70 _____, (b) $70 to $100 _____, (c) over $100 _____.

They sometimes contain unstructured questions of the essay type. A typical example is:

I believe that the important factors in the purchase of a new automobile are _____.

Questions of this type avoid constraining the respondent. They consist of incomplete statements and are often called *open-end* questions. Tests made up exclusively of such questions are *open-end tests.*

Specific-direct-question tests are always objective, in that they ask the respondents to give information about themselves. The questions may be phrased in various ways—the researcher may, for example, ask, "How many gallons of gasoline do you usually purchase every week?"—but they are equire first-person answers. Respondents are asked for explicit descriptions of their own behavior or opinions.

This technique is commonly used in gathering purchase-behavior data in ad hoc surveys and from continuous consumer panels. It seldom makes any demands on the respondent's insight, but frequently taxes his or her memory. Memory decay is a common source of error.

The specific-direct-question test can use any of the data collection media. Personal interviews are preferable when unstructured questions are used; however, a highly trained interviewer is not necessary.

Attitude-Scaling Tests

Attitude-scaling tests confront the respondent with a number of provocative statements and ask him to indicate the extent to which he approves or disapproves of them. For instance, he may be asked to indicate whether he strongly agrees, agrees, disagrees, or strongly disagrees with, or is indifferent to, such statements as, "Brand X is one of the best in its field" or "I would not buy Product Y under any circumstances."

The objective of attitude-scaling tests is to measure, usually quantitatively, consumer attitudes with respect to particular subjects. Since the tests are highly structured, they can be used to evaluate attitudes toward specific brands, particular product characteristics, advertising media, ad copy, or even single words. They can also be used to measure aggregate (overall) attitudes toward broader subjects such as product classes, stores, and manufacturers. Often, they are used to measure attitudes toward each of several related items, such as the color, texture, durability, style, and quality of a particular product. The technique is essentially objective, since the tests normally require a first-person response. However, the questions can be phrased so they elicit a third-person response, and are used projectively.

There are a number of different types of attitude-scaling tests. Although each has the same basic objective, they differ in form and in the way they are prepared. A different test—specifically, a different set of statements—must be prepared for each subject covered by the study. The form and the method of preparation of the tests will determine the nature of the data and the extent to which they can be manipulated. (We shall explore the subject of test preparation in detail in Chapter 15.)

The major advantage of attitude-scaling tests is that they provide a means of collecting attitudinal data that can be quantified. Other methods of collecting behavioral data provide only qualitative statements about attitudes or psychogenic needs; quantification is limited to the distribution of respondents. That is, the researcher can stipulate the number or proportion of respondents expressing a particular attitude or need, but the intensity of the attitude or need itself cannot be expressed quantitatively, except with attitude-scaling tests.

Except for a test called the semantic-differential test, described later in this chapter, all attitude-scaling tests confront the respondent with a scale of verbal options. However, the scale and the statements are prepared so that the respondent's answers can be converted to numerical values. Frequently a numerical scale is constructed to correspond with the verbal scale. Fo example, the scale 2, 1, 0, −1, and −2 might be used in conjunction wit a verbal scale indicating strong approval, approval, neutrality, disapprova and strong disapproval.

Personal interviews are a common medium of data collection whe attitude-scaling tests are used. Sometimes they are essential—for example when the respondent's instructions are a bit complex or more than a fev minutes of the respondent's time are required. Highly trained interviewer are not needed to administer attitude-scaling tests.

Monadic Tests   *Monadic tests* are attitude-scaling tests which ask th respondents to position themselves on a scale between two extremes. Fo example, in taste testing, each respondent might be asked to position him- o herself on the following scale:

Dislike   Like

The method is popular in product-testing. The tests are easy t administer. However, there can be some messy problems in scaling, whicl we'll discuss in the next chapter.

Paired Comparison Tests   *Paired comparison tests* are those asking th respondent to choose between two objects. The objects are typically differen products. Paired comparison tests are often used to see which product i preferred on each of several properties.

In administering the tests, the order of the objects is usually varie to avoid position bias. (People have a slight tendency to choose the objec presented first.) After testing is completed, the researcher simply tallies th votes for each object.

A variation of the paired comparison test is the *triangular compariso test*. This one requires the respondent to choose among three objects.

Error-Choice Tests

Error-choice tests are designed to detect the existence, direction, and th magnitude of respondent bias with respect to a particular subject. They d this by confronting the respondent with a series of values for the produc dimension under study and asking her to indicate the correct value. Fo instance, she may be asked to indicate the coach fare for a round-trip fligh from Los Angeles to Honolulu, given the options $240, $260, $300, $34(and $380. (Current coach fares vary between $280 and $320.) If she select one of the two latter values, she is assumed to have a misconception about th price, or a perceptual bias that is on the high side. If she picks the first answe it suggests a misconception or perceptual bias that is on the low side.

correct, or nearly correct, answer indicates an awareness of the actual price or a lucky guess. If a significant proportion of the respondents, in a sufficiently large ($n > 30$) and random sample, select answers on one side, the researcher is probably safe in concluding that a population bias exists in that direction.

Sometimes the scale of options is constructed using a proxy for the attitude being measured. For instance, the researcher may want to evaluate the market population's attitude toward a corporation—to define its image. One common dimension of this image is greediness. Hence, the researcher may want to know, "Does the population generally perceive the firm as greedy, and if so, to what degree?"

It is poor technique to ask the respondent if he thinks Company X is greedy, and if so, just how greedy. This is particularly true if personal interviews are used to collect the data. The respondents may consider an affirmative response offensive to the interviewer, who is identified with the company, and give biased answers. To prevent this, a proxy term—say, profit—may be substituted for "greed." The respondent may be asked to indicate how large a profit (usually expressed as a percentage of sales or investment) the company made during a given period and shown a series of options ranging from just below to well above the firm's actual earnings. Assuming that the respondent's perception of the firm's greed corresponds to his perception of its profits, the selection of a high value can be taken to imply a greedy image. Selection of a low value would be taken to indicate a "good" image. Selection of the correct, or a moderate value, would indicate an awareness of the firm's actual performance or a neutral attitude.

In order to use a proxy, the researcher must make some assumptions about the correlation between the proxy answers and the respondent's attitude toward the item the proxy represents. If these assumptions are shaky, the test's validity may be impaired. The proxy may not really measure what it is supposed to measure. The solution to this dilemma is redundancy. The researcher confronts the respondent with several questions designed to measure the same thing and compares the answers for consistency. If one question consistently produces answers that conflict with the answers to other questions on the same questionnaire, it should be discarded.

The error-choice test is essentially a projective technique. It has fewer applications than most other methods but is easy to administer and not particularly difficult to analyze. Mail questionnaires or telephone interviews can be used, although personal interviews are preferable. Highly skilled interviewers are not needed. The data can be interpreted by analysts with a modest amount of training in psychological testing and the cost of the study is usually modest.

Semantic-Differential Tests

The *semantic-differential test* is used to determine the connotative meanings of particular words and the intensity of those meanings as perceived by the respondent. It is also used to measure attitudes. The work of Charles E. Osgood, who developed this technique, indicates that a fairly homogeneous population may tend to have similar connotations for familiar words. For instance, Osgood used his technique to test the meaning of the words "good" and "nice" among college students. He discovered that "good" had masculine overtones for the respondents, while "nice" carried a feminine connotation. It may seem nonrational for such simple, genderless words to have sexual implications. However, connotative meanings are not always rational.[5]

The semantic-differential test is used in marketing research to select brand names and key words for advertising copy. The technique is simple. The respondent is asked to rate a particular word in accordance with a series of bipolar adjectives. A scale is inscribed between the members of each adjectival pair, and the respondent selects a point on the scale that represents the direction and intensity of feeling. For instance, the adjectival pair might be "weak" and "strong." If the word under study—say "polite"—connoted strength very intensely, the respondent would select the point at the end of the scale nearest the word "strong." If it carried an intense connotation of weakness, the respondent would select a point on the scale near "weak." If the respondent was indifferent—that is, if the word "polite" did not imply either strength or weakness—a point would be selected in the center of the scale.

The scores—that is, the positions selected on the scale—are averaged for each pair of polar adjectives. The averages are then plotted on a master graph, as in Figure 14-1, which shows the results of Osgood's study of the word "polite." Some meanings will be common and intensely felt, like "smooth," "good," and "relaxed" in the example. Others will not be significantly associated with the word under study. It will be neutral as far as those particular meanings are concerned. For instance, "polite" is a neutral word with respect to the adjectival pairs "small" and "large" and "cold" and "hot."

The reliability of the findings can be tested by drawing two samples of respondents and plotting the average scores for each group on the same graph. If the two plots are similar in shape and location, as they are in Figure 14-2, the findings are probably reliable. This test is, in effect, a graphical application of variance analysis. The means of two supposedly homogeneous samples are compared to test the hypothesis that the findings are the same.

The marketing implications of this technique are fairly obvious. The marketer is interested in identifying words with connotations intensely favorable to the product. Presumably, incorporating these words in a brand name or advertising copy will make the product seem more attractive, and encourage prospects to remember it. Conversely, the marketer is anxious to avoid using words that have unfavorable connotations or will evoke little response from prospects. The semantic-differential test provides a way of identifying such words.

[5] Ernest R. Hilgard and Richard A. Atkinson, *Introduction to Psychology*, 4th ed. (New York: Harcourt Brace Jovanovich, 1967), p. 367.

Figure 14-1   **Osgood's Semantic-Differential Test: Median Responses From Two Groups of 20 Subjects Each**

Source: From *Introduction to Psychology*, 4th Edition, by Earnest R. Hilgard and Richard C. Atkinson, copyright © 1953, 1957, 1962, by Harcourt Brace Jovanoich, Inc., and reproduced with their permission.

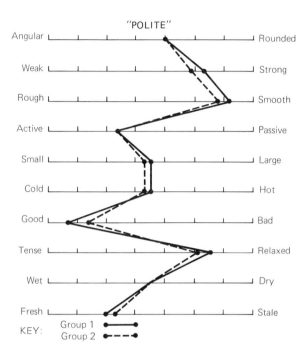

Word-Association Tests

Word-association tests give respondents a list of words and ask them to match each one with a word of their own choosing. Answers are usually timed; hence, personal or phone interviews are used. The objective of these tests is to provoke quick and unrestrained responses that will (hopefully) reveal the respondents' strongest attitudes. The first answer that comes to mind is the important one.

Word association is the oldest and simplest of the projective techniques.[6] It is used in marketing research to identify prevalent attitudes toward a particular subject and to test words that are candidates for brand names or advertising copy. It is also one way of finding words that would be useful for those purposes.

The key words—called *stimulus words*—are buried in a list of 50 to 100 items. Most of the words are padding and are neutral; that is, they have no

---

[6] Word association was discussed in the psychology literature as far back as 1879. See Francis Galton, "Psychometric Experiments," *Brain* **2** (1879), pp. 149–162.

emotional content. The purpose of the padding is to conceal the exact subject of the inquiry from the respondent, thus precluding bias from at least one source. For example, the following list might be prepared to explore attitudes toward cake mixes and find candidates for brand names or advertising copy.

Words	Response	Answer Time in Seconds
1. chair	_____	____
2. soft	_____	____
3. cake	_____	____
4. blue	_____	____
5. cheese	_____	____
6. white	_____	____
7. fluffy	_____	____
* * * * *		
96. mix	_____	____
97. house	_____	____
98. bake	_____	____
99. lamp	_____	____
100. sweet	_____	____

The first response to each word would be the only one recorded. In addition to imposing a short time limit on each response, the interviewer may also record the time it takes the respondent to react to each word. A quick response indicates that a word is a strong stimulus and hence more likely to be noticed and remembered than words that provoke a slow response. Response speed is also indicative of attitude intensity.

A variation of the word-association test is the *homographic free-association test*. A *homograph* is a word that is spelled exactly like another word but has a different meaning and a different derivation. Take, for example, the word "base." "Base," meaning "foundation," is the homograph of the word "base" meaning "wicked."[7]

For this test, words are selected that have two everyday meanings, one social and the other physical, for example, "revolution." The respondent is asked to reply to each word with a synonym or a short phrase. The nature of the response—whether it is social or physical—suggests whether the respondent is oriented toward the social or physical environment and whether he or she interprets words in their interpersonal or literal sense.[8] Due to the scarcity of homographs, the usefulness of this method is limited. However, it is of some value in identifying personality traits and defining

[7] Frank S. Freeman, *Theory and Practice of Psychological Testing*, rev. ed. (New York: Holt, Rinehart & Winston, 1956), p. 550.

[8] Freeman, *Theory and Practice of Psychological Testing*, p. 551.

stereotypes. Data on personality traits are important in studies of persuasibility[9] and in the preparation of advertising directed at a particular class of consumers, such as agricultural innovators or fashion-setters. A knowledge of stereotypes is important in studies of innovation diffusion and the social psychology of consumer group behavior.

Highly trained interviewers are not needed to administer word-association tests. The interviewers simply explain the questionnaire, read the key words, note the respondents' reaction time, and record the replies. However, training in psychology is usually necessary to interpret the data.

Sentence-Completion Tests

The *sentence-completion test* is an elaboration of the word-association test that has the advantage of being able to test ideas as well as words. It is administered in a similar fashion. The respondent is shown the first parts of incomplete sentences and asked to complete them. Each sentence begins with a declarative statement whose completion requires respondents to take a position or express an attitude. The following examples are typical:

1   "My favorite magazine is _____."
2   "When I think of beer I think of _____."
3   "Air travel is _____."
4   "People who buy Cadillacs are _____."

The items can be objective or projective, although sentence completion is usually associated with projective techniques. Sentence-completion tests can be adapted to provide data for a variety of analytical methods. However, like word-association tests, they are generally identified with the Gestalt school, since they tend to reveal conscious attitudes.

Because of the time limit imposed on the answers, personal interviews are the most practical medium for data collection. The interviewer, after explaining the questionnaire, reads the sentence stems and records the answers. As in word-association tests, the object is to provoke an unrestrained response. The first answer is considered the most revealing.

Highly trained interviewers are not required. However, a good deal of specialized knowledge is needed to fully interpret the data. The services of a psychologist are usually required. Pretesting is useful to eliminate confusing sentence stems.

Unstructured Tests

Story-Completion Tests

The *story-completion test* is an extension of the sentence-completion test, but less structured. It is clearly projective. The respondents are given the

---

[9] See Irving L. Janis et al., eds., *Personality and Persuasibility* (New Haven: Yale University Press, 1959), for a detailed exploration of persuasibility's relationship to personality traits.

beginning of a story and asked to complete it. For instance, they may be given a description of a man and woman about to enter an automobile showroom. The details will be skimpy, so as not to encourage a biased response. The couple's family status and income may be given, but little other specific information will be offered. It is hoped that, in completing the story, respondents will reveal preferences, attitudes, anxieties, and beliefs relevant to purchase behavior.

This technique is useful in the exploratory phase of research as an instrument of problem definition. It is useful later in identifying and evaluating specific psychological needs that cannot be uncovered using simpler projective techniques. It can provide data for Freudian analysis, if the test is properly administered. However, this calls for long, in-depth interviews, conducted by highly trained interviewers. Interpretation must be left to psychologists who are skilled in psychoanalysis. The data are qualitative, highly subjective, and not amenable to quantitative evaluation.

Picture-Frustration Tests

The *picture-frustration test* seeks to uncover attitudes toward a subject by inducing the respondent to identify with a cartoon character. The cartoon usually shows two people without facial expressions or other characteristics that would indicate a particular personality. (This neutrality is important, for it helps respondents to identify with a character.) The people are involved in a situation relevant to the subject under study. One has a speech balloon overhead that contains a thought-provoking statement. The other also has a speech balloon overhead, but it is empty. Respondents are asked to provide a statement to fill the second balloon, in hopes that they will take on the role of the character and reveal their own attitude toward the pictured situation. Not only are the characters always neutral, the scene itself is made a bit ambiguous to give respondents latitude in interpreting it. Figure 14-2 is a typical picture-frustration test. One or more such pictures—all related to the same subject—may be used in a given study, and each respondent's reply to each picture noted.

Picture-frustration tests have evolved into a complex projective technique. Gathering the data usually requires a personal interview, conducted by a moderately trained interviewer. The interviewer does not necessarily have to be knowledgeable about psychology or sociology, but must be sufficiently skillful at interviewing so that his or her personal value judgments will not be reflected in the replies. Interpreting picture-frustration data, on the other hand, requires a high level of skill in psychology. For a Freudian interpretation of the results, a trained psychoanalyst is needed. The data are always qualitative and subjective and do not lend themselves to quantitative manipulation.

The picture-frustration test is employed by psychologists and sociologists of a variety of persuasions. Even a superficial analysis of the information it provides may be of some value. For instance, it may serve to expose the more obvious and intense consumer attitudes toward such things as brands, products, prices, and purchasing situations. It can also be subjected to

Figure 14-2   **A Picture-Frustration Test**

Source: From Research Analysis for Marketing Decisions by Chester R. Wasson. Copyright ©
1965 by Meredith Corporation. Reprinted by permission of Appleton-Century-Crofts and
courtesy of the *Chicago Tribune*.

psychoanalysis in an effort to identify the unconscious attitudes that affect
consumer behavior.

Thematic-Apperception Tests

The **thematic-apperception test (TAT)** is an extension of the picture-frustration test. Respondents are again shown a picture or series of pictures, but
these pictures are even more ambiguous than the type used in picture-
frustration tests, containing neither speech balloons nor a half-completed
dialogue. Respondents are asked to explain the scenes, tell what is happening,
and describe the characters. Sometimes they are asked to make up a story
about what is happening now and what may happen later. It is hoped that,
in so doing, they will reveal their own hidden attitudes and suppressed
desires.

This technique is also used in psychoanalysis, frequently in conjunction with psychotherapy. In terms of subjectivity, it is similar to the Rorschach (inkblot) test. The latter, however, is used primarily in psychoanalysis and psychotherapy and virtually never in marketing research.

Administering the TAT requires a lengthy personal interview, conducted by a skilled technician, and the data must be interpreted by a psychologist. For these reasons, and in order to keep the costs of the study within reasonable limits, the samples used are generally small. If the number of respondents is too small to satisfy the requirements for statistical significance, this compromises the validity of any conclusions that are generalized to the market population. Furthermore, since TAT findings are usually interpreted in terms of Freudian psychology, they may be difficult to incorporate into the marketing decision process.

In-Depth Personal Interviews

In-depth personal interviews—often called simply "depth interviews"—can be objective, projective, or a combination of both. Objective interviews are frequently used in exploratory research to define a problem. They are also used to construct complex behavioral models, such as those used to describe markets for highly technical and expensive industrial goods whose purchase must be approved by executives and engineers as well as the firm's purchasing agent. The objective approach is also useful in discovering the virtues and deficiencies customers attribute to complex products—and their importance. It is also a way to discover new applications for the firm's present product line and opportunities for the development of new goods. In conducting an objective in-depth interview, an intimate knowledge of the firm's product, the customer, or the marketplace may be more valuable than a mastery of interviewing skills or a knowledge of psychology.

A projective in-depth interview is a different matter. Here the interviewer's task is to probe the inner thoughts of the respondent in order to reveal suppressed desires, attitudes, and psychoses. Questions are generally, unstructured, and the interviews tend to be long—often lasting several hours—and repetitive. A psychologist is required both to obtain and analyze the data. The samples are necessarily small, and hence an inadequate basis for statistical generalization. In addition to being lengthy and expensive, the process demands a considerable degree of cooperation from the respondents. The data obtained are qualitative, highly subjective, and open to conflicting interpretation. For all these reasons, the projective in-depth interview is of little real value in marketing research.

Role Playing and the Psychodrama

In *role playing*, respondents become, for a short time, actors. The interviewer describes a hypothetical situation and asks each respondent to play a simple part, involving a short monologue but no physical activity. For instance, a male respondent might be asked to play the part of a man advising a close friend on how to go about purchasing a new car—what to look for, who to deal with, and how to bargain over the price. Since the respondent makes up the monologue, he has an opportunity to project his feelings onto the character he portrays. The directions are simple and the response is usually tape recorded; thus, a highly trained interviewer is unnecessary. However, a good deal of skill is needed to evaluate the data if psychogenic needs or suppressed desires are to be uncovered.

Role playing has been useful with children. Children not only influence their parents' purchases, but are buyers themselves. More important they are consumer trainees, representing tomorrow's big spenders.

Children, especially young ones, often lack verbal skills, yet can express themselves in other ways. The trick is to give them the motivation and opportunity for expression in the presence of somebody trained in child psychology. This is done through games and role playing. For example, a female child may be asked to act out her last trip to the supermarket with her mother. Or she might be asked to call a friend on a toy phone and describe a new toy she's just seen advertised or a loaf of bread her mother purchased.[10] An illustration is found in Exhibit 14-2.

The *psychodrama* is an elaboration of role playing. The method was originally developed as an instrument of group therapy.

Several respondents are brought together and asked to act out a marketing situation. In addition, other respondents act as an audience and comment on the roles played by the actors. The direction of the psychodrama and the analysis of the results both require a high level of skill, as well as a considerable knowledge of psychology and sociology, especially in the areas of testing and group dynamics.

Unstructured tests often produce few if any numbers. This inflicts an intolerable burden, both intellectual and emotional, on some researchers. Those who believe in the deity of quantitative methods tend to reject purely qualitative information as little more than organized ignorance: Until one quantifies[11] things, one does not understand the problem.

Although this book pushes the reader toward quantitative techniques, we should also give some attention to qualitative research, which offers some useful tools.

Qualitative Research

Qualitative research is research done without benefit of mathematics or

---

[10] For a discussion of these three examples, see cases 10, 11, and 12, in Walter B. Wentz, ed., *Cases in Marketing Research* (New York: Harper & Row, 1975).

[11] Winston Churchill commented: " 'Quantify,' ever heard that before? I hope you will never hear it again. I believe it was a substitute for 'estimate.' " (The quote is from his acceptance speech for the Nobel Prize for Literature.)

Exhibit 14-2   **Role Playing in Action**

Source: Child Research Services, Inc., New York, NY.

statistics. Practitioners, who sometimes approach the method with missionary zeal, see it as "idea research . . . insight development in its purest form."[12]
One true believer asserts that qualitative research "can yield all the knowledge
and insight that will possibly be useful in marketing."[13] The truth probably
lies somewhere beneath this rhetoric. Qualitative research, like its quantitative counterpart, is both useful and limited.

Limitations

The main limitation to qualitative research is the difficulty in generalizing
the findings to the market population. Qualitative research deals in small
samples, which are rarely claimed to be representative of the universe. However, ideas and insights, not generalizations, are the currency of qualitative
research. These are often sufficient. For instance, two days of qualitative
study revealed enough deficiencies in a prototype trash compactor to scrap
the project. A statistically meaningful survey of homeowners would have
wasted time and money.

With the small and rarely randomized sample comes the limitation of
error specification. One cannot make a rigorous statement about the range

[12] Dale J. Shaw, "Some Comments on Qualitative Methods," unpublished monograph,
1976, p. 1.
[13] Dietz Leonhard, "Can Focus Group Interviews Survive?" *Marketing News* **VIII**:31
(October 10, 1975), p. 6.

of error inherent in the findings. But so long as one avoids the temptation to generalize the findings to the population, this is unimportant.

Qualitative research has the same sort of administrative limitations associated with quantitative research. Time, budgets, schedules, respondent recruiting, and so forth are all problems and constraints. Only the data reduction process is significantly simplified. The data analysis and report preparation may be equally, or even more, difficult.

Applications

Qualitative research is especially suited to exploration. Its uniqueness rests on its ability to produce questions as well as answers. A qualitative study is often authorized to throw a problem into bold relief—to produce hypotheses and questions for further examination. Frequently, it sets the stage for quantitative research. The observations made in the qualitative phase are often evaluated by conventional methods. Then they can be qualified in statistical terms and generalized to the universe.

Qualitative research is often used for concept-testing, idea provocation, and product- and package-testing. Pan Am used it to better understand the traveler's feeling toward skyjacking.[14] Kawasaki invoked it to get consumer reactions to different motorcycle designs. General Motors used it to evaluate a new product concept, the cambered vehicle. Funk & Wagnalls applied it to provoke consumer reactions to a new product line.[15]

Development

The techniques of qualitative research have been contributed mostly by the behavioral scientists, especially the social psychologists. The methods, as they're applied to consumer behavior, grew mainly from studies of group dynamics. Many are similar to techniques used in group therapy.

None of these techniques yields numbers. When numbers are associated with qualitative research, they are confined to sample size and the distribution of responses among participants. Some practitioners argue that even these simple statistics have no place in qualitative research. This position is well founded: If one constructs a frequency distribution, it tends to be inferred to the population.

Projective techniques and unstructured tests are usually used in qualitative research. A common example is role playing, which we discussed earlier.

The most pervasive technique of qualitative research, at least within MR, is the focus group. The focus group is the adaptation of the in-depth interview and group therapy to marketing research. It is currently in high fashion.

[14] Dale J. Shaw, "Pan American World Airways: Skyjacking and Consumer Behavior," in Walter B. Wentz, ed., *Cases in Marketing Research* (New York: Harper & Row, 1975), pp. 77–87.
[15] Alfred Vogel and Herbert Abelson, "Funk & Wagnalls: A Problem in Product Design," in Wentz, ed., *Cases in Marketing Research*, pp. 88–93.

Focus Groups

The *focus group* is a small panel of respondents gathered to discuss a specific subject, such as a new product. The participants are led by a moderator, who motivates the discussion and keeps the group focused on the subject. The format is informal and unstructured.

Objective   The focus group objective is to draw out ideas, feelings, and experiences that would be obscured by conventional methods of data collection. In a successful focus group, respondents unburden themselves. They engage in a spontaneous and uninhibited exchange of thoughts.

According to the method's advocates, this is information that cannot be conveyed over a bridge of antiseptic numbers. Focus groups animate the respondents. According to one user, the technique gives the researcher "a chance to experience a flesh and blood consumer . . . to go into her life and relive with her all the satisfactions, rewards, and frustrations she experiences when she takes the product into her home."[16]

The output of the focus group—the insights and ideas revealed by the participants—is usually recorded on audio or TV tape. Sometimes the groups are secretly observed through one-way mirrors. This variation, however, raises a sticky ethical issue.

Structure   Focus groups consist of eight to 12 respondents. They are usually gathered in a laboratory appointed like the one in Exhibit 14-3. This living-room environment is consistent with the relaxed and informal mood the researcher wants to induce. These qualities are considered so important that some research suppliers insist on holding their focus groups in a real home.

Essentials   Axelrod specified ten essentials for successful focus groups:[17]

a clearly understood objective	a well-prepared moderator
homogeneity within the group	free-flowing dialog
good recruiting	restrained group influence
a relaxed atmosphere	skilled analysis
a moderator who listens	competent researchers

[16] Myril Axelrod, "Marketers Get an Eyeful When Focus Groups Expose Products, Ideas, Images, Ad Copy, etc. to Consumers," Part 1 of 2, *Marketing News* 8:16 (February 28, 1975), pp. 6–7.

[17] Myril D. Axelrod, "10 Essentials for Good Qualitative Research," *Marketing News* VIII: 16 (March 14, 1975), pp. 10–11. The author is indebted to Ms. Axelrod, Vice President, Qualitative Research, Y&R Enterprises, for other material used in this section. He is also indebted to Dr. Dale J. Shaw, consulting psychologist, for his assistance.

Exhibit 14-3   **Focus Group**

Source: Y & R Enterprises Inc., a subsidiary of Young & Rubicam International Inc.

The cornerstone of the focus group is clearly the moderator. The moderator must motivate and control, yet not inhibit or bias the respondents. He or she must assure each respondent's free participation, and must not let the group influence the individuals.

Participants are typically treated to coffee, soft drinks, and snacks. They are individually introduced and often addressed by their first names. They are engaged in small talk—all in an effort to create a relaxed atmosphere and encourage participations. The moderator is usually equipped with a guide to assure that the group is led through all the points of interest to the client.

These mechanics are useful, but are no substitute for empathy, training, and skill. As focus group technology is drawn from psychology, psychologists trained in group dynamics are the preferred moderators.

Output   The output of a focus group is usually a report of the findings, summarizing the observations and analyzing the statements and behavior of the participants. Usually, it is prepared by the moderator. It may contain recommendations and pose hypotheses for testing with quantitative methods. The report may be supplemented with an edited video tape of the proceedings.

Other Methods

In our discussion of data acquisition, we touched on two other methods associated with qualitative research. These were the trip to Delphi and mother-in-law research. Neither should be dismissed out of hand. The first produced the Mustang, one of the most successful cars in Ford's history. The second led to the Polaroid instant camera.[18]

Other qualitative techniques are emerging from the minds of researchers unsatisfied with the traditional forms of inquiry and not content with the inventions of others. Role playing and the psychodrama are past examples.

None of these methods, new or old, is statistically respectable. Yet they can yield important information. Often their findings can be accepted at face value. Great revelations need no statistical props.

Other times the information is unreliable. It must be tested before it can serve as the foundation for a management decision. This brings in the traditional tools of marketing research, namely, the survey and statistics. Qualitative methods assume the role of exploration—a part that they play well. Qualitative research goes first, yielding (hopefully) the right questions. A statistically acceptable survey follows, revealing (it is hoped), the right answers.

Selecting a Method

The Researcher's Orientation

As we mentioned in Chapter 13, a researcher's choice of a particular technique of data collection or analysis is determined largely by the school of psychology or sociology by which he is influenced. For instance, if he subscribes to the Gestalt school of psychology, he will tend to see purchase behavior as a response to conscious, rational needs. Of course, the consumer may be unwilling to reveal many of his motives because they are socially unacceptable or conflict with self-image. Many items, such as Lincoln Continentals and Dior originals, are probably purchased primarily as status symbols by buyers who would not admit to such a motive. In such cases, projective techniques that give the respondent an opportunity to transfer her feelings to a hypothetical third party may relieve her of the inhibitions (imposed by social constraints and her self-image) that prevent her from verbalizing her motives. It is hoped she will expose her own motives by attributing them to the third party.

The Gestalt-trained researcher will look for rationales for behavior. He may even use observational or objective techniques to discover mechanical factors or functional reasons for behavior. (These are often intermixed with psychological factors.) However, he will look primarily for psychogenic causes and rely heavily on projective methods. Although qualitative and largely subjective, the techniques of data collection and manipulation he uses will provide statistically significant samples, require moderately trained

---

[18] The inventor, Edwin Land, attributes the instant camera to an idea he got from one of his children.

interviewers, be moderately complex and expensive, and allow some forms of statistical inference.

If the researcher subscribes to the Freudian school, she will tend to see the consumer as driven by irrational motives, of which he himself is unaware. She will not expect the consumer to be able to verbalize the true causes of his behavior, even if he is relieved of his inhibitions. She will consider the techniques used by those of the Gestalt school as inadequate and their analysis as superficial.

The Freudian-oriented researcher will look for suppressed desires (the id) that conflict with the consumer's socially imposed values (the superego). For example, she is apt to see smoking as the result of a desire for oral gratification and pipes, cigars, or cigarettes as symbolic of the thumb or the mother's breast, either of which the consumer would prefer to suck, were it not for his superego. The symbolic properties of a purchase are most important.

The Freudian depends solely on projective techniques, particularly the picture-frustration, thematic-apperception, and Rorschach tests, for data collection. Her favorite medium for data collection is the in-depth personal interview, her method of analysis is psychoanalysis.

Freudian methods provide very small samples; but practitioners of these techniques argue that basic human drives are sufficiently universal to allow their findings to be generalized to the entire market population. The techniques are both complex and expensive, and require highly trained interviewers and analysts. They offer little opportunity for the rigorous application of quantitative tools.

If the researcher is oriented toward sociology, he will tend to see the behavior of the consumer as a function of her environment, especially her peer group. He will tend to consider the Gestalt and especially the Freudian techniques of data analysis inappropriate, although he may use some of their methods of data collection, including such projective methods as sentence-completion, word-association, and picture-frustration tests. He will make extensive use of personal interviews and the uniquely sociological techniques of sociometry.

The sociologically oriented researcher will look for group norms and interpersonal and intergroup relationships as explanations of consumer behavior. He will stress those psychological needs that are acquired through social involvements. He will seek to identify group leaders and stereotypes that play a role in a particular purchase situation. His methods will be similar to Gestalt techniques in terms of complexity, cost, and amenity to quantitative description and analysis.

Thus, researchers have at their disposal a variety of methods for collecting behavioral data. These serve a variety of information needs. Which they choose depends on their perception of the essential nature of human behavior. Figure 14-3 shows where selected data collection methods fit into the general schemes of behavioral analysis.

Figure 14-3   **Selected Methods of Acquiring Behavior Data**

Source: Adapted from W. B. Wentz and G. I. Eyrich, *Marketing: Theory and Application* (New York: Harcourt Brace Jovanovich, 1970, p. 546) and reproduced with their permission.

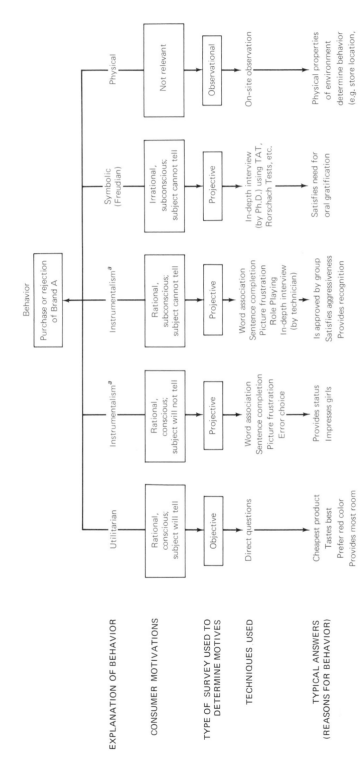

NOTE: [a] *Includes those schools that perceive consumer purchases as instruments for satisfying rational needs, e.g. Gestalt psychology, sociology, social psychology*

Validity and Reliability[19]

The *validity* of a test or questionnaire depends on the extent to which it measures what it purports to measure. For instance, the beer-preference test cited earlier was not valid. The results showed that consumers strongly preferred the light beer, whereas in fact they liked dark beer. The test did not measure what it was supposed to measure. If anything, it measured the relative prestige, or social status, of light and dark beer.

Validity is difficult to ascertain when personality traits are being measured. Unlike IQ, mechanical aptitude, or scholastic ability, there is no standard of performance. Hence, many of the criteria of validity associated with testing are difficult to apply to tests of consumer behavior, especially those involving the measurement of attitudes.

Cross validation is perhaps the most practical way of checking the validity of marketing-research questionnaires used in consumer-behavior analysis. The data collected on the test variable are evaluated by giving a second test to another sample of the same population and comparing the results to those of the original test. If there is no significant difference, then the original test is apparently measuring what it claims to measure. This, however, is not certain. By coincidence, both tests could be measuring the same wrong variable. That is, the responses may be affected in both instances by a factor of which the researcher is unaware.

Another method of checking validity is to compare the results of a market decision with the outcome predicted by the study, assuming of course that the decision was based on the research findings. For instance, if the questionnaire revealed that sales of a brand of soap were low because most consumers disliked the color of the package, and the color was changed, one would expect sales to improve. If they did not, the questionnaire may have been invalid. Of course, any one of many other factors could have produced the same outcome.

The *reliability* of a test is measured by the consistency with which it produces the same results. A reliable test will yield the same answers every time it is given to the same, or comparable, populations, provided that the relevant characteristics of the population have not changed.

Reliability can be checked in three ways: (1) by retesting the same sample of respondents, (2) by testing two homogeneous samples drawn from the same population, or (3) by split-half analysis. The second method is generally the easiest, but also the weakest, way of checking the reliability of consumer-behavior questionnaires.

If the same test is to be given to the same respondents twice, the interval between the first test and the second should be sufficient for memory decay to have nearly cancelled the learning effect. The answers from the first test are compared with those from the second. If there is a significant difference, the questionnaire is assumed to be unreliable.

---

[19] An entire issue of the *Journal of Marketing Research* is devoted mainly to these subjects. See vol. XVI, no. 1, February, 1979.

Testing two homogeneous samples with the same questionnaire simply means administering the test to the entire sample, then making a random division of the questionnaires into two groups. The two sets of questionnaires are then scored and the results compared. If the test is reliable, the two sets of answers should be the same, except for the differences due to chance. An analysis of variance can be used to determine if the difference in the two sets of test scores is sufficient to be attributable to factors other than chance. If so, the test cannot be considered reliable, at least not on the basis of a statistical comparision of the two sets of test scores. (Of course, a larger sample may alleviate this problem, for reasons explained in Chapter 8.)

A graphical comparison of test results can be substituted for an analysis of variance in the evaluation of the sameness of the two sets of answers. (See, for example Figure 14-1, a graph in which the scores of two groups given the same semantic-differential test are averaged, plotted, and compared. If the form and position of the lines are quite similar, as they are in the illustration, the two groups of answers can be considered the same and the test, therefore, reliable.) This method is a bit easier than, but nowhere near as rigorous as, an analysis of variance.

Split-half analysis requires dividing the test itself into two parts and comparing the two sets of answers. Since the two sets of questions (that is,

Table 14-1   **Some Common Sources of Invalidity and Unreliability**

Stage in the Research Process	Mistake and Source of Error	Compromise In
Problem definition	Attacking the wrong problem	Validity
	Inadequately defining parts of the problem	Validity
Project design	Selecting the wrong information sources	Validity and reliability
	Specifying exploratory research procedures for conclusive research goals	Validity and reliability
Data acquisition	Selecting the wrong data collection method	Validity
	Biased sampling	Reliability
	Inadequate sample size	Reliability
	Using objective questions when projective techniques are needed	Validity
	Using improperly structured or confusing questions	Validity
Data reduction	Sloppy work in coding, posting, or tabulating	Validity
	Failure to recognize presence of statistical error	Validity
Data analysis	Improper choice of analytical tools	Validity
	Treating nonparametric as parametric data	Validity
	Misrepresentation of results	Validity

[a] Table is based partially on Robert W. Joselyn, *Designing the Marketing Research Project* (New York: Petrocelli/Charter, 1977), Fig. 5.3, p. 68.

the two halves of the test) must be the same with respect to the variables being measured and the dimensions of the measurement, they may have to be somewhat redundant. This is true if the test is designed to evaluate a number of heterogeneous variables, if the questions are open-ended, or if the answers are scored using different scales. In some cases, these conditions cannot be met, and split-half analysis cannot be used. (An example is the word-association test used to evaluate particular words for their usefulness as brand names or in advertising copy.)

The two sets of answers are compared using the same techniques employed in comparing two sets of scores from a pair of homogeneous samples. If the difference is too great to be attributed to chance, then the test cannot be considered statistically reliable. (If the respondent count is small, an increase in sample size may relieve the problem.)

The issues of validity and reliability extend throughout the research process. Invalidity and unreliability can have many fathers. Some common villains, in addition to those just cited, and listed in Table 14-1.

Media and Costs

Data for consumer-behavior analysis are usually collected through a survey of a sample of the market population, either in the field or in the laboratory. Field surveys are the most common, although consumer juries are sometimes brought into a laboratory to serve as the survey sample.

The personal interview is the most important medium of data collection, although mail questionnaires and telephone interviews are often useful. Personal interviews are essential if the researcher wishes to use complex data collection techniques such as story-completion and picture-frustration tests.

Costs are function of the collection technique, collection medium, and sample size. The data collection technique usually dictates which collection medium will be used and sometimes places a constraint on sample size. Generally, the less sophisticated and more objective the technique, the less the study will cost. Personal interviews are more expensive than telephone interviews by, roughly, a factor of five. Telephone interviews are about three times as costly as mail questionnaires. Variable collection costs interviewer salaries and expenses, telephone charges, printing and postage costs, etc.) are proportional to sample size. To them must be added the semi-variable and fixed costs of recruiting and training interviewers, supervising fieldworkers, coding questionnaires, setting up the project, and tabulating results.

The costs of a study cannot be precisely estimated until the data collection medium is selected. However, experience provides some measure of their order of magnitude. Statistically significant data can seldom be gathered for less than $2,500, considering all costs and assuming a previously prepared population list. With a budget this size, the researcher would probably be limited to using specific, direct questions and a mail questionnaire.

A mail questionnaire can cost from $.50 to $3 per unit in variable costs, depending on the return rate. Telephone interviews will cost from $.80 to $10 per call, depending on the distance of the calls and the length of the interview. Personal interviews can cost from $.75 to many dollars, depending on the level of skill required, the length of the interview, and the location of the respondents.

Occasionally the marginal cost of gathering data can be reduced by combining this function with another activity. For instance, the firm's salespersons may be asked to distribute and collect questionnaires, or even to administer personal interviews. However, this is seldom a good practice, since it limits the researcher's control of the process. Sales people are seldom trained interviewers, and they are usually more interested in maximizing sales than in doing research. An alternative is to combine questionnaires with warranty cards, advertising, or bills. However, this severely limits the researcher's choice of techniques and usually biases the sample.

Problems

1   What method of data collection—structured/unstructured and objective/projective—would be most appropriate in determining the causes for each of the following examples of consumer behavior: (a) commuters not using the local bus line, (b) the association of instant coffee with poor housekeeping, and (c) a decline in the demand for the output of a steel company during a business boom.

2   Suggest a specific test for each of the problems in question 1. Defend your choice.

3   Select a structured test to evaluate a current advertisement. (Select a specific advertisement.) Defend your choice.

4   Describe a specific purchasing situation in which the consumer is responding to psychological or sociological factors that he or she is unlikely to reveal in response to direct objective questions. What might these factors be? Suggest a test which would identify and help evaluate these factors. Defend your choice.

5   Cite a situation where role playing might be useful in the collection of behavioral data. Explain why.

6   Cite a market phenomenon or product which might be studied with the aid of one or more focus groups. Explain why the focus group is relevant.

7   Define "validity" as it applies to tests. Specify some ways to deal with it.

Chapter 15
Scaling and
Data Analysis

Key Concepts

Scaling
Problems and considerations in selecting or creating a measuring standard

Scaling Techniques
Alternative methods of preparing a scale

Data Analysis
More bivariate techniques for determining the relationship between variables

Key Terms

ratio scale	Guttman Attitude Scale
interval scale	multidimensional scaling
ordinal scale	bivariate analysis
nominal values	sign test
dichotomous variable	ranked-sums test
awareness tests	Mann-Whitney test
item analysis	U-test
Thurstone Attitude Scale	rank-correlation coefficient
Likert Attitude Scale	Spearman's coefficient
Q-sort	

Scaling

The preparation of a behavioral questionnaire and the analysis of the resultant data can require a number of skills. These range from common sense to psychoanalysis. The skills needed for a particular study are dictated by the data collection and analytical techniques that have been selected. The choice of techniques depends, in turn, on the objectives of the research project, the project designer's opinion of the consumer's willingness and ability to provide information, and the resources available.

Common sense will generally suffice if a questionnaire is being written to gather objective data on brand preferences or purchasing behavior. Moderate mathematical skills may be needed to prepare a parametric scale for measuring attitudes. A knowledge of psychology is necessary to design a picture-frustration test for identifying suppressed desires. These problems come into bold relief when we confront scaling.

Scaling Problems

Behavioral information tends to take the form of nonmetric data. Much of it is improperly treated as metric data, out of ignorance or convenience. When this happens, the research findings can be inaccurate. In severe cases they can be pure nonsense.

We have incentive to construct tests that will yield metric data. When this is not practical, care must be taken to apply analytical tools that are compatible with nonmetric numbers.

As we learned in Chapter 6, metric data are congenial with mathematical operations. Nonmetric data are alien to direct mathematical operations. (For review, see Table 6-1.)

Distinguishing between metric and nonmetric data is not always easy, since they appear the same (both are expressed numerically). The exception is nominal-scale responses before they are coded. The ultimate test of metricity is the interchangeability of units. This must be determined by examining the variable the data purport to measure, the basis of the measurement scale, and the ways in which the data are to be used.

Most variables associated with consumer-behavior analysis are psychological or sociological; hence, they are inherently qualitative. The only metric data that can emerge from purely qualitative variables are a frequency distribution, where the numbers of respondents giving a particular qualitative response are counted. The resultant data are parametric with respect to the respondents, as long as the respondents themselves are interchangeable. (This would not be the case if some respondents were significantly different with respect to the variable under study. For instance, a minor would not be interchangeable with an adult in a test of beer preferences.) The thing to remember here is that the frequency-distribution data describe the respondent population, not the qualitative variable.

For example, assume that 100 housewives are asked to taste-test a new and unidentified brand of coffee and rate it according to an objective nominal scale: (a) Like it very much _____, (b) Like it _____, (c) Am indifferent _____, (d) Dislike it _____, or (e) Dislike it very much _____. When the survey is completed, the 100 respondents can be distributed among five categories according to their response, as in Table 15-1.

Table 15-1   A Frequency Distribution of Coffee Taste-Testers

Response	Number of Respondents
Like it very much	10
Like it	62
Am indifferent	8
Dislike it	13
Dislike it very much	7
Total	100

This respondent count is metric data and can be treated accordingly. Unfortunately, it does not provide much information, other than the numerical distribution of respondents with respect to five value judgments about the flavor of the coffee.

The next step is to assign numerical values to each of the five ratings on the nominal scale. This would allow scoring and the (questionable) use of mathematical and statistical tools. However, the numerical values assigned will have to be arbitrary, since there is no standard numerical scale for taste-testing. (What is a unit of "liking"?) Worse yet, once the numbers are assigned, their units are not interchangeable since we do not know that the intervals between the five ratings are equal. (Is the difference between "like" and "indifferent" equal to the difference between "indifferent" and "dislike"?) Hence, the response data are not parametric. (The reader is reminded that "parametric" is a common and virtually identical term for "metric." Economists consider it a bit more honest.)

The analytical hazard introduced by assigning numerical values to non-parametric variables is thinking that parametric tools will work with these numbers. The equations associated with mathematics and inferential statistics do not distinguish between parametric and nonparametric data, and hence will provide apparently valid numerical answers and statistical conclusions. In fact, these answers and conclusions may be wholly misleading. In the preceding example, once numerical values are assigned to the purely qualitative responses, averages, dispersions, confidence intervals, and so on can all be calculated by blindly applying the appropriate equations. This would give the study the appearance, but not the substance, of a rigorous analysis. If there are, in fact, considerable differences in intervals between response options, erroneous conclusions (followed by bad marketing decisions) are a likely consequence. For instance, the average response score, assuming that the intervals were equal, would suggest that the sample was favorably disposed toward the new brand. However, if option (a), "Like very much," was the only reaction sufficient to induce brand switching, the new coffee would not meet with the long-run success suggested by the analysis.

The point that the parametric analysis of nonparametric data can lead to serious trouble is stressed because it is a common practice and the temptation to try it is great. The appearance of parametricity can be very seductive. Even the legitimate manipulation of nonparametric data can produce result that can easily be misconstrued as parametric data. The only way to b certain is to trace the quantitative conclusions back to the raw data to determine the basis for assuming the data are parametric.

Fortunately, things are not all bad. Often data that could not withstand a rigorous test of parametricity can, as a pragmatic matter, be treated a parametric. For instance, market shares are treated parametrically, even though brands are seldom perfectly interchangeable within a product class. In addition, there are a number of statistical tools designed especially for the analysis of nonparametric data. We shall discuss the more useful of these in the next section.

Basic Considerations

In preparing any type of scale, two qualitative criteria must be met. The scale must be (1) intelligible to the respondents and (2) discriminatory.[1] (I is discriminatory when it can differentiate between different levels of ir tensity or between different categories of objects or behavior.) These criteri are usually not difficult to meet. However, some pretesting is often require to ensure that no subtle problems exist.

Besides meeting the qualitative criteria, one must choose between ratio, interval, ordinal, or nominal scale. The ratio scale is preferred.

A *ratio scale* is a metric scale with equal intervals and an absolute zer point. The numbers can be added, subtracted, multiplied, or divided. The units of measurement are interchangeable. Thus, the same ratio scale can b used to measure different objects and the results will be directly comparable.

The common systems of measurement for length, volume, weigh speed, and so on—even the common ruler—are all ratio scales. When bot deal with the same dimension, say, length, one form of ratio scale (e.g., fee can be transformed into another (e.g., meters) without distorting the dat. Unfortunately, most behavioral traits cannot be measured by ratio scale which are the ideal form for mathematical manipulation.

An *interval scale* is a metric scale similar in calibration to a ratio scal except that there is no true zero. The zero point is set arbitrarily by th researcher. Intervals are equal, and units of measurement are interchangeabl. The numbers assigned to the different positions on the scale can be adde and subtracted to obtain averages, but they cannot be multiplied and divide in the usual sense. As Crespi points out, one can say that the distance betwee

---

[1] Irving Crespi, *Attitude Research* (Chicago: American Marketing Association, 196. p. 31.

positions 1 and 2 is "as far as" the distance between 4 and 5, but one cannot say that position 8 is twice as favorable as position 4.[2] The scale used in the semantic-differential test for the word "polite" (Figure 14-1) is illustrative. Although the numerical values are not shown on the scale (a common practice in order to avoid confusing the respondents), they are often inserted during coding. This allows one to compute the average position on the line.

An *ordinal scale* is a ranking of alternatives and is nonmetric. It is prepared by the respondent, who assigns an order of preference or priority to each option, using ordinal values—first, second, third, and so on. These rankings show the order, but not the degree, of his or her preferences. There is no meaningful interval between items.

Although the highest-ranked option is preferred above any other alternative, the ordinal scale gives no hint as to how much more preferable it is. For instance, Brands A, B, C, and D may be rated first, second, third, and fourth, respectively, as far as taste is concerned. However, A may be considered only slightly preferable to B, whereas B may be considered far superior to C, which is considered virtually the same as D. Any one or more of the options could be considered not desirable enough to be worth purchasing. None of these things is revealed by the ordinal scale.

There are quantitative methods for dealing with ranked data. However, values assigned using an ordinal scale cannot be subjected to direct mathematical manipulation. Addition, subtraction, multiplication, and division of ordinal values produce nonsensical answers.

The answer options offered the respondent are usually not calibrated on the questionnaire to avoid a possible source of confusion. An array of numbers attached to verbal options can carry misleading connotations. Also, a respondent may mistake one type of scale for another and engage in mental manipulations that are totally inappropriate.

Nominal values are simply identifiers and are nonmetric. A nominal scale is virtually no scale at all. The numbers, usually added during the coding stage, are substituted for words to facilitate data processing.

Nominal data can be converted to metric form by use of dichotomous variables. A *dichotomous variable* is one with two discrete levels, such as "yes/no," "like/dislike," or "male/female." The values are assigned, in coding, allowing the variable to be treated as metric in many types of analysis.

The trouble with this solution to the nominal data problem is the proliferation of variables. A new dichotomous variable is required for every possible answer to a nominally scaled question.

For example, say the question was:

What season do you prefer for your vacation: ☐ *Winter,* ☐ *Spring,* ☐ *Summer, or* ☐ *Fall?*

---

[2] Crespi, *Attitude Research*, p. 32.

Four dichotomous variables would be needed to transform the nominal answer into metric—or what we might better call "parametric"[3]—data:

Winter: Yes = 1,   No = 0
Spring: Yes = 1,   No = 0
Summer: Yes = 1,   No = 0
Fall: Yes = 1,   No = 0

A respondent who checked summer in response to the original question would be coded one for the third dichotomous variable and zero for the others. This can be done very easily on the computer during data processing. However, the process replaces one variable (the original question) with four new ones. If the respondent had been asked to indicate the preferred month, twelve new dichotomous variables would be required.

Of course, the original question can be left in nominal form, coding the four seasons one, two, three, and four. This is fine for frequency distributions and cross tabulations, but good for little else.

Scoring Problems

Many behavioral questionnaires cannot be scored in the same way as IQ, aptitude, and achievement tests, since there are no "right" or "wrong" answers. One exception is *awareness tests*, which measure the knowledge, if any, a consumer has of a product class, a brand or group of brands, or a particular company. Even this type of test often incorporates attitudinal questions that cannot be graded as right or wrong.

The type of scale used sets limits on how the questionnaires can be scored. For instance, with an ordinal scale one can do little more than count responses. For a particular brand, one can tally the number (or percentage) of responses by order value for each question. Brand A might get 50 first-place ratings, 30 second-place ratings, 20 third-place ratings, and no fourth-place ratings for taste, while Brand B got 30 percent of the first-place ratings, 60 percent of the second-place ratings, and so on.

A researcher willing to make some assumptions can aggregate the answers for each questionnaire—that is, total the scores on the individual questions—and then assign a numerical value to the respondent's test as a whole. This is valid if the scale intervals are equal (a very shaky assumption if an ordinal scale has been used). Aggregating the answers also implies that the questions are of equal importance or that their numerical ratings have been properly weighted. This too is a naive assumption, for one can seldom measure the difference in the effect of two psychological variables on consumers' purchase behavior.[4] Besides, the difference in effects will vary between respondents. If a respondent gives top ratings to a product's flavor, texture, and price, and a low rating to its aroma and color, can those grades

---

[3] The reader is reminded that the prefix "para" means "similar to" or "like."

[4] Discriminant analysis is one way of doing this, but it has serious limitations. (See Chapter 21 for an explanation of this technique.)

be legitimately aggregated and then compared with the aggregate score of another respondent's test? Probably not, although it is common practice.

Sometimes assigning algebraic signs to the answers or weighting them will help the problem. Attitude with respect to factors that lessen the desirability of the product—such as the price or hazardous side effects—can be given a minus sign. The more significant factors—such as the taste and nutritional value of food items—can be counted twice or multiplied by an appropriate value. The intervals between answers can also be weighted by varying the distances between points on the scale. Unhappily, weighting forces the analyst to make judgments about the relative importance of the questions or the relative intensity of the answer options. Is price twice as important as convenience? Is a "very favorable" answer worth 1, 2, or 3 points more than a "favorable" answer? Is a first-place position three times as valuable as the third-place position? One can seriously question an analyst's ability to make such distinctions, although many researchers attempt them.

Item analysis is one way of determining the compatibility of questions in order to aggregate the answers. Item analysis tests questions to see if they measure the same dimension as other questions in a group of questions related to the same subject, e.g. the popularity of a brand. The technique is to first compute a total score for each questionnaire by simply summing the scores of the questions. Next, the scores for each question are statistically correlated with the questionnaire scores. Questions with a low correlation are then discarded.[5]

The root of most scoring problems is the coding process. The analyst must somehow transform qualitative responses into quantitative ones. This is inherently an arbitrary process, involving personal judgment and subjective criteria. In order to assign numbers to the respondents' answers, numerical scales must be prepared. These scales are analogous to the common ruler and indicate what numerical values should be assigned to a given answer.

In recognition of the troubles associated with behavioral data, such as the scoring problems, special scaling techniques have been developed.

Scaling Techniques

The Thurstone Attitude Scale

The *Thurstone Attitude Scale*—sometimes called the "method of equal-appearing intervals or the "Thurstone Differential Scale"—is purported to be an interval scale, and hence to provide metric data. While this claim may be a bit shaky, because of certain assumptions it requires, the Thurstone Scale is probably an acceptable approximation of an interval scale. At any rate, there are no significantly superior alternatives.

---

[5] See a basic statistics textbook, such as Boris Parl, *Basic Statistics* (Garden City, N.Y.: Doubleday, 1967), for a discussion of correlation.

Like other attitude scales, it is not universal. A new scale must be constructed every time the subject is changed. For instance, a scale prepared to measure consumer attitudes toward Buick automobiles could not be used to measure attitudes toward Safeway supermarkets. The following is the procedure for preparing a Thurstone Scale:[6]

1   A large number of value-judgment statements relevant to the subject being studied—usually one to two hundred—are prepared, preferably by a number of people.

2   A panel of judges sorts the statements into an odd number of piles—usually eleven—arranged in a series from the most favorable to the most unfavorable. (The middle pile contains statements considered "neutral.") Each judge sorts a complete set of statements. The piles represent the points on the scale and are presumably equal distances apart with respect to degrees of favorability. (This is the key assumption upon which the parametricity of the data rests.)

3   The integers 1, 2, 3, . . . n are assigned to the piles, starting with the most favorable. These numbers are the scale values.

4   The frequency distribution is posted and the mean or median is computed for each statement. Two statements are selected to represent each position (pile) on the scale. (A statement's average scale value determines the position to which it is assigned.) The dispersion of a statement's values is the selection criterion. A narrow dispersion indicates general agreement among the judges as to the statement's meaning, and hence a low probability that respondents will find it ambiguous.

This process produces a scale of both nominal and interval values, which are directly interchangeable. The statements can be in the first or the third person, making it usable for either an objective or a projective test. Obviously the distribution of the statements along the scale depends on the judgment of the individual panel members. Objectivity is important, for a prejudiced judge may bias the distributions and prevent the scale from being a true interval scale. One safeguard against this is to use a large ($n > 20$) panel of judges. This will tend to dampen the effect of one individual's bias, but will escalate the costs, in time and money, of preparing the scale.

The Thurstone Scale is used solely to measure attitudes. Tests employing the scale are generally administered by personal interview. Respondents are shown the statements in random order and without their numerical scale values. They are asked to review them all, then select which statement or statements they agree with. The numerical values of their selections are averaged, and the mean or median value used as their score (position on the attitude scale).

[6] L. L. Thurstone and E. J. Chave, *The Measurement of Attitude* (Chicago: University of Chicago Press, 1929).

The collection of scores represents the distribution of attitudes of the respondent set, which is usually a sample of the market population. If we accept the proposition that the Thurstone method yields an interval scale, the scores can be subjected to the mathematical and statistical manipulations appropriate to parametric data. If the respondents are a representative sample, the tools of inferential statistics can be used to generalize the findings to the population.

The quality of the raw data is suggested by the dispersion of a respondent's answers. If his selection of statements is widely distributed along the scale—say he selects statements valued at 3, 8, and 11 on an 11-point scale— it shows that either his attitude was disorganized, he did not understand the instructions, one or more statements was ambiguous, or the scale was incorrectly calibrated. If only a few respondents react to the test in this way, their scores should be discarded, especially when they have chosen contradictory statements (statements on both sides of the neutral point). If the problem is general, the scale itself had best be examined for ambiguity or miscalibration.

The Likert Attitude Scale

The *Likert Attitude Scale*—also called the "Likert Summated Scale"—is similar in use to the Thurstone Scale, but it is simpler and not as ambitious. The Likert Scale is ordinal; hence, it produces data that are nonparametric and much less amenable to mathematical and statistical manipulation. A different Likert Scale is required for each subject. It may be constructed as follows:

1   A group of 50 to 100 presumably favorable and unfavorable statements is prepared. No attempt is made to ensure an even distribution between extremely favorable and extremely unfavorable positions. The statements are not scaled

2   The statements are presented to a panel—ideally, a small but representative group of respondents drawn from the market population. Each statement is graded by each panel member according to this or a similar scale: (a) Agree strongly, (b) Agree, (c) Am indifferent, (d) Disagree, and (e) Disagree strongly

3   The five grades carry the numerical values $+2$, $+1$, 0, -1, and -2, when a statement is favorable to the subject. The signs are reversed when a statement is unfavorable. (For example, the answer "agree strongly" would be valued $+2$ if the statement was "Brand X is very desirable" and -2 if the statement was "Brand X is inferior to most other brands.")

4   Each respondent's score is computed by adding algebraically numerical values of the grades assigned to the statements by the respondent.

5   The desired number of statements is selected on the basis of the statements' ability to discriminate between respondents who are favorably disposed and those who are unfavorably

disposed toward the subject. Based on their scores, the highest (most favorably disposed) and the lowest (least favorably disposed) quartiles of respondents are identified. For each statement, a mean numerical grade is computed for both the high and the low quartiles. The absolute difference between these two averages is called the *mean difference*. (For example if a statement averaged a grade of 1.5 from the high quartile, and a grade of − 1.0 from the low quartile, the mean difference would be 2.5.) The statements selected for use in the final questionnaire are those with the highest mean differences, hence those best able to discriminate between favorable and unfavorable attitudes.

Tests using a Likert Scale are administered in much the same way as a Thurstone Scale. The only difference is that, since the Likert technique produces an ordinal scale, the answers cannot be treated as parametric data.

The quality of a particular Likert scale can also be judged by the dispersion of a respondent's grades. If they are widely dispersed about their mean (found by dividing the respondent's score by the number of statements), then the researcher should suspect the same problems associated with widely dispersed Thurstone Scale answers. (Note that in making a statistical analysis of the scale itself one is not making a statistical analysis of the nonparametric variables the scale is used to measure.) The solutions are also the same.

The Q-Sort

Q-sort is a method for categorizing respondents on the basis of similarity in attitudes. It does not produce an attitude scale. It posits a simple agreement scale for use in discriminating between respondents.

Once a representative sample of respondents has been selected, preparing a Q-sort survey is relatively simple. There are essentially only two steps:

1   A large number of value-judgment statements relevant to the subject under study—usually 50 to 100—are selected. They range from very unfavorable to very favorable and are usually distributed normally.

2   An agreement scale with an odd number of positions is prepared. The middle position is the indifference (neutral) point. Each position is assigned a numerical value. On a five-point scale, the numerical values might range from + 2 to − 2, with 0 as the indifference point.

Administering a Q-sort survey is a bit involved and usually requires a personal interview sometimes conducted with a group of respondents together. The following procedure is used:

1   The respondent is asked to review all the statements (which are often printed on individual cards for convenience) and

distribute them among the positions on the agreement scale. She is usually required to assign a preset number of statements to each position. This ensures a normal distribution of the statements along the scale, with the midpoint as the median.

2   The answers are tallied by statement and respondent, usually in matrix form. The values in the cells represent the numerical value of the agreement-scale position awarded a particular statement by a particular respondent. If there were 50 statements, n respondents, and a 5-point scale, the matrix might look something like this:

Statement	Respondent					
	1	2	3	4	5	$\cdots n$
1. I will always buy Brand X.	-2	2	1	-2	-2	-2
2. Brand X is the best.	-2	1	2	-2	-2	-1
3. I prefer Brand X.	-1	2	2	-1	-1	-1
4. Brand X is one of the best.	-2	1	2	-1	0	1
* *	*	*	*	*	*	*
* *	*	*	*	*	*	*
* *	*	*	*	*	*	*
48. Brand X is inferior.	2	-1	-1	1	-1	-1
49. Brand X is the worst.	1	-2	-2	2	-1	-1
50. I would never buy Brand X.	1	-2	-2	1	-2	-1

3   The respondents are clustered according to the similarity of their answer patterns. For instance, given the preceding data, respondents 1 and 4 appear to have similar response patterns; hence, they presumably have a similar (favorable) attitude. Respondents 2 and 3 also appear to share a similar attitude, as do respondents 5 and n. Also, the data suggest that there are at least three categories of respondents: (a) those who are favorably disposed toward the subject, (b) those who are neutral, and (c) those who are unfavorably disposed toward the subject.

4   The appropriate analytical tests—such as analysis of variance—is made to see if there is truly a significant difference between categories and no significant difference within categories. For instance, given the preceding data and the three attitudinal categories suggested, an analysis of variance would be appropriate.

A Q-sort is useful when the objective of the survey is simply to group respondents into a small number (two to five) of broad attitudinal categories. If the sample of respondents is representative, then their distribution between categories can be generalized to the market population from which they were drawn. If appropriate additional data have been gathered on the respondents, then discriminant analysis can be utilized to see what, if any, influence selected factors have on attitudes. For example, the researcher might gather information on the respondent's income, social class, reading and viewing habits, or shopping habits. If one or more of these factors turn out to be a significant determinant of attitude, perhaps the firm's marketing policies can be altered to change, accommodate, or exploit them. For example, those respondents with unfavorable attitudes may be members of a particular social class. If so, perhaps the product or the firm's promotional tactics should be altered to conform to the group values associated with that social class.

Of course, this assumes that purchase behavior correlates with attitude. Data on the respondent's purchase history should also be gathered whenever possible and an analysis made to see if a significant correlation exists between sales and attitudinal categories. If not, the researcher may be wasting time examining attitudes.

The Guttman Attitude Scale

The *Guttman Attitude Scale* attempts to measure two components of attitude: value (called "content" by Guttman) and intensity. It is used to evaluate attitudes toward a product or brand in general as well as toward specific properties such as price, appearance, performance, taste, and reliability.

The method uses a questionnaire, normally administered during a personal interview, to provide the initial data. The questionnaire asks the respondent to assign a value judgment—such as "yes" or "no," "like" or "dislike"—to a statement about the product. The respondent is also asked to indicate the intensity of his or her feeling, often by selecting a lower- or upper-case response. The following statements and answer options, drawn from an attitude study made for the Sheaffer Pen Company, are typical.[7]

	Statement	Answers
A	This pen writes smoothly.	YES__, yes__, so:so__, no__, NO__.
B	I like the way the writing looks	YES__, yes__, so-so__, no__, NO__.

The questionnaire itself is usually prepared from ideas that emerge in an exploratory survey using unstructured questions and personal interviews.

After the raw data (responses) are gathered, the following steps are used to produce a Guttman Attitude Scale.

---

[7] Elizabeth A. Richards, "A Commercial Application of Guttman Attitude Scaling Techniques," *Journal of Marketing* **22**, no. 2 (October 1957), p. 170.

1   Two series of arbitrary numerical values are assigned to the answers. One series measures the content (value) component of attitude. In the example, "YES" = 5, "yes" = 4, "so-so" = 3, "no" = 2, and "NO" = 1. The other series measures the intensity component. In the example, "YES" and "NO" = 2, "no" and "yes" = 1, and "so-so" = 0.

2   Total-content and total-intensity scores are computed for each respondent. The pen questionnaire had five questions (statements); hence, a maximum score of 25 was possible for the content component and a maximum score of 10 was possible for the intensity component.

3   Respondent questionnaires are ranked according to their total-content scores. The content answers to individual questions are tabulated and grouped to see if a set of patterns emerges. If less than 90 percent of the individual answers fail to fit into some one of the patterns, a valid Guttman Sscale cannot be constructed. Either the questionnaire must be reconstructed or the project must be abandoned. An example of how response patterns are tabulated is shown in Table 15-2, which gives nine response patterns for the data gathered in the pen study.

4   The number and percentage of respondents fitting each pattern, the midpoint of the cumulative percentage accounted for as we move from the most to the least favorable pattern, and the median intensity score for each group are computed and recorded, giving us a Guttman Attitude Scale in tabular form. (For the pen study, these values are shown in the last four columns of Table 15-2.)

5   A graph is then plotted showing the relationship between median intensity scores (on the vertical axis) and the midpoint of the cumulative percentage of respondents. (This is illustrated in Figure 15-1, using the pen-study example.) This graph is the Guttman Attitude Scale.

Normally, a plot of a Guttman Attitude Scale will have a "U," "J," or "V" shape, with intensity the highest at the extreme content positions ("YES" and "NO" in the example). These denote the most favorable and the most unfavorable valuations. The dividing line between favorable and unfavorable attitudes is found by locating the lowest intensity value, which is usually associated with the point of indifference (the "so-so" answer in the example). In the pen study, the lowest intensity value is 3. Checking the horizontal axis, we see that 82 percent of the respondents have favorable attitudes. Only 18 percent have unfavorable attitudes toward the product.

We can gain further insight into the nature and distribution of respondent attitudes by observing the intensity scores and the shape of the curve. High scores indicate strong feelings, and a curve with steeply sloping sides indicates a wide variation in intensity. A flat curve suggests a consistency in

Table 15-2 **Response Patterns, Respondent Distribution by Pattern and Intensity Scores in a Study of Attitudes Towards Ball Point Pens**

Rank[a]	Response Group	Response Patterns (by Row)					Distribution of Respondents			Median Intensity
		Ques. 1 Y ys-sn N	Ques. 2 Y ys-sn N	Ques. 3 Y ys-sn N	Ques. 4 Y ys-sn N	Ques. 5 Y ys-sn N	Number per Pattern	Percentage per Pattern	Cumulative Percentage (Midpoint)	
1	Pattern A	x	x	x	x	x	49	20%	10%	10
2	Pattern B	x	x	x	x	x	24	10	25	9
3	Pattern C	x	x	x	x	x	34	14	37	8
4	Pattern D	x	x	x	x	x	39	16	52	6
5	Pattern E	x	x	x	x	x	49	20	70	4
6	Pattern F	x	x	x	x	x	10	4	82	3
7	Pattern G	x	x	x	x	x	20	8	86	4
8	Pattern H	x	x	x	x	x	14	6	95	5
9	Pattern I	x	x	x	x	x	5	7	99	10
						Totals	244	100%		

Source: Adapted from Elizabeth A. Richards, "A Commercial Application of Guttman Attitude Scaling Techniques" *Journal of Marketing*, **22**;2 (October 1957), p. 171, published by the American Marketing Association.

[a] Rank 1 = most favorable, 9 = least favorable.

Figure 15-1   **A Guttman Attitude Scale for a Ball-Point Pen Study (Graphical Presentation)**

Source: Prepared from data in Elizabeth A. Richards, "A Commercial Application of Guttman Attitude Scaling Techniques," *Journal of Marketing*, vol. 22 no. 2 (October 1957), p. 171, published by the American Marketing Association.

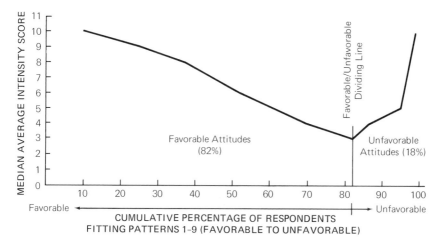

intensity. A flat curve combined with a low-intensity score indicates an attitude of widespread indifference. This situation is rare, for few subjects fail to provoke some feeling among respondents. If a low flat curve is the result of sample survey data, not experimental data, its shape is probably due to ignorance. (Given this condition, the firm would be well advised to examine its promotional strategy.)

The Guttman Attitude Scale can also be used to discriminate between product and promotional alternatives. This is done by preparing a scale for each of the options and comparing their indifference points, their intensities, and the shapes of their curves. In the Shaeffer study, three ball-point pens were evaluated, all by the same group of respondents. Scales for each were plotted on the same graph. The pen ultimately selected for production (which is the one used in the illustration) had an indifference point that showed 82 percent of the respondents to have favorable attitudes toward it, while the other two pens produced enjoyed favorable reactions from only 65 and 58 percent. In addition, the favored pen provoked more intense favorable reactions and less intense unfavorable ones than either of the other pens.

This method can also reveal specific weaknesses in marketing policies. For instance, if the scores are generally favorable for most questions but are unfavorable for one or two statements, the unfavorably rated aspects of the product should perhaps be altered or the promotional program revamped to play them down or change attitudes about them.

Guttman Scale data are also useful in preparing an advertising strategy. If favorable attitudes prevail and the firm has a major share of the market, advertising should be designed to reinforce prevailing attitudes and sustain brand loyalty. If the prevailing attitude is unfavorable, the advertising—supported by appropriate product changes—should concentrate on changing public opinion. The more intense the unfavorable attitude is, the more serious the problem is and the more promotional resources will be required to bring about the desired change.

Preparing the questionnaire is the most difficult task in the construction of a Guttman Attitude Scale. Unless the researcher is attempting to evaluate specific properties—such as color, size, or price options—the first step is usually an unstructured personal interview administered to a few dozen respondents. The respondents are drawn from the market population, although they are not randomly selected in the rigorous statistical sense. These open-ended interviews will help define the problem and will suggest statements that can be used to determine attitudes toward the relevant variables.

The next step is usually to prepare a preliminary questionnaire, using an excessive number of questions (statements). This questionnaire is administered to a selection (usually nonrandom) of respondents and the results are evaluated with a view to selecting the best questions, not determining attitudes. Ambiguous and misleading statements and statements that produce conflicting answers are discarded. The final questionnaire is then prepared.

The last step in the data acquisition process is to administer the questionnaire to a statistically significant sample of respondents. Personal interviews are used, and a minimum of 50 to 200 respondents are randomly selected from the market population to ensure a representative sample. The results are tabulated, plotted, and analyzed, following the procedure described above.

The quality of the data—hence, the reliability, accuracy, and precision of the scale depends on the size and randomness of the sample, the clarity and relevance of the statements, and the skill of the interviewers. Interviewing, however, does not demand a high level of skill once the final questionnaire has been prepared.

Multidimensional Scaling

Multidimensional scaling is a technique, or more precisely, a set of techniques, for measuring objects in a multidimensional space. The objects may be stimuli—such as advertisements, products, tastes, or brands—or respondents. The space itself is defined in terms of two orthogonal (at right angle) axes called "attributes," which describe the objects. The relative distances between objects in this "attribute space" are one-dimensional measurements of the psychological differences between objects. This spatial representation is in sharp contrast to the conventional unidimensional scaling which positions an object on a line. (All scaling methods previously discussed have been unidimensional.)

The hallmark of multidimensional scaling is that it takes a single piece of information and generates multiple measurements. The single piece of information is the ranking or matching of objects based solely on the judgment and personal criteria of the respondents. From this preference— or "similarity"—data, a multidimensional algorithm (there are many) positions the objects in a multidimensional space. The axes of the attribute space are labeled by judgment, after the positioning of the objects. One of the shortcomings of the method is that there is no rigorous criterion for labeling the dimensions (axes) of the multidimensional space.

A study by Green, Maheshwari, and Rao illustrates the method.[8] A group of respondents was given 55 cards, each bearing the names of two automobiles. Each respondent was directed to rank the cards according to the degree of similarity of the pairs of automobiles. (The card with the most similar pair of autos was to be ranked first and the card with the least similar pair of autos was to be ranked last.) The criterion for judging the similarity of the automobiles, and hence the ranking of the cards, was left to the individual respondents. A multidimensional algorithm was then applied to these data to position the automobiles in the two-dimensional attribute space, shown in Figure 15-2.

The labeling of the axes was purely judgmental. The analysts observed that as one moved vertically the objects acquired more of the physical characteristics and image of a sports car and had fewer of the properties

Figure 15-2   **Illustration of a Multidimensional Space**

Source: Adapted from Paul E. Green, Arun Maheshwari, and Vithala R. Rao, "Dimensional Interpretation and Configuration Invariance in Multidimensional Scaling," *Multivariate Behavioral Research,* vol. 4 (April 1969), pp. 159–180, and as shown in Paul E. Green and Donald S. Tull, *Research for Marketing Decisions,* 2nd ed. (Englewood Cliffs, NJ: Prentice-Hall, 1970), p. 215.

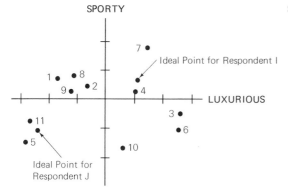

STIMULI—1968 CAR MODELS

1. Ford Mustang 6
2. Mercury Cougar V8
3. Lincoln Continental V8
4. Ford Thunderbird V8
5. Ford Falcon 6
6. Chrysler Imperial V8
7. Jaguar Sedan
8. AMC Javelin V8
9. Plymouth Barracuda V8
10. Buick Le Sabre V8
11. Chevrolet Corvair

    [8] Paul E. Green, Arun Maheshwari, and Vithala R. Rao, "Dimensional Interpretation and Configuration Invariance in Multidimensional Scaling," *Multivariate Behavioral Research* **4** (April 1969), pp. 159–180.

associated with the more conservative family car. Thus the vertical axis was labeled "sporty." The analyst observed that as one moved from left to right the objects took on the properties of luxurious automobiles, and hence the horizontal axis was labeled "luxurious." Thus, from the similarity data emerged the multidimensions "sporty" and "luxurious," which serve to describe the objects.

The study was expanded to include preference data. Each respondent was asked to rank the eleven automobiles in accordance with personal preference. (Again the criterion was solely that of the individual respondent.) By applying the appropriate algorithm, the respondents were then placed in the attribute space. (Two of the respondents, I and J, are shown in Figure 15-2.) The positions of the respondents represent their ideal point—that is, their ideal automobile—with respect to the attributes "sporty" and "luxurious."

By connecting any two points with a line—called a "rod"—we can measure the degree of similarity between the objects. We can also determine, in the example, brand preference. For instance, in our illustration the Ford Mustang and the AMC Javelin (points 1 and 8) are perceived as much more similar than the Mustang and Jaguar sedan (1 and 7). Respondent I clearly prefers the Ford Thunderbird (4) to the Jaguar sedan (7).

A further examination of the attribute space suggests that certain brands may be considered sufficiently similar to be classified as members of the same set, hence highly competitive with one another. (Note stimuli 1, 2, 8, and 9.) Had all the respondents been plotted, we might also have discovered groupings that would represent market segments—segments specified by respondent perception and preference and measured in terms of the two attributes. If there were no stimuli located in or very near a particular respondent cluster, we could assume that we had discovered an unsatisfied market segment. If that unsatisfied segment represented a sufficiently large portion of the buyer population, we would have a strong argument for introducing a product whose properties would place it within that cluster.

The specification of sets (clusters) can be made by judgment once the stimuli and/or respondents are mapped in the attribute space, or the sets can be specified in accordance with one of several statistical criteria. This second alternative involves an analytical tool called "cluster analysis," which we will discuss shortly.

The techniques of multidimensional scaling are varied, and new methods are still being developed. The choice of technique is dependent on the nature of the data—metric or nonmetric[9]—and the judgment of the

---

[9] The terms *metric* and *nonmetric* are used in multidimensional scaling, factor analysis, and cluster analysis to describe data that is essentially parametric and nonparametric, respectively. However, the two sets of terms are not perfectly synonymous. For more detailed explanation, see Paul E. Green and Frank J. Carmone, *Multidimensional Scaling and Related Techniques in Marketing Analysis* (Boston: Allyn and Bacon, 1970), pp. 7–11. The book is also a good introduction to multidimensional scaling, its techniques, potential, and limitations.

analyst. The methods were first developed early in the 1960s by behavioral scientists who were attempting to come to grips with the problems of measuring and interpreting perception and preference. The conventional one-dimensional scales seemed inadequate, and the behaviorists were frustrated by the nonmetric nature of most perception and preference information. They desired a technique which would transform such informato metric data. Multidimensional scaling deals with both of these problems. The techniques are very sophisticated and hence unmanageable without the aid of a computer. Several solution systems are now available in computerized form and more are being developed.[10]

The application of multidimensional scaling to real-world marketing problems has been slight. To date, the thrust has been toward the development of computerized algorithms, but numerous practical applications have been suggested. These include the use of multidimensional scaling to evaluate advertising and vendors, to analyze product life cycles, and to segment markets.[11]

Data Analysis—More Bivariate Methods

Bivariate Analysis

Bivariate analysis is a set of statistical tools used to analyze the relationship between two variables. Most of the analytical techniques examined thus far are bivariate methods. Until the advent of the electronic computer, data analysis was mainly limited to bivariate techniques, which are still the most used tools of analysis. Unfortunately, they often prove inadequate when the phenomena under study involve three or more variables.

Some bivariate methods are especially well suited to behavioral analysis. These are introduced now.

The Sign Test

The sign test uses the algebraic signs of the observed differences between two sets of responses to determine if there is a significant difference between them. Since it does not use means and variances in its calculations, the sign test can be used with nonparametric data. It is also an easy short-cut method to use with parametric data.

In marketing research, the sign test is used frequently with before-and-after data to see if the change in a marketing variable or the application of an experimental treatment has had an effect on a qualitative variable associated

---

[10] Examples are TORSCA, TRICON, MDSCAL, EMD, CEMD, and DEMO. For the source of these algorithms, see the bibliography in Paul E. Green and Frank J. Carmone, "Multidimensional Scaling: An Introduction and Comparison of Nonmetric Unfolding Techniques," *Journal of Marketing Research* **6**:3, (August 1969), pp. 330–341.

[11] For an exploration of such applications see Paul E. Green and Frank J. Carmone, *Multidimensional Scaling and Related Techniques in Marketing Research.*

with the market population. The technique is simple. The analyst determines the algebraic signs of the observed differences, totals the pluses and the minuses (ignoring observations showing no change), and tests the null hypothesis that there is no significant difference between the two sets. Depending on the sample size, either a Z- or a t-distribution is used to test the null hypothesis, using the techniques described in Appendix 2.

For example, suppose that a sample survey reveals certain brand preferences with respect to a particular class of goods and also exposes some attitudes that cause people to reject the firm's brand. An advertising campaign is designed to alter these attitudes and improve the brand's image. After the campaign has been run for a period deemed adequate for it to have an effect, the original respondents are again queried as to their brand preferences. The results of this second survey are shown in Table 15-3, along with a tally of the signs of the observed differences.

If the advertising campaign was ineffective (and there were no exogenous disturbances such as a price cut), the general distribution of brand preferences will be the same as before. Individual changes (indicated by the pluses and minuses) will be caused by random disturbances and cancel one another out. There will be an equal amount of pluses and minuses. That is, 50 percent of the usable observations will be positive and 50 percent will be negative. The probability, P, of getting a plus (or a minus) will be 0.5. That is, $P(+) = 0.5$ and $P(-) = 0.5$. The null hypothesis, H_0, equivalent to the statement that the advertising was ineffective, is $H_0: P(+) = 0.5$.

Chance variation can cause the observed (sample) distribution of pluses to vary from the true (population) distribution. However, the variations will

Table 15-3 **A Change in Brand Preference Induced by an Advertising Campaign**

Respondent	Brand Preference Ranking		Sign of Observed Difference
	Before Campaign	After Campaign	
1	3rd	2nd	+
2	2nd	2nd	0
3	5th	1st	+
4	1st	3rd	$\cdots$
5	1st	2nd	$\cdots$
$\vdots$	$\vdots$	$\vdots$	$\vdots$
96	4th	3rd	+
97	2nd	1st	+
98	3rd	3rd	0
100	3rd	3rd	0
		Totals	37 +
			23 −
			60 Usable observations

be normally distributed, and since we have a large ($n > 30$) sample, we can consult a normal-distribution table to see how many Z-units we can be from the assumed value and still attribute the difference to chance. Assuming that management wants to operate at the 95 percent confidence level (a significance level of 0.05), the critical Z-value for a one-tail test is 1.65. (Note: We are interested only in the chance of getting more pluses than minuses; hence, we are concerned only with the right-hand side of the normal-distribution curve, which covers 50 percent of the possibilities. Since the significance level specified is 0.05, we enter the table at 0.45 [$0.50 - 0.05 = 0.45$].)

The next task is to determine if the total number of pluses falls outside the range of possible values expected at the 0.05 level of significance. As usual, we simply compare the Z-value computed from the observed data with the Z-value found in the normal-distribution table. If the computed Z-value exceeds the table value, the null hypothesis is rejected and we must assume that the advertising was effective.

Since the sign test provides only two possible outcomes ($+$ or $-$), given the usable data, we can use binomial-distribution theory to find the mean, μ_p, and standard deviation, σ_p, both of which are needed to calculate the Z-value. We know that the number of usable observations (n) is 60, the assumed probability (p_0) of a plus is 0.5, and the number (X) of pluses is 37.

$$\mu_p = np_0 \qquad \text{(Formula A1.23)}$$

$$\mu_p = 60(0.5) \qquad \text{(by substitution, } p_0 = p(+) = 0.5\text{)}$$

$$\mu_p = 30 \qquad \text{(by arithmetic)}$$

$$\sigma_p = -\sqrt{np_0(1 - p_0)} \qquad \text{(Formula A2.12)}$$

$$\sigma_p = \sqrt{60(0.5)(1 - 0.5)} \qquad \text{(by substitution)}$$

$$\sigma_p = \sqrt{15} \qquad \text{(by arithmetic)}$$

$$\sigma_p = 3.87 \qquad \text{(by arithmetic)}$$

$$Z = \frac{X - \mu}{\sigma} \qquad \text{(Formula A2.14)}$$

$$Z = \frac{37 - 30}{3.87} \qquad \text{(by arithmetic)}$$

$$Z = 1.81 \qquad \text{(by arithmetic)}$$

Since the computed Z-value, 1.81, is greater than the table Z-value, 1.65, the total number of observed pluses exceeds the number that could be expected at the 95 percent confidence level (*s.l.* $= 0.05$). The null hypothesis must be rejected. Apparently, the advertising campaign changed consumer attitudes sufficiently to induce a favorable shift in brand preferences.

A couple of computational alternatives are available for the sign test. The formula for the Z-statistic for a binomial distribution, $Z = (X - np_0)/\sqrt{np_0(1 - p_0)}$, could be used in place of the three formulas shown here. Or a table of binomial probabilities could be used to determine the probability of getting the observed number of pluses, X, at the assumed probability, p_0. If the probability is sufficiently low—that is, if it is equal to or less than the selected level of significance—the null hypothesis is rejected. This latter method is useful when the total number of observations is small ($n < 15$).

The Ranked-sums Test

The *ranked-sums test*—also called the "Mann-Whitney test" and the "U-test"—uses ranked data from two samples to determine if there is a significant difference between them. It is compatible with nonparametric data and is a useful short-cut in analyzing parametric data. In marketing research, it is often used when observations can be ranked and are not parametric, as is the case with most attitude-scale scores and preference data.

The technique calls for the ranking of observations from the two samples *after* they have been combined. In the event of a tie, each observation is assigned the mean average of the ranks the tied observations, as a group, occupy. (For instance, if four observations were tied for second place, each would be assigned the rank of 3.5, which is the mean average of the second, third, fourth, and fifth places.) Each rank is identified by the source (set) of the observation holding it. The U-statistic is then computed, along with its mean and its standard deviation. Since the U-statistic tends toward a normal distribution, the Z-statistic is also computed and the normal test of significance used to prove or disprove the null hypothesis that there is no significant difference between sets. The formulas needed are

$$U = n_1 n_2 + \frac{n_1(n_1 + 1)}{2} - R_1, \tag{15.1}$$

$$\mu_U = \frac{n_1 n_2}{2}, \tag{15.2}$$

$$\sigma_U = \left[\frac{n_1 n_2(n_1 + n_2 + 1)}{12}\right]^{1/2} \tag{15.3}$$

and

$$Z = \frac{U - \sigma_U}{\sigma_U} \tag{15.4}$$

where

U = the U-statistic

n_1 = the total number of observations in set 1 (the first sample)

n_2 = the total number of observations in set 2 (the second sample)

R_1 = the sum of the rank positions for set 1

μ_U = the arithmetic mean of U

σ_U = the standard deviation of U

Z = the Z-statistic.

It is irrelevant which sample is designated 1 or 2.

To illustrate the technique, suppose we assume that a marketer has been unable to account for the difference in sales between two markets on the basis of demographic or economic data. He suspects that a difference in consumer attitudes is the root of the trouble and conducts an attitude survey in each market to check out this possibility. A Thurstone Differential Scale is used to score each response. Forty-six usable questionnaires are obtained in the first market ($n_1 = 46$) and 50 in the second ($n_2 = 50$). All are used, since the two samples need not be the same size for the ranked-sums test to be valid. The scores are ranked as in Table 15-4.

Having ranked the observations, totaled the number in each set (1 and 2), and summed the ranking positions for the first set ($R_1 = 2 +$

Table 15-4   **A Ranking of Observations from Two Samples for a Ranked-Sums Test**

Rank	Data Source (Set)	Score
1	2	12.51
2	1	12.00
3	2	11.94
4.5	1	11.82
4.5	2	11.82
6	2	11.04
7	2	11.00
⋮	⋮	⋮
91	1	2.87
92	2	2.30
93	2	2.24
94	1	1.25
95	1	0.33
96	1	0.00

$n_1 = 46, n_2 = 50 \qquad R_1 = 3,212$

4.5 + ··· 91 + 94 + 95 + 96 = 3,212), we can use formula 15.1 to compute the U-statistic

$$U = n_1 n_2 + \frac{n_1(n_1 + 1)}{2} - R_1 \qquad \text{(given as equation 15.1)}$$

$$U = 46(50) + \frac{46(46 + 1)}{2} - 3,212 \qquad \text{(by substitution)}$$

$$U = 1,250 \qquad \text{(by arithmetic)}$$

We can use equation 15.2 to find the arithmetic mean of U

$$\mu_U = \frac{n_1 n_2}{2} \qquad \text{(given as equation 15.2)}$$

$$\mu_U = \frac{46(50)}{2} \qquad \text{(by substitution)}$$

$$\mu_U = 1,150 \qquad \text{(by arithmetic)}$$

We can use equation 15.3 to find the standard deviation

$$\sigma_U = \left[\frac{n_1 n_2(n_1 + n_2 + 1)}{12} \right]^{1/2} \qquad \text{(given as equation 15.3)}$$

$$\sigma_U = \left[\frac{46(50)(46 + 50 + 1)}{12} \right]^{1/2} \qquad \text{(by substitution)}$$

$$\sigma_U = 136 \qquad \text{(by arithmetic)}$$

And we can use equation 15.4 to find the Z-statistic

$$Z = \frac{U - \mu_U}{\sigma_U} \qquad \text{(given as equation 15.4)}$$

$$Z = \frac{1,250 - 1,150}{136} \qquad \text{(by substitution)}$$

$$Z = 0.73 \qquad \text{(by arithmetic)}$$

Consulting a table of Z-values (Appendix 4), we see that at the 95 percent confidence level (a 0.05 level of significance) $Z = 1.96$. (Note that this is a two-tailed test and the table shows the areas under only half the curve. Hence, the table is entered at 0.4750, which is one-half the desired 95 percent area.) The computed Z-value, 0.73, is well within this range. Thus, the null hypothesis cannot be rejected, and we must assume that there is no significant difference in attitudes between the two markets, as represented by their respective samples. The researcher will have to look for another explanation—perhaps a difference in the amount of competition—to explain the difference in sales between the two markets.

The Rank-Correlation Coefficient

The *rank-correlation coefficient*, r'—often called "Spearman's coefficient"— has the same meaning as the more conventional coefficient of correlation, r. It tells us how highly correlated one variable is with another variable (0 equals no correlation and 1 equals perfect correlation). It can be used with nonparametric data or as a quick way to analyze parametric data, but it is less precise than r, which is more cumbersome to compute and can be used only with parametric data. Spearman's coefficient is particularly useful in estimating the degree of correlation between qualitative variables common in consumer-behavior analysis.

Like the coefficient of correlation, the rank-correlation coefficient ranges between 0 and ± 1. Perfect positive or negative correlation between two variables is indicated by $r' = \pm 1$. No correlation is indicated by $r' = 0$. Both cases (perfect and zero correlation) are quite rare when real-world market data are used.

The r' value squared, applicable to only two variables, can be interpreted like the coefficient of determination, R^2 (p. 472), which is used with multiple variables. It represents the portion of the total variation in the dependent variable, Y, caused by the independent variable, X. Thus $r' = .92$ means that 84 percent of the variation in Y has been induced by X—a very high degree of correlation. Conversely, $r' = .15$ indicates an insignificant degree of correlation between the two variables.[12]

Determining the correlation between two variables, using Spearman's coefficient, is relatively easy. First, the observed pairs (Y's and X's) are listed and each Y and X observation is ranked. The difference, d, in ranks between the Y and the X in each pair is computed and then squared. The sum of these squared differences, Σd^2, together with the following equation, is used to find the rank correlation coefficient, r'.

$$r' = 1 - \frac{6(\Sigma d^2)}{n(n^2 - 1)} \qquad [15.5]$$

[12] Significance with respect to degrees of correlation is a matter of judgment. Ignoring the sign, a correlation coefficient of over .85 would normally be considered highly significant; .60 to .85, moderately significant; and below .60, insignificant.

where

r' = the rank correlation coefficient (Spearman's coefficient)

d^2 = the difference between the ranks of the paired observations $(X$ and $Y)$, squared

n = the total number of paired observations

For example, assume that a market analyst wants to find the degree of correlation between actual purchase behavior (sales) and attitude, as measured by the Likert Summated Scale. Purchase behavior is a quantitative variable, measured with a ratio scale, and attitude is a qualitative variable, measured with an ordinal scale. (Although the Likert Scale provides numerical scores, these scores should not be construed as parametric data.) An attitude survey is conducted in eight markets, homogeneous with respect to business and demographic factors. Then the average Likert scores for each market are paired with the per-capita sales figures (obtained from consumer-panel data). The results are posted, X and Y are ranked, and the difference between rankings is computed in Table 15-5.

The correlation between sales and attitude is computed using equation 15.5 and the data from the table

$$r' = 1 - \frac{6(\Sigma d^2)}{n(n^2 - 1)} \qquad \text{[given as equation 15.5]}$$

$$r' = 1 - \frac{6(10)}{8(8^2 - 1)} \qquad \text{[by substitution]}$$

$$r' = 0.88 \qquad \text{[by arithmetic]}$$

Table 15-5   Data Needed to Compute a Rank-Correlation Coefficient for Sales and Attitude in Eight Markets

Market (i)	Per Capita Sales (Y)	Mean Attitude Score (X)	Rank of Y	Rank of X	Difference (d)	Difference Squared (d^2)
1	17.1	6.8	5	5	0	0
2	19.8	14.1	2	1	+1	1
3	20.1	12.0	1	2	-1	1
4	16.4	-1.9	6	8	-2	4
5	19.0	11.5	3	3	0	0
6	17.2	9.0	4	4	0	0
7	12.3	3.7	8	6	+2	4
8	10.1	-1.2	7	7	0	0
$n = 8$						$\Sigma d^2 = 10$

Thus, there is a high degree of correlation between actual consumer behavior and attitude. This suggests that the firm's promotional strategy should be directed at reinforcing favorable attitudes and altering unfavorable ones. The latter task is especially important in markets where sales are relatively poor.

Problems

1   What type of scale (nominal, ordinal, interval, or ratio) is represented by each of the following items or series of items: (a) a list of alternative brands of frozen orange juice; (b) a yardstick; (c) a series of value judgments ranging from "unsatisfactory" to "excellent"; (d) a series of value judgments ranging from zero to 100, with zero representing the poorest position and 100 the best.

2   What analytical tools could be used to evaluate data in the forms described in problem 1? How might the data be scored?

3   Describe a psychological variable that could not be measured with a parametric scale but which might affect consumer behavior. Suggest a method for preparing an appropriate nonparametric scale. What questions might be used to obtain data on the variable for manipulation and analysis?

4   Fifty automobile owners were asked to rank Texaco and other brands of gasoline before and after an advertising campaign designed to enhance Texaco's image. The postcampaign interviews revealed that Texaco had been given a better rank by 12 respondents and a worse rank by 7; the remainder ranked it the same way they had before. Was the advertising effective? Defend your answer.

5   An attitude test—using a Likert Summated Scale—has been developed to measure the favorableness of consumer attitudes toward a firm's product. However, the attitudinal data are useful only if they correlate with purchase behavior. To evaluate the test, it is administered to a randomly selected group of buyers, who use the product but not necessarily the firm's brand. The quantity of the brand purchased by each of the 20 respondents is 18, 12, 10, 14, 0, 13, 0, 20, 7, 19, 17, 0, 0, 8, 3, 1, 7, 15, 0, and 19 units, respectively. The test scores—listed in the same order—are 45, 20, 18, 30, 8, 40, 15, 48, 12, 35, 35, 15, 5, 17, 6, 8, 12, 28, 3, and 47. How well does attitude, as measured by the test, correlate with purchase behavior?

Part 6
Summary

Marketing researchers often draw on the theory and techniques of the behavioral sciences to explain the reasons behind consumer behavior. The behavioral sciences seek to explain the causes of market phenomena. These are only defined and specified by other methods of marketing research. The behavioral sciences address themselves to the psychological and sociological factors that influence consumer decisions—especially the psychogenic needs and the attitudes of the buyer.

The methods of behavioral analysis can be divided into two broad categories—objective and projective techniques. Objective techniques are based on the assumption that the respondents are both able and willing to describe their behavioral pattern and articulate the true reasons for their actions. Projective techniques are based on the contrary assumption. Each category embraces a variety of theories and tools, such as different forms of psychological testing. A researcher's selection of a particular method is determined by his or her needs, resources, psychological training, and personal biases.

Behavioral data are usually generated by psychological tests, which often require a personal interview. The tests—objective or projective—may be structured or unstructured. Specific-direct-question, attitude-scaling, error-choice, semantic-differential, word-association, and sentence-completion tests are the basic structured tests. Story-completion, picture-frustration, and thematic-apperception tests, in-depth personal interviews, role playing, and psychodrama are the common unstructured devices for gathering behavioral data.

Test preparation entails scaling and scoring, both of which can be difficult due to the frequently nonmetric quality of the factors being measured. A ratio scale is ideal, but seldom feasible. The researcher must usually settle for an ordinal, an interval, or a nominal scale—each of which has limitations as far as mathematical and statistical manipulation of the data is concerned. The Thurstone Attitude Scale, Likert Attitude Scale, Q-sort, and Guttman

Attitude Scale are popular for scaling and scoring tests. A radically new technique has now emerged, multidimensional scaling.

Since behavioral data are often nonmetric, the conventional tools of mathematical and statistical analysis have only limited applications in this area. Hence, special techniques have had to be devised for analyzing behavioral data. Among them are the sign test, the ranked-sums test, and the rank-correlation coefficient. These are bivariate techniques of data analysis. They often unlock the answers. When they don't, one must turn to the tools of multivariate analysis.

CASE STUDY 6

Leo Burnett U.S.A.: Salvaging Market Share with Psychographics

Joseph T. Plummer (*Joseph T. Plummer, Ph.D., is Vice-President, Special Task Force, Leo Burnet U.S.A.*)

Leo Burnett Company is a worldwide firm, embracing some 38 offices in 24 countries, headquartered in Chicago. It is the fourth-largest advertising agency in both the United States and the world. It is the only agency in the top ten, headquartered outside New York City.

Since its founding, the agency's billings have increased every year. At the end of its first ten years—just after the close of World War II—billings had risen from less than $1 million to $7.4 million. Burnett's United States billings for 1973 were $330 million and worldwide billings were $512 million. Besides its commercial work, the agency does work, free of charge, for worthy nonprofit organizations.

Study Background

One of the agency's clients sells soap. Its product, which has been on the market for 25 years, has been sold as the soap to remove the worst kind of dirt, grease, and grime. The soap did its job very well, yet had been on a slow, 10-year decline in sales and market share.

The client's advertising had stressed the product's ability, through a special ingredient called pumice, to clean the dirtiest hands. It placed emphasis on rugged masculine imagery, featuring men hard at work on dirt-producing jobs. It showed construction workers, auto mechanics, oil riggers, and other men in tough and dirty work.

The advertising was addressed primarily to housewives, however, using media aimed at women. The wives, not the men, were believed to be the soap buyers.

The demographic profile of the heavy users of heavy-duty hand soap indicated the consumers were in the low socioeconomic class. The advertising had been reinforcing this demographic skew. This segment of the population was declining, hence held little hope for more sales.

Management recognized the need for a new marketing strategy. It decided to attract new users to the product rather than to attempt to increase consumption among current users. A new campaign was developed, built on the idea that a heavy-duty hand soap would be ideal around the home for those weekend projects, when hands get extra dirty. The new campaign was titled "Do It Yourself" and portrayed suburban homeowners gardening, fixing bicycles, painting, and so on. As well as anyone could determine, very little happened in the market as a result of the switch in strategy. Sales continued to decline.

After the do-it-yourself campaign had been running for two years, a new creative direction was tried by the agency. This involved a concept called "public dirt"—dirt that one brings into the home from public buildings, buses, playgrounds, and other places. This is the dirt which may not always be visible.

A test commercial, built on the concept of public dirt, was developed from a controlled market test against the do-it-yourself campaign currently on the air. The results of the test did not indicate that either campaign significantly affected sales. A hard look at the consumer was clearly in order.

Research Design

The research on the consumer of heavy-duty hand soap was part of a study done by Leo Burnett, Market Facts, and the University of Chicago, called "life-style research" It was one of the earliest efforts to go beyond traditional consumer attributes, namely demographic and economic variables, in analyzing consumer behavior.

The life-style research reported here was part of a second nationwide survey of people's activities, interests, and opinions (AIOs) on a wide variety of topics. To measure the AIOs, an attitude-scaling test was developed. Three hundred AIO statements were rated on a six-point agreement scale by a representative sample of 1,000 homemakers. Examples of these statements are seen in Table C6-2.

In the past, only demographics and product attitudes were utilized to provide profiles of the target consumer. Life style, through the AIO statements, provides additional information which is more "lifelike" than demographics and helps the advertising specialist better visualize the consumer as a person.

The purpose of life-style analysis—also called "psychographics"—is to determine along what demographic and life-style dimensions the heavy users of a product differ from the light users and non-users. It is these differences that may prove valuable in developing a new advertising strategy which may be more relevant to consumers, hence more likely to improve sales.

How is the portrait of the heavy user constructed from the three sets of data obtained in the survey (AIO statements, demographic characteristics, and product usage)? A profile of the heavy user is made through cross classification and correlation analyses of the AIOs and the demographics with product use. The data processing procedure correlates the levels of agreement on each of the 300 AIO items with usage of heavy-duty hand soap. The higher the correlation between an AIO item and usage, the more likely it is that the item differentiates among heavy users, light users, and nonusers.

The analysis of the heavy users is based on only those AIO and demographic variables whose correlation with product use is significant at the 95 percent confidence level. From the tables indicating the significant items, one can build a life-style portrait of the heavy user by examining the patterns that emerge from all the items. These patterns are developed by putting together several statements which appear to be measuring a similar dimension of one of the user groups.

Table C6-1   **Economic and Demographic Data on Heavy Users**

	Heavy Users, %	Total Sample, %
Age		
Under 25	5	11
25–34	17	20
35–44	22	22
45–54	23	21
55+	29	26
Income		
Up to $3,999	30	23
$4–$5,999	21	17
$6–$7,999	22	19
$8–$9,999	11	15
$10–$14,999	10	18
$15,000+	5	7
Education	19	11
Elementary		
Some high school	24	19
High school grad	42	40
Some college	9	20
College grad	6	11
Region		
East	24	24
E and W North Central	31	30
South	31	29
West	16	18
Family Size		
1–2	35	40
3	24	20
4	19	21
5	11	12
6+	10	8

Table C6-2   AIO Responses of Heavy-Duty Hand Soap Users

Statement Number	AIO Statement	Correlation with Product Use
255	Everyone should use mouthwash.	+.148
143	Soap should have a strong, clean odor.	+.132
232	All medicines sold in drugstores are safe if you use them properly.	+.126
222	I try to arrange my home for my children's convenience.	+.123
189	When making important family decisions, consideration of the children should come first.	+.122
196	I often wish for the good old days.	+.120
150	A person can save a lot of money by shopping around for bargains.	+.120
296	I brush my hair at least twice a day.	+.120
179	The kind of dirt you can't see is worse than the kind you can see.	+.118
20	I spend a lot of time talking with my friends about products and brands.	+.116
244	It is very important for people to wash their hands before eating each meal	+.115
4	A house should be dusted and polished at least three times a week	+.114
140	I dread the future	+.113
31	I like to go camping	+.112
156	I am too generous for my own good	+.112
52	The kitchen is my favorite room	+.111
170	I use one or more household disinfectants	+.110
167	I wish I knew how to relax	+.109
104	Part of each vacation should be educational	+.108
60	In our family we use aspirin for many things	+.108
26	I am happier now than I ever was before	+.108
159	Today most people don't have enough discipline	+.106
77	I like to pay cash for anything I buy	+.106
135	I save recipes from newspapers and magazines	+.104
288	I furnish my home for comfort, not style	+.104
268	A lot of convenience foods on the market today just aren't very tasty	+.104
253	No one should take medicine unless it is prescribed by a doctor	+.104
157	I would rather spend a quiet evening at home than go out to a party	+.104
11	I love to bake and frequently do	+.102
211	I exercise regularly	+.101
128	I often have trouble getting to sleep	+.101

Data

In the sample it was found that 15 percent of all homemakers used heavy-duty hand soap frequently every month, 20 percent used it at least once a month, and 65 percent had not used the product within the past several months. These became the heavy user, light user, and nonuser groups.

The demographic data are listed in Table C6-1. There the percentage of heavy users in each demographic and economic category can be compared to the total sample.

The AIO statements, which correlated significantly with product use, are listed in Table C6-2. Although the correlation coefficients appear small, all of them indicate statistically significant relationships. (Without a large sample of respondents, this would not have been detected.)

Assignment   Construct a portrait of the heavy user of heavy-duty hand soap. Based on this profile, recommend advertising strategies that might halt the sales decline of the client's soap. The recommendation should be supported by analysis of the life-style data against the background of previous campaigns.

Part 7
Multivariate
Analysis

Introduction

    The selection of an executive aircraft is a multidimensional decision. More than one dimension is important.

    When asked to identify the product qualities that determine choice, the buyer will typically cite safety, performance, and cost. But what are these properties? Safety can be broken into several dimensions, such as structural integrity, flight characteristics, and engine reliability. Performance fragments into at least six characteristics: maximum speed, cruise speed, rate of climb, range, service ceiling, and useful load. Cost decomposes into at least three parts: purchase price, fixed operating costs, and variable operating costs. Thus, we have at least twelve dimensions, not to mention such symbolic characteristics as prestige and status.

    There is no monopoly on technology in the general aviation industry. On the contrary, aircraft technology is highly diffused. Aircraft design is mainly a matter of deciding what qualities are most important, then making trade-offs. More payload can be had in exchange for less speed. Both speed and payload can be gained at higher cost, and so forth. The trick is to select the optimum mix of product characteristics—the mix that will yield the greatest amount of total satisfaction to the most prospective buyers.

    The Cessna Aircraft Company has approached the problem in two ways: First, it has proliferated models, offering the public a virtual smorgasbord of airplanes. Second, it has invoked multivariate analysis to identify and rank the aircraft characteristics that are most influential in determining buyer behavior. It designs its products and its promotional material to conform with these findings. Cessna sells 55 percent of all of the civilian airplanes bought in the United States.

Many forces are at work in the marketplace. For instance, a firm's sales are affected by its prices, promotion, distribution, products, and reputation. Sales are also affected by the prices, promotion, and so on of the firm's competitors. To confuse things further, population, income, weather, credit, government regulation, and consumer psychology play a role. Each may influence sales. Each may change without notice. When we observe sales, we see only the net effect of these many forces.

Multivariate methods are a set of statistical tools used to unscramble these simultaneous forces. They are also used to group together objects, such as brands or customers, which have several unique traits in common.

Our excursion into multivariate analysis starts with a survey. Here, in Chapter 16, we look at the basic techniques, their purpose and application. This may be as far as the reader wants to go.

For benefit of the student who wants to apply the more common tools of multivariate analysis, Chapters 17 through 21 go into the details. Three of those chapters focus on regression analysis, by far the most useful and most pervasive of the multivariate methods. Regression analysis has not only the broadest applications, it is also used in many of the other methods.

In the concluding chapters of Part Seven, we examine discriminant analysis and factor analysis. Discriminant analysis is compatible with non-metric dependent variables, such as buy/don't buy, like/dislike, and brand preference. These are not compatible with regression analysis, yet are often crucial in the analysis of marketing problems.

Factor analysis is used to reduce the number of variables in a problem, thus making it more manageable. The technique also allows us to identify groups of things, such as sets of buyers, products, or attitudes which cannot be revealed by other means. This is especially useful in market segmentation studies.

Multivariate analysis takes us to the frontier of marketing research. Many of the techniques are new or were not practical until the electronic computer became part of the researcher's tool kit. Others are still in a state of development. Some might be classified as cures in search of a disease.

Chapter 16
A Survey of Multivariate Methods

Key Concepts

Taxonomy of Analytical Methods
A classification of statistical methods common to MR

Function Methods
Regression analysis and other multivariate tools used to specify dependency among variables

Structural Methods
Factor analysis and other multivariate tools for organizing variables into meaningful groups

Limitations
Data requirements and other constraints on multivariate analysis

Applications
Types of research congenial to multivariate methods and some rules for applying the techniques of multivariate analysis

Key Terms

univariate analysis
multivariate analysis
functional methods
dependence methods
structural methods
interdependence methods
regression analysis
discriminant analysis
multivariate analysis
    of variance (MANOVA)
canonical analysis
factor analysis

cluster analysis
proximity clustering
collinearity clustering
profile analysis
latent structure analysis
conjoint measurement
benefit structure analysis
diagnostic research
prognostic research
strategy research
statistical research

Taxonomy of Methods

Univariate and Bivariate Analysis

Primitive data evaluation is confined to univariate analysis, which is often quite adequate. *Univariate analysis* is analysis confined to one variable. It typically involves computation of the mean and a measurement of dispersion, such as range or standard deviation. Often it involves the preparation of a frequency distribution.

If one is interested in the relationship between variables, then he or she is driven to bivariate analysis. As we observed earlier, *Bivariate analysis* is analysis involving the relationship between two variables, such as sales and price. Cross tabulations and the chi-square test are examples of bivariate methods.

Unfortunately, bivariate techniques break down when multiple variables are interacting simultaneously. This brings us to multivariate analysis.

Multivariate Analysis

Multivariate analysis is the application of one or more statistical techniques used to unscramble the simultaneous effects of multiple forces.

Ideally, we would hold all other variables in the marketing mix and in the marketplace constant, while manipulating the one of interest (such as advertising). We would observe its impact on our dependent variable (usually sales). We'd then apply one of the tools of bivariate analysis (such as the chi-square test) and assess the relationship between the two variables (sales and advertising in our example). Analytically, our job would be simple, and our findings would be reliable.

Except in the laboratory, we seldom have the luxury of using bivariate methods and getting all of the information buried in the data. Too many things happen, all at the same time, in a marketplace that is not a pristine environment. Data are often messy, the variables are often numerous, and only the most powerful analytical tools will make sense out of our observations.

Methods

Multivariate analysis embraces two sets of tools: functional and structural. The *functional*—also called the *dependence*—*methods* seek to specify the relationship between one or more known dependent variables and two or more independent ones. For instance, the researcher might be interested in the relationships among a product's sales and its price, advertising budget, and number of retail outlets. Such information would allow management to more rationally allocate resources among price, advertising, and dealer development.

Structural—also called the *interdependence*—*methods* seek to group things together. They are essentially descriptive. That is, they take a large

Figure 16-1   **Classification of Multivariate Methods**

Source: Reprinted from Jagdish N. Sheth, 'The Multivariate Revolution in Marketing Research," *Journal of Marketing*, vol. 35, no. 1 (January 1971), p. 15, published by the American Marketing Association.

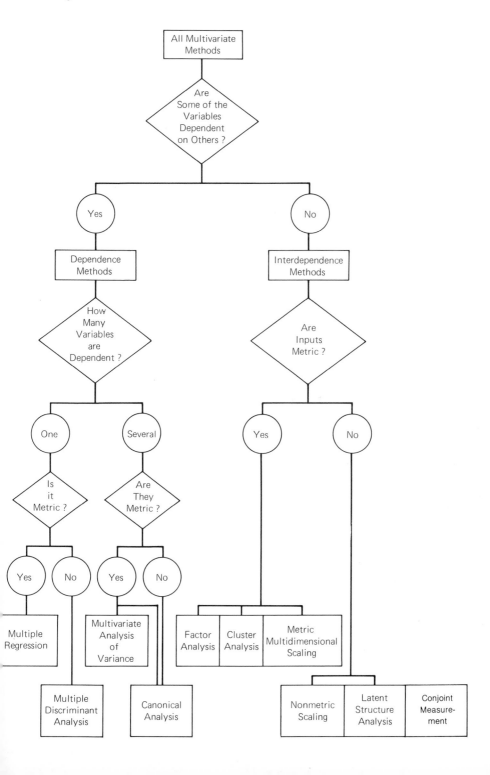

number of items—such as attitudes, life-style characteristics, consumers, or products—and place them into meaningful groups. They reveal relationships and associations not otherwise apparent.

For instance, the researcher may be interested in segmenting a market into clusters of buyers with similar characteristics. Management could then develop a product or promotional strategy uniquely suited to a particular segment. Without the aid of multivariate analysis, the underlying structure of the market—hence, the target segment—might never be revealed.

The more established methods of multivariate analysis are:

Functional Methods	Structural Methods
multiple regression analysis	factor analysis
multiple discriminant analysis	cluster analysis
multivariate analysis of variance	multidimensional scaling
canonical analysis	conjoint measurement
	latent structure analysis

The selection of a method is largely determined by the nature of the variables. In fact, the nature of the variables serves as a convenient device for classifying and choosing multivariate techniques. Figure 16-1 is illustrative.

First, we ask if one or more variables in our data are dependent upon the others: Can we divide our variables into two classes, dependent and independent? If yes, then we will use one of the functional methods.

Functional Methods

Regression Analysis

Regression analysis is a method of estimating the relationship between one dependent variable and one or more independent variables. The dependent variable must be metric. The independent (determinant) variables can be either metric or nonmetric.

In essence, regression analysis fits a line, or its mathematical equivalent, to a scatter of points. The line represents the relationship between the variables in the scatter diagram. Figure 16-2 illustrates.

In part (a) of the figure, we see eleven points. Each point is an observation of the sales that were produced by a particular level of population. Clearly there is a statistical relationship between sales and population: As the population increases, sales increase.

In part (b) of the figure, we see a line fitted to the scatter of points. The line represents an estimate of the relationship between sales and population. It shows how sensitive sales are to a change in population. The line was fitted by regression analysis, which fits the line in accordance with a strict set of rules.

Figure 16-2   **A Scatter Diagram**

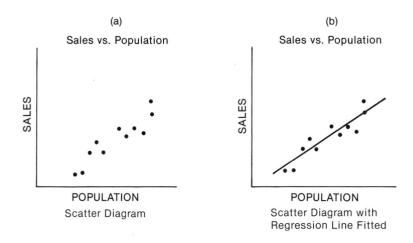

The regression line is probably an imperfect estimate of the sales/ population relationship. If it were perfect, we would expect the line to pass through each of the observed points. If the line is a perfect estimate of the relationship (we cannot tell), the displacement of the points away from the line is explained by outside (extraneous) forces. For instance, consumer income may also influence sales.

The example is bivariate regression analysis—only two variables (sales and population) were involved. This allowed us to draw the two-dimensional graphs shown in Figure 16-2. However, regression analysis can be applied to many independent variables. It is then called "multivariate regression analysis."

We could have regressed sales against population, income, age, season, price, etc., all at the same time. We could not draw a picture of the results, as we did with the bivariate regression analysis. However, we could produce an equation that would estimate how sensitive sales were to each of the determinant (independent) variables. We could also specify the precision and reliability of our findings. We learn how to do this in the next two chapters.

Discriminant Analysis

When the dependent variable is singular, but nonmetric, we can turn to discriminant analysis. Discriminant analysis is similar to regression analysis, but admits nonmetric dependent variables. That is, *discriminant analysis* is a method of estimating the relationship between one nonmetric variable and one or more other variables, metric or nonmetric.

For example, our dependent variable might be brand preference. Our objective would be to determine which of the independent variables—such as price, color, size, and style—influenced brand choice. Discriminant analysis would yield an estimate of the relationship of brand preference to each of these determinants.

If the estimate were valid (there are ways to check validity), management would know which variables to manipulate and how. If color and style determined brand choice, management would focus on those characteristics, choosing the color and style of the most preferred brand. If price were the critical determinant, money would not be spent to change color and style. Instead, management might lower price or offer a price rebate.

Multivariate Analysis of Variance

If two or more dependent variables are involved, multiple analysis of variance or canonical analysis is called for. Sometimes abbreviated as "MANOVA," *multivariate analysis of variance* seeks to test hypotheses concerning responses to different combinations of variables or to different levels of the same variable. As we saw in Chapter 12, MANOVA is commonly used in experimentation to evaluate the responses to multiple treatments or multiple levels of the same treatment.

For example, in Chapter 12, a two-factor experiment was conducted to determine the effect of both price and channel on sales. However, we were also interested in whether the effect of price was different between the two channel treatments (discount house and specialty shop). Thus, we had to cope with the interaction between treatments to determine if a change in channels made sales more or less sensitive to price.

In effect, we had two dependent variables. These were sales and the sales–price relationship. That relationship, as our MANOVA revealed, was dependent upon the channel used.

Canonical analysis is an extension of multiple regression analysis and is applicable to problems involving two or more metric or nonmetric dependent variables. It serves to specify the correlation between two sets of variables: the "criterion set," which consists of the dependent variables, and the "predictor set," which consists of the independent variables. It can also isolate the independent (predictor) variables contributing most significantly to the relationship between the two sets.

Canonical analysis is appropriate when the researcher is interested in the overall relationship between sets of variables. For example, brand loyalty may be measured by several variables—probability of purchase, time interval between purchases, and magnitude of purchases—which can make up the criterion set. This brand loyalty is determined largely by another set of variables, the predictor set, consisting of the brand's attributes (price, size, color, flavor, package, and so on). If the researcher is interested in the relationship between these two sets, brand loyalty and attributes, and is interested in identifying those attributes that play the most significant roles in this relationship, canonical analysis is the appropriate tool. To date, however, the literature contains little evidence of the real-world application of this method. This may be due to its complexity and the current lack of suitable library programs.

Structural Methods

If we cannot divide the variables into dependent and independent classes, then we must defer to structural methods of multivariate analysis.

Factor Analysis

Factor analysis is a set of statistical tools used to redefine a large number of variables as a small number of factors while preserving the essential nature of the original variables. By "essential nature" we mean the essence of the variables so far as those variables serve to describe and distinguish between the objects with which they are associated. The factors can be viewed as synthetic variables which summarize the original variables. Factors can be subjected to the same tools of analysis as conventional variables. However, as the factors are much fewer in number—often just one—they are more manageable than the original set of variables and often much more useful.

For example, assume that a firm wants to know which, if any, of several suggested innovations it should use in its product mix. Each candidate can be measured in terms of many variables. These include the development cost, the fixed manufacturing cost, the variable manufacturing cost, the amount of advertising needed to introduce the innovation and sustain sales, and the potential demand. Other relevant variables may be the item's price elasticity, break-even point, patentability, the new marketing facilities needed to handle it, the risk and profit potential associated with it, its potential cannibalization of present products, and its seasonality. Each variable is important to the commercialization decision, yet none is, by itself, a sufficient basis for accepting or rejecting an idea. (The exception is the case where the value of a particular variable is such that it precludes further consideration—e.g., where the profit potential is negative.) What management needs is a single variable that represents the essence of each innovation as far as its commercial value is concerned. The creation of such a variable—called a *factor*—is the goal of factor analysis.

One solution to the problem would be to specify an equation of the form $F = a_1x_1 + a_2x_2 + \cdots a_nx_n$, where x_j is a variable ($j = 1, 2, \ldots n$), a_j is the coefficient used to weight the variable, and F is the factor representing the commercial value of the innovation. The value of F could then be an index used to distinguish among candidates. That is, it could be used to array them according to their commercial value. It would also serve to identify outstanding, mediocre, or poor product ideas, since the higher the value of F, the greater the commercial value of the innovation.[1]

The simplest way to specify the equation for F would be to set the values of the coefficients intuitively. The coefficients weight the variables, and hence decide their relative importance in determining the value of the

---

[1] For an example of this approach, see W. B. Wentz and G. I. Eyrich, *Marketing: Theory and Application* (New York: Harcourt Brace Jovanovich, 1970) pp. 335–342.

factor. In the example, the researcher might simply canvass a number of executives to get a consensus on the relative importance of each variable. This is a common practice.

Factor analysis is primarily concerned with the analytical (vice judgmental) derivation of weights which allow several variables to be represented by one or a small number of factors. Advocates of factor analysis dismiss the intuitive approach as trivial, concentrating their efforts on the development of mathematical and statistical tools for doing the job.[2] The leadership in the field has been provided primarily by behavioral scientists such as Charles Spearman, Louis Thurstone, and Harold Hotelling, who developed the single-factor solution (using an intercorrelation matrix), the bifactor solution, the centroid method, the rotation-of-the-axis method, and the principal-components technique. New methods are still being developed; modern computer technology has made the use of even very complex factor-analysis alogarithms practical.[3] Each method yields slightly different results. The selection of a particular method is largely judgmental.

To keep things simple, we shall restrict ourselves here to the simple problem of summarizing two variables associated with a particular set of objects, different brands of bread, and to one technique, axial rotation. Each brand has been measured in terms of its protein and vitamin content, represented by axes I and II in Figure 16-3. By rotating the axes, we can measure the brands in terms of a single factor which we could call "nutrition" and which is measured along the new axis, II'. We have reduced the data and summarized the variables, with little loss of information, assuming our interest rests in the essence of the two variables, which is nutrition.

The method of rotation can be visual (intuitive) or mathematical. The mathematical methods are more rigorous, for they align the axes in accordance with a mathematical criterion such as minimizing the sum of the squares of the distances between the points in the scatter and the reference axes. The number of variables can also be reduced, by mathematical methods, in accordance with a selected criterion. Thus, the brands of bread in the example could be measured in terms of many different variables reduced by factor analysis to one or two summary factors.

Factor analysis was, for example, used in a study of coffee taste.[4] Fourteen attributes of coffee taste were summarized into four factors: its "comforting quality," "heartiness," "genuineness," and "freshness." The

[2] For a brief but lucid introduction to these methods, see Howard L. Balsley, *Quantitative Research Methods for Business and Economics* (New York: Random House, 1970), pp. 256–275. For an in-depth introduction, see Theodor Harder, *Introduction to Mathematical Models in Market and Opinion Research* (Dordrecht, Holland: Reidel, 1969), ch. 3. For a tour de force on the subject, see Harry H. Harman, *Modern Factor Analysis* (Chicago: University of Chicago Press, 1960).

[3] An example is the BioMed BMD-X72 code, a common library program. Another example is SPSS's FACTOR procedure.

[4] Bishwa Nath Mukherjee, "A Factor Analysis of Some Qualitative Attributes of Coffee," *Journal of Advertising Research* **5**:1 (March 1965), pp. 35–39.

Figure 16-3   A Factor Analysis Using the Rotation-of-the-Axis Method to Compare Different Brands of Breads

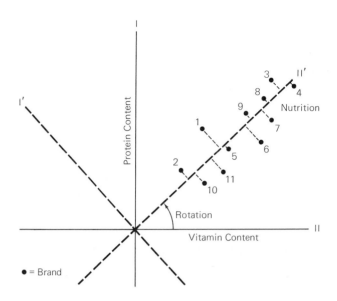

manufacturer selected two of these factors to emphasize in the production and promotion of its coffee.

Another application is described by Harder. Factor analysis was used to reduce 60 characteristic body measurements to 12 for the benefit of the West German clothing industry. Such a reduction is extremely useful in cutting both the manufacturing and the inventory costs of ready-to-wear clothing.[5] (We see more examples in chapter 20.)

Cluster Analysis

Cluster analysis is a set of statistical techniques for grouping objects into internally homogeneous sets on the basis of observed data. It is especially well suited to market segmentation studies. There the objective is to gather consumers into distinctly different, but internally homogeneous, groups. If consumers can be clustered into meaningful groups, management can tailor its marketing mix to be compatible with the traits of a particular group (a market segmentation strategy).

The beauty of cluster analysis is that it allows the researcher to start with nothing but the attributes of the objects that are to be classified. Through cluster analysis, the attributes are allowed to determine which objects should

[5] Harder, Theodor, *Introduction to Mathematical Models in Market and Opinion Research*, pp. 105–106.

be grouped together. The process not only classifies the previously ungrouped objects, it also reveals which attributes discriminate between groups. In the clustering of consumers, the attributes might be age, income, family size, occupation, ethnic class, education, or one or more life-style characteristics. In the clustering of stores or products, the attributes might be location, size, atmospherics, image, cost, performance, color, etc.

Although cluster analysis allows us to make rigorous statistical statements about the associations between the objects within the clusters as well as between clusters, generalizations about the clusters themselves must be intuitive. Cluster analysis does not provide the labels for the clusters. It simply gathers objects into groups according to a prescribed statistical criterion.

There are a number of algorithms for cluster analysis, each using a different criterion to group objects. For example, objects may be clustered according to their interpoint distances (their rods) in an attribute space. For instance, cars 1, 9, 8, and 2 in Figure 15-2 form a fairly homogeneous group. This method, called *proximity clustering*, is illustrated in Figure 16-4(a).

An alternative technique is to cluster objects according to the similarity of the pattern, not the magnitude, of their attribute scores (ratings). Thus the shape of the score profile, not its elevation, becomes the classification criterion. This method, called *collinearity clustering*, is illustrated in Figure 16-4(b). (Note that objects A and C are assigned to one cluster, and B and D to the other.)

Cluster analysis—sometimes called "profile analysis"—embraces other criteria, hence alternative algorithms.[6] This forces some semiarbitrary de-

Figure 16-4   **Alternative Methods of Clustering Objects**

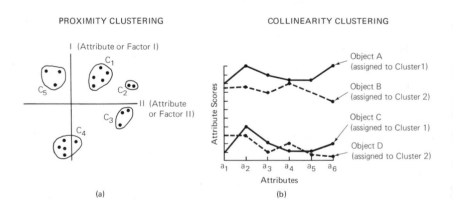

[6] There is no consensus on the taxonomy of cluster analysis. For two classification systems, see Lester A. Neidell, "Discussion and Comments" (on preceding paper by John G. Myers), p. 187; and Lawrence Sherman and Jagdish N. Sheth, "Cluster Analysis and Its Applications in Marketing Research," p. 198, in Jagdish N. Sheth, ed., *Multivariate Methods for Market and Survey Research* (Chicago: American Marketing Association, 1977).

cisions on the researcher. In addition to selecting the clustering criterion, the researcher must make decisions about the number and composition of clusters. He or she must also invent names for the clusters. Thus, cluster analysis is not a purely analytical process: Judgments are required, to say nothing of some messy mathematics. Cluster analysis also has a hearty appetite for computer time. For these reasons, the marketing literature is not rich in examples of the application of cluster analysis.[7]

Latent Structure Analysis

Latent structure analysis has the same goals as factor analysis and cluster analysis, but it admits nonmetric variables. It is a set of alternative methods for finding structure in a mass of seemingly unrelated variables.

The methods have found relatively little application in marketing research. The main inhibitor to the diffusion of latent structure analysis is the lack of readily available computer programs. The tedious mathematical work demanded by the technique makes its use impractical without the computer.

Conjoint Measurement[8]

Conjoint measurement is a method of measuring trade-offs between attributes or between benefits and cost associated with a product. Respondents rank pairwise combinations of attributes according to their preference. Conjoint measurement is then applied to derive a quantitative measurement of utility for each attribute (or benefit).

For example, a person might be asked to express his or her preference for two condominiums. One option has a river view and a high price. The other has a low price, but no river view. Choice will indicate the utility of the river view. Given an adequate sample of condominium buyers, conjoint measurement would yield a ratio-scale value of the utility of a river view. Concurrently, other attributes would be evaluated by the same method. The analysis would reveal a quantitative value for each condominium attribute, such as floor space, air conditioning, and carpeting. It could also yield a scale of utility values for an attribute, such as price, offered at different levels. Presumably, the prospects will select the condominium with the highest aggregate utility value.

---

[7] For a more complete introduction to cluster analysis, see Daniel E. Bailey, *Cluster Analysis and the BC TRY System* (Boulder, Col.: Tryon-Bailey Associates, 1970), or Paul E. Greene and Frank J. Carmone, *Multidimensional Scaling and Related Techniques in Marketing Analysis*, (Boston: Allyn and Bacon, 1970) ch. 5. The second text also explores potential applications in marketing research as does the previously cited article by Sherman and Sheth.

[8] For a more complete, yet nonmathematical, introduction to conjoint measurement, see Jagdish N. Sheth, "What Is Multivariate Analysis?" in Jagdish N. Sheth, ed., *Multivariate Methods for Market and Survey Research*, p. 7. For a rigorous introduction, see Vithala R. Rao, "Conjoint Measurement in Market Analysis," pp. 257–286, in the same book.

By measuring each attribute in utility values, trade-offs are easy to make. For example, if a wet bar had a higher utility value than an automatic garage-door opener, but cost the same, the builder would opt for the wet bar. Management's objective is to emphasize the attributes that will yield the greatest total utility value, hence make the product the most desirable from the viewpoint of the prospective buyers—the marketing concept in action!

Conjoint measurement—also called "benefit structure analysis"—is an extension of multidimensional scaling which we explored in the discussion of scaling (Chapter 15). In fact, we could easily have included it in that discussion. Conjoint measurement, however, goes beyond scaling and allows us to make direct quantitative comparisons of attributes.

Limitations

In marketing research, how well an analytical tool works is the sole measurement of its worth. Sometimes, multivariate analysis works poorly or not at all. There are some brutal limitations which often force us to leave the multivariate methods in the tool kit and fall back on the less sophisticated techniques of analysis.

Data Requirements

Multivariate analysis has an unsatiable appetite for data. A handful of observations—say, fewer than twenty—is seldom adequate. Often hundreds of observations are needed to achieve statistically significant results.

The data problem is especially acute when dealing with a large assortment of variables. As the number of variables increases, so does the need for more observations. Often the researcher is unsure of what attitudes, economic characteristics, life-style dimensions, demographic properties, or whatever are relevant to the problem at hand. The only solution is to include everything that has a reasonable chance of being significant.

In its study of store preferences in the Houston market, Neiman-Marcus's research group considered 112 variables. These included age, household income, occupation, life-cycle position, family size, education, and a bundle of attitudinal and life-style variables. Over 400 respondents were needed to produce an adequate sample size. The final data set consisted of 46,255 pieces of information. Even this would have been inadequate for some of the analysis, had many of the variables not been combined through factor analysis.

Computer Requirements

As a practical matter, one cannot perform multivariate analysis without a computer. The techniques are generally complex, cumbersome and involve a horrendous amount of arithmetic. The tedium of the arithmetic alone would be enough to discourage the most rigorous analyst. A single multivariate procedure often involves over 100,000 mathematical operations. However, when one has access to a machine that can add a pair of ten-digit numbers in one-millionth of a second, arithmetic is no longer a problem.

Preparing the instructions—called the "program"—for the computer is difficult and luckily unnecessary. There are several collections—called "libraries" or "packages"—of multivariate programs readily available. Most academic computer laboratories have one in direct access. All the user need do is enter the data into the computer, then call our the desired program. Different multivariate methods can be invoked, simply by typing a few lines of instruction. For instance, the commonly used Statistical Package for the Social Sciences (SPSS) requires only four short lines of instruction to do a discriminant analysis of the user's data.

Proficiency in computer programming is not a requirement for multivariate analysis. Neither is a firm grasp of the mathematics necessary to apply the techniques. However, one does need an intuitive understanding of the process being used and the ability to interpret the results.

In some areas, there are computer services that will process data and perform the multivariate procedures specified by the client. The client, in this case the market-research person, will still carry the burden of interpreting the results.

Politics

As Ferber pointed out, there is a general awareness of multivariate analysis in the research community, but little familiarity, and even less acceptance.[9] The situation is even less encouraging among line marketers, many of whom prefer to live with their problems rather than accept a solution they do not understand. Ferber related a story analogous to the challenge confronting many of the proponents of multivariate methods:

> . . . reminds me of the story of the college president who was on the school borad of a small southern town. For some years he had been trying to convince the school board to adopt a second language in the elementary schools, and had failed every time. This time he gave a particularly eloquent speech, citing numerous authorities on the value of teaching children a second language early in their school careers. After his speech, there was silence as he sat down and waited for the verdict. Finally, the chairman of the school board, who considered himself somewhat of a scholar, stood up and said, "Personally I am still not convinced; I do not think we need a second language in our schools. After all, if English was good enough for Jesus Christ, it should be good enough for us!"[10]

[9] Robert Ferber, "Antecedent Conditions for Diffusion of Multivariate Methods," in Jagdish N. Sheth, ed., *Multivariate Methods for Market and Survey Research*, pp. 329–30.
[10] Ferber, "Antecedent Conditions for Diffusion of Multivariate Methods," p. 330.

Within the research community itself, there are people, including research managers, with a vested interest in the older forms of analysis. Like pilots and sailors, researchers tend to use the tools and techniques with which they are most familiar. Often they lack the skills or motivation necessary to master new technology. In the meantime, the line marketers do not clamor for that which they do not understand or of which they may never have heard.

The advocate of multivariate analysis may find politics more constraining than any technical or equipment limitations. The researcher's communication and persuasive skills may be as important as his or her technical abilities.

Technology

The technology of multivariate analysis inflicts its own limitations. There is still much that we do not understand. The methods sometimes break down. They can yield findings that are not statistically significant, hence unreliable. They can lead up blind alleys. The information they produce can be valid, but trivial. Some of the techniques, such as factor analysis, lean heavily on subjective judgment.

Multivariate methods can provide information that is statistically valid and operationally useless. Findings can be hard to interpret. The technology can be awkward to explain. Mastering the techniques, especially the more esoteric ones such as multidimensional scaling, can be difficult.

Multivariate analysis, while quite advanced, is still in a state of development. New methods and variants of old ones frequently appear in the scholarly press, such as the *Journal of Marketing*, the *Journal of Marketing Research*, and the *Journal of Consumer Research*.

Especially important to the practitioner is the proliferation of computer programs for applying multivariate methods to practical research problems. These are diffused through the research community via the scholarly journals, research conferences and seminars, and person-to-person exchanges. (One source of such programs is the *Journal of Marketing Research*'s regular feature, "Computer Abstracts.")

Time and Cost

At the margin, multivariate analysis can be very inexpensive in time and money. If adequate data have been collected and entered into the computer for conventional processing (frequency distributions, etc.), the added (marginal) cost of multivariate analysis is cheap.

The Broadway Department Stores' research group gathers survey data on each of its markets. These data are entered into a common IBM computer. A popular statistical library (SPSS) is then applied to produce the descriptive statistics, frequency distributions, and cross tabulations cherished by the less imaginative managers. At this point, the researchers have spent $3,000 to $6,000 in data collection and processing.

The researchers then call out one or more of the library's multivariate programs to identify the variables that determine store selection. The objective is to discover why some buyers patronize the Broadway while others shop at competing stores. This process, the multivariate analysis, takes about one day of a researcher's time and adds $50 to $100 to the computer bill. On the assumption that the other work would have been done regardless (it always was), the multivariate analysis cost the Broadway very little.

Conversely, if a research project is mounted solely to exploit the advantages of multivariate analysis, time and cost become significant. This is especially true if the sponsor does not have the equipment and know-how. Few research suppliers are prepared to do the job beyond data collection and initial processing. Those prepared to handle the entire project will typically charge between $10,000 and $30,000, depending largely on the cost of data collection.

Applications

The applications of multivariate analysis are proliferating as the methods multiply and diffuse through the research community. Today, few areas of inquiry remain untouched by multivariate methods. Table 16-1 offers some examples of the applications of these techniques.

Taxonomy

In Table 16-1, we see another research taxonomy—one that is congenial to multivariate methods. This classification system is similar to a taxonomy introduced in Chapter 1. It takes the managerial viewpoint, focusing on the needs of management. Specifically,

Diagnostic Research   Research designed to provide a snapshot of the marketplace and tell what is going on.

Prognostic Research   Research designed to forecast the future or to estimate current conditions (such as sales potential) where the needed information is unavailable.

Strategy Research   Research designed to estimate the results of a change in the marketing mix.

Statistical Research   Research designed to assess the errors in other research and to devise methods to reduce those errors.[11]

---

[11] Jagdish N. Sheth, "What Is Multivariate Analysis?" in Jagdish N. Sheth, *Multivariate Methods for Market and Survey Research*, p. 8.

Table 16-1   Applications of Multivariate Analysis

Research Needs	Multivariate Methods
A. *Diagnostic Research*	*Structural Methods*
1. Market segmentation	1. Cluster, factor analysis, or latent structure analysis
2. Product or corporate typology	2. Factor, cluster analysis, or latent structure analysis
3. Customer perceptions and preferences	3. Multidimensional scaling or conjoint measurement
B. *Prognostic Research*	*Functional Methods*
1. Sales forecasting	1. Multiple regression or canonical correlation
2. Market potentials	2. Multiple discriminant analysis
C. *Strategy Research*	*Functional Methods*
1. Field experiments	1. MANOVA or discriminant analysis
2. Laboratory simulation	2. MANOVA or discriminant analysis
D. *Statistical Research*	*Structural Methods*
1. Heterogeneity reduction	1. Cluster analysis or factor analysis
2. Measurement errors	2. Factor analysis or multidimensional scaling
3. Indexing or data consistency	3. Factor analysis
4. Normal distributions	4. Factor analysis

Source: Adapted from Jagdish N. Sheth, "What Is Multivariate Analysis?" in Jagdish N. Sheth (Ed.), *Multivariate Methods for Market and Survey Research* (Chicago: American Marketing Association, 1977), p. 9.

Uses

A few examples of multivariate methods in action might throw our discussion into sharper focus and indicate the value of the methods in applied research:

Toyota Motor Sales, U.S.A., Inc. used multiple regression analysis to relate their car and truck sales to economic and demographic variables. The resulting equation was used to predict sales potential for each of the firm's metropolitan markets.

Neiman-Marcus used factor analysis to reduce a large number of buyer characteristics to three factors. These factors represented psychographic dimensions (activities, interests, and opinions). These factors, along with several economic and demographic variables (such as income and age), were then subjected to discriminant analysis. The discriminant analysis identified the psychographic, economic, and demographic characteristics that separated the Neiman-Marcus customers from the customers of the store's major competitors. With this information, management was able to alter the marketing mix to appeal more to the other firms' clientele.

Market Facts, a research supplier, used discriminant analysis and cluster analysis as the basis for its market structure analysis system (MSAS). MSAS is used to find gaps in the marketplace. The gaps (unsatisfied market segments) represent significant new-product opportunities for Market Fact's clients.[12]

Seven Commandments

Sheth suggests seven rules that researchers should follow in applying multivariate methods. They are applicable to most research techniques, but are especially relevant in the esoteric world of multivariate analysis. Specifically,[13]

Do not be technique-oriented   Focus on management's needs, then choose an appropriate analytical tool.

Consider Multivariate Models as Information for Management Multivariate models (equations, perceptual maps, etc.) are an aid to, not a substitute for, managerial judgment.

Do not Substitute Multivariate Methods for Researcher Skill and Imagination   Statistics do not assure causality and are not substitutes for common sense.

Develop Communication Skill   Management will seldom accept findings based on methods they don't understand.

Avoid Making Statistical Inferences about the Parameters of Multivariate Models   We are seldom certain of the distribution of a market population due to nonsampling and measurement errors.

Guard against the danger of making inferences about the market realities when such inferences may be due to the peculiarities of the method   Be sure the statistical findings are consistent with sound theory and common sense.

Exploit the complimentary relationship between functional and structural methods   Use one method to support another, as in the Neiman-Marcus example.

Problems

1   Identify each of the following as univariate analysis, bivariate analysis, or multivariate analysis: (a) the computation of the mean, median,

---

[12] See David K. Hardin, "Market Facts: An Application of Market Structure Analysis," in Walter B. Wentz, ed., *Cases in Marketing Research* (New York: Harper & Row, 1975), pp. 271–281.

[13] Sheth, "Seven Commandments for Users of Multivariate Methods," in Sheth, *Multivariate Methods*, pp. 333–35.

and variance of the income, age, and family size of registered Democrats, (b) the estimation of both main and interaction effects of a factorial design, and (c) the estimation of the price elasticity of Taster's Choice coffee.

2   What do you know, or at least assume, about your data when you apply a functional method of multivariate analysis as opposed to a structural method?

3   Which multivariate method might be useful in analyzing data gathered on 586 small-car buyers, when the objective was to explain brand preference? Assume you have thirteen pieces of information on each buyer.

4   What is regression analysis? Cite a possible application. Name two multivariate methods that produce their own scales. (Enter the analysis with nonmetric data.)

5   A psychographic survey of 218 beer drinkers contained 119 activity, interest, and opinion questions, plus five economic and demographic questions. What multivariate tool(s) might be applied to unscramble meaning from these 27,032 pieces of data? Defend your choice.

6   Assume you are the researcher analyzing the beer-drinker data cited in the previous problem. You must present your findings and recommendations to the director of advertising who thinks statistics is the next worst thing to corporal punishment. What problems would you expect and how would you handle them?

7   A conjoint measurement of riding-lawnmover attributes indicated the ideal product would have these features:

Attribute	Level	Utility
Price	$2,000	.8
Width of cut	48 inches	.5
Horsepower	16	.7
	Total	2.0

Exhibit 16-1   **Example of Utilities for Riding Lawn Mowers**

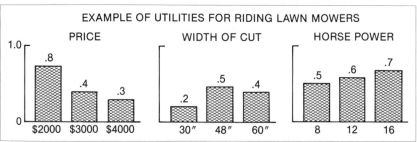

Source: Reprinted from Herbert Hupfer, "Techniques Useful in Planning New Products, Especially Costly Ones," *Marketing News* (Jan. 28, 1977), p. 10, published by the American Marketing Association.

The manufacturer cannot build such a mower at a profit. However, it can profitably build a $3,000 mower with a 30-inch cut and 12 horsepower or a $4,000 mower with a 48-inch cut and 16 horsepower. Both options would yield the same profit at a given volume of sales. Using the conjoint-measurement data in Exhibit 16-1, which option would likely produce the most sales, hence greatest profit? Show your calculations.[14]

[14] This problem is based on Herbert Hupfer, "Technique Useful in Planning New Products, Especially Costly Ones," *Marketing News*, January 28, 1977, p. 10.

Chapter 17
Linear Regression Models

Key Concepts

The Regression Model
The form and meaning of the regression equation

Basic Concepts
The bivariate linear regression model and the method of least squares

Multiple Linear Regression Models
The structure and computation of multivariable models

Key Terms

linear regression analysis
linear regression model
bivariate linear regression
    model
method of least squares
scatter diagram
regression coefficient

intercept
residual
multiple linear regression
    analysis
beta coefficients
standardized valves

The Regression Model

Correct marketing decisions are most easily made when the exact relationships between relevant variables are known. If a marketing manager is confronted with a pricing decision, he or she likes to know just how each alternative price will affect sales. If he or she is contemplating a change in the advertising budget, the manager likes to know just how a given change will affect sales. Determining such relationships is one function of marketing research.

In carrying out this function, the researcher often uses regression analysis. Regression analysis hypothesizes a general, and normally linear, relationship between variables and provides a method for specifying that relationship, as well as for evaluating the reasonableness of the resultant model.[1] The general form of a linear regression model is

$$Y = \alpha + \beta_1 X_1 + \beta_2 X_2 + \cdots \beta_n X_n + u$$

where

Y = the dependent variable

X = an independent variable

α and β are parameters

u = the error, or "disturbance," term

$1, 2, \ldots n$ are subscripts identifying the different variables

It posits a relationship between variables that appears to hold true for many economic (hence, marketing) phenomena. Inclusion of all the relevant independent variables, of course, is virtually impossible, and the information used to specify the model will usually be less than perfect. Hence, the disturbance term, u, is included—evidence of the fact that the other independent terms in the equation do not fully explain the value of the dependent variable, Y.

In marketing-research applications of the regression model, the dependent variable is usually sales. The independent variables are usually factors such as price, advertising, income, or population. Of course, the researcher is not limited to these variables. Taxes, competitors' prices, the number of retail outlets available, weather conditions—any number of factors—find their way into regression models of market phenomena.

In practice, we cannot truly specify the foregoing equation; it is a theoretical model. The actual values of the parameters elude us, for we cannot gather exhaustive data on every relevant variable. Hence, we must settle for something less, which is a regression model of the form

$$\hat{Y} = \hat{\alpha} + \hat{\beta}_1 X_1 + \hat{\beta}_2 X_2 + \cdots \hat{\beta}_n X_n$$

This simply says that the estimated value of a dependent variable, $\hat{Y}$, is related to the actual values of the independent variables $X_1, X_2, \ldots X_n$ as specified by the estimated values of the parameters $\hat{\alpha}, \hat{\beta}_1, \hat{\beta}_2, \ldots \hat{\beta}_n$. Regression analysis enables us to calculate these estimated values, given a quantity of real-world data.

---

[1] Regression analysis is the basic tool of econometrics. Econometrics, a branch of economics, may be defined as "the quantitative analysis of actual economic phenomena based on the concurrent development of theory and observation, related by appropriate methods of inference" (P. A. Samuelson, T. C. Koopmans, and R. N. Stone, "Report of the Evaluation Committee for *Econometrica*," *Econometrica* **22**:2 [April 1954], p. 141).

By specifying the preceding equation, we create an apparent cause-and-effect model that provides insight into the relationships between the variables and serves to predict the value of the dependent variable. For instance, a trailer manufacturer used regression analysis to specify the following model of the demand for a particular class of recreational vehicles:

$$\hat{Y} = 73.61 + .00136X_1 - .00105X_2 + 1.66X_3$$

The model shows an estimated relationship—based on available data—between sales, $\hat{Y}$, and husband-and-wife households, X_1, the population over 55 years of age, X_2, and the number of trailer parks, X_3 in a particular market area. Although the firm could not control the independent variables, it did use the model to estimate the sales in states where vehicle-registration lists were unavailable. These estimates were crucial to its distribution plans and the geographic allocation of its promotional resources.

Of course, a cause-and-effect relationship is only implied by the model. Regression analysis determines the statistical correlation, if any, between variables. Remember, correlation is not causation. The model must withstand certain statistical tests and be consistent with economic theory and common sense before it can be accepted as a reasonable analogue of reality.

Basic Concepts

Definition

Linear regression analysis is a statistical method of estimating a linear[2] relationship between a dependent and one or more independent variables. A general linear regression model has the following form

$$\hat{Y} = \hat{\alpha} + \hat{\beta}_1 X_1 + \hat{\beta}_2 X_2 + \cdots \hat{\beta}_n X_n \qquad [17.1]$$

where

$\hat{Y}$ = the estimated value of the dependent variable (sometimes called the calculated value and represented by Y_C)

$\hat{\alpha}$ = the estimated value of the intercept

$\hat{\beta}$ = the estimated value of the coefficient specifying the relationship between $\hat{Y}$ and X

X = an independent variable

1, 2, ... n are subscripts identifying the different variables

---

[2] A linear function is an equation of the first order. In other words, it is a function in which no term has an exponent greater than 1. For example, $y = 4x$ and $y = 30 + 0.2x - 3z$ are linear functions. All other functions are nonlinear—or curvilinear. For example, $y = x^2$ and $y = 6 + 5x - 7z^2$ are second-order nonlinear equations; $y = x^3$ and $y = 3 + 2x + 4x^3$ are curvilinear third-order equations.

The model's parameters (the $\hat{\alpha}$ and $\hat{\beta}$'s that specify the relationships) are estimates (the use of the carets over the symbols indicate this). Their true values are never known. The independent variables are observed or assumed values. The property of linearity—the hallmark of the linear regression model—pertains only to the parameters. The variables themselves may be nonlinear (X^2, X^{-1}, etc.), as we shall see when we discuss curvilinear models.

The linearity of the equation makes it relatively easy to compute the parameters and evaluate the model statistically. As a pragmatic accommodation, linearity is often assumed when real-world relationships are not truly linear. Although this does distort the results somewhat, the extent of the distortion can be estimated.

A Bivariate Linear Regression Model

The *bivariate linear regression model*—sometimes called the "bivariant" or "simple" linear regression model—is a two-variable linear equation of the form

$$\hat{Y} = \hat{a} + \hat{\beta}X \qquad\qquad [17.2]$$

where

$\hat{Y}, \hat{\alpha}, \hat{\beta}$, and X are defined as before

This equation is a special case of the general linear regression equation (formula 17.1). The bivariate model represents the simplest form of regression. It is a convenient way of introducing regression analysis, for it is easily understood, and it illuminates principles that are also applicable to the more complicated—and more powerful—models that follow.

The bivariate model is often sufficient to describe a market phenomenon, especially when most of the variation in the dependent variable is caused by a single independent variable. It is the mathematical expression of a straight line fitted to the scatter of points in a two-dimensional space (a plane). The two dimensions are Y and X, the dependent and independent variables, respectively. The points represent the paired values of Y and X. Each point reflects a different combination of the two variables.

The model is specified (that is, values are determined for the parameters, $\hat{\alpha}$ and $\hat{\beta}$) by the process of fitting the line to the distribution of paired values. The statistical technique used is called the *method of least squares*.

The Method of Least Squares

Observed data plotted on a two-dimensional graph are called a *scatter diagram*. Using this diagram, we can draw a line approximating the relationship between the two variables represented by the Y and X axes. The line may be erratic, straight, or curved, depending on the distribution—called "scatter"—of the points and the criterion used to draw it. It can be drawn freehand or in accordance with a mathematical rule. In linear regression analysis, the line is straight and the criterion used to fit it to the scatter of Y-and-X points is that of least squares. The points themselves may represent time-series or cross-sectional data.

The criterion of least squares is met when the sum of the squares of the residuals is minimum. The residuals are the distances between the observed values of the dependent variable, Y, and the estimated values, $\hat{Y}$ (represented by the line). Using the symbol e to represent the distances (the vertical deviations of the points from the line, hence the residuals or "errors"), we can state the least-squares criterion as follows

$$\sum_{i=1}^{n} e_i^2 \text{ is minimum} \tag{17.3}$$

where

$$e_i = Y_i - \hat{Y}_i (\text{the "residual"}) \tag{17.4}$$

$Y =$ the observed value of the dependent variable

$\hat{Y} =$ the estimated value of the dependent variable

$n =$ the total number of observations

$i =$ the number of the observation

All this may seem a bit confusing, but an example should clarify things. Assume that an analyst has recorded ten observations of sales and advertising for a particular product and posted these data in Table 17-1.

Table 17-1   **Sales and Advertising Expenditures**

Observations (i)	Sales (Y)	Advertising (X)
1	155 units	180 units
2	120	100
3	220	290
4	120	160
5	230	400
6	225	370
7	170	220
8	195	240
9	220	320
10	120	200

[a] Advertising can be expressed in dollars, say, as the cost of advertisements or allowances made to dealers for cooperative advertising. Or it can be expressed in units—the number of ads, inches of advertising, or commercials used.

Inspection of the data suggests that there may be a positive correlation between sales and advertising. This apparent relationship is more obvious when the data are plotted in the form of a scatter diagram, as in Figure 17-1. The apparent relationship between sales and advertising can be represented by a straight line fitted to the scatter of points by the method of least squares, as in Figure 17-2. A straight line is expressed mathematically as

$$Y = \alpha + \beta X \qquad\qquad [17.5]$$

where

$Y =$ the variable on the vertical axis

$X =$ the variable on the horizontal axis

$\alpha =$ the y-axis intercept (called simply "intercept"), which is the value of Y when X is at the origin, i.e., when $X = 0$

$\beta =$ a coefficient representing the slope of the line, and hence the sensitivity of Y to changes in X

Equation 17.5 is identical to equation 17.2, the general form of the bivariate linear regression model, except for the absence of the carets over Y, α, and β. The caret simply signifies that the values in equation 17.2 are estimates. Mathematically, the two equations are the same. Thus the method of least squares specifies the bivariate model.

The method of least squares allows us to compute the $\hat{\alpha}$ and $\hat{\beta}$ values that are the parameters of the equation, while meeting the condition of a minimum

$$\sum_{i=1}^{n} e_i^2.$$

By specifying the parameters, we specify the relationship between the variables, in this case sales and advertising. This, of course, is the practical objective of regression analysis.

Once the parameters are known, we can easily draw a line that minimizes the sum of the squares of the vertical deviations, e. We simply select a value for X and substitute it into the equation to obtain a companion Y value. This pair of X and Y values represents a point on the line. By selecting another X value, we can generate another Y value, and hence have a second point on the line. By constructing a straight line through these two points, we can replicate the function expressed by the equation. That is, we can represent the mathematical regression model graphically.

If the equation is an estimate of the relationship between Y and X, a caret is placed over Y and the parameters α and β. This symbolizes the fact that the line is only an approximation of the true relationship. Notice that

Figure 17-1   **Sales and Advertising Expenditures**

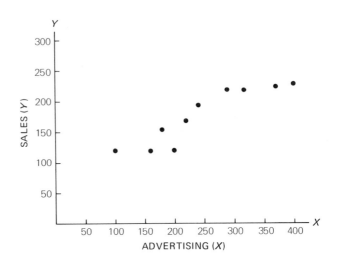

Figure 17-2   **A Linear Estimate of the Relationship Between Sales and Advertising for a Hypothetical Product**

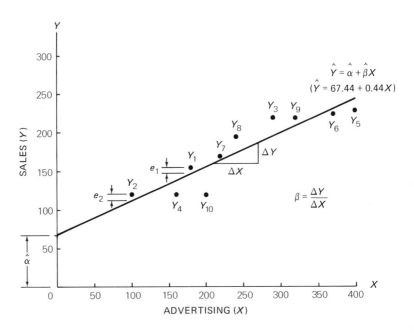

the true values of Y for the ten observations in Figure 17-2 do not rest *on* the line. If the equation were a perfect expression of the Y-and-X relationship the line would pass through each observed point. Such a line would be erratic and would represent an extremely complex equation. Hence, we must settle for something less accurate, but far more manageable, than an exact model.

Computing Parameters

The parameters $\hat{\alpha}$ and $\hat{\beta}$, which define the Y-and-X relationship, are computed by the following formulas. (The i's identifying the observations have been left off to make the notation less cumbersome.)

$$\hat{\beta} = \frac{n(\Sigma XY) - (\Sigma X)(\Sigma Y)}{n(\Sigma X^2) - (\Sigma X)^2} \qquad [17.6]$$

and

$$\hat{\alpha} = \bar{Y} - \hat{\beta}\bar{X} \qquad [17.7]$$

where

$\hat{\beta}$ = the slope of the line (the *regression coefficient*)

$\hat{\alpha}$ = the *intercept*

Y = the observed values of the dependent variable

$\bar{Y}$ = the mean of the observed values of the dependent variable

X = the observed values of the independent variable

$\bar{X}$ = the mean of the observed values of the independent variable

n = the total number of observations

Table 17-2   Observed Values and Preliminary Calculations for a Bivariate Linear Regression Model

Observation (i)	Sales (Y)	Advertising (X)	Preliminary Calculations (X^2)	(XY)
1	155	180	32,400	27,900
2	120	100	10,000	12,000
3	220	290	84,100	63,800
4	120	160	25,600	19,200
5	230	400	160,000	92,000
6	225	370	136,900	83,250
7	170	220	48,400	37,400
8	195	240	57,600	46,800
9	220	320	102,400	70,400
10	120	200	40,000	24,000
	$\Sigma Y = 1,775$	$\Sigma X = 2,480$	$\Sigma X^2 = 697,400$	$\Sigma XY = 476,750$
$n = 10$	$\bar{Y} = 177.5$	$\bar{X} = 248$		

These equations may be solved by simple arithmetic, although i practice a computer is often used. The data drawn from Table 17-1—tl observed pairs of Y and X values—is subjected to the manipulations show in Table 17-2 and the resultant totals and means substituted into equatic 17.6 and 17.7 to find the value of $\hat{\alpha}$ and $\hat{\beta}$. Substituting these parametr values into the equation for a straight line gives us the function plotted i Figure 17-2. This function is our estimate of the relationship between tl firm's sales and its advertising.

$$\hat{\beta} = \frac{n(\Sigma XY) - (\Sigma X)(\Sigma Y)}{n(\Sigma X^2) - (\Sigma X)^2}$$
(given as equation 17.

$$\hat{\beta} = \frac{10(476,750) - (2,480)(1,775)}{10(697,400) - (2,480)^2}$$
(by substitutio:

$$\hat{\beta} = \frac{4,767,500 - 4,402,000}{6,974,000 - 6,150,400}$$
(by arithmeti

$$\hat{\beta} = 0.44378$$
(by arithmeti

$$\hat{\beta} = 0.44$$
(by roundin

$$\hat{\alpha} = \bar{Y} - \hat{\beta}\bar{X}$$
(given as equation 17.

$$\hat{\alpha} = 177.5 - 0.44378(248)$$
(by substitutio

$$\hat{\alpha} = 67.44296$$
(by arithmeti

$$\hat{\alpha} = 67.44$$
(by roundin

$$\hat{Y} = \hat{\alpha} + \hat{\beta}X$$
(given as equation 17.

$$\hat{Y} = 67.44 + 0.44X$$
(by substitutio

Again, the inclusion of the caret symbolizes the fact that values of tl parameters, and hence the computed value of the dependent variable, a estimates. The formula $\hat{Y} = 67.44 + 0.44X$ is not an exact expression of tl relationship between the firm's sales, Y, and its advertising, X. Is the mod sufficiently precise to enable the firm to make the right advertising decisioi Fortunately, there are techniques for evaluating such equations that can t(the advertising manager, very specifically, just how reliable it is.

This kind of model is common in causal research. Data are acquired perhaps from a store audit or a consumer panel and an examination of tl irm's advertising records—and subjected to linear regression analysis. The esult is an explicit mathematical equation describing the cause-and-effect elationship between the firm's sales and its advertising. We call it a model •ecause it is a replica of the sales–advertising relationship. It tells us that he firm can expect approximately 67.44 units of sales if it does no advertising $X = 0$). It tells us that sales will increase by approximately half a unit (0.44))r every additional unit of advertising or, conversely, will decrease by pproximately the same amount for every unit of advertising cut, at least 'ith the range of observed values.

The problem is illustrative of regression analysis. First, empirical data re gathered on presumably related marketing variables, sales and advertis- ıg. Then, perhaps concurrently, an underlying relationship is hypothesized, amely that $Y = \alpha + \beta X + u$. The disturbance term, u, is included in rec- ·gnition of the fact that advertising, X, does not fully account for the value f sales, Y. Since sufficient data are not available to specify the true values •f the parameters (all possible pairs of sales–advertising values have not •een observed), the model form $\hat{Y} = \hat{\alpha} + \hat{\beta} X$ is assumed and its parameters stimated. This yields an explicit model that gives the marketer the informa- ion needed to make the advertising budget decision. Before we discuss how ıch a model can be evaluated to determine the reasonableness of the ypothesized relationship and the quality of the estimated parameters, we hall explore multiple linear regression analysis, which relieves us of the onstraint of having only one independent variable in our model.

Multiple-Linear Regression Models

'requently, the dependent variable is influenced by more than one inde- endent variable. For instance, sales may be influenced by the seller's price, dvertising, and personal selling. Sales may also be influenced by the size f the market population, personal income, weather, and competitors' prices. ' any of these factors change during the period under study, sales may vary s a result. In fact, the variation in sales caused by these various factors may e so great as to make a two-variable model useless.

If analysts are trying to estimate the explicit relationship between sales nd a particular marketing instrument, say price, they would be wise to ıclude other active variables in their equation. It is seldom possible to lentify and include every related variable. Fortunately, most of them are ot significant, either because they do not vary during the period of the study r their effect on the dependent variable is slight. However, the significant ıes must be included if the equation is to be meaningful.

Multiple-linear regression analysis is used to estimate, simultaneously, ıe linear relationship between a dependent variable and two or more in- ependent variables. The solution system is analogous to that of simple wo-variable) linear regression analysis. The mathematical theory underlying ıe derivation of the multivariable model is an extension of the reasoning behind the bivariate model. The methods of interpreting and evaluating the models are also quite similar. However, the mathematical manipulations required become progressively more complex as the number of variables in the model increases. If there are more than three variables, a computer is virtually essential.[3]

If a third variable, X_2 (a second independent variable), is added to a bivariate model, the result is a linear equation of the form $\hat{Y} = \hat{\alpha} + \hat{\beta}_1 X_1 + \hat{\beta}_2 X_2$. This equation expresses the relationship between Y and two independent variables X_1 and X_2. It can be portrayed graphically as a plane in a three-dimensional space. If more variables are added, the equation cannot be shown graphically. However, the mathematical properties of the model remain the same whether the equation is a straight line, a plane, or the linear equivalent in an undrawable n-dimensional space.

A regression equation with three or more variables, including the dependent variable, is called a "multivariate," "multivariant," "multivariable," or "multiple regression" model. As shown earlier, the general form of the multivariate linear regression equation is

$$\hat{Y} = \hat{\alpha} + \hat{\beta}_1 X_1 + \hat{\beta}_2 X_2 + \cdots \hat{\beta}_n X_n \qquad \text{(given as equation 17.1}$$

where

$\hat{Y}, \hat{\alpha}, \hat{\beta},$ and X are defined as before

Ceteris Paribus

Before we proceed to the specification of the multivariate model, a brief reminder is in order. The condition *ceteris paribus* is especially appropriate to models of market phenomena. It is implicit in all regression equations. Although the relationships described by a regression model may hold true for a wide range of exogenous conditions, the estimated value of the dependent variable may be influenced by factors not included in the equation. Thus, the effect of a change in an independent variable may be exactly as specified by the equation, but the actual value of the dependent variable may be very different than the one predicted.

In the previous example, an increase in advertising would clearly induce an increase in sales, *ceteris paribus*. However, if this condition were violated—say, a competitor drastically lowered its price—the effect of the increase in advertising might be offset and the net result could be a decrease

---

[3] Standard computer programs are readily available and not difficult to use. Examples are IBM's "Stepwise Multiple Regression Program" (Program No. 360D136001), GE's "MREG (Publication No. 807232), BioMed's "BMD 02R," MIT's "Time Series Processor" and SPSS' "REGRESSION".

in the firm's sales. One of the virtues of multivariate linear regression is that more marketing and economic variables can be included in the model; hence, the chance of *ceteris nonparibus* is smaller.

Computing Parameters

The parameters, α, β_1, β_2, ... β_n, of the multivariate model are estimated by conventional algebraic formulas and arithmetic, by the solution of systems of simultaneous equations by conventional methods, or by matrix algebra.[4] Matrix algebra is the most convenient method if the calculations must be done manually. However, any manual method becomes extremely time-consuming when there are more than three variables. Fortunately, computer programs are available that will solve extremely complex regression problems. These programs require as input only the observed values of Y and the selected X's, plus some simple instructions regarding the form of the output. Because of them, regression analysis is a practical tool for business and economic research. They are useful even for the solution of simple bivariant problems.

The conventional algebraic formulas for finding the parameters of the multivariate model are given below. They perform the same task as the formulas for finding the parameters of the bivariate model (and conform to the same least-squares criterion), but they are more complex due to the additional variable. Only the formulas for the three-variable model are shown, since, as we have pointed out, when there are more than three variables matrix algebra or a standard computer program is more appropriate.

The conventional algebraic solution of a three-variable problem requires summing the observations of Y, X_1, and X_2, some multiplying and squaring, summing the products and squares, and solving the following system of three equations. (Again, the i's identifying the observations have been dropped to make the notation less cumbersome.)

$$\hat{\beta}_1 = \frac{\Sigma(x_1 Y) \cdot \Sigma x_2{}^2 - \Sigma(x_2 Y) \cdot \Sigma(x_1 x_2)}{\Sigma x_1{}^2 \cdot \Sigma x_2{}^2 - [\Sigma(x_1 x_2)]^2} \qquad [17.8]$$

$$\hat{\beta}_2 = \frac{\Sigma(x_2 Y) \cdot \Sigma x_1{}^2 - \Sigma(x_1 Y) \cdot \Sigma(x_1 x_2)}{\Sigma x_1{}^2 \cdot \Sigma x_2{}^2 - [\Sigma(x_1 x_2)]^2} \qquad [17.9]$$

$$\hat{\alpha} = \bar{Y} - \hat{\beta}_1 \bar{X}_1 - \hat{\beta}_2 \bar{X}_2 \qquad [17.10]$$

---

[4] *Matrix algebra* is that branch of mathematics concerned with the manipulation of arrays—that is, rows and columns of numbers such as a table of data. It is extremely useful in solving many business and economic problems. For a good introduction to this topic, see Dennis E. Grawoig, *Decision Mathematics* (New York: McGraw-Hill, 1967), chs. 1 and 2. For an in-depth exploration, see S. R. Searle and W. H. Hausman, *Matrix Algebra for Business and Economics* (New York: Wiley, 1970).

where

$\hat{\beta}$ = the estimated value of a regression coefficient

$\hat{\alpha}$ = the estimated value of the intercept

x = the deviation of an independent variable ($x = X - \bar{X}$)

Y = the dependent variable

$\bar{Y}$ = the mean of the dependent variable

X = an independent variable

$\bar{X}$ = the mean of the independent variable

1 and 2 are subscripts identifying the independent variable and its associated regression coefficient

The solution of these three equations allows us to specify the three-variable-linear regression model $\hat{Y} = \hat{\alpha} + \hat{\beta}_1 X_1 + \hat{\beta}_2 X_2$.

Applying Multiple-linear Regression Analysis

To see the application of multivariate-linear regression analysis, assume that the sales of a certain product have fluctuated over time. This fluctuation is presumed to be a result of changes in the firm's price and advertising. Sales at various levels of price and advertising are shown in Table 17-3.

The analyst's task is to estimate the relationship between the dependent variable, sales, and the two presumably determinant (independent) variables, price and advertising. Assuming, for the present, that a linear regression equation is a realistic replica of this relationship, the analyst can specify the model as follows.

Table 17-3   **Data for a Multivariate Linear Regression Model**

Observation (*i*)	Sales (*Y*)	Price (X_1)	Advertising (X_2)
1	2,298 units	$12.50	$2,000
2	1,814	10.00	550
3	1,647	9.95	1,000
4	1,496	11.50	800
5	969	12.00	000
6	1,918	10.00	1,500
7	1,810	8.00	800
8	1,896	9.00	1,200
9	1,715	9.50	1,100
10	1,699	12.50	1,300

Table 17-4 Data and Preliminary Calculations for Specifying a Multivariate Linear Regression Model

i	Y	X_1	x_1	x_1^2	x_1Y	X_2	x_2	x_2^2	x_2Y	x_1x_2
1	2,298	12.50	2.005	4.020	4,607.49	2,000	975	950,625	2,240,550	1,954.88
2	1,814	10.00	−.495	.245	−897.93	550	−475	225,625	−861,650	235.13
3	1,647	9.95	−.545	.297	−897.61	1,000	−25	625	−41,175	13.63
4	1,496	11.50	1.005	1.010	1,503.48	800	−225	50,625	−336,600	−226.13
5	969	12.00	1.505	2.265	1,458.35	000	−1,025	1,050,625	−993,225	−1,542.63
6	1,918	10.00	−.495	.245	−949.41	1,500	475	225,625	911,050	−235.13
7	1,810	8.00	−2.495	6.225	−4,515.95	800	−225	50,625	−407,250	561.38
8	1,896	9.00	−1.495	2.235	−2,834.52	1,200	175	30,625	331,800	−261.62
9	1,715	9.50	−.995	.990	−1,706.43	1,100	75	5,625	128,625	−74.63
10	1,699	12.50	2.005	4.020	3,406.50	1,300	275	75,625	467,225	551.38

$\Sigma Y = 17,262$ $\Sigma X_1 = 104.95$ $\Sigma x_1^2 = 21.552$ $\Sigma(x_1Y) = -826.03$ $\Sigma X_2 = 10,250$

$\bar{Y} = 1,726.2$ $\bar{X}_1 = 10.495$ $\Sigma x_2^2 = 2,666,250$ $\Sigma(x_2Y) = 1,439,350$ $\Sigma(x_1x_2) = 976.25$

$\bar{X}_2 = 1,025$

$n = 10$

First, he or she calculates the mean, deviations, squared deviations, products, and sums for each data set. The results of these simple but laborious manipulations are shown in Table 17-4. Second, he or she substitutes the computed data into the appropriate equations to obtain numerical values for the model's parameters, $\hat{\alpha}$, $\hat{\beta}_1$, and $\hat{\beta}_1$:

$$\hat{\beta}_1 = \frac{\Sigma(x_1 Y) \cdot \Sigma x_2{}^2 - \Sigma(x_2 Y) \cdot \Sigma(x_1 x_2)}{\Sigma x_1{}^2 \cdot \Sigma x_2{}^2 - [\Sigma(x_1 x_2)]^2} \qquad \text{(given as equation 17.8)}$$

$$\hat{\beta}_1 = \frac{(-826.02)(2,666,250) - (1,439,350)(976.25)}{(21.552)(2,666,250) - (976.25)^2} \qquad \text{(by substitution)}$$

$$\hat{\beta}_1 = \frac{-2,202,375,825 - 1,405,165,438}{57,463,020 - 953,064} \qquad \text{(by arithmetic)}$$

$$\hat{\beta}_1 = -63.84 \qquad \text{(by arithmetic)}$$

$$\hat{\beta}_2 = \frac{\Sigma(x_2 Y) \cdot \Sigma x_1{}^2 - \Sigma(x_1 Y) \cdot \Sigma(x_1 x_2)}{\Sigma x_1{}^2 \cdot \Sigma x_2{}^2 - [\Sigma(x_1 x_2)]^2} \qquad \text{(given as equation 17.9)}$$

$$\hat{\beta}_2 = \frac{(1,439,350)(21.552) - (-826.02)(976.25)}{(21.552)(2,666,250) - (976.25)^2} \qquad \text{(by substitution)}$$

$$\hat{\beta}_2 = \frac{31,020,871 + 806,402}{57,463,020 - 953,064} \qquad \text{(by arithmetic)}$$

$$\hat{\beta}_2 = 0.56 \qquad \text{(by arithmetic)}$$

$$\hat{\alpha} = \bar{Y} - \hat{\beta}_1 \bar{X}_1 - \hat{\beta}_2 \bar{X}_2 \qquad \text{(given as equation 17.10)}$$

$$\hat{\alpha} = 1,726.2 - (-63.84)(10.495) - (0.56)(1,025) \qquad \text{(by substitution)}$$

$$\hat{\alpha} = 1,726.2 + 670.0 - 577.3 \qquad \text{(by arithmetic)}$$

$$\hat{\alpha} = 1,818.90 \qquad \text{(by arithmetic)}$$

Thus, the regression model for estimating the product's sales, $\hat{Y}$, as determined by its price, X_1, and the firm's advertising, X_2, is

$$\hat{Y} = 1,818.90 - 63.84 X_1 + 0.56 X_2$$

Interpreting the Model

The foregoing model gives the researcher a device for estimating the sales that will occur at a given price with a given advertising budget. It also implies that sales are relatively insensitive to price. A $1 increase in price will decrease sales by only 63.83 units. Thus, a price increase of nearly 10 percent lowers sales less than 3 percent.[5] At least within the observed range, the product's price is clearly inelastic. Thus, an increase in price will increase revenue while reducing the firm's costs (by slightly decreasing sales).[6] A high price is clearly feasible, assuming, of course, that there are no exogenous constraints.

The model also implies that sales are responsive to advertising. An additional unit is sold for every $1.79 spent on advertising ($1 of advertising increases sales by 0.56 units). If the marginal profit (excluding the advertising cost) of the product is greater than $1.79, the advertising should be increased.

In making recommendations, the researcher must bear in mind the linearity of the model. Both economic theory and common sense tell us that the relationship between sales and price and between sales and advertising is never linear throughout the entire range of possible prices and advertising outlays. There must be some price that will drive away every customer; similarly, there must be some point at which additional advertising outlays will no longer increase sales. The model does not tell us when these conditions will be encountered.

A prudent analyst would suggest a moderate increase in price—say, to $13.50 if the present price is $12.50—and a moderate increase in advertising. An advertising budget of $2,500 might be reasonable. Sales could then be observed at these new levels of price and advertising to see if the model holds up, since both these values are outside the range of values used in constructing the model. If it does, a second round of price and advertising increases may be in order, again followed by a reexamination of the model to see if its prediction has been realized.

Another fact that must be remembered is that the model produces only an *estimate* of the sales–price–advertising relationships. This estimate may be a very good or a very bad approximation of the actual relationships. The model's true quality can never be known exactly. However, there are techniques for evaluating it, and these techniques should be invoked before any recommendations (or decisions), based on the model, are made.

---

[5] These percentages will vary with the base value. For instance, a $1 increase from a price of $10 would be a 10 percent increase. However, a $1 increase from a price of $8 would be a $12\frac{1}{2}$-percent increase, and a $1 increase from a price of $12 would be an $8\frac{1}{3}$-percent increase. Consequently, elasticity (the ratio of a percentage change in quantity induced by a percentage change in price) will generally vary over the range of prices.

[6] Price is defined as inelastic when a relative change in price will induce a proportionately smaller relative change in sales. For instance, a product would be judged price inelastic if a 10 percent increase in its price resulted in a 5 percent decrease in the quantity sold. When a a good is price inelastic, an increase in price will increase revenue. (Note that revenue equals price times quantity sold and quantity will decline proportionally less as the price increases, given inelasticity.) Concurrently, the cost of production presumably falls as output decreases and a new equilibrium is reached. The net effect of these changes in revenue and cost is an increase in profit.

Standardizing the Data

The size of the regression coefficient (β) tells us how sensitive $\hat{Y}$ is to a particular X. However, a coefficient's size is meaningless unless we know how the X is scaled.

For example, one might have the term $+.023X_5$ in a regression model, where X_5 is defined as the number of households. $\hat{Y}$ would increase .023 every time another household was added to the population. If X_5 was defined as thousands of households, a common way of recording and entering census data, the term would become $23X_5$. The relationship between $\hat{Y}$ and X_5 would be the same—an additional household would still increase $\hat{Y}$ by only .023 units. However, the larger coefficient might imply a greater sensitivity of $\hat{Y}$ to X_5 than did the smaller one.

Frequently we want to compare the relative power of each independent variable (X) in influencing $\hat{Y}$. We can do this if we keep in mind the scale of each X, when comparing their coefficients. However, this is a bit sloppy—something like comparing apples and oranges, thanks to the different scales used for the various X's.

A solution to this dilemma is to standardize the data before performing the regression. *Standardizing the data* means converting each observation to its Z-value. In fact, the Z-statistic is often called the "standardized value."

The Z-value is computed with formula A2.14, found in the appendix. Converting each observation to its Z-value puts the Y and all the X's on the same scale. The resulting regression coefficients can then be directly compared. For instance, if the standardized coefficient for X_3 is twice as large as the standardized coefficient for X_1, we can say $\hat{Y}$ is twice as sensitive to X_3 as it is to X_1. For instance, a 10 percent change in X_3 would have twice the effect as a 10 percent change in X_1.

When standardized data are used, the resulting regression coefficients are called "standardized regression coefficients," "beta weights," or "beta coefficients." Sometimes the Arabic letter "B" (or "b") is used to symbolize unstandardized coefficients, while the Greek letter "β" is used to denote standardized ones. We have been following the opposite convention, using "β" to symbolize unstandardized (conventional) regression coefficients.

Standardizing the data and producing standardized regression coefficients are quick and easy once the original data are in the computer. In fact, some programs, such as SPSS's REGRESSION, automatically compute and output the standardized coefficients along with the unstandardized ones. Of course there is no standardized α. The intercept is always zero when standardized data are used.

Problems

1   The management of a chain of shoe stores needs a method of estimating the total (industry) demand, by city, for its product class. The firm's market researcher believes that this demand is a function

of population, personal income, and the propensity to consume—all of which are represented by a city's total retail sales. Total-retail-sales data are published by the Bureau of the Census for each SMSA. Thus, if the relationship between shoe-industry sales and total retail sales can be specified, estimating the demand for shoes in a local market should be simple. Retail-store audits are purchased for nine SMSA's and matched with total-retail-sales data as follows:

SMSA	Total Shoe Sales (in millions)	Total Retail Sales (in billions)
Milwaukee, Wis.	$30	$2.2
Portland, Ore.	24	1.6
Phoenix, Ariz.	22	1.5
Dayton, Ohio	20	1.2
Syracuse, N. Y.	15	1.0
Richmond, Va.	13	0.9
Fresno, Calif.	12	0.8
Orlando, Fla.	8	0.7
Austin, Tex.	5	0.4

Construct a linear regression model of the relationship between the demand for shoes and total retail sales.

2 Prepare a graph of the data given in question 1 and the model constructed in response to it. Indicate on the graph any of the terms and symbols in Figure 17-2 that are applicable.

3 A market researcher has collected data on his firm's sales, advertising, and personal selling in six local markets. These cross-sectional data are shown below:

Market	Sales (in units)	Advertising	Personal Selling (no. of salespersons)
1	140	$20,000	30
2	82	10,000	20
3	68	8,000	15
4	118	20,000	20
5	45	4,000	10
6	132	14,000	22

Construct a multivariate linear regression model of sales as a function of advertising and personal selling. (Save your work sheets and model for use in the next chapter.)

4 Interpret the model you have just developed in terms of its implications for the firm's marketing policy. Assume that the fixed cost of maintaining a sales office is $2,000 and that each sales person's pay for the period covered by the data is $800.

Chapter 18
Evaluating Regression Models

Key Concepts

Need and Criteria for Model Evaluation
Why a regression model is evaluated

Tools of Evaluation
Important statistical tests and other tools for evaluating regression models

Key Terms

t-test
F-test
F-ratio
standard error of the regression coefficient

two-tail test
coefficient of determination
tightness of fit
standard error of the residual
goodness of fit

Need and Criteria for Model Evaluation

Need

Linear regression analysis allows us to fit a line—or its mathematical equivalent, in an n-variable model—to any combination of variables. Thus, an analyst could derive an equation specifying a relationship that is manifestly untrue—say, a relationship between Ford sales in Ohio and the Pigmy population of Borneo. Even where common sense or economic theory supports the existence of a relationship between variables—say, our model equated Ford's Ohio sales with the state's income and population—the model may still be misleading.

As long as the number of observations equals or exceeds the number of variables in a model, the model can be specified. However, the relationship it posits may be unreal or distorted. The existence of a specific model does not, in itself, guarantee a real-world relationship between the variables or reliable estimates of the dependent variable. Often the real-world relationship is obscure and can be verified only by using common sense and applying rigorous statistical tests. Occasionally, common sense alone will suffice, as in the case of the Ford-Pigmy model. However, even if common sense confirms the existence of a relationship, rigorous tools are needed to evaluate the statistical quality of the model that purports to represent this relationship.

Criteria

Market researchers invoke regression analysis for two reasons. First, they may be interested in the relationship between a dependent variable and one or more presumably determinant variables. In other words, they may be interested in a cause-and-effect relationship between variables. For instance, the researchers may want to estimate the sensitivity of sales to price and advertising, as in the example in the preceding chapter. In this case they are interested primarily in the coefficients—the β's—of the model, for these represent the sensitivity of one variable to another. However, before accepting the coefficients, and hence the model, as a realistic statement of the cause-and-effect relationship, they should question the coefficients' significance, precision, and rationality. These are the criteria by which we evaluate the model's parameters. The tools used are the t-test, the F-test, the standard error of the regression coefficient, common sense, and economic theory.

Second, researchers may be interested in predicting (or forecasting) the value of the independent variable, Y. For example, they may want to predict sales, given a particular population size or level of buying power. If so, they are primarily interested in the amount of change in the independent (predicted) variable accounted for by the model. A model that accounted for only a small portion of the change would be of little value. In this case, the most important evaluative criterion is the amount of explained variation. The primary criterion of evaluation is the coefficient of determination.

The coefficient of determination may be supported by the tools mentioned above, especially the F-test. The rationality of the cause-and-effect relationship, however, is seldom relevant in prediction. Hence, the test of compatibility with common sense and economic theory may often be ignored. In fact, variables may be employed that are statistically correlated but between which there is obviously no cause-and-effect relationship. In such cases, the independent variables are simply proxies of the true determinants— a phenomenon we shall discuss more fully in the next chapter.

The standard error of the residual and the size of the residuals may also be relevant in evaluating the predictive quality of a regression model. The mechanics of evaluation become very complicated—that is, awkward mathematical formulas must be used—with multivariate models. Thus, they are generally handled using computers and standard library programs.

Tools of Evaluation

The *t*-Test

The *t-test* is a test of significance. It is used to determine if a significant relationship exists between *Y* and each of the *X*'s. (The *t*-test is applied separately to each *X*.) Essentially, it asks if the variation in *Y* that appears to be induced by variations in a particular *X* is greater than the variation that could be induced by chance. In other words, how likely is it that the apparent correlation between *Y* and X_j was caused by coincidental variations in the sample data? (The subscript *j* is used to identify a particular *X*.)

If *Y* and X_j are unrelated, the true regression coefficient, β_j, will equal zero. It is this null hypothesis (H_0) we are concerned with. If the *t*-test forces rejection of the hypothesis, we assume that β_j does not equal zero and *Y* and X_j are significantly related. However, should the test fail to force rejection of H_0, we then lack sufficient statistical evidence to support the claim that *Y* and X_j are significantly related. (At this point we are talking only about a statistical relationship.)

This latter condition suggests, but does not require, that X_j be removed from the regression model. Obviously, the model should be purged of any independent variable not significantly related to the dependent variable. However, the failure of the *t*-test to disprove H_0 does not prove that *Y* and X_j are unrelated. It only demonstrates that the linear relationship posited between them is not supported by the available statistical evidence. Common sense or economic theory may support such a relationship and justify the retention of X_j.

The *t*-test uses the *t*-distribution to determine if $\hat{\beta}_j$ is close enough to β_j (which is assumed to be zero) for the difference between them to be the result of random error. If it is not, H_0 is rejected, and we assume that β_j does not equal zero and *Y* and X_j are significantly related.[1]

Our first step is to determine the maximum distance (at a given significance level) that the estimated value of the parameter, $\hat{\beta}_j$, can be expected to vary from the true value, β_j. This distance is the product of the standard deviation of $\hat{\beta}_j$ (symbolized as $s_{\hat{\beta}_j}$ and called the *standard error of the regression coefficient*) and the *t*-statistic $t_{T, j}$. This *t*-statistic is found by consulting a table of *t*-statistics such as that in Appendix 4.[2]

---

[1] Implicit in the *t*-test is the assumption that the possible values of $\hat{\beta}_j$ are normally distributed about the true value, β_j. Thus, the difference between $\hat{\beta}_j$ and β_j is presumed to be due to random error. (Statistical theory tells us that random error will cause the estimated values of a statistical parameter to be normally distributed about the true value.) The *t*-distribution (a special case of the normal distribution) represents a range of values about the true (or an assumed) value of the parameter. We can expect, at a given level of confidence, that any estimated value of the parameter (such as $\hat{\beta}_j$) will be within this range. If it is not, then we must reject the hypothesis that the assumed value (in this case, zero) is the true value of the estimated parameter.

[2] Many of the terms in this chapter, including the *t*-statistic, are explained in Appendix 2. Many of the tables referred to can be found in Appendix 4.

Next, the actual variation $(\hat{\beta}_j - \beta_j)$ is compared to the maximum variation due to random error $(s_{\hat{\beta}_j} \cdot t_{T,j})$. Note that the actual variation is simply the difference between the estimated value of the parameter, $\hat{\beta}_J$, and and the true value, β_J, which is assumed to equal zero for purposes of the test. (β_J will equal zero if Y and X_J are truly unrelated.) If the actual variation is greater than the presumed maximum, the null hypothesis ($\beta_J = 0$) must be rejected. There is apparently a statistically significant relationship between Y and X_J. Stated symbolically, H_0: $\beta_J = 0$ *is rejected if*

$$\left| \hat{\beta}_j - \beta_j \right| > \left| s_{\hat{\beta}_j} \cdot t_{T,j} \right| \qquad [18.1]$$

or

$$\left| \frac{\hat{\beta}_j - \beta_j}{s_{\hat{\beta}_j}} \right| > \left| t_{T,j} \right| \qquad [18.2]$$

Note that the sign of each term is ignored. That is, absolute values are used in comparing the left- and right-hand side of the inequality.[3]

Equation 18.2 is simply a rearrangement (by algebraic manipulation) of equation 18.1. The left-hand term is the computed *t*-statistic, $t_{C,j}$. The right-hand term is the table *t*-statistic, $t_{T,j}$. Thus, the equation can also be written

$$\left| t_{C,j} \right| > \left| t_{T,j} \right| \qquad [18.3]$$

This is the most convenient form in which to visualize the *t*-test.

Given the use of a computer—the only practical way to handle regression analysis—the execution of the *t*-test is simple: One compares the value of $t_{C,j}$ provided by the computer with the value of $t_{T,j}$ found by consulting a table of *t*-values. (The tabular *t*-value cannot be generated by the computer since it involves a judgment decision—namely, the selection of a significance level.)

If the computer program fails to provide for the computation of $t_{C,j}$, it should at least provide for the computation of the standard error of the regression coefficient, $s_{\hat{\beta}_j}$. Given $s_{\hat{\beta}_j}$, $t_{C,j}$ can be readily determined using formula 18.4, which is also appropriate if the regression model is being specified and evaluated manually. In short,

$$t_{C,j} = \frac{\hat{\beta}_j - \beta_j}{s_{\hat{\beta}_j}} \qquad [18.4]$$

---

[3] The absolute value of a number is the number without its sign; it is indicated by a pair of vertical lines, as in the example.

where

$t_{C,j}$ = the computed value of the t-statistic

$\hat{\beta}_j$ = the estimated value of the regression coefficient

β_j = the true value of the regression coefficient (in this case, assumed zero)

$s_{\hat{\beta}_j}$ = the standard deviation of $\hat{\beta}_j$

j = the number of the parameter being tested

The formulas for $s_{\hat{\beta}_j}$ are equations 18.14, 18.15, and 18.16, shown shortly.
The table t-statistic, $t_{T,j}$, is found by consulting a table of t-statistics after we have determined the degrees of freedom and the significance level, appropriate to the problem. For this particular use of the t-distribution, the following formulas apply:

$$d.f. = n - K \qquad\qquad\qquad [18.5]$$

where

$d.f.$ = degrees of freedom

n = the number of observations

K = the number of variables, including the dependent variable

$$s.l. = 1 - c.l. \qquad\qquad\qquad [18.6]$$

where

$s.l.$ = the significance level (two-tail test)[4]

$c.l.$ = the confidence level

Let us now return to our example, the multivariate linear regression equation developed in Chapter 17. We are now in a position to test β_1 and β_2 to see if X_1 and X_2 are significantly related to Y. β_1 is tested first, although the order of testing is arbitrary.

$$t_{C,1} = \frac{\hat{\beta}_1 - \beta_1}{s\hat{\beta}_1} \qquad\qquad \text{(given as equation 18.4)}$$

$$t_{C,1} = \frac{-63.84 - 0}{34.58} \qquad\qquad \text{(by substitution)}$$

---

[4] The two-tail test, and its attendant probability (significance level) is relevant because we are concerned with the chance of exceeding the table t-statistic in either direction. Again, see Appendix 2 for further explanation.

$t_{C,1} = -1.8462$ (by arithmetic)

$d.f. = n - K$ (given as equation 18.5)

$d.f. = 10 - 3$ (by substitution)

$d.f. = 7$

$s.l. = 1 - c.l.$ (given as equation 18.6)

$s.l. = 1 - 0.80$ (by substitution, $c.l.$ of 80 percent is chosen by judgment)

$s.l. = 0.20$ (by arithmetic)

$t_{T,1} = 1.415$ (by consulting a table of t-values)

$|-1.8462| > |1.415|$, hence $|t_{C,1}| > |t_{T,1}|$, and the null hypothesis must be rejected. Thus, at the 80 percent confidence level (0.20 level of significance), we must assume that sales, Y, and price, X_1, are significantly related. However, at a confidence level of 90 percent, the null hypothesis could not be rejected. (At $s.l. = 0.10$, $t_{T,1} = 1.895$, which makes $t_{C,1}$ slightly less than $t_{T,1}$.)

Thus, the model is a bit shaky as far as its description of the relationship between sales and price is concerned. The relatively small regression coefficient (a significant price change does not induce a large change in sales) and the weak significance test imply that sales are not very sensitive to price. In fact, at the 90 percent confidence level, we cannot claim that sales and price are statistically related. However, economic theory and common sense tell us that there is some correlation, although slight, between the two variables. Some goods, such as cigarettes (the product class, not individual brands) are very price inelastic, but they are not entirely insensitive to price.

From a pragmatic viewpoint, we would do well to retain the price term $(-63.84X_1)$ in our model, while recognizing its weakness. At the moment, it is the only, hence the best, statement we have of the sales–price relationship. It does yield useful information, namely, the apparent price inelasticity of the product. Its defense will have to rest on economic theory and its use on necessity.

On the basis of the available data, -63.84 is still the most likely value of β_1. The failure of the t-test at $c.l. = .90$ tells us that we have not established a good statistical relationship between sales and price. Of course, had common sense and economic theory not supported the assumption of a negative correlation relationship between sales and price, the term would have been rejected and a new model specified.

The t-test of the specified relationship between sales and advertising is very good. The computed t-value is 5.729, which means the null hypothesis must be rejected even at the 99 percent confidence level. There is obviously a significant relationship between the product's sales and its advertising. However, before we make a final judgment, some other tests are in order.

The *F*-Test

The *F-test* is another test of significance. It is used to determine if a significant relationship exists between *Y* and the *X*'s taken as a whole. Essentially it asks if the explained variance in *Y* is truly induced by the *X*'s or is probably a result of random variation in the sample data. Unlike the *t*-test, the *F*-test treats the independent variables as a unit, uses a different frequency distribution, and uses a different statistical measurement—the *F*-ratio. The method is analogous to the analysis of variance techniques explained in Chapter 12.

The *F-ratio* is a ratio between variances. The *F*-test compares the computed *F*-statistic, F_C, with the table *F*-statistic, F_T, to test the hypothesis that no significant relationship exists between *Y* and the *X*'s. If F_C is greater than F_T, then the hypothesis is rejected and we assume that *Y* and the *X*'s (taken as a whole) are truly related. At the selected level of confidence, $F_C > F_t$ indicates that the computed *F*-value rests outside (to the right) of the region of *F*-values that would probably result were the variation in *Y* due to chance. We assume that this variation was induced by *X*'s, and hence that the two sides of the equation are truly related.

The computed *F*-statistic is found by dividing explained variance (explained by the *X*'s) by the unexplained variance. The formula used is

$$F_C = \frac{\Sigma(\hat{Y} - \bar{Y})^2/(K - 1)}{\Sigma(\hat{Y} - Y)^2/(n - K)} \qquad [18.7]$$

or

$$F_C = \frac{R^2/(K - 1)}{(1 - R^2)/(n - K)} \qquad [18.8]$$

where

F_C = the computed *F*-statistic

R^2 = coefficient of determination (see equation 18.12)

K = the number of variables including the dependent variable

n = the number of observations

Y, $\hat{Y}$, and $\bar{Y}$ are defined as before

The table *F*-statistic is found by consulting a table of *F*-values (Appendix 4), after having determined the degrees of freedom (for the numerator and the denominator) and the significance level. The following equations are used:

$$d.f._n = K - 1 \qquad [18.9]$$

and

$$d.f._d = n - K \tag{18.10}$$

where

$d.f._n$ = the degrees of freedom for the numerator

$d.f._d$ = the degrees of freedom for the denominator

K and n are defined as before

$$s.l. = 1 - c.l., \tag{18.11}$$

where

$s.l.$ = the significance level

$c.l.$ = the confidence level

The application of the F-test can be illustrated using the data developed for the example in the preceding section. Since R^2 is normally computed in the course of evaluating the model—as we shall see in the next section—formula 18.8 is generally the most convenient way of calculating F_C:

$$F_C = \frac{R^2/(K - 1)}{(1 - R^2)/(n - K)} \qquad \text{(given as equation 18.8)}$$

$$F_C = \frac{0.8296/(3 - 1)}{(1 - 0.8296)/(10 - 3)} \qquad \text{(by substitution)}$$

$$F_C = \frac{0.4148}{0.0243} \qquad \text{(by arithmetic)}$$

$$F_C = 17.06 \qquad \text{(by arithmetic)}$$

$$F_T = 4.74 \qquad \text{(by consulting a table of } F\text{-values;}$$

$$d.f._n = 2, d.f._d = 7, \text{ and } s.l. = .05)$$

Obviously, 17.06 is considerably larger than 4.74; hence, $F_C > F_T$, and the hypothesis that no statistical relationship exists between Y and the X's (taken as a whole) must be rejected at the 0.05 level of significance (a confidence level of 95 percent).

Were we to compare F_C and F_T, for $d.f._n = 2$ and $d.f._d = 7$, at different levels of significance, we would find that the hypothesis must be rejected even at a level of significance of 0.01, hence every level below that. Thus, the null hypothesis must be rejected even at the 99 percent confidence level, and we can be quite confident that the two sides of the equation are related.

The F-value is very sensitive to degrees of freedom. As n approaches K, $d.f.$ become very small ($d.f. = 0$ when $n = K$). A small $d.f.$ will encourage a low F_C and ensure a high F_T. Almost invariably, this will result in an F_C less than F_T, and the F-test will not disprove the hypothesis that Y and the X's are unrelated.

If the F-test does not disprove the hypothesis, we cannot be certain that the Y and the X's are unrelated. We can only state that there is insufficient statistical evidence to allow us to claim (operating at or above the the selected significance level) that there is a relationship.

If the F-test fails to support a relationship between Y and the X's, we have three alternatives. First, we can discard the model as meaningless. However, this may leave us with nothing but conjecture upon which to base the marketing decision. An imperfect model may be better than none at all. Second, we can try using common sense or economic theory to defend the proposition that the X's are truly determinants of Y, especially if the results of the other evaluation tests are satisfactory. Third, we can try to increase the value of the computed F-statistic. This alternatively, which we shall explore later, is not always open to us. Its feasibility is restricted by the availability of data and our willingness to make certain compromises with respect to the model.

Conversely, if the F-test does disprove the null hypothesis, we can assume (operating at or below the selected level of significance) that Y and the X's are statistically related. (The reader is reminded that a lower level of significance means at a larger significance level value. Thus $s.l. = 0.10$ is a lower level of significance than $s.l. = 0.05$. This is because at the lower level of significance there is a greater chance—$0.10 > 0.05$—that we will be wrong.)

Coefficient of Determination

The *coefficient of determination*, R^2, is the ratio of the explained variation in Y (caused by all X's) to the total variation. This term, called the "coefficient of determination," represents the percentage of the change in Y explained by the regression equation. For instance, if $R^2 = 0.86$, then the independent variables, $X_1, X_2, \ldots X_n$, are responsible for 86 percent of the observed variation in Y. If $R^2 = 1$, then all the observed variation in Y is caused by the X's and the equation contains every variable that has influenced Y. An R^2 of 1 is rare when the researcher is using real-world data, for it is virtually impossible to identify and quantify every determinant of Y. However, an R^2 in excess of 0.75 is common. When it occurs, the accompanying regression equation may be viewed as a fairly inclusive model. (The total range of R^2 is between 0 and 1.)

R^2 is sometimes described as measuring the tightness of fit. *Tightness of fit*—also called, *goodness of fit*—is the degree to which the model fits the data. Figure 18-1 is illustrative. Where the regression line passes through

Figure 18-1   **R^2 and Tightness of Fit**

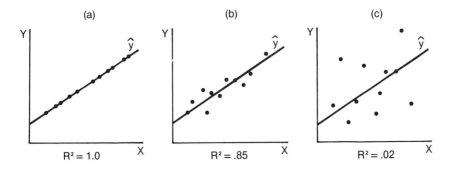

all of the observed values, as it does in 18-1(a), $R^2 = 1.0$. We have a perfect fit: All of the residuals equal zero. Where the regression model comes close to the observed values of Y as in 18-1(b), we have a high R^2 value. The fit is fairly tight, but not perfect. Where the fit is very loose, as in 18-1(c), we have a low R^2 value. Our model is explaining very little of the variation in Y.

The coefficient of determination is found by the following formulas:

$$R^2 = \frac{\Sigma y^2 - \Sigma e^2}{\Sigma y^2} \qquad\qquad [18.12]$$

or

$$R^2 = 1 - \frac{\Sigma e^2}{\Sigma y^2} \qquad\qquad [18.13]$$

where

$R^2 =$ the coefficient of determination

$y =$ the deviation of Y from $\bar{Y}$ ($y = \bar{Y} - Y$)

$e =$ the unexplained deviation ($\hat{Y} - Y$), called the "residual"

In our example R^2 is 0.8296.

$$R^2 = 1 - \frac{\Sigma e^2}{\Sigma y^2} \qquad\qquad \text{(given as equation 18.13)}$$

$$R^2 = 1 - \frac{177{,}389}{1{,}040{,}787} \qquad\qquad \text{(by substitution)}$$

$$R^2 = 0.8296 \qquad\qquad \text{(by arithmetic)}$$

Thus, the regression equation explains 82.96 percent of the variation in sales. Obviously one or more other variables, which have been excluded from the model, are influential in determining the product's sales. (Otherwise, 17.04 percent of the variation in sales would not be unexplained.) Nevertheless, on the basis of this test, the equation appears to be a reasonable approximation of the sales function.

In some cases, however, the coefficient of determination can be misleading. For example, if the number of observations equals the number of variables (including the dependent variable), R^2 will equal one even if there is no relationship at all between Y and the X's. This is because the solution of simultaneous equations always produces unique answers when the number of observations, n, equals the number of variables, K. With unique answers, there are no residuals; that is, $e = 0$. An examination of the formulas 18.12 and 18.13 shows R^2 becomes one if $e = 0$ for each observation, regardless of the values of y.

Another way of looking at the model is to say that when $n = K$ the degrees of freedom, $d.f.$, equal zero ($d.f. = n - K$) and the system is fully constrained. A fully constrained system has unique answers and no residuals.

If the number of observations is greater than, but close to, the number of variables, R^2 will still be large. (The regression is unsolvable if the condition $n \geq K$ is not met.) Consequently, the F-test must be used to determine if there is a statistically significant relationship between Y and the independent variables taken as a whole. Only after the existence of a significant relationship between the two sides of the equation has been established can the coefficient of determination be viewed with confidence.

Standard Error of the Regression Coefficient

The *standard error of the regression coefficient*, $s_{\hat{\beta}_j}$, mentioned earlier, is a measure of the precision of the regression coefficient, $\hat{\beta}_j$. It tells us the amount by which the true value of a parameter may be expected to vary from the estimated value due to random error. Since it is also the standard deviation of $\hat{\beta}_j$, it can be used to specify the confidence interval about that parameter at a given confidence level. For instance, if $s_{\hat{\beta}_1} = 2$, $\hat{\beta}_1 = 60$, and $n \geq 30$, then the probability is 0.68 that the true value of β_1 is between 58 and 62. At the 95 percent confidence level, the true value of β_1 would be between 56 and 64. (Generally, this would be considered a good estimate.) As always, the confidence level must be specified by judgment.

In a bivariate model, the standard error of the regression coefficient can be specified by the following equation. (The subscript j is dropped because there is only one β in the bivariate model.)

$$s_{\hat{\beta}} = \left(\frac{n}{n\Sigma X^2 - (\Sigma X)^2} \right)^{1/2} \cdot s_e \qquad [18.14]$$

where

$s_{\hat{\beta}}$ = the standard error of the regression coefficient for a bivariate model

s_e = the standard error of the residual (see formula 18.17)

n and X are defined as before

With a three-variable model, the computations are considerably more laborious. The formulas needed are

$$s_{\hat{\beta}_1} = \left[\frac{n\Sigma X_2{}^2 - (\Sigma X_2)^2}{n[\Sigma X_1{}^2\Sigma X_2{}^2 - (\Sigma X_1 X_2)^2] + \Sigma X_1[\Sigma X_2\Sigma X_1 X_2 - \Sigma X_1\Sigma X_2{}^2]} \right.$$
$$\left. \overline{\phantom{n[\Sigma X_1{}^2\Sigma X_2{}^2]} + \Sigma X_2[\Sigma X_1\Sigma X_1 X_2 - \Sigma X_2\Sigma X_1{}^2]} \right]^{1/2} \cdot s_e \quad [18.15]$$

and

$$s_{\hat{\beta}_2} = \left[\frac{n\Sigma X_1{}^2 - (\Sigma X_1)^2}{n[\Sigma X_1{}^2\Sigma X_2{}^2 - (\Sigma X_1 X_2)^2] + \Sigma X_1[\Sigma X_2\Sigma X_1 X_2 - \Sigma X_1\Sigma X_2{}^2]} \right.$$
$$\left. \overline{\phantom{n[\Sigma X_1{}^2\Sigma X_2{}^2]} + \Sigma X_2[\Sigma X_1\Sigma X_1 X_2 - \Sigma X_2\Sigma X_1{}^2]} \right]^{1/2} \cdot s_e \quad [18.16]$$

where

$s_{\hat{\beta}_1}$ = the standard error of the first regression coefficient

$s_{\hat{\beta}_2}$ = the standard error of the second regression coefficient

s_e = the standard error of the residual (see formula 18.17)

X_1, X_2, and n are defined as before

With larger multivariate models, the conventional algebraic formulas become unmanageable manually, and we are driven to the use of a computer to find $s_{\hat{\beta}_j}$. The importance of computers in regression analysis cannot be overemphasized.

Suppose we return now to our example. By checking our computer output (or, if necessary, laboring through formula 18.15), we see that $s_{\hat{\beta}_1} = 34.58$. Since we started with only ten observations, the t-statistic is the appropriate multiplier to find the magnitude of possible error. Nine degrees of freedom ($d.f. = n - 1$) and a desired confidence interval of 0.90 gives us a table t-value of 1.833. Thus, the true value of the regression coefficient is within 63.39 units ($1.833 \cdot 34.58$) of the estimated value at the 90 percent confidence level. Since $\hat{\beta}_1 = -63.83$, β_1 can lie anywhere within the confidence interval -127.22 to -0.44. This confirms our earlier finding, based on the *t*-test, that the equation is a very imprecise estimate of the relationship between sales and price.

The precision of the first regression coefficient, β_1, is so poor that management would be ill-advised to blindly rely on it when making pricing decisions. In fact, it is so bad that at the 95 percent confidence level the confidence interval would extend past zero, making the upper limit of its range positive. A positive β_1 would mean that sales increase as price increases, which is patently absurd. Caution is in order.

There are four possible causes for the poor estimate of β_1: (1) erroneous data, (2) an insufficient number of observations, (3) extraneous forces, and (4) poor correlation between the variables. Each should be investigated. The first warrants a review of the data collection procedure and a check on the correctness of the observations. The second appears possible, since $n = 10$ is a small number of observations for a three-variable equation, especially if there is very little correlation between Y and X_1. A large number of observations may be needed to get a precise estimate (i.e., a small $s_{\hat{\beta}_1}$).

Extraneous forces too may be a factor, especially in view of the size of R^2 (it is only 0.8296). Poor correlation between the variables is also highly likely, for the evidence thus far indicates the product's price is inelastic (hence, Y is insensitive to X_1). This in itself is useful information for the decision-maker. In other words, sales and price are poorly correlated, at least within the range of observed prices. This is frequently the case with certain product classes, such as gasoline, cigarettes, and liquor. It is relatively rare with product brands, except where the firm enjoys a monopoly or has a highly differentiated product.

Computing the standard error, the magnitude of possible error, and the confidence interval for the second regression coefficient yields far more encouraging results: $s_{\hat{\beta}_2} = 0.098, E = 0.18 (@ c.l. = 0.90)$, and $0.38 < \beta_2 < .74$ $(@ c.l. = 0.90)$. Hence, $\hat{\beta}_2$ is a moderately precise, although far from perfect, estimate of β_2, and the model is probably an adequate basis for advertising decisions.

Generally speaking, the standard deviation should be less than half the value estimated for the parameter. Otherwise, the estimate is very imprecise. Of course, what constitutes real precision is still a matter of judgment.

The Standard Error of the Residual

We need to know the standard error of the residual, s_e, in order to compute the standard error of the regression coefficient algebraically. (The residual itself is also useful as a measure of the precision of the estimate of the independent variable, $\hat{Y}$. (For this reason, it is sometimes labeled the *standard error of the estimate* on computer printouts.)

The *standard error of the residual* is also a standard deviation. Unfortunately, it is useful only for specifying the confidence interval about the mean value of $\hat{Y}$. This is because the magnitude of possible error associated with $\hat{Y}$ increases the further one moves from the mean. The further out one goes (in either direction) in estimating Y values, the more cautious one must be in using the estimates, especially in making predictions.

The formula for specifying the standard error of the residual is the same for all regression models, irrespective of the number of variables they contain. It is

$$s_e = \left(\frac{\Sigma e^2}{n-K}\right)^{1/2} \tag{18.17}$$

where

s_e = the standard error of the residual

e, n, and K are defined as before

Applying this formula to our example gives us

$$s_e = \left(\frac{\Sigma e^2}{n-K}\right)^{1/2} \qquad \text{(given as equation 18.17)}$$

$$s_e = \left(\frac{177{,}389}{10-3}\right)^{1/2} \qquad \text{(by substitution)}$$

$$s_e = 159.19 \qquad \text{(by arithmetic)}$$

This value suggests that the estimates of sales, $\hat{Y}$, are fairly precise and that the model should be useful in predicting sales. Of course, we must point out again that this precision will deteriorate the further the estimates are from $\bar{Y}$, especially if they extend beyond the observed range of Y values. Again, caution is in order in using the results.

The Size of the Residuals

The relative size of the residuals is a measure of the accuracy of the model. If the residuals are small—say, less than 10 percent of the observed values of Y—then the equation is estimating values close to the true values, at least within the range of observations, and can be considered accurate. Of course, what constitutes accuracy is a value judgment; what seems accurate to one marketer in one situation may seem sloppy to another marketer in another situation. The sensitivity of a decision's outcome to the estimate of Y will often influence the researcher's definition of acceptable accuracy.

In evaluating residuals, the analyst may examine individual e's, the range of e's, the average of their absolute values,[5] and their standard

---

[5] The mean of the residuals, $\bar{e}$, will always equal zero when signs are included in its calculation. (See Table 18-1.)

Table 18-1 **The Residual Calculations for a Multivariable Linear Regression Problem**

Observation (i)	Actual Sales (Y)	Estimated Sales ($\hat{Y}$)	Residual (e)
1	2298	2147.33667	150.66333
2	1814	1490.27319	323.72681
3	1647	1746.91187	−99.91187
4	1496	1535.31787	−39.31787
5	969	1052.82642	−83.82642
6	1918	2025.32764	−107.32764
7	1810	1758.75562	51.24438
8	1896	1920.20239	−24.20239
9	1715	1831.96118	−116.96118
10	1699	1753.08618	−54.08618

$$\Sigma e = 00.00000$$
$$\Sigma |e| = 1051.26887$$
$$\overline{|e|} = 105.12689$$

deviation. The dispersions of the residuals is important if a single bad estimate of Y can be disastrous.

Returning to our example, we see that the average magnitude of the residuals (using the absolute values of e) is 105.12, which is not excessive. The range, shown in Table 18-1, is from −116.96 to 323.72. The standard deviation is 160, which shows that the residuals are widely dispersed. However, a really large residual (large relative to the size of the estimate of Y) is unlikely; hence, we can claim moderate accuracy for the model. Sales predictions, based on price and advertising values, within the range used to construct the model, should be accurate enough for most marketing decisions.

An examination of the residuals, like the other tests used in model evaluation, is not sufficient in itself. For instance, as the number of degrees of freedom decreases, the residuals will become smaller. In the extreme case (when $n = K$, hence $d.f. = 0$) e will equal zero for each observation; that is, Y will equal $\hat{Y}$. Thus, other tests, especially the t- and F-tests, should be tried before any important decisions are based on the model.

The Size of the Intercept

Regression may explain much of the variation in Y, but say little about why Y is as large or as small as it is through the range of observed values. For example, say sales (Y) were largely determined by price. Yet if price were constant throughout the observations, we would not have a hint of its power over Y. Still, we might get a tight-fitting model, explaining most of the observed variation in Y. (Perhaps we correlated Y with advertising expenditures and the number of retail outlets.) We might also get excellent F-test and t-test results.

Figure 18-2   **Regression Model with Large Intercept**

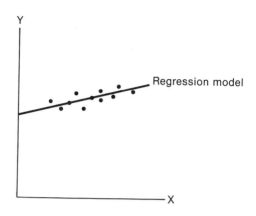

A large intercept, such as seen in Figure 18-2, suggests that Y is determined mainly by something other than the X's in the model. (Again, we illustrate with a bivariate model so we can draw a graph.)

A large intercept should motivate the analyst to look for other variables to enter into the model. If one or more of the likely candidates has varied little over the course of the observations, it should be considered a possible determinant of Y. Should the entry of still other variables yield a small intercept and a tight-fitting model, then the candidate that had held constant can be dismissed. (The possibility that the variable is important will still exist. However, the probability can be considered low.)

Common Sense and Economic Theory

Regression equations can be seductive. Even if they survive all the statistical tests of validity, they may still be a poor reflection of the real relationships between the variables. If the results of the equation do not make sense, or are not compatible with economic theory, then they cannot be trusted as a basis for decision-making.

Common sense must also be used in interpreting a regression model. For instance, the model itself will not indicate the direction of the relationship between variables. If regression analysis produces an excellent equation showing that beer sales are a function of the size of the adult population, it will also produce an equally good equation showing that the size of the adult population is a function of beer sales. The absurdity of the latter proposition is clear, but it would not be revealed by statistical tests.

A regression analysis may also produce a coefficient with an illogical sign. For instance, the $\hat{\beta}$ value in a sales–price equation might be positive, suggesting that sales would increase as price increased. Although such a model would probably fail one or more of the statistical tests, the researcher might have to depend on knowledge of economic theory to spot the fallacy and reject the model.

The are just two examples of the need for good judgment in using regression analysis. It is a powerful tool, but one that must be used with care.

Problems

1   Suggest some relationships, specifiable by linear regression analysis, that might seem reasonable but which you would suspect as not significant. How would you confirm or deny your suspicion?

2   The following regression model, derived from consumer-panel data and company records, purportedly shows the sensitivity of sales, Y, to advertising (in dollars) in newspapers, X_1; on radio, X_2; and on television, X_3: $\hat{Y} = 5392 + 0.55X_1 + 0.50X_2 + 0.60X_3$. Coefficients $\hat{\beta}_1$ and $\hat{\beta}_2$ pass the t-test at the 0.02 level of significance and have a standard deviation of 0.05 and 0.04, respectively. $\hat{\beta}_3$ cannot pass the t-test above the 0.10 level of significance and has a standard deviation of 0.08. The coefficient of determination is 0.743, and the computed value of the F-statistic is larger than the table value at the 0.02 level of significance. Evaluate the model. What recommendations would you make to the advertising director with respect to the reallocation of his budget between the three media?

3   Using the data on page 453, evaluate the model $\hat{Y} = 67.44 + 0.44X$, which is derived from this data.

4   Evaluate the multiple regression model you constructed in answer to problem 3 in the preceding chapter.

Chapter 19
Special Problems and Curvilinear Regression Models

Key Concepts

Special Problems
Spurious correlation and other villains in regression analysis

Improving the Model
Remedies for poor test performance

Time-Series versus Cross-Sectional Data
How data differ with respect to the relative time of observation

Curvilinear Regression Models
Some partial solutions to the problem of functions which are not linear

Key Terms

spurious correlation	autocorrelation
nonsense correlation	von Neuman ratio
identification problem	K-statistic
noninclusiveness	Durbin-Watson test
covariance	lagged relationship
multicollinearity	heterogeneity
dummy variable	isolation
time-series data	curvilinear
cross-sectional data	parabolic bivariate model
noise	exponential model

Special Problems

Regression analysis has its villains. Some can do considerable harm without being noticed. If present, they give us little incentive to believe what our regression model tells us.

Spurious Correlation

A *spurious correlation*—sometimes called a "nonsense correlation"—is an apparent correlation between variables not causally related. For instance, the textbook sales may appear to correlate with the price of diamond rings, even though there is obviously no real relationship between the two variables. What has probably happened is that the student population grew at the same time and at nearly the same rate as diamond prices inflated. Unfortunately, not all cases of spurious correlation are obvious.

Lack of Variance

A lack of variance in a significant variable will hide the effect of that variable. Regression analysis depends on change. It will show no correlation between two variables if one of them remains unchanged during the period under study. For instance, if sales of a particular brand and promotional expenditures on its behalf vary over time, but its price remains constant, regression will show sales as a function of promotion, insensitive to price. In fact, sales may be very sensitive to price, but we have no way of knowing this if the price has never been varied.

Identification

The *identification problem* (a term commonly used by econometricians) arises in regression analysis when the data used to specify the model are the result of two different functions operating simultaneously.

For instance, in a competitive market a price represents the intersection of supply and demand curves. If the price of a good, the quantity sold, or both change, obviously one or both of the curves has shifted. The supply and/or the demand function has changed—but which one? A line fitted to the scatter of observed prices could be a supply curve, a demand curve, or a meaningless combination of both functions. The improper labeling (i.e., identification) of such a curve would mean an erroneous interpretation of the price–quantity relationship. Managerial reliance on the model could lead to disastrous pricing decisions.

If the supply curve alone shifts, it will inscribe a series of price–quantity points along the demand curve. If these points are observed, quantity can be regressed against price—that is, a regression equation can be derived with quantity as the dependent variable—to reveal the demand curve. This is precisely what a firm does when it experiments with price in a test market. However, the experiment may not be tightly controlled, and the analyst may be uncertain which curve has shifted. Finding out may be difficult—even using econometrics' rules of identification[1]—and a meaningful regression may be impossible.

---

[1] Any good econometrics textbook, such as Lawrence R. Klein, *An Introduction to Econometrics* (Englewood Cliffs, N.J.: Prentice-Hall, 1962), or J. Johnston, *Econometric Methods* (New York: McGraw-Hill, 1970), contains an exposition of the identification problem. (Of the two suggested books, the Klein is the easier and the Johnston the more rigorous.)

Noninclusiveness

Another problem in this type of analysis is the difficulty of including all the significant variables. A regression model may seem excellent in every other way yet still produce a low coefficient of determination. A low R^2 indicates that something important has been left out—that we need one or more additional independent variables in the equation—but it does not tell us what that something is. To find out the researcher will have to rely on his experience, his common sense, and his knowledge of economic theory and the market.

Covariance

Covariance is a correlation of two unrelated variables (no cause-and-effect relationship) caused by both variables being dependent upon a common variable. It is a frequent source of spurious correlation. For instance, the demand for gin correlates nicely with the money spent on education. This does not mean education drives people to drink (we hope not), only that gin sales and educational budgets both vary with population.

Another, more subtle example, is the high correlation between fishing tackle and fishing licenses. There is no cause-and-effect relationship here. The purchase of fishing tackle is motivated by the desire to go fishing, not by the possession of a license. Both variables, however, are determined largely by the number of active fishermen.

When suspected, the presence of covariance can sometimes be verified. First, the analyst must identify the independent variable that may be concurrently determining the value of the two suspected covariant variables. Each of the covariant variables is then regressed against the common independent variable. If both correlate well with the common independent variable, covariance is likely. Common sense and economic theory will generally tell the researcher the direction of the dependency between the variables and help assess the validity of the relationship.

Covariance is actually very useful in marketing research. Often the true determinant of the dependent variable is known, but cannot be measured. If a measurable covariant is available, it can serve as a proxy for the actual determinant.

Again, we can use the fishing-tackle example. It is impractical to count the number of active fishermen in each state, but data on the number of fishing licenses in force are usually available from such state agencies as fish and game departments, statistical bureaus, or the U.S. Department of the Interior. These data are nearly as useful as a census of fishermen, for estimating the demand for fishing tackle. The analyst simply regresses tackle sales against the license count for those states where sales data are available. This should produce a good equation. If not, the addition of per capita personal income (also available by state) as a second independent variable should do the job. Given a model of tackle sales as a function of two easily determined independent variables—fishing licenses and personal income—the analyst can estimate the sales potential of various geographic markets. The model will work, even though it is constructed on the unrealistic (but convenient) assumption that tackle sales are a function of fishing licenses.

Multicollinearity

Multicollinearity, "collinearity," or "joint correlation," is a linear or near-linear relationship between two independent variables. (The variables are "independent" with respect to the dependent variable in the regression model, but not with respect to each other.) Collinearity is a technical problem that can be hard to detect and difficult to remedy. It can seriously distort the model, since the offending variables will appear to act in unison. This makes the separation of their effects—and hence the specification of parameters—a precarious task. When collinearity exists, the method of least squares—the basis of regression analysis—is not a reliable way of allocating the sum of the explained variation among the independent variables.

Multicollinearity is common in economic data, particularly data that have been drawn from the marketplace *in vivo* rather than generated by experimentation. In an experiment, the researcher controls one or more independent variables, and hence has the opportunity to prevent their changing in unison. One indication of collinearity is the existence of inordinately large standard deviations, particularly large standard errors for the regression coefficients. Sensitivity of parameters to minor changes in model specification or small changes in observed data also suggests the presence of collinearity.[2]

If collinearity is suspected, it can often be detected by comparing the data on the two offending variables graphically and inspecting the two curves visually to see if they are moving in unison. A more rigorous test would be to regress one of the offending variables against the other. The correlation between the two independent variables can then be compared to the correlation between the dependent variable and each of the independent variables. Generally, if the coefficient produced by regressing one X against the other is larger than the sum of the regression coefficients of the two X's in the original model, multicollinearity is present.

Collinearity can be reduced or eliminated by several methods. An increase in the number of observations is useful, provided the new observations are not collinear. Another remedy is to change variables. For instance, if income is believed to be an important component of the regression model but collinearity is suspected, analysts might use a different income measurement—say, GNP instead of personal income or personal income instead of personal disposable income. They might also compress the data, that is, combine the two offending (or suspected) variables. For instance, they might substitute a buying power index for personal income and population statistics or GNP for two of its subaccounts.

Kane suggests the transformation of the offending data to ordinary or logarithmic first differences. This serves as a means of ameliorating the

---

[2] Edward J. Kane, *Economic Statistics and Econometrics* (New York: Harper & Row, 1968), p. 278.

oblem when it is induced by the operation of common influences.[3] Un-
rtunately, none of these techniques is foolproof. The analysts may have to
y several remedies before they discover the cure—if any—for their partic-
ar problem.

mproving the Model

emedies for Poor Test Performance

a regression model fails to pass one or more statistical tests, there are often
chniques that will correct the problem. The most common and effective
medies—excluding a change in the mathematical structure of the equa-
on—are more sets of observations and a change of variables. Gathering
ore observations is a good idea when the problem is a lack of significance
the desired confidence level. However, time or budgetary constraints may
eclude the collection of additional observations in some cases; in others,
ore data may be unavailable.

If certain independent variables produce weak t-tests, have very small
gression coefficients, or have large standard deviations (standard errors of
e regression coefficient), a change in variables is indicated. When an in-
pendent variable is weak—that is, it is imprecise or does little to explain
e variation in Y—it should be replaced with a better one or sometimes
opped. This may not be easy, especially if data are scarce and the remaining
's are little better.

Sometimes a change in the dependent variable will correct the problem.
or instance, if Y is changed from unit sales to revenue, a much better, and
ually useful, equation may result.

If R^2, the coefficient of determination, is low, more explanatory vari-
les are needed. This does not mean that the original variables should be
scarded. On the contrary, they may be very significant. If they stand up
ll under the other statistical tests they should be retained, even if they
plain only a moderate portion of the variation in Y.

If the absolute value of a residual (the difference between a predicted
d an observed value) is high, the researchers may be justified in discarding
at set of observations. Recalculating the regression equation without the
averick observation set will invariably improve the apparent quality of the
odel. In fact, if the number of observations is large enough so that degrees
freedom are no problem, the equation can be made to order simply by
lecting observations that support one's preconceptions. This is, however,
dishonest use of statistics.

A set of observations should be discarded only when an extraneous,
ique, and nonrepetitive factor has substantially disturbed the Y value. For
stance, suppose the data consist of eight sets of sales, price, and advertising
ures drawn from eight retail stores. If one set shows unusually low sales

---

[3] Kane, *Economic Statistics and Econometrics*, p. 280.

combined with a low price and a high advertising outlay, this will mean
high residual for that data set, which will hardly enhance the quality of th
regression model. However, if an examination of background data show
that that store—and only that store—had been involved in a serious lab
dispute or was closed for several days because of a fire, its set of observatior
can justifiably be deleted. The new equation will be a substantial improv
ment over the previous regression, and the integrity of the analysis will nc
have been compromised. On the contrary, the model will be more, not les
representative of the true relationship among sales, price, and advertisin
once the disturbance has been removed.

If the disturbance factor is common—that is, if it occurs frequently—tl
best solution may be to incorporate it into the regression model as an i
dependent variable. The dimension of the variable will depend on its measu
ability. Weather, for instance, can be specified in degrees of temperature
inches of precipitation. Sometimes a proxy variable is useful. For exampl
the Dow–Jones average may be used as a proxy of the public's confiden
in the economy—a factor that often influences the sale of high-priced good

Factors such as labor strife, political upheavals, war, and the season
the year can be represented by dummy variables. A *dummy variable* is a var
able that uses a number to represent a qualitative condition. Dummies a
usually zero-or-one variables. For instance, $X_3 = 1$ could represent lab
peace, and $X_3 = 0$ a strike.

Dummy variables are normally treated like other variables in tl
specification and interpretation of the model. However, they may be i
corporated into the model *after* regression analysis has produced an equ
tion. For example, regressing the sale of automobiles, Y, against populatio
X_1, and personal income, X_2, might yield an excellent equation of the for
$\hat{Y} = \hat{\alpha} + \hat{\beta}_1 X_1 + \hat{\beta}_2 X_2$. However, what happens when automobile produ
tion stops, hence $Y = 0$, during an industrywide strike? This factor can
accommodated by altering the equation, using a dummy variable, X_3,
follows: $\hat{Y} = X_3(\hat{\alpha} + \hat{\beta}_1 X_1 + \hat{\beta}_2 X_2)$. X_3 is defined as before, Y becomes ze
in times of labor strife. (Note: The observations made during strikes wou
be ignored in computing the regression equation, for they would distort tl
parameters. Besides, the special condition, a strike, is accounted for by tl
dummy variable.)

An Example

If the F-test showed no significant relationship between the variables in
model at the 95 percent confidence level, this would certainly make it
rather shaky basis for an important marketing decision. However, rath
than discarding the model, which may otherwise be sound, the research
may opt to gather more data. If the degrees of freedom are low, this would
a likely solution. For example, if the regression model developed in Chapt
17 had been computed using only the first six observations, it would not ha
passed the F-test at the 95 percent confidence level (0.05 significance leve
However, the inclusion of four more observations brings the F_T value

the same confidence level) down from 9.55 to 4.74, which is well below the computed F-value. On the basis of only six observations, the analyst could not claim that there was a statistically significant relationship between the Y and the X's. The model would have been unreliable, although not necessarily useless to management. With ten observations, the relationship between the variables becomes statistically significant, even at the 99 percent confidence level. Thus, the additional observations allow management to accept the model with confidence.

Reflecting further on our illustrative regression model, we can see other opportunities for improvement. For example, the R^2 value is impressive, yet might be improved by introducing some additional explanatory variables. Competitors' prices or promotional expenditures (if they can be estimated), consumer income, the market population, and a dummy variable for consumer tastes are logical candidates. Adding new variables and evaluating their effect on the equation is essentially a trial-and-error process, hence a good task for a computer. If manual calculations are required, a trial-and-error approach becomes too cumbersome.

Even when ten observations are used, the model's price component is still very weak. Again, the situation can perhaps be remedied by using more observations or including more explanatory variables. It may also help to drop some of the observations or remove the price term completely. Adding more observations or more explanatory variables is the best solution, but it is not always possible. Excluding observations is hazardous, since it can reduce the degrees of freedom to the point where none of the significance tests hold up. If extreme care is not taken in purging observations, the data may be biased and the model's description of reality distorted. Observations should never be deleted simply because their residuals are high, but only when unique circumstances have induced the exceptional values.

Discarding the price term is a very drastic solution and one that treats the symptom rather than the problem. Price is an important factor in determining the sales of most products, even those whose prices are moderately inelastic. However, if nothing else works and the model's price component cannot pass significance tests at a respectable level of confidence, has a high standard of error, and has a relatively low coefficient, then surgery may be the only answer. The price component in our example is probably not bad enough to warrant its expulsion. Although it is statistically a marginal factor, its inclusion is logically defensible. Economic theory assures us that sales and price are related. Besides, it provides us with at least one piece of information, namely, that price elasticity is low. Exactly how low, however, we cannot really tell from the model.

Time-Series versus Cross-Sectional Data

Time-Series Data

Time-series data are data obtained through observations made at different points in time. For example, sales may be recorded daily, weekly, monthly, or yearly. Time-series data are often the only kind of information available, or usable, especially when there are only one or two points of observation or markets are located close to one another. Unfortunately, it is especially vulnerable to exogenous disturbances and autocorrelation.

Exogenous Disturbances   Changes over time in factors exogenous to (outside) the model can disturb the observed values of the dependent variable, thus distorting the model. These disturbances are called *noise*. If not detected, they can cause the entire equation to fail various statistical tests. On the other hand, if they are in phase with one or more of the independent variables included in the model, they can distort the effect of those variables without compromising the apparent quality of the equation. The longer the observation period is, the more vulnerable the model is to exogenous disturbances.

   Variations in weather, population, income, tastes, and the strength and number of competitors all occur over time. In fact, the list of possible time-series disturbances is endless. Most of these time-variable factors have little influence or tend to cancel one another out. However, some cannot be ignored. They must be incorporated explicitly into the model, or the data must be corrected to eliminate their effect before the regression is made. Unfortunately, doing either may be difficult or impossible.

   One method of reducing time-related disturbances is to narrow the time span of the observations. The longer the observation period is, the less homogeneous the set of observations from which the data is drawn will be. It is this lack of homogeneity that causes trouble in analyses of time-series data. Unfortunately, compression of the observation period also has drawbacks, the most critical of which is the usual reduction in the number of observations obtainable and the resultant decrease in degrees of freedom. Whether the analyst is willing to accept this depends on his or her estimation of the seriousness of the disturbances and need for data.

   A visual inspection of the residuals will often expose time-related disturbances. However, it will not reveal disturbances that are in phase with one or more of the explanatory variables. Researchers simply plot the changes in the residuals over time on arithmetic graph paper[4] and draw freehand curve through the scatter of points. They then examine the curve for unique fluctuations or a pattern of some kind. A unique fluctuation suggests the possibility of an exceptional event at that point in time. something out of the ordinary did occur during the observation period, might well account for the extreme value of the residual. For instance, large negative residual may be caused by exceptional weather, a national calamity, a strike, or an action of a competitor such as a special promotional campaign.

   If the source of a unique fluctuation can be identified and its effect estimated, the observed value of Y may be adjusted accordingly. This would

---

[4] Some regression programs, such as MIT's "Time Series Processor," will perform this task.

reduce or eliminate the residual and improve the overall quality of the equation. The unexplained variation in particular would be reduced, thus producing a higher R^2. An alternative is to eliminate the observation set associated with the extreme residual, as long as this does not bring the number of degrees of freedom below the critical level. This would also improve the overall quality of the model. However, we must again emphasize that these adjustments should be made with care. It is all too easy to rationalize the discarding of information that does violence to the model or the analyst's preconceptions.

A pattern in the residual data suggests the existence of a repetitive factor that should be included in the model or whose effect should be removed from the data. Seasonal variations are typical. If the residual curve consistently dips or climbs in a particular month, a seasonal factor is present. For example, the toy sales invariably get a great boost in December from the cultural habit of gift giving at Christmas. If a firm's retail toy sales were regressed against price and promotion without correcting for this seasonal factor, the residuals for the December observations would be gigantic. This would suggest that sales were correlated with an important seasonal variable and could not be fully explained by price and advertising. This variable, Christmas, should be included in the model (using a dummy variable), or the seasonal fluctuation removed from the data before the regression equation is specified.

If a pattern is detected but its cause cannot be identified, the effect should still be incorporated into the model or removed from the data. If it is not incorporated, the analyst should make note of it and advise the decision-maker of its existence.

Autocorrelation   Another problem associated with time-series data is autocorrelation, or "serial correlation." *Autocorrelation* is a correlation between observations of a variable over time. It is the result of a dependency between observations of the variable in a time series. For example, sales in January may affect sales in February, or the Wednesday price may influence the Thursday price. The value of the variable in one period influences its value in a following period. If autocorrelation is present in the dependent variable, it may be difficult to isolate the effect of the independent variables. A change in Y attributed to the X's may actually have been partly induced by the previous value of Y. Autocorrelation also affects the results of the F-test and the t-test used in model evaluation, for both are based on the assumption that the residuals are normally distributed about their mean—a condition violated by autocorrelation.

Several tests can be used to check for autocorrelation. One method is to graph the residuals during consecutive periods and compare them. Normally, one year's residuals are compared to the preceding year's residuals. If the points are connected by a freehand curve, its shape should be revealing. An erratic curve indicates no autocorrelation. A curve with a pattern (other than a horizontal line) suggests the presence of autocorrelation. However, this visual test is not wholly reliable.

The preceding analysis can be made more rigorous by regressing each residual against its predecessor using a bivariate model. The values used in specifying the equation are shown in Table 19-1. Generally speaking, auto-correlation is assumed to be present if the *t*-test of $\hat{\beta}$ indicates significance at the 0.05 level.

The *von Neumann ratio*—commonly called the *K-statistic*—is another statistical test of autocorrelation. It is similar to the *F*-test and the *t*-test in that it compares a computed value to a table value to determine if an apparent effect can be attributed to chance. The table value of *K* is actually a range of values between two extremes, *K* and *K'*. *K* is the low value and *K'* is the high value at a given significance level. If the computed value, K_C, is less than *K*, positive autocorrelation is assumed. If K_C is greater than *K'*, negative autocorrelation is assumed. If K_C is between *K* and *K'*, the apparent autocorrelation effect is assumed to be due to chance.

The table values, *K* and *K'*, are found by consulting a table of von Neumann ratios. The computed value is found by the following formula:

$$K_C = \frac{m^2}{s^2} \qquad\qquad\qquad [19.1]$$

where

$$m^2 = \frac{\Sigma(e_{i+1} - e_i)^2}{n-1}$$

$$s^2 = \frac{\Sigma e_i^2}{n}$$

K_C = the computed value of the *K*-statistic

m^2 = the summation of the squares of the differences between successive residuals, divided by $n - 1$

s^2 = the arithmetic mean of the residuals, squared

e = a residual

n = the number of observations

i = the number of an observation in a series of consecutive observations

The *Durbin-Watson test* is yet a fourth satistical method for detecting autocorrelation.[5] Essentially, it is equivalent to the von Neumann test, but has a different form. It is mentioned here only because the Durbin-Watson

---

[5] For an explanation of the Durbin-Watson test and its applications, see Ronald J. and Thomas H. Wonnacutt, *Econometrics* (New York: Wiley, 1970), p. 142; or Arthur S. Goldberger, *Econometric Theory* (New York: Wiley, 1964), p. 243.

Table 19-1 **Values Used in Regression of Time-Series Residuals**

Dependent Variable (Y)	Independent Variable (X)
e_{i+1}[a]	e_i
e_{i+2}	e_{i+1}
e_{i+3}	e_{i+2}
$\vdots$	$\vdots$
e_n	e_{n-1}

[a] e = a residual and i = the number of an observation in a series of consecutive observations.

statistic is provided by some computer programs for regressing time-series data.[6]

Autocorrelation, once identified, can usually be reduced or eliminated by the introduction of an additional independent variable that is lagged with respect to Y. For instance, if there is autocorrelation in the series of Y values—that is, if Y_i is partially determined by its preceding value, Y_{i-1}—Y_{i-1} would be included on the right-hand side of the regression equation as one of the explanatory variables. To avoid confusion, we would probably define the new independent variables as $Y_{i-1} = X_i$. Thus the regression coefficient $\hat{\beta}_1$ would represent the sensitivity of Y_i to its predecessor. The term $\hat{\beta}_i X_i$ would represent the influence of autocorrelation in the model.

Lagged Relationships   A significant advantage of time-series data is that they allow the specification of lagged relationships. In *a lagged relationship*, the value of one variable is influenced by the value of another variable at an earlier point in time. We have just seen an example of this in the discussion of autocorrelation, which is a special—and usually troublesome—case of a lagged relationship between two observations of the same variable. More conventional examples of this phenomenon are the influence of advertising on sales, income on consumption, and building permits on construction. Lagged variables are often important and often should be included in a model. For example, sales of electrical appliances are partially determined by the price of electricity. However, the full effect of a reduction in the price of electricity will not be felt for many months, possibly years; certainly families will not immediately scrap good gas appliances simply to replace them with electrical ones. Another example is advertising, which frequently has a cumulative effect. Thus, sales at time t may be a function of advertising at times $t - 1, t - 2, t - 3$, and so on.

A lagged variable is introduced into the regression equation just like any other variable. Notationally, it may be identified by a subscript such

[6] MIT's "Time Series Processor" is one such program.

as "$t - 1$." Or it may simply be defined as X_i, the observed value of X at time $t - 1$. Time t is the time the Y observation is made. The 1 represents one unit of time, which is the interval between observations. For example, sales of building supplies, Y, regress nicely against the issuance of building permits, X, provided the dependent variable (sales) is lagged three months behind the independent variable (building permits). Thus Y_t is a function of X_{t-3} or X_i where $i = t - 3$.

Cross-Sectional Data

Cross-sectional data consist of observations made simultaneously. For instance, sales on a particular day may be recorded for each store, SMSA, or state in a given region. Using cross-sectional data enables the researcher to avoid some of the problems associated with time-series data, but they create other problems.

Heterogeneity   One big problem with cross-sectional data is the lack of homogeneity between observational units. This problem is called "heterogeneity." For instance, even if a set of retail stores approximately the same size are used, each will have different characteristics—different clienteles, different locations, and different marketing philosophies. These factors will influence the dependent variable by different amounts. They will probably not be included in the model, but their differences will be reflected in the residuals, where their effect will be inseparable from statistical error.

A good researcher will minimize this problem by selecting similar units or by adjusting the observations for the differences in units. One device is to use an index or a proportion instead of an absolute value for the dependent variable. For example, an area's market share might be used in lieu of unit sales or revenue, thus moderating differences in population and income between observational units. However, such decisions must be made prior to the collection of the data. In fact, anticipating the heterogeneity problem is part of the job of research design.

Another technique for dealing with heterogeneity is to weight the variables to compensate for differences in observational units. For instance, if one store normally sells twice as much merchandise any other store in a group of test stores, its sales may be reduced by half in specifying a regression model of the sales-price relationship.

Once the observational units—the stores, cities, SMSA's, and so on— are chosen, the complete set should be retained and all the data used. Only extraordinary circumstances excuse the purging of one or more observations.

Isolation   Another problem that can be acute with cross-sectional data is that of isolating the observational units.[7] The value of an independent

[7] Isolation can also be a problem with time-series data when the results in one time period are affected by conditions in a previous period.

variable in one unit can influence the value of the dependent variable in another. For example, a low price in one store may attract sales away from another store.

Observational units are especially vulnerable to changes in key variables, particularly promotion at adjoining units. Often the effect is delayed. A special display in one store may influence buyers, but they may not cross the purchase threshold until later, at which time another store—one without the special display—is more convenient. Thus, the no-display unit will receive credit for the sales induced by the display at the other store. If the purpose of the regression is to estimate the effect of the display on sales, this lack of isolation will obviously distort the model.

Such incidents will, with luck, be randomly distributed and cancel one another out. This assumption is implicit in many research designs, but will not always withstand careful scrutiny. Increasing the number of observational units and the distance between them will help relieve the problem, but will seldom eliminate it. Modern communications and the high mobility of today's consumers virtually ensures some isolation problems.

Advantages of Cross-Sectional Data   The chief virtue of cross-sectional data is that it is presumably impervious to changes in time-related variables. Since all the observations are simultaneous, the effects of changes in extraneous factors—such as economic and demographic variables—is presumably excluded. Actually this assumption is a bit naive, for cross-sectional data usually involve values generated over time, such as monthly sales, weekly revenue, or daily receipts. Ths observations are seldom instantaneous, and the observational units rarely respond equally to changes in exogenous forces. However, the period measured is usually brief and is the same for all the observations. Unless a major political or economic event occurs, important external factors should not change enough to significantly influence the observed data.

Common Problems and Joint Uses of Time-Series and Cross-Sectional Data

One problem common to both types of data is a shortage of observations. When this occurs, there are few satisfactory solutions. One possibility—if there are only a few observations—is to reduce the number of variables in the model. As the number of variables, K, is reduced, the degrees of freedom increase (generally, $d.f. = n - K$). However, a reduction in explanatory variables also increases the size of the unexplained variation in Y, causing R^2 to deteriorate.

If analysts are desperate for observations, they can pool the time-series and cross-sectional data, as long as redundant observations are eliminated and they are prepared to assume that the relationships between the variables are constant with respect to time and place. The result will be a heterogeneous set of observations, and the resultant model probably will not survive all the tests or lend itself to all the remedies associated with the two forms of data.

However, circumstances may provide no other options. The analyst will simply have to rely heavily on personal judgment in using the pooled data and evaluating the model.

Occasionally, cross-sectional data can be used to support time-series data and vice-versa. An analysis made using one kind of data can be checked against an analysis made using the other kind. If the two contradict each other, statistical tests should reveal the superior model. If they agree, the best model should still be chosen. The fact that its findings have been reinforced by the other model will give the analyst and the decision-maker even more confidence in it.

Caution

Regardless of which type of data are employed, the researcher should be alert for problems. A suspicious nature, if not outright paranoia, can be an asset in multivariate analysis. Regression is no exception. In addition to the usual suspicions about the bias and randomness of the data, one should be wary of the problems we've just reviewed. Namely:

spurious correlation	multicollinearity
identification	autocorrelation
noninclusiveness	heterogeneity
covariance	isolation

Computerized regression algorithms typically provide the common tests of model quality, such as the t-statistic, F-ratio, standard error of the regression coefficient, and R^2. Some, such as SPSS's REGRESSION, also offer residuals (in tabular or graphic form) and the Durbin-Watson statistic. Beyond that, the researcher is left to his or her own devices. And once a problem is identified, the remedy will have to come out of the brain of the researcher, not a mindless machine.

Curvilinear Regression Models

A *curvilinear* model is one that has one or more nonlinear variables.[8] That is, it has one or more variables with an exponent other than one. It derives its name from the fact that it plots as a curved line (a two-variable model)

---

[8] The terms nonlinear and curvilinear are often used interchangeably. However, econometricians generally make a distinction: A *nonlinear* function is any function with one or more exponents not equal to one. That is, either the parameters or the variables can be nonlinear. Thus $Y = \alpha + \beta X^3$, $Y = \alpha + \beta^2 X$, $Y = \alpha + \beta^2 X^4$, and $Y^2 = \alpha + \beta X$ are all nonlinear functions. *Curvilinearity* is a special case of nonlinearity in which one or more variables are nonlinear, but all the parameters are linear. Thus $Y = \alpha + \beta X^3$, $Y^2 = \alpha + \beta X$, and $Y = \alpha + \beta \sqrt{X}$ are all curvilinear. The method of least squares will not work if the model being specified has any nonlinear parameters.

or a curved surface (a three-variable model), or has the mathematical properties of curvilinearity (an *n*-variable model).

The relationships between the variables encountered in the market are seldom linear. Yet, a linear model is frequently a close enough approximation of an actual relationship to be useful in decision-making. This is fortunate, for the linear model is much more manageable than its nonlinear counterpart. Curvilinear regression analysis is more complicated, less advanced, and far more limited than linear regression analysis.

There are times when a linear equation is such a poor approximation of reality that analysts have no choice but to discard it and attempt a curvilinear model. If they are willing to use one of several special types of curvilinear models, they can transform the equation into linear form and use the techniques of linear regression analysis in their computations and statistical tests. Otherwise, they must employ complex methods beyond the scope of this book or forego regression entirely and look for another, perhaps qualitative, method of analysis.

Parabolic Bivariate Models

Occasionally a second-degree polynomial equation best describes the relationship between two variables. Such an equation inscribes a parabolic curve when plotted on arithmetic graph paper. By treating the second-degree component of the model as a third variable (a second independent variable), we can treat the model as linear for purposes of computation. Unfortunately, this technique works only for bivariate models.

The general form of a parabolic vibariate model is

$$\hat{Y} = \hat{\alpha} + \hat{\beta}_1 X + \hat{\beta}_2 X^2 \qquad\qquad [19.2]$$

where

$\hat{Y}$ = the estimate of the dependent variable

$\hat{\alpha}$ = the estimate of the intercept

$\hat{\beta}_1$ = the estimate of the first regression coefficient

$\hat{\beta}_2$ = the estimate of the second regression coefficient

X = and independent variable

The parameters of equation 19.2 can be specified using the techniques of multivariate linear regression analysis explained in Chapter 17. However, the formula must first be transformed into an equation that conforms to the general model of a linear regression. This is accomplished by defining two independent variables, X_1 and X_2, as X and X^2, respectively. Thus equation 19.2 becomes $\hat{Y} = \hat{\alpha} + \hat{\beta}_1 X_1 + \hat{\beta}_2 X_2$, which can be specified by conventional methods. We simply substitute the value of X for X_1 and the value of X^2 for X_2 for each observation of the Y and X pair. Once the parameters

Figure 19-1 **A Parabolic Bivariate Regression Model**

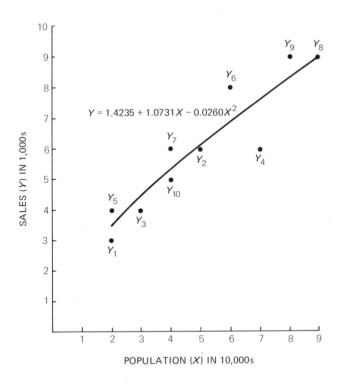

are computed, the model can be transformed back to its original form (equation 19.2) by substituting X for X_1 and X^2 for X_2.

Parl provides an example of parabolic bivariate regression in the construction of a second degree polynomial model of a product's sales, Y, as a function of market population, X.[9] The resultant equation, $\hat{Y} = 1.4235 + 1.0731X - 0.0260X^2$, is plotted in Figure 19-1. Once specified, the parabolic bivariate regression model is interpreted in the same way as linear regression models. However, a bit more caution may be in order in using $\hat{Y}$ values well outside the domain of $\hat{Y}$ values generated by X's within the observed range. In short, be careful in extrapolating the curve. The curvature of the parabolic model can lead to curious results at the extremities. This is especially true of the portion of the curve at the far right, where the squared term is dominant.

Since the model has the same form as a multivariate linear model, the same evaluative criteria apply. The separation of the squared component into a term with its own regression coefficient, $\hat{\beta}_2 X^2$, reduces the degrees of freedom to one less than in the linear bivariate model. In the

[9] Boris Parl, *Basic Statistics* (New York: Doubleday, 1957), pp. 246–247.

parabolic model, X^2 is counted as another variable. Hence, the total number of variables is 3 ($K = 3$).

Exponential Models

An *exponential*, or "semilogarithmic," model is one in which the dependent variable, Y, is related geometrically to the independent variables, X_1, $X_2, \ldots X_n$. This kind of relationship is typical of certain growth curves (e.g., population size as a function of time) and production functions (e.g., output expressed as a function of capital and labor inputs). Such relationships can be specified by regression analysis if the model can be put in linear form. The only precondition is that the parameters of the model be related multiplicatively, not additively. Otherwise the equation cannot be restated linearly.

The transformation to linearity is accomplished by converting the equation into logarithmic form. This does not alter the essential mathematical structure of the model, but does make it amenable to linear regression analysis. For example, the following is a typical multivariate exponential model:

$$\hat{Y} = \hat{\alpha} \cdot \beta_1^{X_1} \cdot \beta_2^{X_2}, \ldots \beta_n^{X_n} \qquad [19.13]$$

The same equation in its logarithmic (and linear) form is

$$\log \hat{Y} = \log \hat{\alpha} + \log \beta_1 \cdot X_1 + \log \beta_2 \cdot X_2 + \cdots \log \beta_n \cdot X_n \qquad [19.4]$$

After the transformation is made and the observed values of Y are converted to their logarithms, linear regression techniques can be used to specify the parameters. We simply substitute the logarithmic values of Y and the natural values of the X's in the equation. This gives us the logarithms of the parameters (α and the β's). The model can be left in logarithmic form or put back into exponential form, using the natural values of the parameters. (The natural values of α and the β's can easily be found with a computer or a table of logarithms. Many pocket calculators do this conversion.)

Again, Parl has developed an illustration, using population as the dependent variable, Y, time as the determinant, X, and 1900 as a base year (i.e., $X_{1900} = 0$). By regressing the logarithmic values of the observed Y's against the natural values of the observed X's, he produced the following exponential model[10]

$$\log \hat{Y} = 1.89732 + 0.05832X \qquad [19.5]$$

or

$$\hat{Y} = 78.9(1.144)^X \qquad \text{(equation 19.5 restated in natural form)}$$

---

[10] Parl, *Basic Statistics*, pp. 284–285. Parl uses simultaneous algebraic equations to solve the regression. This is a slightly different approach than the one we have used, which employs independent algebraic equations. Matrix algebra could also have been used.

Figure 19-2   A Bivariate Exponential Regression Model (Arithmetic Scales)

Source: From *Basic Statistics* by Boris Parl. Copyright © 1967 by Doubleday & Company, Inc.
Reproduced by permission of Doubleday & Company, Inc.

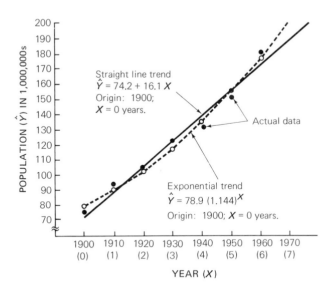

Figure 19-3   A Bivariate Exponential Regression Model (Logarithmic Vertical Scale)

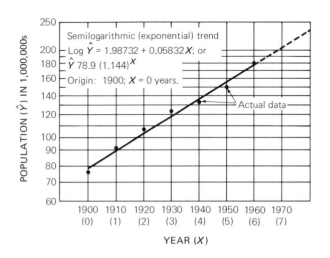

The observed (actual) Y and X values used in the regression and the resultant exponential equations are shown in Figure 19-2. A straight-line (i.e., linear) model–derived from the same data–is also shown.

A useful peculiarity of a bivariate exponential function is that it plots as a straight line on semilogarithmic graph paper. The natural values of $\hat{Y}$ are plotted on the vertical axis, which is a logarithmic scale. The natural values of X are plotted on the horizontal axis, which is an arithmetic scale. The observed values, Y, can also be plotted this way, but they will not inscribe a straight line unless the equation explains all the variation in the dependent variable. This is extremely unlikely; however, should it happen, the Y values would coincide with the $\hat{Y}$ values.

Figure 19-3 shows Parl's exponential model plotted on a semilogarithmic graph, along with the observed values of Y. One advantage of the semilogarithmic plot is that it can be inscribed using only two points by connecting them with a straight line extending through the desired range of X. Estimated values of the dependent variable can easily be read from the graph.

A useful variant of the exponential model, which can also be specified by regression analysis, is

$$\hat{Y} = \hat{\alpha} X_1^{\hat{\beta}_1} X_2^{\hat{\beta}_2}, \ldots X_n^{\hat{\beta}_n} \qquad [19.6]$$

The same equation in logarithmic form is

$$\log \hat{Y} = \log \hat{\alpha} + \hat{\beta}_1 \cdot \log X_1 + \hat{\beta}_2 \cdot \log X_2 + \cdots \hat{\beta}_n \cdot \log X_n \qquad [19.7]$$

Once the model has been put in logarithmic form, the equation is specified by the usual regression techniques. This time, however, we end up with the logarithmic value of $\hat{\alpha}$ and the natural values of the $\hat{\beta}$'s. If the analyst wishes, the specified logarithmic model can easily be transformed back to the natural form.

An interesting property of this variant of the exponential model, for the market researcher, is that the $\hat{\beta}$'s represent elasticities. For instance, if one variable is price, then its parameter, $\hat{\beta}$, represents price elasticity. Another of its properties is the fact that the dependent variable becomes zero if any independent variable goes to zero. In some cases, this makes it a much more realistic model, especially when population is one of the independent variables and demand is the dependent variable.

Other Compatible Curvilinear Models

Many curvilinear models are compatible with regression analysis. The test of compatibility is the linearity of the parameters. Any curvilinear model can be specified by linear regression analysis *if* it can be transformed into a linear equation by algebraic manipulations or by using logarithms.

The objective of the algebraic manipulations is to break the model down into a set of one or more linearly related terms, isolate the parameters from the rest of the terms, and substitute a single variable, X_i, for each term (exclusive of its parameter). The following cases are illustrative. (The independent variables have arbitrarily been identified as P, Q, and R, and the parameters as α, $\hat{\beta}_1$, $\hat{\beta}_2$, $\hat{\beta}_3$, etc.)

(a) Curvilinear model

$$\hat{Y} = \hat{\alpha} + \frac{3\hat{\beta}_1}{P} \qquad\qquad [19.8]$$

Linear form

$$\hat{Y} = \hat{\alpha} + \hat{\beta}_1 X_1 \qquad\qquad [19.9]$$

where

$$X_1 = \frac{3}{P}$$

(b) Curvilinear model

$$\hat{Y} = \hat{\alpha} + \hat{\beta}_1 \sqrt{P} + \hat{\beta}_2(Q + R^2) \qquad\qquad [19.10]$$

Linear form

$$\hat{Y} = \hat{\alpha} + \hat{\beta}_1 X_1 + \hat{\beta}_2 X_2$$

where

$$X_1 = \sqrt{P}$$
$$X_2 = (Q + R^2)$$

Logarithms may be used to deal with geometric relationships.

(c) Curvilinear model

$$\hat{Y} = \hat{\alpha} P^{\hat{\beta}_1} \qquad\qquad [19.12]$$

Linear form

$$\log \hat{Y} = \log \hat{\alpha} + \hat{\beta}_1 \log P \qquad\qquad [19.13]$$

or

$$\log \hat{Y} = \log \hat{\alpha} + \hat{\beta}_1 \log X_1 \qquad\qquad [19.14]$$

where

$$X_1 = P$$

(d) Curvilinear model

$$\hat{Y} = \frac{P^{\beta_1}}{Q^{\beta_2}}$$ [19.15]

Linear form

$$\log \hat{Y} = \log \hat{\alpha} + \hat{\beta}_1 \log P - \hat{\beta}_2 \log Q$$ [19.16]

or

$$\log \hat{Y} = \log \hat{\alpha} + \hat{\beta}_1 \log X_1 - \hat{\beta}_2 \log X_2$$ [19.17]

where

$$X_1 = P$$

and

$$X_2 = Q$$

The model specified by regression analysis will always have an inter-cept, $\hat{\alpha}$. Of course $\hat{\alpha}$ could be zero, but this is highly unlikely. In writing the transformed equations, the intercept is included as a matter of convention. If regression reveals it to be zero it is simply ignored in transforming the specified linear model back to the curvilinear form. Of course $\hat{\alpha}$ cannot equal zero in multiplicative models such as equations 19.12 and 19.15. If it did, $\hat{Y}$ would always be zero. When $\hat{\alpha}$ is omitted from a multiplicative model, as in equation 19.15, it is presumed to equal one and to have been left out as a matter of notational convenience.

Before we can use regression analysis to specify the model, the values of the X's must be computed from the observed data. For instance, in equation 19.8, if the ninth observation showed Y to be 30 and P to be 5, the values $Y = 30$ and $X_1 = 0.6$ would be used for that particular observation ($i = 9$) in equation 19.9. When logarithms are used in the linear form, the raw data must be converted to its logarithmic equivalents before proceeding with the regression. The conversion of the raw data to logarithmic equivalents, as well as the conversion of the answers to natural numbers, can be done automatically by a computer. If manual solutions are used, a table of logarithms and a bit more paperwork will be needed. (Relief can be found in the better pocket calculators.)

The statistical tests described in Chapter 18 apply only to the linear form of the model. If the linear form happens to be logarithmic, then certain test measures—such as the residuals—will also be logarithmic values. However, once they are computed they can easily be transformed to natural numbers.

Once the model is specified in linear form, it can easily be restored to its original curvilinear form by reversing the algebraic processes used to accomplish the first transformation. Of course, the retransformed model will have specified parameters, and hence can be used to predict values of the dependent variable, Y. We simply substitute the natural values of the independent variables–P, Q, and R in our examples–in the model and solve for Y.

Problems

1   What special problems might you encounter in attempting to derive a regression model for each of the following: (a) the relationship between Campbell's Soup sales and its advertising; (b) the sensitivity of Ford sales to advertising by Chevrolet and Plymouth; and (c) the relationship between the aggregate demand for pleasure boats and population, personal income, and the number of marinas in operation. Suggest some remedies.

2   Suggest remedies for each of the following conditions: (a) a high R^2 and an unsatisfactory F-test for a regression model with three independent variables; (b) one poor t-test, an excellent F-test, and an R^2 of 0.863 for a regression model with three independent variables; and (c) an R^2 of 0.437 when all other tests are satisfactory for a regression model with two independent variables.

3   Discuss the advantages and disadvantages of using time-series and cross-sectional data in the regression models described in question 1.

4   Construct a curvilinear regression model for sales as a function of price, using the following data.

Observation	Sales (units)	Price
1	55	$10
2	45	$11
3	32	$12
4	26	$13
5	23	$14
6	20	$15

Chapter 20
Factor Analysis*

Key Concepts

Fundamentals
Factors, factor scores, and other basic ideas

The Process
The steps from data entry to using the factor scores

Alternative Methods
Different algorithms producing different results

Applications
Four basic uses of factor analysis

Key Terms

principle of parsimony
factor
factor score
R-analysis
Q-analysis
factor loading
factor loading matrix
communality

common factors
unique factors
factor-score coefficient
factor-score coefficient matrix
principal components analysis
classical factor analysis
attribute map

Fundamentals

Occasionally we are inundated with variables—so many that they are unmanageable. For instance, a researcher for the Broadway Department Stores studied the Tuscon market in hopes of learning why her firm did poorly

---

* The author is especially indebted to Jagdish N. Sheth for his assistance in preparing this chapter.

there. Her questionnaire had 26 store-image questions. Each image question had to be asked about the Broadway and each of its five competitors. With 652 telephone interviews, she had to cope with 101,712 pieces of image data (26 × 6 × 652). For relief, she turned to factor analysis.

Purpose

As we observed in our survey of multivariate analysis, factor analysis is a set of techniques for analyzing interdependence among variables. The main objective of factor analysis is to redefine a large set of variables as a smaller set. The new variables are indexes called "factors." Each factor represents two or more of the old variables.

As the factors are fewer in number than the original variables, they are much more manageable. In the Broadway study, the original variable set was reduced to three factors. The data were thus reduced from 101,712 to 11,736 pieces (3 × 6 × 652). Further analysis was made easier.

This reduction of data is consistent with the principle of parsimony common to all scientific theory. The *principle of parsimony* holds that a model should be simpler than the data upon which it is based. One should generally strive for parsimony throughout the research process, especially after entering the data analysis phase.

Factors

A *factor* is essentially a linear combination of the observed variables. Specifically,

$$F_j = a_1 X_1 + a_2 X_2 + a_3 X_3 \cdots + a_n X_n, \qquad [20.1]$$

where

$F_j =$ the *j*th factor ($j = 1, 2 \ldots m$)

$a =$ a coefficient

$X =$ an observed variable (usually in standardized form)

$1 \ldots n =$ number (identifier) of the observed variable and its coefficient

Ideally, the chosen algorithm yields factors upon which some variables load very heavily and other variables load very lightly, or not at all. For instance, say we had seven original variables which we reduced to two factors. We'd like to see something like:

| *Var 1* | *Var 2* | *Var 3* | *Var 4* | *Var 5* | *Var 6* | *Var 7* |

$$F_1 = a_{1,1} X_1 + a_{1,2} X_2 \qquad\qquad\qquad\qquad\qquad\qquad + a_{1,6} X_6 + a_{1,7} X_7$$

$$F_2 = \qquad\qquad\qquad\qquad + a_{2,3} X_3 + a_{2,4} X_4 + a_{2,5} X_5$$

Factor One (F_1) is an index of variables 1, 2, 6, and 7. Factor Two (F_2) summarizes variables 3, 4, and 5. We hope the variables associated with a particular factor have more in common than merely their statistical relationship. If the variables do not share some common essence, their factor will prove useless and we cannot even give it a name.

Factor Scores

A *factor score* is the score a respondent gets on a particular factor. This value is derived from equation 20.1.

For example, assume Factor Two was made up mainly of variables 3, 4, and 5. A respondent rated high on each of these variables would have a high Factor-Two score. That score would become part of the data set associated with that respondent. It would probably replace variables 3, 4, and 5 in future analysis.

Factor scores are treated like any other metric variable. For instance, the researcher might regress a dependent variable, say purchases, against one or more factor scores. The objective would be to estimate the sensitivity of purchases to each of the factors.

Labeling the Factors

Factor analysis does not name the factors it produces. This burden falls on the researcher who must select a label he or she deems appropriate. Thus, the labeling process introduces nonstatistical judgments into the analysis. Of course, this problem is often encountered in other statistical techniques.

If factor analysis works well, the names will be fairly obvious. In the Broadway study, one factor was made up mainly of the variables price, quality, sales, credit, and return privileges. This factor was labeled "economics," for it clearly represented the economic dimension of the store as perceived by the Tucson respondents.

R-Analysis versus *Q*-Analysis

Most factor-analysis programs produce factors which are combinations of the observed variables. Focusing on the variables is called "*R*-analysis." It is by far the most common.

A few factor-analysis algorithms produce factors which are combinations of respondents (also called "subjects"). Focusing on the subjects is called "*Q*-analysis." *Q*-analysis is seldom used for three reasons: First, the available algorithms[1] cannot handle even moderately large samples. Second, the factors have proven unstable, hence unreliable, between samples from the same universe. And third, the algorithms have a ferocious appetite for computer time. *Q*-analysis is expensive.

The shortcomings of *Q*-analysis are unfortunate. Grouping respondents into meaningful clusters is appealing, especially in market segmentation

---

[1] One such program is found in P. Horst, *Factor Analysis of Data Matricies* (New York: Holt, Rinehart and Winston, 1965).

analysis. After all, market segments are made up of people, not incomes, ages, attitudes, and so forth.

Penalties

One pays several penalties for the use of factor analysis. First, one must accept some subjectivity. One source is the labeling process. There are other sources of subjectivity, such as the need to choose between alternative methods.

Second, one must accept the loss of information. The amount of loss is dictated by the interdependency of the variables and the amount of reduction. Variables that are highly correlated can be combined neatly into a common factor with little loss of information. If the observed variables are combined into one or two factors, there will be a greater loss of information than if three or four factors are used.

Third, there is no statistical method for fully evaluating the results of factor analysis. The final assessment must rest mainly on common sense and economic or behavioral theory.

Four, there are many ways one can perform a factor analysis, even within a given algorithm. Each method and each option will produce different results. There is no consensus on which is the best method. Choice rests on the judgment of the researcher, and one must accept more subjectivity.

Sometimes factor analysis proves useless. The loss of information is too great or the grouping of variables makes little sense. Under these circumstances, one must try different algorithms or abandon factor analysis.

The Process

Steps

The factor-analysis process typically runs through the following steps:

1	Enter the raw data into the computer.
2	Convert the observations to standardized values.[2]
3	Produce a correlation matrix.
4	Produce a factor loading matrix.
5	Evaluate the results.
6	Start over at step 3 if the results are unsatisfactory.
7	Label the factors.
8	Produce a factor-score coefficient matrix.
9	Compute the factor scores for each case (respondent or object).
10	Add the factor scores to the data file.
11	Continue on to the next analysis, e.g., attribute mapping, regression analysis, discriminant analysis, etc..

---

[2] The standardized value is simply the Z-statistic calculated with formula A2.14. See Appendix 2 for a discussion.

The raw data are entered in the computer by the usual media—punch cards, keyboard, magnetic tape, or floppy disk. This step typically transpires early in the data processing phase in preparation for the initial data reduction. With a computer-library package, such as BioMed or SPSS, the data are usually left on file in the system. They are then called into the computer memory, usually from disk storage, when an analysis is to be performed.

When data consist of a diverse set of measurements, they must be standardized before factor analysis begins. The conversion of the observations to their standardized values (Z-values) is part of most factor-analysis algorithms. However, it is not always mandatory. (The conversion to Z-values is automatic in most library programs.)

The next step, preparation of the correlation matrix, is done automatically by the algorithm. The algorithm usually offers the option of having the correlation matrix printed with the other output. This is a useful feature as the correlation matrix is handy for other purposes, such as identifying pairs of highly correlated variables.

The Factor Loading Matrix

The production of the factor loading matrix is the key step—the very heart—of factor analysis. This is also where the most important, and unfortunately the most subjective, decisions must be made.

Factor Loadings   The relationship between the observed variables and the newly produced factors is revealed in the form of the factor loading matrix. A *factor loading* is a coefficient indicating the importance of a factor in determining the value of a variable. Specifically,

$$X_n = a_{n,1}F_1 + a_{n,2}F_2 \cdots + a_{n,j}F_j + e_{n,j} \qquad [20.2]$$

X_n = the nth variable

$a_{n,j}$ = the factor loading for the nth variable on the jth factor

F_j = the jth factor

$e_{n,j}$ = the error term[3]

As different factor-analysis algorithms are available, one can produce different sets of loadings from the same data. This is one of the drawbacks of factor analysis: Researchers can argue all night over which algorithm is most relevant, hence which set of loadings is the most appropriate.

If the data are transformed into Z-values before the loading are computed, the factor loadings will represent the correlation between the variables and the factors. Hence, the *factor loading matrix* can be interpreted as a matrix of correlations between the variables and the factors.

---

[3] The error term does not appear when principal components analysis is used. (This is discussed shortly.)

In Table 20-1 we see the factor loadings (.8023, .1015, etc.) which indicate the correlation between the factors and the observed variables. We also see the communality values which indicate the extent the variables are summarized by the two factors. Specifically, *communality* (h^2) is the percentage of total variance summarized in common factors. A *common factor* is one shared by at least two variables. A low communality says the variable is statistically independent and cannot be combined with other variables. In the terminology of factor analysis, the variable is "unique." If communality is low for all or most of the variables, the factor analysis has failed.

Interpretation   The statistics in Table 20-1 indicate that factor analysis has worked moderately well. Factor One nicely summarizes variables 1, 3, 4, 9, and 10. Factor Two nicely summarizes variables 2, 5, 6, and 8. Both factors are distinctly different, except for variable 6, which loads on both of them. (Variable 6 is ambiguous.) Variable 7 loads poorly on both factors, and has a communality of only 18 percent. Variable 7 is therefore unique.

Unique variables, like variable 7, are often excluded—that is, they are not considered part of any factor. But what is "unique"? Some researchers feel that any variable with a communality below .40 is unique and should be dropped. (In our example, they would exclude variables 7, 8, 9, and 10.) Other researchers believe all variables should be included. Using all the variables in the computation of factor scores is called the "complete estimation method" as opposed to the "shorthand method." The SPSS algorithm FACTOR uses the complete estimation method, although it offers the option of excluding selected variables.[4] Again, the researcher is driven to a judgmental decision.

If we had several variables behaving like number 7, we might try the analysis again. On the next run, we would call for three factors, instead of

Table 20-1   **A Factor Loading Matrix: Motorcycle Study**

Variable	Factor One	Factor Two	Communality $(h^2)^a$
1. Speed	.8023	.1015	.79
2. Price	.1105	.7246	.68
3. Acceleration	.8438	.0966	.89
4. Handling	.4943	.0492	.64
5. Fuel economy	−.1023	−.4831	.27
6. Payload	.3821	.4261	.46
7. Comfort	.1231	.0713	.18
8. Maintenance cost	.1803	.3291	.31
9. Braking distance	.2100	−.0823	.34
10. Riding ease	−.2731	−.0728	.25

[a] Communalities are not part of the factor loading matrix. They are shown here for convenience.

[4] For a discussion, see Norman H. Nie et al., *Statistical Package for the Social Sciences*, 2nd ed. (New York: McGraw-Hill, 1975), pp. 488–489.

two. We hope the third factor would collect our errant variables and yield a high communality for each of them. If it does not, we could try a different algorithm or accept the notion that some of our variables cannot be combined. This in itself is useful information, because it says that each of these variables has little in common with the other variables and their underlying factors.

Graphical Presentation   We can picture our factors and their components (the variables) graphically. In fact, many computerized algorithms do this for us.[5] We see an example in Figure 20-1. The two factors constitute an attribute space. The variables are represented as vectors, whose length

Figure 20-1   **An Attribute Space: Motorcycle Study**

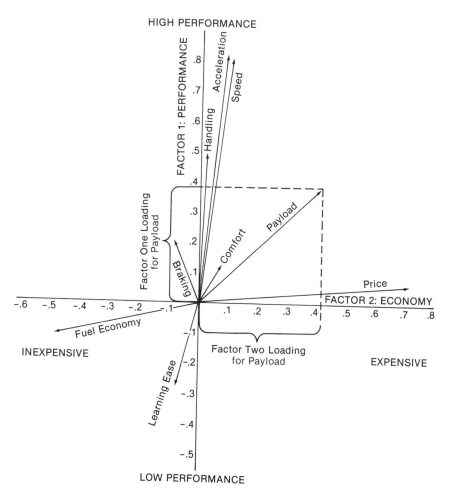

[5] SPSS's FACTOR is an example.

represents their relative importance. The angle of the vectors indicates direction, or how they are loaded on the factors.

Labeling   An examination of Figure 20-1 suggests labels for the two factors—"Performance" and "Economy." If a motorcycle received high scores on speed, acceleration, handling, and braking, it would rank high on performance. If it had a low price and high fuel economy (m.p.g.), it would rank high on economy. A good comfort-rating would have little effect on either factor.

Excluding Variables   The factor loading matrix helps one decide which variables to associate with a given factor. If a variable is rejected, one excludes it later when constructing the factor-score equation (formula 20.1).

In our example, the ambiguous nature of payload and its relatively low communality suggest it not be included as part of either factor. This is a judgmental decision. One might include only those variables with a significant loading in a given factor. Thus, acceleration would be included in Factor One, but excluded from Factor Two. Again, this is a judgmental, hence subjective, decision. Having to make such judgments is one of the problems that make many researchers uncomfortable with factor analysis.

The Factor-Score Coefficient Matrix

The factor-score coefficient matrix is produced from the factor loading matrix. The *factor-score coefficients* are regression-parameter coefficients used to convert the original variables into factors. (They are symbolized as "a" in equation 20.1.) Each factor will have a factor-score coefficient for each variable. The coefficient represents the variable's contribution to the generation of the factor. Ideally, the coefficient will be high (near unity when standardized data are used) on some variables and very low (zero or near zero) on others.

Once we have the factor-score coefficients, we can specify equation 20.1. We can then use the equations (one for each factor), to compute the factor scores for each respondent or object.

For example, the motorcycle study yielded an equation for Factor One of

$$F_1 = .7219X_1 + .0961X_2 + .6954X_3 \cdots -.2201X_{10},$$

where X_1, X_2, etc. are variables 1, 2, etc. (speed, price, etc.) and F_1 is the Factor One score for a given object (motorcycle).

A motorcycle with a high speed, and fast acceleration, etc., would get a high score on Factor One, which was named "performance."

The factor-score coefficients are calculated from the factor loadings. The method varies, depending on which technique of factor analysis is being

Table 20-2   **A Factor-Score Coefficient Matrix: Motorcycle Study**

Variable	Factor One	Factor Two
1. Speed	.7219	.1302
2. Price	.0961	.8109
3. Acceleration	.6954	.0899
4. Handling	.5231	−.1081
5. Fuel economy	−.0893	−.3962
6. Payload	.2041	.3811
7. Comfort	.1604	−.0012
8. Maintenance cost	.1463	.4618
9. Braking distance	.1072	−.1038
10. Riding ease	−.2201	−.0046

applied. The mechanics involve matrix algebra.[6] Except for the most trivial problems, the number of arithmetic calculations is horrendous. Again, a computer is essential.

The output of this process is the factor-score coefficient matrix. The *factor-score coefficient matrix*—also called the "factor-estimate matrix"—is simply the set of factor-score coefficients. We see an example in Table 20-2.

Fortunately, the availability of library programs relieves us of the need to master the intricacies of matrix algebra. The availability of computers relieves us of the tedium, which would make factor analysis virtually unusable.

In applying factor analysis, we must remember to distinguish between the factor loading matrix and the factor-scores coefficient matrix, as they look somewhat alike. The factor loading matrix is used to evaluate and label the factors. It tells us how well the factors group and summarize the variables. It tells us if further factor analysis—using a different algorithm, different options, or possibly extracting a different number of factors—is in order. We hope the factor loading matrix also reveals hidden relationships, hence structure.

---

[6] For the reader familiar with matrix algebra: When the principal-components method is being used, the factor-score coefficient matrix ($\mathbf{F}$) is computed from the factor loading matrix ($\mathbf{A}$) as follows:

$$\mathbf{F} = (\mathbf{A}^T\mathbf{A})^{-1}\mathbf{A}^T$$

If classical factor analytic methods are being used:

$$\mathbf{F} = \mathbf{A}^T\mathbf{R}^{-1},$$

where $\mathbf{R}$ is the correlation matrix. See Henry F. Kaiser, "Formulas for Component Scores," *Psychometrika* **27**:1 (March 1962), pp. 83–87, and Harry H. Harman, *Modern Factor Analysis* (Chicago: University of Chicago Press, 1967), p. 352.

The factor-score coefficient matrix is used to compute the factor scores for each of our cases (respondents or objects). This allows us to reduce the number of variables, hence shrink our data set.[7] As we'll see shortly, that has a number of advantages.

Evaluation and Labeling

The typical computerized algorithm produces the factor loading matrix and the factor-score coefficient matrix in the same run. These are evaluated and labeled by the researcher. If some unrelated variables load heavily against a common factor, there are a lot of ambiguous variables, or few variables have significant loadings, a return to step three is in order. By switching to a different algorithm or selecting different options within a given algorithm, results may be improved. They may also get worse. Factor analysis may not work.

Often the researcher thinks any one of several approaches may work. Many computerized algorithms allow different analyses to be performed during the same run. This saves time and lowers computer charges.

Once factors are produced that are unique as well as consistent with both theory and common sense, labels can be attached. We saw an example earlier.

Factor Scores

Once the researcher is comfortable with the results of the factor analysis, he or she will likely want factor scores. One can compute factor scores for each case (respondent or object) using the full set of factor-score coefficients and their variables for each factor. This way, each of the observed variables will play some part, however small, in determining each factor score. If this is acceptable, the scores can likely be computed and assigned to their appropriate case by the same program that did the basic analysis. In fact, many computerized algorithms offer this option during, or subsequent to, the basic analysis.

The researcher may elect to purge certain variables from some factors. An ambiguous variable, or one with a weak factor loading, is a candidate for exclusion. Again, this is a subjective decision.

If variables are to be excluded from select factors, they and their factor-score coefficients must be removed from equation 20.1. This will require the rewriting of the equation and its reentry into the computer. This is required for each select factor.

Once the factor scores are computed for each case, they can be used like any other variable. For instance, in our motorcycle study, they were

---

[7] For the reader familiar with matrix algebra the relationships between the original data matrix (**X**), the factor scores matrix (**F**), and the factor loadings matrix (**A**) is:

$$\mathbf{X} \simeq \hat{\mathbf{X}} = \mathbf{AF}$$

where $\hat{\mathbf{X}}$ is the matrix of the estimate values of **X**.

used to compare competing brands and models in terms of performance (Factor One) and economy (Factor Two).

Updating the Data File

The next step in the factor-analysis process is usually to add the factor scores to their respective cases in the original data file. Each case will now contain the original variables plus the new factors. As further analysis is invoked, those variables represented by the new factors will likely be ignored. Only the factors will be used.

Alternative Methods

Popular Algorithms

Factor analysis is not a unitary concept. Like most multivariate methods, it embraces a number of independent solution systems. Some of the more popular algorithms are:

> Principal components analysis[8]
> Classical factor analysis
> > Rao's canonical factoring
> > Alpha factoring
> > Image factoring

   Although each algorithm serves the same objective—the production of a few factors from a lot of variables—their assumptions and mechanics vary. Also, each algorithm offers options that allow the solution system to be varied even more.

   In practice, one typically tries two or three algorithms and different options on the same data. One then takes the output that is most consistent with common sense, economic and behavioral theory, and the objectives of the study.

Principal Components Analysis

Principal components analysis is geometric in nature. The method creates one or more axes in space which summarize the original dimensions (variables) of the respondents or objects.

   We saw an example back in Chapter 16 (Figure 16-3), which listed eleven brands of bread. Each object (brand) had two important dimensions: protein content and vitamin content. Each dimension (variable) was scaled on an axis, with the two axes forming an attribute space. Each brand was then plotted in this space. The plot was analogous to a map. Only instead of a pair of north–south/east–west axes we have a pair of protein-content/

---

[8] Principal components analysis is sometimes considered separately from other methods of factor analysis. However, as its objective is the same, we collect it under the general heading of factor analysis.

vitamin-content axes. The concept was the same. In fact, the attribute space is often called an "attribute map."

If one wanted to compare or rank the objects, having them positioned on a single dimension would be very helpful. Principal components analysis creates such a dimension—called a "principal component," "principal axis," or "factor"—by rotating the axes. Figure 16-3 illustrated: The rotated axis (II) became the new dimension summarizing the original two dimensions. Each brand was positioned on this single factor which we labeled "nutrition." The space, number of variables (dimensions), and data have all been reduced.

The principal components algorithm seeks to retain as much of the interpoint distance information, or variance, as possible. In fact, the amount of variance retained in the factor (principal component) is an indication of the success of the analysis. If that statistic is high, say 90 percent, we've lost little information in the space-reduction process.

We cannot graphically illustrate the method with more than three variables. Even a three-dimensional space is awkward to draw. However, we can apply the technique mathematically with n-number of variables. The SPSS program[9] admits up to 100 variables, which it reduces to whatever number of factors is desired by the user.

Classical Factor Analysis

Principal components analysis seeks to retain as much interpoint distance between objects as possible. Classical factor analysis seeks to produce the most distinct and interpretive factors. The outputs of both techniques are similar. However, if we emphasize one property, such as interpoint distance, we must make some sacrifice in the other one.

Classical factor analysis decomposes each variable into one or more factors and an error term. (This is illustrated by equation 20.2.) The error term is produced only by classical analysis and includes all residual variation in the variable not explained by the factors. It is similar in meaning to the error term, hence residual, in regression analysis.

A portion of the error term (we don't know how much) is presumed to be another factor. The remaining factors—those specified in the equation—are common factors.

Where principal components analysis is essentially geometric in its generation of factor loadings, classical factor analysis is statistical. Principal components analysis starts with the data and generates a model. Classical factor analysis starts with a model (there are several) and sees how well the data fit. It then estimates the parameters (factor loadings) of the model. In classical factor analysis, one is forced to make a priori assumptions about the underlying structure of the data.

Selection

Principal components analysis is probably the most common method of factor analysis. The researcher who has little experience with factor analysis

---

[9] FACTOR, found in the Statistical Package for the Social Sciences.

is well advised to stick with this method. As he or she becomes more comfortable with factor analysis, the classical techniques may be applied.[10]

Principal components analysis is the most straightforward method of transforming a set of variables into a new and smaller set of factors. It requires neither the faith or number of judgments demanded by classical factor analysis. The method also consumes less computer time—a significant consideration when the budget is short or the que is long.

Principal components analysis does not produce an error term because the variables are transformed directly into factors. There is no estimation process, as we have in classical factor analysis. Some of the variation is simply lost. This is a disadvantage of the method: It makes the factor loadings less precise, hence the factors are less unique and more difficult to interpret. This is motivation for going to classical factor analysis. Classical factor analysis tends to yield the most unique and interpretable factors.

Applications

Factor analysis has four applications:

Data condensation and simplification   The number of original variables can be reduced and summarized in a smaller number of factors.

Structural analysis   The latent factors (hidden dimensions) which determine the relationship between objects can be revealed.

Analysis of relationships between variables   Hidden relationships between variables can be revealed.

Clustering   Groupings of objects can be revealed that were previously obscure.

An Example

Again the Broadway study serves as an example.[11] First, the data were condensed and simplified: Three factors were extracted from the original 26 variables.[12] The factor loading matrix, seen in Table 20-3, was used to identify the components of each factor. An examination of the

---

[10] For a discussion, see Jae-On Kim, "Factor Analysis," in Norman H. Nie et al. *SPSS: Statistical Package for the Social Sciences*, 2nd ed. (New York: McGraw-Hill, 1975), p. 480. This article, pp. 468–508, is an excellent introduction to the theory and practical application of factor analysis.

[11] The author is indebted to Elizabeth Siegel, formerly of the Marketing Research Department, Broadway Department Stores, for use of the material in our example. These data were slightly altered in recognition of the proprietary nature of the study. The alteration does not change the essential nature of the problem, however.

[12] As each respondent rated each of the six stores, each respondent produced six sets of observations (one set for each store). Thus, 3,912 cases were available for the factor analysis. (Several hundred were thrown out because of nonresponse to questions on some stores.) The stores, not the respondents, thus became the objects.

Table 20-3   **A Factor Loading Matrix: Department Store Study**

No. Variables: Consumer Ratings	Factor One	Factor Two	Factor Three	Communality
1. Price	.6493	.0312	.1248	.73
2. Section	.1109	.0895	.8501	.80
3. Sales	.5813	.0934	−.2033	.42
4. Quality	−.1910	.1711	.5211	.58
5. Value	.6349	.1402	.3012	.77
6. Style	−.1979	.0018	.7014	.81
7. Salespersons—friendliness	.1010	.6205	.1879	.55
8. Salespersons—knowledge	−.0984	.5415	.3891	.69
9. Salespersons—availability	−.1389	.7290	.2081	.68
10. Salespersons—appearance	−.0021	.0128	.0815	.08
11. Credit policy	.4892	.1799	.1025	.42
12. Merchandise-return policy	.1806	.3584	−.0956	.32
13. Delivery service	.1022	.3631	.1171	.40
14. Gift wrapping	−.1568	.3217	.2015	.41
15. Atmosphere	−.1038	.2112	.4800	.50
16. Parking	.0012	.2655	.1992	.28
17. Reliability of advertising	.1161	.0421	.2815	.41
18. Quality of Advertising	.1231	.0188	.4132	.53
19. Attractiveness	.0977	.1243	.1082	.10
20. Prestige	−.2866	.3177	.3812	.56
21. Patronage by friends	.0283	.1861	.2056	.23
22. Ease of locating merchandise	−.1092	.1272	.0065	.12
23. Crowdedness	.0568	−.1922	.0181	.09
24. Convenience	.1231	.0293	.1336	.18
25. Youthfulness	.0813	.1028	.0099	.09
26. Progressiveness	.1084	.1266	.1126	.19

Table 20-4   **Main Components of Factors: Department Store Study**

Factor One: Economic Image	Factor Two: Service Image	Factor Three: Merchandise Image
Price	Salespersons—friendliness	Selection
Sales	Salespersons—knowledge	Quality
Value	Salespersons—availability	Style
Credit Policy	Merchandise-return policy	Atmosphere
	Delivery service	Quality of advertising
	Gift wrapping	Prestige
	Prestige	

components set, shown in Table 20-4, suggested the labels "economic image," "service image," and "merchandise image" for the three factors. (Variables which loaded weakly or ambiguously were excluded.) As we are focused on the variables, not the respondents, this is *R*-analysis.

Second, the variables (components) assigned each factor were scrutinized to identify hidden relationships. The variables which load heavily on the same factor tend to move together. That is, they're correlated. Often they are considered proxies for one another. In this case, we see an interesting relationship between the quality of advertising and other merchandise-related variables. Atmosphere and prestige are also part of the merchandise image—a finding that is consistent with the multidimensional concept of the product.[13] These revealed relationships have important implications for store management: Namely, the merchandise image is sensitive to things besides the physical goods.

Third, the structure of the market was described, and the stores were positioned. This was done by using the factors to construct the attribute maps seen in Figures 20-2 and 20-3. The six stores were then positioned in the spaces by computing their scores for each of the axes (factors) forming the spaces.[14]

The individual factor scores were computed by entering the means of the variables, for each store, in the equation for each factor. For example, Factor One contains four variables, each with a coefficient drawn from the factor-score coefficient matrix. (Weak loading and ambiguous variables were excluded.)

$$F_1 = .6813X_1 + .5421X_3 + .7100X_5 + .2829X_{11},$$

where F_1 = Factor score for Factor One, "Economic Image"

X_1 = Price rating

X_3 = Sales rating

X_5 = Value rating

X_{11} = Credit-policy rating

The ratings are the values awarded the store by the respondents on a semantic differential scale of one to five. The average ratings (transformed to standardized values) for store A, a popular discount house, are .44, .23, −.10, and −.31 for price, sales, value, and credit policy. Hence, store A gets a mean Factor One score of .27, computed as follows:

$$F_1 = .6813X_1 + .5421X_3 + .7100X_5 + .2829X_{11}$$
$$\text{(Factor One Equation)}$$

$$F_{1,\text{Store A}} = .6813(.44) + .5421(.23) + .7100(-.10) + .2829(-.31)$$
$$\text{(by substitution)}$$

$$F_{1,\text{Store A}} = -.27$$
$$\text{(by arithmetic)}$$

---

[13] This concept holds that a product has many significant dimensions, only a few of which are physical properties. For instance, psychological dimensions can be important.

[14] Do not confuse this with *Q*-analysis. The factor analysis algorithm was used to combine variables, not respondents. We have simply used the new variables (the factors) to compare stores.

Figure 20-2   **A Two-Dimensional Attribute Map: A Department Store Study**

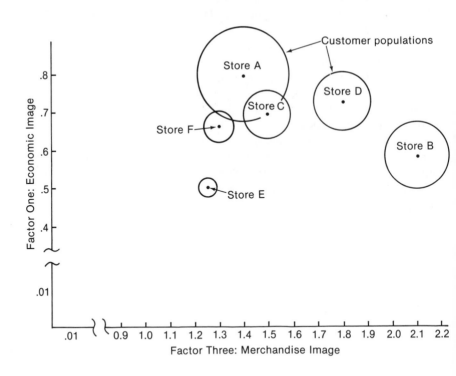

Figure 20-3   **A Three-Dimensional Attribute Map: A Department Store**

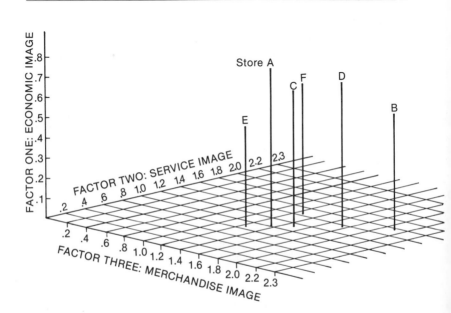

Table 20-5 **Factor Scores: Department Store Study**

| | Mean Factor Scores[a] | | |
Store	Factor One Economic Image	Factor Two Service Image	Factor Three Merchandise Image
A	.87	.990	1.41
B	.58	1.58	2.10
C	.69	1.12	1.52
D	.73	1.32	1.81
E	.50	.83	1.26
F	.66	1.40	1.30

[a] A constant was added to each score (F_j) to make all scores positive, hence forcing them into the upper right quadrant on the graph. This facilitated plotting and made interpretation easier for the line managers. It did not change the relative standings.

These ratings are tallied in Table 20-5. Notice we now have the stores scaled in three dimensions. We started with 26. Now we can easily compare the stores.

Negative Scores and Data Presentation

Almost always, we standardize our variables (step 2). Consequently, we get some negative values for each X. We can also expect some negative factor-score coefficients. As a result, we will get some negative factor scores for some of our cases. This is normal. As factors are indexes, not absolute values, we should not be disturbed by the minus signs. Our interest rests in the order of, and the interval between, our cases on each dimension (factor).

These negative values can confuse the layperson. So, rather than digress on an explanation of the subtleties of factor analysis, many researchers confront management with all positive values. They simply add a constant to each factor score. If one is drawing a two-axes (2-factor) attribute map, this will drive all of the objects into the upper-right quadrant. In a three-axes space, this will avoid extending the axes beyond the origin, which can be a bit messy.

In the Broadway study, 0.6 was added to each Factor One score, 1.2 was added to each Factor Two score, and 1.5 was added to each Factor Three score. This did nothing to the essence of the findings, but made the information more digestible for line management. The store comparisons quickly made sense.

The comparisons are especially vivid in Figure 20-3. Each store has been enclosed by a circle representing its customer population.[15] The market is

---

[15] Again, do not confuse this with Q-analysis. The relative size of each respondent group is shown simply to indicate the popularity of the stores. Respondents had already been grouped by their store preference. Factor analysis was not used to group respondents. It was used to summarize many variables into a few factors which in turn were used to position the stores.

clearly segmented. One group of buyers—mainly store A's customers—clearly prefers good economics to high-quality merchandise. These people are sensitive to price, sales, value, and credit. This is the biggest segment. There is another important segment—mainly store B's customers—preferring quality over bargains. In between, there appears a segment where economics are compromised with quality. Stores C, E, and F indicate there are very small segments for the store with a poor image in both economics and merchandise. These stores need to reposition themselves in the direction of store A or B. The shift toward store A is clearly the shortest and probably the easiest and most profitable.

How does management shift position? It adjusts its marketing mix. It comes down hard on those elements, such as price and credit policy, that strongly affect factor scores.

Our attribute maps, coupled with our information on the relative performance of each store, reveal the structure of the Tucson department store market. However, to reveal further why the Tucson consumers behave the way they do, Broadway researchers turned to discriminant analysis.

Problems

1   What is the main objective of factor analysis?
2   What is a factor score?
3   What is a factor loading?
4   What are some of the penalties encountered in factor analysis?
5   In the motorcycle study, cited in the chapter, the following factor scores were produced for some popular street bikes:

		Factor One	Factor Two
1	BMW R100/7	.788	.872
2	BMW R60/7	.581	.709
3	Honda Gold Wing	.710	.712
4	Honda 750K	.771	.647
5	Honda 400 TI	−.032	.315
6	Honda 200	−.189	−.113
7	Harley Davidson E/G	.531	.811
8	Harley Davidson Sportster	.709	.755
9	Kawasaki KZ1000	.842	.685
10	Kawasaki KZ650	.511	.490
11	Kawasaki KZ400	−.102	.309
12	Kawasaki KZ200	−.210	−.105
13	Suzuki GS750	.705	.681
14	Suzuki GS550	.415	.481
15	Yamaha XS1100	.839	.698
16	Yamaha XS650	.498	.320
17	Yamaha SR500	.401	.265

Construct an attribute map and position each object in the attribute space. Analyze the map: Do you see any hole that might be worth filling? What would you do to improve the relatively weak sales of the two Harley Davidson bikes?

6 The Broadway researcher chose principal components analysis to produce the factor loading matrix. This method promised the greatest interpoint distances (distances between stores in the attribute space). Unfortunately, it produced some messy loadings and factors that were not as unique as they might have been. How could more unique, hence cleaner, factors have been produced? What would be the penalty?

Chapter 21
Discriminant Analysis

Key Concepts

Fundamentals
Definitions, objectives, and other basic ideas

Model Building
Alternative ways to construct a linear discriminant model

Dealing with Multilevel Dependent Variables
Problems and solutions when the dependent variable has more than two levels

Applications
Classification and analysis with discriminant analysis

Key Terms

categorical variable	discriminators
linear discriminant analysis (LDA)	boundary function
	dichotomous variable
multilinear discriminant analysis	n-variable
	k-variable
linear discriminant function	step-wise discrimant analysis
	classification function
discriminant score	group centroid
discriminant function	confusion matrix
critical value	classification results matrix

Fundamentals

Marketing researchers are often asked to explain or predict a phenomenon represented by a categorical variable. A *categorical variable* is one that divides into nominal levels. An example is buyer behavior which could be divided into two levels (also called "categories," "classes," or "groups"), such as buy and do-not-buy. Another example is store preference, which might be divided into multiple levels, such as Sears/J. C. Penney/Montgomery Ward/other. When confronted with a dependent variable that is categorical, the researcher often invokes discriminant analysis.

Definitions

As we said earlier in our survey of multivariate methods, *discriminant analysis* is a method for estimating the relationship between a nominal (categorical) variable and one or more independent variables. Of course, the nominal variable is the dependent one and the independent variables are the explanatory variables. In discriminant analysis, these explanatory variables are often called "discriminating variables" or simply "discriminators." The discriminators must be metric before entry into the analysis. However, nonmetric variables can usually be transformed into metric ones by use of dichotomous variables. Unfortunately, as we saw in Chapter 17, the transformation causes a proliferation of variables. The additional variables may be difficult to manage, especially if one is limited to a relatively small sample size.

Linear discriminant analysis (LDA) is a method for estimating a linear relationship between a categorical variable and one or more discriminators. Multilinear discriminant analysis, a special case of LDA, is a method of estimating a linear relationship between a categorical variable and two or more discriminators.

Objectives

Discriminant analysis has two objectives: analysis and classification. Analysis refers to the identification and evaluation of the discriminators. For example, a chain store used LDA to analyse the performance of store managers. The categorical variable, performance, had three levels: superior, average, and below average. The independent variables were age, education, retail experience, marital status, family size, and test scores. The analysis revealed which of these variables were statistically important in determining the level of performance. It told management what to look for in job candidates.

Classification refers to the use of the discriminant model (produced by the LDA) to classify respondents or objects. This is sometimes referred to as "prediction." In the chain store case, the model was used to classify candidates for store manager jobs as a superior, average, or below average performer. When the model classified (predicted) a candidate as below average, he or she was dropped or subject to further evaluation. Those candidates classified as superior were hired or promoted into the job, unless information not included in the model (such as a criminal record) indicated they should not be hired.

Often prediction (classification) is of no interest. Neiman-Marcus did a LDA on data collected on patrons of Houston specialty stores such as

Sak's, Lord and Taylor, Sakowitz, Foley's, and itself. The analysis revealed those characteristics which discriminated among the Neiman-Marcus customers and the customers of each of the competing stores. (The dependent variable was store patronage.) Neiman-Marcus's management was then able to focus on these characteristics and disrupt some of the established loyalties in the Houston market. There was no purpose in using the model to classify customers who had not revealed their store preference.

Models

There are several common algorithms for use in discriminant analysis. Each yields slightly different results in slightly different forms, as we'll see shortly. However, each produces some kind of a discriminant function and a classification function.

Discriminant Function   *A linear discriminant function* is a linear combination of discriminant variables in the general form:

$$D = d_1 X_1 + d_2 X_2 \cdots + d_n X_n,$$ [21.1]

where

D = the discriminant value

d = a parameter specifying the relationship between D and X

X = a discriminating variable

$1, 2, \ldots n$ = identifiers for the discriminating variables

Analysis focuses on the discriminant function. The discriminant function tells us how powerful each discriminator is in determining the classification of a respondent (or object). For instance, if d_1 was large and d_2 was small, we'd conclude that X_1 was more powerful than X_2 in determining the level of our categorical variable. Of course, the discriminators must be measured against similar scales, or standardized as is usually done, for such comparisons to be valid.

The discriminant function allows us to compute the discriminant value—often called *discriminant score*—for each respondent. Respondents in the same category will tend to have similar scores. For instance, if we have two categories—say, buyer and nonbuyer—the buyers might have scores near .837 and the nonbuyers scores near −.635. This brings us to classification.

Classification Functions   To assign unclassified respondents (or objects) to a level within the categorical variable, we need a criterion. There are several, depending on which algorithm is used. For example, we might have a group mean for each level. A respondent would then be assigned to the group (level) with the mean closest to his or her discriminant score.

In a two-level model—one with a categorical variable of two levels, such as buyer and nonbuyer—we might have a critical value. A *critical value* is the boundary between a pair of adjoining levels. Respondents scoring above the critical value would be assigned to one level. Respondents with discriminant scores below the critical value would be assigned to the other level.

The critical value is found in the boundary function which is produced by the algorithm. A *boundary function* is a simple formula specifying the critical value. An example is seen in equation 21.3.

Another alternative to the classification problem is to have a set of classification functions that calculate the probability of group membership for each level (group) of the categorical variable. The respondent is then assigned to the level for which he or she has the highest probability of membership.

Rarely will LDA provide a model that will properly classify each respondent or object. Some buyers will be classified as nonbuyers, some Sears patrons will be classified as J. C. Penney customers, and so forth. In fact, one way we evaluate a LDA model is to see what portion of our cases (respondents or objects) it correctly classifies. Occasionally it does little better than we would expect to do by random assignment. Like other multivariate methods, discriminant analysis sometimes works poorly or not at all. Marketing research can still produce problems more readily than solutions.

Model-building

Our perception of linear discriminant analysis is enhanced if we can see a graphical replica of an LDA model. Better yet, we should walk through the construction of a model, then build one ourselves. (The end-of-the-chapter problems offer the reader the latter opportunity.)

To these ends, we have chosen a simple problem with a two-level categorical variable and two discriminant variables. Our solution system is the Massy LDA algorithm which yields to conventional algebra. This algorithm produces a discriminant function and a critical value.

LDA Graph

Figure 21-1 shows a linear discriminant model of a consumer group divided into two categories, buyers and nonbuyers, on the basis of two independent variables, X_1 and X_2. The critical value of the categorical variable, Y_C, is 30. (Note: The dependent variable, Y, is not represented on either axis, since both are needed to measure independent variables.) The critical-value line—the boundary function—is an isoquant[1] of Y. Specifically, it is the set

---

[1] An isoquant is a line of constant value.

Figure 21-1   A Linear Discriminant Model Showing Buyers and Nonbuyers

Source: Adapted from William F. Massy, "Discriminant Analysis of Audience Characteristics," *Journal of Advertising Research*, vol. 5, no. 1 (March 1965), p. 40.

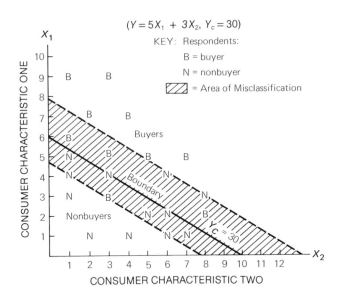

of all positive $X_1 X_2$ pairs that, when substituted into the equation, will yield the critical value of Y (30, in the example). Thus, any member of the population whose Y score falls below the line is assigned to the nonbuyer category, and any member whose score falls above the line is assigned to the buyer category. A member who scores exactly 30 is neither a buyer or a nonbuyer, and hence is nonclassifiable.

The discriminant function relating the categorical variable, Y, to the two independent variables, X_1 and X_2, is $Y = 5X_1 + 3X_2$. The critical value, $Y_C = 30$, forms the boundary between the two levels of the categorical variable. However, several misclassifications have occurred: The equation placed one buyer in the nonbuyer category and two nonbuyers in the buyer category. This indicates that the correlation between the categorical variable and the independent variables is less than perfect; thus, the model is not wholly reliable. This is hardly surprising, since some degree of uncertainty is typical even in the most rigorous areas of marketing research.

There is an alternative to the model just described. Instead of a system of equations consisting of a discriminant function and a boundary function, we can use a set of probability functions, one for each level of the categorical variable. Given the necessary data, we can compute the probability that a given element of the population belongs to a particular category. The category with the highest probability gets the element. If the probability that an individual is a buyer is 0.81 and the probability that he or she is a nonbuyer is 0.19, the individual is assigned to the buyer category. (The probabilities must sum to unity for each element.)

Specifying the Model

A linear discriminant model can be specified intuitively. For instance, the decision to commercialize or not to commercialize a product may be a function of the profit, the fixed cost, the probable volume of business, the capital and resources needed, and such qualitative variables as its compatibility with the current product line, its marketability, and its probable effect on the corporate image. The independent variables are scaled and the coefficients are determined by executive judgment. The coefficients are in effect weights, placing the desired emphasis on each of the determinants. The judgment process often involves a number of executives and marketing specialists, with the scale calibrations and coefficients being decided by a consensus. This is not rigorous, but it will work in some cases.

Specifying a discriminant model rigorously usually requires sophisticated statistical techniques and advanced mathematics. The complexity of the computations varies with the number of levels in the categorical variable and the number of independent variables. A categorical variable with two levels, sometimes called a *dichotomous variable*, involves relatively simple mathematics. A categorical variable with three or more levels, called an *n-variable* or a *k-variable*, requires more complicated handling.

Unfortunately, linear regression analysis cannot be used in this case, because of the nonmetric nature of the dependent variable. A discriminant model frequently resembles a linear regression model and has similar applications. However, the two models are significantly different and should not be confused.

In order to specify a linear discriminant model, we need certain raw data: We need a sample, preferably random, of population elements distributed between the two or more nominal categories (levels) in proportion to the relative size of those categories in the population as a whole. Thus, if 80 percent of the population are nonbuyers, 80 percent of the sample should be nonbuyers. In addition, values for each independent variable to be incorporated into the model are needed. These are obtained by observing or questioning the sample elements.

The researcher should try to include in the model all the independent variables that have a significant influence on an element's classification. Those that prove insignificant can be dropped, but their insignificance should be noted since this information may be of value to the line marketer.

Often the researcher has a large assortment of independent variables and can only guess at which ones would be strong discriminators. There are four solutions to this dilemma.

First, one can enter all likely variables into the model. As this will require a large sample size, this solution may be impractical.

Second, one can use trial-and-error, performing LDA on likely combinations of variables. This is time-consuming, expensive, and likely to lead to an inferior solution.

Third, one can first apply factor analysis to reduce a large portion of the variables to a few factors, then enter the factors into the LDA. This option is useful when many of the variables are similar, as is often the case with life-style dimensions. Of course, the researcher must sacrifice information as well as lump together both strong and weak discriminators.

A fourth solution is stepwise discriminant analysis. This procedure is analogous to stepwise regression analysis. In a stepwise algorithm, discriminating variables are entered in the model one at a time in order of their discriminating power. (The stepwise option is offered by both the SPSS and BioMed programs.) The procedure keeps adding new discriminators until additional discriminators make little or no contribution to the model's discriminating power. Of course, the researcher can choose a model with anywhere from one discriminating variable to as many as are ultimately entered by the stepwise procedure. The researcher can also suppress selected variables if there is some reason for their exclusion. When one has more than five or six independent variables in the data set, stepwise LDA is usually the preferred method.

The Massy Algorithm[2]

The Massy solution system, adapted from an algorithm first developed by R. A. Fisher, is easier than most methods. Unfortunately, it works only for two-level models with two independent variables.

The algorithm produces two equations: The first is the discriminant function, which expresses the discriminant value, Y, of a population element, i, as a function of two independent variables, X and Z. The discriminant value is compared to the critical value, Y_C, to determine which category an element is in.

The second equation is the boundary function and specifies the critical value, Y_C, as a constant. This constant is the boundary between the categories. If the discriminant value, Y, of an element, i, is larger than Y_C, then the element is assigned to one category. If Y_i is less than Y_C, the element is assigned to the other category. The further Y_i is from Y_C, the more likely it is that the element i is being properly classified.

The general forms of the discriminant and boundary functions that constitute the model are

$$Y_i = c_X X_i + c_Z Z_i \tag{21.2}$$

[2] William F. Massy, "Statistical Analysis of Relations Between Variables," in R. E. Frank, A. A. Kuehn, and W. F. Massy, eds., *Quantitative Techniques in Marketing Analysis* (Homewood, Ill.: Irwin, 1962), pp. 95–100.

and

$$Y_C = k \qquad\qquad [21.3]$$

where

Y_I = the discriminant value of the ith element of the population
c_X = a parameter specifying the relationship between Y and X
c_Z = a parameter specifying the relationship between Y and Z
X_i = an explanatory variable
Z_i = an explanatory variable
Y_C = the critical value (i.e., the boundary between the two categories)
k = a constant
(Note: X and Z are used in lieu of X_1 and X_2 to avoid double subscripts.)

The parameters c_X and c_Z are specified by the following equations:

$$c_X = \frac{S_{ZZ}d_{\bar{X}} - S_{XZ}d_{\bar{Z}}}{S_{ZZ}S_{XX} - (S_{XZ})^2} \qquad\qquad [21.4]$$

$$c_Z = \frac{S_{XX}d_{\bar{Z}} - S_{XZ}d_{\bar{X}}}{S_{ZZ}S_{XX} - (S_{XZ})^2} \qquad\qquad [21.5]$$

S_{XX}, S_{ZZ}, and S_{XZ} are sample moments,[3] found by substituting the observed data into the following equations

$$S_{XX} = \sum_{i=1}^{n} (X_i - \bar{X})^2 \qquad\qquad [21.6]$$

$$S_{ZZ} = \sum_{i=1}^{n} (Z_i - \bar{Z})^2 \qquad\qquad [21.7]$$

and

$$S_{XZ} = \sum_{i=1}^{n} (X_i - \bar{X})(Z_i - \bar{Z}) \qquad\qquad [21.8]$$

---

[3] A moment is a statistical measurement, similar in this case to the variance and covariance of X and Z.

where

X_i = the observed value of the independent variable X for element i

$\bar{X}$ = the mean of the observed values of X

Z_i = the observed value of the independent variable Z for element i

$\bar{Z}$ = the mean of the observed values of Z

The d's in equations 21.4 and 21.5 are the differences between the means of X and Z in the two categories:

$$d_{\bar{X}} = \bar{X}^* - \bar{X}^\circ \qquad\qquad\qquad [21.9]$$

and

$$d_{\bar{Z}} = \bar{Z}^* - \bar{Z}^\circ, \qquad\qquad\qquad\qquad [21.10]$$

where

$d_{\bar{X}}$ = the difference between the means of X in the two categories

$d_{\bar{Z}}$ = the difference between the means of Z in the two categories

$\bar{X}$ and $\bar{Z}$ are defined as before

* and ° represent the two categories

The critical value of Y, Y_C, can be determined in several ways. One method is to average the two extremes of the range of overlapping elements. Often an analyst who arrays the elements in order of their Y values finds that some of the elements falling into the first category are sandwiched between elements falling into the second category. This indicates that the model misclassifies some of the elements, which is to be expected. If this range of overlap is small, the model is considered precise. If there is no overlap—if the model is very precise—Y_C can be specified as the average of the Y values of the two closest first- and second-category elements. Often, judgment is the best basis for specifying Y_C. The analyst simply selects a value (usually one midway between two adjoining, but categorically different, observations) that minimize the number of observed misclassifications.

Solution Procedure   The solution procedure for finding the parameters and specifying the Massy model is as follows:

1   Tally the data, preferably using a matrix.
2   Sum the observed values of each explanatory variable, X and Z.
3   Compute the mean of X and Z.
4   Compute the deviations and then the squared deviations of X_i and Z_i for each observation i.
5   Use formulas 21.6, 21.7, and 21.8 to compute S_{XX}, S_{ZZ}, and S_{XZ}.

6   Compute the average X and Z value for the two categories of the dependent variable.

7   Use formulas 21.9 and 21.10 to compute $d_{\bar{x}}$ and $d_{\bar{z}}$.

8   Use formulas 21.4 and 21.5 to specify parameters c_X and c_Z.

9   Specify the discriminant function by substituting these values in equation 21.2.

10   Specify the boundary function, equation 21.3, by averaging the Y_i values of the elements within the area of misclassification, or by judgment.

You are now prepared to classify the elements of the population whose Y values have not been observed and must be predicted. You are also in a good position to judge the sensitivity of group membership to each of the explanatory variables.

Example   An example will help to clarify the application of this algorithm. Suppose we assume that a firm has developed an industrial process that is radically different from established methods and fairly expensive to install. To use promotional resources efficiently during the new process's introductory phase, the marketer must identify the innovators and early adopters in the market population.[4] The cost and novelty of the new process suggests that prospects' financial resources and technical progressiveness will be the primary determinants of demand. Revenue data on various firms is available from *Moody's Industrial Manual*. Memberships in major trade and technical societies are a practical proxy for technical progressiveness.[5] The seller too belongs to these organizations, and has little difficulty in obtaining membership lists.

Revenue, X, and memberships, Z, are determined for a cross section of 20 prospects, each of whom is subjected to an intensive sales campaign. Six of the prospects become buyers. Linear discriminant analysis is then used to determine if the two variables, X and Z, are useful in distinguishing between buyers and nonbuyers.

The data are tallied in matrix form, and the appropriate sums, deviations, squares, and products computed in accordance with steps 2, 3, and 4 in the solution procedure. S_{XX}, S_{ZZ}, S_{XZ} are then computed, along with $d_{\bar{x}}$ and $d_{\bar{z}}$ (steps 5 through 7), and the parameters c_X and c_Z specified (step 8). The data needed for the analysis and the computations involved are shown in Table 21-1.

The discriminant function is specified simply by substituting the values found for c_X and c_Z (0.0014 and 0.0494) in equation 21.2. The boundary

---

[4] See Everett M. Rogers, *Diffusion of Innovations* (New York: Free Press, 1962), for a discussion of the introduction of innovative products and classes of prospective buyers.

[5] See C. F. Carter and B. R. Williams, "The Characteristics of Technically Progressive Firms," *Journal of Industrial Economics* 7:2 (March 1959), p. 59, for a list of qualities associated with innovative firms. Or see Walter B. Wentz, *Marketing* (St Paul, MN: West Publishing Co., 1979), p. 140.

Table 21-1   Sample Calculations for Linear Discriminant Analysis

Obs. (i)	Behavior (Buy/Do not buy)	Revenue (in \$ millions) (X)	Deviations of X (X − X̄)	Squares of Deviations of X (X − X̄)²	Memberships in Trade Assoc., etc. (Z)	Deviations of Z (Z − Z̄)
1	N	4	−14	196	3	−1
2	B	20	2	4	7	3
3	B	8	−10	100	3	−1
4	N	12	−8	64	0	−4
⋮	⋮	⋮	⋮	⋮	⋮	⋮
18	N	7	−11	121	3	−1
19	B	26	8	64	6	2
20	N	18	0	0	1	−3
		$\Sigma X = 360$		$\Sigma(X - \bar{X})^2 = 1{,}630$	$\Sigma Z = 80$	
		$\bar{X} = 18$		$S_{XX} = 1{,}630$	$\bar{Z} = 4$	

Buyers   = 6
Nonbuyers = 14
     Total   20

$$c_X = \frac{S_{ZZ}d_{\bar{X}} - S_{XZ}d_{\bar{Z}}}{S_{ZZ}S_{XX} - (S_{XZ})^2} \qquad \text{(given as equation 21.4)}$$

$$c_X = \frac{120(7.1) - 87(6.7)}{120(1{,}630) - (87)^2} \qquad \text{(by substitution)}$$

$$c_X = 0.0014 \qquad \text{(by arithmetic)}$$

function is specified by selecting a value midway between prospects 3 and 18 that minimizes the number of observed misclassifications (see Table 21-2). Hence the linear discriminant model for the firm's prospects is

$$Y_i = 0.0014X_i + 0.0494Z_i$$

$$Y_C = 0.1587$$

Two observations out of 20 are misclassified (prospects 8 and 14). The range of observed misclassifications is 0.1399 to 0.1683; untested prospects which the model places within that range ($0.1399 \le Y_i \le 0.1683$) would be considered ambiguously or unreliably classified. On the whole, however, the model appears to be an effective instrument for distinguishing between good and bad prospects. Thus, it should help the firm in allocating its promotional resources, especially its sales force, more efficiently.

To apply the model, the analyst simply takes a new prospect's revenue (sales) and the number of memberships it holds in trade associations and technical societies, and substitutes these figures for X_i and Z_i in the equation. The resultant Y_i value is compared to the boundary value, Y_C, to determine whether the firm is a good or bad sales prospect. The Y_i value can also be used to array prospects according to their purchase probabilities. For instance, a prospect with a Y_i value of 0.3824 would be a good prospect and would be ranked above prospects with a lower Y_i. A firm whose revenue and

Squares of Deviations of Z $(Z - \bar{Z})^2$	Products of X and Z Deviations $(X - \bar{X})(Z - \bar{Z})$	Tallies of Buyers and Nonbuyers			
		Buyers (X^*)	Nonbuyers (X°)	Buyers (Z^*)	Nonbuyers (Z°)
1	14		4		3
9	6	20		7	
1	10	8		3	
16	32		12		0
$\vdots$	$\vdots$	$\vdots$	$\vdots$	$\vdots$	$\vdots$
1	11		7		3
4	16	26		6	
9	0		18		1
$(Z - \bar{Z})^2 = \overline{120}$	$\Sigma(X - \bar{X})(Z - \bar{Z}) = \overline{87}$	$\Sigma X^* = \overline{168}$	$\Sigma X^\circ = \overline{292}$	$\Sigma Z^* = \overline{52}$	$\Sigma Z^\circ = \overline{28}$
$S_{ZZ} = 120$	$S_{XZ} = 87$	$\bar{X}^* = 28$	$\bar{X}^\circ = 20.9$	$\bar{Z}^* = 8.7$	$\bar{Z}^\circ = 2$

$$d_{\bar{X}} = \bar{X}^* - \bar{X}^\circ \qquad d_{\bar{Z}} = \bar{Z}^* - \bar{Z}^\circ$$
$$d_{\bar{X}} = 28 - 20.9 \qquad d_{\bar{Z}} = 8.7 - 2$$
$$d_X = 7.1 \qquad d_{\bar{Z}} = 6.7$$

$$c_Z = \frac{S_{XX}d_{\bar{Z}} - S_{XZ}d_{\bar{X}}}{S_{ZZ}S_{XX} - (S_{XZ})^2} \qquad \text{(given as equation 21.5)}$$

$$c_Z = \frac{1{,}630(6.7) - 87(7.1)}{120(1{,}630) - (87)^2} \qquad \text{(by substitution)}$$

$$c_Z = 0.0494 \qquad \text{(by arithmetic)}$$

membership statistics yielded a value below the boundary, Y_C (0.1587), would be rejected as a bad prospect. Of course, the new prospect could be mis-classified, especially if its Y_i value were near the boundary. The model is hardly perfect, but it is certainly more reliable than an arbitrary ranking procedure. If the firm has special information about a particular prospect that contradicts the model, its classification can always be changed.

Cooley-Lohnes Algorithm   This is a more complex and general solution method, using a classification system based on probabilities. Whichever category a population element is most likely to belong to is the one to which it is assigned. Thus, if the probability is 0.56 that the ith element is a member of the jth category, it is assigned to that category. This is called the *maximum likelihood criterion.*

An element's probability of membership in a particular category is determined by equation 21.11,[6] which is based on Bayesian statistics and solved by matrix algebra.

$$P_{i_j}(H_j | \mathbf{X}_i) = \frac{(p_j/|\mathbf{D}_j|^{1/2})[e - (\chi_j^2/2)]}{\sum (P_K/|\mathbf{D}_K|^{1/2})[e - (\chi_k^2/2)]} \qquad [21.11]$$

---

[6] William W. Cooley and Paul R. Lohnes, *Multivariant Procedures for the Behavioral Sciences* (New York: Wiley, 1962), p. 138. See pp. 146–149 for a computer program, CLASSIF, that solves the equation.

Table 21-2   **A Prospect Array Based on a Linear Discriminant Model**
$(Y_C = 0.0014X_C + 0.0494Z_I, \ Y_C = 0.1587)$

Observed Prospect (i)	Discriminant Value (Y_i)	Actual Behavior (Buy/Do not buy)	Category Predicted by Model
$\vdots$	$\vdots$	$\vdots$	Buyer
2	.3738	B	
19	.3328	B	
11	.2446	B	
8	.1683	N (Misclassification)	
3	.1594	B	
——————— Boundary (Y_C)———————			Range of Misclassifications (.1399 to .1683)
18	.1580	N	
1	.1538	N	
14	.1399	B (Misclassification)	
7	.1023	N	
15	.0985	N	
20	.0746	N	
12	.0321	N	
4	.0168	N	
$\vdots$	$\vdots$	$\vdots$	Nonbuyer

where

$P_{i_j}(H_j|\mathbf{X}_i)$ = the probability of hypothesis j, given the score vector, $\mathbf{X}$, of element i. H_j states that element i is a member of group j

p = an *a priori* or posterior probability of an element's membership in a particular category, j or k; the relative proportion of the population in category j or k

$\mathbf{D}$ = the dispersion (variance-covariance) matrix of category j or k

e = the Napierian number, 2.71828

χ^2 = the chi-square statistic of category j or k

$\chi^2 = \mathbf{X}_i'\mathbf{D}^{-1}\mathbf{X}_i$

where

$\mathbf{X}$ = m-element vector of deviation scores,
$\mathbf{X}_i = [X_{1i} - \bar{X}_1, X_{2i} - \bar{X}_2, \ldots X_{mi} - \bar{X}_m]$

$\mathbf{D}^{-1}$ = inverse of the dispersion (variance-covariance) matrix of category j or k. Matrix is of order m

i = the number of an element in the population; $i = 1, 2, \ldots N$, where N = population size

j = a category of the dependent variable

k = a category of the dependent variable $k = 1, 2, \ldots j, \ldots g$, where g = the total number of categories

With the Cooley–Lohnes system, one set of probabilities is required for each element in the population being classified. Once the probabilities are known, classification is easy. Using the maximum-likelihood criterion, we simply assign the element to the category with the highest probability. However, solving the algorithm itself requires a knowledge of statistics and mathematics beyond the scope of this book. An analyst unfamiliar with matrix algebra will need the help of a mathematician, unless he has access to a packaged computer program that can handle the manipulations.[7]

Dealing with Multilevel Dependent Variables

Instead of a two-way classification (buyer/nonbuyer, etc.), the dependent variable may have three or more levels. An example would be brand preference, such as GM/Ford/Chrysler/AMC/Toyota/Datsun/other. This makes LDA more difficult. The problems of computation and interpretation gets much messier as the levels of the categorical (dependent) variable increase beyond two.

The greater complexity of the computational processes should not be intimidating if library programs are available. Programs such as SPSS's "DISCRIMINANT"[8] handle multilevel problems as conveniently as two-level ones. Unfortunately, the interpretation of the multilevel-problem output cannot be handled so easily.

A value for a given discriminant function can be computed for each case (respondent or object) in the study. One can then group similar cases (those at the same level) and compute their means. For a single group, the mean discriminant score is called the "group centroid." A group centroid can be thought of as the center of gravity of its group.

---

[7] For an introduction to matrix algebra, see any good business-mathematics text such as Dennis E. Grawoig, *Decision Mathematics* (New York: McGraw-Hill, 1967), chs. 1 and 2. The BioMed Series includes packaged computer programs for LDA such as 'BMD07M'. IBM's "DMATX" and "DISCR" are also applicable.

[8] See William R. Klecka, "Discriminant Analysis," in Norman H. Nie, *SPSS: Statistical Package for the Social Sciences*, 2nd ed. (New York: McGraw-Hill, 1975), pp. 434–467, for an introduction to discriminant analysis and a guide to the use of SPSS's DISCRIMINANT program.

Figure 21-2   **Discriminate Spaces**

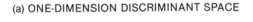
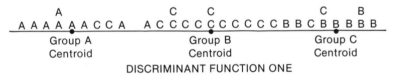
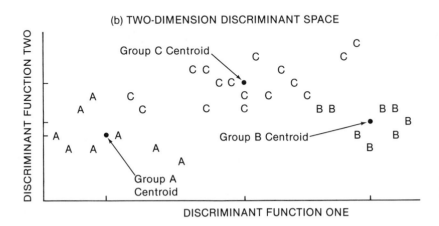

(a) ONE-DIMENSION DISCRIMINANT SPACE

DISCRIMINANT FUNCTION ONE

(b) TWO-DIMENSION DISCRIMINANT SPACE

DISCRIMINANT FUNCTION ONE

The group centroid can be plotted on an axis. By comparing the positions of the centroids (one for each group) on a single axis, we can see how well that particular discriminant function separates each group. Figure 21-2(a) illustrates.

We note in Figure 21-2(a) that there is some overlapping of members of the three groups. This suggests we invoke a second discriminant function, hence a second axis, to further separate the several groups (levels) within our categorical variable. These levels are denoted by A, B, and C. They cluster rather neatly, with no overlapping, in the two-dimensional space. (See Figure 21-2(b).) Note, however, that discriminant function number two is a rather weak discriminator. If it alone were used, we'd have a rather confused jumble of objects, with considerable overlapping of groups.

The computer program typically orders the discriminant functions from best (strongest) to worst (weakest). It also provides some tests, such as the *t*-statistic, to evaluate each function's significance.

With more than two discriminant functions, we cannot draw diagrams like those we saw in Figure 21-2. Assigning an object to a particular level (group) with one or two functions is easy. We simply assign it to the group whose centroid is closest to the discriminant-function score of the object. (With two functions, we could plot the object in the discriminant space and assign it to the group with the nearest centroid.) Unhappily, this method breaks down when we have three or more discriminant functions. Of course, we could base our assignment exclusively on the first (best) or on the first and second functions. This would cause us to sacrifice some useful information, for we would have fewer discriminant functions. It would also increase the chance of misclassification.

Classification Functions

The solution to the preceding dilemma rests with classification equations. These can be specified several ways.[9] They take the form:

$$C_i = k + c_{i,1}V_1 + c_{i,2}V_2 \cdots + c_{i,n}V_n, \tag{21.12}$$

where

C_i = the classification score for group (level) i

k = a constant

$c_{i,n}$ = a classification coefficient

V_n = the raw (unstandardized score) of a discriminant variable

n = the identifier of the variable

There is a separate equation for each group. Hence, a classification score must be computed for each group for each case being assigned: If there were four groups, four equations would be used to compute four scores for a given case. That case would then be assigned to the group whose equation produced the highest score.

Again, one can ignore the mathematics if a computer and library program are available. The classification equations and the classification scores for each case can be produced during the basic discriminant-analysis run.

The Confusion Matrix

Some discriminant-analysis programs, such as SPSS's DISCRIMINANT and BioMed's BMD05M, will produce a confusion matrix. A *confusion matrix* is a two-way classification table showing how many cases were classified correctly and how many cases were classified incorrectly. Table 21-3 illustrates.

The confusion matrix—also called a "classification results matrix"— suggests the quality of the discriminant function(s). A high portion of misclassifications would imply a low level of discriminating power.

---

[9] See Nie, *SPSS: Statistical Package*, pp. 445–446, for discussion and for an explanation of the traditional method.

Table 21-3   **A Confusion Matrix**

Actual Groups	Number of Cases	LDA Classifications				Portion Correctly Classified, %
		Brand X Buyers	Brand Y Buyers	Brand Z Buyers	Other Brand Buyers	
Brand X Buyers	50	46	2	0	2	92
Brand Y Buyers	80	7	68	2	3	85
Brand Z Buyers	40	3	10	25	2	63
Other Brand Buyers	38	4	2	3	29	76

Total cases: 80.8% correctly classified

The confusion matrix produced by the typical library program is based on the same cases used to specify the LDA model. Thus, the results are biased in favor of correct classifications.

Ideally, the LDA model should be tested with a set of cases not used in specifying the model. (Those cases should be drawn from the same population as the ones used to build the model.) If the researcher is rich in observations, he or she might do a split-half analysis: Half the cases, randomly selected, are used to specify the model. The other half are used for the confusion matrix. Unfortunately, the researcher seldom has this luxury and is unwilling to reduce sample size in return for some independent test cases.

Applications

Classification

In prediction the objective of LDA is to classify (by categorical level) unclassified objects. For example, two scholars used discriminant analysis to identify innovators and noninnovators in a market population.[10] The identification of innovators and their special characteristics is necessary to the understanding of innovation diffusion.

A food processing company used discriminant analysis to predict which snack food formulations would be most liked.[11] The findings guided management in new product development.

---

[10] Thomas S. Robertson and James N. Kennedy, "Prediction of Consumer Innovators: Application of Multiple Discriminant Analysis," in David A. Aaker, *Multivariate Analysis in Marketing: Theory and Application* (Belmont, Calif.: Wadsworth, 1971), pp. 142–153.

[11] James H. Myers and Edward Tauber, *Market Structure Analysis* (Chicago: American Marketing Association, 1977), pp. 57–67.

Analysis

In analysis, the objective is to learn which independent variables determine the classification of an object. For example, Cessna used discriminant analysis to determine why some buyers chose turboprop aircraft and others selected small jet aircraft. (Cessna built a small jet plane, but no turboprop aircraft at the time.) The two types were very similar in price. The findings were used in formulating the firm's promotional strategy and product line. One result was the addition of a turboprop aircraft to the product line.

A researcher used discriminant analysis to learn what social and economic characteristics determined FM station choice in the Boston SMSA.[12] Such information made media selection more objective for local FM advertisers.

In its Tucson study, the Broadway Department Stores invoked discriminant analysis to analyze the effect of perceived store characteristics and shopper demographic qualities on store preference. The initial study was supplemented later by a psychographic study of the original respondents. The psychographic traits were distilled to three life-style factors by factor analysis. Discriminant analysis was then applied to see how powerful the life-style factors were in determining store patronage. The two analyses allowed Broadway merchandisers to adjust their product mix and promotion to better satisfy the target segments of the Tucson market.

One of the earliest, and perhaps classic, applications of discriminant analysis was Evans' study of Ford and Chevrolet buyers. For years, the folklore of the auto industry held that Ford and Chevrolet owners had had different personalities. Evans demonstrated that personality characteristics were virtually useless in classifying these buyers as Ford or Chevrolet customers.[13]

In short, discriminant analysis is a powerful tool. The technique belongs in the repertoire of the serious marketing researcher.

Problems

1   Define the following terms:

        categorical variable
        linear discriminant analysis
        discriminant function
        group centroid
        classification function

[12] William F. Massy, "Discriminant Analysis of Audience Characteristics," in Aaker, *Multivariate Analysis in Marketing: Theory and Application*, pp. 122–126.

[13] Franklin B. Evans, "Psychological and Objective Factors in the Prediction of Brand Choice: Ford vs. Chevrolet," *Journal of Business* (October 1959), pp. 340–369.

2   Suggest several marketing-research problems that could be solved by linear discriminant analysis. Explain why this method of analysis is more appropriate than other techniques.

3   Family size and income appear to be the most significant determinants of repeat purchases of a particular class of high-priced recreational goods. Data have been gathered on ten repeat-buyer households, each of which traded up to a larger unit. Data have also been gathered on ten households that did not make repeat purchases. The family size and income of each of the ten repeat-buyer households is 4, $15,000; 3, $20,000; 2, $12,000; 5, $16,000; 4, $18,000; 3, $22,000; 5, $16,000; 4, $20,000; 2, $10,000; and 6, $14,000. The data for non-repeat buyers are 3, $9,000; 2, $15,000; 3, $12,000; 4, $15,000; 2, $13,000; 3, $11,000; 4, $10,000; 2, $15,000; 3, $18,000; and 2, $17,000. Construct a model that will identify repeat and nonrepeat buyers, using as inputs the family size and income of present owners. Evaluate the sensitivity of repeat purchases to each of the two determinants and evaluate the accuracy of the model.

4   What are the problems in dealing with a categorical variable of three or more levels?

Part 7
Summary

Multivariate analysis is a set of statistical tools used to find meaning in the simultaneously occurring effects of multiple variables. The techniques fall into two classes. First is the functional (dependence) methods which deal with dependency between one or more dependent variables and multiple independent (determinant) variables. These techniques include regression analysis, discriminant analysis, multivariate analysis of variance, and canonical analysis.

The second class of methods is the structural (interdependence) methods which deal with the grouping of variables and the describing of their underlying relationships (structure). These techniques include factor analysis, cluster analysis, multidimensional scaling, nonmetric scaling, conjoint measurement, and latent structure analysis.

Regression analysis is the most pervasive tool in multivariate analysis. It is a statistical method of estimating the explicit relationship between a dependent variable and one or more independent variables.

The bivariate regression model is the simplest and can be specified using conventional algebra. Multivariate linear regression models (which have two or more independent variables) are usually specified by matrix algebra, although conventional algebra can be used if the equation is small. A computer is normally used in model specification and is virtually essential when there are more than three independent variables or a large number of observations.

A formal statistical evaluation of regression models is important, for the models can be very misleading. The tools used for this purpose are the t-test, the coefficient of determination, the F-test, the standard errors of the parameters, the residuals, the intercept, common sense, and economic theory.

Special problems, unique to regression analysis—such as spurious correlation, lack of variance, identification problems, covariance, and multicollinearity—can distort the model. Fortunately, these and other problems can usually be detected and often remedied or reduced to a tolerable level.

Both time-series and cross-sectional data are used in regression. Time-series data are sometimes more accessible than cross-sectional data, but are more vulnerable to exogenous disturbances. In addition, they're subject to autocorrelation. Autocorrelation can usually be identified with the aid of the von Neumann ratio (the K-statistic) and eliminated by introducing an additional (and lagged) variable. Cross-sectional data are not affected by the time-related disturbances associated with time-series data, but they entail other problems such as heterogeneity and isolation.

Curvilinear regression analysis produces more realistic models when real-world relationships are nonlinear. Unfortunately, the techniques are not well developed, and the construction and statistical evaluation of a meaningful curvilinear model is not always possible. Some curvilinear models, such as parabolic bivariate and exponential models, can be transformed into linear equations for computational purposes.

Although not so common as regression analysis, factor analysis and discriminant analysis are being diffused in marketing research. Factor analysis seeks to reduce a large number of observed variables to a small number of factors. When the method works, each factor contains the essence of the variables it represents. The factors, being few in number, are much easier to manage than the original data.

Discriminant analysis seeks to specify the relationship between a dependent categorical (hence nonmetric) variable and multiple independent variables. Discriminant analysis is used to predict the classification (group membership) of unclassified objects, such as store patrons. It is also used to analyze relationships—to identify those variables that influence classification.

Multivariate analysis allows us to draw meaning out of a crazy quilt of data. When it works, it lets us confront a swirl of forces and make sense out of what is going on.

Case Study 7

Jurgensen's Grocery Company: A Store Location Problem

Walter B. Wentz

The Jurgensen's Grocery Company is a 44-year-old firm currently consisting of 23 retail food stores supported by a warehouse, bakery, and corporate office. The company caters mainly to the older, smaller, and more affluent households. It offers personalized service, home delivery, charge accounts, superb foods and beverages (many are house brands), accessories, and high prices. One of its units is seen below.

A Jurgensen's Store

Source: Courtesy Jurgensen's Grocery Company.

One store is near a university, hence is denied a liquor license. The others carry a broad line of liquors at regulated prices and the best selection of wines in the state. Seventeen are full-line stores. The rest do not carry fresh produce and some staples. Several are in resort areas.

The young president, son of the founder, is smart, Stanford-educated, and aggressive. He is ambitious and dissatisfied with recent growth—sales have held near $14 million annually—and the declining earnings. He wants to prune the chain of its perennial losers and establish new stores in profitable trading areas. He is willing to attempt salvaging the losers by installing new managers and injecting extra promotional effort, provided the exogenous determinants of store sales will yield a reasonable probability of success. Where the exterior conditions are bad, he wants to shut down. He also wants a more rigorous method for selecting new-store locations to avoid repeating past disasters.

Marketing Decisions

1   Select stores to be closed.
2   Select money-losing stores to be salvaged (hopefully) with new managers and an infusion of recuperative promotion.
3   Decide where new stores should be installed.

Information Needs

1   The identification and evaluation of the exogenous determinants of sales.
2   The identify of stores that cannot survive profitably in their trading areas.
3   The identity of stores now losing money, which might be salvagable.
4   An estimate of the expected revenues that would be yielded by new stores at several prospective sites.

Data

To be profitable, a full-line store must yield a minimum revenue of $600.000 yearly. A limited-line store must have sales of at least $400,000.

A geographic plot of a random selection of each store's charge account customers suggests that 72 percent of their customers are within two miles of the store. (This finding is consistent with other grocery studies found in the literature.) Hence, the natural trading areas are defined as areas in a two-mile radius from the stores. These circular trading areas are altered, however, where geographic or cultural features warrant. For

Table C7-1   Jorgensen's Grocery Company: Store Location Data

No.	Established-store Locations	Sales (× 1000)	Full-line	Resort Area	In Shopping Center	Total Population (× 1000)	Population ≥ 35 (× 1000)	Population ≥ 45 (× 1000)	Median Income (× $1000)	Families with Income $15,000–24,999	Families with Income ≥ $25,000	Professional and Tech. Workers	Officials and Managers	Houses $35,000–49,000	Houses > $49,000	Competitors A[b]	Competitors B[c]
1.	Glenfield	$890	✓			60.1	30.7	28.1	13.2	1,672	1,899	3,317	3,202	2,022	2,418	1	1
2.	Las Flores	629	✓	✓		52.2	27.1	19.5	12.8	1,531	1,419	2,682	2,701	2,239	2,045	0	1
3.	Ocean View	522	✓[a]			17.6	9.2	7.1	9.7	582	205	498	510	1,472	923	0	1
4.	University City	748	✓		✓	99.3	47.6	37.0	11.2	1,382	1,861	2,987	3,105	2,674	7,538	0	0
5.	Elmwood	577	✓			78.5	30.9	21.8	10.9	2,168	1,482	2,768	2,922	2,015	5,648	1	0
6.	Halmark No. 1[d]	654				147.3	79.1	74.1	13.6	1,783	2,562	3,210	3,100	4,896	10,195	1	0
7.	San Pasqual	705	✓			68.1	36.7	29.2	15.1	1,932	1,764	2,873	2,805	2,633	2,446	1	0
8.	Halmark No. 2	928	✓			147.3	79.1	74.1	13.6	1,783	2,562	3,210	3,100	4,896	10,195	0	0
9.	Pasadores	134			✓	109.0	40.5	28.2	10.1	948	218	914	1,191	1,609	451	1	0
10.	Los Toros	644	✓	✓		263.0	147.6	11.9	13.9	1,682	1,580	3,890	3,701	3,478	2,596	0	1
11.	Seascape	660	✓			20.4	11.2	9.1	9.9	1,200	513	1,048	1,030	977	1,258	1	0
12.	Harbor City	433		✓		59.1	23.4	17.1	11.8	1,481	402	1,021	1,121	3,024	1,279	0	1
13.	Carmel No. 1[e]	776	✓	✓		28.1	15.4	12.1	12.9	1,373	1,038	596	671	3,564	2,197	0	0
14.	Carmel No. 2	383		✓		28.1	15.4	12.1	12.9	1,373	1,038	596	671	3,564	2,197	0	0
15.	Spaville	420	✓	✓		25.2	13.8	11.7	11.9	1,262	260	518	627	789	729	0	0
16.	Mountainside	466		✓		N/A	N/A	N/A		N/A	N/A	N/A	N/A	N/A	N/A	0	0
17.	Arroyo Seco	756				85.9	34.9	27.6	12.9	1,720	1,989	3,289	3,461	2,785	4,590	0	0
18.	Jefferson	686			✓	180.1	91.4	72.0	11.2	1,923	1,421	3,162	3,321	614	2,260	0	1
19.	Balboa	613	✓			78.1	34.3	29.1	9.9	879	125	428	861	379	175	0	0
20.	Tootsville	800			✓	59.8	32.9	27.0	10.9	1,621	2,001	2,817	2,761	1,961	2,619	1	2
21.	Porterton	414	✓			205.1	81.1	69.2	10.8	1,041	4,991	1,401	2,001	1,231	648	0	1
22.	Carryville	593		✓		82.2	44.6	29.9	11.3	1,201	259	1,418	1,980	914	461	0	0
23.	Appleton	210				170.1	81.1	70.1	11.0	1,489	185	193	482	919	203	0	0
Prospective-store Locations																	
a	Willington	Option Open				70.2	35.6	31.4	10.9	1,293	410	1,683	1,598	1,492	941	0	1
b	Surfside			✓		26.1	13.2	10.9	9.8	1,010	921	469	1,009	2,982	1,012	0	0
c	Isota				✓	106.1	46.3	38.9	9.1	1,842	402	981	2,105	481	195	0	2
d	Forrest Valley					48.2	27.9	18.7	14.3	1,425	2,309	3,861	4,194	2,160	3,950	1	1

a No liquor.
b Very similar to Jurgensen's.
c Similar, but without all services offered by Jurgensen's.
d 2 blocks from store number 8.
e Next to store 14.

Note: The data have been disguised. However, this does not change the reality of the case, nor the conclusions that will be reached by the analysis.

example, one store has a narrow, but very long, body of water separating it from some households within the two-mile limit. These households are therefore excluded. Another store has a group of households outside its two-mile limit, but perched on a mountainside with no grocery stores closer than the Jurgensen's store. This tract is included.

Those exogenous factors that seemed to be likely determinants, or statistical proxies, of sales were listed. Their magnitude was then determined by reference to census tract data or on-site observation. Sums were tallied from all the tracts within each of the prescribed trading areas. The data are posted in Table C7-1.

Assignment   Provide the information required by management and make specific recommendations for each decision. Prepare a criterion or, better yet, a mathematical model for evaluating store locations. Explain how the model is to be used by the decision-maker.

Part 8
Forecasting

Introduction

Long before the first Volkswagen Rabbit reached a dealer's showroom, millions of deutsche marks had to be spent on tooling and committed to the procurement of raw materials and purchased parts. As the model changeover approached, employee requirements had to be specified and transportation resources had to be allocated. Financing had to be arranged.

All of these decisions rested on the firm's forecast of Rabbit sales. If the forecast was high, unsold automobiles would accumulate at the factory, in distributors' yards, and on dealers' lots. Millions of marks and dollars would be lost by the factory in extra tooling, in financing unsold inventory, and by the dealers in extra flooring costs. Volkswagen would again experience the trauma of terminating thousands of employees. On the other hand, if the forecast proved low, millions of marks and dollars in opportunity costs would be lost as disappointed car buyers turned to Toyota and Datsun.

Forecasting is a high-stakes game. It is also a science and a black art.

Formal methods of forecasting, including algorithms applicable to business and economics, date back to well before the birth of Christ. Methods of divination prescribed over 3,000 years ago—some using mathematical jargon similar to that found in current management-science journals—are still in publication and presumably in use.[1] Of course, these ancient tools are

---

[1] One of the best-known examples is the Chinese *Book of Changes*, the *I Ching*, which goes back to approximately 1150 B.C. and which has become very popular in recent years. One of the more recent translations, currently in print, is by John Blofeld, ed. (New York: Dutton, 1965).

associated primarily with astrologists, palmists, witches, warlocks, sorcerers, wizards, and sundry occult philosopers. In deference to convention, we shall confine the discussion here to the more traditional statistical methods of divination. However, we are not so presumptuous as to claim that they are superior to metaphysical techniques. A marketing-research department might find a resident wizard a significant asset.

The terms prediction and forecasting are commonly used interchangeably. We shall follow that custom. However, some researchers make a distinction between the two: They define *prediction* as the estimation of the *present* value of a variable. For instance, one might predict the potential demand in a new market, the current sales of a product in a particular SMSA, or a competitor's present advertising budget. They define *forecasting* as the estimation of a *future* value of a variable. For instance, one might forecast the future demand for consumer durables, a firm's 1985 sales, or the growth of the mobile-home market.

In Chapter 22, we survey the common methods of forecasting and confront some of its problems. We'll examine both quantitative and qualitative techniques, emphasizing the former. We shall also discuss the challenge of aggregate data and the technique of purging them of cyclical, seasonal, and irregular variation.

In Chapter 23, we study growth models. Growth models are probably the most pervasive statistical methods of forecasting future values.

Finally, in Chapter 24, we examine nonstatistical methods and the practical application of forecasting. Nonstatistical forecasting is necessary for innovations. One seldom finds historical data of similar products to suggest future demand for a true innovation.

A look at applications is important because the forecast is usually part of a complex decision process. The development and use of a forecast is shaped by many forces, not the least of which is politics.

The words of Lord Kenneth Clark may also be in order: "There is no intellectual activity more dishonest than forecasting the future."[2]

---

[2] As quoted from his *Civilization* on the *Today Show*, June 27, 1978.

Chapter 22
Forecasting: The Basic Concepts

Key Concepts

Assumptions
Three important postulates

Common Methods
Some popular techniques of forecasting

Analyzing Aggregated Data
Dealing with the four components of observed data

Reintroducing Seasonal Variation
Reentering the seasonal component for short-run forecasts

Measuring Statistical Significance
Applying the U-test

Key Terms

judgment forecast
poll forecast
casual-model forecast
regressive forecast
analytical forecast
time-series model
growth model
simulation forecast
growth curve
trend
secular trend
cyclical variation
seasonal variation

irregular variation
noise
erratic fluctuation
residual variation
smoothing
semiaverage
moving average
ratio-to-moving-average
percentage-of-moving average
seasonal index
U-value
run

Assumptions

A Relationship Between Variables

Forecasts depend on several assumptions. The first is that a relationship exists between the variable being forecast and one or more other variables that can be measured or estimated. The former is called the "dependent" variable and the latter "independent", "explanatory", or "determinant" variables (or simply "determinants").

Often a relationship is purely statistical, with little or no cause and effect between the dependent and independent variables. For example, growth curves express the dependent variable as a function of time. An equation that relates such variables as income, consumption, or revenue with time is not really saying that their value is determined by time, only that there is a convenient statistical relationship here. National income, for instance, is determined by, among other things, the amount of capital investment, the size and quality of the labor force, government monetary and fiscal policies, and business's expectations as to the future of the economy—and not by time. However, because it correlates well with time, time is a convenient assumed determinant.

Frequently an independent variable is selected because it is a good proxy of the real determinant, which cannot easily be measured, estimated, or forecast. Automobile-drivers' licenses are a nearly perfect proxy for the number of automobile drivers, which in turn is one of the determinants of the demand for automobiles and car insurance. Building permits are a good proxy for the number of new houses going up, which in turn is a key determinant of the demand for construction supplies and services. The number of licenses and permits is easily found. Hence, they are useful proxies.

Stability

The second assumption underlying forecasts is that the relationship between the variables will remain relatively stable over time and from one locale to another, or will alter in a way that can be anticipated. This is probably the shakiest assumption, for if anything is characteristic of the marketplace, it is change.

Manageability

The third assumption—required only by the more rigorous methods of forecasting—is that the relationship between the variables can be approximated by mathematical forms which are sufficiently manageable and explicit to be of practical use to the analyst. Complex curvilinear equations may serve to explain market phenomena or defend economic theories, but they are of little use in applied research if the values of the parameters cannot be specified. The computer has partially remedied the data manipulation problem, but not the data acquisition problem, inherent in these techniques. Forecasting models are developed from real-world data, and the quality of that data largely determine the quality of the model. If the data are inaccurate or nonrepresentative, the model will be poor.

Common Methods

The taxonomy of forecasting methods is rather loose. The one shown in Table 22-1 is probably as representative as any, but should not be considered as the definitive list.

Although Table 22-1 highlights the salient properties of the basic techniques, a bit more detail is in order for some common methods. This is especially true of certain time-series techniques (growth models), explored in Chapter 23, and nonstatistical forecasting, explored in Chapter 24.

Judgment Forecasts

Judgment forecasts are based on intuition and subjective evaluations. Although they are the least rigorous, they are frequently a powerful factor in decision-making. Intuition is often the only tool the researcher has, and it can be spectacularly successful. Witness the Ford Mustang, the Xerox machine, and the Piper airplane, all products that were introduced primarily on the basis of executive judgment.

Acceptance of a judgment forecast is based mostly on the reputation of the forecaster, since there are no statistical ways of evaluating it. Very often, a champion is needed to push through recommendations based on such forecasts. For example, a vice-president of the Cessna Aircraft Co. felt strongly that there was a big unexploited demand for a twin-engine airplane with its power plants mounted in tandem instead of laterally as in conventional designs. (This would prevent asymmetrical thrust, thereby reducing the hazards of flying with one engine out.) His judgment conflicted with forecasts made by more rigorous methods. Nevertheless, the company committed itself to the idea. The product was introduced, but sales fell far short of the level he estimated. Instead of backing down, the executive insisted that his analysis of demand, hence potential sales, was correct and that the fault lay in the design of the aircraft. He won his point, and the model was not dropped. An alteration in the design (the incorporation of retractable landing gear) made the product acceptable to the market, and sales rose to the level he forecast. The model became—for a time—the most successful product in the firm's line.

As was the case with the Cessna example, judgment forecasts usually require an advocate, for they seldom can stand on their own for lack of supporting data and objective analysis. Their inputs are experience and partial (usually qualitative) knowledge; their analytical tools are intuition and common sense; their evaluation is a function of faith. They are frequently ill-received, especially when they suggest a future that is substantially different from the present or involves a radically different product or promotional scheme. Chester Carlson, the inventor of the electrostatic copier, is a classic example. He was rejected by twenty potential sponsors of his Xerox machine, none of whom would accept his judgment forecast of the potential demand for his invention.

Table 22-1   Basic Forecasting Techniques

A. Qualitative Methods

Technique	1. Delphi Method	2. Market Research	3. Panel Consensus
Description	A panel of experts is inter-rogated by a sequence of questionnaires in which the responses to one questionnaire are used to produce the next questionnaire. Any set of information available to some experts and not others is thus passed on to the others, enabling all the experts to have access to all the information for forecasting. This technique eliminates the bandwagon effect of majority opinion.	The systematic, formal, and conscious procedure for evolving and testing hypotheses about real markets.	This technique is based on assumption that several ex can arrive at a better forec than one person. There is secrecy, and communicati is encouraged. The forecas are sometimes influenced social factors, and may no reflect a true consensus.

Accuracy
    Short term
    (0–3 months)
    Medium term
    (3 months–2 years)
    Long term
    (2 years & up)
	Fair to very good
	
	Fair to very good
	
	Fair to very good
		Excellent
		
		Good
		
		Fair to good
			Poor to fair
			
			Poor to fair
			
			Poor

Identification of **turning points**	Fair to good	Fair to very good	Poor to fair
Typical applications	Forecasts of long-range and new-product sales, forecasts of margins.	Forecasts of long-range and new-product sales, forecasts of margins.	Forecasts of long-range an new-product sales, forecas of margins.
Data required	A coordinator issues the sequence of questionnaires, editing and consolidating the responses.	As a minimum, two set of reports over time. One needs a considerable collection of market data from question-naires, surveys, and time series analyses of market variables.	Information from a panel experts is presented openl group meetings to arrive a consensus forecast. Again minimum is two sets of re over time.

Cost of forecasting[a]
    With a computer
    Is calculation possible
    without a computer?
	$2,000+
	Yes
		$5,000+
		Yes
			$1,000+
			Yes

Time required to develop
    an application and
    make a forecast
	2 months+	3 months+	2 weeks+

References	North & Pyke, "Probes' of the Technological Future." HBR May–June 1969, p. 68.	Bass, King & Pessemeier, *Applications of the Sciences in Marketing Management.* [New York: Wiley, 1968].	———

le 22-1   Basic Forecasting Techniques (*cont'd.*)

ualitative Methods (cont.'d)		*B. Time Series Analysis and Projection*	
4. Visionary Forecast	*5. Historical Analogy*	*1. Moving Average*	*2. Exponential Smoothing*
>phecy that uses personal its, judgment, and, when ole, facts about different rios of the future. It is cterized by subjective work and imagination; in al, the methods used are cientific.	This is a comparative analysis of the introduction and growth of similar new products, that bases the forecast on similarity patterns.	Each point of a moving average of a time series is the arithmetic or weighted average of a number of consecutive points of the series, where the number of data points is chosen so that the effects of seasonals or irregularity or both are eliminated.	This technique is similar to the moving average, except that more recent data points are given more weight. Descriptively, the new forecast is equal to the old one plus some proportion of the past forecasting error. Adaptive forecasting is somewhat the same except that seasonals are also computed. There are many variations of exponential smoothing: some are more versatile than others, some are computationally more complex, some require more computer time.
	Poor Good to fair Good to fair	Poor to good Poor Very poor	Fair to very good Poor to good Very poor
	Poor to fair	Poor	Poor
:asts of long-range and product sales, forecasts rgins.	Forecasts of long-range and new-product sales, forecasts of margins.	Inventory control for low-volume items.	Production and inventory control, forecasts of margins and other financial data.
of possible scenarios the future prepared by a xperts in light of past i.	Several years' history of one or more products.	A minimum of two years of sales history, if seasonals are present. Otherwise, less data. (Of course, the more history the better.) The moving average must be specified.	The same as for a moving average.
t	$1,000+ Yes	$.005 Yes	$.005 Yes
k +	1 month +	1 day −	1 day −
———	Spencer, Clark & Hoguet, *Business & Economic Forecasting.* (Homewood, Ill.: Irwin, 1961).	Hadley, *Introduction to Business Statistics.* (San Francisco: Holden-Day, 1968).	Brown, "Less Risk in Inventory Estimates." HBR July–August 1959, p. 104.

Continued on Next Page →

Table 22-1   Basic Forecasting Techniques (*cont'd.*)

Time Series Analysis and Projection (*cont'd.*)

Technique	3. Box-Jenkins	4. X-11	5. Trend Projections
Description	Exponential smoothing is a special case of the Box-Jenkins technique. The time series is fitted with a mathematical model that is optimal in the sense that it assigns smaller errors to history than any other model. The type of model must be identified and the parameters then estimated. This is apparently the most accurate statistical routine presently available but also one of the most costly and time-consuming ones.	Developed by Julius Shiskin of the Census Bureau, this technique decomposes a time series into seasonals, trend cycles, and irregular elements. Primarily used for detailed time series analysis (including estimating seasonals); but we have extended its uses to forecasting and tracking and warning by incorporating other analytical methods. Used with special knowledge, it is perhaps the most effective technique for medium-range forecasting— three months to one year— allowing one to predict turning points and to time special events.	This technique fits a trend to a mathematical equation and then projects it into the future by means of this equation. There are several variations: the slope-characteristic method, polynomials, logarithms, and so on.

Accuracy
   Short term
     (0–3 months)
   Medium term
     (3 months–2 years)
   Long term
     (2 years & up)
	Very good to excellent
	
	 Poor to good
	
	 Very poor
		Very good to excellent
		
		 Good
		
		 Very poor
			Very good
			
			 Good
			
			 Good

Identification of turning points	Fair	Very good	Poor
Typical applications	Production and inventory control for large-volume items, forecasts of cash balances.	Tracking and warning, forecasts of company, division, or department sales.	New-product forecasts (particularly intermediate-long-term).
Data required	The same as for a moving average. However, in this case more history is very advantageous in model identification.	A minimum of three years' history to start. Therefore, the complete history.	Varies with the technique. However, a good rule of thumb is to use a minimum five years' annual data to start. Therefore, the complete history.

Cost of forecasting[a]
   With a computer
   **Is calculation possible
   without a computer?**
	$10.00
	 Yes
		$10.00
		 No
			Varies with application
			 Yes

Time required to develop an application and make a forecast	1–2 days	1 day	1 day –
References	Box-Jenkins, *Time Series Analysis, Forecasting & Control*. (San Francisco: Holden-Day, 1970).	McLaughlin & Boyle, "Time Series Forecasting." American Marketing Association Booklet, 1962, Marketing Research Technique Series No. 6.	Hadley, *Introduction to Business Statistics*. (San Francisco: Holden-Day, 1 Oliver & Boyd, "Technique Production Control," Imperial Chemical Industr 1964.

ble 22-1   Basic Forecasting Techniques (*cont'd.*)

'ausal Methods

1. Regression Model	*2. Econometric Model*	*3. Intention-to-buy and Anticipation Surveys*	*4. Input-output Model*
functionally relates sales .her economic, competitive, ternal variables and nates an equation using the -squares technique. tionships are primarily yzed statistically, although relationship should be ted for testing on a ınal ground.	An econometric model is a system of interdependent regression equations that describes some sector of economic sales or profit activity. The parameters of the regression equations are usually estimated simul-taneously. As a rule, these models are relatively expensive to develop and can easily cost between $5,000 and $10,000, depending on detail. However, due to the system of equations inherent in such models, they will better express the causali-ties involved than an ordinary regression equation and hence will predict turning points more accurately.	These surveys of the general public (a) determine intentions to buy certain products or (b) derive an index that mea-sures general feeling about the present and the future and estimates how this feeling will affect buying habits. These approaches to forecasting are more useful for tracking and warning than forecasting. The basic problem in using them is that a turning point may be signaled incorrectly (and hence never occur).	A method of analysis con-cerned with the interindustry or interdepartmental flow of goods or services in the economy or a company and its markets. It shows what flows of inputs must occur to obtain certain outputs. Considerable effort must be expended to use these models properly, and additional detail, not normally available, must be obtained if they are to be applied to specific businesses. Corporations using input-output models have expended as much as $100,000 and more annually to develop useful applications.
d to very good d to very good	Good to very good Very good to excellent Good	Poor to good Poor to good Very poor	Not applicable Good to very good Good to very good
good	Excellent	Good	Fair
casts of sales by product ?s, forecasts of margins.	Forecasts of sales by product classes, forecasts of margins.	Forecasts of sales by product class.	Forecasts of company sales and division sales for industrial sectors and subsectors.
al years' quarterly history ıtain good, meaningful onships. Mathematically ssary to have two more ırvations than there are ıendent variables.	The same as for regression.	Several years' data are usually required to relate such indexes to company sales.	Ten or fifteen years' history. Considerable amounts of information on product and service flows within a corpora-tion (or economy) for each year for which an input-output analysis is desired.
	$5,000+ Yes	$5,000 Yes	$50,000+ No
ınds on ability to identify ionships.	2 months+	Several weeks	6 months+
ınd, de Cani, Brown, & Murray, *Basic* ttics *with Business Appli-* ıs. (New York: Wiley, .	Evans, *Macro-economic Activity: Theory, Forecasting & Control.* (New York: Harper & Row, 1969).	Publications of Survey Re-search Center, Institute for Social Research, University of Michigan, and of Bureau of the Census.	Leontief, *Input-Output Economics.* (New York: Oxford University Press, 1966).

Continued on Next Page →

Table 22-1   Basic Forecasting Techniques (*cont'd.*)

C. *Causal Methods* (*cont'd.*)

Technique	5. Economic Input-output Model	6. Diffusion Index	7. Leading Indicator	8. Life-cycle Analysis
Description	Econometric models and input-output models are sometimes combined for forecasting. The input-output model is used to provide long-term trends for the econometric model; it also stabilizes the econometric model.	The percentage of a group of economic indicators that are going up or down, this percentage then becoming the index.	A time series of an economic activity whose movement in a given direction precedes the movement of some other time series in the same direction is a leading indicator.	This is an analysis and forecasting of new-product growth rates based on *S*-curves. The phases of product acceptance by the various groups such as innovators, early adapters, early major, late majority, and laggards are central to the analysis.
Accuracy **Short term** (0–3 months)	Not applicable	Poor to good	Poor to good	Poor
Medium term (3 months–2 years)	Good to very good	Poor to good	Poor to good	Poor to good
Long term (2 years & up)	Good to excellent	Very poor	Very poor	Poor to good
Identification of turning points	Good	Good	Good	Poor to good
Typical applications	Company sales for industrial sectors and subsectors.	Forecasts of sales by product class.	Forecasts of sales by product class.	Forecasts of new-product sales.
Data required	The same as for a moving average and *X*-11.	The same as an intention-to-buy survey.	The same as an intention-to-buy survey + 5 to 10 years' history	As a minimum, the annual sales of the product being considered or of a similar product. It is often necessary to do market surveys.
Cost of forecasting[a] **With a computer** **Is calculation possible without a computer?**	$100,000 No	$1,000 Yes	$1,000 Yes	$1,500 Yes
Time required to develop an application and make a forecast	6 months +	1 month +	1 month +	1 month +
References	Evans & Preston, "Discussion Paper 138." Wharton School of Finance & Commerce, The University of Pennsylvania.	Evans, *Macro-economic Activity: Theory, Forecasting & Control.* (New York: Harper & Row, 1969).	Evans, *Macro-economic Activity: Theory, Forecasting & Control.* (New York: Harper & Row, 1969).	Bass, "A New Product Growth Model for Consumer Durables" *Management Science*, January 1969.

[a] These estimates are based on the experience of Chambers, Mullick, and Smith using this machine configuration: an IBM 360-40, 2 system and a Univac 1108 Time-Sharing System, together with such smaller equipment as G. E. Time-sharing and IBM 360-30's and 11 *Source:* John C. Chambers, Satinder K. Mullick, and Donald Smith, "How to Choose the Right Forecasting Technique." *Harvard Business Review*, 49:4 (July–August 1971), p. 54. Copyright © 1971 by the President and Fellows of Harvard College. All rights reserved.

The Delphi Method.[1] The Delphi method of forecasting is the canvassing of experts for their opinions. In essence, this is the same technique discussed in our exploration of surveys in Chapter 5. The method has become fairly sophisticated in the hands of its more zealous practitioners.

Frequently, in fact ideally, each expert is given all of the information available to every other expert. Often a feedback system is provided to inform the participants of the conclusions of their fellow experts. As a result, the Delphi process can take several months. At no time are the experts brought together (ideally). This is to avoid dominance by one or more outspoken participants and the bandwagon effect.

The Delphi method can involve a few participants or thousands. It can become institutionalized. For instance, the McGraw-Hill Company regularly surveys executives to gather forecasts of investment, sales, and capacity. The Security and Exchange Commission conducts a similar survey. A summary of their findings are then published.

Some people, individually or collectively, seem to have an uncanny intuition for what is going to happen. Professor Gerald Eyrich illustrates the potential efficiency and accuracy of the Delphi method with this anecdote:

> I was asked by a client, Santa Anita Race Track, to build an econometric model to forecast track attendance. The model was to be used for short-run predictions of daily gate receipts. It was to guide management in staffing the track.
>
> During my preliminary study I discovered that the employees had organized a betting pool. The daily pool was won by the employee whose attendance estimate came closest to the day's receipts. The estimates were submitted nearly a week in advance. The mean estimate invariably fell within a few hundred units of the actual attendance figures—an error of less than 2 percent. I advised the client that the firm already had a superb forecasting system operating right under its nose and not to spend its money with me. Econometrics has not yet reached the advanced state of the betting pool.[2]

Poll Forecasts

Poll forecasts are based on the expressed intentions of members of the market population, who have been polled by one of the conventional survey techniques—mail questionnaires, or telephone or personal interviews. A *poll* is a collection of individual forecasts from the elements sampled in the survey. If the respondents were randomly selected, then the tools of inferential statistics can be used to evaluate the data. However, the researcher and the

---

[1] An introduction to the basics of the Delphi method is found in Marvin A. Jolson and Gerald L. Rossow, "The Delphi Process in Marketing Decision Making," *Journal of Marketing Research* **8**:4 (November 1971), pp. 443–448. For a *tour de force*, see Harold A. Linstone and Murray Turoff, *The Delphi Method: Techniques and Applications* (Reading, MA: Addison-Wesley, 1975).

[2] As related by Gerald I. Eyrich to the author.

decision-maker must remember that the mean, dispersion, and standard error of the estimate and the confidence interval about it all pertain to the population's estimate of the future value of the variable, not its true value.

For instance, assume that a sample survey of purchasing agents reveals an average estimate of 153 million tons of steel to be consumed during the coming calendar year. The range of possible error is computed to be 145 million to 153 million tons at the 90 percent confidence level. What the analyst is saying is that the true value of the average *estimate* rests between 145 million and 153 million tons. The actual value for the year's steel consumption may be considerably different. The decision-maker will have to pass judgment on the collective wisdom of the purchasing agents before making any decisions based on the poll.

He or she may get some help from the researcher, if a similar poll has been taken in past years. In that case, the previous years' estimates can be compared to the actual values and an estimate made of the range of error possible at a given confidence level. The residuals from the previous polls simply are tallied, and their mean and standard deviation computed. The magnitude of error (possible at the desired confidence level) can then be computed, using either the t- or the Z-statistic, depending on the number of residuals. Given the magnitude of possible error, the confidence interval can be easily found. (The statistical techniques for performing this evaluation are explained in Appendix 2.)

Poll forecasts—often called "market-research forecasts"—are susceptible to all the errors that plague statistical surveys, plus those due to bad judgment, ignorance, and uncertainty among the respondents. The respondents' judgment, especially with respect to future events such as purchase behavior, can be very poor, as various consumer and voter polls have demonstrated.[3] Even a broad consensus can be misleading, although the advocates of polling would argue that many of the fiascoes—such as the poll forecasts of the Landon and Dewey presidential election victories in 1936 and 1944—were caused by a bad research design or poor execution, not by any inherent deficiency in the method.

Poll forecasting is quite popular, and some commercial research organizations such as Nielsen, Gallup, and Harris specialize in this field. Many periodicals, among them *Fortune, Business Week, Forbes,* and a number of special-interest trade journals, also use polls. Even universities have gotten into the act. Among the best known of the academic poll-takers are the Survey Research Center at the University of Michigan and the Survey Research Center at UCLA.

Poll forecasts are very common in business firms. For instance, surveys are often made of, or by, a company's sales force to get a consensus of future demand. (Such a poll may be a collection of judgment forecasts.) Poll forecasts are often used as a basis for the prior probabilities associated with Bayesian statistics.

---

[3] Witness the Harris poll forecast of a substantial Labor Party victory in the 1970 British election. Of course, voters are notorious for changing their minds at the last minute.

The U.S. Department of Commerce samples over 9,000 business firms quarterly to gather data on actual capital expenditures for the preceding period and anticipated expenditures for the following period. With two decades of experience behind it, the department is generally able to detect seasonal variation, bias, and other sources of error. This has enabled it to adjust the respondents' estimates as well as to generalize the findings to the aggregate U.S. market. The result is now a very accurate poll forecast of future capital expenditures—one of the key variables in many models of the national economy and an important index of future business activity.

Poll forecasts often provide the data for causal forecasting models. For instance, a firm may have a model that shows its sales as a function of capital expenditures. Using the figures published by the Department of Commerce, it can quickly forecast the demand for its products.

Causal-Model Forecasts

Causal-model forecasts—also called "regressive forecasts" or "analytical forecasts"—are based on a statistical relationship between the forecast (dependent) variable and one or more explanatory variables. Time-series models, or "growth models," are a special case of causal models where time is the independent variable. (These are examined in detail in the next chapter.)

As we mentioned earlier, there need not be a cause-and-effect relationship between the dependent variable and the independent variables. A statistical correlation alone is a sufficient basis for causal-model forecasting. The real test of a model is whether it works. The firm's sales could be specified as a function of something as irrelevant as sunspots; if this resulted in accurate, reliable forecasts, the model would be acceptable.

In general, a causal model is constructed by finding variables that explain, statistically, the changes in the variable to be forecast. Such variables must have the following properties: (1) They must be related statistically to the dependent variable, (2) data on them must be available, and (3) there must be some way of forecasting them, or their relationship with the dependent variable must be lagged.

The statistical relationship is estimated and verified with the tools of descriptive and inferential statistics. The selection of variables depends on the imagination and resources of the researcher. With the aid of a computer, dozens of candidates can be tested, easily and quickly, once the structure—that is, the mathematical form—of the model has been decided. This, too, may be selected by trial and error.

The availability of data is largely determined by the time and resources the researcher has. Data are the key to specifying the model. Once the model has been specified (that is, once the parameters have been assigned numerical values), data are then needed to calculate the forecast variable.

Given unlimited data, causal models can be constructed that explain almost any marketing phenomenon. Unfortunately, this is seldom a realistic assumption. Shortages of time, money, and personnel; limits on the accessibility of data; and deficiencies in measurement techniques all impose serious restraints on data availability. Often, researchers must be content with secondary data, proxy variables, outdated observations, and inaccurate information. The result is usually an imperfect model, although not necessarily a useless one.

Forecastability or a lagged relationship with the dependent variable is essential for fairly obvious reasons. It does little good to construct a forecasting model if the future values of the explanatory variables are as difficult to estimate as those of the dependent variable. The only alternative is to use independent variables whose present values determine the dependent variable's future values.

The most common technique for constructing causal models—and perhaps the most powerful—is linear regression analysis. Although the topic has already been covered in some detail, there are some problems associated with regression equations used in forecasting that still should be examined.

Regression models are linear estimates of statistical relationships that existed within the range of observations at the times when (or places where) they were made. For instance, if sales are regressed against population sizes of 1.5 to 4 million and per capita average incomes of $2,400 to $4,500, the model will reflect relationships that apparently exist between these extremes. If sales are forecast using values of population or income that fall outside these ranges, the relationships expressed by the model may not hold. The assumption of linearity may break down if the extreme values, used in the specification of the model, are exceeded. Once a certain threshold value is passed, the relationship between variables may change appreciably. For instance, food consumption becomes relatively insensitive to income when the latter exceeds $8,573 per year. The same is true for tobacco products when income exceeds $6,710 annually.[4]

Simulation Forecasts

Simulation forecasts are made by simulating the behavior of a market over time. A model—usually mathematical and computerized—is prepared that replicates the operation of the market over the period of the forecast. The changing values of the forecast variables—which are included in the model— are observed at various points in time, during the operation of the model. This technique is especially useful when complex phenomena, such as transition processes, play an important role in determining future values of the forecast variables. It is, for example, valuable in forecasting sales and market shares of brands of convenience goods, such as cigarettes, which are strongly influenced by the brand-loyalty/brand-switching phenomenon.

Simulation is a complex subject with several important applications, including prediction and forecasting, in marketing research. We shall, therefore, defer further discussion of the topic until Part Nine, which is devoted entirely to the anatomy and application of market simulation.

---

[4] Richard D. Millican, "A Re-examination of Engel's Laws Using BLS Data (1960–61)," *Journal of Marketing* **31** no. 4 (October 1967), p. 19. One must correct these numbers for inflation if they are to make sense in today's market.

Time-Series Models

Time as an Independent Variable   Time-series models show the dependent variable as a function of a single independent variable, time. They can be specified by regression analysis or by fitting one of a number of common functions to observed data. These functions, called *growth curves*, can take a variety of forms, both linear and curvilinear. Like many models, time-series models are based on a statistical correlation that does not necessarily reflect a real cause-and-effect relationship between the dependent and the independent variable.[5]

The values of the dependent variable are determined by four time-related factors:

long term phenomena	such as population, economic development, and culture
cyclical phenomena	principally the business cycle
seasonal phenomena	such as weather and customs (e.g., Christmas)
irregular or unique phenomena	such as strikes, wars, and acts of God

These four factors induce, respectively, the follow types of behavior in the dependent variable:

trend
cyclical variation
seasonal variation
irregular fluctuations

These types of variation are encountered frequently in the literature of market and economic forecasting and warrant close examination. Graphical examples of each, together with a sample of the composite variation they produce, are given in Figure 22-1.

Trend   A *trend*—sometimes called a "secular trend"—is a long-run tendency to change with time. A variable's trend is a reflection of its statistical relationship with time, exclusive of cyclical, seasonal, and irregular disturbances. Trend functions are described by growth curves, which express—both graphically and mathematically—the underlying pattern of time-related changes. This pattern is usually induced by such factors as population, GNP, industrialization, technology, and taste. It can be inherently positive, as in the demand for food. It can be negative, as in the demand for anthracite coal. It can reverse direction, as did the demand for passenger rail service. Or it can be erratic, as in the demand for clothing styles.

The time period specified for a particular trend function varies considerably. Economists frequently define it as any period in excess of that required for a complete business cycle (these cycles average about 4.5 years).

---

[5] Many physical and biological variables, such as radioactivity, plant size, and cellular growth, are actually affected by time. Certain psychological variables, such as learning, are also largely dependent on time. Few marketing variables are a direct function of time, but many change in a fixed or predictable way over time, thus producing a statistical correlation.

Figure 22-1   **Time-Related Changes in a Dependent Variable (Sales)**

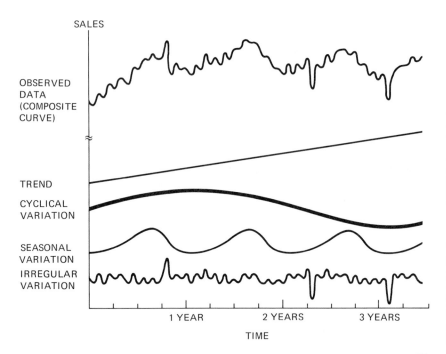

Marketers tend to specify a trend period as equivalent to the expected life-time of the product. This can vary from a few months for a fad item, such as the hula hoop or a pop record, to a couple of years for a fashion item, such as the mini-skirt, to an indefinite period for an essential, such as electricity.

Cyclical Variation   *Cyclical variation* is the variation of the forecast variable due to the business cycle. The business cycle is the wave-like fluctuation in the level of economic activity that has been associated with the economies of the developed nations since the early years of the Industrial Revolution. The business cycle has never been fully explained by economists, adequately controlled by governments, or satisfactorily predicted by business analysts. However, the phenomenon is apparent if any of the common economic indicators (such as GNP, employment, stock prices, corporate profits, or capital investment) are plotted over time. The period of individual cycles varies, although they usually last well beyond a year—measured from peak to peak or valley to valley. In the United States, cycles range from one to ten years. Four to five years is normal. The magnitude of the fluctuations, measured vertically from peak to valley (or vice versa), varies enormously and thus far has defied precise forecasting.

The business cycle has a conspicuous effect on sales of luxury goods, machine tools, and automobiles and on the demand for new housing and capital goods. It has a slight effect on sales of food, clothing, and tobacco products, except during extreme downward movements such as the Great

Depression of the 1930s. In the short run, unless there has been a major economic disturbance, cyclical variation can often be ignored.

Seasonal Variation   *Seasonal variation* is the variation of the forecast variable associated with the time of the year. It is aptly named, for it is a function both of the weather and of the social customs associated with the four seasons. For instance, the high birth rate and increasing affluence of the post-World War II period induced an increasing trend in the consumption of toys. However, toy sales invariably peak in December, due to heavy Christmas buying, and suffer a large decline in January. (Although the trend may decline due to the recent decrease in the birth rate, the seasonal variation will remain.) Seasonal fluctuations in the demand for such product classes as recreational goods, air conditioners, and cars are pronounced. Seasonal fluctuations in sales of goods such as cigarettes and most food products are negligible.

Irregular Variation   *Irregular variation*—also called "noise," "erratic fluctuation," and "residual variation"—includes all the variation in the forecast variable that cannot be attributed to a trend, cyclical variation, or seasonal variation. It has two subsets: (1) random variation and (2) variation due to special events.

Random variation is produced by chance fluctuations in the forecast variable due to a variety of small unidentified factors. The frequency and magnitude of disturbances in a given time interval are randomly distributed about their means. Hence, their effects tend to cancel one another out. In the long run, the average magnitude of truly random disturbances is zero. The expected value of random variation, therefore, is also zero. The dispersion of random disturbances can be estimated using inferential statistics. Hence, the confidence interval about the forecast variable with respect to random variation, can readily be computed.

Variation due to special events is a singular change in the forecast variable induced by the occurrence of a significant and readily identifiable event. Wars, political upheavals, severe storms, and strikes are examples. Although the disturbance factor is easily identified and the magnitude of its effect can usually be estimated, it can seldom be forecast. Variation due to special events is normally purged from the data used in constructing a growth model.

Such noise can be treated as random variation. This will make the forecasting model less precise, but the confidence interval more realistic. Of course, if researchers believe they can predict special events, this kind of variation can be explicitly incorporated into the model using a dummy variable.

Analyzing Aggregate Data

The composite, or "aggregate," line in Figure 22-1 represents the raw observations collected by the researchers. One of their first tasks is to break down these data into their four components—the trend, cyclical variation, seasonal variation, and irregular variation. The basic time-series forecasting model estimates the trend when the absolute, percentage, or exponential change in the variable remains constant during the period under study. Some typical trends are shown in Figure 22-1. Figure 22-3, and Figure 23-4. More complex trend functions are possible but are extremely difficult to devise.

The composite curve can easily be purged of seasonal variation. Cyclical variation is a bit harder to remove. Irregular variation due to major disturbances can easily be identified and often estimated (and hence purged from the composite values). Irregular variation due to minor events and random disturbances can be estimated statistically. Random disturbances should, over the long run, average out to zero. When all these disturbances are removed from the data, what is left is the trend line.

Purging Cyclical Variation

Cyclical variation can be removed by performing two tasks. The first is the most crucial and the most difficult, namely, estimating the relationship between the forecase variable and the business cycle. An appropriate index—such as GNP, capital investment, or the Dow Jones average—is selected to represent the business cycle. The elasticity of the forecase variable with respect to the business-cycle index is then estimated subjectively or by regression analysis. The objective is to determine how much of the fluctuation in the variable was induced by the business cycle. For instance, if the index drops 10 percent, how much will the forecase variable change? Once this is determined, the observations of the forecast variable—the values that make up the composite curve—can be adjusted. This is the analyst's second task. He or she simply subtracts algebraically the cyclical variation, computed for each point in time, from each observation. What remains is a time series free of cyclical variation.

A sensible alternative is to leave the cyclical variation in the data. This will increase the dispersion of the forecast variable's actual values about the growth curve, making the model less precise. However, the model will also be more realistic, since the confidence interval about the dependent variable will also reflect the uncertainty induced by the business cycle.

Management is interested in the quantity of sales it can expect in future periods and the range of possible error it can expect at the selected confidence level. The underlying causes for variations in sales are of little interest to decision-makers, unless they are in a position to influence them. However, growth curves represent the sales that will probably result if the endogenous variables (those controlled by the firm) remain fixed. The variation in the actual values of the forecast variable are often a significant indication of changing conditions in the marketplace and should not, as a rule, be ignored.

Purging Seasonal Variation

Seasonal variation is eliminated by a process called *smoothing*. The most common instruments for this purpose are freehand lines, semiaverages, moving averages, and the method of least squares. Freehand lines are a convenient way of smoothing out fluctuations in data, but they are necessarily

Table 22-2   **Observed Data versus Moving Averages**

Period (i)	Observed Data (Y)	3-Period Moving Average (Y')	4-Period Moving Average (Y'')	4-Period Moving Average Centered (Y''')
1	51			
2	65	64		
			63.8	
3	76	68		66.6
			69.5	
4	63	71		72.0
			74.5	
5	74	74		74.0
			73.5	
6	85	77		76.0
			78.5	
7	72	80		81.4
			84.2	
8	83	84		84.1
			84.0	
9	97	88		
10	84			

imprecise and the resultant function cannot be expressed mathematically unless the analyst has constructed a straight line through the scatter of points or fitted the curve of a known nonlinear equation to the data. Even then the model cannot be evaluated statistically, since the underlying assumptions and mathematically properties necessary for the application of inferential statistics are missing.

Using *semiaverages* to smooth out a curve is only slightly more rigorous than using freehand lines. The analyst simply divides the time series into two equal parts—its first and second halves—and then computes the arithmetic mean of each part. The two means are plotted and a straight line drawn through the two points. This line represents the dampened (smoothed) curve. It can be expressed mathematically, but the function cannot be evaluated by statistical testing.

The *moving average*—also called the "ratio-to-moving-average" and the "percentage of the moving average"—is computed by finding the mean of adjoining observations. This average then replaces the observations used in its calculation. This is done for each observation in the series, except those at the beginning and the end. If a three-observation moving average were to be used to smooth out a series and the first three observations were 51, 65, and 76, the first moving average would be 60. If the fourth observation were 63, the second moving average would be $[(65 + 76 + 63)/3 = 68]$. Thus, 64 and 68 would be the first two values in the moving-average series. For example, assume that there are ten observations, as in Table 22-2. By using the moving averages, we can generate a new series of points in which the fluctuations associated with the three-observation range are dampened. The original series and the moving-average series are plotted in Figure 22-2.

Note the absence of a moving average for the first and last periods. This is because we cannot compute a moving average without knowing the value of the observation preceding and following the observation being replaced. As the number of periods used to calculate the moving-average increases, the new curve will become smoother, but shorter.

Figure 22-2   **Time-Series Curves**

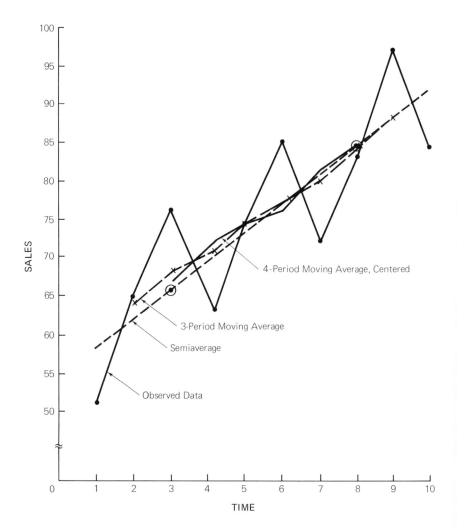

A moving average can also be computed using an even number of observations. The computation procedure is essentially the same. For instance, using the data from Table 22-2, the first four-period moving average would be 63.8 $[(51 + 65 + 76 + 63)/4 = 63.8]$, which plots midway between periods two and three. However, the even-period moving average can be centered—that is, it can be plotted at the same point in time as observed data. The analyst simply takes the mean of two consecutive moving averages and assigns it to the period it straddles. However, the range of the curve is reduced as the number of observations in the moving average is increased.

The correct number of periods for finding a moving average depends on the length of the seasonal cycle, the frequency of the observations, and the willingness of the analyst to sacrifice the tails of the curve. Most seasonal variations have a one-year cycle. Hence, a three-period moving average is appropriate for data gathered at four-month intervals. A four-period moving average is useful for quarterly data. If monthly observations are recorded, then a twelve-period moving average will remove seasonal variation.

The method of least squares (explained in Chapter 17) can be used to fit a straight line to the scatter of data. When the objective is to eliminate seasonal fluctuations, it should be used to compute the midpoints in the seasonal cycles. These midpoints can then be plotted and connected by straight lines or a freehand curve to portray the time series free of its seasonal variation. Or a growth curve can be fitted to the data using one of several methods to be discussed shortly.

Purging Irregular Variation   Irregular variation is eliminated in the smoothing-out process used to get rid of seasonal fluctuations. However, this prevents the researcher from obtaining a precise estimate of the seasonal effect. Isolating the seasonal effect is important if the analyst plans to forecast seasonal values of the dependent variable. For instance, management may need monthly sales forecasts as well as annual sales forecasts. He or she will have to reintroduce the seasonal effect into the monthly estimate provided by the trend curve.

Noise introduced by random variations can only be eliminated by smoothing. The more of it there is, the broader the confidence interval about the estimate of the forecast variable will be. This is one of the reasons the confidence interval is important. Any forecast is a shaky basis for decision-making if it is not accompanied by a statistical evaluation, including a confidence interval.

To truly purge random variation from the data—thus purifying the forecasting model and reducing the width of the confidence interval to zero— the analyst must identify its causes and precisely measure their effect. This is usually extremely difficult, or impossible.

Variation introduced by a major special event, such as a natural disaster or a strike, can be identified and usually measured, or at least estimated with reasonable accuracy. Either an adjustment can be made in the observed values or the observations taken during the event can be deleted. For instance, an evaluation of the long-run trend in the demand for consumer durables would exclude the data for the years 1942 through 1945, when the nation's military needs forced the government to drastically curtail the output of such goods.

When adjustments or deletions are made, the fact should be noted. The decision-maker should be made aware of the effect of these events and the probability of their recurrence. When the effects are severe and there is a possibility that they will recur, management can sometimes make provisions for them.[6]

---

[6] Insurance is the most common way of protecting the firm against the effects of distur- bances due to special events, especially those falling into the category of natural disasters or criminal acts. Losses due to labor strife, political upheavals, and wars, which are not normally covered by insurance, can often be handled by risk-sharing agreements among members of the same industry (a practice common in oligopolistic industries confronted with big labor unions) or by establishing a contingency account.

The usual order of removing unwanted variation is to first remove fluctuations due to special events, then cyclical variation (business-cycle effects), and finally seasonal variation. The residual variation is a combination of the true trend and unpurged random variation. These data can then be plotted and an appropriate curve drawn through, or fitted to, the scatter of points. Often, if one or more significant economic or marketing variables have varied during the time period, the residual data can be used for a regression analysis. The unpurged data can also be used in a regression model if the influence of the business cycle, seasonal fluctuations, and irregular special events are accommodated by introducing additional explanatory variables. These additional variables will likely be dummies representing the month or season and the occurrence or nonoccurrence of a special event. However, this approach not only complicates the model, but also reduces the number of degrees of freedom. It may be unacceptable if the number of observations is relatively small.

Reintroducing Seasonal Variation

Short-Run versus Long-Run Forecasts[7]

Short-run forecasts are generally more accurate and precise than long-run forecasts because the underlying determinants and the relationships between variables tend to change less in the short run than in the long run. However, short-run forecasts are vulnerable to seasonal variations that, if unaccounted for, can make them unrealistic.

A long-run model is ideally a trend model, affected only by irregular random variation. A trend model is usually the primary objective of the analyst, for management is interested essentially in the growth characteristics of the product. Major manufacturing- and marketing-resource allocations are usually long-term decisions; plants and equipment, for instance, cannot be acquired quickly or disposed of easily.

A long-run model may include cyclical variation, but it excludes seasonal variation. Hence, in order to make a short-run forecast, the analyst will have to reintroduce seasonal fluctuations by using seasonal indexes.

Computing Seasonal Indexes

A *seasonal index* is a relative measure of seasonal variation, usually expressed as a percentage. Its base is the average value of the dependent variable for the seasonal period, usually a month. For instance, if the long-term forecast predicted sales of 6,000 units during a particular year, the monthly average predicted for that year would be 500 units. Thus, the base (100%) would equal 500. If the seasonal index for October were 120, then the sales predicted for

---

[7] *Short-run* and *long-run* are relative terms whose actual length varies tremendously between product classes. In forecasting, it is convenient to define the long run as equivalent to the product's cycle or the time from product introduction to maturity. Short-run forecasts are usually for one year or less.

that month would be 600 units (120% · 500). In other words, a seasonal index is really a set of indexes—one for each period in the year, giving the sales of that period as a percentage of the sales for an average period.

The Ratio-to-Moving-Average Method   There are several ways of computing a seasonal index. The most common is the *ratio-to-moving-average*, or *percentage-of-moving-average*, method. Here, the researcher isolates seasonal variation by a process of elimination. Irregular variation due to special events is removed from the data first, then trend and cyclical variation. This leaves only seasonal and irregular random variation combined in a figure representing monthly sales[8] as a percentage of the average sales for the twelve

Figure 22-3   **Sales of Women's Apparel**

Source: John E. Freund and Frank J. Williams, *Elementary Business Statistics: The Modern Approach,* © 1964. Reprinted by permission of Prentice-Hall, Inc., Englewood Cliffs, New Jersey.

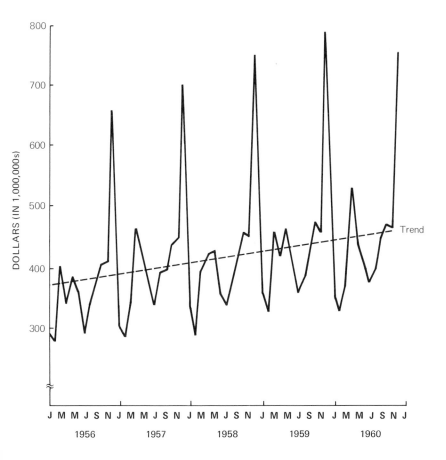

8 Monthly periods are used for purposes of illustration since they are by far the most common. However, other intervals, such as weeks or quarters, can also be used.

months in which each month is centered. The irregular random variation is then removed by taking the average value for each January, February, March, and so on through December. These twelve averages (one for each month) are then adjusted so that they add up to 1200 percent. Thus, the base value (the mean of the adjusted averages) becomes 100, and the adjusted monthly values become the seasonal indexes for their respective months. The following example from Freund and Williams illustrates this method nicely.[9]

A graph of sales of women's apparel reveals both a noticeable trend and a pronounced seasonal variation. There is a consistent and very high peak in December and a persistent dip in both January and July. If monthly sales were forecast on the basis of trend data alone, the estimates would seldom be even close to the real values, as Figure 22-3 shows.

Using the ratio-to-moving-average method, the raw data—purged only of special irregular variation due to special events—is arrayed as in Table 22-3, column 1. Twelve-month moving totals are then computed and centered, in column 2. The 12-month moving total is simply the total sales for 12 consecutive months. As subsequent totals are computed, the first month in each series is dropped and a new last month added. Since each 12-month moving total is centered, six months at the beginning and six months at the end of the aggregate time series is lost.

To realign the moving totals and subsequent data, 2-year moving totals are computed and centered between the pairs of 12-month moving totals used in their computation, as in column 3. Next, a centered 12-month moving average is computed for each month in the series, excluding the first and last which are lost. This new average is found by dividing the 2-year moving total (column 3) by 24. (Note that the 2-year moving total includes data for 24 months.) The centered 12-month moving averages are recorded in column 4. These contain both trend and cyclical variation.

Finally, the percentage of the 12-month moving average (ratio-to-moving-average) is computed by dividing the original monthly data by the centered 12-month moving averages (column 1 by column 4). These values are recorded in column 5. This fifth step eliminates the trend and cyclical variation, leaving only seasonal and irregular random variation.

After computing the percentage of 12-month moving average for each month, the researcher must still eliminate the irregular random variation. Since this variation is evenly distributed about the mean or median of each month's moving average (column 5), we can use this mean or median as the basis for the seasonal index. The computations are shown in Table 22-4.

A seasonal index is defined as the percentage of average monthly sales expected in a given month. The mean month is 100 percent. Thus, the total of the 12 months' index should equal 1,200. This is not always the case. In the illustration, the total of the 12 medians is 1,202.4. To adjust these monthly averages so that they can be used as the seasonal indexes, the analyst simply multiplies each one by 1,200 divided by their sum. In the example, each

---

[9] John E. Freund and Frank J. Williams, *Elementary Business Statistics: The Modern Approach* (Englewood Cliffs, N.J.: Prentice-Hall, 1964), pp. 336–339.

Table 22-3   **Data and Computations for a Ratio-to-Moving Average for Sales of Women's Apparel (millions of dollars)**

Year	Month	Sales (1)	12-Month Moving Total (2)	2-Year Moving Total (3)	Centered 12-Month Moving Average (4)	Percentages of 12-Month Moving Average (5)
1956	January	292				
	February	278				
	March	403				
	April	344				
	May	388				
	June	364	4,540			
	July	290	4,558	9,098	379.1	76.5
	August	338	4,563	9,121	380.0	88.9
	September	374	4,507	9,070	377.9	99.0
	October	405	4,626	9,133	380.5	106.4
	November	410	4,660	9,286	386.9	106.0
	December	654	4,677	9,337	389.0	168.1
1957	January	310	4,725	9,402	391.8	79.1
	February	283	4,777	9,502	395.9	71.5
	March	347	4,801	9,578	399.1	86.9
	April	463	4,830	9,631	401.3	115.4
	May	422	4,863	9,698	404.1	104.4
	June	381	4,915	9,783	407.6	93.5
	July	338	4,946	9,861	410.9	82.3
	August	390	4,941	9,887	412.0	94.7
	September	398	4,983	9,929	413.7	96.2
	October	434	4,945	9,933	413.9	104.9
	November	448	4,943	9,893	412.2	180.7
	December	701	4,925	9,873	411.4	170.4
1958	January	341	4,921	9,846	410.2	83.1
	February	278	4,904	9,825	409.4	67.9
	March	394	4,924	9,828	409.5	96.2
	April	420	4,947	9,871	411.3	102.1
	May	425	4,950	9,897	412.4	103.1
	June	358	4,993	9,943	414.3	86.4
	July	334	5,011	10,004	416.8	80.1
	August	373	5,055	10,066	419.4	88.9
	September	418	5,116	10,171	423.8	98.6
	October	457	5,113	10,229	426.2	107.2
	November	451	5,149	10,262	427.6	105.5
	December	744	5,201	10,350	431.2	172.5
1959	January	359	5,223	10,424	434.3	82.7
	February	322	5,228	10,451	435.5	73.9
	March	455	5,238	10,466	436.1	104.3
	April	417	5,252	10,490	437.1	95.4
	May	461	5,252	10,504	437.7	105.3
	June	410	5,284	10,536	439.0	93.4
	July	356	5,288	10,572	440.5	80.8
	August	378	5,286	10,574	440.6	85.8
	September	428	5,211	10,497	437.4	97.9

Table 22-3   **Data and Computations for a Ratio-to-Moving Average for Sales of Women's Apparel (millions of dollars)** (*cont'd.*)

Year	Month	Sales (1)	12-Month Moving Total (2)	2-Year Moving Total (3)	Centered 12-Month Moving Average (4)	Percentages of 12-Month Moving Average (5)
	October	471		10,531	438.8	107.3
	November	451	5,320	10,614	442.2	102.0
	December	776	5,294	10,584	441.0	176.0
			5,290			
1960	January	363		10,594	441.4	82.2
	February	320	5,304	10,624	442.7	72.3
	March	380	5,320	10,655	444.0	85.6
	April	526	5,335	10,666	444.4	118.4
	May	435	5,331	10,675	444.8	97.8
	June	406	5,344	10,661	444.2	91.4
	July	370	5,317			
	August	394				
	September	443				
	October	467				
	November	464				
	December	749				

Source: John E. Freund and Frank J. Williams, *Elementary Business Statistics: The Modern Approach* © 1964. Reprinted by permission of Prentice-Hall, Inc., Englewood Cliffs, New Jersey.

median is multiplied by 0.998 (1,200.0 ÷ 1,202.4). The seasonal indexes can now be used to multiply the monthly trend values to set realistic estimates.

If the analyst is recording monthly observations and wants to purge them of seasonal disturbances, the procedure is simply reversed. The monthly observations are divided by the monthly seasonal indexes to obtain seasonally adjusted monthly trend-cyclical values. Unfortunately, this reintroduces the random variation as well as the variation from the trend and business-cycle effects. The pattern is usually clear, nonetheless.

Census Method II   In 1954, the Bureau of the Census prepared a comprehensive computer program to deal with seasonal variation. This program followed the procedure for seasonal adjustments used by the Federal Reserve System. The program, designated *Census Method I*, was soon upgraded to include techniques for purging irregular variation and computing other time-series statistics such as trend and cyclical variation. The refined program, called *Census Method II*, is available to other government agencies and private users through the Office of the Chief Economic Statistician of the Bureau of the Census in Washington, D.C.[10]

Census Method II is illustrative of the applications of computers in marketing research. Sophisticated mathematical manipulations that would

[10] For an excellent lay introduction to the program and its commercial applications, see R. L. McLaughlin, *Time Series Forecasting*, Marketing-Research Technique Series, no. 6, (Chicago: American Marketing Association, 1962).

Table 22-4   **Computed Monthly Medians and Seasonal Indexes**

Month	1956	1957	1958	1959	1960	Median	Seasonal Index
January		79.1	83.1	82.7	82.2	82.4	82.2
February		71.5	67.9	73.9	72.3	71.9	71.8
March		86.9	96.2	104.3	85.6	91.6	91.4
April		115.4	102.1	95.4	118.4	108.8	108.6
May		104.4	103.1	105.3	97.8	103.8	103.6
June		93.5	86.4	93.4	91.4	92.4	92.2
July	76.5	82.3	80.1	80.8		80.4	80.2
August	88.9	94.7	88.9	85.8		88.9	88.7
September	99.0	96.2	98.6	97.9		98.2	98.0
October	106.4	104.9	107.2	107.3		106.8	106.6
November	106.0	108.7	105.5	102.0		105.8	105.6
December	168.1	170.4	172.5	176.0		171.4	171.1
						1,202.4	1,200.0

Source: John E. Freund and Frank J. Williams, *Elementary Business Statistics: The Modern Approach* © 1964. Reprinted by permission of Prentice-Hall, Inc., Englewood Cliffs, New Jersey.

take many hours manually (even using a desk calculator) are performed quickly, and the computations are error-free. Like all the firm's resources, the time of the analysts is both limited and rationed. By relieving them of the drudgery, the computer allows them to concentrate their energies on data collection and analysis.

Measuring Statistical Significance: The *U*-Test

There is the possibility that the forecast variable has no significant statistical relationship to time and that the apparent time-related variations are due to chance. Hence, it is sometimes appropriate to test the relationship statistically to determine the existence or nonexistence of a trend line. The *U*-test is good for this purpose.

The *U-test*, as we saw in Chapter 15, compares the number of runs—called the *U-value*—in a sequence of observations, with the minimum number of runs shown in a *U*-distribution for a specific confidence level. A *run* is a sequence of numbers, each sharing a common characteristic, preceded and followed by a number with the opposite characteristic or no number at all. The characteristic used to group a sequence of numbers into a run is whether the number is above or below the median of the entire series.

A *U*-distribution, (Appendix 4) shows the number of runs—the *U*-value—that could occur by chance in a given number of observations. This distribution—which is simply a statement of the probabilities of getting *U*-values by chance—was developed by Swed and Eisenhart in their work on

Table 22-5   **Domestic Lumber Shipments**

Year	Millions of Board-Feet	Below (a) or Above (b) Median	
1957	33,142	a	} 1st a-run
1958	33,715	a	
1959	36,770	b	} 1st b-run
1960	32.223	a	
1961	32,665	a	} 2nd a-run
1962	33,327	a	
1963	34,410	b	
1964	37,143	b	
1965	37,749	b	} 2nd b-run
1966	36,482	b	

Sources: Adapted from National Industrial Conference Board, *Economic Almanac* 1967–1968 (New York: Macmillan, 1968), p. 366. Figures are based on U.S. Department of Commerce and National Forest Products Association Statistics.

random grouping.[11] The computed U-value[12] is compared to the table U-value to test the null hypothesis that the observed arrangement of observations below and above the median is random, and not due to an underlying trend. We reject the null hypothesis when the calculated U-statistic is less than the table value.

For example, the observations in Table 22-5 relate to shipments of lumber by domestic firms. Assuming that sales are equal to shipments, suppose we use the U-test to determine if there is a significant trend in the demand for domestic lumber.

The median in this time series is 34,062. With an even number of observations, there is no middle value. Hence, the average of the fifth and sixth values—with the observations arrayed in ascending or descending order—is used for the median; $(33,715 + 34,410)/2 = 34,062$. Thus, half the observations (designated "a" observations) will be below and half (designated "b" observations) will be above 34,062. Labeling the observations accordingly, we can see that there are two a-runs and two b-runs, for a total of four runs. Hence, $U = 4$.

Checking a table of U-values (Appendix 4) tells us that $U_{.05} = 3$, for $a = b = 5$.[13] Since the observed U-value is greater than the table value, we cannot reject the null hypothesis that the grouping of a and b observations occurred by chance. Hence, we cannot honestly claim, on the basis of the statistical evidence, a trend in the demand for domestic lumber at the 0.05 level of significance (a 95 percent confidence level).

---

[11] F. S. Swed and C. Eisenhart, "Tables for Testing Randomness of Grouping in a Sequence of Alternatives," *Annals of Mathematical Statistics* **14** (1943), p. 66.

[12] The formula for computing the U-statistic was discussed in Chapter 15.

[13] The a or b count (a and b must be equal) is used instead of the total number of observations because an odd number of observations would make one of the observations the median; hence, it could not be counted in any of the runs.

There are also other ways to test the statistical significance of an apparent trend. For example, the observed (or purged) data could be regressed against time and the t-test or F-test used to see if there was a significant relationship. Although more rigorous, regression analysis is more cumbersome than the U-test—particularly if manual methods of computation are employed. If the U-test confirms the existence of a trend at the desired confidence level, there is no need to reconfirm it by regression analysis.

Problems

1   What variables might be useful, and what assumptions necessary, in performing the following tasks: (a) predicting the demand in Oregon and Washington for a brand of beer sold previously only in California, (b) forecasting the total (industry) sales for household appliances through 1985, and (c) forecasting the U.S. population through 1990?

2   What method would you use to obtain the following forecasts: (a) steel sales for the coming year, (b) the winners of an upcoming election, and (c) expenditures for recreational goods and services through 1990? Defend your choice.

3   The following data have been recorded on the sales of the firm's product:

	Quarter	Units		Quarter	Units
1975	1st	300	1977	1st	390
	2nd	350		2nd	400
	3rd	375		3rd	470
	4th	450		4th	520
1976	1st	340	1978	1st	400
	2nd	360		2nd	420
	3rd	400		3rd	420
	4th	480		4th	540

The total sales for this particular product class are moderately sensitive to the business cycle. A 2 percent change in the Dow Jones average induces a 1 percent change in sales. Compute the firm's quarterly sales when the effects of the business cycle are removed. (Use actual or hypothetical Dow Jones values.) Plot the original data and the new curve. On the same graph, plot the effects of the business cycle.

4   Compute and plot the trend line for sales of the product discussed in question 3. (The line will have to include noise, since there is insufficient information to purge the data in this respect.)

5   Using the trend line constructed in response to problem 4, and reintroducing seasonal variation, forecast sales for the first quarter in 1983. What assumption did you make with respect to the business cycle?

Chapter 23
Growth Models

Key Concepts

Growth Functions
Ways to express time-series models

Linear Models
Fitting a straight line to time-related data

Curvilinear Models
Alternative ways of fitting curves to time-related data

Modified Exponential Models
Fitting the Gompertz function and other more-complex models
time-related data

Selecting and Improving a Model
Choosing the most appropriate model and making it better

Key Terms

Growth Functions

As we said in Chapter 22, *growth functions* are mathematical expressions of the relationship between a dependent variable (usually sales, in marketing research) and time. Since they contain only two variables (e.g., sales and time), they can easily be graphed. A *growth curve* is really a graphical portrait of a growth function, although the two terms are used interchangeably.

Growth curves assume a number of forms, from straight lines to complex curvilinear functions. The selection of a particular function depends on which one best fits the observed (or purged) data and the analyst's perception of the essential character of the true trend. For example, the characteristic trend of the demand for an energy source such as petroleum or atomic power is likely to be considerably different from that of the demand for consumer fashion items.

Before examining specific growth curves, we need to recognize and clarify a possible source of confusion. Growth models (time-series models) can express the dependent variable either incrementally or cumulatively. For instance, a product's sales can be expressed in terms of units sold during a given period (e.g., 23,000 units during 1978) or in terms of the total number of units sold as of a particular time (e.g., 318,000 units as of December 31, 1978). If the growth function for a cumulative value is specified, the function for the incremental value can be found by taking the first derivative. For example, if the cumulative growth function is $Y_t = 1290 + 830t$ (where $Y_t =$ cumulative sales at time t and $t =$ the number of periods that have elapsed since the base period), then $dY/dt = 830$. We could also use a slightly different notation, saying $\Delta Y_t = 830$, where ΔY_t is sales during year t.

Conversely, if the incremental growth function is known, the cumulative growth function will be its integral. For example, if sales in year t equal 9,438 ($\Delta Y_t = 9,438$), then the cumulative growth curve will be $y_t = a + 9,438t$. Integral calculus does not specify the constant, a, which is the value of the intercept. (a is the cumulative total of Y as of the base time.) However, in practical applications, finding the value of a is not difficult.

We can avoid using calculus in going from the cumulative to the incremental function, or vice versa, by substituting graphical techniques. If the cumulative curve can be plotted, incremental values can be measured, using the vertical scale, Y, for any selected period. (Time is measured on the horizontal, or X, axis.) If the incremental function is known, the cumulative values can be plotted simply by summing the incremental values up to and including each point in time. These points, connected by a freehand curve, represent the cumulative function.

Both calculus and graphs can be avoided by aggregating (summing.) the incremental values, ΔY, to get the cumulative total value, Y_t, at the desired point in time

$$\left(Y_t = \sum_{i=0}^{t} \Delta Y_i \right)$$

Conversely, if cumulative totals are known, incremental values can be found by disaggregating the total values ($\Delta Y_t = Y_t - Y_{t-1}$). Often an analyst will discover a growth curve to fit the cumulative data when he or she cannot find a function to fit the incremental data. The reverse may also occur.

Fortunately, the growth functions can be specified with either cumulative or incremental data, as the mathematical structure of the equations remains the same.

Preparing the Observed Data

The raw data—that is, the unaltered observations—should usually be purged of cyclical and seasonal variation, as well as irregular variation due to any special events, before the growth model is selected and fitted. This will reduce the average size of the residuals and generally improve the quality of the model, assuming that it is a realistic replica of the actual trend. When the purging is complete, the reduced data should reflect only the trend and possibly some random disturbances. The U-test can then be used to determine if there is a significant statistical relationship between the dependent variable and time. If not, there will be no point in trying to construct a growth model.

Complete purging is not always practical. Sometimes the analyst must be satisfied with dirty data containing some unwanted variations and disturbances. When long-run forecasts—say, for four years or longer—are being made, cyclical variation should probably be left in the data. The causes of cyclical variation (primarily population and income changes) are often powerful determinants of the forecast variable. When they are, they should be incorporated into the model. Since growth models have only one independent variable (time), these forces can be included only by not adjusting the data to compensate for their effects.

Once they are purged, the data should be tabulated and graphed. This will help the researcher to make accurate intuitive judgments about the nature of the underlying growth function and select an appropriate model.

Linear Models

Linear growth models are those that specify a linear relationship between the dependent variable and time. They are naive in that they assume that what happens tomorrow will be identical to what happened yesterday, with respect to the direction and rate of change. This assumption is rarely true, although it is often a convenient and workable approximation of the truth.

In mathematical terminology, linear growth functions are *first-degree polynomials*, since every variable has an exponent of one. (By convention, an exponent of one is not shown; thus, $X^1 = X$ and so on.) The general form of the linear growth model is

$$Y_t = a + bt \qquad\qquad [23.1]$$

and

$$\Delta Y_t = b = Y_t - Y_{t-1} \qquad\qquad [23.2]$$

where

Y_t = the cumulative value of the dependent variable at time t

ΔY_t = the incremental value of the dependent variable at time t

a = the intercept, which is equal to Y_t at $t = 0$ (the base period)

b = a parameter equal to the slope of the growth curve

t = the number of periods that have elapsed since base period ($t = 0$)

For example, assume that annual sales, ΔY_t, have been averaging 2,000 units, and a linear growth model is required to forecast future sales. The year 1979 has been selected as the base year; hence, $Y_{1972} = Y_0$. Cumulative sales up to and including 1979 were 5,000 units; hence, $a = 5,000$. Substituting these values in formulas 23.2 and 23.1 gives us the following growth model:

$\Delta Y_t = 2,000$ (by substitution)

$Y_t = 5,000 + 2,000t$ (by substitution)

ΔY is always 2,000. In 1979, when $t = 0$; $Y = 5,000$; in 1980, when $y = 1$, $Y = 7,000$; and so on. The resultant growth function is shown in Figure 23-1. By extending the curve, or simply by substituting the appropriate value for t, we can theoretically forecast sales at any time in the future. However, it would be foolish to assume that this linear relationship between sales and time will prevail indefinitely.

In order to specify a general model, the analyst needs data. The parameters, a and b, must be assigned numerical values. The analyst can use either empirical data or estimates. For instance, if the product has been sold for a number of periods, there will be a cumulative figure that will represent the intercept, a, if the base period, Y_0, is specified as the last period covered by the cumulative figure.

Estimating the other parameter, b, is more difficult. If data are available for one or more previous periods, then the incremental value of one of those periods, ΔY_t, can be assigned to b. If there are several observations—ΔY_t, ΔY_{t-1}, and so on—they will probably not be equal and the analyst will have to select a value intuitively, by averaging the available figures, or by fitting a line to the data. Ideally the observations should be purged of unwanted variation before a value for b is selected.

If the analysts decides to fit a line to the data, he or she can get values for both the intercept, a, and the coefficient, b. The line is constructed using two or more observations of cumulative sales. The intercept, a, is then read off the vertical axis. The coefficient b is found by measuring the change in Y, ΔY, for a one-unit change in t, Δt, as in Figure 23-1(A). The linear growth model is then specified by substituting these values for a and b in formulas 23.1 and 23.2.

Figure 23-1   **Cumulative and Incremental Linear Growth Models**

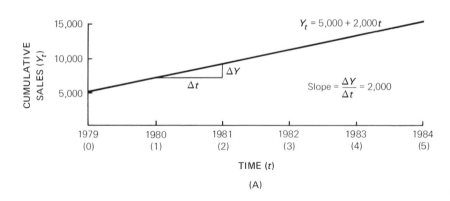

(A)

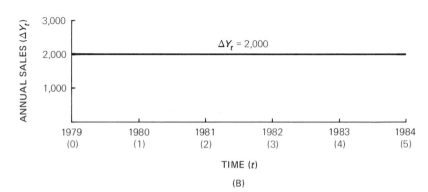

(B)

The graphical method is easy and fast, but it is not precise; nor does the resultant model lend itself to statistical evaluation. Visual inspection of the dispersion of the observed values about the line gives us some indication of the quality of the model, but this subjective estimate is seldom sufficient. Linear regression analysis is a more rigorous way of obtaining values for a and b. A line is fitted, using the method of least squares explained in Chapter 17, with inferential statistics used to evaluate the corresponding equation.

Curvilinear Models

Curvilinear growth models are those that specify a curvilinear relationship between the dependent variable and time. A perfectly accurate model would inscribe a growth curve through every historical value of the forecast variable. Unless these observations fell coincidentally along a relatively simple curve—an extremely unlikely event—this "perfect" growth function would be so complicated as to be unmanageable. Among other things, the usual tools of statistical evaluation would not work, We must settle, then, for a curvilinear growth function that is a reasonable approximation of reality.

There are several that are quite manageable and have proven to be acceptable approximations of real-world growth functions. These are:

  second-degree polynomials
  logarithmic functions
  modified basic exponential functions
  Gompertz functions
  logistic functions

Second-Degree-Polynomial Growth Models

The second-degree-polynomial equation is the simplest of the curvilinear growth models. Its general forms are

$$Y_t = a + bt + ct^2 \qquad\qquad [23.3]$$

and

$$\Delta Y_t = Y_t - Y_{t-1} \qquad\qquad [23.4]$$

where

  Y_t = the cumulative value of the dependent variable at time t

  ΔY_t = the incremental value of the dependent variable at time t

  a = the intercept, which is equal to Y_t at $t - 0$ (the base period)

  b = a perameter

  c = a perameter

  t = the number of periods that have elapsed since base period ($t = 0$)

The introduction of the third term, ct^2, induces a bow in the curve and forces it to eventually reverse direction. Unlike a first-degree-polynomial (linear) equation, where the slope of the curve is constant throughout the range of t, the second-degree-polynomial model has a continually changing slope. By changing the signs and the magnitudes of the parameters b and c, the curve can be made concave or convex to the horizontal axis, peaked or broad. By varying the sign and the value of the intercept, a (which is also a parameter), the curve can be shifted in either direction any distance from the origin ($t = 0$).

Two forms of second-degree polynomials are applicable to marketing research. The first is a curve convex to the horizontal axis. The intercept, a, is zero or positive; b is usually negative, and c is positive. The curve moves downward at a decreasing rate, bottoms out, then moves upward at an increasing rate. Two examples of this kind of function are given in Figure 23-2. Note that only the values in the upper-right quadrant (where sales and time are both positive) are meaningful. Occasionally the values in the upper-left quadrant are also meaningful—for example, when the origin ($t = 0$) has been assigned to the middle year in the observation period.

Figure 23-2   **Typical Convex Second-Degree-Polynomial Growth Curves**

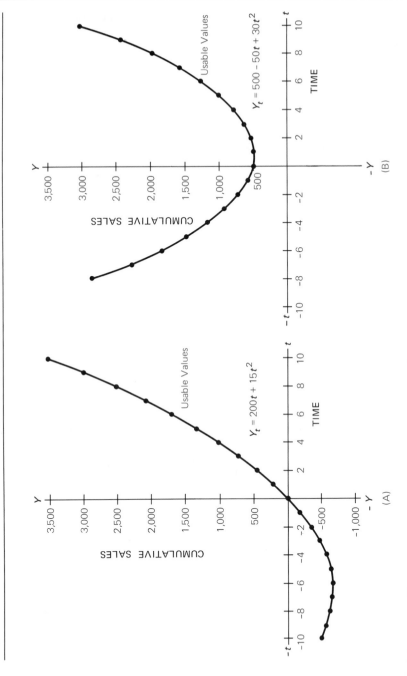

The left-hand, declining, portion of the curve makes no sense when the dependent variable is cumulative sales. It implies that the firm is repurchasing its own output. However, the right-hand portion is typical of the first half of the life cycle of many products. It depicts total sales as low and growing slowly, a common phenomenon during the introductory phase of a product, when only the innovators are purchasing. As we move further from the base year, total sales become larger and grow more rapidly. This is typical of the next phase in the product's life, when the early adopters and then the early majority are buying.

Nevertheless, even the right-hand portion of the curve must be ignored beyond a certain range. It will continue to bend upward until it is nearly vertical and total sales are increasing at a ferocious rate. In reality, the converse is usually true. Total sales tend to increase less and less rapidly as the late majority and then the laggards begin buying and their predecessors switch to new brands or products.[1]

The other form of second-degree polynomial used in marketing research is a curve concave to the horizontal axis. The parameters a and b are positive, and c is negative. Hence, the curve moves upward at a decreasing rate, peaks, and moves downward at an increasing rate. An example of such a function is given in Figure 23-3.

The declining portion of this curve is meaningless when the dependent variable is cumulative sales. The only way cumulative sales will decline with time is if the firm buys back a portion of its own output. Such an assumption is patently ridiculous. However, the left-hand portion of the curve is often useful. Many products experience large incremental sales that decline at an increasing rate until they reach zero (the peak of the cumulative sales curve). The result is a total sales curve similar to the useful portion of Figure 23-3.

An alternative application of the second-degree polynomial is to define Y_t as incremental sales. The curve then represents annual—or monthly, weekly, or daily—sales. In this case, the entire curve above the X-axis is meaningful, since incremental sales normally do increase, peak, and then decline to (or approach) zero. When a second-degree polynomial is used to express the incremental-sales function, cumulative sales are found by aggregating the incremental values. The equation formerly used to find the incremental values, ΔY_t, becomes an expression of the periodic change in them.

Computing cumulative sales by aggregating incremental sales is feasible with any growth model. We simply define the dependent variable, usually written Y_t, as incremental sales, ΔY_t; compute the incremental sales for each period in the desired range of t; then sum these values. (We shall demonstrate this process shortly in the discussion of the logarithmic growth models.)

---

[1] For a discussion of product life cycles and the buyer categories, see Thomas A. Stuadt and Donald A. Taylor, *A Managerial Introduction to Marketing* (Englewood Cliffs, N.J.: Prentice-Hall, 1965), ch. 8, and Everett M. Rogers, *The Diffusion of Innovations* (New York: Free Press, 1962).

Figure 23-3   **A Typical Concave Second-Degree-Polynomial Growth Curve**

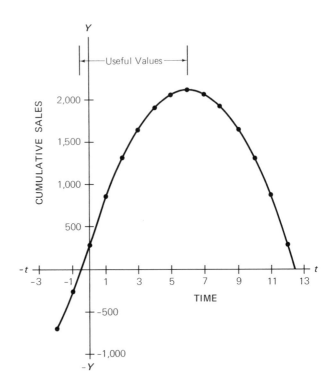

One outstanding advantage of a second-degree polynomial is that it can be transformed into a linear equation and subjected to linear regression analysis. The algebraic procedure described in Chapter 19 is the most popular method of transforming equations. However, we could also tabulate the data and solve the following system of simultaneous equations

I. $\Sigma Y = Na + b\Sigma t + c\Sigma t^2$

II. $\Sigma tY = a\Sigma t + b\Sigma t^2 + c\Sigma t^3$

III. $\Sigma t^2 Y = a\Sigma t^2 + b\Sigma t^3 + c\Sigma t^4$

where

N = the number of observations Y, t, a, b, and c are defined as before

The arithmetic involved can be simplified by making the midpoint in the observed range of time the base ($t = 0$), or "origin." This distributes the periods symmetrically about $t = 0$. As a result, the sums of all odd powers of t (i.e., Σt and Σt^3) become zero and drop out of the equations. The system is reduced to the following form

    I. $\Sigma Y = Na + c\Sigma t^2$

    II. $\Sigma t Y = b\Sigma t^2$

    III. $\Sigma t^2 Y = a\Sigma t^2 + c\Sigma t^4$

Once the variables are aggregated and substituted into the equations, the system can be solved for a, b, and c, by the usual methods. The model itself is then specified by substituting the explicit values of the three parameters (a, b, and c) into the polynomial equation.

    A third, less rigorous, method of specifying second-degree growth models is sometimes used when there are no observed values of Y and the analyst must rely solely on individual judgment. First, we estimate the value of Y at three points—designated t_1, t_2, and t_3—in the range of t to be covered by the model. We then substitute these values, along with the corresponding t values, into the following system of simultaneous equations and solve for a, b, and c.

    I. $Y_{t_1} = a + bt_1 + ct_1{}^2$

    II. $Y_{t_2} = a + bt_2 + ct_2{}^2$

    III. $Y_{t_3} = a + bt_3 + ct_3{}^2$

Given the explicit values of the three parameters, we can quickly specify the model.

    All models specified with judgment estimates, or with a small number of observed values, should be examined carefully to see if they make sense. A graph of the model is gnerally very useful. The curve should be plotted through the entire range of t; if some of the Y values are illogical or suspicious-looking, then the model should be respecified using different assumptions or another type of curve should be fitted to the values.

    Polynomial equations higher than the second degree ($Y = a + bt + ct^2 + dt^3 + \cdots xt^n$) can be used, but they are seldom appropriate as growth models. The higher the largest exponent is, the more times the curve reverses direction and the smaller the useful portion becomes. (The declining portions of the curves cannot be used when Y_t is cumulative sales). Such functions are occasionally used for prediction models, where time is never a variable. They too can be transformed into linear equations and specified by linear regression analysis.

Logarithmic Growth Models

The *logarithmic growth model* is the simplest of the exponential functions—a family of curves so named because the independent variables are exponents. It specifies an exponential relationship between the dependent variable and time and is based on the assumption that the dependent variable keeps

Figure 23-4   **A Typical Logarithmic Growth Model: Incremental Sales (Arithmetic Scale)**

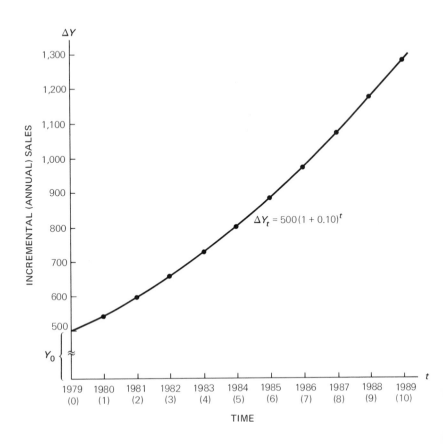

changing by a fixed percentage. If t is one year, the dependent variable will change annually by a fixed percentage. The absolute value of the annual change is not constant, however. It is the product of the fixed percentage times the value of the dependent variable in the preceding year, which is changing. If the trend measured is upward (it usually is), the dependent variable, and hence the annual increment of change, will become larger, producing a curve like that in Figure 23-4. If the model is plotted as on semilogarithmic paper, however, the result will be a straight line like that in Figure 23-5.

The general form of the logarithmic growth model is

$$\Delta Y_t = \Delta Y_0 (1 + b)^t \tag{23.5}$$

and

$$Y_t = \sum_{i=0}^{t} \Delta Y_i \tag{23.6}$$

***Figure 23-5*   A Typical Logarithmic Growth Model: Incremental Sales (Semilogarithmic Scale)**

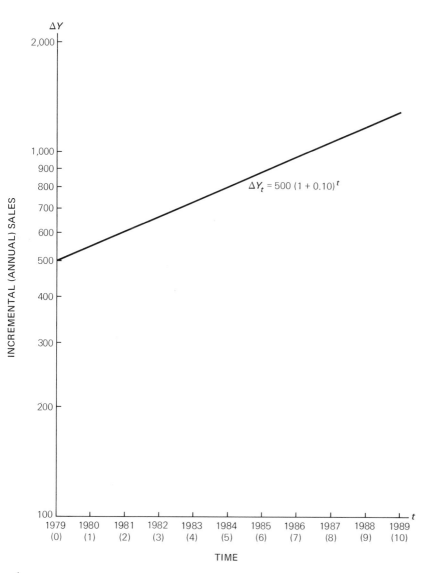

where

ΔY_t = the incremental value of the dependent variable at time t

ΔY_0 = the value of the dependent variable at $t = 0$

b = the rate of change in each period

t = the number of periods that have elapsed since period, Y_0 and

Y_t = the cumulative value of the dependent variable at time t

(*Note:* Substitute Y_t for ΔY_t and Y_0 for ΔY_0 if equation 23.5 is to be used to fit a logarithmic curve directly to cumulative sales vice incremental sales.)

The logarithmic function is usually defined in terms of incremental values (annual, monthly, or weekly sales, etc.) and the cumulative value found by aggregating them. However, it could be defined in cumulative terms (Y vice ΔY) and the incremental values found by disaggregation ($\Delta Y_t = Y_t - Y_{t-1}$).

For example, assume that 1979 is the base year ($t = 0$) and sales are expected to increase at a rate of 10 percent per year ($b = 0.10$). The first year, 500 units were sold ($\Delta Y_0 = 500$). To find the incremental sales, ΔY, for each annual period, t, from 1979 through 1989, we simply substitute the appropriate values in equation 23.5:

1979	$\Delta Y_0 = 500(1 + .10)^0$	(by substitution)
	$\Delta Y_0 = 500$	(by arithmetic)[2]
1980	$\Delta Y_1 = 500(1 + .10)^1$	(by substitution)
	$\Delta Y_1 = 550$	(by arithmetic)
1981	$\Delta Y_2 = 500(1 + .10)^2$	(by substitution)
	$\Delta Y_2 = 605$	(by arithmetic)

$$. \quad . \qquad\qquad .$$
$$. \quad . \qquad\qquad .$$
$$. \quad . \qquad\qquad .$$

1989	$\Delta Y_{10} = 500(1 + .10)^{10}$	(by substitution)
	$\Delta Y_{10} = 1{,}296.7$	(by arithmetic)

To find the cumulative sales, Y, through 1989 ($t = 10$), we use formula 23.6:

$$1989 \quad Y_{10} = \sum_{i=0}^{10} \Delta Y_i \qquad\qquad \text{(by substitution)}$$

$$Y_{10} = \Delta Y_0 + \Delta Y_1 + \Delta Y_2 + \Delta Y_3 + \Delta Y_4 + \Delta Y_5 + \Delta Y_6$$
$$+ \Delta Y_7 + \Delta Y_8 + \Delta Y_9 + \Delta Y_{10} \qquad \text{(by expansion)}$$

$$Y_{10} = 500 + 550 + 605 + 665.5 + 732 + 805.2 + 885.7$$
$$+ 974.2 + 1{,}071.6 + 1{,}178 + 1{,}296.7 \quad \text{(by substitution)}$$

$$Y_{10} = 9{,}264.7 \qquad\qquad \text{(by arithmetic)}$$

---

[2] Any term raised to the zero power equals one. Thus, $X^0 = 1$, $5^0 = 1$, $(20 + X^3)^0 = 1$, and so on.

Incremental growth curves are illustrated in Figures 23-4 and 23-5. In Figure 23-4, the model is plotted on a conventional (arithmetic) scale, and hence has the shape characteristic of a logarithmic function. In Figure 23-5, the model is plotted on a semilogarithmic scale, where it inscribes a straight line. This allows us to draw the curve over its entire range, after computing and plotting only two values of ΔY_t.

A cumulative logarithmic growth curve is illustrated in Figure 23-6, using an arithmetic scale. It too has a characteristic shape, due to the exponential relationship between incremental sales and time. However, the cumulative model does not plot as a straight line on semilogarithmic graph paper. This is because, when formula 23.6 is used, cumulative sales are an additive, not an exponential, function of ΔY.

Figure 23-6   **A Typical Logarithmic Growth Model: Cumulative Sales (Arithmetic Scale)**

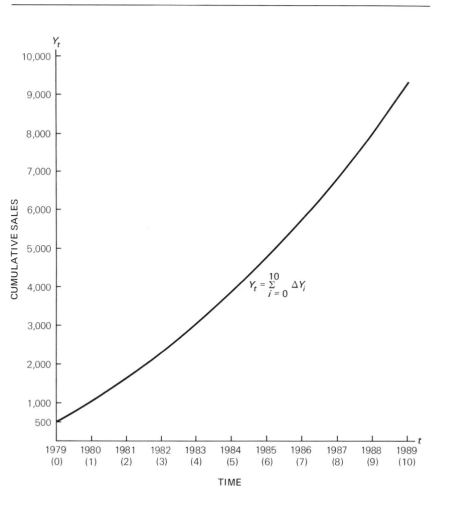

$$Y_t = \sum_{i=0}^{10} \Delta Y_i$$

Specifying the Model   A logarithmic growth model can be specified using empirical data or by estimating the parameter, b, by judgment. By estimating the parameter, the base period, ΔY_0, is usually the first observed period; thus, ΔY_0 equals the intercept. When the equation has been specified, the observed values of ΔY_t will not equal the estimated values, except occasionally by chance. This is because the curve is a line of best fit and can pass through every observed value of ΔY_t only if ΔY_t correlates perfectly with time and it is specified precisely. Both these conditions are extremely unlikely. If they appear to have occurred, the equation should be evaluated carefully. Apparently perfect correlation ($R^2 = 1$) suggests an inadequate number of observations—not a perfect model, which is a bit too much to expect in the real world. Checking the degrees of freedom and using appropriate significance tests should quickly enable the analyst to confirm or deny this suspicion.

The easiest and quickest way of constructing a logarithmic growth curve is to plot any two points (pairs of ΔY_t and t values) on semilogarithmic graph paper, then inscribe a straight line through them. ΔY_t is measured on the vertical axis and t on the horizontal axis, as in Figure 23-5.

The most rigorous way of specifying the parameter is by linear regression analysis of the logarithmic form of the model. The criterion used to determine the line of best fit for a scatter of logarithmic values is slightly different from that used when the values are natural numbers. Normally, the sum of the squares of the deviations of the observed values from the estimate (line) values must be a minimum. Thus, $\Sigma(\Delta Y_i - \Delta Y_i)^2$ must be a minimum. With logarithmic values, we need to minimize the sum of the difference in logarithms. $\Sigma(\log \Delta Y - \log \Delta Y)^2$ must be a minimum. In terms of the original data (prior to their transformation into logarithms), we minimize the sum of the relative (percentage) differences between observed and estimated values of the dependent variable, ΔY.

This method exploits two essential properties of logarithms: first, the fact that adding logarithms is equivalent to multiplying the natural numbers they represent, and second, the fact that multiplying a logarithm by a natural number is equivalent to raising the antilog to that power. For example, $\log X + \log Z$ is equivalent to XZ and $3 \log X$ is equivalent to X^3.

Thus equation 23.5, in cumulative terms, $Y_t = Y_0(1 + b)^t$, can be expressed as

$$\log Y_t = \log Y_0 + t \log (1 + b) \qquad [23.7]$$

A more convenient form of this equation, easily recognizable as a bivariate linear regression model, is

$$\log Y_t = \log Y_0 + \log B \cdot t \qquad [23.8]$$

where

$\log Y_t$ = the dependent variable

$\log Y_0$ = the intercept

$\log B$ = the regression coefficient $(B = 1 + b)$

t = the independent variable, time

Given a series of observations, we can easily obtain their logarithmic values from a table of logarithms or a computer, and substitute them, along with their accompanying t-values, in equation 23.8. The result will be a system of simultaneous equations, each containing two unknowns, $\log Y_0$ and $\log B$. These unknowns are equivalent to the parameters α and β in equation 17.2, the general form of the bivariate linear model. The equations can be solved by any of the methods outlined in Chapter 17. (Y_i represents the variable $\log Y_t$ and X represents t. The solutions for α and β are thus the solutions from $\log Y_0$ and $\log B$.)

By getting the natural numbers for these logarithms (via table or computer) we can return the linear regression equation to its original curvilinear form, with the parameters specified. First, we compute b, using the following formula, and substitute it in equation 23.5. (This is easy, once B has been specified.)

$$b = B - 1, \qquad\qquad\qquad\qquad\qquad\qquad [23.9]$$

where

b and B are defined as before

Next, we find the natural value of the intercept and substitute it for Y_0 in formula 23.5. We now have a logarithmic growth model specified in natural numbers and curvilinear form.

Evaluating the Model   To evaluate the model, we must use the linear form. The coefficient of determination, the t-statistic, and the F-statistic will be natural numbers. The other important statistics (such as the standard error of the estimate, the standard error of the regression coefficient, and the various confidence intervals) will be logarithms. However, they can easily be converted to natural numbers. Either the logarithmic or the natural form of the model can be used for forecasting.

A word of caution to the practitioner is appropriate. The logarithmic model increases the absolute value of the dependent variable by larger and larger increments as time is projected into the future. This may be far more realistic than a linear model in the short run or, for that matter, for a considerable time in the future. It is especially realistic for the introductory and initial growth phases of most products and brands. However, during the latter growth phase and the maturity phase (frequently followed by a decline phase) the simple logarithmic model is extremely misleading. Hence, the logarithmic curve should seldom be used past the anticipated mid-point of the product's or the brand's life cycle. To do so will forecast continually increasing increments of sales into a period which will probably have a continually declining demand. If the absolute value of incremental demand does not decline, it will probably become stabilized once the good has entered into its maturity stage. At that time, a linear function would be appropriate. There are several forces that tend to induce a linear or a declining curve, once the item reaches its maturity. They are the marginal utility of the product, declining economies of scale in both production and marketing, market saturation combined with a constant need for replacement due to mortality or physical consumption, and technological change.

Modified Exponential Growth Models

A *modified exponential function* is simply a logarithmic model, whose mathematical structure has been altered to give it properties that make the forecasts more realistic in certain situations. The dependent and explanatory variables (usually sales and time) are still exponentially related. There are numerous modified exponential functions, many of which have little or no use in marketing. However, three models—the basic model, the Gompertz model, and the logistic model—do have important applications.

The Basic Form

The basic form of the modified exponential function portrays nicely the sales curve associated with certain products, such as specific models of commercial airliners. In addition, it provides a convenient introduction to some special properties common to other modified exponential functions. It relates the dependent and independent variables exponentially; the dependent variable increases, but at a constantly decreasing rate. The graph of this function is a curve that moves upward, but whose slope declines as it moves to the right, as in Figure 23-7.

This model, like all exponential models, is asymptotic. That is, the dependent variable approaches, but never reaches, a constant value. Graphically, the curve approaches a straight line. The incremental increases keep getting smaller, but will not reach zero until the independent variable reaches infinity, which in practice means never.

The concept of an *asymptote*—a constant value that is approached but never reached—is especially appropriate to marketing research. The asymptote is analogous to 100 percent market saturation, the condition that exists when every potential buyer has purchased the product. Complete market saturation rarely occurs, except among certain product classes such as diesel locomotives and personal radios. (These exceptions hold only in the U.S. market.)

Figure 23-7   **A Modified Exponential Growth Model: The Basic Form**
$(Y_t = K - ab^t)$

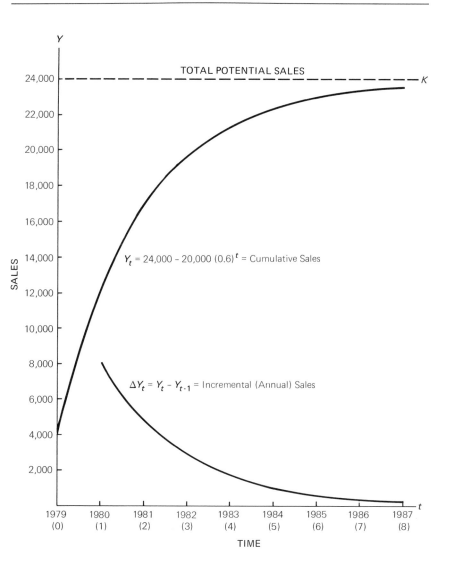

An estimate of total potential sales is often used as an asymptote in marketing models, especially by consumer-goods firms.

The general form of the basic modified exponential function is

$$Y_t = K - ab^t \qquad\qquad [23.10]$$

and

$$\Delta Y_t = Y_t - Y_{t-1} \qquad\qquad \text{(given as equation 23.4)}$$

where

> Y_t = cumulative sales through period t
>
> K = the asymptote of Y_t (i.e., the limit that Y_t will approach, but never reach), which must exceed zero
>
> a = the value of K minus the intercept (the value on the Y-axis at $t = 0$): $a = K - Y_0$. a is always a constant greater than zero
>
> b = the percentage by which the growth rate is decreasing; a constant greater than zero and less than one
>
> t = the number of periods that have elapsed since the base period
>
> ΔY_t = the incremental value of sales

We have defined the exponential function in terms of cumulative sales. The incremental sales are found by disaggregating total sales. This is the conventional approach. However, there is no reason why the exponential function cannot be defined in terms of incremental sales and the total sales found by aggregation. The analyst should use whichever approach best fits the situation.

A mathematical example will help to illustrate the model. Assume that maximum potential sales, K, is 24,000 units. The first year, $t = 0$, 4,000 units were sold; hence, a is 20,000. An estimate of the expected decline in incremental sales suggests that the growth rate (the slope of the curve) will decrease 60 percent per year ($b = 0.6$). By substituting these values for the parameters in formula 23.10, we can specify the modified exponential growth model for this particular product: $Y_t = 24,000 - 20,000 (0.6)^t$. This allows us to forecast the value of Y at any time, t, in the future. If the base period, $t = 0$, is 1979, we can easily forecast sales for the following decade:

	$Y_t = K - ab^t$	(given as equation 23.10)
1979	$Y_0 = 24,000 - 20,000(0.6)^0$	(by substitution)
	$Y_0 = 4,000$	(by arithmetic)
1980	$Y_1 = 24,000 - 20,000(0.6)^1$	(by substitution)
	$Y_1 = 12,000$	(by arithmetic)
1981	$Y_2 = 24,000 - 20,000(0.6)^2$	(by substitution)
	$Y_2 = 16,800$	(by arithmetic)
1982	$Y_3 = 19,680$	(by substitution and arithmetic)
1983	$Y_4 = 21,408$	(by substitution and arithmetic)
1984	$Y_5 = 22,445$	(by substitution and arithmetic)
1985	$Y_6 = 23,067$	(by substitution and arithmetic)
1986	$Y_7 = 23,440$	(by substitution and arithmetic)
1987	$Y_8 = 23,664$	(by substitution and arithmetic)

We can compute the incremental value, ΔY_t, for every period except the base period by using formula 23.4. Both Y_t and ΔY_t are plotted in Figure 23-7.

	$\Delta Y_t = Y_t - Y_{t-1}$	(given as equation 23.4)
1980	$\Delta Y_1 = 12{,}000 - 4{,}000$	(by substitution)
	$\Delta Y_1 = 8{,}000$	(by arithmetic)
1981	$\Delta Y_2 = 16{,}800 - 12{,}000$	(by substitution)
	$\Delta Y_2 = 4{,}800$	(by arithmetic)
1982	$\Delta Y_3 = 2{,}880$	(by substitution and arithmetic)
1983	$\Delta Y_4 = 1{,}728$	(by substitution and arithmetic)
1984	$\Delta Y_5 = 937$	(by substitution and arithmetic)
1985	$\Delta Y_6 = 622$	(by substitution and arithmetic)
1986	$\Delta Y_7 = 373$	(by substitution and arithmetic)
1987	$\Delta Y_8 = 224$	(by substitution and arithmetic)

Unfortunately, equation 23.10 cannot be restated in logarithmic form because the two right-hand terms, K and ab^t, are not multiplicatively related and there is no way natural numbers can be added or substracted in their logarithmic form.[3] However logarithms can be used to simplify the arithmetic.

Putting the second term in logarithmic form reduces considerably the amount of multiplication involved. Instead of multiplying b by itself t times (e.g., $abt = a \cdot b \cdot b \cdot b \cdot b \cdot b$ when $t = 5$), the logarithm of b is simply multiplied by the exponent ($\log ab^5 = \log a + 5 \log b$). The result is converted to a natural number to solve for Y_t. (This is especially handy with many pocket calculators.)

We can get around any problems caused by our inability to transform equation 23.10 into a linear equation by working with formula 23.4 instead. By a bit of manipulation, we can derive an equation that will lend itself to regression analysis

$\Delta Y_t = Y_t - Y_{t-1}$	(given as equation 23.4)
$\Delta Y_t = (K - ab^t) - (K - ab^{t-1})$	(by substitution from equation 23.10)
$\Delta Y_t = ab^t \, (-1 + 1/b)$	(by algebraic manipulation)
$\Delta Y_t = a \, (1/b - 1)b^t$	(by algebraic manipulation)
$\log \Delta Y_t = \log [a(1/b - 1)] + t \cdot \log b$	(by conversion to logarithmic form)

---

[3] Adding and subtracting logarithms is equivalent to multiplying and dividing their natural numbers.

This last equation can be restated as a bivariate regression model as follows:

$$\log \Delta Y_t = \alpha + \beta t \qquad\qquad [23.11]$$

where

$$\alpha = \log \left[a(1/b - 1) \right]$$
$$\beta = \log b$$

ΔY_t and t are defined as before

Now, it can be specified and evaluated by using the tools of linear regression analysis.

Gompertz Models

The *Gompertz model* is another example of a modified exponential function; it too relates the dependent and explanatory (independent) variables exponentially. In the kind of Gompertz model used in market research, the dependent variable, Y, increases first at an increasing rate, then at a decreasing rate.[4] The point of change is called the *inflection point*. The Gompertz function produces an S-shaped growth curve that describes the rate of market penetration over time. Four historical growth curves that fit this pattern are in Figure 23-8.

The Gompertz model gets its shape from a constant ratio of successive first differences[5] of the logarithmic values of the dependent variable, Y, that causes the first differences of the natural values of the dependent variable to have a skewed distribution about the inflection point of the independent variable. The inflection point is that part of the curve where the slope is neither increasing nor decreasing.[6] Infinitesimally small, it may be viewed

---

[4] There are four forms of the Gompertz function. Each is distinguished by the position of its asymptote and its slope. See Frederick E. Croxton and Dudley J. Cowden, *Applied General Statistics*, 2nd ed. (Englewood Cliffs. N.J.: Prentice-Hall, 1955), p. 302, for a description of all four forms.

[5] A *first difference* is the difference between two consecutive values in a series. For instance, if $Y_4 = 60$ and $Y_3 = 50$, their first difference would equal 10. A *second difference* is the difference between two consecutive first differences, and so on. For example:

(i)	Y_i	First Differences	Second Differences
1	35		
		7	
2	42		1
		8	
3	50		2
		10	
4	60		2
		12	
5	72		

[6] The inflection point is also defined—in differential calculus—as the point at which the second derivative of the function equals zero.

Figure 23-8   **Market Penetration Over Time by Four Products**

Source: Adapted from Everett M. Rogers, *Diffusion of Innovations*, reprinted with permission of The Macmillan Company, © The Free Press of Glencoe, 1962; and from Edwin Mansfield, "Technical Change and the Rate of Innovation," *Econometrica*, vol. 29, no. 4 (October 1961), p. 743.

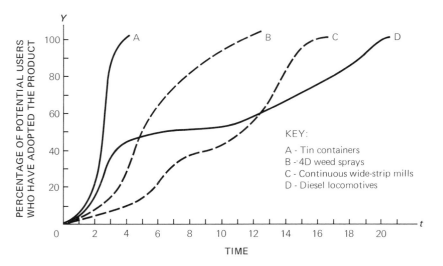

as the junction of the portion—called "limb"—of the curve with an increasing slope and the limb with a decreasing slope. Since the incremental values, ΔY_t, are the first differences of the dependent variable ($\Delta Y_t = Y_t - Y_{t-1}$), their distribution is skewed, as in Figure 23-12.

The Gompertz growth model has two asymptotic limits: The lower (left) limb of the curve approaches but never reaches zero. The upper (right) limb of the curve approaches but never reaches a constant, K, which is usually specified as the total potential market.

The first half (left limb) of the Gompertz curve is shaped like a logarithmic function and has the same properties. The second half of the curve is shaped like the basic form of the modified exponential function and has its properties. Thus, the Gompertz model would seem to offer us the best of two worlds—a logarithmic model of the introductory and initial growth phases of the product's life cycle and a basic modified exponential model of the later growth and maturity phases. The general form of the Gompertz function used in marketing research is

$$Y_t = Ka^{b^t} \qquad\qquad [23.12]$$

and

$$\Delta Y_t = Y_t - Y_{t-1} \qquad\qquad \text{(given as equation 23.4)}$$

where

Y_t = cumulative sales through period t

K = the upper asymptotic limit of Y

a = a parameter

b = a parameter

t = the number of periods that have elapsed since the base period

ΔY_t = the incremental value of sales (the first difference of Y_t)

Formula 23.12 can easily be restated in logarithmic form; as usual, this greatly reduces the amount of arithmetic involved

$$\log Y_t = \log K + (\log a) \cdot b^t \qquad\qquad [23.13]$$

where

Y_t, K, a, b, and t are defined as before

The parameters K, a, and b can be estimated intuitively on the basis of experience or an examination of the historical performance of similar products. Or, a Gompertz curve can be fitted to the data. When sales figures are unavailable (as in the case of a brand new product) the findings of innovation-diffusion studies should help the researcher make some kind of estimate.[7] (Many of these works include very useful models of product life cycles; an example of one such model is shown in Figure 23.10.)

A product's life cycle—defined as the consumption of the good over time—is typically an S-shaped function. Cumulative sales, Y_t, increase slowly at first as the product is tried by the innovators in the market population. If these people are satisfied with it, sales will grow more rapidly as the early adopter class follows their lead. The growth curve reaches its inflection point as the early adopter segment of the market is saturated and the late adopters begin to buy the product. During this stage, Y_t is still increasing significantly but at a steadily declining rate (incremental sales, ΔY_t, are decreasing).

As the late-adopter group approaches saturation, the market enters maturity. Sales to laggards will sustain ΔY_t, but at a very low level once the late adopters have completed their purchases. At this stage, cumulative sales will continue to increase (as they must, so long as ΔY_t is greater than zero) but at a very low and diminishing rate.[8] Practically speaking, the firm has now saturated the market, although Y_t will continue to grow, approaching but never reaching its theoretical limit, K. These phenomena—

---

[7] For a detailed exploration of innovation diffusion, see Rogers, *Diffusion of Innovations*; and Edwin Mansfield, "Technical Change and the Rate of Innovation," *Econometrica* **29**:4 (October 1961), p. 743.

[8] This argument does not take into account the replacement market, which is relevant to many product classes. We shall discuss this subject later in the book.

Figure 23-9   An Adoption Pattern of a Successful Innovation: Cumulative Sales

Source: Reprinted with permission of The Macmillan Company from *Diffusion of Innovations* by Everett M. Rogers. © by The Free Press, 1962.

Figure 23-10   A Typical Adoption Pattern: Incremental Sales

Source: Reprinted with permission of The Macmillan Company from *Diffusion of Innovations* by Everett M. Rogers. © by The Free Press, 1962.

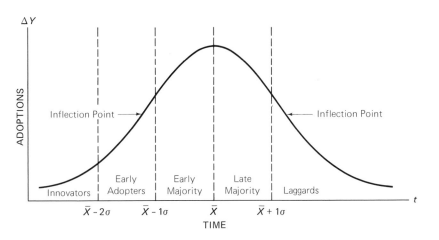

the characteristic growth patterns of cumulative and incremental sales for most products and brands—are shown in Figures 23-9 and 23-10.

Specifying the Model Intuitively   The first task of the analyst in specifying the model intuitively is to estimate the parameter K, the total potential market. One can use historical data, market surveys, regression analysis or any combination of these methods. The parameter a is then specified by, first, estimating the volume of sales expected during the base period, Y_0. This will probably be the most intuitive judgment the analyst will have to make. The estimate of Y_0 should reflect experience, the history of similar products, and the level of production and marketing effort the firm will probably put forth during the base period (usually one year).

Having estimated K and Y_0, one can use formula 23.12 to compute a. The parameter b can be unspecified in this calculation, since any value raised to the zero power is equal to one.

$$Y_t = Ka^{b^t} \qquad \text{(given as equation 23.12)}$$

$$Y_0 = Ka^{b^0} \qquad \text{(by substitution)}$$

or

$$Y_0 = Ka \qquad \text{(Note: } b^0 = 1 \text{; hence } a\text{'s exponent becomes 1 and need not be shown)}$$

$$a = \frac{Y_0}{K} \qquad \text{(by algebraic manipulation)}$$

Now that K and a have been specified, only the parameter b is without a numerical value. We can remedy this situation, first, by estimating the length of time, m, required for the product to reach maturity and the percentage of the total potential market, K, that will be saturated by that time. The history of similar products is the best indicator of what these two values should be. However, historical data should not be used alone, but in conjunction with an appraisal of future trends in the determinants of demand and the peculiarities of the product and market under study.

Cumulative sales at maturity are represented by Y_t when $t = m - 1$. (The base period is designated $t = 0$ and m represents the total number of periods to maturity.) Cumulative Y_{m-1} is the estimated percentage of total market the analyst foresees the firm capturing by that point, times K. For instance, if the analyst foresees that the firm will capture 80 percent of the total potential market by the time the product reaches maturity, and that market is estimated as 100,000 units ($K = 100,000$), then Y_{m-1} will equal 80,000. Given this information, one can solve formula 23.12 for b. Due to the complexity of the exponent, it is more convenient to use the logarithmic form of the equation.

$$Y_t = Ka^{b^t} \qquad \text{(given as equation 23.12)}$$

$$Y_{m-1} = Ka^{b^{m-1}} \qquad \text{(by substitution)}$$

$$Y_{m-1}/K = a^{b^{m-1}} \qquad \text{(by algebraic manipulation)}$$

$$\log(Y_{m-1}/K) = (\log a)b^{m-1} \qquad \text{(by transformation to logarithms)}$$

$$b^{m-1} = \frac{\log(Y_{m-1}/K)}{\log a} \qquad \text{(by algebraic manipulation)}$$

$$b = \left[\frac{\log(Y_{m-1}/K)}{\log a} \right]^{1/(m-1)} \qquad \text{(by algebraic manipulation)}$$

The solution of *b* completes the specification of the model. The analyst can compute *Y* at any point in the product's life cycle simply by substituting an appropriate value for *t*. A series of such calculations produces an S-shaped curve, the Gompertz function for that product, on arithmetic graph paper.

Specifying the Model by Fitting a Curve to the Data   If a product has been on the market for a number of periods, a Gompertz curve can be fitted to its historical sales record. First, the data are purged, as far as possible, of unwanted variation. The cumulative figures are then plotted on arithmetic graph paper and the result subjected to a visual inspection to see if it has the profile of an emerging S-shaped curve. If so, a Gompertz model is probably appropriate. The observed data are divided into three equal parts, and the following formulas used to specify the parameters. *b* is computed first, then *a*, and finally *K*:

$$b = \left(\frac{\Sigma_3 - \Sigma_2}{\Sigma_2 - \Sigma_1}\right)^{1/(n/3)} \tag{23.14}$$

$$a = \log^{-1}\left[(\Sigma_2 - \Sigma_1)\frac{b - 1}{(b^{n/3} - 1)^2}\right] \tag{23.15}[9]$$

and

$$K = \log^{-1}\left[\frac{1}{n/3} \cdot \frac{(\Sigma_1 \cdot \Sigma_3) - \Sigma_2{}^2}{\Sigma_1 + \Sigma_3 - 2\Sigma_2}\right] \tag{23.16}$$

where *b*, *a*, and *K* are the parameters of equation 23.12

n = the number of observations used (*n* must be divisible by 3)

$$\Sigma_1 = \sum_{i=1}^{n/3} \log Y_i$$

$$\Sigma_2 = \sum_{i=(n/3)+1}^{2n/3} \log Y_i$$

$$\Sigma_3 = \sum_{i=(2n/3)+1}^{n} \log Y_i$$

For example, suppose we assume that data are available for 23 consecutive years on the consumption of microfilm readers by the library market.[10] After a visual inspection of the data, we then choose a Gompertz

---

[9] The superscript "-1" signifies the logarithm's natural number. For example, if $\log X = \log Z$, then $X = \log^{-1} Z$.

[10] W. B. Wentz and G. I. Eyrich, *Marketing: Theory and Application* (New York: Harcourt Brace Jovanovich 1970), pp. 561–564.

Table 23-1   **Sales of Microfilm Readers to Libraries**

Year	Annual Sales (in units)	Cumulative Sales (in units)
1948	95	95
1949	125	220
1950	165	385
1951	210	595
1952	290	885
1953	305	1,190
1954	505	1,695
1955	500	2,195
1956	655	2,850
1957	585	3,435
1958	785	4,220
1959	760	4,980
1960	1,060	6,040
1961	975	7,015
1962	1,265	8,280
1963	1,355	9,635
1964	1,380	11,015
1965	1,505	12,520
1966	1,565	14,085
1967	1,550	15,635
1968	1,555	17,190

Source: Marketing: Theory and Application by W. B. Wentz and G. I. Eyrich, copyright ©
1970, by Harcourt Brace Jovanovich, Inc. and reproduced with their permission.

function to forecast future sales. Since, the number of observations, n, used in
the computations must be divisible by three, we drop two sets of observations and tally the remaining 21, as in Table 23-1.

Their next step is to find Σ_1, Σ_2, and Σ_3. The calculations required are
shown in Table 23-2.

Having prepared the data, converted the observations to their loga-
rithmic values, and found Σ_1, Σ_2, and Σ_3, we are now in a position to apply
formulas 23.14, 23.15, and 23.16.

$$b = \left(\frac{28.619963 - 25.282131}{25.282131 - 18.932023}\right)^{1/(21/3)} \qquad \text{(by substitution in}$$
$$\text{equation 23.14)}$$

$$b = (0.525634)^{1/7} \qquad \text{(by arithmetic)}$$

$$b = 0.912216 \qquad \text{(by arithmetic)}$$

$$a = \log^{-1}\left[(25.282131 - 18.932023) \cdot \frac{(0.912216 - 1)}{(0.525634 - 1)^2}\right]$$

$$\text{(by substitution in equation 23.15)}$$

Table 23-2   **Calculations Needed to Find Σ_1, Σ_2, and Σ_3 in Specifying a Gompertz Function**

Year	Number Observation (i)	Period (t)	Cumulative Sales (Y_i)	Log Y_i
1948	1	0	95	1.977748
1949	2	1	220	2.342452
1950	3	2	385	2.585493
1951	4	3	595	2.774552
1952	5	4	885	2.946980
1953	6	5	1,190	3.075586
1954	7	6	1,695	3.229210

$$\Sigma_1 = \sum_{i=1}^{7} \log Y_i = 18.932023$$

Year				
1955	8	7	2,195	3.341476
1956	9	8	2,850	3.454888
1957	10	9	3,435	3.535971
1958	11	10	4,220	3.625358
1959	12	11	4,980	3.697276
1960	13	12	6,040	3.781084
1961	14	13	7,015	3.846076

$$\Sigma_2 = \sum_{i=8}^{14} \log Y_i = 25.282131$$

Year				
1962	15	14	8,280	3.918080
1963	16	15	9,635	3.983902
1964	17	16	11,015	4.042035
1965	18	17	12,520	4.097656
1966	19	18	14,085	4.148809
1967	20	19	15,635	4.194151
1968	21	20	17,190	4.235329

$n = 21$

$$\Sigma_3 = \sum_{i=9}^{21} \log Y_i = 28.619963$$

Source: Marketing: Theory and Application by W. B. Wentz and G. I. Eyrich, copyright © 1970 by Harcourt Brace and Jovanovich, Inc. and reproduced with their permission.

$$a = \log^{-1}\left[6.350108 \cdot \frac{(-0.087784)}{(-0.474366)^2}\right] \qquad \text{(by arithmetic)}$$

$$a = \log^{-1}(-2.477248) \qquad \text{(by arithmetic)}$$

$$a = 0.003332 \qquad \text{(by consulting a table of logs)}$$

$$K = \log^{-1}\left[\frac{1}{21/3} \cdot \frac{(18.932023) \cdot (28.619963) - (25.282131)^2}{18.932023 + 28.619963 - 2(25.282131)}\right]$$

(by substitution in equation 23.16)

$$K = \log^{-1}\left[\frac{1}{7} \cdot \frac{541.833798 - 639.186148}{47.552986 - 50.56426}\right] \qquad \text{(by arithmetic)}$$

$$K = \log^{-1}(4.616934) \qquad \text{(by arithmetic)}$$

$$K = 41,393.68 \qquad \text{(by consulting a table of logs)}$$

The numerical values of b, a, and K are inserted in equation 23.12 to obtain an explicit growth model:

$$Y_t = (41,393.68)(0.003332)^{(0.912216)^t} \quad \text{(by substitution in equation 23.12)}$$

Figure 23-11   **A Gompertz Growth Model: Cumulative Sales ($Y_t = Ka^{bt}$)**

Source: *Marketing: Theory and Application*, by W. B. Wentz and G. I. Eyrich, copyright © 1970 by Harcourt Brace Jovanovich, Inc., and reproduced with their permission.

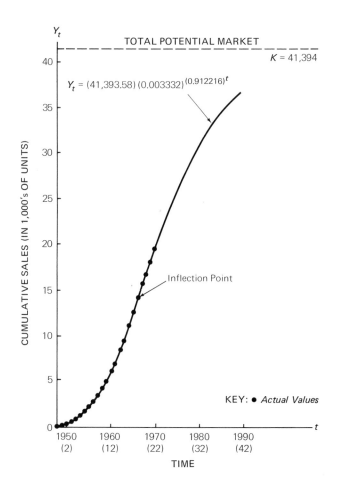

Figure 23-11, a graph of this model, uses actual and projected values through 1990.

Equation 23.4 gives us the figures for incremental sales, ΔY_t, plotted in Figure 23-12. Again, both actual and projected values are shown.

Logistic Models

The *logistic*—or "Pearl-Reed"—*model* is a modified exponential function similar to the Gompertz model. It too relates the dependent and explanatory variables exponentially. In the form used in market research, it has a dependent variable that increases first at an increasing rate and then at a decreasing

Figure 23-12   Incremental Sales Using a Gompertz Growth Model
$(\Delta Y_t = Y_t - Y_{t-1})$

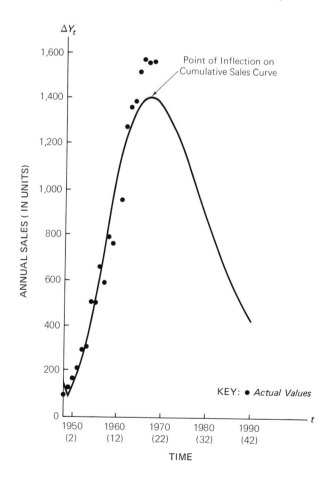

Figure 23-13   **A Logistic Growth Model of the U.S. Population (Continental United States) (Data from Table 23-3)**

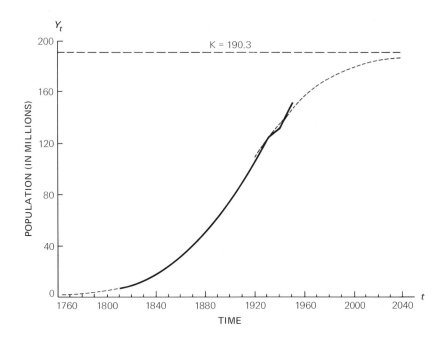

rate. The logistic function also produces an S-shaped growth curve, like that in Figure 23.13.

Like the Gompertz model, the logistic model has two asymptotic limits. The lower limb of the curve is asymptotic to zero and the upper limb

Figure 23-14   **Annual Increases in Population Size Predicted by a Logistic Growth Model of the United States Population**

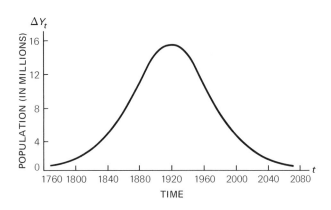

to a constant, *K*, usually the total potential market. Unlike the Gompertz function, however, the logistic model gets its shape from a constant ratio of 'successive first differences of the *reciprocal* of the dependent variable, $(1/Y)$. As a result, the first differences of the natural values of the dependent variable are symmetrically distributed about their inflection point. Thus incremental values such as annual sales are also distributed symmetrically about an inflection point, halfway between the upper and lower asymptotes (see Figure 23-14). This pattern, which contrasts with the skewed distribution of the incremental values in a Gompertz model, is one factor that should be considered in choosing between the two functions.

The general form of the logistic model used in market research is

$$Y_t = \frac{K}{1 + e^{a+bt}} \qquad\qquad [23.17]$$

and

$$\Delta Y_t = Y_t - Y_{t-1} \qquad\qquad \text{(given as equation 23.4)}$$

where

Y_t = the cumulative value of the dependent variable (usually sales)

K = the upper asymptotic limit of Y

e = a constant, usually the Napierian number (2.71828) or ten[11]

a = a parameter

b = a parameter

t = the independent variable, always time in a growth model ($t = 0$ in the base period)[12]

ΔY_t = the incremental value, hence the first difference, of the dependent variable (usually annual sales for year *t*)

Due to the additive relationship in the denominator, the function cannot be transformed into a logarithmic linear equation. Hence, the parameters cannot be specified by linear regression analysis.

Although the inflection point is apparent in a graph of the model (see Figure 23-13), it can, if necessary, be computed by the following equation:

$$t_c = \frac{\log_e a}{b} \qquad\qquad [23.18]$$

---

[11] The constant *e* is usually specified as 2.71828, due to the unique mathematical properties of the Napierian number. Any positive rational number will work, although the values of the *a* and *b* parameters will be different, they will still yield the same curve for given data.

[12] The independent variable is often represented by *X*.

where

t_c = the value of the independent variable at the inflection point

a and b are defined as before

Specifying the Model   There are a number of ways of specifying a logistic growth model.[13] The method of selected points, which we shall use here, is an algorithm prescribed by Croxton and Cowden.[14]

First, we select three points in time—three t-values—that are equidistant and cover most of the range of t. These are designated t_0, t_1, and t_2; t_0 becomes the origin on the horizontal axis of the graph.

Second, we identify the observed (actual) Y values associated with t_0, t_1, and t_2. These are designated Y_0, Y_1, and Y_2. The logistic growth curve will pass through these points.

Third, we solve the following equations for the parameters K, a, and b of the logistic function:

$$K = \frac{(2 \cdot Y_0 \cdot Y_1 \cdot Y_2) - Y_1^2(Y_0 + Y_2)}{(Y_0 \cdot Y_2) - Y_1^2} \qquad [23.19]$$

$$a = \log \frac{K - Y_0}{Y_0} \qquad [23.20]$$

and

$$b = \frac{1}{n} \left[\log \frac{Y_0(K - Y_1)}{Y_1(K - Y_0)} \right] \qquad [23.21]$$

where

n = the number of periods, t, between t_0 and t_1 (hence, between t_1 and t_2)

K, a, b, Y_0, Y_1, and Y_2 are defined as before

Logistic functions are most often used to fit a growth curve to population data, although they can be used as models of phenomena unrelated to population statistics. For this reason, and because population is probably the single most important marketing variable, we shall use a population model to illustrate the specification of a logistic function. Croxton and Cowden provide the following example.[15]

---

[13] See K. R. Nair, "The Fitting of Growth Curves," in Oscar Kempthorne *et al.* eds., *Statistics and Mathematics in Biology* (Ames: University of Iowa Press, 1954), pp. 119–132.

[14] Croxton and Cowden, *Applied General Statistics*, pp. 310–315.

[15] Croxton and Cowden, *Applied General Statistics* pp. 311–316.

We are given a series of 15 decennial observations (1810 through 1950); three points—1820, 1880, and 1940—are selected and designated t_0, t_1, and t_2, respectively. The number of periods between each t is 6; hence, $n = 6$. The corresponding Y-values are 9.6, 50.2, and 134.6; these are designated Y_0, Y_1, and Y_2, respectively. The appropriate formulas are then used to specify the logistic growth model:

$$K = \frac{(2 \cdot Y_0 \cdot Y_1 \cdot Y_2) - Y_1^2(Y_0 + Y_2)}{(Y_0 \cdot Y_2) - Y_1^2} \qquad \text{(given as equation (23.19)}$$

$$K = \frac{2(9.6)(50.2)(134.6) - (50.2)^2(9.6 + 134.6)}{(9.6)(134.6) - (50.2)^2} \qquad \text{(by substitution)}$$

$$K = 190.293 \qquad \text{(by arithmetic)}$$

$$a = \log \frac{K - Y_0}{Y_0} \qquad \text{(given as equation 23.20)}$$

$$a = \log \frac{190.293 - 9.6}{9.6} \qquad \text{(by substitution)}$$

$$a = \log 18.822188 \qquad \text{(by arithmetic)}$$

$$a = 1.274670 \qquad \text{(by consulting a table of logarithms)}$$

$$b = \frac{1}{n} \left[\log \frac{Y_0(K - Y_1)}{Y_1(K - Y_0)} \right] \qquad \text{(given as equation 23.21)}$$

$$b = \frac{1}{6} \left[\log \frac{9.6(190.293 - 50.2)}{50.2(190.293 - 9.6)} \right] \qquad \text{(by substitution)}$$

$$b = \frac{1}{6} \cdot \log 0.148266 \qquad \text{(by arithmetic)}$$

$$b = \frac{1}{6} (9.171042 - 10) \qquad \text{(by consulting a table of logarithms)}$$

$$b = \frac{1}{6} (-0.828958) \qquad \text{(by arithmetic)}$$

$$b = -0.138159 \qquad \text{(by arithmetic)}$$

Ten is selected as the value of the constant e, since it makes the computations a bit easier. This does not affect the curve, or the Y values, which are calculated as follows:

$$Y_t = \frac{K}{1 + 10^{a+bt}}$$ (given as equation 23.17)

$$Y_t = \frac{190.293}{1 + 10^{(1.274670 - 0.138159t)}}$$ (by substitution)

The graph of this model is shown in Figure 23-13. The first differences—that is, the incremental values, ΔY_t—are shown in Figure 23-14. They represent the annual increases in population and are normally distributed about the inflection point, 1920. ($t_c = 10$, which is the year 1920.)

The dependent variable, Y, can be estimated for any year, t, simply by substituting the appropriate t value in the model. Of course, the manipulations are a bit cumbersome without a computer. Manually, the easiest solution is to use the variable μ, defined as the second term in the denominator of equation 23.17

$$\mu_t = e^{a+bt}$$ [23.22]

hence

$$Y_t = \frac{R}{1 - \mu}$$ [23.23]

where

μ = a variable used to compute Y_t

$e, a, b, t,$ and Y are defined as before

μ can also be written in logarithmic form, which makes the computations much more manageable

$$\log \mu = \log e \cdot (a + bt)$$ [23.24]

or

$$\log \mu = \log e \cdot (a) + \log e \cdot (bt)$$ [23.25]

where

$\mu, e, a, b,$ and t are defined as before

Using the parametric values from the previous example, we can specify formula 23.25 as follows. (Again we have set the constant e equal to 10, for convenience. We could also use 2.71828 and get the same results.)

log μ = log 10 $\cdot$ (1.274670) + log 10 $\cdot$ ($-0.138159t$)

(by substitution)

log μ = 1.274670 $-$ 0.138159t

(by consulting a table of logarithms, log 10 = 1.000, and arithmetic)

We are now ready to forecast Y_t for any period, t. The calculations are shown in Table 23-3. First, we multiply the desired t value (column 3) by 0.138159. The product (column 6) is the second term in the preceding equation. Next, we solve the equation for log μ (column 7). We then convert log μ into the natural value of μ (column 8), add one (column 9), and solve for Y_t (column 10).

The solutions for Y_t through the range $t = -1$ to $t = 13$, inclusive, are shown in Table 23-3. Notice the excellent fit of the model—how closely the estimated (computed) values of Y match the observed (actual) values and how tiny the residuals are. The fit can also be judged by examining the estimated and actual curves visually and noting their proximity. In this case, the model falls virtually on top of the true curve (see Figure 23-13).

Like other growth curves, the logistic model is fitted to historical data determined by such factors as population, income, taste, competition, laws, strikes, and wars. As soon as we extrapolate the curves into the future, we bet on a continuation or repetition of past conditions—or at least a specified rate of change. This is a naive assumption, which becomes more naive the further we project the curve into the future. The logistic model described here demonstrates this clearly. Its fit is outstanding. It expresses the statistical relationship between population and time with great precision within the range of observed values (1810–1950). However, it tells us that the population of the continental United States will never exceed 190.3 million—a figure exceeded in 1969. Of course, a critical eye would have caught the disturbance in the historical curve and the abrupt upswing in 1945, and the model would have been adjusted or discarded.

Discrepancies between actual and observed values are most apparent in a graph, such as Figure 23-13. Their existence suggests that reality may be changing in a way not specified by the model, and they should be analyzed. They could be merely the result of a special event, but they could also be the bellwether of a significant change in the true relationship between the dependent and explanatory variables. In that case, neither the analyst nor the decision-maker will be able to rely on the model for long-range forecasts—at least not until the parameters have been respecified or the model itself restructured to reflect the new relationship.

Model Variations   The logistic model just described is by far the most common. However, it can be varied by expanding the exponent of the second term in the denominator as follows:

$$y_t = \frac{K}{1 + e^{a + bt + ct2 + \cdots xt^n}}$$ [23.26]

Table 23-3   Raw Data and Computations for Specifying a Logistic Growth Model by the Method of Selected Points

Year (1)	t (2)	t (3)	Population in millions Y (4)	Y (5)	0.1381596t (6)	Log μ = 1.274670 − 0.1381596t (7)	μ (8)	1 + μ (9)	$Y_t = \dfrac{190.293}{1+\mu}$ (10)
1810	⋯	−1	7.2	⋯	−0.138160	1.412830	25.87	26.87	7.1
1820	t_0	0	9.6	9.6(Y_0)	0	1.274670	18.82	19.82	9.6
1830	⋯	1	12.9	⋯	0.138160	1.136510	13.69	14.69	13.0
1840	⋯	2	17.1	⋯	0.276319	0.998351	9.962	10.962	17.4
1850	⋯	3	23.2	⋯	0.414479	0.860191	7.248	8.248	23.1
1860	⋯	4	31.4	⋯	0.552638	0.722032	5.273	6.273	30.3
1870	⋯	5	39.8	⋯	0.690798	0.583872	3.836	4.836	39.3
1880	t_1	6	50.2	50.2(Y_1)	0.828958	0.445712	2.791	3.791	50.2
1890	⋯	7	62.9	⋯	0.967117	0.307553	2.030	3.030	62.8
1900	⋯	8	76.0	⋯	1.105277	0.169393	1.477	2.477	76.8
1910	⋯	9	92.0	⋯	1.243436	0.031234	1.075	2.075	91.7
1920	⋯	10	105.7	⋯	1.381596	−0.106926	0.7818	1.7818	106.8
1930	⋯	11	122.8	⋯	1.519756	−0.245086	0.5687	1.5687	121.3
1940	t_2	12	131.7	134.6(Y_2)	1.657915	−0.383245	0.4138	1.4138	134.6
1950	⋯	13	150.7	⋯	1.796075	−0.521405	0.3010	1.3010	146.3

Column (7)–(10) fall under the spanning header **Computation of Trend Values**.

Source: Frederick E. Croxton and Dudley J. Cowden, *Applied General Statistics*, © 1955. Reprinted by permission of Prentice-Hall, Inc., Englewood Cliffs, New Jersey.

Note: the Y values of column 5 are geometric means of three values centered at t_0, t_1, and t_2. The negative logarithms in column 7 must be rewritten in their alternative forms with negative characteristic and positive mantissa (e.g. −0.106926 = 9.893074 − 10) before the values of μ can be obtained.

where

$c \ldots x$ are parameters and

y_t, K, e, a, and b are defined as before

Expanding the exponent skews the curve so that the inflection point is no longer midway between the two asymptotes, zero and K. Thus, the two limbs of the curve are no longer mirror images of each other and the first differences are not normally distributed. This loss of symmetry may be desirable, however, if the new curve fits the data better.

Selecting and Improving the Model

Selecting a Growth Model

Common sense and trial and error are the best guides in selecting a model. Logic helps to narrow the choice to a few alternatives, and experimentation helps to identify the best one. For instance, if products similar to the firm's have an S-shaped growth curve and management wants a long-range forecast, a Gompertz or logistic function is clearly in order. If the analysts have access to a computer, they can easily experiment with several models and sets of data in order to see which one provides the best fit.

Once a model is selected, they may want to experiment with different parametric values to see how sensitive the dependent variable is to changes in underlying assumptions. For instance, they might vary the value of K to see how sensitive total, as well as incremental, sales are to estimates of the total potential market. If the dependent variable is highly sensitive to changes in a particular parameter, the assumptions underlying that parameter, and the estimate of it, may be in need of scrutiny. In fact, a special research project may be needed just to evaluate the assumptions.

After the raw data have been tabulated and purged of nonrecurring disturbances, they should be plotted on arithmetic graph paper and the points connected with a freehand curve to simulate the historical growth pattern. A curve that is straight, or close to it, suggests a linear function. The shape of the right-hand limb is especially important, since it is this portion of the curve that will be extended to produce the forecasting model.

If the curve suggests a nonlinear function, the data (including the curve) should also be plotted on semilogarithmic graph paper. If the result is a straight line, a logarithmic model is in order. If not, some other kind of curvilinear model is appropriate and the data should be examined further to narrow the choice.

If visual inspection of the arithmetic and logarithmic graphs fails to suggest an appropriate model, the analysts can compute and tabulate the first and second differences and transform the data into logarithms. They should then be able to use one of the rules of thumb suggested in Table 23-4.

Table 23-4 **Rules of Thumb for Selecting a Growth Model**

1. If the first differences tend to be constant, use a straight line.
2. If the second differences tend to be constant, use a second-degree curve.
3. If the first differences tend to decrease by a constant percentage, use a modified exponential model.
4. If the approximate trend, plotted on arithmetic paper, is a straight line, use a straight line.
5. If the approximate trend, plotted on semilogarithmic paper, is a straight line, use an exponential curve.
6. If the approximate trend, plotted on semilogarithmic paper, resembles a modified exponential function, use a Gompertz curve.
7. If the approximate trend, plotted on a grid with a reciprocal vertical scale and an arithmetic horizontal scale, resembles a modified exponential, use a logistic curve. Alternatively, $1/Y_C$ and X may be plotted on an arithmetic grid.
8. If the first differences resemble a skewed frequency curve, use a Gompertz curve or a more complex logistic curve, such as formula 23.26.
9. If the first differences resemble a normal frequency curve, use a logistic curve.
10. If the first differences of the logarithms are constant, use an exponential curve.
11. If the second differences of the logarithms are constant, fit a second-degree curve to the logarithms.
12. If the first differences of the logarithms are changing by a constant percentage, use a Gompertz curve.
13. If the first differences of the reciprocals are changing by a constant percentage, use a logistic curve.
14. If the approximate trend values (or the original data), expressed as percentages of a selected asymptote, appear linear on arithmetic probability paper, use a logistic curve.

Source: Adapted from Frederick E. Croxton and Dudley J. Cowden, *Applied General Statistics,* ©1955. Reprinted with permission of Prentice-Hall, Inc., Englewood Cliffs, New Jersey.

Improving the Model

The various growth functions, like all mathematical models, are ideal forms. They are smooth, often symmetrical (aside from the fact that the right-hand limb extends indefinitely), and free of the multitudinous disturbances that occur in the marketplace. Because they are trend lines representing the underlying relationship between sales and time, they are generally devoid of cyclical, seasonal, and irregular variation. This hardly nullifies their usefulness as models, but the analysts should recognize the need to adjust specific forecasts to accommodate these disturbances and to estimate confidence intervals.

Allowing for Replacement Sales   Sales figures generally have two components: (1) original and (2) replacement purchases. Replacement purchases are induced by product consumption and mortality. Manufacturers of some product classes—such as food, gasoline, and raw materials—depend almost exclusively on the replacement market. Others—such as education, dams, and wedding dresses—depend almost solely on original, or one-time, purchases. Brand sales, even of a mature product that depends primarily on replacement sales, are largely dependent on original purchases. The exception is a monopoly, where the brand and the product are synonymous, giving buyers no opportunity to switch.

The models developed thus far have not explicitly provided for replacement sales. If they are specified using historical data from a long enough period, the effects of consumption and mortality will be left and Y_t and ΔY_t will reflect the replacement market. However, because the replacement market lags behind the original-purchase market (frequently by several years), projections tend to understate the replacement demand. This defect in the model can be remedied by breaking down the forecast into two components: (1) original sales, Y, and (2) replacement sales, Y'. Combined sales, S, will then be

$$S_t = Y_t + Y_t' \qquad [23.27]$$

and

$$\Delta S_t = \Delta Y_t + \Delta Y_t' \qquad [23.28]$$

where

S_t = the cumulative combined sales for period t

Y_t = the cumulative original sales for period t

Y_t' = the cumulative replacement sales for period t

ΔS_t = the incremental combined sales in period t

ΔY_t = the incremental original sales in period t

$\Delta Y_t'$ = the incremental replacement sales in period t

The original sales can be estimated by any appropriate growth model. Replacement sales are a lagged function of original sales and can be expressed as a percentage of original sales in some previous period. Thus

$$\Delta Y_t' = c\,\Delta Y_{t-x} \qquad [23.29]$$

where

$\Delta Y_t'$ and ΔY_t are defined as before

c = the portion of original purchases that is replaced

x = the average life expectancy of the product (or the average length of time the product is kept by its original owner)

For example, original purchasers of automobiles retain their cars for an average of three years ($x = 3$). Since some of these purchasers will have died, the replacement market three years from now will not equal the original-sales market today. This fact is taken into account, in the model, by the coefficient c, which is always less then one.

The significance of the replacement component in the combined-sales equation depends on the product. In some cases—say, the product is tickets for a particular sports or theatrical event—it is zero, or so negligible that it can safely be ignored. With products such as shoes, tires, or home appliances, however, it must be included in the forecast.

Allowing for Variation in the Potential Market   Up to now we have assumed, in discussing exponential models, that the asymptote, K, remains constant. Unless the product has a short life cycle—say, less than five years—this is usually unrealistic. Even in the short run, K will probably vary, although not enough to affect short-range forecasts very much.

The principal factors that determine the total potential market, population and income, have a positive trend. Hence, K tends to increase from year to year, although major disturbances such as wars and recessions will occasionally disrupt this growth. The variable character of K suggests a modification of the exponential growth models to bring them closer to reality and hence make them more reliable as forecasting instruments. This is done by substituting K' for K in the equations. K' represents the present potential market, K, adjusted for growth over the life cycle of the product. The adjustment is made as follows

$$K_t' = (1 + \alpha)^t \cdot K \qquad\qquad\qquad [23.30]$$

where

K' = the total potential market in period t

α = the growth rate of the total potential market

t = the period

K = the total potential market at the time the product is introduced

The use of a variable, K', instead of a constant for the parameter specifying the total potential market may seem trivial to some. However, it is a very significant and realistic modification. Figure 23-15 shows the effect market growth can have on cumulative sales, Y_t; Figure 23-16 shows the effect it can have on incremental sales, ΔY_t. The bottom curve in each graph is a typical Gompertz function with K held constant. The upper two curves show the same Gompertz function when K increases at an annual rate of 3 and 6 percent, respectively.

If K is static, incremental sales will decline to virtually nothing once the product has reached maturity. Unless there is a substantial replacement market, there will be little reason for the firm to retain the product beyond this point. However, if population and other factors are increasing the potential market, then incremental sales, exclusive of replacement purchases, may sustain a product well past the beginning of the maturity stage. In fact, an annual increase in K of 6 percent ($\alpha = 0.06$) will provide continually increasing sales—both in the original and the replacement market. This is the delightful situation that confronts the automobile and construction

Figure 23-15   **Market Forecasts When *K* Varies: Cumulative Sales**

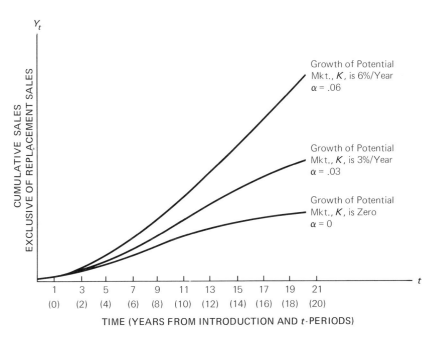

Figure 23-16   **Market Forecasts When *K* Varies: Annual Sales**

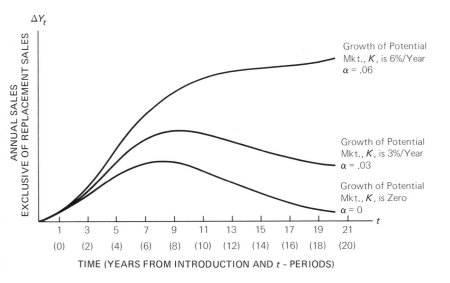

industries, whose products have been in the maturity state for many years.

In a dynamic economy, such as that of an industrialized nation, the forces that determine K and the other parameters of the growth models are constantly changing. Regardless of the goodness of fit of the original curve, the analysts should be alert for variations between forecast and actual values and be prepared to alter their models.

Problems

1   What kind of growth model, if any, would be appropriate for each of the following forecasts: (1) a 10-year forecast of color-television sales, (b) a 30-day forecast of Pillsbury cake-mix sales, and (c) a 20-year forecast of the demand for new housing? Defend your choice.

2   During the introductory stage of a new brand that was launched in a mature market for an established product class, 2,192 units were sold. Since that time, t_0, monthly sales of 400, 380, 420, 400, 350, and 450 units have been recorded. Construct an appropriate growth model, and use it to forecast cumulative sales two years from t_0. What doubts would you have about a forecast of sales ten years from t_0, and what additional information would you need to lessen these doubts?

3   Construct a growth model by fitting an appropriate curve to the following series of sales figures for consecutive periods: 140, 155, 173, 192, 209, 230. Comment on the model as a forecasting instrument.

4   A firm is introducing a new model that is a variation of a well-established product. Experience has led the marketing-research department to estimate a total potential market of 100,000 units and a model life cycle of 5 years. First-year sales of other models of the product have averaged 10 percent of the total sales. Total sales have averaged 80 percent of estimates of the total potential market. Construct a Gompertz model, and use it to forecast cumulative and annual sales for each of the next five years. Graph both curves.

5   In spite of its excellent goodness of fit, the Gompertz growth model of the U.S. (continental) population (Figure 23-13) failed to forecast accurately the population beyond 1960. What happened? Is there anything on the graph that suggests that the forecast was going astray? Compare this projection with the updated projection in Croxton and Cowden's 3rd or 4th edition of *Applied General Statistics*.

Chapter 24
Nonstatistical Methods and Other Matters

Key Concepts

Nonstatistical Forecasting
Building a model without benefit of historical data

Updating the Model
Improving yesterday's model with today's information

Applications
Practical problems in building and using forecasts

Key Terms

planning horizon

Nonstatistical Forecasting[1]

Traditional methods of marketing research are often inadequate for forecasting the demand for radically new products. Historical sources, surveys, and experimentation may fail to provide the information needed to specify a conventional model. Where, for example, could the electronics industry have found relevant sales data before introducing television? What kind of survey information could the container industry have gotten prior to introducing the tin can? How could a market experiment have been designed to test the acceptance of the diesel locomotive, prior to its production? Each of these goods was once a revolutionary new-product idea with a promising

---

[1] This section draws heavily on W. B. Wentz and G. I. Eyrich, "Product Forecasting Without Historical, Survey, or Experimental Data," in Robert L. King, *Marketing and the New Science of Planning* (Chicago: American Marketing Association, 1968), pp. 215–221.

but highly uncertain market. Each required substantial resources for its development, tooling, and introduction.

Product commercialization generally depends on the estimated profitability of an item and the associated risk, which are frequently combined into an expected value. An estimate of profitability requires cost and revenue information which in turn depends on an estimate of demand. Both total-demand and market-penetration rates are needed before management can allocate rationally.

When the traditional methods of data acquisition and analysis are inadequate, the researcher must try a less orthodox approach. Nonstatistical forecasting uses both marketing and innovation-diffusion theory to construct a demand model free of dependency on empirical data. Three steps are involved. First, a general model is constructed identifying the determinants of demand. Second, the general model is upgraded by estimating the parameters to provide an equation that will yield an estimate of the total potential demand for the product. Third, innovation-diffusion theory is used to estimate the rate of market penetration, and hence the product's annual sales.

If the firm does not have—or cannot maintain—a monopoly position, then the annual sales estimates must be adjusted to reflect its market share. In addition, the model can be made stocastic by explicitly including a probabilistic factor. Later, as experience accumulates, the forecasting model can be altered to reflect the realities of the marketplace.

Constructing a General Model

The most important and difficult task in constructing a general model—within the context of nonstatistical forecasting—is the selection of the independent variables. (Sales are normally the dependent variable.) These variables represent the basic determinants of total (industry) demand. They do not include factors such as price and advertising that are associated exclusively with the firm's demand and which act primarily as determinants of market share.

In searching for the basic determinants of demand, the researcher should think in terms of the new product's potential applications. For instance, if the item is useful in the medical field, then hospitals, doctors, or patients are probable determinants of demand. The number of hospitals, their total capacity (the number of beds), or the doctor or patient population may be appropriate variables.

An independent variable should have two properties. First, it should be measurable, or at least estimable with precision. Second, it should be forecastable. Without these qualities, a variable is useless as part of a forecasting model. The search for demand determinants and the variables to represent them usually begins with the originator of the new product. Presumably, he or she had one or more specific applications in mind when the idea was developed. Often the idea itself results from the perception of a need, and hence an application in the marketplace. Management is well advised to discover some practical applications before it commits substantial resources to the further development and introduction of the product. Many companies assign a market researcher to work with the product's developers early in the evaluation and development of the idea.

After the possible applications have been defined and the demand determinants and their companion variables have been isolated, a simple model can be constructed based on the following general form:

$$D = f(X_1, X_2, \ldots X_n) \tag{24.1}$$

where

D = the total potential demand

X = independent variables representing the determinants of demand $1, 2, \ldots n$

For example, assume that the firm is evaluating a device which would give users direct access to published material. The device is a computerized closed-circuit television system providing remote terminals with random access to a data bank of published documents. The most likely sources of demand are public libraries, secondary schools, colleges, and major business firms and institutions with large collections of reference material. In constructing the equation, these factors are represented by the number of libraries, secondary schools, colleges, corporations with sales over $100 million, and independent research organizations in the firm's market area. These five variables are labeled X_1, X_2, X_3, X_4, and X_5, respectively. Thus, the general model is $D = f(X_1, X_2, X_3, X_4, X_5)$. The total potential demand, D, is a function of the number of libraries, secondary schools, colleges, and so on.

Constructing an Explicit Model

Now that the forecasting problem has been reduced to manageable dimensions, the researcher can focus on specific factors, such as the demand generated by libraries, in upgrading the model. The explicit form of the forecasting equation is derived by estimating the potential demand associated with each determinant. Summing these separate elements gives us the estimate of total potential demand

$$\hat{D} = \hat{\gamma}_1 X_1 + \hat{\gamma}_2 X_2 + \cdots \hat{\gamma}_n X_n \tag{24.2}$$

where

$\hat{D}$ = the estimate of total potential demand

$\hat{\gamma}$ = the estimate of the parameter of demand determinant X

$1, 2, \ldots n$ are the numbers of the demand determinants

For example, we can extend the previous example by assuming that demand is measured by the number of remote terminals ordered. A study of the product's applications in public libraries indicate that the average library could justify three units. Since X_1 represents the number of libraries, the parameter $\hat{\gamma}_1$ becomes 3. Thus, the term specifying the relationship between total demand, $\hat{D}$ and the library population is $3X_1$.

Estimating the parameters—$\hat{\gamma}_1, \hat{\gamma}_2, \ldots \hat{\gamma}_n$ in the forecasting model— requires a thorough analysis of the product's applications with respect to each of the demand determinants identified in step one. This analysis may be performed within the firm when security is important or with the aid of potential customers. Potential users frequently provide insights with respect to both applications and limitations that elude the firm. In fact, in the industrial-goods field, customers are a prime source of new-product ideas. Interviews with customers can also provide insights with respect to promotional tactics and modifications of the product itself, if it is commercialized.

The case for customer involvement was illustrated not too long ago in a study of the aggregate demand for helicopters in the petroleum industry. One of the applications suggested for the product was pipeline patrols. (Pipeline patrols were previously made on foot, on horseback, or with land vehicles or fixed-wing aircraft.) Discussions with pipeline operators and helicopter pilots provided a good estimate of the number of miles of pipeline that could be patroled by a single helicopter. A forecasting model was constructed using the reciprocal of that value as the parameter and inter-terminal pipeline mileage (published data) as the variable for the term representing that particular product application.

Once all the parameters have been estimated, the explicit equation can be specified. In the preceding example, the equation might be $\hat{D} = 3X_1 + 2X_2 + 5X_3 + 2X_4 + 2X_5$, where $\hat{D}$ is the estimate of total potential demand expressed in terms of the number of terminal units and $X_1, X_2, \ldots X_5$ are the demand determinants.

Like most equations derived in this way, the function is linear and additive. Usually each variable represents a particular market segment or customer group. We hope the variables will be exclusive. If they are not, a compensating term should be incorporated into the equation. This would be necessary, for example, if there were joint applications. Many colleges operate research institutes and hence would be included in the count for both X_3 and X_5, thus inflating the total-demand figure. This could be corrected by adding to the equation the term $-\hat{\gamma}_6 X_6$, where X_6 equals the number of college research bureaus.

One of the virtues of this approach is that the market segments are defined at an early stage. Even if the estimated values for the parameters are a bit shaky, there is still an advantage in formally defining the independent variables that represent the potential markets. This is a major step toward the efficient allocation of research resources.

Estimating the Market-Penetration Rate

The explicit equation for $\hat{D}$ yields an estimate of the total potential demand for the new product. This is a static model; that is, it makes no allowance for changes in the parameters over time. Static models are unrealistic in that few marketing phenomena or processes occur instantaneously. The innovation-diffusion process takes time—often many years. Even a spectacular and extremely beneficial product, such as the Salk antipolio vaccine, is not immediately accepted by every potential user.

In the consumer-goods field, total market penetration is seldom achieved. Ignorance, stubbornness, disinterest, religious or philosophical beliefs, or cultural biases may prevent potential buyers from crossing the purchase threshold. Even today there are Amish and Mennonites in Indiana and Pennsylvania who prefer horses and buggies to automobiles for religious reasons. Likewise, there are many people, especially in the cities, who have given up automobiles in favor of older but nonpolluting forms of transportation, such as bicycles. Even when the barriers to complete market penetration can be overcome, the cost is usually prohibitive. The additional promotional expenditures necessary to push the last of the laggards across the purchase threshold are seldom exceeded by the added revenue they would produce. Thus, total sales may approach, but seldom equal, $\hat{D}$.

The market-penetration rate is usually nonlinear. As the product histories in Figures 23-8 and 23-9 indicate the penetration rate—that is, sales per unit of time—varies over the life cycle of the product. Market penetration (cumulative sales) at any point in time is usually described by an S-shaped curve such as the Gompertz function described earlier. This kind of model is especially useful when nonstatistical forecasting is required.

Using the Gompertz Function

When the Gompertz function is applied to nonstatistical forecasting, K is equivalent to $\hat{D}$. The estimate of the total potential demand, $\hat{D}$, provided by the explicit equation, is the asymptotic limit, K, in the Gompertz function. The other values needed to solve the function (equation 23-2) are determined by the methods suggested in Chapter 23. Once these values are specified, the equation will yield a value for cumulative sales, Y_t, for each period, t, in the product's life cycle.

Formula 23.4 can be used to compute the anticipated sales in each period. If K remains constant over time, these incremental sales will increase, peak, and then decline. However, if K depends on GNP, personal income, or population, it will probably continue to increase over time. Incremental sales may remain stable or increase even after the product has entered the maturity stage. This phenomenon is illustrated in Figures 23-15 and 23-16. Of course, the introduction of another innovation—one that makes the present product obsolete—can terminate this process, causing incremental sales to decline sharply as the original good gives way to the improved version.

The point of obsolescence is often forecastable, especially when the innovation is not radical. For instance, automobile body styles go out of fashion after three years, women's clothing after one or two. When an innovation is a radical departure from anything in its product class or creates a totally new product class—as did the automobile, radio, and television when they were first introduced—the obsolescence point cannot be forecast. Under these circumstances, we simply assume that obsolescence will not occur during the period covered by the forecast.

The forecast period is usually determined by the firm's planning horizon. The *planning horizon* is the time limit imposed on projections of revenues, costs, profit, and on budgets. It is the time period covered by the plan, forecast, etc. Ten years is usually the maximum; a three-year planning horizon is common in the processed-foods industry, a one-year horizon in retailing and high-fashion industries.

In all prediction and forecasting methods, the initial estimates are altered as new information is accumulated. Once the product is on the market and empirical data filter in, more conventional techniques can be used and nonstatistical forecasts discontinued.

Updating the Model

The job of forecasting is a rather precarious task at best. The uncertainty inherent in market behavior underscores the need for rigorous research. It also ensures that the outcomes which occur in the marketplace will not coincide exactly with those forecast. Some error must be expected. In fact, the absence of error is unnatural, for the true determinants of demand do change over time and their relationship with sales does alter. No researcher can consistently forecast these changes and alterations.

Using New Information

Time not only shows up forecasting errors, it also provides new information. This information can be useful in updating the model and improving research techniques. For instance, additional observations will usually increase the precision of the model, especially when linear regression analysis or similar methods of fitting a line have been used. Even if the method of data collection has been nonrandom (thus precluding the use of statistically determined confidence intervals) or the model was constructed by drawing a freehand curve, a comparison of the new observations and the forecast values will tell the researcher something about the quality of the model.

Time also provides an opportunity for refining the model. Plotting new observations of the forecast variable against the forecast provides a quick test of the model's quality. If the actual values are near those predicted, the model is performing well, and the only reason for respecifying it is to narrow the confidence interval.

Respecifying the Model

If the new observations are far from the forecast values, the model should be respecified, if not completely restructured. The actual values, both old and new, should be examined to see if a pattern is emerging. Patterns are easiest to detect in two-variable time-series models portrayed graphically. Multivariate models, such as three- and four-variable causal models, may present a problem. An inspection of the data will not always disclose a meaningful pattern. A curvilinear relationship may seem to be emerging when the model assumes linearity, or vice versa. A modified exponential curve may emerge when a logarithmic function has been used for the model. These conflicts can often be resolved only by restructuring the model to conform with the emerging pattern.

If the pattern of the observations appears to match that of the model, but there is a large discrepancy between the observed and the forecast values, it is time to reestimate the parameters. The structure of the model is left unaltered, but the parameters are recomputed using the new data (as well as the original observations). These new calculations should displace the curve of forecast values, or alter its slope, so that it conforms more closely to the new data.

Repurging the Data

Occasionally time will reveal information that allows the analyst to do a better job of purging unwanted variations and disturbances from the original data. Purifying the earlier data can lead to a better forecasting model, but it can also lead to distortion if the purging is not done consistently and honestly. The model's apparent quality may be enhanced while its real value deteriorates. It is very tempting to make adjustments when they bring the observed data closer to the forecast values and ignore adjustments when they increase the dispersion of the observations.

Improving Research Skills

Time also gives the firm's research department a chance to improve its skills, especially when a particular type of product or market is being researched repeatedly. Researchers should keep a tally of forecast values and estimates of parameters, as well as observations gathered after the forecast and updated parametric values. This information can be used to construct distribution curves and compute standard deviations, hence confidence intervals. The estimated value that is the most likely, or mean, outcome, can be pinpointed. The standard deviation can be computed from previous forecasting experience and used to calculate the range of possible error at the desired confidence interval.

For instance, a firm competing in a market with a good deal of new-brand competition—such as the cigarette, breakfast-food, and detergent markets—may have to estimate K and m parameters for Gompertz growth models frequently. Its own experience and its observation of the performance of competing brands will soon reveal a distribution of these parameters about their means. This information can then be used to judge the precision of forecasts.

Multiple Forecasts

A more sophisticated forecast may contain three estimates of Y. The middle estimate is the forecast value produced by the model when the expected, or mean, values are used for the parameters. The other two estimates are produced when the high and low values of the parameters, at a given confidence level, are used. For instance, suppose the number of periods to product maturity, m, is 5, with 90 percent of the observed values resting between 4 and 6. Sales can be forecast with $m = 4$, $m = 5$, and $m = 6$ to obtain the highest, lowest, and expected values at the 90 percent confidence level. Variations in the other parameters can be handled in the same manner.

The model need not be constructed with randomized data in order to obtain multiple forecasts. Only the observations used to estimate the range of error of the parameters must be selected at random. (As a practical matter, all the observations are generally used.) The difficulty, of course, is that a series of models and observations must have been made previously. There is no way to specify statistically the confidence intervals for the first couple of models unless they are based on randomly gathered data.

Applications

Forecasting and the Decision Process

As Figure 24-1 suggests, the forecasts often fit into a complex process of intelligence-gathering, data reduction and analysis, and decision-making. Politics can also play a role. Machiavelli, rather than a rigorous forecast, is sometimes the chief inspiration for the line manager.

Successful forecasting, like other forms of marketing research, rests largely on technical skill and good communications. Brilliant technique is wholly for naught if line management does not understand and believe, or simply ignores, the forecast.

The information conduit should flow two ways, not just from the forecaster to the manager. Managers not only carry the burden of decision, many have sharp noses for the marketplace. They can be a gold mine of ideas and insights. Managers should be involved in the forecasting process, especially in the problem definition stage.

Problem Definition

At the Xerox Corporation and the Corning Glass Works, they are confronted with the following questions by their forecasters:[2]

How is the forecast to be used?

What decision will be based on the forecast and when must this decision be made?

The decision is also the key to level of precision required. Some decisions can tolerate a forecasting error of 20 to 30 percent. Others are sensitive to a 5 to 10 percent error. The precision requirement will significantly influence the method, time, and cost of the forecast.

---

[2] John C. Chambers, Satinder K. Mullick, and Donald D. Smith, *An Executive's Guide to Forecasting* (New York: Wiley, 1974), p. 17.

Figure 24-1   **The Role of the Forecast in the Decision Process**

Source: John C. Chambers, Satinder K. Mullick, and Donald D. Smith, *An Executive's Guide to Forecasting* (New York: Wiley, 1974), p. 15.

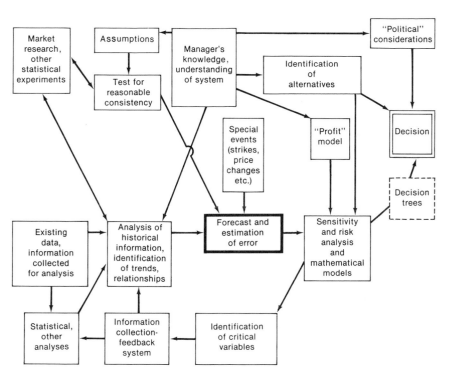

Research Design

The research design focuses mainly on the selection of forecasting methods. In selecting the method, the forecaster should ponder the

> nature and timing of the marketing decision
> error tolerance
> time and budget
> value of historical data
> data availability
> forecast horizon
> technical properties of alternative methods (see Table 24-1)

Product Life Cycle

The application of forecasting is somewhat governed by the product's life cycle. Forecasting needs, error tolerance, and data availability all vary over the life of the product. A research design appropriate to one stage may be inappropriate to another. Table 24-1 illustrates.

Table 24-1 **Forecasting and the Product Life Cycle**

State of life cycle	Preproduct	Product Development	Market Testing and Early Introduction	Rapid Growth	Steady State	Phasing Out
Typical decisions	Allocation of R&D Distribution system needs Personnel needs Acquisitions	Amount of development effort Product design Business strategies	Optimum facility size Marketing strategies, including distribution and pricing	Facilities expansion Marketing strategies Production planning	Promotions specials Pricing Production planning Inventories	Transfer of facilities Marketing effort Production planning
Forecasting techniques	Delphi method Progress functions Panel consensus Trend analysis Historical analogy Tracking for signals	Delphi method Historical analysis of comparable products Priority pattern analysis Input-output analysis Panel consensus	Consumer surveys Tracking-and-warning systems Market tests Experimental designs **Sales**	Statistical techniques for identifying turning points Tracking-and-warning systems Market surveys Intention-to-buy surveys	Time-series analysis and projection Causal and econometric models Market surveys for tracking and warning Life-cycle analysis	Slope characteristic Statistical tracking and market research Historical analogy and regression analysis

Source: John C. Chambers, Satinder K. Mullick, and Donald D. Smith, *An Executive's Guide to Forecasting* (New York: Wiley, 1974), p. 73.

Examples

Short of the Concorde supersonic transport, where politics overrode economics, forecasting's biggest failure was probably the Ford Edsel. The Edsel disaster was fathered by sloppy forecasting. The forecast rested not on a poll of what consumers wanted, but on a study of preferences toward cars the industry already offered.[3] Then, as perhaps now, industry research was largely directed toward validating management's preconceptions.

Spectacular successes are more difficult to cite than disasters, because good forecasting is seldom credited for a marketing success. However, there are some yeoman examples.

The Corning Glass Works has forecasting well integrated into its management system. Corning's forecasting procedure admits both macro and micro data. It includes an econometric model to forecast key economic determinants of demand. It includes simulation models to predict consumer requirements. The forecast is instrumental in determining production schedules, inventory levels, and marketing plans.[4]

Cessna has successfully used forecasts to determine the level of resources allocated to particular products. One of its best forecasts was the estimated demand for its Model 150 during the airplane's first year of production. Demand was estimated at 3,000. By year's end, sales were within a few aircraft of that number. The company experienced no opportunity cost and no surplus inventory cost on that product, thanks to a precise forecast accepted by Cessna management.

The Research and Planning Division of the United California Bank predicts the values of key economic indicators for California and the nation. These annual forecasts are used by the bank management and by the bank's clients. Over the past eleven years, they have been in error an average of 0.9 percent.[5]

The *raison d'être* of forecasting rests on a simple fact: Major business decisions are made on the basis of management's perception of the future. That perception can mirror intuition or rigorous analysis.

Problems

1 Name a recent product innovation that has just been introduced or is not yet on the market, and explain how you would estimate its demand. Prepare an equation for the computation of this demand.

---

[3] Theodore A. Levitt, "Marketing Myopia," *Harvard Business Review* **38**:4 (July–August 1960), p. 45.

[4] John C. Chambers, Satinder K. Mullick, and Donald D. Smith, "How To Choose the Right Forecasting Technique," *Harvard Business Review* **48**:4 (July–August 1970), p. 52.

[5] Research and Planning Division, UCB, *1978 Forecast* (Los Angeles: United California Bank), p. 4.

If you must limit the equation to its general form, explain how you would go about specifying the parameters.

2   Explain how you would update the model you have just developed as market experience accumulated. What data should you gather after the product had been introduced?

3   How would you estimate the annual (or monthly) and cumulative sales of the innovation, using the model developed in response to question 1?

4   Cite some industries where forecasting is extremely important. Explain why.

Part 8
Summary

Forecasts are among the most important products of marketing research. Major business decisions often rest on them.

Forecasts depend on several assumptions. These include the existence of a statistical relationship between the forecast variable and one or more determinants. Another key assumption is that this relationship will remain stable over time or between places, or that its changes can be anticipated.

There exist a broad assortment of forecasting methods. There are the essentially qualitative techniques such as the Delphi method, poll, and judgment forecasts. There are the time-series (growth model) methods which treat the dependent variable as a function of time. And there are the causal methods which search for a statistical relationship between the forecast variable and one or more determinants, other than time. Each has its own bundle of characteristics: accuracy, data requirements, cost, and time.

Researchers are typically confronted with composite data. To reveal the trend, these data must be disaggregated by removing cyclical variation, seasonal variation, and irregular fluctuation (noise). Later, in making monthly or seasonal forecasts, seasonal variation is often reintroduced.

Formal forecasting is often done with growth curves. These vary from simple linear models to complex curvilinear ones. The latter include second-degree-polynomials, logarithmic functions, modified basic exponential functions, Gompertz functions, and logistic functions.

A true innovation, such as television or the electronic calculator may confront the forecaster with little or no relevant data. Such a situation drives the researcher to nonstatistical forecasting where a quantitative answer must be produced from mainly qualitative input.

The application of forecasting varies with the nature and timing of management decisions. The forecast is often part of a complex process, where many factors impinge on its construction and acceptance. Not the least of these is politics, the researcher's technical skills, and his or her ability to communicate with management.

Case Study 8

Cessna Aircraft Company: How High Will Citation Fly?

Walter B. Wentz

The Cessna Aircraft Company was once described by a member of the Piper family as "the best-managed company in general aviation." If longevity, sales, growth, and profit are the criteria, Mr. Piper was—and still is—correct. Cessna has built over half of the general aviation airplanes produced in the United States in the past two decades. It has survived over 40 years of depression, recessions, booms, and wars in an industry that has been a grave-yard for hopes and fortunes.

The general aviation industry is an oligopoly, dominated by three old firms: Cessna, Beech, and Piper. More than 100 other airframe companies have entered the industry since its founding in the 1920s. Few have survived. Except for the big three, virtually none have made money, at least not over many years. The business is exciting and glamorous, however. In fact, these may be the qualities that have attracted many promoters and investors.

Cessna management has succeeded in finding the magic mix of product and promotion and of commitment and constraint that has eluded most other entrants. It has developed a keen sense of timing and an uncanny nose for holes in the marketplace. Thus, it has brilliantly positioned new products, satisfying large demands that were being ignored by its competitors.

This is not to suggest the firm has been infallible. On the contrary, it has an impressive assortment of product blunders. Examples are its four-engine transport and its civilian helicopter, both of which absorbed considerable earnings. However, Cessna management has seldom allowed ego to take priority over the sound of the cash register. It has willingly scrapped new products, thus writing off millions of dollars of investment, when data and judgment indicated the market was illusionary.

Management has also faced its corporate responsibilities, long before such behavior was fashionable. For instance, when it canceled its helicopter program, it repurchased every unit that had been sold. This prevented customers from owning orphan aircraft that would have no ready source of spare parts or engineering support.

Except for its unsuccessful excursion into the helicopter market, Cessna had developed its civilian product line around half-a-dozen basic models of single- and twin-engine airplanes. These used conventional piston engines with propellers. Its military line, however, included a small jet-engine trainer, the T-37. (Military sales varied dramatically but never exceeded 20 percent of the output, except during World War II.) Business aviation provided most of the firm's revenue.

Dr. Leslie Thomason developed for Cessna the largest, as well as the best, marketing research group in the industry. He was the first researcher to demonstrate empirically what many aircraft marketers long suspected: that there is a high degree of brand loyalty among airplane owners. Thomason also showed that there was a strong tendency for owners to trade up and that the entry vehicle was typically a small single-engine airplane. This behavioral pattern held for both pleasure and business airplane buyers. Thus, the probability of a prospect purchasing a particular airplane was largely determined by the brand and size of airplane he or she currently (or previously) owned.

Thomason's findings rationalized Cessna's strategy of proliferating models. A consumer could start with a model 150 (about $10,000) and then move, by relatively small increments, all the way to a deluxe model 421 (about $450,000) without ever leaving the Cessna line. However, stepping beyond the 421 led out of the Cessna line and into a turbine-powered airplane, either a turboprop or a pure-jet aircraft. Beech with its King Air, Gates with its Learjet, and Mitsubishi with its MU-2 were being fed customers by Cessna. By 1968, several hundred of these small turbines were being sold annually. Their market, although sensitive to the economy, was growing. (Sales are inferred from deliveries. Deliveries normally lag sales by three to nine months, but are used as a sales proxy because they are recorded and published by the FAA.)

Cessna clearly had incentive to push its line upward, which meant the addition of a turbine-powered twin-engine airplane—an executive jet. The firm responded with Citation This is a pure-jet aircraft initially priced, completely equipped, at $695,000.

That price made Citation the least costly pure-jet airplane, yet positioned the product next to the turboprop airplanes. In fact, the Citation was conceived through an exercise in product positioning. Management saw a gap between the turboprops, then topping off at a price of $650,000, and the jet, starting at $900,000. It also saw a demand for a plane with pure-jet performance but with the ability to operate from

A Cessna Citation

Source: Courtesy Cessna Aircraft Company.

small fields. It perceived the demand for a pure jet that an experienced piston-twin pilot could easily learn to fly. (Hence, the Cessna piston-twin pilot could easily make the transition into the new jet.) The Citation met these criteria nicely, except that it was 80 knots slower than any other pure jet.

Citation was seen as a trade-up aircraft, thus defining its market as mainly owners of piston-twin and turboprop airplanes, particularly Cessnas. Citation was a logical extension of the present line. Thus, it seemed like an easy product to adapt to the firm's manufacturing and marketing facilities, both of which were the biggest—and probably the best—in the industry.

In a business that is characterized by inbreeding, Cessna has been unique in that it has hired executives from outside the industry. It has even gone so far as to ignore the rule "pilot first, businessman second." Thus, James B Taylor, formerly a vice-president of Pan American World Airways Corporation, was recruited in 1969 to head the Citation program.

Taylor soon discovered he was not in agreement with Cessna management on many major issues. The most controversial one was the use of the established distribution system.

Taylor wanted, and finally got, his own marketing organization, the "Commercial Jet Marketing Division" (CJMD). CJMD
was a radical departure from Cessna tradition, for it was designed
by Taylor to sell Citations directly to the consumers. Thus, it
bypassed one of the firm's most important assets, Cessna's
network of more than 800 domestic and foreign dealers. Many
general aviation marketers saw this as sheer folly. A few saw it
as the final error in a series of mistakes that started with a bad
product concept: Neither Citation nor CJMD would fit into the
general aviation market.

The marketplace of general aviation has often been described as a "village bazaar"—a place where sellers lay out their
wares and wait sleepily for customers. Taylor arrived in Wichita
with the expressed intention of leading at least one seller into
the twentieth century. He also expected to sell 1,000 Citations in
the coming decade.

Under Taylor's leadership the Commercial Jet Marketing
Division became very independent and very different from
Cessna's established marketing organization. More important,
it sold airplanes—lots of them.

By July 1973, Cessna was deep into the executive jet segment of the aviation market. In the prior year, it had delivered
more business jets than any of its competitors. CJMD and Citation were Number One.

Production was running at nine units per month, ordered to
to go to 12 early in 1974. These numbers had been set by intuition
and presumably would match Citation sales. They reflected the
best judgment of Cessna's president and the chairman of its
board.

Taylor likes to hear, but does not always accept, the findings
and opinions of outsiders. Thus, he sometimes employs the
services of consultants. So do several of his key executives, including E. J. Brandreth, Jr., general sales manager. Mr. Brandreth
asked a member of the American Research Institute to forecast
Citation sales.

Forecasting in the airframe industry is a high-stakes game.
If management accepts a forecast that proves low, it experiences
heavy opportunity costs. That is, it forgoes sales and profits
because of its inability to deliver enough product. If it goes with a
forecast that proves, high, it incurs heavy losses supporting an
inventory of costly airplanes.

Marketing Decisions

Management must establish a budget, hire marketing and
manufacturing personnel, write production releases and purchase
orders, and prepare for a cash flow, all based on the number of

airplanes it will sell. Some of these commitments, such as the purchase orders for jet engines, must be made 12 to 18 months prior to aircraft delivery.

Information Needs

Management needs an accurate forecast of Citation sales for the next 24 months. It would like a reasonable forecast for the following four years.

Data[1]

The history of Citation sales, from formal introduction to the time the forecast was requested, is shown below. The numbers include both foreign and domestic sales, with foreign sales rather consistently accounting for 25 percent of the total.

1971		1972		1973	
Sept.	2	Jan.	3	Jan.	13
Oct.	0	Feb.	4	Feb.	16
Nov.	1	Mar.	3	Mar.	14
Dec.	0	Apr.	6	Apr.	15
		May	4	May	16
		June	5	June	13
		July	6		
		Aug.	8		
		Sept.	9		
		Oct.	11		
		Nov.	8		
		Dec.	12		

Assignment   Forecast Citation's cumulative total sales from July 1973 through June 1980.

Note: The reader might be tempted to invoke hindsight by reading currently available publications that contain data on Citation deliveries during the critical forecast period. However, this will not only spoil the fun, but may be misleading. Sales are seldom in phase with deliveries in this industry.

---

[1] The data in this case have been disguised to maintain the security of proprietary information. However, this does not alter the essence of the case.

Part 9
Simulation

Introduction

> *At the General Foods Corporation, a new product manager raised the wholesale price of instant coffee to $14.85 per case. To offset the price increase and maintain market share, he increased the first year's advertising budget $11,500,000. The changes were implemented immediately. Market share dropped nearly one-quarter and profit declined $543,601.*
>
> *In an effort to salvage market share and regain lost earnings, price was lowered $1.00 and the advertising budget was reduced $1,800,000. The marketplace responded with little enthusiasm. A portion of the lost market share was regained, but earnings dropped another $631,905.*
>
> *Further changes in the marketing mix were ordered. Both market share and profit improved, but remained below their original level. The manager was beginning to recognize his mistakes.*
>
> *Although the profit-and-loss statements for the product (Maxim) indicated the manager's errors had cost General Foods over $1.4 million, he retained his job. His boss didn't even reprimand him. The manager had been simulating.*

Simulation is the manipulation of a symbolic, analogical, or iconic model to determine the changes in one or more dependent variables induced by changes in one or more independent variables. If the model is a reasonably accurate replica of reality—or at least those aspects of reality that are relevant—the results of the simulation can be assumed to represent real-world outcomes. For instance, an economist might construct a model of aggregate consumer behavior with respect to expenditures for recreation. The model would likely include personal disposable income as one of the independent variables. The effect of changes in consumer income on recreational expenditures could then be determined by manipulating the income variable and observing the different levels of recreational expenditures that resulted.

In a broad sense, the term *market simulation* describes the manipulation of nearly any model of a marketing phenomenon, including consumer panels or test markets, representative of the market population. In fact, we might even call market experimentation a special case of market simulation. Marketing-research literature, however, generally confines its discussion of simulation to models with no live elements and where the data generated are artificial; that is, no changes actually occur in the real marketplace. In this narrower context, all the elements of the simulation model are artificial. Business gaming, where competing firms are frequently represented by live players, is one exception. However, even business games frequently provide artificial players whose moves are determined probabilistically. The single live player is the decision-maker for one of the competing firms, who represents the home team.

Simulation minimizes the effort, cost, and risk involved in manipulating market conditions and trying out alternative courses of action. However, it is not a substitute for logic or the decision process, both of which are needed to prepare and use a model. The five applications of market simulation—defined for pedagogical convenience—are:

business gaming
experimentation
the analysis of transition processes
forecasting
heuristic programming

We shall discuss each of these applications after we have explored the anatomy of market simulation.

Chapter 25
Anatomy of Market Simulation

Key Concepts

Simulation Systems
Nomenclature and design problems of simulation

Virtues and Limitation
The advantages and constraints of simulation

Market Models
The basic components of models designed to simulate markets

Players
The real-world people or institutions and their roles in the simulation process

Data
The sources and nature of the data that go into and come out of the model

Key Terms

symbolic model	iteration
analogical model	program
iconic model	artificial data
stochastic model	Monte Carlo methods
dynamic model	programming
operating characteristic	

Simulation Systems

System Components

A simulation system requires:

a model
players
input data
output data

Figure 25-1   **A Simulation System**

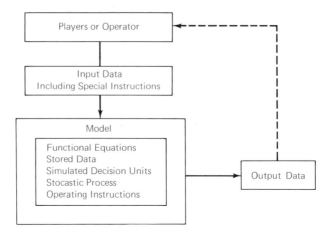

Computers are generally associated with simulation and are often essential to the manipulation of the more sophisticated models. However, the concept of simulation was understood long before the age of the computer.[1] Even today many models are manipulated manually or with the aid of a good pocket calculator. The computer may facilitate simulation but it is not a theoretical prerequisite. The simulation system in Figure 25-1 is typical of the types—often computerized—used in marketing research.

Types of Models

Simulation models can be symbolic, analogical, or iconic, depending on whether they are, respectively, equations, analogues, or physical replicas of reality. A *symbolic model* uses numbers and other symbols to represent properties of the process or object being simulated. Its heart is a system of one or more mathematical equations describing a relationship between variables of the model. An *analogical model* uses one or more of its (the analogue's) physical properties to represent a property of a process or an object. The continuous scale on a dial—such as the tuning scale representing a band of broadcast frequencies and the fuel meter representing quantities of gasoline—are illustrative. An *iconic model* is a smaller (or larger), but exact, replica of a real object, at least with respect to the feature being studied. It is usually a scale model and operative to some extent. A model airplane is an example.

Simulation is used in both physical and social sciences. An easily recognized example is the wind tunnel testing of small-scale iconic models

---

[1] For example, the ancient game of chess is a simulation of two opposing forces on the field of battle; it was once used as a military training game.

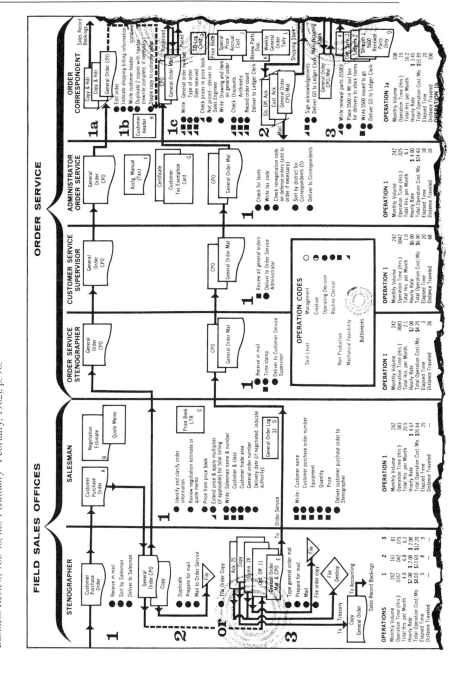

of airplanes. Much of the performance data are determined by simulating flight in a wind tunnel. These data would otherwise have to be gathered by full-scale flight tests or estimated by elaborate mathematical analysis using cumbersome systems of equations.

In business and economic research, the symbolic model is the most common. However, there are exceptions. For example, A. W. Phillips of the London School of Economics built a hydraulic apparatus which he used to estimate the effect of government monetary policies on British income flows.[2] William R. King built a simple mechanical analogue of customer locations which he used to solve warehouse-location problems.[3] Market Facts, Inc., uses consumer panels as iconic models of national market populations.[4] Flow charts and small-scale replicas of floor plans and equipment are occasionally used to simulate order or product flows, customer traffic, and store or warehouse layouts. In business logistics (a field peripheral to marketing, since it deals with physical-distribution problems), analogical and iconic models are common.

Figure 25-2 shows an analogical model of part of a firm's order booking, processing, and billing procedure. Such charts are very useful in the analysis of distribution problems, especially when the objective is to streamline the flow of paperwork or the handling of merchandise, since they help to identify bottlenecks, redundancy, and waste.

Figure 25-3 shows an iconic model, a three-dimensional replica of an office, complete with desks, cabinets, equipment, and miniature people.

Although we may not have said so, we have engaged in the construction of symbolic models throughout much of the book. Any time we write an equation specifying the relationship between two or more marketing variables, we are constructing a symbolic model of a marketing phenomenon. Of course, such models have many purposes, only one of which is simulation.

Although a single-equation model may be used for simulation, multiple-equation models are far more common. In fact, one of the strengths of simulation is that it allows any number of equations, different in structure and parametric specifications, to be incorporated into the model.

Design Considerations

Market-simulation models can be very simple or extremely complex. For instance, we might use the equation $Q = 4700 - 85P$ as a model of a sales-price relationship. To determine the sales, Q, at any given price, P, we would simply substitute the price value for P and solve for Q. Simulating the effect

[2] A. W. Phillips, "Mechanical Models in Economic Dynamics," *Economica* **17**:67 (August 1950), pp. 283–305.

[3] William R. King, *Quantitative Analysis for Marketing Management* (New York: McGraw-Hill, 1967), p. 539.

[4] Jack Abrams, "A New Method for Testing Price Decisions," *Journal of Marketing* **28**:2 (July 1964) pp. 6–9; and "Reducing the Risk of New Product Marketing Strategies Testing," *Journal of Marketing Research* **6**:2 (May 1969), pp. 216–220.

Figure 25-3   **An Iconic Model**

Source: Marshall K. Evans and Lou R. Hague, "Master Plan for Information Systems." Reprinted with permission of *Harvard Business Review*, vol. 40, no. 1 (January-February, 1962), p. 100.

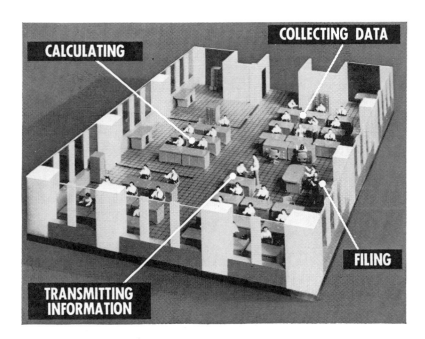

of price on sales in this way is far easier, cheaper, and safer than manipulating price in the marketplace.

Obviously, such a model is naive—or we could say, "not comprehensive"—for it ignores any number of important factors. The output value generated will be realistic only so long as these factors remain constant or change in such a way that their effects cancel one another out. This is an unrealistic assumption.

The model's shortcomings can be corrected by incorporating more significant factors. For example, the equation might be expanded to $Q = 4700 - 85P + 0.5A + 4.8S + 234R$, where A, S, and R represent advertising expenditures, personal selling (in person-hours), and the number of retail outlets for the product. The model would then be more sophisticated, but it would still exclude many factors that affect sales, such as consumer income, population, and tastes, as well as the prices, advertising expenditures, sales forces, distribution channels, and products of the firm's competitors. Nor does the expanded model make any allowance for uncertainty or changes in the effect of variables over time. Simulation offers an answer to these problems.

If the researcher needs a model of the profit process, a cost function can be added to the revenue function already suggested. Models that contain dozens of independent variables and go far beyond the analytical techniques, such as regression analysis, discussed previously, can be constructed. The Brookings Institute's model of the national economy contains over 2,000 variables, and more are gradually being added.[5]

Aggregate output data—such as the total sales for a firm or an industry—can be generated without an aggregate equation specifying relationships between the dependent variable and each independent variable. Instead of attempting to develop a purely analytical model containing several dozen variables—say, a regression equation or a curvilinear demand function—we can construct a market-simulation model that specifies the purchase behavior of individual consumers, simulates this behavior, and sums the results. The total is the aggregate behavior of the population represented by the consumers (the artificial decision units) simulated in the model. For instance, the market population may be represented by 3,000 simulated decision units, each of which is a household with a set of economic and demographic characteristics and a history of purchase behavior. Of course, these characteristics will be distributed among the decision units in the same proportion as they are among the real market population.

In designing a simulation model, the first task is to identify the relevant significant variables. The second, and most difficult, task is to determine the functional relationships between them. The third task, which usually goes hand in hand with the second, is to gather data on the exogenous variables (those outside the control of the firm). The fourth task is to organize this information (the functional relationships and the data) and prepare a procedure for inputting new data—such as higher or lower prices and advertising budgets—and generating output. The fifth and final task is to evaluate the model and update it to conform to changes in the real market. The evaluation and updating process should be repeated periodically for as long as the model remains in use.

Virtues and Limitations of Simulation

Feasibility

Simulation is often more feasible than other forms of marketing research. First, it avoids the extremely complicated problem of using conventional mathematical analysis to specify aggregate functions. A large number of variables can be introduced without having to incorporate them all into a single equation. This is especially important when the key dependent variable—say, profit—is a function of many independent variables and when relationships are nonlinear.

[5] For an in-depth explanation of the model, see J. S. Duesenberry, G. Fromm, L. R. Klein, and E. Kuh, eds. *The Brookings Quarterly Econometric Model of the United States Economy* (New York: Rand McNally, 1965); or Gary Fromm and Paul Tauban, *Policy Stimulations with an Econometric Model* (Washington, D.C.: Brookings Institute, 1968).

Second, simulation avoids many of the practical problems associated with market surveys and experiments. There is usually no need to prepare questionnaires, select samples, conduct interviews, set up test markets, or supervise field operations.

Third, simulation does not put the heavy demand on the firm's resources that large and complex surveys or market experiments do, particularly when management needs to know the effect of changes in many variables or the effects of numerous levels of one or two variables.

Fourth, simulation is often the only way of measuring the effects of postulated changes in variables over which the firm has no control, such as population, income, and the marketing tactics of competitors.

Cost Benefits

Simulation can be more economical than other forms of research. Surveys and experiments can be very expensive, particularly if they must be repeated in order to gather data under different conditions. In simulation, one or more variables (e.g., a price, a distribution channel, or a competitor's advertising budget) can easily be changed and a new set of output data (e.g., sales, market share, or profit) gotten immediately. Once the model is constructed, programmed, and in the computer, the marginal cost of rerunning the problem, using different values for the variables or the parameters, is a tiny fraction of what the information would have cost had it been gotten by more traditional means.

Time Savings

The time savings in simulation is considerable because the variables and parameters are changed only on paper, not in the field, and the revised problem is usually processed by computer. A marketer can change a price, for example, and within a minute or two have new data on sales. The same thing could be accomplished by other means, but it would take weeks.

Safety

Simulation is also a safe way of manipulating variables. If the results of a decision—say, an increase in price—are disastrous, they are disastrous only on paper. Hence, the marketer can try all sorts of wild changes in the marketing mix and lose nothing more than a dollar or two of computer time. Furthermore, he or she can estimate the effect of these changes without tipping off competitors about the plans.

Limitations

In spite of these significant advantages, market simulation is not widely used. Its unpopularity stems primarily from the difficulty of constructing models that are satisfactory replicas of real-world marketing processes. A model that is not a valid replica of the phenomenon being simulated will produce invalid results.

In the model-building stage of market stimulation, it is often necessary to use other methods of research to specify internal relationships among the variables. Consumer-panel data may be needed to determine the probabilities required for a brand-shifting model. A market experiment may be necessary to specify the price-elasticity functions for a sales-forecasting model. Historical data may be needed to determine the distribution of demographic characteristics needed for a consumer-behavior model.

The time and expense involved in gathering this information often nullifies the advantages of simulation. In addition, the only way to test the validity and reliability of a model is to manipulate real-world variables in the same way that the variables in the model are manipulated. If there is a significant discrepancy in the two sets of results, then the model cannot be used—at least not in its present form. As soon as analysts begin manipulating the real-world variables, they start to forfeit the advantages associated with simulation. Of course, once the model is properly structured and specified and has been validated in the marketplace, it can be used for far more experiments than could be conducted in the marketplace. Far more data can be computed by simulation than by real-world experimentation or observation. The model can also be used to train marketing personnel.

Market Models

Basic Properties

In marketing research, the simulation model is almost always a mathematical replica of a market phenomenon or process. The model is the heart, brain, and nervous system of simulation. It contains information on the relationships between variables and the values of those variables, and it responds to stimuli—the input or self-generated data. Market-simulation models are essentially symbolic and are usually prepared in a format digestible by a computer. The designer ordinarily prepares a schematic diagram of the model first. This diagram is then transformed into a computer program using an appropriate computer language.[6] An example of such a diagram and a computer program is shown in Exhibits 25-2 and 26-2.

Model Components

Generally speaking, models have five components: functional equations, stored data, simulated decision units, a stochastic process, and operating instructions. Only the first component—or its analogical or iconic equivalent—is really necessary. In fact, a symbolic model can consist of nothing

---

[6] BASIC, FORTRAN, and PL-1 are the most common general-purpose languages used in marketing-research applications. FORTRAN is the most popular. Several languages, such as GPSS and SIMSCRIPT, have also been developed especially for simulation. Exhibits 25-2 and 26-2 use BASIC. Exhibit 25-1 uses FORTRAN.

more than a simple two-variable linear equation. However, large numbers of relationships and variables can be handled only by complex models.

Functional Equations   *Functional equations* are statements of the relationships between the variables incorporated in a model. The simplest model has only one functional equation. More sophisticated models have dozens. Preparing these equations is the toughest part of market simulation. Normally, conventional analytical methods are used. Differential calculus is used to derive maximizing and minimizing functions, determine rates of change, and derive optimum-output equations. Integral calculus is used to derive total-revenue and total-cost equations when unit revenue or unit cost varies with output. Linear programing is used to optimize resource allocations or input mixes. Regression analysis is used to specify the sensitivity of a dependent variable to one or more independent variables. Statistics—both classical and Bayesian—is used to test the validity of relationships.

In order to use these mathematical and statistical tools, however, the researcher must have data. If the equations are to be representative of real-world relationships, they must be based on empirical findings. In gathering these data and in structuring and specifying the functional equations, the analyst may well need all the tools of marketing research discussed thus far. In fact, the paradox of market simulation is that it seeks to avoid the handicaps of other research methods, but is based on them. This has severely limited the practical applications of the technique. The technology of market simulation has progressed dramatically in the past two decades, thanks to the work of people like Massy, Olcutt, Greenlaw, Shubik, and Mize.[7] However, the practical problems associated with the preparation of the functional equations have prevented its widespread use.

Once they are prepared, the functional equations are simply recorded on worksheets, in the case of manual models. If the model is to be computerized, the equations must be transcribed into a computer language (similar to conventional mathematical notation) and recorded on punch cards or magnetic tape or put directly into a memory drum via a keyboard.

Stored Data   The *stored data* consist of real-world information, information generated by the model during the simulation process, and hypothetical data entered by the model operator or players. The real-world data are usually the current values of variables exogenous to the firm, that play a role in the market process replicated by the model. They may include economic, demographic, and business data such as income, employment, and population statistics and the prices, advertising expenditures, and market shares of competitors.

The information generated by the model is usually the predicted values of endogenous variables when other variables or model parameters are

---

[7] For an extensive introduction into simulation see Joe H. Mize and J. Grady Cox, *Essentials of Simulation* (Englewood Cliffs, N.J.: Prentice-Hall, 1968).

manipulated. The variables that are changed may be those controlled by the firm or exogenous to it. For example, researchers might alter the population variable to represent the market in 1990. Or they might change a competing brand's price in anticipation of a change in that competitor's marketing strategy. These manipulations can induce changes in many other variables. For example, an increase in population will probably increase employment, retail sales, and GNP. These new data are stored in the model, which is then used to simulate the market process under the new conditions.

Parameters can be altered to reflect a possible alteration in the structure of market processes. For instance, researchers may notice a change in the market population's reading habits, leisure-time activities, or shopping patterns. This change in turn could alter the relationships between certain variables and hence the parameters of the functional equations. Sales could become less sensitive to advertising in certain media, the cross elasticity of demand could change, and revenues could become more or less sensitive to increases in certain types of retail outlets. Such parametric changes could induce changes in stored data.

New information is also generated by adding a stochastic process to the model. Mortality among individuals, households, and business firms will alter the values of some exogenous variables. Births, marriages, and new business undertakings will have a comparable, but opposite, effect. The time and distribution of such events are determined by chance and approximated by the stochastic process. The information it generates provides a more accurate simulation of future markets and transition processes.

Simple worksheets are used to tabulate stored data when the model is manipulated manually. Computerized models use punch cards, magnetic tape, disks or internal memory for information storage.

Simulated Decision Units   The *simulated decision units* are the actors or players of the model. They are the artificial representatives of the individuals, households, and government or business institutions that have a role in the market processes being copied. Their characteristics are those of their real-world counterparts and are distributed in the same way. Thus, if the model depicts a market where the average household income is $17,235, the average income of the simulation units will be $17,235. If one-fifth of the real households have four members, then one-fifth of the units will have four members. In short, the units are a mirror of the real-world population. The quality of the model depends heavily on the representativeness of this hypothetical sample.

The simulation units are usually hypothetical in that no one of them represents a specific individual or household. However, taken as a group, they do represent a specific population. Exceptions are made for units representing specific institutions, such as government agencies, large customers, and competitors. These units assume the relevant properties of their real-world counterparts and are identified with them.

The units represent the decision-makers in the real-world process. The unique and most significant property of market simulation is its ability to simulate the behavior of thousands of individual units, aggregate that behavior, and measure its effect on important market variables. The behavior of the individual units is simulated by the researcher, real-life players (in business gaming), or the model itself. In the latter case, the individual unit's reactions are governed by a probabilistic functional equation (sometimes called an *operating characteristic*) and a stochastic process. The operating characteristic specifies the probability that the unit will behave in a particular manner.

For instance, the probability that a given household, i, will purchase a new automobile, $P(A)_i$, may be specified as a function of income, I; family size, F; savings, S; and the age of its present car, C. Or $P(A)_i = f(I_i, F_i, S_i, C_i)$. If a new car is purchased, the probability that it will be a particular brand— say, Brand B—is a function of the market share, M, of that brand. Thus, $P(B/A) = M_B$. Once the necessary probabilities are calculated, the stochastic process is invoked to determine the outcome—namely, whether the unit buys a new car, and if so, what model. These calculations are repeated for every unit in the model. The outcomes are then aggregated to get the total number of new-car purchases for the period.

By repeating this operation, with each iteration representing a consecutive period, we can simulate the market process over time. After each repetition, the stored data are updated to reflect the behavior of the simulation decision units. For instance, if unit number 1,835 ($i = 1,835$) buys a new car, ownership of that brand and model year becomes one of the properties of that simulated household.

The operating characteristics and the stochastic process can be applied to each simulation unit manually. The computations are not complicated, but when we multiply the time required to determine the behavior of one unit by the number of units in the model, the workload can become very great indeed. The more sophisticated models include thousands of such units. Again, the only practical solution is computerization. A computer can perform individual calculations in a matter of microseconds, and an entire iteration, including the updating and printing of output data, can be accomplished in a few minutes. If a data printout is not required until the last iteration has been made, dozens of iterations are possible in about the same length of time. This allows the researcher to "age" the market or to allow one or more transition processes to run their full course and still have the answers almost immediately.

The Stochastic Process   A realistic model of an actual market or a marketing phenomenon must include all the significant variables (or be appropriately qualified) and replicate the relationships between those variables accurately. Ideally, the model should also be stochastic and dynamic. A *stochastic model* is one that explicitly includes uncertainty (or risk). A *dynamic model* is one that explicitly includes time.

A stochastic process, or chance, can be introduced into the model if the researcher can estimate the probability distribution associated with a particular variable. For instance, if brand choice is a variable, the probability that a buyer will select one of the various brands can be determined from consumer-panel data. If the sex of newborn children is a variable, the distribution of boys and girls can be gotten from Census Bureau statistics. Once the probability distribution is known, it can be simulated using random numbers.

A table of random numbers, or a random-number generator, provides a series of digits, from 0 to 9, inclusive, each with an equal (hence, random) chance of selection. Since each digit is selected independently, a particular digit—say, 2—has as much chance of appearing in a given position as any other digit. This is true even if that digit already occupies the preceding position. Each digit has a probability of 0.1 of occupying a position in the series.

A probability distribution is simulated by assigning single digits or larger numbers to the possible events in proportion to the probabilities of their occurrences. For example, we know that the probability of getting heads from a coin flip is 0.5. The probability of getting tails, of course, is also 0.5. Thus, half the digits—say, 0 through 4 or all the odd digits—should be assigned to heads and the other half to tails. We can then simulate flipping a coin by drawing a series of random numbers. Ten numbers represent ten flips, and the distribution between heads and tails will be the same as if we had actually flipped a balanced coin.

The same technique is used with more complicated frequency distributions. For example, if we needed to simulate brand choice and empirical data revealed that the probability distribution of brand choices was $P(A) = 0.21$, $P(B) = 0.15$, $P(C) = 0.09$, $P(D) = 0.04$, and $P(E) = 0.51$, with A, B, and C being the most important brands, D being all other brands, and E being no purchase, we could select random numbers, two digits at a time, with those in the ranges $00-20$, $21-35$, $36-44$, $45-48$, and $49-99$ assigned to events A, B, C, D, and E, respectively.

During the simulation, in order to find out which of the possible events has occurred, we simply draw a number from a table of random numbers. If the model has been computerized, we would draw the number from a bank of random numbers stored in the computer or use a random-number generator contained in a subroutine.[8]

Monte Carlo methods are a group of techniques for simulating probabilistic processes. The term encompasses a variety of methods, including the random-number method for determining outcomes governed by chance. The name is taken from the famous gambling casino on the French Riviera, which uses techniques such as craps and roulette to simulate stochastic processes. In fact, the mechanical equipment of the gambler—the dice, the spinning wheel or pointer, and the deck of cards—has often been used in simulating human behavior, such as queueing. (It is usually more practical, however, to use random numbers.)

---

[8] One such subroutine is General Electric's D/NORM1 (Pub. 807231).

In simulation models, the stochastic process is used to determine which of the possible events occurs. First, an appropriate functional equation— the operating characteristic—is used to compute the probability of each possible event. Say that the probability that unit 853 will purchase a new refrigerator is 0.2. Next, the stochastic process is used to determine if the event occurred. If the digit 0 or 1 is drawn, unit 853 purchases a new refrigerator (a fact duly recorded as part of 853's history and characteristics), and total refrigerator sales are increased by one. If the digit 2, 3, 4, 5, 6, 7, 8, or 9 is drawn, unit 853 does not buy a refrigerator during the iteration, and total sales remain unchanged.

Dynamic Property   A model can be made dynamic in two ways. We can include time as a variable, or we can use iterations. The first approach is feasible when the change in time-dependent variables can be specified by a growth model. For instance, innovation diffusion, which is important in studies of products' life cycles and rates of market penetration, can be approximated by a Gompertz function. A Gompertz model specifies sales or market share as a curvilinear function of time, the total potential market, and the product's rate of acceptance. A variety of other growth models relevant to market phenomena were explained in Chapter 23. In each, time is the independent variable.

There are often time-related changes in other independent variables, such as population and income. These relationships, too, can sometimes be specified and incorporated into the model. For example, a simulation may start with a set of values assigned to the time-dependent independent variables at $t = 0$ (the starting time). As t is increased, simulating the passage of time, these variables will change according to the patterns specified for them. They are independent with respect to the output variables (sales, etc.), but they are dependent with respect to time. All these relationships can easily be incorporated into the model as separate equations.

Iteration is another way of making the model dynamic. Each *iteration*— that is, each operation or cycle of the model—alters the data according to a time-related stochastic process. For instance, if a single iteration represents one year of market activity, then five iterations will cover five years of market activity. At the end of the fifth iteration, the model should be in the same condition (approximately) as the real market five years hence. Household 853 (as well as each other simulated decision unit) will have had five opportunities to buy a refrigerator, increase or decrease its size, shift brands, and do all the other things associated with its real-market counterparts, which are included in the model. Even the operating characteristics will change from "year" to "year" as the values of the variables change.

Operating Instructions   The operating instructions, as the term implies, tell the human operator (in a manual simulation) or the computer what to do. In the more complex simulation models, where manual manipulation is impractical, the operating instructions are written in a language and a form

Exhibit 25-1   A Segment of a Computer Program Using Probability Functions and Stochastic Process to Simulate Purchase Behavior

```
    ⋮
130 DO 200  I = 3000
131 PA(I) = .003*AINC(I) − 8.*FAM(I) + .006*SAV(I) + 10.*(YEAR-CAR(I) )
132 RAND = RANGEN(X)
133 IF  (RAND-PA(I) )  140,140,200
*140 RAND = RANGEN(X)
142 IF  (RAND-22.)  145,145,150
*145 CHEV = CHEV + 1.
147 GO TO 175
*150 IF  (RAND-40.)  155,155,160
*155 FORD = FORD + 1.
157 GO TO 175
*160 IF  (RAND-48.)  165,165,170
*165 PLYM = PLYM + 1.
168 GO TO 175
*170 OTHER = OTHER + 1.
*175 CAR(I) = YEAR
190 TOTCAR = TOTCAR + 1.
*200 CONTINUE
    ⋮
```

Explanation of program segment by numbered statements: 130 tells the computer to cycle every household (I), one through 3,000, through the sequence of instructions 130 to 200. After a household is run through the "loop," I is increased by one and the cycle is repeated. 131 tells it to compute the probability that the Ith household will purchase a new automobile. PA (I) is a function of the annual income, family size, savings, and age of the present car of the Ith household. It is expressed as a percentage (03.21, 40.56, etc). 132 invokes a subprogram called "RANGEN (X)." RANGEN (X) is a random-number generator—a separate program stored in the computer that produces a randomly chosen number between 00 and 99. This number becomes the value of "RAND." 133 tells the computer to determine if the random number falls between 00 and PA (I). If so, I purchases a new car, and we go statement 140 to determine which brand. If not (RAND > PA (I)), no car is purchased and the program branches to statement 200. 140 invokes RANGEN (X) again to generate another random number. (This is necessary to avoid the bias that would result if the previous RAND value was used, since if RAND > PA (I), 140 is bypassed by branching to 200.) 142 instructs the computer to determine if RAND is less than or equal to 22 (percent), which is Chevrolet's market share. If it is, I purchases a Chevrolet and the program branches to statement 145, which increases total Chevrolet sales by one unit. If it is not, the program branches to statement 150 to decide if I purchases a Ford. Since all values of RAND ≤ 22 have been assigned Chevrolet, only those falling between 23 and 40 inclusive (Ford's market share is 18 percent) will cause I to purchase a Ford and the program to branch to 155. If RAND > 40 at statement 150, the program branches to 160, which offers I a choice between a Plymouth or an unnamed "other" brand. Once a brand is chosen and its total sales have been increased by one, the program will go to statement 175. 175 tells the computer to change I's car to the current model year. 190 tells it to increase total car sales by one unit. 200 completes the loop, and the routine starts all over again at statement 130. (I is increased by one to represent the next household.) When all 3,000 households have been through the loop, the program continues onward from 200.

The numbering of statements is arbitrary. In fact, it is unnecessary, unless the statement is referred to in another statement. Each statement that requires a number is indicated by an asterisk. This is for the reader's convenience and not part of the program. The year of the iteration (YEAR = 1980, 1981, etc.) and the values of the other independent variables (AINC (I), FAM (I), etc.) are stored in the computer's memory unit, having been recorded from input data or generated by an earlier phase of the program. Many of these values change during the course of the program. The new values—along with the computed values of the dependent variables—can be included in the data printout simply by giving the appropriate instructions later in the program. The market shares, shown as constants, could be specified as variables. Their values would then be recomputed near the end of each iteration.

that is digestible by a computer. The process of preparing instructions for the computer is called *programming*. A set of such instructions—written in computer language and recorded on punch cards or magnetic tape—is called a *program*.

The operating instructions explain the simulation procedure step by step. They specify the sequence of operations to be performed. There is no essential difference between operating instructions prepared in plain English and those prepared in computer languages. However, the computer program must conform to a strict format, follow a special set of grammatical rules, and use only the vocabulary and symbols permitted.

The program tells the computer when to read input information, when to apply functional equations to decision units, when to use a stochastic process, when to compute data, what formulas to use, what data to store, what information to print as output data, and when to print it. Instructions can also be conditional. That is, a preceding calculation or an input (a value provided by a player during the simulation) can determine which of several operations is performed at a certain point.

For instance, if the functional equation for the probability that a household will purchase a new automobile is 0.19 for simulation decision unit number 2,465 and the stochastic process yields a random number within the range 00 to 19, inclusive, then household 2,465 buys a new car. If the random number falls outside this range, no new car is purchased by unit 2,465 during that particular iteration.

If a purchase is indicated, a brand choice is the next step. Again, a stochastic process is used. The data are then recorded. Unit 2,465 is credited with a new car, the brand is specified, and total sales of that brand—say, Chevrolet—are increased by one. Total car sales are also increased by one. The cycle is then repeated for the next household (decision unit number 2,466) and so on until all the households—say, there are 3,000 units in the model—have been given an "opportunity" to buy a new car. This segment of the operating instructions is shown in computer language in Exhibit 25-1.

Constructing a Model

Model-building starts with a statement of objectives. This may be little more than a definition of the dependent variables. For instance, one objective might be a forecast of sales or a specification of price. Next, the designers must identify all the determinants they want to include in the model and assign an order of priority to them. They should also discriminate between those that are necessary to the model and those that are merely desirable. If they cannot specify the relationships between certain variables, they may be unable to use them. Of course, one of the great virtues of simulation is that the model can be expanded as more information becomes available. More determinants can always be added later.

Their third task is to prepare the functional equations—the heart of the model. They may start with a simple verbal description, followed by a logical-flow diagram. In other words, they may go from a prose (symbolic)

Exhibit 25-2 Three Models of a Competitor's Reaction to a Firm's Price Cut

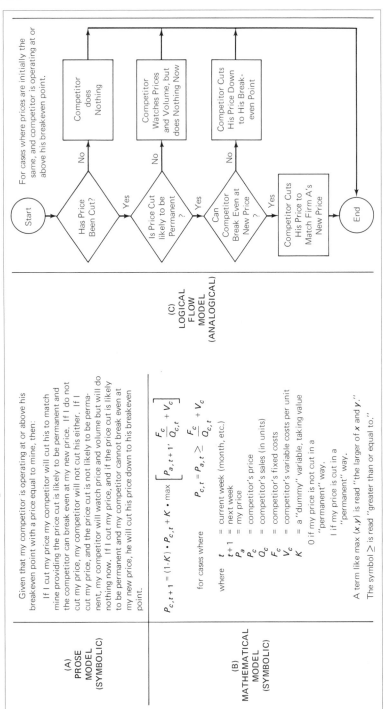

(A) PROSE MODEL (SYMBOLIC)

Given that my competitor is operating at or above his breakeven point with a price equal to mine, then:

If I cut my price my competitor will cut his to match mine providing the price cut is likely to be permanent and the competitor can break even at my new price. If I do not cut my price, my competitor will not cut his either. If I cut my price, and the price cut is not likely to be permanent, my competitor will watch price and volume but will do nothing now. If I cut my price, and if the price cut is likely to be permanent and my competitor cannot break even at my new price, he will cut his price down to his breakeven point.

(B) MATHEMATICAL MODEL (SYMBOLIC)

$$P_{c,t+1} = (1-K) \cdot P_{c,t} + K \cdot \max\left[P_{a,t+1}, \frac{F_c}{Q_{c,t}} + V_c\right]$$

for cases where

$$P_{c,t} = P_{a,t} \geq \frac{F_c}{Q_{c,t}} + V_c$$

where
- t = current week (month, etc.)
- $t+1$ = next week
- P_a = my price
- P_c = competitor's price
- Q_c = competitor's sales (in units)
- F_c = competitor's fixed costs
- V_c = competitor's variable costs per unit
- K = a "dummy" variable, taking value
  - 0 if my price is not cut in a "permanent" way.
  - 1 if my price is cut in a "permanent" way.

A term like max (x,y) is read "the larger of x and y."
The symbol $\geq$ is read "greater than or equal to."

(C) LOGICAL FLOW MODEL (ANALOGICAL)

For cases where prices are initially the same, and competitor is operating at or above his breakeven point.

Start → Has Price Been Cut?
- No → Competitor does Nothing
- Yes → Is Price Cut likely to be Permanent?
  - No → Competitor Watches Prices and Volume, but does Nothing Now
  - Yes → Can Competitor Break Even at New Price?
    - No → Competitor Cuts His Price Down to His Breakeven Point
    - Yes → Competitor Cuts His Price to Match Firm A's New Price → End

Source: William F. Massey, *Model Building In Marketing: An Overview,* Working Paper No. 162 (Stanford, CA: Graduate School of Business: July 1969), p. 7a. Used by permission.

model, to an analogical model, to a mathematical (symbolic) model. Exhibit 25-2 shows three forms of a model designed to predict a competitor's behavior with respect to price. The designers need not follow this procedure exactly, of course. In some cases, they may go directly to the construction of the equations, depending on the complexity of the problem and their familiarity with the variables.

Having prepared the necessary functional equations, the designers will probably want to embellish the basic model with stored data, simulated decision units, a stochastic process, and whatever operating instructions are required. They can then transcribe the model into a computer language and record it on punch cards, disk, or magnetic tape.

Players

The players in market simulation represent real-world people or institutions that have some role in the market process under analysis. Usually, they represent the firm, its competitors, and the members of the market population. They can be either live or simulated. The player representing the firm is usually a real person. The members of the market population—the individuals, households, or establishments that are the actual or potential customers—are usually simulated. Competitors may be represented by live players or simulated decision units, depending on the objectives and design of the model.

The term operator is occasionally more appropriate than player, since the individual providing input data to the model does not always represent a real-world person or institution. He or she may be a researcher asking questions, or, in the case of business gaming, the umpire or a noncompetitive manipulator who changes such exogenous variables as weather, population, and income. If the players are novices, the operator may be an instructor or an intermediary between them and the computer.

The more sophisticated simulation systems are less likely to have an operator as a noncompetitor, instructor, or go-between. Changes in exogenous variables are programmed into the model, usually along with a stochastic process. Instructions are also programmed into the model. In some cases, the players simply turn on a typewriter-like terminal, enter the name of the simulation program, and watch the terminal print out instructions and questions. The terminals themselves are usually so simple that supervision of the players is unnecessary.

If the players (whom we might view as actors) play their roles realistically, they will make the same decisions and respond in the same way as their real-world counterparts. The player representing the firm, of course, may make decisions contrary to company practice in order to determine their consequences. In fact, such experimentation is frequently the whole point of the simulation.

Simulated versus Live Players

Simulated players are incorporated into the model as decision units. They make decisions, when appropriate, based on a probability distribution and a stochastic process. The probability distribution is expressed as one of the functional equations in the model. The gut problem in modeling is to derive equations that reflect precisely the real-world probability distributions they represent.

There are several advantages to having simulated players rather than live ones. First, if the market population is large and the sample must be big in order to be representative, it may be impossible to gather, instruct, and manage enough live players. There is virtually no limit to the number of simulated players that can be used, at least not if the simulation is computerized.

Second, a simulated player can be programmed so that its responses match exactly the known past performance of its real-world counterpart. In addition, it has none of the emotional or interpretive problems associated with live players.

Third, if all the players are simulated, the model can be operated at any time, without waiting for participants to assemble.

Fourth, simulated players do not tire. This is important when a transition process is being studied or forecasts are being made that require numerous iterations. Live players grow fatigued, slow down the iterations, and delay the outcomes.

Characteristics and Functions of Players

A player, live or simulated, starts with a given set of characteristics that correspond to those of the real-world counterpart. For instance, a player representing a competitor will have the same product line, prices, market share, distribution system, sales force, and advertising budget. As the simulation process progresses, these properties will change in response to changing conditions and decisions made by the player. Changes in such conditions as population size or other firms' prices alter the player's market share, sales, revenues, profit, and so on in the manner specified by the functional equations.

Hopefully, the live players will immerse themselves in the role of their real-world counterparts, making their decisions within the context of specified objectives, such as profit maximization or market domination, and incomplete information. (The model is usually capable of providing complete information, but does not do so to be realistic.) The players analyze the market data provided at the start of the simulation or as output, and make decisions which become input data for the simulation.

A simulated player has fewer options, being restricted, naturally, to the alternatives specified by the designer. Which of the alternatives it chooses depends on the probability distribution for each and the results of the stochastic process.

For example, assume that a live player—one representing the firm—has increased his or her price. Prior to constructing the model, the designer noted that a particular competitor always responded in one of three ways: It raised its price (option A), it increased its advertising (option B), or it made no changes (option C). The probabilities of these three alternatives appear to be 0.5, 0.2, and 0.3, respectively. These choices, and their companion probabilities, are incorporated into the model. When the live player increases the firm's price, the simulated competitor responds. The operating instructions invoke the appropriate stochastic process and, depending on its outcome, the simulated player increases the price, increases the advertising, or makes no changes. If alternative A or B is the outcome, then the appropriate functional equations must be used to calculate the effect on the dependent variables—the sales (hence, market shares) of the live player as well as each of the other simulated competitors.

Input and Output Data

Input data are entered into the model during the course of the simulation. They consist of decision options (such as prices and advertising budgets) chosen by live players, changes in exogenous variables (such as population and income) made by the operator, and changes in parameters, also determined by the operator. Normally, each iteration represents an accounting period—say, a month or a quarter. The operator (researcher) and the live players are allowed to change the values of the variables they control only once during each iteration.

If, during an iteration, the value of any independent variable is changed, then one or more functional equations must be used to determine the new value of the one or more dependent variables affected. In the more sophisticated simulations, many changes are generated by the model itself, primarily through the operation of the simulated decision units and the stochastic process. Even routine random variations in the weather are sometimes included in the model; hence, changes occur in every iteration even if there are no new input data. Such models never reach a state of perfect equilibrium. Like real-world markets, they are continually changing. Every iteration produces a slightly different arrangement of market shares, sales, and so on.

Input data for computerized models, like operating instructions, require a special format. Since they are usually quantitative, however, the users need not master a computer language. Often the data are recorded by live players on a prepared form and then given to an operator, who transcribes them onto punch cards or other media acceptable to the computer.

Many simulation models require the players or operator merely to enter the input data via an electric typewriter tied directly into the computer. Some simulation models are designed so that the typewriter will automatically type the questions—such as "WHAT IS YOUR NEW PRICE"—and then wait for the player (or operator) to type the answers.[9]

The *output data* are the new values of the dependent variables after one or more iterations. They are generated by the model and include such

---

[9] General Electric's GAME1$, GAME2$, GAME3$, and GAME4$, for example, use this format.

information as the current values of each firm's sales, costs, profit, and market share, as well as the values of exogenous variables that would normally be accessible to the firm. In business gaming, live players get only the information to which they would be privy in the real world. Thus, a player representing Company A would not receive profit data on Companies B, C, or D. In other applications of simulation, all the output data are available to the players.

With computerized models, data printouts are economical and take little time. Consequently, the program often calls for the reprinting of all relevant data, including the last set of input data, at various points. This gives the operator (and if necessary the live players) a check on the simulation process, a convenient recapitulation of the position of the firm, and the current state of the market being simulated. Programs written for the more sophisticated business games usually provide a printout of complete profit-and-loss statements and balance sheets, at the end of each iteration, for each firm represented in the simulation. The output data are also retained within the model as stored data. They represent the set of conditions that prevail at the start of the next iteration.

Output data—sometimes called "artificial data"—may be printed at the completion of each iteration. However, if the model is dynamic and the researcher wants to forecast conditions *n* periods in the future, the appropriate number of iterations are made before a printout is generated. For instance, a single iteration may represent one week of activity in the marketplace—an appropriate period for food items and convenience goods. If the researchers want to forecast the structure of the market two months hence, they will run through eight iterations before requesting a printout.

The output data are not only useful in themselves, they are also valuable in measuring and improving the model's performance. By comparing the actual events with those predicted by the simulation, the researchers can evaluate the model's accuracy and gain insights into its deficiencies. Of course, the stored data and the original inputs must reflect the situations that existed in the marketplace when the simulation began, or a comparison of real-world and output data would be meaningless.

Problems

1   What type of model would you use, what would you do for players, where would you find (or how would you generate) input data, and what form of output data would you produce in a simulation of the U.S. automobile market? Defend your choices.

2   Discuss the components you would include in a model of (a) the market for frozen vegetables, (b) the behavioral pattern of doctors selecting prescription drugs, and (c) the market for aluminum food and beverage containers.

3   In simulating the market for instant coffee, how many simulated players would you use and whom would they represent? How would you introduce the element of chance into the model, with respect to the behavior of the players?

4   Devise some unspecified functional equations appropriate to the preceding model. List the kind of input data you would use, and describe how it could be obtained. List the data that would be stored in the model and the output data you would ask for.

Chapter 26
Applications of Market Simulation

Key Concepts

Business Gaming
Simulation as a training aid

Experimentation
Producing data by simulation

Analysis of Transition Processes
Markov chains and other iterative models

Estimating and Forecasting
Predicting present values and forecasting future ones through Simulation

Heuristic Programming
Using rules-of-thumb to simulate a decision process

Key Terms

Markov chain
steady state
heuristic programming

Business Gaming

Business gaming uses simulation as a training device to allow novice managers to practice decision-making.[1] In marketing games, the players mani-

---

[1] The modern use of simulation as an instrument of gaming can be traced to the Prussian generals who developed war games in the late nineteenth century. By the early twentieth century, war games had become a standard training aid at the European and American war colleges. War gaming is still used, though it is now computerized.

pulate one or more of the firm's marketing instruments—price, promotion (advertising and personal selling), distribution, the product, and marketing research. Ideally, the conditions of the game and the consequences of the decisions should resemble closely those of the real market. Of course, the realism of the game is inherently limited, in part because the psychological pressures associated with real-world decision-making are lacking. (Some psychological pressure can be induced by giving the player a limited time to make decisions.) Errors in judgment show up only in the output of the simulation, not on the profit-and-loss statement of the firm. Even if the model is a close replica of the real-world process, the fear and anxiety associated with the real marketing decisions are absent. Freedom from real consequences can induce a cavalier approach to decision-making that is not normal in the real world. Thus, the decision processes may not parallel the ones the players would employ in the discharge of their regular duties.

The typical simulation model designed for business gaming places several firms in competition. The actions of each firm can be directed by a different player, each of whom manipulates the variables normally controlled by that firm. The objective of each player is to maximize some dependent variable (usually profit) associated with the firm.

Players start with certain information that would be available to each were they really in the position they have assumed. This normally includes the firm's cost function, prices, product characteristics, distribution channels, sales force, advertising budget, present inventory, and past sales, as well as competitors' product characteristics and prices. The data on the firm's market share and the state-of-nature data are sometimes provided. Additional information, classified as market-research data, is usually available, but must be purchased by the player. As in the real world, knowledge has a price tag and can be increased only by increasing the firm's costs.

The value of each variable at the starting point is stored in the model, which also contains the functional equations specifying the relationships between them. Of course, the players do not have complete access to the model, and hence must deduce these relationships by observing changes in the variables as the game progresses.

Each player starts with a current balance sheet and a profit-and-loss statement. These data are also stored in the model. They can manipulate those variables that in reality would be controlled by their firm. The manipulations (i.e., the new values of the player-controlled variables) are entered into the model as they occur. In addition, the umpire (operator) may manipulate exogenous variables associated with "nature," such as the population, personal disposable income, or the weather.

Once a set of new input data has been fed into the model, the functional equations are used to compute a new set of values for the dependent variables. Obviously, changes in the player-controlled variables—such as prices, product characteristics, and advertising—will induce changes in sales, costs, revenues, market shares, profits, and so on. A new set of output data is then provided for each player. However, information that is confidential (such as profit-and-loss data) is given only to the appropriate firm. Each player then analyzes the information received, contemplates the effects of previous decisions, and decides which of the controllable variables should be changed and by how much.

The players' decisions become the next set of input data, and the process of recalculating and disseminating new output data is repeated, in a cycle called an iteration, defined previously. The game can continue through an unlimited number of iterations, until all but one player (firm) goes broke or until a preset time limit is reached.

Like their real-world counterparts, the players operate in a state of partial ignorance. Much of the information they would like to have—such as data on the price elasticity of their products and the sensitivity of their sales to advertising expenditures and sales-force size—is hidden in the model. Some of this information may be purchased as "market research." Some information—such as the probable responses of competing firms or the psychological characteristics of fellow players—can only be guessed at. Some facts can be estimated by analyzing the series of data that emerges in successive iterations. All this is as it should be, since one of the purposes of business gaming is to challenge the analytical skills of the participants.

Often the individual players are replaced by teams. This is convenient when there is a large group of participants. It is also appropriate when the game is complex, there is a wealth of data available, and there are opportunities for sophisticated analyses preparatory to decision-making.

A number of computerized games are available from companies such as IBM and General Electric.[2] For instance, IBM offers the PURDUE SUPERMARKET MANAGEMENT GAME (Program No. 360D151002), a mathematical model of a business economy in which two to five supermarkets compete. The players (two to five), who "manage" the respective stores make marketing decisions and enter them in the computer. The computer invokes the model and simulates one week of business activity. It then prints the output data—the week's revenue, costs, profit, market share, and so on—for each store. The players analyze the new information, reflect on their previous decisions, make new decisions, and proceed with the next iteration.

In computerized games, a single iteration can be completed in only a few minutes. If the players are willing to make snap decisions, five to ten iterations can be completed in an hour. However, such speed defeats the purpose of business gaming. Players (or teams) should be given time to analyze the output data and use the marketing skills they are attempting to acquire or improve. In some cases, several hours or days should be allowed between iterations.

One deficiency of business gaming is the tendency of the players (or teams) to compete against one another instead of pursuing the specified goal.

---

[2] The GE games, cited in Chapter 25, are GAME1$, GAME2$, GAME3$, and GAME4$. GAME2$ is primarily marketing-oriented, and all four games require marketing decisions. These games are especially designed for use with a remote terminal. Other popular market-simulation games are Greenlaw and Kniffin's MARKSIM and Boone's MARKETING STRATEGY.

Decisions made to further the one objective are not always the ones that would have been made had the other goal been the primary concern. Of course, competition among players is not entirely unrealistic. Marketing executives are sometimes more concerned with outperforming their competitors than they are with, say, maximizing profit, especially when the firm's profit is already high enough to satisfy its directors and stockholders. A partial solution to this problem is to use simulated (artificial) players for everyone except the hometeam player. The game can then be played solo, and the issue of outperforming outher participants need not arise.

Experimentation

Experimentation is used to produce data for analytical models, to select the best of a group of explicit alternatives, and to perform sensitivity analysis. In simulated experiments—also called "experimental gaming" and "operational gaming"—the values of dependent variables are determined by trial and error. The methods used are conceptually the same as those of conventional market experiments, discussed in Part Five, and the output is analyzed with the same mathematical and statistical tools. Conventional experiments subject live members of the market population to real changes in one or more marketing variables. Experimental gaming subjects artificial members of the market population (whose behavior is simulated by the model) to hypothetical changes in marketing variables.

Deriving Data for Analytical Models

In deriving data for analytical models, such as regression equations, by experimental gaming, the researchers follow the same procedure they would use for conventional experiments. They manipulate the independent variables, observe what happens to the dependent variable, and invoke the appropriate analytical tools to specify a relationship. They use the output data in the same way they would use information from historical sources, surveys, or actual test markets.

For instance, they might alter the price variable in each iteration, thus generating a series of values for sales. These output values could then be regressed against the input values (the experimental prices) to obtain an estimate of the relationship between the two variables. Of course, the validity of the equation—the analytical model of the sales–price relationship—depends on the realism of the simulation model.

If the model is comprehensive—that is, if it is rich in independent variables and interrelationships—the sales values will not be based solely on a simple price-elasticity equation, but will take into account the probable reactions of competitors to the firm's price changes and the effect of those reactions on sales. Thus, the sales–price relationship specified with the simulation data will be more realistic than the original price-elasticity function incorporated in the model. It will certainly be more helpful to the decision-maker, who must take all known factors into account in selecting a price strategy. Given the single-equation analytical model derived from the simulation data and the product's cost function (provided by the firm's accounting department), the researchers can use differential calculus to determine the optimum price and manufacturing output.

Selecting the Best Alternative

In using simulation to select the best of two or more explicit alternatives, the researchers simply try each alternative in a separate iteration and choose the one that comes closest to producing the results they want. This kind of experimentation is especially useful when a number of variables must be manipulated simultaneously and conventional optimization techniques fail. This is typically the case when an inclusive marketing strategy is being prepared.

For instance, in preparing a promotional strategy involving an elaborate media mix, it is not possible to optimize the mix by the usual methods.[3] The interaction between advertisements placed in different media—many with overlapping audiences—make differential calculus and linear programing ineffective. Simulation does not generate alternatives, but it lets us compare existing (specified) options. Alternative media mixes can be prepared and run through the simulation model to see which produces the most sales, the largest aggregate audience, and so on. In this case, the simulation model would have to include the reading, listening, and viewing habits of the hypothetical purchasing units. We hope their habits will parallel those of the real-market population they represent.

Simulation will seldom yield an optimum answer in complex decision situations, for it is unlikely that the alternative with the optimum value for each decision variable will be included in the group of specified options. The possible combinations of decision values can easily run into the tens of thousands, and it is improbable that the analyst will hit upon the perfect combination. If the alternatives are all bad, the simulation cannot produce good results. However, if the model is computerized, a very large number of alternatives can be tried quickly and cheaply.

Sensitivity Analysis

Simulation can also be used to determine the sensitivity of dependent variables—such as profit, costs, and market share—to particular independent variables or parameters. Sensitivity analysis is useful in making marketing decisions and in planning marketing research. Like other applications of simulation, it takes advantage of the method's ability to handle a large number of variables and relationships.

---

[3] Simulation has proven very useful in media-mix decisions. For a good survey article on this subject, see Dennis H. Gensch, "A Computer Simulation Model for Selecting Advertising Schedules," *Journal of Marketing Research* **6**: 2 (May 1969), pp. 203–214.

Sensitivity analysis aids the decision maker by identifying the factors that have the most effect on the outcomes in the marketplace. It answers such questions as, "How sensitive is profit to changes in output?" "How sensitive is total readership to rearrangements in the media mix?" and "How sensitive are sales to changes in personal income?"

Often, such questions can be answered by examining the structure and parameters of single-equation analytical models. For instance, the sensitivity of sales to advertising expenditures, for a particular product, can be determined by examining the regression equation on page 454. However, the problem is not always so straightforward, due to the complexity of the many real-world relationships that impinge on advertising effectiveness over the range of possible advertising expenditures. A simulation model can include all these relationships, or at least as many of them as can be identified and specified.

Resource-allocation decisions can be improved by sensitivity analysis when the problem is too complex for conventional optimization procedures. For instance, if the marketers know that the firm's sales are significantly more sensitive to personal selling than to advertising, they can shift their available resources in that direction and increase sales. If total delivery time is insensitive to changes in shipping methods, the cheapest alternative should be used. If the firm's sales are insensitive to changes in competitors' promotional strategies, then there is little reason to spend research time gathering data on competitors' promotional plans and activities.

The Maxim Marketing Planning Model[4]

The *Maxim Marketing Planning Model*—called "MAXIM1" for short—is a good example of market-simulation models in general and experimentation through simulation in particular. MAXIM1 is a computerized model designed to be operated solo by a single player from a remote computer terminal. The simulation system thus consists of the operator, input data entered via a keyboard on the computer terminal, the model itself, and output data printed by the terminal.

The mechanics of the system are simple. The player sits in front of a computer terminal such as the one in Figure 26-1, where he exchanges input for output data. He engages the program by typing "RUN MAXIM1." The computer acknowledges the instruction by repeating the name of the program, printing some accounting information, and asking a series of questions. The first question, "DO YOU WISH THE SHORT FROM—1 IF YES, 2 IF NO?" gives the player the option of using an abbreviated format that dispenses with most of the printed material and allows the input data to be entered more quickly.

The player responds to the questions by typing his answers (the input data) on the terminal. When the long form is used, the questions, the input

---

[4] The material in this section was provided by Prof. William F. Massy of the Graduate School of Business, Stanford University.

Figure 26-1   **A Remote Computer Terminal (General Electric Terminet 300)**

Source: Used by permission of General Electric Co.

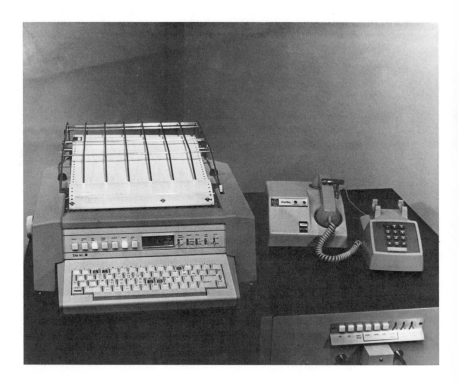

data, and the output data are all printed on the roll of paper in the terminal. This printout is called a *tab run*. A sample run is shown in Exhibit 26-1. (The information provided by the player is underlined.)

The Player   The player in this model represents a product manager for the Maxwell House Division of General Foods. His product is Maxim, a freeze-dried instant coffee introduced in 1969. The model allows him to try various marketing plans—manipulating such variables as promotion and price—and see the results, in terms of sales, costs, and profit, immediately. In addition, he can manipulate certain variables—such as market size, market growth, and the discount rate—that are exogenous to the firm to determine their effect on his product's market performance. Thus, the player (who is also the operator in this case) can forecast performance values and make sensitivity analyses, as well as judge the relative merits of alternative marketing plans.

The Input Data   The input data in MAXIM1 consists of the values of the marketing variables (such as promotion and price) controlled by the product manager and certain market statistics (such as the potential-buyer population). Since these statistics are specified by the player, conditions can be set to match those of any given market.

The input data are prepared in three stages. First, the player enters the values of promotion in awareness (CP*), household impressions (ΣAHI), and copy execution (CE). These are three dimensions of promotion. They are based on judgment and empirical data on such factors as the type of promotions, the promotional value of various media, the number of households covered, the reach of various kinds of advertising, the duration (in weeks) of promotional campaigns, the freshness and appropriateness of ads, the effectiveness of demonstrations (if they are used), and the quality of the ad copy. The scales used for the three dimensions were derived from experience with 40 new brands of various food and drug products, all with short repurchase cycles and priced below a dollar.[5] The calibration of the scales is suggested by the means and standard deviations (except for ΣAHI) of the three dimensions for the 40 brands: $\overline{CP^*}$ = 20.5 with σ = 35.7; $\overline{\Sigma AHI}$ = 3,162,000; and $\overline{CE}$ = 0.60 with σ = 0.11.

Given the first batch of promotional-input data (the estimates of the three dimensions), the computer—in accordance with the operating instructions programmed into it—invokes the model's functional equations to compute (and print) a value for awareness. *Awareness* is defined as the percentage of potential buyers (households) able to recall the advertising claims of the new brand.

The second batch of required input data includes information on family brand (yes or no), price, the total market size, the estimated growth rate of sales (optional), the planning horizon, the advertising budget (costs), and the loss due to cannibalization. The output printed in return includes such vital statistics as the first year's market share, yearly sales (in units), annual revenue, gross margin, marketing costs, profit, and cash flow.

The third batch of input data is concerned with the discount rate. The single best criterion for judging the marketing plan is its *net present value*—that is, the stream of profits (and losses) that will accrue during the planning period, discounted to their present value. Net present value is sensitive to the discount rate (which is similar, and often equal, to the expected interest rate). MAXIM1 allows the player to vary the discount rate and responds immediately with a new present value.[6]

The Model   The heart of the MAXIM1 model is the functional equations that relate the output variables to the various input variables and the stored data. Many are based on work of N.W. Ayer and Sons, Inc.. These formula

---

[5] This work was done by N. W. Ayer and Sons, Inc. (a New York advertising agency) and is described in Henry J. Claycamp and Lucien E. Liddy, "Prediction of New Product Performance: An Analytical Approach," *Journal of Marketing Research* **6**, no. 4 (November 1969), pp. 414–420.

[6] For an explanation of these and other accounting terms, see W. B. Wentz and G. I. Eyrich, *Marketing: Theory and Application* (New York: Harcourt Brace Jovanovich, 1970), chs. 4 and 5.

Exhibit 26-1   A Sample Run of MAXIM1, Market-Simulation Model[a]

```
RUN MAXIM1

MAXIM1              15:04      07/3/68       WEDNESDAY        SFO


DO YOU WISH THE SHORT FORM- 1 IF YES, 2 IF NO? 2
YOUR VALUE OF PROMOTION IN AWARENESS IS? 30
YOUR VALUE OF AVERAGE HOUSEHOLD IMPRESSIONS IS? 260 000 000
YOUR VALUE OF COPY EXECUTION IS? .60
THE VALUE OF AWARENESS IS 63.0475


YOUR VALUE OF PROMOTION IN INITIAL PURCHASES IS? 60
IS THIS A FAMILY BRAND- 1 IF YES, 0 IF NO? 1
THE VALUE OF INITIAL PURCHASES IS 20.429


YOUR PRICE IS? 13.50
REPEAT RATE IS .304275
THE FIRST YEAR MARKET SHARE IS 6.52364   %


WHAT IS THE SIZE OF THE MARKET IN UNITS? 55 000 000


WHAT ARE YOUR COMPETITIVE AND GROWTH ASSUMPTIONS?
YOUR SECOND YEAR SALES FACTOR IS? 1.2
YOUR THIRD YEAR SALES FACTOR IS? 1.3
THIS WILL CONTINUE UNTIL THE END OF WHAT YEAR (MAX 20)? 9
WHAT WILL BE THE RESIDUAL VALUE AT THE END OF THAT YEAR? 3 000 000


                     YEARLY SALES IN UNITS
                 YEAR                SALES
                   1                3587998
                   2                4305596
                   3                4664398
                   4                4804328
                   5                4948456
                   6                5096908
                   7                5249813
                   8                5407305
                   9                5569522


WHAT ARE ADVERTISING COSTS IN YEAR 1? 10 000 000
WHAT ARE CONSUMER PROMOTION COSTS IN YEAR 1? 14 000 000
WHAT ARE ADVERTISING COSTS IN YEAR 2? 4 000 000
WHAT ARE ADVERTISING COSTS IN YEAR 3 AND BEYOND? 8 000 000
WHAT IS THE LOSS IN GROSS MARGIN DUE TO CANNIBALIZATION
IN YEAR 1, YEAR 2, YEAR 3 AND BEYOND? 10 000 000 ,8,000 000
                                       8 000 000,5,
                                          5 000 000[b]
```

forecast the performance of new brands in the product class, given the values of the independent variables.[7] In MAXIM1, these values are provided by the player (who determines the input data) and by the simulation

---

[7] See Henry J. Claycamp and Lucien E. Lidely, "Prediction of New Product Performance: An Analytical Approach."

Exhibit 26-1   A Sample Run of MAXIM1, Market-Simulation Model[a] (cont'd.)

PRO FORMA PROFIT AND LOSS STATEMENT

	YEAR 1	YEAR 2	YEAR 3
SALES ($)	4.84380E 07[c]	5.81255E 07	6.29694E 07
GROSS MARGIN	2.16177E 07	2.59412E 07	2.81030E 07
MARKETING COSTS	2.92000E 07	7700000	11700000
DEPRECIATION	2836561	2836561	2836561
GROSS CONTRIBUTION	− 10418881	15404655	13566431
CANNIBALIZATION	− 10000000	− 8000000	− 5000000
INCREMENTAL PROFIT	− 2.04189E 07	7404655	8566431

ESTIMATED ANNUAL SALES AND CASH FLOW

YEAR	UNIT SALES	CASH FLOW
0	0	− 2.55291E 07
1	3587998	− 1.75823E 07
2	4305596	10241216
3	4664398	11402992
4	4804328	11895056
5	4948456	12763440
6	5096908	13657856
7	5249813	14579104
8	5407305	15528000
9	5569522	1.75860E 07

WHAT IS THE DISCOUNT RATE? .20
NET PRESENT VALUE = $58173
DO YOU WISH TO TRY ANOTHER RATE- 1 IF YES, 2 IF NO? 1
? .25
NET PRESENT VALUE = $ − 6544327
DO YOU WISH TO TRY ANOTHER RATE- 1 IF YES, 2 IF NO? 1
? .15
NET PRESENT VALUE = $9031025
DO YOU WISH TO TRY ANOTHER RATE- 1 IF YES, 2 IF NO? 1
? .10
NET PRESENT VALUE = $2.14610E 07
DO YOU WISH TO TRY ANOTHER RATE- 1 IF YES, 2 IF NO? 1
? .075
NET PRESENT VALUE = $2.94705E 07
DO YOU WISH TO TRY ANOTHER RATE- 1 IF YES, 2 IF NO? 2

TIME   0 MINS.   1 SECS.

Source: Prof. William F. Massy, Graduate School of Business, Stanford University.
[a] The underlining has been added to indicate information provided by the player (the input data).
[b] Notice that two errors have been made (unwanted commas) and corrected by the player.
[c] This is scientific—also called "exponential" notation. The number right of the "E" tells us where the decimal goes. Thus 4.84380E 07 is 48,438,000. Scientific notation is used to save space and, in some cases, simplify calculations.

model (which contains certain stored data). The simulation model also contains functional equations for computing revenues, marketing costs, depreciation, cash flows, new present values, and other important output data.

The data stored in the MAXIM1 model include measures of product uniqueness, effectiveness of promotions, the percentage of all commodity distribution that will probably be achieved after 13 weeks (this is the percentage of retailers stocking the brand, weighted according to the amount of shelf facings and displays), the impact of advertising graphics on awareness, and several other marketing factors—all of which are needed to solve Ayer's equations. In addition, it includes probabilities of repeat purchases for the range of possible prices; a 3 percent rate of market growth (subject to change by the player); a plant cost of $5 per unit of capacity; an initial trade-promotion expense of $3,500,00; a recurring trade-promotion expense of $2,000,000 per year; a personal-selling expense of $1,700,000 per year; a unit-production cost of $5.72; a retailer margin of 13 percent of the retail price; a depreciation rate; and other exogenous data needed to solve the functional equations and not provided by the player. The stored data are exogenous in that they are not controlled by the product manager. Some of the factors are within the control of the firm (such as production costs and retailer margins), but the product manager does not have the authority to manipulate them.

MAXIM1 is written in BASIC, a popular computer language, and the stored data are recorded on punch cards or magnetic tape. A portion of the model is reproduced in Exihibit 26-2. Much of it can be interpreted using only common sense and a bit of imagination, even by a reader unversed in BASIC.[8] As company policy, manufacturing technology, and market conditions change, the stored data can be altered by calling in a computer programmer.

The operating instructions are integral to the model and are explained in a six-page manual given to the player. A portion of these instructions are reproduced in Exhibit 26-2. Many of these require little or no explanation to be intelligible. For instance, Line 1001 instructs the computer to ask the the player which format he wants. Line 1002 tells him to enter the answer. Line 1003 interprets the answer, telling the computer to skip to Line 8100 if the short form (answer "1") is requested. MAXIM1 contains no simulated players. It is thus a relatively simple model, although the functional equations represent some fairly sophisticated analytical work. Also it involves a stochastic process to randomly vary some of the stored data according to the distribution of values observed in the market place.

The Output Data   The output data in MAXIM1 consists of the market-performance statistics, a profit-and-loss statement, and figures for the cannibalization (opportunity) costs, the cash flow, and the net present values

---

[8] Readers who feel they need help should consult the key to the earlier FORTRAN print-out, Exhibit 25-1, since the languages are in many ways similar.

Exhibit 26-2 A Computerized Market-Simulation Model (BASIC Language Program for MAXIM1)

```
LIST MAXIM1

MAXIM1          16:19       07/3/68      WEDNESDAY       SFO


0006 REM MAXIM1 PROGRAM
0100 READ U,D,K
0200 READ M,A1,B,R2
0400 READ G
1000 REM AYER MODEL OF TRIAL AND AWARENESS
1001 PRINT "DO YOU WISH THE SHORT FORM- 1 IF YES, 2 IF NO";
1002 INPUT X
1003 IF X = 1 THEN 8100
1010 PRINT "YOUR VALUE OF PROMOTION IN AWARENESS IS";
1020 INPUT P1
1030 PRINT "YOUR VALUE OF AVERAGE HOUSEHOLD IMPRESSIONS IS";
1040 INPUT H
1050 PRINT "YOUR VALUE OF COPY EXECUTION IS";
1060 INPUT C
1070 LET A = − 62.25 + .83*U + .12*P1 + 14.24*(LOG(H)/LOG(10))*C
1080 PRINT "THE VALUE OF AWARENESS IS"; A
1090 PRINT
1100 PRINT "YOUR VALUE OF PROMOTION IN INITIAL PURCHASES IS";
1110 INPUT P2
1120 PRINT "IS THIS A FAMILY BRAND- 1 IF YES, 0 IF NO";
1130 INPUT F
1140 LET P = − 14.9 + .14*P2 + .19*A + .0022*D*K + 7.24*F
1150 PRINT "THE VALUE OF INITIAL PURCHASES IS"; P
1160 PRINT
2000 REM CALCULATION OF FIRST YEAR SHARE
2010 PRINT "YOUR PRICE IS";
2020 INPUT P5
2030 LET T = 1.5*P
2040 LET R1 = M/(1 + EXP(− (A1 + B*P5)))
2041 PRINT "REPEAT RATE IS"; R1
2050 LET S = T*R1*R2
2060 PRINT "THE FIRST YEAR MARKET SHARE IS"; S "%"
2070 PRINT
3000 REM DEFINITION OF MARKET IN UNITS
3010 PRINT "WHAT IS THE SIZE OF THE MARKET IN UNITS";
3020 INPUT M1
3030 PRINT
4000 REM CALCULATION OF UNIT SALES
4010 REM SALES IN YEAR 1
4015 DIM S(20)
4020 LET S(1) = M1*(S/100)
4021 IF X = 1 THEN 8400
4030 PRINT "WHAT ARE YOUR COMPETITIVE AND GROWTH ASSUMPTIONS?"
4040 REM SALES IN YEAR 2
4050 PRINT "YOUR SECOND YEAR SALES FACTOR IS";
4070 INPUT F2
4080 LET S(2) = S(1)*F2
4090 REM SALES IN YEAR 3
4100 PRINT "YOUR THIRD YEAR SALES FACTOR IS";
4110 INPUT F3
4120 LET S(3) = S(1)*F3
```

Source: Prof. William F. Massy, Graduate School of Business, Stanford University.

associated with the marketing plan and the set of market data received as input. The output data are generated by the functional equations and are printed on the tab run in accordance with the operating instructions. They can be readily identified by examining Exhibit 26-1, the sample tab run. It is this information that is used to judge the marketing plan specified by the player (operator).

Applications   MAXIM1 can be used to test alternative marketing plans by entering different values for promotion and price. Of course, each mix requires another run. (If the analyst is in a hurry, he can use the short form of the program.) Although the player can try dozens of alternative plans in about the same number of minutes, random selection of marketing mixes is both inefficient and self-defeating. Like most simulation models, MAXIM1 only identifies the best option among the alternatives offered. In a sense, then, it forces the player to think about his promotional strategy before sitting down at the computer terminal. He must make explicit decisions regarding the type and extent of promotion he wants, the media mix, the effectiveness of ad copy, the positioning of ads, and his budget. He must also set a price and determine (probably from historical data) the size and growth rate of his potential market. He must make judgments about his competition, the rate at which his brand will cannibalize sales from other brands in the Maxwell House product line, and the effect of this cannibalization on the advertising and promotional budgets of these other products. In short, he must make the same judgments and decisions as the real product manager. MAXIM1—like other simulation models—reveals only the results of a course of actions. It is not a substitute for thinking, nor does it provide a means for checking the logic and consistency of the judgments and decisions.

The model also serves to generate experimental data. For example, the player may want to know the price elasticity over a broad range. Eight to ten model runs, using a different price each time, will provide enough price-quantity pairs to estimate the function, given the market conditions specified in the model. (Linear regression analysis may be the best way to fit a line to these data.)

MAXIM1 can also be used for sensitivity analysis. For instance, the player can readily determine the sensitivity of profit to various changes in the discount rate. He can also determine the sensitivity of the firm's market share, unit sales, revenue, and profit to changes in promotion, price, market size, and the market growth rate. Of course, these sensitivities may vary with market conditions, but this too can be determined simply by changing the appropriate variables and rerunning the model.

The simulation model is also useful for business gaming. In this capacity, it pits the player against nature, for there are no provisions for more than one player, either simulated or real. Of course, consecutive real players can be allowed to play and their scores compared. (The net present value of their plans would be the best basis for scoring.) However, this introduces an element of unreality, since the players would not be competing against one another in the simulated marketplace. Hence, the decisions of one player would not affect the market shares, sales, or revenue of another, as they would in most models designed specifically for business gaming.

The speed and economy of market simulation, once the model has been developed, is suggested by the last line in the sample tab-run. This is an accounting statement telling the player how much computer time is being charged to his account for that particular run. In this case, it is one second. The cost is probably less than $2.[9]

Analysis of Transition Processes

Simulation is used in the study of market transition processes, such as the redistribution of market shares. The simulation model serves to replicate the behavior that induces the transition. An understanding of such processes is often a prerequisite to accurate forecasting or the optimum manipulation of marketing instruments, especially advertising. Phenomena that take months or even years to reach completion in the marketplace can be simulated in minutes by a computerized model. The results of the simulated transition can be very close to those of the actual transition.[10] Furthermore, not only are transition processes simulated for their own sake, but they are often a necessary addition to simulation models constructed for other purposes, such as business gaming and experimentation.

Constructing a Model

Realistic models of transition processes can be constructed when two properties of consumer behavior are known or can be estimated accurately. First, analysts must have a probability distribution for the alternative actions of each consumer. For example, if the instant-coffee market is being studied, they need to know the probability that a housewife will buy a given brand. Second, they must know the average period between successive acts. In the coffee study, they must know the average time between purchases. With this information, they can construct a dynamic model of the behavioral pattern and simulate the transition process.

Markov Chains

In simulating transition processes, consumer behavior is sometimes represented by a Markov chain. A *Markov chain* is a series of iterations in which each successive state is determined by the probabilities in the previous state. Behavior during a given iteration is determined by the probabilities

---

[9] Charges are usually based on the time the central processing unit (CPU) is used (one second in the illustration). The CPU is the heart of the computer system and by far the most expensive component. There also may be a fixed monthly rental for peripheral equipment, such as the terminal.

[10] For example, see William F. Massy, "Forecasting the Demand for a New Convenience Product," *Journal of Marketing Research* **6**: 4 (November 1970), pp 405–412.

of the alternatives and a stochastic process. The method was first developed by a Russian mathematician, A. A. Markov, to study transition processes in physical matter and only later adapted to studies of human behavior. It is especially useful to market researchers studying the effect of brand loyalty and brand shifting on market shares.

Markov chains are conceptually attractive, for they provide a means for studying transition processes that elude definition by conventional analytical techniques. By constructing a Markov chain, we can simulate a transition process up to any point. Thus, we can determine the "state of nature" (e.g., the distribution of market shares) at any point in the future, at least so far as that state is determined by the transition phenomenon.

Unfortunately, the basic Markov model requires certain assumptions that do not always hold up in the marketplace. One such assumption is homogeneity among customers with respect to purchase behavior. Each customer is presumed to respond the same way to a given set of conditions. Hence, if the probability that one customer who previously purchased Brand A will purchase Brand B during the next purchase cycle is 0.4, the probability that all other Brand A buyers will purchase B the next time around is also 0.4. Another questionable assumption is the proposition that the purchase probabilities remain constant over time.[11] These constraints have been modified by the development of more elaborate models, many of which are adaptations of the basic Markov model, such as the quasiheterogeneous Markov model and the higher-order Markov models.[12]

A first-order Markov chain—or "model"—assumes that the probability that a consumer will buy a particular brand depends solely on the identity of the brand purchased previously. This is a conditional probability, which remains constant over time. Although empirical studies have shown that a constant conditional probability is often an unrealistic assumption, a first-order chain serves nicely to explain the essence of transition models. For example, suppose that there are two brands, A and B, from which the buyer must choose. Consumer-panel data reveal that the probability of A being purchased, given the previous purchase of A, is 0.7: $P(A/A) = 0.7$. There are three other possibilities: $P(B/A) = 0.3$, $P(A/B) = 0.5$, and $P(B/B) = 0.5$. The possible outcomes in each of four iterations (repurchase cycles) are illustrated in Figure 26-2, a tree diagram of a consumer's options if he or she starts with Brand A.

The probability of reaching a particular point in the chain—say, the top A_3 in the third iteration—is a joint probability. It is the product of the probability of the preceding event times the conditional probability

[11] See William F. Massy, "Order and Homogeneity of Family Specific Brand Switching Processes," *Journal of Marketing Research* **3**: 1, (February 1966), p. 53.

[12] See Donald G. Morrison, "New Models of Consumer Loyalty Behavior: Aids to Setting and Evaluating Marketing Plans," in Peter D. Bennet, ed., *Marketing and Economic Development* (Chicago: American Marketing Association, 1965), pp. 323-337; Donald G. Morrison, "Testing Brand-Switching Models," *Journal of Marketing Research* **3**: 4 (November 1966), pp. 401–409; and James F. Engel, David T. Kollat, and Roger D. Blackwell, *Consumer Behavior* (New York: Holt, Rinehart and Winston, 1968), pp. 595–608.

Figure 26-2   **First-order Markov Chain with Four Iterations**

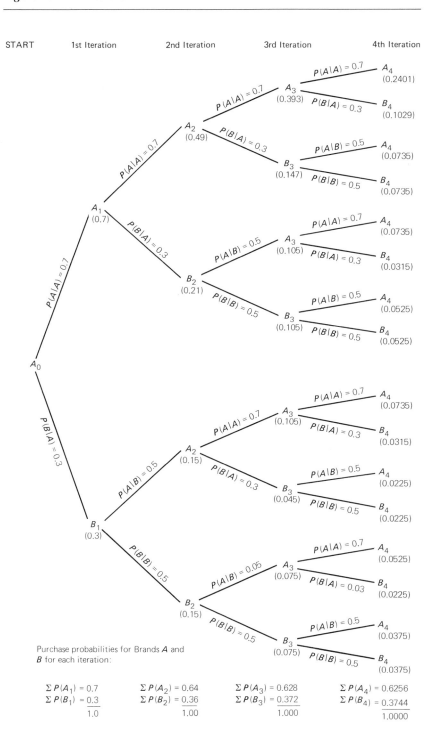

START	1st Iteration	2nd Iteration	3rd Iteration	4th Iteration

Purchase probabilities for Brands *A* and
B for each iteration:

$\Sigma P(A_1) = 0.7$ $\Sigma P(A_2) = 0.64$ $\Sigma P(A_3) = 0.628$ $\Sigma P(A_4) = 0.6256$
$\Sigma P(B_1) = 0.3$ $\Sigma P(B_2) = 0.36$ $\Sigma P(B_3) = 0.372$ $\Sigma P(B_4) = 0.3744$
$\overline{\quad 1.0 \quad}$ $\overline{\quad 1.00 \quad}$ $\overline{\quad 1.000 \quad}$ $\overline{\quad 1.0000 \quad}$

of the even itself.[13] Thus, the probability of reaching the top A_2 is 0.49, $(0.7) \cdot (0.7)$, and the probability of reaching the top A_3 is 0.343, $(0.49) \cdot (0.7)$.

The probability that a given brand will be purchased during a particular iteration is the sum of the probabilities of each possible event involving that brand.[14] Thus, the probability that Brand B will be purchased during the third iteration is 0.372, the sum of 0.147, 0.105, 0.045, and 0.075.

Consumer behavior with respect to the transition process (the redistribution of market shares among the two brands) is simulated by following a path through each iteration. The probabilities are stated as functional equations in the model. At each iteration, the simulated consumer is routed along a path indicated by the appropriate functional equation and a stochastic process. For instance, in the first iteration, a customer who had originally purchased Brand A would purchase it again if a random number between 0 and 6, inclusive, were generated by the stochastic process. If a random number between 7 and 9, inclusive, was generated, a purchase of Brand B would be recorded. By repeating this process for each simulated customer, the total purchases of A and B (hence, their respective market shares) in each iteration can be estimated. The iterations can be translated into points in time by computing the average time required for a repurchase cycle. The period between repurchases can be learned from continuous consumer panels or other forms of surveys.

Given the sales data for one purchase cycle and the conditional probabilities for the purchase of each alternative, the brand sales in the next cycle (iteration) can be computed. We simply add up the products of the conditional probabilities and the first set of brand sales:

$$Q_{i_{(t+1)}} = \sum_{j=1}^{n} P(i|j)\, Q_{j_{(t)}} \qquad [26.1]$$

where

$Q_{i_{(t+1)}}$ = the sales of the ith brand at time $t + 1$

$P(i|j)$ = the conditional probability that the ith brand will be purchased given the previous purchase of Brand j

$Q_{j_{(t)}}$ = the sales of the jth brand at time t

Thus, if there were three competing brands—A, B, and C—the sales of A at $t + 1$ would equal $P(A|A) \cdot Q_{A_{(t)}} + P(A|B) \cdot Q_{B_{(t)}} + P(A|C) \cdot Q_{C_{(t)}}$.

Suppose we go a step further and follow the change in sales and market shares of the three brands through four purchase cycles. We need to know the conditional purchase probabilities, shown in Table 26-1, and the starting

---

[13] See almost any introductory statistics text for the rules of probability.
[14] The additive formula applies here since the events that may occur during a given iteration are mutually exclusive and independent with respect to the other events in that iteration.

Table 26-1   Conditional Purchase Probabilities for Brands A, B, and C

Brand A	Brand B	Brand C
$P(A\mid A) = 0.5$	$P(A\mid B) = 0.4$	$P(A\mid C) = 0.4$
$P(B\mid A) = 0.3$	$P(B\mid B) = 0.4$	$P(B\mid C) = 0.3$
$P(C\mid A) = 0.2$	$P(C\mid B) = 0.2$	$P(C\mid C) = 0.3$
$\overline{1.0}$	$\overline{1.0}$	$\overline{1.0}$

sales (S_t when $t = 0$), shown in the second column of Table 26-2. By using formula 26.1, we can then compute the total sales for each brand during the first iteration.

For instance, Table 26-1 tells us that the conditional probabilities of the purchase of Brand A, given the previous purchase of A, B, or C, are 0.5, 0.4, and 0.4, respectively. Table 26-2 gives the sales of Brands A, B, and C during the period $t = 0$ as 300, 400, and 300 units, respectively. Thus, the total sales of Brand A during the first iteration ($t + 1$) can be computed as follows:

$$Q_{i_{(t+1)}} = \sum_{j=1}^{n} P(i\mid j)Q_{j_{(t)}} \qquad \text{(given as equation 26.1)}$$

$$Q_{A_{(t+1)}} = P(A\mid A)Q_{A_{(t)}} + P(A\mid B) \cdot Q_{B_{(t)}} + P(A\mid C) \cdot Q_{C_{(t)}} \quad \text{(by expansion)}$$

$$Q_{A_{(t+1)}} = 0.5(300) + 0.4(400) + 0.4(300) \qquad \text{(by substitution)}$$

$$Q_{A_{(t+1)}} = 150 + 160 + 120 \qquad \text{(by arithmetic)}$$

$$Q_{A_{(t+1)}} = 430 \qquad \text{(by arithmetic)}$$

The total sales for each brand form the basis for the next round of computations, and so on until sales through the desired iteration have been estimated. If the average purchase cycle lasts three months and a forecast of brand sales (thus market shares) one year hence is needed, four iterations will be required. The entire transition process is illustrated in Table 26-2.

The effect of the transition process, as indicated by the Markov chain, is obvious. Brands A, B, and C, which started with market shares of 30 percent, 40 percent, and 30 percent, respectively, finished the year holding 44.4 percent, 33.3 percent, and 22.3 percent of the market. There has been a substantial change in the sales of each competitor; A has usurped the dominant position, at the expense of B and C.

This example is a gross simplification compared to the transition processes that occur in the marketplace. However, it does illustrate a method by which these processes can be incorporated into a simulation model. Simulation is the only way in which the more complex transition phenomena can be analyzed and their effects on sales forecast.

Table 26-2   **Sales of Brands A, B, and C Through
Four Purchase Cycles Using a First-Order Markov Chain**

First-Iteration Sales
(Period $t + 1$)

Sales During Period $t = 0$		Sales During Period $t + 1$		
Brand	Quantity	A	B	C
A	300	150	90	60
B	400	160	160	80
C	300	120	90	90
	Totals	430	340	230

Second-Iteration Sales
(Period $t + 2$)

Sales During Period $t + 1$		Sales During Period $t + 2$		
Brand	Quantity	A	B	C
A	430	215	129	86
B	340	136	136	68
C	230	92	69	69
	Totals	443	334	223

Third-Iteration Sales
(Period $t + 3$)

Sales During Period $t + 2$		Sales During Period $t + 3$		
Brand	Quantity	A	B	C
A	443	221	133	89
B	334	134	133	67
C	223	89	67	67
	Totals	444	333	223

Fourth-Iteration Sales
(Period $t + 4$)

Sales During Period $t + 3$		Sales During Period $t + 4$		
Brand	Quantity	A	B	C
A	444	222	133	89
B	333	133	133	67
C	223	89	67	67
	Totals	444	333	223

Market Equilibrium

Many transition processes approach equilibrium—also called "steady state"—after a number of iterations. Sales or market shares tend to stabilize, even though brands-switching or other phenomena continue. For example, the first-order Markov model tends toward equilibrium after the third iteration. In the preceding example, brand sales—and hence brand shares— become constant after period $t + 3$. The disturbances (the changes in market shares, etc.) also lessen with each successive iteration. Perfect equilibrium is rare, but if the transition process tends toward a steady state and disturbances are minimal, the variations become so small after a number of iterations that they may be ignored and the market considered stable.

One of the virtues of simulation is the ease with which the effects of disturbances can be estimated, especially if the model has been computerized. For instance, suppose we want to evaluate the effects of changes in promotional strategy. Different strategies will have different effects on the various conditional purchase probabilities. If these effects can be estimated, the redistribution of sales and market shares induced by the changes in strategy can easily be forecast.

Selecting and Adapting a Model

There are a variety of transition models appropriate to market simulation. The first-order Markov chain is probably the simplest, but it is limited by the assumptions that conditional probabilities remain constant, that there is no mortality among consumers, and that the aggregate market does not grow. Of course, these conditions can be manipulated during the simulation.

Another alternative is to retain the basic Markov model but expand the purchase-probability equations to include two parameters—a retention factor and a merchandising-attraction factor. The *retention factor*, r_i, represents the number of purchases made by habitual buyers of brand i. The *merchandising-attraction factor*, a_i, represents the number of purchases made by buyers of other brands who are attracted to brand i. Thus, if 40 percent of Brand B's sales are made to habitual customers ($r_B = 0.4$), 60 percent of its sales ($1 - 0.4$) will be vulnerable to wooing by A. If A has the power to attract 0.30 percent of the available sales ($a_A = 0.3$), it will capture 18 percent ($0.6 \cdot 0.3$) of B's total market during the following purchase cycle. If 18 percent of B's sales will go to A in the next purchase cycle, then, according to the rules of probability, the likelihood that a Brand B buyer will purchase Brand A is 0.18 $[P(A|B) = 0.18]$. In other words, $P(A|B) = (1 - r_B)a_A$.

Alfred Kuehn, the developer of this model, argues that the portion of brand i's sales which are vulnerable to wooing by other brands are also vulnerable to being reattracted to i.[15] This assumption is a bit shaky, since some of the disloyalty to i is presumably induced by dissatisfaction with it.

---

[15] Alfred E. Kuehn, "A Model for Budgeting Advertising," in Frank M. Bass et al., eds., *Mathematical Models and Methods in Advertising* (Homewood, IL: Irwin, 1961), pp. 302–353.

However, following Kuehn's logic, the total proportion—and hence the probability of repurchase—of brand i's sales in one period that will be retained in the next will equal the proportion retained by loyalty or habit (r_i) plus the proportion reattracted $[(1 - r_i)a_i]$. Using Brand A as an example, we would say that $P(A|A) = r_A + (1 - r_A)a_A$. If there are three competing brands in the market—A, B, and C—the conditional-purchase probabilities can be expressed as follows:

Brand A:
$$P(A|A) = r_A + (1 - r_A)a_A \quad P(A|B) = (1 - r_B)a_A \quad P(A|C) = (1 - r_C)a_A$$

Brand B:
$$P(B|A) = (1 - r_A)a_B \quad P(B|B) = r_B + (1 - r_B)a_B \quad P(B|C) = (1 - r_C)a_B$$

Brand C:
$$P(C|A) = (1 - r_A)a_C \quad P(C|B) = (i - r_B)a_C \quad P(C|C) = r_C + (1 - r_C)a_C$$

$P(A|A)$, $P(B|B)$, and $P(C|C)$ represent sales that will be retained by each brand as repurchases. The other probabilities represent sales taken away from competing brands.

Instead of fixed conditional purchase probabilities, such as those in Figure 26-2, Kuehn uses probabilities that can vary over time. The variation is induced by changes in the parameters, r_i and a_i; changes in their values can be made by the operator or included in the model itself. For instance, the model may include an equation specifying a_A as a function of Brand A's price and advertising budget and the prices and advertising budgets of competing brands. As any of these independent variables are changed—by either live players or simulated decision units—during the course of the simulation, the value of a_A will change. This in turn will alter the transition processes that are reallocating market shares and sales.

The basic Markov model can be expanded to a second-, third-, or higher-order function if sufficient market data are available to specify the conditional probabilities. In a second-order Markov chain, a purchase probability would be conditional upon the two preceding purchases; in a third-order chain, it would be conditional on the three preceding purchases; and so on. Although more realistic, the higher-order chains complicate both the specification and the operation of the model. A long history of the transition process and a large number of consumers are needed to estimate the the more elaborate probabilities with an acceptable level of confidence. If the model is computerized, however, the manipulations will not be a problem.

Markov chains, as well as most other transition models, can be adapted to accommodate virtually any kind of behavioral alternatives. For instance, the no-purchase option can be represented by a dummy variable. If three alternative brands are available, the no-purchase option can be represented by a fourth "brand." Thus, the consumer (usually represented by a simulated decision unit) will have four alternatives—say, A, B, C, and D, with D being the decision not to buy.

Table 26-3   **Some Characteristics of Major Brand-Loyalty Models**

Assumed Determinants of Transition Probabilities	Assumed Behavior of Transition Probabilities Over Time	
	Constant	Time Variant
No previous purchases and no other influences	Bernoulli Models	Dynamic Bernoulli models
Brand purchased last	Homogeneous first-order Markov models	Quasiheterogeneous first-order Markov models
Two or more brands purchased previously	Higher-order Markov models	
Two or more brands purchased previously and other factors		Learning model Learning-Markov model

Source: From *Consumer Behavior* by James F. Engel, David T. Kollat, and Roger D. Blackwell. Copyright © 1968 by Holt, Rinehart and Winston, Inc. Reproduced by permission of Holt, Rinehart and Winston, Inc.

Other behavioral models have also been designed or adapted to accommodate transition processes. Among the better known are Farley and Kuehn's learning model of brand loyalty,[16] the Bernoulli models,[17] and the quasiheterogeneous Markov models. The special characteristics of each are summarized in Table 26-3.

Estimating and Forecasting

Simulation is used in estimating and forecasting to establish the value of a variable that cannot easily be specified by conventional analytical techniques such as regression equations and growth models. Transition processes in particular, as we have seen, often defy description by purely analytical techniques but lend themselves to simulation.

Estimates

Estimates—sometimes called "predictions"—are obtained by entering the conditions of the market for which the prediction is being made into a model

[16] John U. Farley and Alfred E. Kuehn, "Stocastic Models of Brand Switching," in George Schwartz, ed., *Science in Marketing* (New York: Wiley, 1965), p. 452.
[17] See George Brown, "Brand Loyalty—Fact or Fiction," *Advertising Age* **23** (January 26, 1953), pp. 75–76; Ross Cunningham, "Brand Loyalty—What, Where, How Much, *Harvard Business Review* **34** (January–February 1956), pp. 116–128; Ross Cunningham, "Customer Loyalty to Store and Brand," *Harvard Business Review* **39** (November–December 1961), pp. 127–137; and Ronald A. Howard, "Dynamic Inference," *Research in the Control of Complex Systems*, Technical Report No. 10, Operations Research Center (Cambridge: Massachusetts Institute of Technology Press, 1964).

simulating that market. If the actual conditions are unknown, they are estimated. Estimation is a relatively infrequent application of simulation. Generally, analytical models can be developed that are simpler and equally satisfactory. Linear regression analysis, using cross-sectional data, is especially useful for this purpose. It produces practical analytical models that are good predictors and can be operated manually. Simulation is relatively cumbersome as an instrument of prediction.

Forecasts

Forecasts can be obtained by iteration or by entering conditions at the forecast time into the model. If iteration is not used, time must be included as an independent variable in the appropriate functional equations. Iteration is the more powerful of the two alternatives because it allows transition processes to be incorporated in the model. Since they are time-dependent, transition processes often have a significant influence on the future values of the forecast variables. For instance, brand-switching, by inducing a reorganization of the market over time, can have an extremely important effect on market shares and the sales of competitors. Its effect during the forecast period can be reproduced using consecutive iterations. Analytical models can be made to include transition processes also, but the equations are difficult to construct and awkward to solve. When future values are strongly influenced by transition processes, simulation is the most practical method of forecasting.

Heuristic Programming[18]

Heuristic programming is the simulation of human decision-making by copying the logical process and decision rules used by live problem-solvers. *Heuristic programs,* or "models," consist of a series of steps leading to various alternatives. The selection of steps, and hence the ultimate selection of alternatives, is determined by a group of intuitive decision rules.

Heuristic programming is used to find satisfactory solutions to problems that resist optimization by known techniques such as differential calculus or linear programming or do not have an optimum (ideal) solution. For example, consider the game of chess: One can define every possible move. Theoretically, we could specify every possible combination of moves. Having done so, we could prepare an algorithm—a solution system—that would select the optimum move in every situation. Equipped with this algorithm, we would never lose and the game of chess would be reduced to trivia. Unfortunately, there are billions upon billions (approximately 10^{180}) of possible move combinations. Thus, the solution system is a theoretical possibility but a practical impossibility.

---

[18] "Heuristic" is defined by Webster as "serving to guide, discover, or reveal . . . valuable for empirical research but unproven or incapable of proof." See *Webster's Seventh New Collegiate Dictionary* (Springfield, Mass.: Merriam, 1961), p. 391.

Or consider the missionary-cannibal problem, another classic example: Three missionaries are escorting three cannibals to church. Before arriving at the church and receiving religious enlightenment, the cannibals persist in their traditional eating habits. If they outnumber the missionaries at any time en route, they will eat them. The party reaches a river and finds only one boat that will carry no more than two people. How does the party get to the far side of the river without one or more missionaries being eaten? (Remember, somebody has to row the boat back from the far side of the river.) There is no optimum solution, but there are several workable ones.[19]

In both these cases, heuristic programming can be used to find a satisfactory solution. In the case of the chess game, we can specify the opponent's most likely moves with respect to a given move option open to our player. Using a computer, we can then try various combinations of moves and countermoves until we find one that produces a satisfactory result—say, it enables us to capture an opponent's piece—even if it is not the optimum move from the point of view of speedily winning the game.[20] In fact, this is the basis upon which computers have been programmed to play chess. They are beaten, but only occasionally.

The missionary-cannibal problem has also been solved by heuristic programming. Simulated river crossings are made using different combinations of travelers. Trial and error soon yields a system that gets all three missionaries across safely. The system may not be optimum in terms of the number of boat trips, but it works in terms of the major criterion—namely, ensuring the safe arrival of all the missionaries.

The Method

A heuristic program is a procedure for arriving at a satisfactory solution in accordance with a set of decision rules. The procedure takes the form of a network of paths, similar to a maze, that lead from the starting condition to two or more final decisions. The choice of a final decision depends on which path is followed. Each path leads to only one decision, although many paths may lead to the same decision. The selection of paths is determined by using the appropriate decision rule at each junction (step) in the network. The outcome of a particular decision rule depends on the conditions existing at that junction. For instance, in Figure 26-3, a heuristic program for a pricing decision, one of the first steps is to decide if the good in question is a basic item—a judgment decision. If the answer is "YES," the decision path branches to the instruction box "USE STANDARD PRICE." If the answer is "NO," the decision path branches to the question "DOES ITEM HAVE SPECIAL AESTHETIC APPEAL?" Whichever path is taken, we eventually wind up with a "FINAL SALE PRICE."

[19] Robert Ferber and P. J. Verdoorn, *Research Methods in Economics and Business* (New York: Macmillan, 1967), p. 200.
[20] The move chosen may, coincidentally, be the optimum move. However, its selection would be the result of chance, not logic.

Figure 26-3   **A Heuristic Model of a Sale-Pricing Decision**

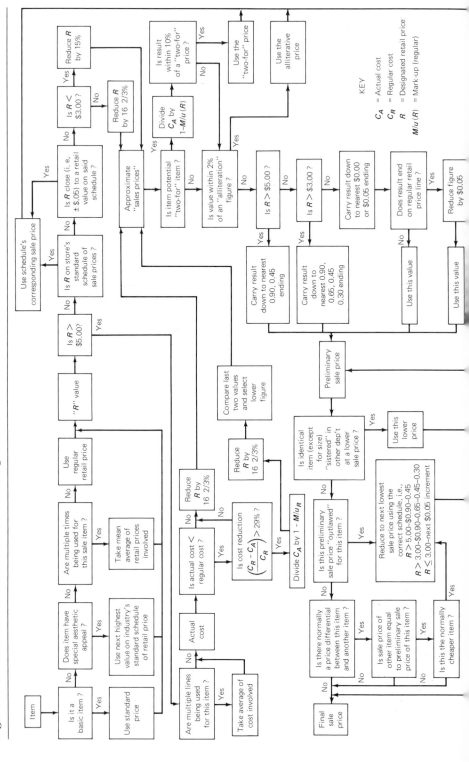

A heuristic program is normally prepared in two forms: First, a schematic diagram is drawn depicting every possible step in the decision process and showing the route segments. The route segments connect the various steps in the decision process and form the network of paths leading to the final decision alternatives. Decision rules are specified for each junction to determine which route segments will be selected, and hence which path will be followed in solving a particular problem.

Second, a computer program is prepared by transcribing the schematic diagram into a form digestible by a computer. Any one of several languages may be used, depending on the skills of the researcher or programmer and the type of equipment available. BASIC, FORTRAN, and PL-1 are all common choices.

Applications

A typical heuristic program is illustrated in Figure 26-3. By tracing our way from the beginning to the end of the flow chart, using arbitrary values or conditions at each decision point, we can easily see how the program works. It can be computerized by transcribing the schematic diagram into an appropriate computer language. The chart represents the sale-pricing decision process of a department of a major retail store. (A cost–price table was used to set the original prices, since the sotre has a cost-plus-fixed-markup pricing policy.) Few of the decision rules were specified by the store management; most were intuitive processes used by department personnel and observed by the researchers who designed the program.

The model was tested with an unrestricted random sample of 197 invoices. It correctly predicted the price of 188 of the items. A correct prediction was defined as a price equal (to the penny) to the price actually assigned to the article by the human decision-maker.[21]

Figure 26-3 is typical of heuristic programs designed to handle categorical variables. When the input information needed to apply the decision rules is all quantitative—or can be assigned a numerical value—a mathematical model may be possible. All that is required is an appropriate scaling technique and some dummy variables.

A heuristic program in mathematical form has the appearance of an analytical model. Inspection will not reveal its true nature, although the observer should suspect that the model is heuristic if it is complex, nonlinear, and especially if it contains many independent variables.

A mathematical model is heuristic if the relationships between the variables are estimated intuitively rather than by mathematical or statistical analysis. One such model, developed for a large manufacturer of synthetic fibers, is shown in Exhibit 26-3. It simulates the allocation of the firm's advertising budget among the various synthetic fiber markets.

---

[21] R. M. Cyert, J. G. March, and C. G. Moore, "A Model of Retail Ordering and Pricing by a Department Store," in Ronald E. Frank, Alfred A. Kuehn, and William F. Massy, *Quantitative Techniques in Marketing Analysis* (Homewood, IL: Irwin, 1962), p. 521.

Exhibit 26-3 **A Mathematical Heuristic Model of an Advertising Allocation Decision**

$$
A_i = \frac{A_T E_i \left[Fk_i \dfrac{S_i}{F_i} + \dfrac{F_i}{F}(1 - k_i)(P_i - S_i) \right]^{1/2}}{\displaystyle\sum_{i=1}^{N} E_i \left[Fk_i \dfrac{S_i}{F_i} + \dfrac{F_i}{F}(1 - k_i)(P_i - S_i) \right]^{1/2}}
$$

where

A_i = advertising dollars to be allocated to the ith market

E_i = margin \$/lb, for ith market

A_T = total advertising dollars available for allocation

$k_i = \dfrac{\text{current sales level in } i\text{th market in pounds}}{\text{target sales level in } i\text{th market in pounds}}$

F_i = sensitivity to the firm's advertising factor for the ith market expressed as a rating from 1 (very insensitive) to 100 (very sensitive) (These factors were derived from the judgmental estimates of the advertising executives.)

$\bar{F}$ = average sensitivity to advertising for all markets under consideration.

P_i = annual potential sales to the ith market (total market size, in pounds)

S_i = current annual sales to the ith market (in pounds)

N = number of markets in allocation group

Source: Paul E. Green and Donald S. Tull, *Research for Marketing Decisions,* © 1966. Reprinted by permission of Prentice-Hill. Inc., Englewood Cliffs, New Jersey.

Heuristic programming is relatively new, having emerged as a useful marketing-research tool only in the 1960s. It has been successfully applied to a number of practical marketing problems where purely analytical techniques have not worked, and has been particularly helpful in resolving distribution problems involving store location, warehouse operation, and inventory control.[22] Heuristic programs are useful in studying complex behavioral processes and predicting their outcomes, since they provide a means for incorporating judgment into a formal decision procedure and evaluating that judgment with respect to its influence on the final outcome.

A collateral application is the use of heuristic programs in sensitivity analysis. Once a program—preferably computerized—has been prepared,

[22] For more examples of the application of heuristic programming, see William F. Massy and J. D. Savvas, "Logical Flow Models for Marketing Analysis," *Journal of Marketing* **28**: 1 (January 1964), pp. 32–37; Fred Tonge, *A Heuristic Program for Assembly Line Balancing* (Englewood Cliffs, NJ: Prentice-Hall, 1961); Patrick J. Robinson, "Simulation in Operations Research," *Canadian Oil/Gas World* (November 1957), pp. 39–44; and William A. Morgenroth, "A Method for Understanding Price Determinants," *Journal of Marketing Research* **1**: 3 (August 1964), pp. 17–26.

the analyst can easily determine the sensitivity of the final outcome to changes in one or more decision rules. For example, in the advertising-budget problem (Exhibit 26-3), the outcome, A_i (i.e., the allocation for the ith market) is more sensitive to the gross (profit) margin in the ith market, E_i, than to the current annual sales, S_i. If the decision process is very cumbersome and time-consuming, the heuristic program may reveal opportunities for condensing and streamlining it.

A heuristic program will accommodate both judgment and analytical decision rules. The method by which a rule is derived has little to do with its operation in the program. The steps in the program can be simple conditional statements (e.g., "Given condition B, go to step 8.") or complex mathematical equations. If the model is computerized, an input option—say, a possible warehouse location—can be evaluated in a few seconds. Thus, hundreds of decision alternatives can be evaluated in a short time. A computerized program can also be expanded to array various options in terms of their effect on a specific criterion such as cost or delivery times.[23]

Designing a Program

The basic design objective of heuristic programming is to construct a model that conforms to the procedure, rules, and outcomes of the human decision process being simulated. If no satisfactory decision system exist, the objective may be to develop one. Sometimes, unsatisfactory human decision processes are duplicated so that they can be studied and improved.

In Figure 26-3, the objective was to construct a model of the decision process for determining the retail price of sale goods at a major department store. The analyst simulated the sale-pricing process and determined the outcome (i.e., a good's sale price) by selecting an item and following the program to the last step (the "FINAL SALE PRICE").

In Exhibit 26-3, the objective was to construct a model of the decision process for allocating a firm's total advertising budget, A_T, among various end-use markets, i. The model includes several judgment factors, such as target-sales levels and a measure of sensitivity to advertising. Each variable is assigned a numerical value, since the model is mathematical. However, advertising sensitivity, which is nonparametric, is measured by an arbitrary scale. To simulate the decision process and determine the outcome (i.e., the advertising budget for a particular medium), we simply substitute the appropriate values in the equation and solve for A_i, the dependent variable.

Models of human behavior must be based on observation of that behavior, and heuristic programs are no exception. The researcher usually interviews the participants in the decision process, observes the process in motion, traces the prodecure from start to finish, and records the outcomes. This is how the models described above were developed.

---

[23] For example, see Alfred A. Kuehn and Michael J. Hamburger, "A Heuristic Program for Locating Warehouses," in Ronald E. Frank, Alfred A. Kuehn, and William F. Massy, *Quantitative Techniques in Marketing Analysis* (Homewood, IL: Irwin, 1962), pp. 523–596.

Like all simulation models, a heuristic program can only select from among the alternatives suggested by its operators. Hence, the optimum choice may be overlooked. However, even when a very large number of alternatives is theoretically possible (e.g., when the firm is considering warehouse locations for a national market), the number of realistic possibilities is usually manageable. If the decision-makers are at all knowledgeable, they should be able to identify the more feasible options.

Problems

1   How might market simulation be used (a) to train brand managers at General Mills, (b) to choose between an advertising theme that stressed brand loyalty and one that encouraged brand-switching, and (c) to select a new store site for Sears Roebuck?

2   Outline a schematic diagram of a simulation model appropriate to one of the applications mentioned in question 1.

3   Consumer-panel data reveal the following purchase probabilities for three brands, *A, B,* and *C,* assuming a previous purchase of each brand:

$$P(A|A) = 0.5 \quad P(A|B) = 0.3 \quad P(A|C) = 0.4$$
$$P(B|A) = 0.3 \quad P(B|B) = 0.6 \quad P(B|C) = 0.4$$
$$P(C|A) = 0.2 \quad P(C|B) = 0.1 \quad P(C|C) = 0.2$$

At present, *A* has 30 percent of the market, *B* has 50 percent, and *C* has 20 percent. Assuming that all three are competing brands of a consumer convenience good and that replacement purchases are made on an average of once a month, forecast their respective market shares four months from now. Would you consider the market in equilibrium at that point?

4   Construct a heuristic model of the decision process you would use in one of the following situations: (a) purchasing a tank of gasoline, (b) buying a new automobile, or (c) investing in stocks.

Part 9
Summary

Simulation is the manipulation of a model to determine the changes in one or more dependent variables induced by changes in one or more independent variables. A market-simulation system has four components: a model, players, and input and output data. A computer is generally associated with this kind of simulation, but it is not essential unless the model is so complex that manual manipulation is impractical. Models can be symbolic, analogical, or iconical. Most market-simulation models are symbolic.

Because it is quick, economic, and safe, market simulation is often more feasible than other forms of research. However, it is sometimes difficult, or even impossible, to construct accurate models of real-world processes. Hence, simulation is not common.

A market-simulation model has five components: functional equations, stored data, simulated decision units, a stochastic process, and operating instructions. Only the first component—or its analogical of iconical equivalent—is necessary. The functional equations are the heart of the model, and their specification is the most difficult part of model building.

The stored data consist of real-world information, information generated by the model itself, and hypothetical data entered by the players or operators. Players can be live (as in most business games) or simulated decision units—artificial representatives of the individuals, households, business firms, and institutions that have a role in the market process being simulated.

A stochastic process is essentially a probability distribution, coupled with a random-number generator, that is used to simulate the element of chance normally associated with a variable. Operating instructions tell the human operator or the computer what to do at each point in the program. For the live players, they are the rules of the game.

Input data are entered into the model during the simulation. They consist of the decision values (such as prices) selected by the live players and the changes in exogenous variables (such as personal income) made by them or the operator. Output data are generated by the model. They consist of the new values of the dependent variables (such as profit and market share), which change during each iteration.

Market simulation is used most often in business gaming, experimentation, analyzing transition processes, prediction and forecasting, and heuristic programming. Business gaming is a form of management training in which live players compete against other live players or against simulated decision units.

Simulation is used in experimentation to derive the values of dependent variables by trial and error. The method is similar to that of conventional experimentation, but the test market used is only a copy of the real market. The output data are analyzed in the same way as the results of real-market experiments.

Simulation is used in analyzing transition processes to replicate the behavior that induces the transition. Processes (such as a redistribution of market shares) that may take months in the marketplace can be reproduced in minutes by a simulation model. The Markov chain is the most common transition model.

Simulation is used frequently in forecasting and occasionally in prediction. By using iterations to simulate the passage of time, we can include transition processes, which frequently play an important role in determining the future value of a forecast variable, in the model.

Simulation is used in heuristic programming to replicate a decision process. It uses the same rules a human decision-maker would to reach a satisfactory—although not necessarily optimum—solution to a complex problem. This kind of technique is especially useful in dealing with problems that do not lend themselves to solution by conventional forms of analysis.

As useful as it may be, simulation is but one of many devices that belong in the compleat researcher's tool kit. As new tools are developed, they should be added to that kit, and obsolete ones should be discarded. Perhaps we should even heed the words of Thoreau who suggested: "If you are to understand the fern you must first forget your botany."

CASE STUDY 9

Ajax Advertising Agency: Building a New-Product Evaluation Model

David A. Aaker (*David A. Aaker, Ph.D., is Associate Professor of Marketing, University of California at Berkeley.*)

As a model-builder in the marketing services group in a large advertising agency, you are pondering your latest assignment. The task is to develop a model that will predict the success of new frequently purchased consumer products. Many clients rely heavily on new products and need to be able to predict the likelihood of success before undertaking expensive test markets. They also need guidance in developing products and marketing programs that will be successful in the test market, and ultimately in national distribution.

Preliminary discussions with a set of client representatives and other agency people have already provided some tentative conclusions:

First, it has been decided that to support the model developing and testing process, a panel of 1,200 households would be established in a city often used as a test market. Thus, as new products were introduced into this city, the panel could be used to monitor their performance. Over a period of three years, it was expected that 50 or 60 products could be observed.

Second, it was suggested that product success depends on obtaining consumer knowledge of the product, enticing people to try the product, and then achieving respectable levels of repurchase. Thus, it was concluded that a useful model would be one that was capable of predicting and explaining the following three variables: (1) product knowledge, (2) trial, and (3) repeat purchase.

Operationally, these variables would be measured by taking a consumer survey covering 250 housewives randomly selected from the 1,200-member panel. These housewives would be contacted by telephone. The variables would be defined as follows:

1   *Product knowledge* Percent of housewives who were able to accurately recall advertising claims at the end of 13 weeks.
2   *Trial* Percent of housewives who made one or more purchases of the product during the first 13 weeks.
3   *Repeat purchases* Percent of housewives who had purchased and used the product, who had repurchased it, or were planning to do so.

The immediate task was to develop three sets of explanatory or independent variables that would explain and predict the three dependent variables. In addition, it would be necessary to specify the nature of the causal relationship—whether it would be, for example, additive or multiplicative and/or linear or nonlinear.

One variable seemed obvious. Product knowledge should depend on the level of advertising. Advertising could be measured in several ways. It would be possible, by monitoring local and national media, to estimate the average number of media impressions (advertisement exposures) per household. It was not clear, however, if advertising's impact on product knowledge was linear.

Several other tasks must be faced eventually. For instance, the model will need to be tested and validated. The data base to be collected could be used for this purpose. The variables to be included in the data base will need to be specified soon. Also, thought will have to be given to how and when managers should use the model.

Assignment 1   Develop a model of product knowledge. Specify variables, indicating precisely how they should be measured in any test application of the model. Indicate how such a model could be tested. Prepare a one-page paper a summarizing your model.

Assignment 2   Develop a model of trial purchase and one of repeat purchase. Indicate how you would use such a set of models if you were coming out with a new type of packaged cake mix.

Appendixes

Appendix 1
Mathematical Terms

Constants and Variables

A *constant* is a value that is fixed—that is, does not vary. It may be represented symbolically by an Arabic or a Greek letter or have a numerical value. A familiar example is the ratio between the area and the squared radius of a circle, which is symbolized by the Greek letter pi (π) and equal numerically to 3.1416. Constants are common in marketing formulas, where they are frequently used to specify the relationships between variables or to fix a minimum or maximum value. For instance, the total-cost equation is $C = F + VQ$, where V is a constant specifying the relationship between output, Q, and total cost, C, and F is a constant specifying the fixed (as well as minimum) cost.

A *variable* is a value that is subject to change. It is represented in the same way as a constant. The symbols C and Q in the total-cost equation are examples. A *dependent variable* is one whose value is determined by the value of one or more other variables or by a variable and a constant. It is normally placed on the left side of the equation. In the preceding formula, total cost, C, is the dependent variable.

An *independent variable*—also called a "determinant"—is a variable whose value is not influenced by the other variables or constants in the equation. In the total-cost equation, output, Q, is an independent variable.

Variables are often subject to constraints that limit their values. These constraints are imposed when the relationships specified by the equation do not hold true in every case. For instance, if the total-cost formula did not yield correct answers when output exceeded 5,000 units, the independent variable, Q, would be constrained to the range zero (since output could not be negative) to 5,000. This constraint could be expressed symbolically as $0 \leq Q \leq 5,000$, which would be read "zero is equal to or less than Q, which is equal to or less than 5,000."

The term *domain* describes all the acceptable values for an independent variable. The term *range* describes all the acceptable values for a dependent variable. Thus, the domain of the output, Q, were it constrained as suggested above, would be zero to 5,000. If the variable R depended on Q—say, $R = 5Q$—then the range of R would be zero to 25,000.

Parameters

A *parameter* is a value that specifies the relationship between a dependent and an independent variable. It is represented in general form by a letter— usually one from the first part of the Greek alphabet, such as α, β, or β_3, or by a lower case letter from the Arabic alphabet, such as a, b, t, or e. It is represented in specific form as a number, such as 12, 1.43, or 0.005.

A parameter is usually a constant as far as a given equation or model is concerned. However, it may vary if it depends on one or more extraneous (outside) factors. For example, assume that the sales, S, of a mail-order house are a function of its advertising, A. Thus, $S = f(A)$, or $S = s(A)$. This relationship might be specified by the parameter β. Thus, $S = \beta A$, if the equation is in the general form. If every $1 spent on advertising produces $3 in sales, then $\beta = 3$ and $S = 3A$ in the specific form. If a bright advertising manager developed a new and more effective advertising strategy, sales would become more sensitive to advertising, and the parameter would change (in this case becoming larger).

The term "parameter" is also used by statisticians, but in a different context. In statistics, the word "parameter" is often used to refer to a population value, as opposed to a sample value. The latter is sometimes distinguished by the term "statistic." Thus, the mean, μ, of a population would be a parameter, whereas the mean, $\bar{X}$, of a sample would be a statistic.

Isoquants

An *isoquant* is a line of fixed value. For instance, if sales (S), advertising (A), and number of salespersons (P) were related $S = 2A + 50P$, an isoquant of S would represent all possible combinations of A and P which would yield a particular value of S. Usually an infinite number of isoquants are possible. A familiar example of an isoquant is a contour line on a map. The contour line is a line of equal elevations. That is, each point on the isoquant is the same height above sea level.

Summation (Σ)

Summation means "the addition of . . ." It is symbolized by the capital form of the Greek letter sigma, Σ. In an equation, Σ serves as an operational symbol telling us to add up all the values to the right. Thus, if the sales at each individual store in a food-market chain were represented symbolically by X, ΣX would indicate the sum of all the stores' sales.

Sometimes, subscript values are used to identify the units included in the summation. For instance,

$$\sum_{i=5}^{15} X_i$$

means the sum of the sales, X, for stores 5 through 15. This is obviously more convenient than writing $X_5 + X_6 + X_7 \cdots X_{15}$. If subscript values are not used, each unit in the set (in this case, each store) is included in the summation.

Sometimes, the notation becomes a bit involved, as when the sum of a set of sums is desired. For instance, the analyst may want the total sales, S_T, for all the food-market chains in an area, or

$$\sum_{i=1}^{n} \sum_{j=1}^{m} X_{i,j}.$$

To get S_T, he or she would sum the sales for all the stores, i, in each chain, j, then sum the totals for each chain.

The rules of summation are

(1) $\quad \displaystyle\sum_{i=1}^{n} X_i = X_1 + X_2 + \cdots X_n$

(2) $\quad \displaystyle\sum_{i=1}^{n} (X_i \pm Y_i) = \sum_{i=1}^{n} X_i \pm \sum_{i=1}^{n} Y_i$

(3) $\quad \displaystyle\sum_{i=1}^{n} k \cdot X_i = k \cdot \sum_{i=1}^{n} X_i$

(4) $\quad \displaystyle\sum_{i=1}^{n} k = k \cdot n$

(5) $\quad \displaystyle\sum_{i=1}^{n} \sum_{j=1}^{m} X_{i,j} = \sum_{i=1}^{n} X_{i,1} + \sum_{i=1}^{n} X_{i,2} + \cdots \sum_{i=1}^{n} X_{i,m}$

Logarithms

Logarithms–or "logs"–are exponents used to represent real numbers. The logarithm (log) of a number (X) is the value (Y) to which a base number (b) must be raised to equal that number (X). If the base number (b) is 10 and the real number (X) is 1,000, the logarithm (Y) of X is 3 ($1,000 = 10^3$). The log to the base b of X is Y, and the log to the base 10 of 1,000 is 3.0000:

$$\log_b X = Y$$

$$\log_{10} 1,000 = 3.0000$$

Any positive number other than one can be used as the base ($b \neq 1$). To change a logarithm from one base, say b, to another base, say a, we would use the following formula:

$$\log_a X = \log_b X \cdot \log_a b$$

Most systems of logarithms use either 10 or 2.718281828 as the base. Logs with the base 10 are called *common logarithms* and are written "$\log_{10}$" or simply "log." When the base of a log is not specified, it is usually 10. Logs with the base 2.71828 . . . are called *natural* or *Napierian logarithms* and are written "$\log_e$" or "ln." However, when logarithms are incorporated into an equation, the word "log" is often used, and the selection of a base is left to the discretion of the user. Due to the peculiar mathematical properties of the Napierian number, natural logarithms are generally preferred in marketing research.

Logarithms have several unique properties. Adding them is equivalent to multiplying their natural values. (A log's "natural" value, or "antilog," is the real number it represents; i.e., X is the antilog of $\log_b X$.) Conversely, subtracting one logarithm from another is equivalent to dividing their natural numbers. Multiplying a logarithm by a constant (r) is equivalent to raising the log's natural value to that power. Dividing a logarithm by a constant (r) is equivalent to taking that root of its natural value. These four properties are summarized by the following rules:

(1) $\log_b (X \cdot W) = \log_b X + \log_b W$

(2) $\log_b \left(\dfrac{X}{Y}\right) = \log_b X - \log_b Y$

(3) $\log_b (X^r) = r \cdot \log_b X$

(4) $\log_b (\sqrt[r]{X}) = (\log_b X)/r$

Since addition and subtraction are much easier than multiplication and division, since a single multiplication is far easier than raising a number to a power, and since a single division is considerably easier than taking a root, the use of logarithms can considerably simplify mathematical manipulation—especially when large numbers or exponents are involved.

To convert a number to its logarithmic value, or vice versa, one consults a table of logarithms. Or one enters the appropriate symbol in a computer program or punches the appropriate button on a pocket calculator. Thanks to the proliferation of both devices, we rarely struggle with the table.

Variations in Notation

Although there are prevailing conventions, there are also frequent variations in mathematical notation. For example, one may encounter almost any kind of Greek, Arabic, or Roman symbol representing a variable, constant, or parameter. Also, there are different ways of representing mathematical relationships. Choice is usually dictated by the need for compactness. Some common examples follow:

$$\sqrt[n]{X} = X^{(1/n)} = X^{1/n}$$

$$\frac{a + b}{c - d} = (a + b)/(c - d)$$

$$\frac{1}{X^n} = X^{(-n)} = X^{-n}$$

Other Notation

The following symbols are commonly encountered:

$<$	less than, e.g., $3 < 7$
$\leq$	less than or equal to, e.g., $3 \leq 4$ or $4 \leq X$
$\geq$	greater than or equal to, e.g., $5 \geq 4$ or $4 \geq 4$
$>$	greater than, e.g., $9 > 8$
$\simeq$	approximately equal to, e.g., $3.987 \simeq 4$
$\wedge$	estimated value, e.g., $\hat{Y}$ is the estimated value of Y

Expected Value

The *expected value*, $E(X)$, of an alternative is the sum of the products of each possible outcome associated with that alternative times its probability.

$$E(X) = \sum_{i=1}^{n} P(x_i) \cdot x_i \qquad \text{[A1.1]}$$

where

$E(X) =$ the expected value of alternative X

$P(x) =$ the probability of outcome x

$x =$ an outcome x

$i =$ the number of an outcome associated with alternative X

For example, in Table A1-1 a marketing manager has three alternatives with respect to price. In a decision, he or she must consider four possible events: The competitor may lower its price, increase its price, offer a premium, or make no change in his present marketing strategy. Experience has enabled the marketing manager to assign probabilities to each event and to estimate the value of each outcome. The probabilities are shown in parentheses, and the outcome values are shown in the cells of the matrix. The competitor's choices are not conditional on the manager's action. Since alternative 3 has the greatest expected value, it is the most logical choice.

***Table A1-1*   A Market Decision Matrix**[a]

Decision Alternatives (X)		Lower Price (0.1)	Raise Price (0.3)	Offer Premium (0.1)	No Change (0.5)
		Events (Possible Competitive Reactions)			
1	Lower Price 10¢	$ 2,000	$4,000	$2,500	$3,000
2	Increase Price 10¢	$ −1,000	$4,500	$3,000	$3,500
3	Make No Change	$ 000	$5,000	$3,500	$4,000

$E(1) = (0.1)(\ \$2,000) + (0.3)(\$4,000) + (0.1)(\$2,500) + (0.5)(\$3,000) = \$3,150$
$E(2) = (0.1)(-\$1,000) + (0.3)(\$4,500) + (0.1)(\$3,000) + (0.5)(\$3,500) = \$3,250$
$E(3) = (0.1)(\ \$\ 000) + (0.3)(\$5,000) + (0.1)(\$3,500) + (0.5)(\$4,000) = \$3,850$

[a] Cells contain outcomes, e.g., a $2,000 profit for the decision maker's firm.

Binomial Probability Distributions

A *binomial probability distribution*–often called the "Bernoulli distribution" or simply the "binomial distribution"–is a distribution of the probabilities of getting x successes in n independent trials when there are only two possible outcomes, such as true or false, yes or no, and buy or do-not-buy. It is useful in marketing research, especially in the area of consumer-behavior analysis.

The general form of a binomial distribution is expressed mathematically as

$$P(x\,|\,n) = \left[\frac{n!}{x!\,(n-x)!}\right] p^x\,(1-p)^{n-x} \qquad [\text{A1.2}]$$

where

$P(x\,|\,n) =$ the probability of getting x successes given n trials

$x =$ the number of successes

$n =$ the number of trials (and the total number of outcomes)

$p =$ the probability of outcome x given a single trial

! indicates a factorial[1]

---

[1] The factorial notation, !, signifies the number of possible permutations of n distinct objects taken together. The value is found by multiplying the series of numbers starting with n and ending with 1. $n! = n \cdot (n-1) \cdot (n-2) \cdots \ldots 1$. For example; $6! = 6 \cdot 5 \cdot 4 \cdot 3 \cdot 2 \cdot 1 = 720$; $3! = 3 \cdot 2 \cdot 1 = 6$; and $2! = 2 \cdot 1 = 2$.

Suppose that we want to know the probability of getting 3 heads, x, given 5 flips, n, of a balanced coin. Obviously, the probability, p, of getting a head on a single flip of a balanced coin is 0.5. $P(3|5)$ is found as follows

$$P(x|n) = \left[\frac{n!}{x!\,(n-x)!} \right] p^x\,(1-p)^{n-x} \qquad \text{(given as formula A1.2)}$$

$$P(3|5) = \left[\frac{5!}{3!\,(5-3)!} \right] .5^3(1-.5)^{5-3} \qquad \text{(by substitution)}$$

$$P(3|5) = \left[\frac{5 \cdot 4 \cdot 3 \cdot 2 \cdot 1}{3 \cdot 2 \cdot 1(2 \cdot 1)} \right] .125(.5)^2 \qquad \text{(by arithmetic)}$$

$$P(3|5) = .3125 \qquad \text{(by arithmetic)}$$

The probability of getting x successes (heads, in the example) given n trials, when the probability of success given a single trial is known, can also be found by consulting a binomial-distribution table.

The probability that the number of successes will equal or exceed x' is simply the sum of the probability of x' and the probability of each possible number of successes between x' and the total number of trials, n

$$P(x \geq x'|n) = \sum_{x=x'}^{n} \frac{n!}{x!\,(n-x)!} \cdot p^x(1-p)^{n-x} \qquad [\text{A1.3}]$$

where

$P(x \geq x'|n) =$ the probability of a number of successes, x, equal to or greater than x', given n trials

$x' =$ the lowest value in the range of success x' through n

$p =$ the probability of success given a single trial x and n are defined as before

The probability that the number of success, x, will be less than x' is simply one minus the probability that the number of successes will be equal to or greater than x'

$$P(x < x'|n) = 1 - P(x \geq x'|n) \qquad [\text{A1.4}]$$

where

$P(x < x'|n) =$ the probability of a number of successes, x, less than x', given n trials

x, x', and n are defined as before

If x' and n are fairly large—say, greater than 5—the arithmetic becomes cumbersome and a computer or a cumulative binomial-distribution table had best be used.

The mean (average) of the binomial distribution, μ_p, is equal to the product of the number of trials, n, and the probability of a success given a single trial, p

$$\mu_p = np \qquad\qquad [A1.5]$$

This value is a useful short cut in computing the expected value of an alternative, A, when the possible outcomes are normally distributed.[2] We simply multiply the payoff value of a success by μ_p. To get the net expected value, we subtract the cost of the alternative from its expected value.

For instance, the mean of the binomial distribution in the preceding coin-flip problem is 2.5, ($\mu_p = 5(0.5)$). Thus, if we are paid \$1 for each head, the expected value of the game is \$2.50. If it costs \$2 to play the game, its net expected value is 50 cents.[3]

---

[2] For an explanation of normal distributions, see Appendix 2.

[3] This is the basis upon which insurance companies and professional gamblers set their premiums and prices for playing their games (or the payoffs). Their expected value must always be positive if they are to avoid going broke. Hence, the insuree or the amateur gambler's expected value will always be negative.

Appendix 2
Statistical Skills

The term "statistics" has several meanings, all of which are encountered in the marketing research literature. *Statistics* can be defined as: (1) The science of collecting, organizing, analyzing, interpreting, and presenting numerical information; (2) a collection of numerical information; and (3) a set of statistical measurements based on a sample. In the latter case, *statistic* is the correlate of *parameter*, which is a statistical measurement based on a population. For instance, if we recorded the age of every member of a community, then computed the average age, that average would be a population parameter. However, if we recorded the ages of a sample of members—say, 100 members out of a population of 3,000—and computed the average age based on our sample, that average would be a sample statistic. Statistics, used in this sense, are estimates of parameters. (Do not confuse the use of "parameter" here with the use of "parameter" in the mathematical sense as explained in Appendix 1.)

As a pedagogical convenience, statistics is divided into two sets; descriptive statistics and inductive statistics (also called "statistical inference"). First we shall examine descriptive statistics.

Descriptive Statistics

Descriptive statistics are the data about a particular universe based on a measurement or count of the elements in that universe. They describe a universe, such as the population of San Diego, in terms of one or more of its characteristics. These characteristics might be the number of adult males, the per capita food consumption, the average weekly retail sales, or the distribution of personal income. The information may be detailed or summarized. It may be obtained by a population count (by observing every element in the universe) or a sample. *Sample data* are information taken by observing a portion of the elements in a universe. Conversely, *census data* are information taken by observing every element in the population.

Gathering descriptive statistics by checking historical sources or running surveys is usually one of the first steps in marketing research. The data

are often summarized by giving the averages and distributions of the characteristics being examined. Such summaries are called *statistical descriptions*.

Averages

The three common averages—also called "measures of central tendency"—
are the arithmetic mean, the median, and the mode. The *arithmetic mean*—or
simply the "mean"—is the sum of all the observations divided by the number
of observations. If every element in the universe is observed, it is called a
population mean. Expressed mathematically

$$\mu = \frac{\Sigma X}{N} \qquad\qquad\qquad [A2.1]$$

where

$\mu =$ the population mean

$X =$ the value of each element observed

$N =$ the total number of observations, hence the total number of
elements in the universe

If only a portion of the elements is observed, the average is called a
sample mean. The sample means serves as an estimate of the population
mean. It is computed in essentially the same way as the population mean, but
different symbols are used to distinguish it as representative of sample data.

$$\bar{X} = \frac{\Sigma X}{n} \qquad\qquad\qquad [A2.2]$$

where

$\bar{X} =$ the sample mean

$X =$ the value of each element observed

$n =$ the total number of observations in the sample (i.e., the sample
size)

The *median* is the middle value when all the observations are arrayed
in ascending or descending order.

The *mode* is the value that occurs most frequently. It is often used in
stipulating consumer preferences. For example, if the most popular color in
men's shoes were brown, brown would be the modal color. In some cases,
there may be more than one modal value. For instance, in the numerical

series 3, 2, 5, 5, 3, 7, either 3 or 5 could be the mode. (This series would be called "bimodal.")

Proportions

A *proportion* is the percentage of a population or sample having a particular characteristic. Since it is a relative measurement, it is expressed as a percentage between 0 and 100 or as a fraction or decimal value between zero and one inclusive.

More specifically, proportion is the ratio between the number of elements in a population (or sample) with a particular characteristic, property, or attribute and the total number of elements in the population (or sample). It may also be defined as the ratio between the number of times a particular event occurs and the number of trials (or total events) in a sample. A population proportion is defined mathematically as

$$\Pi_i = \frac{N_i}{N} \qquad [A2.3]$$

where

Π_i = the proportion of the population with attribute i

N_i = the number of elements in the population with attribute i

N = the total number of elements in the population (the population size)

A sample proportion is defined mathematically as

$$\pi_i = \frac{n_i}{n} \qquad [A2.4]$$

where

π_i = the proportion of the sample with attribute i (sometimes symbolized as "$\hat{\Pi}_i$")

n_i = the number of elements in the sample with attribute i, and

n = the total number of elements in the sample (the sample size)

If i is an event

$$\pi_i = \frac{x_i}{n} \quad \text{or} \quad \pi_i = \frac{n_i}{n} \qquad [A2.5]$$

where

x_i = the number of occurrences of event *i*, or the number of "successes"

π_i and *n* are defined as before, with *n* being called "number of trials"

$n_i = x_i$

The probability that any one element will have a particular attribute, *A*, is equal to the proportion of elements with that attribute in the population

$$P(A) = \Pi_A \qquad\qquad\qquad [A2.6]$$

where

$P(A)$ = the probability that any one element will have attribute *A*

Π_A = proportion elements with attribute *A* in the population

For instance, if 75 percent of the households in a given community have color television sets, the probability that a given household will have one is 0.75.

Often, such probabilities are estimated from samples. For example, had the true proportion of color sets, Π_i, been unknown, a sample could have been drawn. Had the sample proportion, π_i, been 72 percent, then the probability of color-TV ownership would have been estimated as 0.72. (There is usually some discrepancy between the true and estimated probability, since sample data are seldom perfectly representative.)

Dispersion

Dispersion—sometimes called "variability," "variation," or "scatter"—is the spread of observed values in a distribution. The most common measures of dispersion are the range, quartile deviation, variance, and standard deviation.

The *range* is the difference between the highest and the lowest of a group of values.

The *quartile deviation*—also called the "semiinterquartile range" or "QD"—is half the difference between the second and third quartile. The first quartile, Q_1, is the value below which 25 percent of the data fall. The third quartile, Q_3, is the value above which 25 percent of the data fall. When the data are symmetrically distributed about their mean, half of them fall within one quartile deviation to each side of the mean.

The *variance* is the average of the squares of the deviations from the mean. (A deviation is simply the difference between an observed value, *X*, and the mean, μ.) A population variance is defined mathematically as

$$\sigma^2 = \frac{\Sigma(X - \mu)^2}{N} \qquad\qquad\qquad [A2.7]$$

where

σ^2 = the population variance

X, μ, and N are defined as before

The variance of a sample is defined mathematically as

$$s^2 = \frac{\Sigma(X - \bar{X})^2}{n - 1} \quad \text{or} \quad s^2 = \frac{\Sigma(X - \bar{X})^2}{n - 1} \cdot \left[\frac{N - n}{N - 1}\right]^{1/2} \qquad \text{[A2.8]}$$

where

s^2 = the sample variance, hence the estimate of the population variance (sometimes symbolized as "$\hat{\sigma}^2$")

X, $\bar{X}$, N, and n are defined as before[1]

The second form of A2.8 should be used when the sample size, n, is large relative to the population size, N—say, when $n \geq 0.1N$. Obviously the two forms yield different results. However, the difference is trivial when n is relatively small.

The right-hand term in the second form of A2.8

$$\left[\frac{N - n}{N - 1}\right]^{1/2}$$

is called the "finite population correction factor," or simply the "finite multiplier." Its purpose is to account for the effect of a comparatively large sample. It should be applied to any calculation of a variance or standard deviation when that calculation is based on a relatively large sample. That is, it should be used whenever $n \geq 0.1N$. Otherwise it can be ignored.

The *standard deviation* is the square root of the variance. Unlike the variance, it is expressed in the same units as the observations and mean used to compute it. The standard deviation is the most popular measure of dispersion. It is defined mathematically as

$$\sigma = \sqrt{\sigma^2} \qquad \text{[A2.9]}$$

or

$$\sigma = \left[\frac{\Sigma(X - \mu)^2}{N}\right]^{1/2} \qquad \text{[A2.10]}$$

---

[1] The denominator $n - 1$ is used rather than n because one degree of freedom was lost in computing $\bar{X}$.

where

σ = the population standard deviation

σ^2, X, μ, and N are defined as before

The estimate of the standard deviation, based on data from a random sample, is

$$s = \left[\frac{\Sigma(X - \bar{X})^2}{n - 1}\right]^{1/2} \quad \text{or} \quad s = \left[\frac{\Sigma X^2 - n\bar{X}^2}{n - 1}\right]^{1/2} \qquad [A2.11]$$

where

s = the sample standard deviation, hence the estimate of the population standard deviation (sometimes symbolized as "$\hat{\sigma}$")

X, $\bar{X}$, and n are defined as before

Both forms of A2.11 yield identical results. However, the second form is more convenient with some pocket calculators.

If the estimate, s, of the standard deviation, σ, is based on a relatively large sample ($n \geq 0.1N$), the finite multiplier should be used. This would change A2.11 to

$$s = \left[\frac{\Sigma(X - \bar{X})^2}{n - 1}\right]^{1/2} \cdot \left[\frac{N - n}{N - 1}\right]^{1/2}$$

or

$$s = \left[\frac{\Sigma X^2 - n\bar{X}^2}{n - 1}\right]^{1/2} \cdot \left[\frac{N - n}{N - 1}\right]^{1/2}$$

The standard deviation of the binomial distribution is

$$\sigma_p = \sqrt{np_0(1 - p_0)} \qquad [A2.12]$$

where

σ_p = the standard deviation of the mean of a binomial distribution

n = the number of trials

p_o = the probability of success given a single trial

The standard deviation of a sample proportion, based on data from a random sample, is

$$s_\pi = \left[\frac{\pi(1-\pi)}{n}\right]^{1/2} \cdot \left[\frac{N-n}{N-1}\right]^{1/2}$$

or

$$s_{x/n} = \left[\frac{\frac{x}{n}\left(1-\frac{x}{n}\right)}{n}\right]^{1/2} \cdot \left[\frac{N-n}{N-1}\right]^{1/2} \qquad [A2.13]^2$$

where

s_π and $s_{x/n}$ = the standard deviation (also called the "standard error") of the sample proportion, hence the estimate of the standard deviation of the population proportion

π = the proportion of elements with attribute A, in sample n

n = the number of elements in the sample

N = the population size

x = the number of sample elements with attribute A.

Both forms of A2.13 yield identical results. The reader may be more comfortable with the second form because it is more descriptive. It reminds us that the sample proportion, π, equals the number of sample elements with a particular attribute (A) divided by the sample size. That is, $\pi = x/n$. (Note that π is also the probability that any one element drawn from the sample will have that particular attribute. Thus π serves as an estimator of $P(A)$.)

In both forms of A2.13, the second term will be recognized as the finite multiplier. It can be dropped if n is less than 10 percent of N.

The standard deviation has a number of useful properties. For instance, if it is small relative to the mean, we know that the observed values are grouped closely about the mean. If it is large, then we know that the observed values are widely scattered about the mean.

The Normal Distribution

The *normal distribution* is a bell-shaped frequency distribution whose values are distributed symmetrically about their mean. Hence, the mean, median, and mode of the distribution are equal. A graph of a normal distribution is called a "normal" or "Gaussian" curve.

---

[2] The second term is the finite multiplier.

Figure A2-1   **A Normal Distribution Curve**

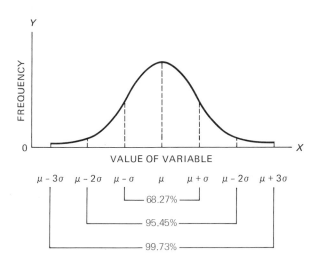

A normal distribution is typical of the distribution of characteristics of many populations, especially physical or biological ones. The actual weights of a case of "one-pound" cans of coffee, the dress sizes of a class of freshmen women, the intelligence quotients of a group of businesspeople, the aptitude-test scores of a group of job candidates, the productivity of members of a sales force, and the magnitude of errors made in measuring a series of TV audiences will all tend toward a normal distribution.

If the characteristic being studied is normally distributed, the standard deviation will reveal the portion of values within a given range. For example, 68.27 percent of all values will be within $\pm$ one standard deviation from the mean; 95.45 percent of all the values will be within $\pm$ two standard deviations from the mean.

Figure A2-1 is a typical normal curve. If the standard deviation were smaller, the curve would be more peaked—that is, it would be tall and thin. If the standard deviation were larger, the curve would be less peaked—that is, it would be lower and wider.

All normal distributions are symmetrical and have the same mathematical properties. However, the peakedness of the curve and the calibration of the two axes will vary from one population to another. A distribution of dress sizes and a distribution of test scores will obviously be different, even though each is normal. If we plot the number of times each dress size or each test score is observed, a bell-shaped curve will emerge, but the same curve will not fit both sets of data.

Fortunately, it is unnecessary to plot the curve or compute the distribution function for each normally distributed population. Instead, we simply convert the unit of measurement for the relevant characteristic to a standard unit called a "Z-statistic," using the following formula:

$$Z = \frac{X - \mu}{\sigma} \qquad \text{[A2.14]}$$

where

Z = the standard unit of measurement for a normal distribution and is the number of standard deviations between X and μ.

X, μ, and σ are defined as before[3]

The *Z-value* for a binomial distribution is

$$Z_b = \frac{x - np_0}{\sqrt{np_0(1 - p_0)}} \qquad \text{[A2.15]}$$

where

Z_b = the Z-statistic for a binomial distribution

x = the number of success

n = the number of trials

p_0 = the probability of a success given a single trial

If the sample is large ($n \geq 30$), the binomial distribution will be very similar to the normal distribution. Hence, Z_b can be used in the same way as Z.

Given a normal-distribution table (a table of Z-values), an analyst can quickly determine the portion of a population or sample above or below a particular level, X, with respect to some characteristic or between two levels of the characteristic, X_1 and X_2. The numbers in the body of the table represent the percentage of the population (or sample) with characteristic values between the mean and X. Since 50 percent of the values are on each side of the mean, the portion of the population of interest to the analyst can be computed by simple addition or subtraction.

For example, assume that an analyst wants to know what portion of a market population has an annual personal income, X, of \$8,500 or more. Descriptive statistics reveal a mean income, μ, of \$7,000 and a standard deviation, σ, of \$2,000. Hence, $Z = 0.75$. Consulting the table of Z-values in Appendix 4, (p. 727) gives us a value of 0.2734. Thus, 27.34 percent of all

---

[3] This formula is for population data. For sample data, we would simply substitute $\bar{X}$ for μ and s for σ.

Figure A2-2   **The *Z*-Statistic and Areas Under a Gaussian Curve**

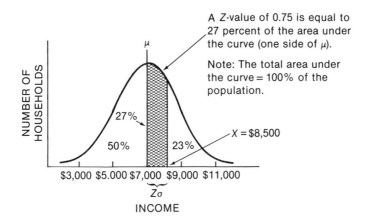

incomes are between $7,000 ($\mu$) and $8,500 ($X$). Since 50 percent of all incomes are above μ ($7,000), 50 percent less 27 percent, or 23 percent must be above $8,500. Figure A2-2 is a graph of this distribution.

If the analyst wanted to know what portion of the population had incomes below $5,000 ($X = \$5,000$), the appropriate *Z*-statistic would be -1. Consulting the table again would give us a value of 0.3413. Since the sign of the *Z*-statistic is negative, we are talking about the area to the left of μ. Since 34 percent of the population rests between μ and X, 16 percent (50%–34%) must be to the left of X. Hence 16 percent of the incomes are below $5,000.

Having computed the *Z*-statistic for $X = \$5,000$ and $X = \$8,500$, the analyst can easily calculate the area under the curve (and the portion of the population) with incomes in the $5,000–$8,500 range. It is 61 percent (0.2734 + 0.3413).

Statistical Inference

Often, especially in marketing research, it is impossible or very impractical to observe every element in a population. Instead, sample data are collected and the results generalized to the total population. Statistical inference—also called "inductive statistics"—provides a body of techniques based on probability theory for generalizing sample data and for qualifying the conclusions inferred about the population as a whole.

Confidence Levels and Intervals

Unless the analysts measure and count *every* element in a universe, they cannot make statistical generalizations about that universe with absolute certainty. For instance, they cannot say absolutely that the mean household income of the population of Denver is X dollars per year simply because that is the mean of the sample data. However, if their sample is randomly selected, they can say that the true population mean will be within a specified range—called a "confidence interval"—at a given level of confidence. A *confidence level* is simply the probability that one is correct; it is usually expressed as a percentage. For instance, if the analysts say the true mean is within a confidence interval of $5,725 to $6,350 at a confidence level of 95 percent, they are telling us that they are 95 percent certain that the true mean will be between those two values. Statistically speaking, if they repeat the research (including the collection of the sample data) again and again, 95 out of every 100 times the true mean will be within the specified range. In other words, confidence level is the probability that the parameter rests within the confidence interval.

The relationship between the confidence level and the confidence interval has a frustrating quality. They go up and down together. Increase the confidence level and the confidence interval gets wider. Lower the confidence level and the interval shrinks.

Normally the analyst selects a confidence level first, and then computes a confidence interval. However, the procedure can be reversed. Confidence levels and intervals can be found for virtually every parameter estimated by random sampling.[4]

Degrees of Freedom

The *degrees of freedom* ($d.f.$) in a numerical system are the number of observations that can be varied without changing the constraints or assumptions associated with that system. Usually, the $d.f.$ equal the total number of observations, n, less the number of constraints or assumptions. (Once a statistical measurement is specified, it becomes a constraint.) For instance, if 10 observations are made ($n = 10$) and their mean, $\bar{X}$, is computed, one degree of freedom is lost. Hence, 9 degrees of freedom remain ($d.f. = 10 - 1$). That is, as long as $\bar{X}$ is to remain constant, nine of the observations can vary freely, but one must be controlled to ensure that the mean remains fixed.[5] Degrees of freedom are frequently used in statistical computations, especially to remove the estimating bias from sample data. A number of specific applications are discussed in the text.

---

[4] The randomization of sample data is discussed in detail in Chapter 8. A random sample is one in which every element in the population had a known—usually, equal–chance of being selected for the sample.

[5] A reader who is uncomfortable with the concept of degrees of freedom might try the following experiment, preferably with a partner: Take any number of observations, say, 5, and compute their mean. The system now has four degrees of freedom. No matter how his partner changes the value of any 4 of the observations, by controlling the one remaining observation the reader can produce the same mean. (Negative values are allowed.)

Statistical Errors

Statistical errors are errors in sample data caused by having only a portion of the population members included in the sample. They're always present in sample data. They should not be confused with errors caused by sloppy mathematics or the misuse of statistical techniques during the manipulation of the data. There are two general categories of statistical error: (1) statistical bias and (2) random error. (Both are discussed in detail in Chapter 8.)

Random errors are errors resulting from chance and are subject to the laws of probability. They are always present in sample data. If the sample observations are made at random, then the random errors will be normally distributed and we can define their range at a given confidence level.

Statistical bias is caused by improper sampling techniques and small samples. The method of selecting respondents from a market population may exclude a particular group, or a questionnaire or interviewer may unconsciously encourage respondents to favor a particular answer. Bias is usually present in a nonrandom sample. Unfortunately, it is not predictable. If it is not detected and measured, it can distort the analysis.

In small samples ($n < 30$), there is a downward bias—that is, values tend to be low—in the estimate of the standard deviation. However, this estimating bias can be eliminated by adjusting the estimates for the degrees of freedom in the system. The use of the term $n - 1$ instead of n in equations A2.8 and A2.11 is illustrative. Estimating bias is also present in large-sample data, but to a much more limited extent. Bias is never present in the estimate of a mean, even for small samples, if random sampling is used.

Estimating Random Error

We can compute the range of random error for estimates of statistical parameters when those estimates are based on randomly selected observations, or when the observations include every element in the population. Defining the range of error tells us how precise the estimate is and enables us to test the correctness of hypotheses. In each case, we assume a particular distribution of the estimated values of the parameter about the true value. For example, if the true mean of a population is μ and a number of unbiased, random samples are drawn from that population, the sample means, the $\bar{X}$'s, will be normally distributed about μ. Depending on the size of the sample, we can predict how close its mean will be to the population mean. Thus if we have a sample mean, $\bar{X}$, and know the sample size, n, we can estimate the standard error of the sample mean. The *standard error of the sample mean*, $s_{\bar{X}}$, is an estimate of the standard error of the population mean, σ_X, which is a measure of how much the samples means, $\bar{X}$'s, vary from the true value of the population mean, μ, due to random error. (For this reason, $s_{\bar{X}}$ is often shown as $\hat{\sigma}_X$, with the caret symbolizing "estimate.") The following formula applies

$$s_X = \frac{s}{\sqrt{n}} \cdot \sqrt{\frac{N - n}{N - 1}} \qquad \text{[A2.16]}$$

where

s_X = the standard error of the sample mean ($\hat{\sigma}_{\bar{X}}$)

s = the standard deviation of the sample

n = the number of elements in the sample

N = the population size

The second term in formula A2.16 is the finite multiplier. As always, it can be ignored when $n \leq 0.1N$. Note that the finite multiplier, hence $s_{\bar{X}}$, approaches zero as n approaches N. When we observe every element in the population, n will equal N and the finite multiplier, hence the standard error will be zero.

Given the standard error of the sample mean, we can easily compute the magnitude of possible random error for a given confidence level. Given a sample equal to or greater than 30 ($n \geq 30$), we can use the following formula

$$E = Z_{c.l.}\hat{\sigma}_{\bar{X}} \qquad\qquad [A2.17]$$

where

E = the magnitude of possible random error of the mean (measured in both directions from the sample mean)

Z = the Z-statistic

$c.l.$ = the confidence level

$\hat{\sigma}_{\bar{X}}$ = the standard error of the sample mean (also symolized $s_{\bar{X}}$)

The standard error of a sample proportion, s_π, is substituted for s_X in computing the magnitude of possible error, E_Π, of a proportion

$$E_\Pi = Z_{c.l.}s_\pi \qquad\qquad [A2.18]$$

where

E_Π = the magnitude of possible random error of a proportion (measured in both directions from the sample proportion)

s_π = the standard deviation (also called the "standard error") of the sample proportion (computed with equation A2.13)

$Z_{c.l.}$ = the Z-statistic for the selected confidence level

In this case, Z is a multiplier—or a *confidence coefficient*—that tells us how many standard deviations are contained in the correct confidence interval for the selected confidence level.

Given E, we can easily specify the confidence interval of the estimated mean. (The true population mean, μ, will lie in the range $\bar{X} \pm Z_{c.l.}s_{\bar{X}}$.) Expressed more conventionally,

$$\bar{X} - E < \mu < \bar{X} + E \qquad\qquad\qquad\qquad\qquad [\text{A2.19}]$$

where

$\bar{X}$, E, and μ are defined as before

Given E_{Π}, we can specify the confidence interval for the proportion. (The true proportion, Π, will lie in the range $\Pi \pm Z_{c.l.}s_{\pi}$.) Expressed more conventionally,

$$\pi - E_{\Pi} < \Pi < \pi + E_{\Pi} \qquad\qquad\qquad\qquad\qquad [\text{A2.20}]$$

where

π = sample proportion

Π = population proportion

E_{Π} is defined as before

The confidence level, *c.l.*, is selected by judgment. It tells us what percentage of the time the confidence interval is expected to include the true mean. The confidence interval is an area under a normal curve. (The curve shows the distribution of the sample means, the $\bar{X}$s, about the true mean, μ.) The values in a normal-distribution table (a table of Z-values) are areas on one side of the mean, expressed as a percentage. In this case, we want the area on both sides of the mean. Since the curve is symmetrical, we simply enter the table with a value equal to half the total area. Thus for a confidence level of 0.95, we enter the table with 0.475, $[0.5(0.95) = 0.475]$, and get a Z-value of 1.96.

If an analyst had 36 observations ($n = 36$), a mean, $\bar{X}$, of 70, and a standard deviation, s, of 18, then the standard error of the sample mean, $s_{\bar{X}}$, would be 3. If he chose a 90 percent confidence level, Z would equal 1.65. The magnitude of possible error, E, would be 4.95 $[1.65(3) = 4.95]$, measured in either direction from the mean. Hence the confidence interval would be 9.9, or 65.05 to 74.95. The analyst could be 90 percent sure that the true mean was between 65.05 and 74.95 ($65.05 < \mu < 74.95$ @ *c.l.* = 0.90).

When the sample is small ($n < 30$), the same technique is used, but the *t*-statistic is substituted for the Z-statistic. The resulting E value is slightly larger than it would have been had the Z-statistic been used; hence the confidence interval is slightly larger for any given $\bar{X}$, s, and *c.l.* A small sample provides a less precise estimate of parameters than a large sample.

Figure A2-3   **A Comparison of the *t*-Distribution and a Normal Distribution**

Source: From *Basic Statistics* by Boris Parl. Copyright © 1967 by Doubleday & Company, Inc. Reproduced by permission of Doubleday & Company, Inc.

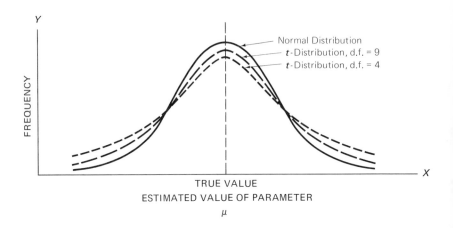

The *t*-Distribution

The *t-distribution* is a bell-shaped frequency distribution with its values symmetrically distributed about its mean and whose size is dependent upon degrees of freedom. It is very similar to the normal distribution, but it is influenced by sample size, or, more precisely, by the degrees of freedom. In fact, for any given mean and standard deviation there is a series of *t*-distributions, one for each degree of freedom. As Figure A2-3 shows, the curve representing the *t*-distribution is lower and wider than a normal curve would be for the same $\bar{X}$ and *s*.

The *t*-statistic may be computed using the following formula:

$$t = \frac{\bar{X} - \mu}{\dfrac{s}{\sqrt{n}}} \qquad [A2.21]$$

where

t = the *t*-statistic

$\bar{X}$ = the sample mean

μ = the population mean

s = the standard deviation of the sample

n = the number of elements in the sample

Like the Z-statistic, the t-statistic is as a confidence coefficient that tells us how many standard error (deviation) units—such as the standard error (deviation) of the mean—should be used in calculating the range of the possible random error of the estimate of a parameter.

For instance, in a sample of only 10 observations, the t-statistic at the 90 percent confidence level would be 1.833 ($d.f. = 9$). If the sample had a mean of 70 and a standard error of 3(as in the previous example), substituting the t-statistic for the Z-statistic would give us a magnitude of possible error of 5.5. Hence, the confidence interval would be 11 (64.5–75.5). This is a significantly broader range than that obtained when the analyst had the advantage of a large sample and could use the Z-statistic.

Tables of t-statistics (see Appendix 4) show the t-values for different significance levels and degrees of freedom. A *significance level* (*s.l.*) represents the portion of the X-values outside the t-value. It can also be thought of as the probability of drawing an X-value beyond the point on the X-axis represented by the t-value. Thus, the significance level can be viewed as the converse of the confidence level, which represents the probability of drawing an X-value between a pair of points on the X-axis. For instance, an *s.l.* of 0.05 is equivalent to a *c.l.* of 0.95.

If an analyst wanted to operate at the 95 percent confidence level, he would select a significance level of 0.05. The confidence interval for the estimate of the parameter would be equivalent to the unshaded area in Figure A2-4. The significance level is not unique to t-distributions; it is also used with other curves, such as the F-distribution.

If we are interested in the probability of exceeding the t-value in just one direction, then we'd want a single-tail test. If we're interested in the probability of exceeding the t-value in either direction, we would want a two-tail test. Table A4-2, in Appendix 4, is calibrated for both the single-tail and two-tail tests. Note that the probabilities double for the two-tail test.

The desired significance level (and hence the confidence level) is selected first—a judgment decision. The degrees of freedom are then computed (normally, $d.f. = n - 1$), and the appropriate t-value read from the

Figure A2-4   **A Typical t-Distribution Curve**

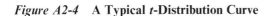

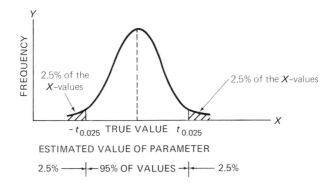

table. Of course, we can never be absolutely certain that the true parameter will be within the associated confidence interval.

F-Distribution

The *F-distribution* is a lopsided function expressing the distribution of *F*-ratios. The *F-ratio*—or the "variance ratio"—is the ratio between the variances of two samples. Specifically:

$$F = \frac{s_1{}^2}{s_2{}^2}$$ [A2.22]

where

F = the *F*-ratio

$s_1{}^2$ = the variance of the first sample

$s_2{}^2$ = the variance of the second sample

If both samples were drawn from the same universe, their variances will tend to be equal and F will approach one. It will seldom equal one, because of random error. If the samples (and thus the degrees of freedom) are small, the difference between their variances will tend to be large and F will be large also. (F will always be greater than one since the larger s^2 is always assigned to the numerator.)

The *F*-distribution shows the frequencies, hence probabilities, that different *F*-values may be expected. As these frequencies vary with the size of the two samples, there is a different *F*-distribution for every pair of sample sizes. The curves became virtually identical as the samples (and hence the degrees of freedom) became larger.

Figure A2-5   A Typical *F*-Distribution Curve

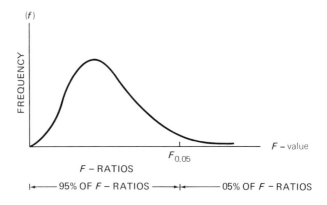

If the samples are both drawn from the same universe (the same with respect to the characteristic being studied) the probability of getting a large F-value diminishes as n increases. For instance, if both samples have 16 elements (hence, the $d.f.$ for each sample, after computing the variance, is 15), the probability of getting an F-ratio over 2.40 is .05. In other words, the chance of an F-ratio exceeding 2.40 is only 5 percent. If the F-ratio does exceed this value, it is very likely that the two samples were drawn from different populations (different with respect to the property being studied).

Figure A2-5 shows a typical F-distribution. The subscript attached to the F indicates the significance level.

Testing Hypotheses

There are two steps in testing hypotheses: framing a statement and determining whether it is probably true or false at a given confidence level. For instance, we might assert that the true mean of a population is 240 and then use statistical techniques to see if the statement can be accepted or rejected at the 95 percent confidence level. Or we might hypothesize that a product's sales do not depend on personal income and run a statistical test to evaluate our assumption. Testing hypotheses is necessary only when we are dealing with sample data. If observations of the entire population are available, then we do not need inferential statistics.

A hypothesis, H, can be affirmative or negative. In either case, it can be assumed to be true or false. A statistical test of the assumption has four possible outcomes, shown in Table A2-1.

Rejecting a true hypothesis is a *Type I error*—or an "alpha (α) error." Accepting a false hypothesis is a *Type II error*—or a "beta (β) error." An assumption is usually accepted or rejected on the basis of probability distributions such as those just discussed. Whether it is better to test the assumption that H is true or the assumption that H is false depends on the relative costs of making a mistake. If a Type II error would be more costly than a Type I error, then we should test the assumption that H is true.

One way of testing hypotheses is to compare two values of a statistic, such as a mean or a proportion. A classic example is the balanced coin. We know that in the endless universe of coin flips, balanced coins will land heads-up 50 percent of the time. Hence, the probability of getting a head, $\Pi_H = 0.5$. The standard deviation, σ, has been proven to be .05. If we suspect

Table A2-1   **Possible Outcome of Testing Hypotheses (H)**

	H is True	H is False
Accept H	Correct Decision	Type II Error $[\beta]$
Reject H	Type I Error (α)	Correct Decision

that a particular coin is unbalanced, we can perform a simple test. We hypothesize that the coin is evenly balanced—hence, $\Pi_H = 0.5$. To test this assumption, we flip the coin a number of times and compute π_H, the proportion of heads in our sample of flips. Since the sample proportions of heads encountered in flipping balanced coins is known to be approximately normally distributed about the true proportion, .5, given a large enough number of trials, we can use the normal distribution curve (assuming $n > 30$) to determine the probability of getting any particular π value.

If we flip the coin 100 times and get 62 heads ($\pi = .62$), our Z-statistic (using the formula A2.15) is 2.4. Entering a normal-distribution table with this value, we see that only .1 percent $(0.50 - 0.4918)$ of the sample proportions of heads flipped with balanced coins are equal to or greater than 0.62. It is highly unlikely that the coin is balanced and that the discrepancy between Π and π is due to random error. Even at the 99 percent confidence level, we would reject the hypothesis that the coin is balanced (i.e., $\Pi = 0.50$). If we are wrong, and the coin actually is balanced, then we will have committed a Type I error. The probability of a Type I error (.01 in our example) is often called the "significance level."

The *F-test* is another way of evaluating hypotheses, particularly the assumption that two samples are from the same universe with respect to a given characteristic. For example, we might assume that household purchasing habits are the same for two market populations. After obtaining a random sample of purchase behavior in both markets (perhaps by observing weekly grocery purchases) and calculating the variance of the two samples, we compute the *F*-ratio. We then select a significance level and consult a table of *F*-values associated with that level of significance. If we want to be 95 percent sure that the difference in variances (if any) is not due to chance variation, we select a significance level of .05. The table is entered with the degrees of freedom for the two sample variances (the numerator and denominator). The resultant *F*-value indicates the point on the curve separating 95 percent of the possible *F*-values from the remaining 0.05 percent. (See Figure A2-5)

If the computed *F*-statistic is larger than the table value, there is at most a 5 percent chance that the samples are from the same universe, and the hypothesis can be rejected at the 0.05 level of significance. (The assumption may be acceptable at a lower level of significance, since the table value would be smaller.) Conversely, if the computed *F*-value is less than the table value, the hypothesis can be accepted at the 0.05 level of significance. The fact that a hypothesis passes the *F*-test at a given significance level is not proof that it is correct. However, it cannot be rejected on the basis of the evidence at hand.

Bayesian Statistics

Bayesian statistics differs from classical statistics (which we have been discussing up to now) in that subjective probabilities are substituted for objective probabilities when the latter are unavailable. The subjective probabilities are then altered as sample data are obtained. Whereas classical methods predict the outcome when the *probabilities* are known, Bayesian techniques estimate the probabilities when the *outcome* is known.

Bayesian statistics is applicable to a great number of problems for which the classical approach cannot be used. Unfortunately, it entails compromises that preclude an objective determination of the magnitude of possible error, the testing of hypotheses, and the estimation of the confidence intervals for various confidence levels. The method derives its name from the Reverend Thomas Bayes (1702–1761), although it has been expanded to include considerably more than the work of this English clergyman.

Bayes' Theorem

Bayes' single greatest contribution to the body of work bearing his name is a theorem that appeared in a posthumously published article, "Essay Toward Solving a Problem in the Doctrine of Chances." *Bayes' theorem*—also called "the Rule of Bayes"—is a formula for computing conditional probabilities when the outcome is known. Given the outcome, the theorem estimates the probability that a particular series of events occurred. The theorem is

$$P(A_i|B) = \frac{P(B|A_i) \cdot P(A_i)}{P(B|A_1) \cdot P(A_1) + P(B|A_2) \cdot P(A_2) + \ldots P(B|A_n)P(A_n)} \quad [A2.23]$$

where

A_i = a particular event from a set of mutually exclusive events A_1, $A_2, \ldots A_n$, and

B = an outcome that can be reached via (i.e., it is conditional upon) event A_i

Subjective Probabilities

Subjective probabilities—also called "personal," "judgment," "a priori," and "prior" probabilities—are probabilities estimated without the benefit of sample data. Frequently, they are the best guesses of managers or analysts whose personal experience has given them an intuitive ability to estimate probabilities. Given a condition of pure uncertainty (thus excluding even an educated guess), Bayes' postulate is invoked.

Bayes' Postulate

Bayes' Postulate—also called "the rule of ignorance" and "the equal-distribution-of-ignorance rule"—assigns an equal probability to each possible event $A_1, A_2, \ldots A_n$ when there is no other basis for estimating the likelihood of

Figure A2-6   **A Tree Diagram of a Bayesian Model**

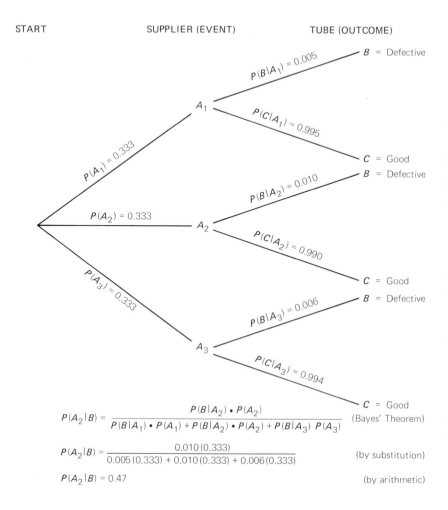

$$P(A_2|B) = \frac{P(B|A_2) \cdot P(A_2)}{P(B|A_1) \cdot P(A_1) + P(B|A_2) \cdot P(A_2) + P(B|A_3) \, P(A_3)} \quad \text{(Bayes' Theorem)}$$

$$P(A_2|B) = \frac{0.010\,(0.333)}{0.005\,(0.333) + 0.010\,(0.333) + 0.006\,(0.333)} \quad \text{(by substitution)}$$

$$P(A_2|B) = 0.47 \quad \text{(by arithmetic)}$$

their occurance. It is a useful rule, even if logically inconsistent. An alternative is to guess the probabilities, for even a guess is bound to reflect some degree of experience and judgment.

Applications of the Bayesian Approach

The use of subjective probabilities and Bayes' Theorem can easily be illustrated by an example. Assume that a TV manufacturer has been purchasing identical tubes from three sources, A_1, A_2, and A_3. The rate of defects up to now has been 0.005, 0.010, and 0.006, respectively, for the three suppliers. Thus, the conditional probability of getting a bad tube, B, from a particular source, A_i, is $B|A_i : P(B|A_1) = 0.005, P(B|A_2) = 0.010,$ and $P(B|A_3) = 0.006$.

Now, assume that a tube from an unidentified batch has been subjected to destructive testing and found defective. (Operating life is the criterion of defectiveness.) What is the probability that the tube, and hence the entire batch, came from supplier A_2, whose tubes are unacceptable because of the high rate of defects?

The tree diagram and equation in Figure A2-6 illustrates how the problem would be solved using Bayes' Theorem. Note that the rule of ignorance has been used to assign values to $P(A_1)$, $P(A_2)$, and $P(A_3)$, which are the prior probabilities that the defective tube has been produced by a particular supplier.

Thus, the conditional probability that A_2 was the supplier, given outcome B, a defective tube, is 0.47. This is considerably different from the original probability of 0.333. The subjective, or "prior," probability (0.333) has been modified by the sample data (outcome B was observed) to produce a posterior conditional probability (0.47).

Appendix 3
Common Secondary
Data Sources

Table A3-1 **Common Secondary Data Sources**

Periodical and Newspaper Indexes
Business Periodicals Index
Funk & Scott Index of Corporations & Industries
Psychological Abstracts
Public Affairs Information Service Bulletin
Wall Street Journal Index

Periodicals and Newspapers
Advertising Age
Barron's
Business Week
Dun's Review
Forbes
Fortune
Industrial Marketing
Journal of Advertising Research
Journal of Marketing
Journal of Marketing Research
Journal of Retailing
Merchandising Week
Sales and Marketing Management
Wall Street Journal
Wall Street Transcript

Dictionaries, Handbooks, Bibliographies, etc.
Encyclopedia of Associations
Handbook of Marketing Research
Marketing and Communications Media Dictionary
Reference Guide to Marketing Literature

Consumer and Market Information Sources
N. W. Ayer & Son's Directory of Newspapers and Periodicals
Editor & Publisher Market Guide
Guide to Consumer Markets
Rand McNally Commercial Atlas & Marketing Guide
Survey of Buying Power

Table A3-1   **Common Secondary Data Sources** (*cont'd.*)

Industry Information Sources
Barometer of Small Business
Fairchild's Financial Manual of Retail Stores
Predicasts (also Predicasts Source Directory)
Robert Morris Annual Statement Studies
Standard & Poor's Industry Surveys
Troy's Almanac of Business & Industrial Financial Ratios

Corporate Information Sources
Dun & Bradstreet's Million Dollar Directory
Fortune Double 500 Directory
Moody's Industrial Manual (also Transportation Mannual, etc.)
Standard & Poor's Corporation Records
Standard & Poor's Register of Corporations, Directors & Executives
Thomas Register of American Manufacturers

Advertising Information Sources
Bacon's Publicity Checker
Daniel Starch and Staff reader audience reports (various titles)
Standard Directory of Advertisers
Standard Rate and Data Service publications (various titles)

U.S. Government Information Sources
American Statistics Index
Monthly Catalog of U.S. Government Publications
Statistical Abstract of the United States
County and City Data Book
Census of Population
Census of Business
Census of Manufacturers
Census of Retail Trade
Census of Transportation
Handbook of Economic Statistics
Federal Reserve Bulletin
Statistic of Income
Monthly Labor Review
Economic Report of the President
Survey of Current Business

Source: Professor Robert F. Hoel, Colorado State University

Appendix 4
Mathematical and
Statistical Tables

Table A4-1 A Cumulative Normal Distribution

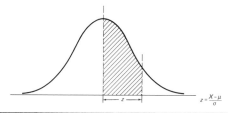

$z = \dfrac{X - \mu}{\sigma}$

z or $\dfrac{X-\mu}{\sigma}$	.00	.01	.02	.03	.04	.05	.06	.07	.08	.09
0.0	.00000	.00399	.00798	.01197	.01595	.01994	.02392	.02790	.03188	.03586
0.1	.03983	.04380	.04776	.05172	.05567	.05962	.06356	.06749	.07142	.07535
0.2	.07926	.08317	.08706	.09095	.09483	.09871	.10257	.10642	.11026	.11409
0.3	.11791	.12172	.12552	.12930	.13307	.13683	.14058	.14431	.14803	.15173
0.4	.15542	.15910	.16276	.16640	.17003	.17364	.17724	.18082	.18439	.18793
0.5	.19146	.19497	.19847	.20194	.20540	.20884	.21226	.21566	.21904	.22240
0.6	.22575	.22907	.23237	.23565	.23891	.24215	.24537	.24857	.25175	.25490
0.7	.25804	.26115	.26424	.26730	.27035	.27337	.27637	.27935	.28230	.28524
0.8	.28814	.29103	.29389	.29673	.29955	.30234	.30511	.30785	.31057	.31327
0.9	.31594	.31859	.32121	.32381	.32639	.32894	.33147	.33398	.33646	.33891
1.0	.34134	.34375	.34614	.34850	.35083	.35314	.35543	.35769	.35993	.36214
1.1	.36433	.36650	.36864	.37076	.37286	.37493	.37698	.37900	.38100	.38298
1.2	.38493	.38686	.38877	.39065	.39251	.39435	.39617	.39796	.39973	.40147
1.3	.40320	.40490	.40658	.40824	.40988	.41149	.41309	.41466	.41621	.41774
1.4	.41924	.42073	.42220	.42364	.42507	.42647	.42786	.42922	.43056	.43189
1.5	.43319	.43448	.43574	.43699	.43822	.43943	.44062	.44179	.44295	.44408
1.6	.44520	.44630	.44738	.44845	.44950	.45053	.45154	.45254	.45352	.45449
1.7	.45543	.45637	.45728	.45818	.45907	.45994	.46080	.46164	.46246	.46327
1.8	.46407	.46485	.46562	.46638	.46712	.46784	.46856	.46926	.46995	.47062
1.9	.47128	.47193	.47257	.47320	.47381	.47441	.47500	.47558	.47615	.47670
2.0	.47725	.47778	.47831	.47882	.47932	.47982	.48030	.48077	.48124	.48169
2.1	.48214	.48257	.48300	.48341	.48382	.48422	.48461	.48500	.48537	.48574
2.2	.48610	.48645	.48679	.48713	.48745	.48778	.48809	.48840	.48870	.48899
2.3	.48928	.48956	.48983	.49010	.49036	.49061	.49086	.49111	.49134	.49158
2.4	.49180	.49202	.49224	.49245	.49266	.49286	.49305	.49324	.49343	.49361
2.5	.49379	.49396	.49413	.49430	.49446	.49461	.49477	.49492	.49506	.49520
2.6	.49534	.49547	.49560	.49573	.49585	.49598	.49609	.49621	.49632	.49643
2.7	.49653	.49664	.49674	.49683	.49693	.49702	.49711	.49720	.49728	.49736
2.8	.49744	.49752	.49760	.49767	.49774	.49781	.49788	.49795	.49801	.49807
2.9	.49813	.49819	.49825	.49831	.49836	.49841	.49846	.49851	.49856	.49861
3.0	.49865	.49869	.49874	.49878	.49882	.49886	.49889	.49893	.49897	.49900
3.1	.49903	.49906	.49910	.49913	.49916	.49918	.49921	.49924	.49926	.49929
3.2	.49931	.49934	.49936	.49938	.49940	.49942	.49944	.49946	.49948	.49950
3.3	.49952	.49953	.49955	.49957	.49958	.49960	.49961	.49962	.49964	.49965
3.4	.49966	.49968	.49969	.49970	.49971	.49972	.49973	.49974	.49975	.49976
3.5	.49977									
3.6	.49984									
3.7	.49989									
3.8	.49993									
3.9	.49995									
4.0	.49997									

Source: Adapted from *Outline of Theory and Problems of Statistics* by M. R. Spiegel. Copyright © 1961 by McGraw-Hill, Inc. Used by permission of McGraw-Hill Book Company.

Table A4-2   The *t*-Distribution

Student's t-Distribution

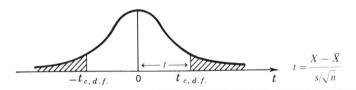

$$t = \frac{X - \bar{X}}{s/\sqrt{n}}$$

Degrees of Freedom	Probability of a (Absolute) Value Greater than the Table Entry[a]					
	0.005	0.01	0.025	0.05	0.10	0.15 Single-tail
	0.010	0.02	0.050	0.10	0.20	0.30 Two-tail
1	63.657	31.821	12.706	6.314	3.078	1.963
2	9.925	6.965	4.303	2.920	1.886	1.386
3	5.841	4.541	3.182	2.353	1.638	1.250
4	4.604	3.747	2.776	2.132	1.533	1.190
5	4.032	3.365	2.571	2.015	1.476	1.156
6	3.707	3.143	2.447	1.943	1.440	1.134
7	3.499	2.998	2.365	1.895	1.415	1.119
8	3.355	2.896	2.306	1.860	1.397	1.108
9	3.250	2.821	2.262	1.833	1.383	1.100
10	3.169	2.764	2.228	1.812	1.372	1.093
11	3.106	2.718	2.201	1.796	1.363	1.088
12	3.055	2.681	2.179	1.782	1.356	1.083
13	3.012	2.650	2.160	1.771	1.350	1.079
14	2.977	2.624	2.145	1.761	1.345	1.076
15	2.947	2.602	2.131	1.753	1.341	1.074
16	2.921	2.583	2.120	1.746	1.337	1.071
17	2.898	2.567	2.110	1.740	1.333	1.069
18	2.878	2.552	2.101	1.734	1.330	1.067
19	2.861	2.539	2.093	1.729	1.328	1.066
20	2.845	2.528	2.086	1.725	1.325	1.064
21	2.831	2.518	2.080	1.721	1.323	1.063
22	2.819	2.508	2.074	1.717	1.321	1.061
23	2.807	2.500	2.069	1.714	1.319	1.060
24	2.797	2.492	2.064	1.711	1.318	1.059
25	2.787	2.485	2.060	1.708	1.316	1.058

Source: Adapted from J. E. Freund and F. J. Williams, *Elementary Business Statistics: The Modern proach.* Copyright © 1964. Reprinted by permission of Prentice-Hall, Inc. Table is taken from Table of Fisher: *Statistical Methods for Research Workers,* published by Oliver & Boyd Limited, Edinbu and used by permission of the author and publishers.

[a] This probability is often called "level of significance."

ble A4-2   The *t*-Distribution (*cont'd.*)

egrees of eedom	Probability of a (Absolute) Value Greater than the Table Entry					
	0.005 0.010	0.01 0.02	0.025 0.050	0.05 0.10	0.10 0.20	0.15 Single-tail test 0.30 Two-tail test
26	2.779	2.479	2.056	1.706	1.315	1.058
27	2.771	2.473	2.052	1.703	1.314	1.057
28	2.763	2.467	2.048	1.701	1.313	1.056
29	2.756	2.462	2.045	1.699	1.311	1.055
30	2.750	2.457	2.042	1.697	1.310	1.055
∞	2.576	2.326	1.960	1.645	1.282	1.036

Table A4-3   **Values of the F-Distribution**

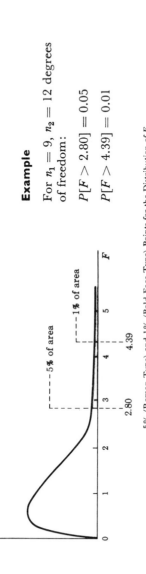

Example

For $n_1 = 9$, $n_2 = 12$ degrees of freedom:

$$P[F > 2.80] = 0.05$$
$$P[F > 4.39] = 0.01$$

5% (Roman Type) and 1% (Bold Face Type) Points for the Distribution of F

Degrees of freedom of denominator

n_1 degrees of freedom (for greater mean square) of numerator

n_2	1	2	3	4	5	6	7	8	9	10	11	12	14	16	20	24	30	40	50	75	100	200	500	∞	n_2
1	161 / **4,052**	200 / **4,999**	216 / **5,403**	225 / **5,625**	230 / **5,764**	234 / **5,859**	237 / **5,928**	239 / **5,981**	241 / **6,022**	242 / **6,056**	243 / **6,082**	244 / **6,106**	245 / **6,142**	246 / **6,169**	248 / **6,208**	249 / **6,234**	250 / **6,258**	251 / **6,286**	252 / **6,302**	253 / **6,323**	253 / **6,334**	254 / **6,352**	254 / **6,361**	254 / **6,366**	1
2	18.51 / **98.49**	19.00 / **99.00**	19.16 / **99.17**	19.25 / **99.25**	19.30 / **99.30**	19.33 / **99.33**	19.36 / **99.34**	19.37 / **99.36**	19.38 / **99.38**	19.39 / **99.40**	19.40 / **99.41**	19.41 / **99.42**	19.42 / **99.43**	19.43 / **99.44**	19.44 / **99.45**	19.45 / **99.46**	19.46 / **99.47**	19.47 / **99.48**	19.47 / **99.48**	19.48 / **99.49**	19.49 / **99.49**	19.49 / **99.49**	19.50 / **99.50**	19.50 / **99.50**	2
3	10.13 / **34.12**	9.55 / **30.82**	9.28 / **29.46**	9.12 / **28.71**	9.01 / **28.24**	8.94 / **27.91**	8.88 / **27.67**	8.84 / **27.49**	8.81 / **27.34**	8.78 / **27.23**	8.76 / **27.13**	8.74 / **27.05**	8.71 / **26.92**	8.69 / **26.83**	8.66 / **26.69**	8.64 / **26.60**	8.62 / **26.50**	8.60 / **26.41**	8.58 / **26.35**	8.57 / **26.27**	8.56 / **26.23**	8.54 / **26.18**	8.54 / **26.14**	8.53 / **26.12**	3
4	7.71 / **21.20**	6.94 / **18.00**	6.59 / **16.69**	6.39 / **15.98**	6.26 / **15.52**	6.16 / **15.21**	6.09 / **14.98**	6.04 / **14.80**	6.00 / **14.66**	5.96 / **14.54**	5.93 / **14.45**	5.91 / **14.37**	5.87 / **14.24**	5.84 / **14.15**	5.80 / **14.02**	5.77 / **13.93**	5.74 / **13.83**	5.71 / **13.74**	5.70 / **13.69**	5.68 / **13.61**	5.66 / **13.57**	5.65 / **13.52**	5.64 / **13.48**	5.63 / **13.46**	4
5	6.61 / **16.26**	5.79 / **13.27**	5.41 / **12.06**	5.19 / **11.39**	5.05 / **10.97**	4.95 / **10.67**	4.88 / **10.45**	4.82 / **10.27**	4.78 / **10.15**	4.74 / **10.05**	4.70 / **9.96**	4.68 / **9.89**	4.64 / **9.77**	4.60 / **9.68**	4.56 / **9.55**	4.53 / **9.47**	4.50 / **9.38**	4.46 / **9.29**	4.44 / **9.24**	4.42 / **9.17**	4.40 / **9.13**	4.38 / **9.07**	4.37 / **9.04**	4.36 / **9.02**	5
6	5.99 / **13.74**	5.14 / **10.92**	4.76 / **9.78**	4.53 / **9.15**	4.39 / **8.75**	4.28 / **8.47**	4.21 / **8.26**	4.15 / **8.10**	4.10 / **7.98**	4.06 / **7.87**	4.03 / **7.79**	4.00 / **7.72**	3.96 / **7.60**	3.92 / **7.52**	3.87 / **7.39**	3.84 / **7.31**	3.81 / **7.23**	3.77 / **7.14**	3.75 / **7.09**	3.72 / **7.02**	3.71 / **6.99**	3.69 / **6.94**	3.68 / **6.90**	3.67 / **6.88**	6
7	5.59 / **12.25**	4.74 / **9.55**	4.35 / **8.45**	4.12 / **7.85**	3.97 / **7.46**	3.87 / **7.19**	3.79 / **7.00**	3.73 / **6.84**	3.68 / **6.71**	3.63 / **6.62**	3.60 / **6.54**	3.57 / **6.47**	3.52 / **6.35**	3.49 / **6.27**	3.44 / **6.15**	3.41 / **6.07**	3.38 / **5.98**	3.34 / **5.90**	3.32 / **5.85**	3.29 / **5.78**	3.28 / **5.75**	3.25 / **5.70**	3.24 / **5.67**	3.23 / **5.65**	7
8	5.32 / **11.26**	4.46 / **8.65**	4.07 / **7.59**	3.84 / **7.01**	3.69 / **6.63**	3.58 / **6.37**	3.50 / **6.19**	3.44 / **6.03**	3.39 / **5.91**	3.34 / **5.82**	3.31 / **5.74**	3.28 / **5.67**	3.23 / **5.56**	3.20 / **5.48**	3.15 / **5.36**	3.12 / **5.28**	3.08 / **5.20**	3.05 / **5.11**	3.03 / **5.06**	3.00 / **5.00**	2.98 / **4.96**	2.96 / **4.91**	2.94 / **4.88**	2.93 / **4.86**	8
9	5.12 / **10.56**	4.26 / **8.02**	3.86 / **6.99**	3.63 / **6.42**	3.48 / **6.06**	3.37 / **5.80**	3.29 / **5.62**	3.23 / **5.47**	3.18 / **5.35**	3.13 / **5.26**	3.10 / **5.18**	3.07 / **5.11**	3.02 / **5.00**	2.98 / **4.92**	2.93 / **4.80**	2.90 / **4.73**	2.86 / **4.64**	2.82 / **4.56**	2.80 / **4.51**	2.77 / **4.45**	2.76 / **4.41**	2.73 / **4.36**	2.72 / **4.33**	2.71 / **4.31**	9
10	4.96 / **10.04**	4.10 / **7.56**	3.71 / **6.55**	3.48 / **5.99**	3.33 / **5.64**	3.22 / **5.39**	3.14 / **5.21**	3.07 / **5.06**	3.02 / **4.95**	2.97 / **4.85**	2.94 / **4.78**	2.91 / **4.71**	2.86 / **4.60**	2.82 / **4.52**	2.77 / **4.41**	2.74 / **4.33**	2.70 / **4.25**	2.67 / **4.17**	2.64 / **4.12**	2.61 / **4.05**	2.59 / **4.01**	2.56 / **3.96**	2.55 / **3.93**	2.54 / **3.91**	10

Table A4-3   Values of the F-Distribution (cont'd.)

5% (Roman Type) and 1% (Bold Face Type) Points for the Distribution of F

n_1 degrees of freedom (for greater mean square) of numerator

n_2	1	2	3	4	5	6	7	8	9	10	11	12	14	16	20	24	30	40	50	75	100	200	500	∞
11	4.84 **9.65**	3.98 **7.20**	3.59 **6.22**	3.36 **5.67**	3.20 **5.32**	3.09 **5.07**	3.01 **4.88**	2.95 **4.74**	2.90 **4.63**	2.86 **4.54**	2.82 **4.46**	2.79 **4.40**	2.74 **4.29**	2.70 **4.21**	2.65 **4.10**	2.61 **4.02**	2.57 **3.94**	2.53 **3.86**	2.50 **3.80**	2.47 **3.74**	2.45 **3.70**	2.42 **3.66**	2.41 **3.62**	2.40 **3.60**
12	4.75 **9.33**	3.88 **6.93**	3.49 **5.95**	3.26 **5.41**	3.11 **5.06**	3.00 **4.82**	2.92 **4.65**	2.85 **4.50**	2.80 **4.39**	2.76 **4.30**	2.72 **4.22**	2.69 **4.16**	2.64 **4.05**	2.60 **3.98**	2.54 **3.86**	2.50 **3.78**	2.46 **3.70**	2.42 **3.61**	2.40 **3.56**	2.36 **3.49**	2.35 **3.46**	2.32 **3.41**	2.31 **3.38**	2.30 **3.36**
13	4.67 **9.07**	3.80 **6.70**	3.41 **5.74**	3.18 **5.20**	3.02 **4.86**	2.92 **4.62**	2.84 **4.44**	2.77 **4.30**	2.72 **4.19**	2.67 **4.10**	2.63 **4.02**	2.60 **3.96**	2.55 **3.85**	2.51 **3.78**	2.46 **3.67**	2.42 **3.59**	2.38 **3.51**	2.34 **3.42**	2.32 **3.37**	2.28 **3.30**	2.26 **3.27**	2.24 **3.21**	2.22 **3.18**	2.21 **3.16**
14	4.60 **8.86**	3.74 **6.51**	3.34 **5.56**	3.11 **5.03**	2.96 **4.69**	2.85 **4.46**	2.77 **4.28**	2.70 **4.14**	2.65 **4.03**	2.60 **3.94**	2.56 **3.86**	2.53 **3.80**	2.48 **3.70**	2.44 **3.62**	2.39 **3.51**	2.35 **3.43**	2.31 **3.34**	2.27 **3.26**	2.24 **3.21**	2.21 **3.14**	2.19 **3.11**	2.16 **3.06**	2.14 **3.02**	2.13 **3.00**
15	4.54 **8.68**	3.68 **6.36**	3.29 **5.42**	3.06 **4.89**	2.90 **4.56**	2.79 **4.32**	2.70 **4.14**	2.64 **4.00**	2.59 **3.89**	2.55 **3.80**	2.51 **3.73**	2.48 **3.67**	2.43 **3.56**	2.39 **3.48**	2.33 **3.36**	2.29 **3.29**	2.25 **3.20**	2.21 **3.12**	2.18 **3.07**	2.15 **3.00**	2.12 **2.97**	2.10 **2.92**	2.08 **2.89**	2.07 **2.87**
16	4.49 **8.53**	3.63 **6.23**	3.24 **5.29**	3.01 **4.77**	2.85 **4.44**	2.74 **4.20**	2.66 **4.03**	2.59 **3.89**	2.54 **3.78**	2.49 **3.69**	2.45 **3.61**	2.42 **3.55**	2.37 **3.45**	2.33 **3.37**	2.28 **3.25**	2.24 **3.18**	2.20 **3.10**	2.16 **3.01**	2.13 **2.96**	2.09 **2.89**	2.07 **2.86**	2.04 **2.80**	2.02 **2.77**	2.01 **2.75**
17	4.45 **8.40**	3.59 **6.11**	3.20 **5.18**	2.96 **4.67**	2.81 **4.34**	2.70 **4.10**	2.62 **3.93**	2.55 **3.79**	2.50 **3.68**	2.45 **3.59**	2.41 **3.52**	2.38 **3.45**	2.33 **3.35**	2.29 **3.27**	2.23 **3.16**	2.19 **3.08**	2.15 **3.00**	2.11 **2.92**	2.08 **2.86**	2.04 **2.79**	2.02 **2.76**	1.99 **2.70**	1.97 **2.67**	1.96 **2.65**
18	4.41 **8.28**	3.55 **6.01**	3.16 **5.09**	2.93 **4.58**	2.77 **4.25**	2.66 **4.01**	2.58 **3.85**	2.51 **3.71**	2.46 **3.60**	2.41 **3.51**	2.37 **3.44**	2.34 **3.37**	2.29 **3.27**	2.25 **3.19**	2.19 **3.07**	2.15 **3.00**	2.11 **2.91**	2.07 **2.83**	2.04 **2.78**	2.00 **2.71**	1.98 **2.68**	1.95 **2.62**	1.93 **2.59**	1.92 **2.57**
19	4.38 **8.18**	3.52 **5.93**	3.13 **5.01**	2.90 **4.50**	2.74 **4.17**	2.63 **3.94**	2.55 **3.77**	2.48 **3.63**	2.43 **3.52**	2.38 **3.43**	2.34 **3.36**	2.31 **3.30**	2.26 **3.19**	2.21 **3.12**	2.15 **3.00**	2.11 **2.92**	2.07 **2.84**	2.02 **2.76**	2.00 **2.70**	1.96 **2.63**	1.94 **2.60**	1.91 **2.54**	1.90 **2.51**	1.88 **2.49**
20	4.35 **8.10**	3.49 **5.85**	3.10 **4.94**	2.87 **4.43**	2.71 **4.10**	2.60 **3.87**	2.52 **3.71**	2.45 **3.56**	2.40 **3.45**	2.35 **3.37**	2.31 **3.30**	2.28 **3.23**	2.23 **3.13**	2.18 **3.05**	2.12 **2.94**	2.08 **2.86**	2.04 **2.77**	1.99 **2.69**	1.96 **2.63**	1.92 **2.56**	1.90 **2.53**	1.87 **2.47**	1.85 **2.44**	1.84 **2.42**
21	4.32 **8.02**	3.47 **5.78**	3.07 **4.87**	2.84 **4.37**	2.68 **4.04**	2.57 **3.81**	2.49 **3.65**	2.42 **3.51**	2.37 **3.40**	2.32 **3.31**	2.28 **3.24**	2.25 **3.17**	2.20 **3.07**	2.15 **2.99**	2.09 **2.88**	2.05 **2.80**	2.00 **2.72**	1.96 **2.63**	1.93 **2.58**	1.89 **2.51**	1.87 **2.47**	1.84 **2.42**	1.82 **2.38**	1.81 **2.36**
22	4.30 **7.94**	3.44 **5.72**	3.05 **4.82**	2.82 **4.31**	2.66 **3.99**	2.55 **3.76**	2.47 **3.59**	2.40 **3.45**	2.35 **3.35**	2.30 **3.26**	2.26 **3.18**	2.23 **3.12**	2.18 **3.02**	2.13 **2.94**	2.07 **2.83**	2.03 **2.75**	1.98 **2.67**	1.93 **2.58**	1.91 **2.53**	1.87 **2.46**	1.84 **2.42**	1.81 **2.37**	1.80 **2.33**	1.78 **2.31**
23	4.28 **7.88**	3.42 **5.66**	3.03 **4.76**	2.80 **4.26**	2.64 **3.94**	2.53 **3.71**	2.45 **3.54**	2.38 **3.41**	2.32 **3.30**	2.28 **3.21**	2.24 **3.14**	2.20 **3.07**	2.14 **2.97**	2.10 **2.89**	2.04 **2.78**	2.00 **2.70**	1.96 **2.62**	1.91 **2.53**	1.88 **2.48**	1.84 **2.41**	1.82 **2.37**	1.79 **2.32**	1.77 **2.28**	1.76 **2.26**
24	4.26 **7.82**	3.40 **5.61**	3.01 **4.72**	2.78 **4.22**	2.62 **3.90**	2.51 **3.67**	2.43 **3.50**	2.36 **3.36**	2.30 **3.25**	2.26 **3.17**	2.22 **3.09**	2.18 **3.03**	2.13 **2.93**	2.09 **2.85**	2.02 **2.74**	1.98 **2.66**	1.94 **2.58**	1.89 **2.49**	1.86 **2.44**	1.82 **2.36**	1.80 **2.33**	1.76 **2.27**	1.74 **2.23**	1.73 **2.21**
25	4.24 **7.77**	3.38 **5.57**	2.99 **4.68**	2.76 **4.18**	2.60 **3.86**	2.49 **3.63**	2.41 **3.46**	2.34 **3.32**	2.28 **3.21**	2.24 **3.13**	2.20 **3.05**	2.16 **2.99**	2.11 **2.89**	2.06 **2.81**	2.00 **2.70**	1.96 **2.62**	1.92 **2.54**	1.87 **2.45**	1.84 **2.40**	1.80 **2.32**	1.77 **2.29**	1.74 **2.23**	1.72 **2.19**	1.71 **2.17**
26	4.22 **7.72**	3.37 **5.53**	2.98 **4.64**	2.74 **4.14**	2.59 **3.82**	2.47 **3.59**	2.39 **3.42**	2.32 **3.29**	2.27 **3.17**	2.22 **3.09**	2.18 **3.02**	2.15 **2.96**	2.10 **2.86**	2.05 **2.77**	1.99 **2.66**	1.95 **2.58**	1.90 **2.50**	1.85 **2.41**	1.82 **2.36**	1.78 **2.28**	1.76 **2.25**	1.72 **2.19**	1.70 **2.15**	1.69 **2.13**

Degrees of freedom of denominator

Table A4-3 Values of the *F*-Distribution (cont'd.)

5% (Roman Type) and 1% (Bold Face Type) Points for the Distribution of *F*

Degrees of freedom of denominator

Each cell shows the 5% point (Roman) / 1% point (Bold).

ϕ_2	ϕ_1 degrees of freedom (for greater mean square) of numerator																								ϕ_2
	1	2	3	4	5	6	7	8	9	10	11	12	14	16	20	24	30	40	50	75	100	200	500	∞	
27	4.21/**7.68**	3.35/**5.49**	2.96/**4.60**	2.73/**4.11**	2.57/**3.79**	2.46/**3.56**	2.37/**3.39**	2.30/**3.26**	2.25/**3.14**	2.20/**3.06**	2.16/**2.98**	2.13/**2.93**	2.08/**2.83**	2.03/**2.74**	1.97/**2.63**	1.93/**2.55**	1.88/**2.47**	1.84/**2.38**	1.80/**2.33**	1.76/**2.25**	1.74/**2.21**	1.71/**2.16**	1.68/**2.12**	1.67/**2.10**	27
28	4.20/**7.64**	3.34/**5.45**	2.95/**4.57**	2.71/**4.07**	2.56/**3.76**	2.44/**3.53**	2.36/**3.36**	2.29/**3.23**	2.24/**3.11**	2.19/**3.03**	2.15/**2.95**	2.12/**2.90**	2.06/**2.80**	2.02/**2.71**	1.96/**2.60**	1.91/**2.52**	1.87/**2.44**	1.81/**2.35**	1.78/**2.30**	1.75/**2.22**	1.72/**2.18**	1.69/**2.13**	1.67/**2.09**	1.65/**2.06**	28
29	4.18/**7.60**	3.33/**5.42**	2.93/**4.54**	2.70/**4.04**	2.54/**3.73**	2.43/**3.50**	2.35/**3.33**	2.28/**3.20**	2.22/**3.08**	2.18/**3.00**	2.14/**2.92**	2.10/**2.87**	2.05/**2.77**	2.00/**2.68**	1.94/**2.57**	1.90/**2.49**	1.85/**2.41**	1.80/**2.32**	1.77/**2.27**	1.73/**2.19**	1.71/**2.15**	1.68/**2.10**	1.65/**2.06**	1.64/**2.03**	29
30	4.17/**7.56**	3.32/**5.39**	2.92/**4.51**	2.69/**4.02**	2.53/**3.70**	2.42/**3.47**	2.34/**3.30**	2.27/**3.17**	2.21/**3.06**	2.16/**2.98**	2.12/**2.90**	2.09/**2.84**	2.04/**2.74**	1.99/**2.66**	1.93/**2.55**	1.89/**2.47**	1.84/**2.38**	1.79/**2.29**	1.76/**2.24**	1.72/**2.16**	1.69/**2.13**	1.66/**2.07**	1.64/**2.03**	1.62/**2.01**	30
32	4.15/**7.50**	3.30/**5.34**	2.90/**4.46**	2.67/**3.97**	2.51/**3.66**	2.40/**3.42**	2.32/**3.25**	2.25/**3.12**	2.19/**3.01**	2.14/**2.94**	2.10/**2.86**	2.07/**2.80**	2.02/**2.70**	1.97/**2.62**	1.91/**2.51**	1.86/**2.42**	1.82/**2.34**	1.76/**2.25**	1.74/**2.20**	1.69/**2.12**	1.67/**2.08**	1.64/**2.02**	1.61/**1.98**	1.59/**1.96**	32
34	4.13/**7.44**	3.28/**5.29**	2.88/**4.42**	2.65/**3.93**	2.49/**3.61**	2.38/**3.38**	2.30/**3.21**	2.23/**3.08**	2.17/**2.97**	2.12/**2.89**	2.08/**2.82**	2.05/**2.76**	2.00/**2.66**	1.95/**2.58**	1.89/**2.47**	1.84/**2.38**	1.80/**2.30**	1.74/**2.21**	1.71/**2.15**	1.67/**2.08**	1.64/**2.04**	1.61/**1.98**	1.59/**1.94**	1.57/**1.91**	34
36	4.11/**7.39**	3.26/**5.25**	2.86/**4.38**	2.63/**3.89**	2.48/**3.58**	2.36/**3.35**	2.28/**3.18**	2.21/**3.04**	2.15/**2.94**	2.10/**2.86**	2.06/**2.78**	2.03/**2.72**	1.98/**2.62**	1.93/**2.54**	1.87/**2.43**	1.82/**2.35**	1.78/**2.26**	1.72/**2.17**	1.69/**2.12**	1.65/**2.04**	1.62/**2.00**	1.59/**1.94**	1.56/**1.90**	1.55/**1.87**	36
38	4.10/**7.35**	3.25/**5.21**	2.85/**4.34**	2.62/**3.86**	2.46/**3.54**	2.35/**3.32**	2.26/**3.15**	2.19/**3.02**	2.14/**2.91**	2.09/**2.82**	2.05/**2.75**	2.02/**2.69**	1.96/**2.59**	1.92/**2.51**	1.85/**2.40**	1.80/**2.32**	1.76/**2.22**	1.71/**2.14**	1.67/**2.08**	1.63/**2.00**	1.60/**1.97**	1.57/**1.90**	1.54/**1.86**	1.53/**1.84**	38
40	4.08/**7.31**	3.23/**5.18**	2.84/**4.31**	2.61/**3.83**	2.45/**3.51**	2.34/**3.29**	2.25/**3.12**	2.18/**2.99**	2.12/**2.88**	2.07/**2.80**	2.04/**2.73**	2.00/**2.66**	1.95/**2.56**	1.90/**2.49**	1.84/**2.37**	1.79/**2.29**	1.74/**2.20**	1.69/**2.11**	1.66/**2.05**	1.61/**1.97**	1.59/**1.94**	1.55/**1.88**	1.53/**1.84**	1.51/**1.81**	40
42	4.07/**7.27**	3.22/**5.15**	2.83/**4.29**	2.59/**3.80**	2.44/**3.49**	2.32/**3.26**	2.24/**3.10**	2.17/**2.96**	2.11/**2.86**	2.06/**2.77**	2.02/**2.70**	1.99/**2.64**	1.94/**2.54**	1.89/**2.46**	1.82/**2.35**	1.78/**2.26**	1.73/**2.17**	1.68/**2.08**	1.64/**2.02**	1.60/**1.94**	1.57/**1.91**	1.54/**1.85**	1.51/**1.80**	1.49/**1.78**	42
44	4.06/**7.24**	3.21/**5.12**	2.82/**4.26**	2.58/**3.78**	2.43/**3.46**	2.31/**3.24**	2.23/**3.07**	2.16/**2.94**	2.10/**2.84**	2.05/**2.75**	2.01/**2.68**	1.98/**2.62**	1.92/**2.52**	1.88/**2.44**	1.81/**2.32**	1.76/**2.24**	1.72/**2.15**	1.66/**2.06**	1.63/**2.00**	1.58/**1.92**	1.56/**1.88**	1.52/**1.82**	1.50/**1.78**	1.48/**1.75**	44
46	4.05/**7.21**	3.20/**5.10**	2.81/**4.24**	2.57/**3.76**	2.42/**3.44**	2.30/**3.22**	2.22/**3.05**	2.14/**2.92**	2.09/**2.82**	2.04/**2.73**	2.00/**2.66**	1.97/**2.60**	1.91/**2.50**	1.87/**2.42**	1.80/**2.30**	1.75/**2.22**	1.71/**2.13**	1.65/**2.04**	1.62/**1.98**	1.57/**1.90**	1.54/**1.86**	1.51/**1.80**	1.48/**1.76**	1.46/**1.72**	46
48	4.04/**7.19**	3.19/**5.08**	2.80/**4.22**	2.56/**3.74**	2.41/**3.42**	2.30/**3.20**	2.21/**3.04**	2.14/**2.90**	2.08/**2.80**	2.03/**2.71**	1.99/**2.64**	1.96/**2.58**	1.90/**2.48**	1.86/**2.40**	1.79/**2.28**	1.74/**2.20**	1.70/**2.11**	1.64/**2.02**	1.61/**1.96**	1.56/**1.88**	1.53/**1.84**	1.50/**1.78**	1.47/**1.73**	1.45/**1.70**	48

Table A4-3 Values of the F-Distribution (cont'd.)

5% (Roman Type) and 1% (Bold Face Type) Points for the Distribution of F

Degrees of freedom of denominator

n_1 degrees of freedom (for greater mean square of numerator)

n_2	1	2	3	4	5	6	7	8	9	10	11	12	14	16	20	24	30	40	50	75	100	200	500	∞
50	4.03 / **7.17**	3.18 / **5.06**	2.79 / **4.20**	2.56 / **3.72**	2.40 / **3.41**	2.29 / **3.18**	2.20 / **3.02**	2.13 / **2.88**	2.07 / **2.78**	2.02 / **2.70**	1.98 / **2.62**	1.95 / **2.56**	1.90 / **2.46**	1.85 / **2.39**	1.78 / **2.26**	1.74 / **2.18**	1.69 / **2.10**	1.63 / **2.00**	1.60 / **1.94**	1.55 / **1.86**	1.52 / **1.82**	1.48 / **1.76**	1.46 / **1.71**	1.44 / **1.68**
55	4.02 / **7.12**	3.17 / **5.01**	2.78 / **4.16**	2.54 / **3.68**	2.38 / **3.37**	2.27 / **3.15**	2.18 / **2.98**	2.11 / **2.85**	2.05 / **2.75**	2.00 / **2.66**	1.97 / **2.59**	1.93 / **2.53**	1.88 / **2.43**	1.83 / **2.35**	1.76 / **2.23**	1.72 / **2.15**	1.67 / **2.06**	1.61 / **1.96**	1.58 / **1.90**	1.52 / **1.82**	1.50 / **1.78**	1.46 / **1.71**	1.43 / **1.66**	1.41 / **1.64**
60	4.00 / **7.08**	3.15 / **4.98**	2.76 / **4.13**	2.52 / **3.65**	2.37 / **3.34**	2.25 / **3.12**	2.17 / **2.95**	2.10 / **2.82**	2.04 / **2.72**	1.99 / **2.63**	1.95 / **2.56**	1.92 / **2.50**	1.86 / **2.40**	1.81 / **2.32**	1.75 / **2.20**	1.70 / **2.12**	1.65 / **2.03**	1.59 / **1.93**	1.56 / **1.87**	1.50 / **1.79**	1.48 / **1.74**	1.44 / **1.68**	1.41 / **1.63**	1.39 / **1.60**
65	3.99 / **7.04**	3.14 / **4.95**	2.75 / **4.10**	2.51 / **3.62**	2.36 / **3.31**	2.24 / **3.09**	2.15 / **2.93**	2.08 / **2.79**	2.02 / **2.70**	1.98 / **2.61**	1.94 / **2.54**	1.90 / **2.47**	1.85 / **2.37**	1.80 / **2.30**	1.73 / **2.18**	1.68 / **2.09**	1.63 / **2.00**	1.57 / **1.90**	1.54 / **1.84**	1.49 / **1.76**	1.46 / **1.71**	1.42 / **1.64**	1.39 / **1.60**	1.37 / **1.56**
70	3.98 / **7.01**	3.13 / **4.92**	2.74 / **4.08**	2.50 / **3.60**	2.35 / **3.29**	2.23 / **3.07**	2.14 / **2.91**	2.07 / **2.77**	2.01 / **2.67**	1.97 / **2.59**	1.93 / **2.51**	1.89 / **2.45**	1.84 / **2.35**	1.79 / **2.28**	1.72 / **2.15**	1.67 / **2.07**	1.62 / **1.98**	1.56 / **1.88**	1.53 / **1.82**	1.47 / **1.74**	1.45 / **1.69**	1.40 / **1.62**	1.37 / **1.56**	1.35 / **1.53**
80	3.96 / **6.96**	3.11 / **4.88**	2.72 / **4.04**	2.48 / **3.56**	2.33 / **3.25**	2.21 / **3.04**	2.12 / **2.87**	2.05 / **2.74**	1.99 / **2.64**	1.95 / **2.55**	1.91 / **2.48**	1.88 / **2.41**	1.82 / **2.32**	1.77 / **2.24**	1.70 / **2.11**	1.65 / **2.03**	1.60 / **1.94**	1.54 / **1.84**	1.51 / **1.78**	1.45 / **1.70**	1.42 / **1.65**	1.38 / **1.57**	1.35 / **1.52**	1.32 / **1.49**
100	3.94 / **6.90**	3.09 / **4.82**	2.70 / **3.98**	2.46 / **3.51**	2.30 / **3.20**	2.19 / **2.99**	2.10 / **2.82**	2.03 / **2.69**	1.97 / **2.59**	1.92 / **2.51**	1.88 / **2.43**	1.85 / **2.36**	1.79 / **2.26**	1.75 / **2.19**	1.68 / **2.06**	1.63 / **1.98**	1.57 / **1.89**	1.51 / **1.79**	1.48 / **1.73**	1.42 / **1.64**	1.39 / **1.59**	1.34 / **1.51**	1.30 / **1.46**	1.28 / **1.43**
125	3.92 / **6.84**	3.07 / **4.78**	2.68 / **3.94**	2.44 / **3.47**	2.29 / **3.17**	2.17 / **2.95**	2.08 / **2.79**	2.01 / **2.65**	1.95 / **2.56**	1.90 / **2.47**	1.86 / **2.40**	1.83 / **2.33**	1.77 / **2.23**	1.72 / **2.15**	1.65 / **2.03**	1.60 / **1.94**	1.55 / **1.85**	1.49 / **1.75**	1.45 / **1.68**	1.39 / **1.59**	1.36 / **1.54**	1.31 / **1.46**	1.27 / **1.40**	1.25 / **1.37**
150	3.91 / **6.81**	3.06 / **4.75**	2.67 / **3.91**	2.43 / **3.44**	2.27 / **3.14**	2.16 / **2.92**	2.07 / **2.76**	2.00 / **2.62**	1.94 / **2.53**	1.89 / **2.44**	1.85 / **2.37**	1.82 / **2.30**	1.76 / **2.20**	1.71 / **2.12**	1.64 / **2.00**	1.59 / **1.91**	1.54 / **1.83**	1.47 / **1.72**	1.44 / **1.66**	1.37 / **1.56**	1.34 / **1.51**	1.29 / **1.43**	1.25 / **1.37**	1.22 / **1.33**
200	3.89 / **6.76**	3.04 / **4.71**	2.65 / **3.88**	2.41 / **3.41**	2.26 / **3.11**	2.14 / **2.90**	2.05 / **2.73**	1.98 / **2.60**	1.92 / **2.50**	1.87 / **2.41**	1.83 / **2.34**	1.80 / **2.28**	1.74 / **2.17**	1.69 / **2.09**	1.62 / **1.97**	1.57 / **1.88**	1.52 / **1.79**	1.45 / **1.69**	1.42 / **1.62**	1.35 / **1.53**	1.32 / **1.48**	1.26 / **1.39**	1.22 / **1.33**	1.19 / **1.28**
400	3.86 / **6.70**	3.02 / **4.66**	2.62 / **3.83**	2.39 / **3.36**	2.23 / **3.06**	2.12 / **2.85**	2.03 / **2.69**	1.96 / **2.55**	1.90 / **2.46**	1.85 / **2.37**	1.81 / **2.29**	1.78 / **2.23**	1.72 / **2.12**	1.67 / **2.04**	1.60 / **1.92**	1.54 / **1.84**	1.49 / **1.74**	1.42 / **1.64**	1.38 / **1.57**	1.32 / **1.47**	1.28 / **1.42**	1.22 / **1.32**	1.16 / **1.24**	1.13 / **1.19**
1000	3.85 / **6.66**	3.00 / **4.62**	2.61 / **3.80**	2.38 / **3.34**	2.22 / **3.04**	2.10 / **2.82**	2.02 / **2.66**	1.95 / **2.53**	1.89 / **2.43**	1.84 / **2.34**	1.80 / **2.26**	1.76 / **2.20**	1.70 / **2.09**	1.65 / **2.01**	1.58 / **1.89**	1.53 / **1.81**	1.47 / **1.71**	1.41 / **1.61**	1.36 / **1.54**	1.30 / **1.44**	1.26 / **1.38**	1.19 / **1.28**	1.13 / **1.19**	1.08 / **1.11**
∞	3.84 / **6.64**	2.99 / **4.60**	2.60 / **3.78**	2.37 / **3.32**	2.21 / **3.02**	2.09 / **2.80**	2.01 / **2.64**	1.94 / **2.51**	1.88 / **2.41**	1.83 / **2.32**	1.79 / **2.24**	1.75 / **2.18**	1.69 / **2.07**	1.64 / **1.99**	1.57 / **1.87**	1.52 / **1.79**	1.46 / **1.69**	1.40 / **1.59**	1.35 / **1.52**	1.28 / **1.41**	1.24 / **1.36**	1.17 / **1.25**	1.11 / **1.15**	1.00 / **1.00**

The function, $F = t$ with exponent $2z$, is computed in part from Fisher's table VI (7). Additional entries are by interpolation, mostly graphical.

Source: Reprinted by permission from *Statistical Methods*, 5th edition, by George W. Snedecor, © 1956 by The Iowa State University Press, Ames, Iowa.

Table A4-4 Chi-Square Distribution

example
for $\phi = 8$ degrees
of freedom:
$P[\chi^2 > 13.36]$
$= .10$

Percentage Points of the χ^2 Distribution

ϕ \ P	0.995	0.99	0.975	0.95	0.90	0.75	0.50	0.25	0.10	0.05	0.025	0.01	0.005	P \ ϕ
1	0.0^4393	0.0^3157	0.0^3982	0.0^23	0.0158	0.102	0.455	1.323	2.71	3.84	5.02	6.63	7.88	1
2	0.0100	0.0201	0.0506	0.103	0.211	0.575	1.386	2.77	4.61	5.99	7.38	9.21	10.60	2
3	0.0717	0.115	0.216	0.352	0.584	1.213	2.37	4.11	6.25	7.81	9.35	11.34	12.84	3
4	0.207	0.297	0.484	0.711	1.064	1.923	3.36	5.39	7.78	9.49	11.14	13.28	14.86	4
5	0.412	0.544	0.831	1.145	1.610	2.67	4.35	6.63	9.24	11.07	12.83	15.09	16.75	5
6	0.676	0.872	1.237	1.635	2.20	3.45	5.35	7.84	10.64	12.59	14.45	16.81	18.55	6
7	0.989	1.239	1.690	2.17	2.83	4.25	6.35	9.04	12.02	14.07	16.01	18.48	20.3	7
8	1.344	1.646	2.18	2.73	3.49	5.07	7.34	10.22	13.36	15.51	17.53	20.1	22.0	8
9	1.735	2.09	2.70	3.33	4.17	5.90	8.34	11.39	14.68	16.92	19.02	21.7	23.6	9
10	2.16	2.56	3.25	3.94	4.87	6.74	9.34	12.55	15.99	18.31	20.5	23.2	25.2	10
11	2.60	3.05	3.82	4.57	5.58	7.58	10.34	13.70	17.28	19.68	21.9	24.7	26.8	11
12	3.07	3.57	4.40	5.23	6.30	8.44	11.34	14.85	18.55	21.0	23.3	26.2	28.3	12
13	3.57	4.11	5.01	5.89	7.04	9.30	12.34	15.98	19.81	22.4	24.7	24.7	29.8	13
14	4.07	4.66	5.63	6.57	7.79	10.17	13.34	17.12	21.1	23.7	26.1	29.1	31.3	14
15	4.60	5.23	6.26	7.26	8.55	11.04	14.34	18.25	22.3	25.0	27.5	30.6	32.8	15

	-2.58	-2.33	-1.96	-1.64	-1.28	-0.674	0.000	0.674	1.282	1.645	1.960	2.33	2.58	
16	5.14	5.81	6.91	7.96	9.31	11.91	15.34	19.37	23.5	26.3	28.8	32.0	34.3	16
17	5.70	6.41	7.56	8.67	10.09	12.79	16.34	20.5	24.8	27.6	30.2	33.4	35.7	17
18	6.26	7.01	8.23	9.39	10.86	13.68	17.34	21.6	26.0	28.9	31.5	34.8	37.2	18
19	6.48	7.63	8.91	10.12	11.65	14.56	18.34	22.7	27.2	30.1	32.9	36.2	38.6	19
20	7.43	8.26	9.59	10.85	12.44	15.45	19.34	23.8	28.4	31.4	34.2	37.6	40.0	20
21	8.03	8.90	10.28	11.59	13.24	16.34	20.3	24.9	29.6	32.7	35.5	38.9	41.4	21
22	8.64	9.54	10.98	12.34	14.04	17.24	21.3	26.0	30.8	33.9	36.8	40.3	42.8	22
23	9.26	10.20	11.69	13.09	14.85	18.14	22.3	27.1	32.0	35.2	38.1	41.6	44.2	23
24	9.89	10.86	12.40	13.85	15.66	19.04	23.3	28.2	33.2	36.4	39.4	43.0	45.6	24
25	10.52	11.52	13.12	14.61	16.47	19.94	24.3	29.3	34.4	37.7	40.6	44.3	46.9	25
26	11.16	12.20	13.84	15.38	17.29	20.8	25.3	30.4	35.6	38.9	41.9	45.6	48.3	26
27	11.81	12.88	14.57	16.15	18.11	21.7	26.3	31.5	36.7	40.1	43.2	47.0	49.6	27
28	12.46	13.56	15.31	16.93	18.94	22.7	27.3	32.6	37.9	41.3	44.5	48.3	51.0	28
29	13.12	14.26	16.05	17.71	19.77	23.6	28.3	33.7	39.1	42.6	45.7	49.6	52.3	29
30	13.79	14.95	16.79	18.49	20.6	24.5	29.3	34.8	40.3	43.8	47.0	50.9	53.7	30
40	20.7	22.2	24.4	26.5	29.1	33.7	39.3	45.6	51.8	55.8	59.3	63.7	66.8	40
50	28.0	29.7	32.4	34.8	37.7	42.9	49.3	56.3	63.2	67.5	71.4	76.2	79.5	50
60	35.5	37.5	40.5	43.2	46.5	52.3	59.3	67.0	74.4	79.1	83.3	88.4	92.0	60
70	43.3	45.4	48.8	51.7	55.3	61.7	69.3	77.6	85.5	90.5	95.0	100.4	104.2	70
80	51.2	53.5	57.2	60.4	64.3	71.1	79.3	88.1	96.6	101.9	106.6	112.3	116.3	80
90	59.2	61.8	65.6	69.1	73.3	80.6	89.3	98.6	107.6	113.1	118.1	124.1	128.3	90
100	67.3	70.1	74.2	77.9	82.4	90.1	99.3	109.1	118.5	124.3	129.6	135.8	140.2	100
z_x	-2.58	-2.33	-1.96	-1.64	-1.28	-0.674	0.000	0.674	1.282	1.645	1.960	2.33	2.58	z_x

Source: Abridged from "Table of percentage points of the χ^2 distribution" by Catherine M. Thompson, Biometrika, 32 (1941), pp. 187–191, and is reprinted here by permission of the author and editor of Biometrika.

Table A4-5 Random Numbers

6063	2353	8531	8892	4109	5782	2283	1385	0699	5927
6305	1326	4551	2815	8937	2908	0698	5509	4303	9911
0143	0187	8127	2026	8313	8341	2479	4722	6602	2236
1031	0754	7989	4948	1804	3025	0997	9562	3674	7876
2022	3227	2147	5613	2857	8859	4941	7274	9412	0620
9149	0806	9751	8870	9677	9676	1854	8094	7658	7012
5863	0513	1402	3866	8696	9142	6063	2252	7818	2477
8724	0806	9644	8284	7010	0868	9076	4915	5751	9214
6783	4207	2958	5295	3175	3396	8117	5918	1037	4319
0862	1620	4690	0036	9654	4078	1918	8721	8454	7671
9394	2466	6427	5395	9393	0520	7074	0634	5578	4023
3220	3058	7787	7706	4094	5603	3303	8300	6185	8705
1491	3503	0584	7221	6176	0116	0309	1975	0910	3535
4368	5705	8579	5790	7244	6547	8495	7973	1805	7251
2325	4026	2919	8327	0267	2616	6572	8620	8245	6257
0591	1775	5134	8709	7373	3332	0507	5525	7640	2840
3471	1461	1149	6798	6070	9930	1862	3672	6718	3849
2600	9885	6219	3668	1005	5418	5822	0416	4220	4692
9572	7874	6034	4514	2628	1693	0628	2200	9006	3795
0822	2790	9386	5783	2689	2565	1565	0349	3410	5216
4329	3028	2549	2529	9434	3083	6800	8569	9290	8298
9289	5212	2355	9367	1297	1638	9282	3720	7178	2695
3932	9960	3399	1700	8253	1375	4594	6024	1223	5383
2282	0648	7561	7528	5870	7907	0713	8608	9682	8576
9933	3416	5957	2574	5553	5534	4707	3206	0963	2459
9015	6416	6603	2967	7591	5013	2878	8424	5452	4659
1539	0719	2637	9969	8450	4489	3528	3364	1459	9708
6849	5595	7969	2582	5627	1920	9772	8560	0892	6500
2523	7769	3536	9611	1079	1694	1254	4195	5799	5928
0701	7355	0587	8878	3446	1137	7690	0647	1407	6362
2163	8543	4594	6022	0496	8648	2999	1262	6702	0811
0327	5727	1070	5996	8660	9024	2135	9799	8414	9136
2169	3160	8707	6361	6339	4054	3251	7397	3480	5805
8393	8147	5360	4150	2990	3380	1789	7436	4781	0337
9726	9151	2064	0609	5878	9095	9737	2897	6510	8891
0515	2296	2636	9756	5313	7754	0916	6066	3905	1298
0649	8398	5614	0140	3155	2211	4988	3674	7663	0620
0026	9426	8005	8579	5774	7962	5092	5856	1626	0980
3422	0092	1626	1298	2475	1997	9796	7076	1541	1731
8191	1983	9164	1885	5468	8216	4327	8109	5880	9804
7408	0486	7654	4829	2711	6592	4785	5901	7147	9314
8261	9440	8118	6338	8157	9052	9093	8449	4066	4894
9274	8838	8342	3114	0455	6212	8862	6701	0099	0501
2699	0383	1400	3484	1492	4683	5369	3851	5870	0903
8740	0349	3502	3971	9960	6325	6727	4715	2945	9938
0247	2372	0424	0578	0036	1619	4479	7108	8520	1487
5136	9444	8343	1152	3615	1420	8923	7307	3978	5724
4844	8931	0964	2878	8212	9328	2656	1965	4805	0634
0205	8457	4333	2555	5353	9201	1606	2715	4014	1877
2517	5061	7642	3891	7713	7066	5435	1200	7455	5562

2271	2572	8665	3272	9033	8256	2822	3636	7599	0270
3025	0788	5311	7792	1837	4739	4552	3234	5572	9885
3382	6151	1011	3778	9951	7709	8060	2258	8536	2290
7870	5799	6032	9043	4526	8100	1957	9539	5370	0046
1697	0002	2340	6959	1915	1626	1297	1533	6572	3835
3395	3381	1862	3250	8614	5683	6757	5628	2551	6971
6081	6526	3028	2338	5702	8819	3679	4829	9909	4712
3470	9879	2935	1141	6398	6387	5634	9589	3212	7963
0432	8641	5020	6612	1038	1547	0948	4278	0020	6509
4995	5596	8286	8377	8567	8237	3520	8244	5694	3326
8246	6718	3851	5870	1216	2107	1387	1621	5509	5772
7825	8727	2849	3501	3551	1001	0123	7873	5926	6078
6258	2450	2962	1183	3666	4156	4454	8239	4551	2920
3235	5783	2701	2378	7460	3398	1223	4688	3674	7872
2525	9008	6997	0885	1053	2340	7066	5328	6412	5054
5852	9739	1457	8999	2789	9068	9829	1336	3148	7875
0440	3769	7864	4029	4494	9829	1339	4910	1303	9161
0820	4641	2375	2542	4093	5364	1145	2848	2792	0431
7114	2842	8554	6881	6377	9427	8216	1193	8042	8449
6558	9301	9096	0577	8520	5923	4717	0188	8545	8745
0345	9937	5569	0279	8951	6183	7787	7808	5149	2185
7430	2074	9427	8422	4082	5629	2971	9456	0649	7981
8030	7345	3389	4739	5911	1022	9189	2565	1982	8577
6272	6718	3849	4715	3156	2823	4174	8733	5600	7702
4894	9847	5611	4763	8755	3388	5114	3274	6681	2657
2676	5984	6806	2692	4012	0934	2436	0869	9557	2490
9305	2074	9378	7670	8284	7431	7361	2912	2251	7395
5138	2461	7213	1905	7775	9881	8782	6272	0632	4418
2452	4200	8674	9202	0812	3986	1143	7343	2264	9072
8882	3033	8746	7390	8609	1144	2531	6944	8869	1570
1087	9336	8020	9166	4472	8293	2904	7949	3165	7400
5666	2841	8134	9588	2915	4116	2802	6917	3993	8764
9790	2228	9702	1690	7170	7511	1937	0723	4505	7155
3250	8860	3294	2684	6572	3415	5750	8726	2647	6596
5450	3922	0950	0890	6434	2306	2781	1066	3681	2404
5765	0765	7311	5270	5910	7009	0240	7435	4568	6484
8408	1939	0599	5347	2160	7376	4696	6969	0787	3838
8460	7658	6906	9177	1492	4680	3719	3456	8681	6736
4198	7244	3849	4819	1008	6781	3388	5253	7041	6712
9872	4441	6712	9614	2736	5533	9062	2534	0855	7946
6485	0487	0004	5563	1481	1546	8245	6116	6920	0990
2064	0512	9509	0341	8131	7778	8609	9417	1216	4189
9927	8987	5321	3125	9992	9449	5951	5872	2057	5731
4918	9690	6121	8770	6053	6931	7252	5409	1869	4229
8099	5821	3899	2685	6781	3178	0096	2986	8878	8991
1901	4974	1262	6810	4673	8772	6616	2632	7891	9970
8273	6675	4925	3924	2274	3860	1662	7480	8674	4503
2878	8213	3170	5126	0434	9481	7029	8688	4027	3340
6088	1182	3242	0835	1765	8819	3462	9820	5759	4189
5773	6600	5306	0354	8295	0148	6608	9064	3421	8570

Source: Donald B. Owen, *Handbook of Statistical Tables*, 1962, Addison-Wesley, Reading, Ma. Courtesy of U.S. Atomic Energy Commission.

Table A4-6   Critical Values of μ (Runs)

Number of a's = Number of b's	$\mu_{.05}$	$\mu_{.01}$	Number of a's = Number of b's	$\mu_{.05}$	$\mu_{.01}$
5	3	2	20	15	13
6	3	2	25	19	17
7	4	3	30	24	21
8	5	4	35	28	25
9	6	4	40	33	30
10	6	5	45	37	34
11	7	6	50	42	38
12	8	6	60	51	47
13	9	7	80	70	65
14	10	8	100	88	84
15	11	9			
16	11	10			
17	12	10			
18	13	11			
19	14	12			

Source: John E. Freund and Frank J. Williams, *Elementary Business Statistics: the Modern Approach,* © 1964. Reprinted by permission of Prentice-Hall, Inc., Englewood Cliffs, NJ, p. 445, based on F. S. Swed and C. Eisenhart, "Tables for testing randomness of grouping in a sequence of alternatives," *Annals of Mathematical Statistics,* 14 (1943), p. 66.

Table A4-7   Critical Values of r

n	$r_{.025}$	$r_{.010}$	$r_{.005}$	n	$r_{.025}$	$r_{.010}$	$r_{.005}$
3	0.997			18	0.468	0.543	0.590
4	0.950	0.990	0.999	19	0.456	0.529	0.575
5	0.878	0.934	0.959	20	0.444	0.516	0.561
6	0.811	0.882	0.917	21	0.433	0.503	0.549
7	0.754	0.833	0.875	22	0.432	0.492	0.537
8	0.707	0.789	0.834	27	0.381	0.445	0.487
9	0.666	0.750	0.768	32	0.349	0.409	0.449
10	0.632	0.715	0.765	37	0.325	0.381	0.418
11	0.602	0.685	0.735	42	0.304	0.358	0.393
12	0.576	0.658	0.708	47	0.288	0.338	0.372
13	0.553	0.634	0.684	52	0.273	0.322	0.354
14	0.532	0.612	0.661	62	0.250	0.295	0.325
15	0.514	0.592	0.641	72	0.232	0.274	0.302
16	0.497	0.574	0.623	82	0.217	0.256	0.283
17	0.482	0.558	0.606	92	0.205	0.242	0.267

Source: Abridged from Table VI of R. A. Fisher and F. Yates, *Statistical Table for Biological, Agricultural, and Medical Research,* published by Oliver and Boyd, Ltd., Edinburgh, by permission of the author and publishers.

Table A4-8   Values of the K-Statistic (Von Neumann Ratio Values at Different Levels of Significance, P)

Values of $\dfrac{\delta^2}{s^2}$ for Different Levels of Significance

Values of k			Values of k'		Values of k			Values of k'	
n	P = .01	P = .05	P = .95	P = .99	n	P = .01	P = .05	P = .95	P = .99
4	.8341	1.0406	4.2927	4.4992	31	1.2469	1.4746	2.6587	2.8864
5	.6724	1.0255	3.9745	4.3276	32	1.2570	1.4817	2.6473	2.8720
6	.6738	1.0682	3.7318	4.1262	33	1.2667	1.4885	2.6365	2.8583
7	.7163	1.0919	3.5748	3.9504	34	1.2761	1.4951	2.6262	2.8451
8	.7575	1.1228	3.4486	3.8139	35	1.2852	1.5014	2.6163	2.8324
9	.7974	1.1524	3.3476	3.7025					
10	.8353	1.1803	3.2642	3.6091	36	1.2940	1.5075	2.6068	2.8202
					37	1.3025	1.5135	2.5977	2.8085
11	.8706	1.2062	3.1938	3.5294	38	1.3108	1.5193	2.5889	2.7973
12	.9033	1.2301	3.1335	3.4603	39	1.3188	1.5249	2.5804	2.7865
13	.9336	1.2521	3.0812	3.3996	40	1.3266	1.5304	2.5722	2.7760
14	.9618	1.2725	3.0352	3.3458					
15	.9880	1.2914	2.9943	3.2977	41	1.3342	1.5357	2.5643	2.7658
					42	1.3415	1.5408	2.5567	2.7560
16	1.0124	1.3090	2.9577	3.2543	43	1.3486	1.5458	2.5494	2.7466
17	1.0352	1.3253	2.9247	3.2148	44	1.3554	1.5506	2.5424	2.7376
18	1.0566	1.3405	2.8948	3.1787	45	1.3620	1.5552	2.5357	2.7289
19	1.0766	1.3547	2.8675	3.1456					
20	1.0954	1.3680	2.8425	3.1151	46	1.3684	1.5596	2.5293	2.7205
					47	1.3745	1.5638	2.5232	2.7125
21	1.1131	1.3805	2.8195	3.0869	48	1.3802	1.5678	2.5173	2.7049
22	1.1298	1.3923	2.7982	3.0607	49	1.3856	1.5716	2.5117	2.6977
23	1.1456	1.4035	2.7784	3.0362	50	1.3907	1.5752	2.5064	2.6908
24	1.1606	1.4141	2.7599	3.0133					
25	1.1748	1.4241	2.7426	2.9919	51	1.3957	1.5787	2.5013	2.6842
					52	1.4007	1.5822	2.4963	2.6777
26	1.1883	1.4336	2.7264	2.9718	53	1.4057	1.5856	2.4914	2.6712
27	1.2012	1.4426	2.7112	2.9528	54	1.4107	1.5890	2.4866	2.6648
28	1.2135	1.4512	2.6969	2.9348	55	1.4156	1.5923	2.4819	2.6585
29	1.2252	1.4594	2.6834	2.9177					
30	1.2363	1.4672	2.6707	2.9016	56	1.4203	1.5955	2.4773	2.6524
					57	1.4249	1.5987	2.4728	2.6465
					58	1.4294	1.6019	2.4684	2.6407
					59	1.4339	1.6051	2.4640	2.6350
					60	1.4384	1.6082	2.4596	2.6294

Source: Reproduced by permission of the editors, from B. I. Hart, "Significance levels for the ratio of the mean square successive difference to the variance," *Annals of Mathematical Statistics*, **13**:4 (1942), pp. 445–447.

Glossary

a priori probabilities   *see* subjective probabilities.

ad hoc research   research that is done just once, as opposed to being done continuously; also called "problem study."

algorithm   a solution system.

alpha error   *see* Type I error.

alpha factoring   one of several algorithms for factor analysis.

analogical model   a model that uses one or more of its physical properties to represent a property of the process or object being simulated. An example is the scale on a fuel gauge.

analytical forecast   *see* causal forecast.

area sampling   a method of cluster sampling in which the clusters are defined as geographic areas.

asymptotic   the property of approaching but never quite reaching a fixed value (asymptote).

attitude   the predisposition to act in a certain way in particular situations or toward particular persons or things.

attitude-scaling test   a structured test which confronts the respondents with provocative statements and then asks them to indicate the extent of their agreement or disagreement.

autocorrelation   a correlation between observations of a variable over time. That is, the value of the variable at one time is partially determined by the value of the same variable at an earlier time; also called "serial correlation."

awareness test   a test which measures the degree of knowledge a person has on a particular subject.

Bayes' postulate   the assumption that all possible events have an equal probability of occurrence. The postulate is applicable when one has no other basis for estimating the probabilities. The postulate is also called the "rule of ignorance" and the "equal distribution of ignorance rule."

Bayes' theorem   a formula for computing conditional

probabilities when the outcome is known; also called the "Rule of Bayes."

Bayesian statistics that branch of statistics which admits subjective probabilities and which also estimates probabilities when the outcome is known. Bayesian statistics rest on the work of Rev. Thomas Bayes (1702–1761).

beta error *see* Type II error.

biological needs the basic drives one is born with, such as hunger, thirst, pain avoidance, and sex.

Bio-med *see* Bio-medical Computer Programs.

Bio-medical Computer Programs a package of computer programs for statistically analyzing data; also called "Bio-Med" and "BMD." BMD is maintained by, and available through, the Health Sciences Computing Center, University of California at Los Angeles.

bivariate involving only two variables.

bivariate analysis data analysis involving the relationship between two variables; also called "bivariant analysis."

BMD *see* Bio-medical Computer Programs.

canonical analysis a group of statistical tools for estimating the relationship between sets of variables. Canonical analysis admits two or more dependent variables, which may be metric or nonmetric.

causal-model forecast a forecast based on a statistical relationship between variables; also called

an "analytical forecast" and a "regressive forecast."

causal research research that seeks to explain the relationship between variables.

census a survey which includes every member of the population; also called a "population survey."

Census Method II a Bureau of the Census computer program designed to analyze time series data, extracting trend, seasonal variation, cyclical variation, and noise.

central limit theorem the concept that a statistic tends to get closer to its parameter as sample size increases.

ceteris paribus a Latin term meaning "all things remaining equal."

checklist a list of items that must be considered or included, or a list of tasks that must be done to complete a job.

chi square test a test of statistical significance used to tell if there is a significant difference between frequency distributions.

classification results matrix *see* confusion matrix.

cluster a subset of a population.

cluster analysis a set of statistical techniques for grouping objects into internally homogeneous sets; also called "profile analysis."

cluster sampling sampling by first dividing the population into clusters, then randomly selecting a number of clusters from which to draw the sample elements. (This is one form of multistage sampling.)

code book a guide assigning labels (usually numbers) to

code book (*continued*) answers, e.g., 1 = YES; 2 = NO.

coding the categorization of respondent answers (or other information) by assigning labels (usually numbers) to them.

coefficient of determination a measure of the amount of variance in the dependent variable explained by the model.

cognition a person's awareness with respect to a particular thing; the act of knowing.

collinearity *see* multicollinearity.

collinearity clustering a method of cluster analysis which uses the similarity of the pattern of their attribute scores to group objects into clusters.

commercial marketing marketing in the pursuit of profit.

common factor a factor shared by at least two variables (factor analysis).

communality the percentage of total variance summarized in common factors (factor analysis).

comparative scale a scale upon which objects are placed as a function of their comparison with other objects on the scale. (This is the converse of the conventional procedure of placing each object on the scale according to an independent assessment.)

concept sorting a method of identifying new or unique relationships between objects: Respondents are given a set of objects and asked to group them into what they think are internally homogeneous subsets.

conditional probability the probability that event A has occurred, given the fact (or assumption) that event B has occurred.

confidence interval the range of possible random error at a given confidence level.

confidence level the probability that an answer is correct or is within the confidence interval. For example, a confidence level of .95 would mean the probability is 95 percent that a value, such as an estimate of a population mean, is within the specified confidence interval

confusion matrix a two-way classification table showing how many cases were correctly classified and how many were incorrectly classified; also called a "classification results matrix." Confusion matrices are commonly used in discriminant analysis.

conjoint measurement a statistical method for measuring the trade-offs between attributes or between benefits and cost associated with a product; also called "benefit structure analysis."

consumer behavior model a symbolic or diagrammatic description of the purchase process.

consumer panel a group of people (members of a market population) who are used to provide information on purchase behavior, media habits, or product usage, usually over a period of time.

contingency table a cross tabulation of data on two variables, such as sales and price; also called a "two-way classification table," "cross break," "cross tabulation," and "cross tab."

control unit a test unit which is not subjected to the experimental treatment(s); also called a "test control unit."

convenience sample a nonrandom sample composed of members who entered by accident or just happened to be at the location where the sampling was done.

correlation analysis the analysis of the statistical relationship between two or more variables. The objective is to estimate the degree to which the variables move (change) together.

cost-benefit analysis a system for evaluating alternatives without use of the profit criterion; also called "cost-utility analysis" and "cost-effectiveness analysis."

cost-effectiveness analysis *see* cost-benefit analysis.

cost-utility analysis *see* cost-benefit analysis.

covariance a correlation between two unrelated variables caused by both variables being related to a common variable.

cross break *see* contingency table.

cross-sectional data data gathered for the same point in time.

cross stratification the designation of strata by two parameters, such as age and income.

cross tabulation *see* contingency table.

cross validation a method of checking validity: The same test as used on the original sample is applied to a second sample

drawn from the same universe. Test results are then compared.

curvilinear a special case of nonlinear: A curvilinear function is one in which a variable(s) has an exponent not equal to one. For example: $Y = \alpha + \beta X^2$.

cyclical variation variation caused by the business cycle.

data acquisition the locating and collecting of information.

data bank an information storage center (MIS term). "Data bank" also refers to a collection of information.

data processing the conversion of raw data to useful information.

data reduction the summarization information.

decision tree a tree diagram of a decision process; see tree diagram.

degrees of freedom the number of observations that can be changed without changing the constraints or assumptions (statistics); degrees of freedom increase with and are mainly determined by sample size.

Delphi method a technique of data collection and forecasting based on information gathered from a panel of experts.

demographics the statistics of population, such as age, income, occupation, education, and family status.

depth interview *see* in-depth interview.

descriptive data data used mainly to describe rather than explain market (or other) phenomena.

descriptive research research that seeks to define or describe a subject.

deviation   the difference between an observation and the mean.

diary   a record of media viewing, purchases, or product usage maintained by a panel member.

dichotomous variable   a variable having two discrete levels, such as yes/no, like/dislike, or one/zero.

discriminant analysis   a statistical method of estimating the relationship between one nonmetric variable and one or more other variables which can be metric or nonmetric. The method is used to analyze relationships and to classify respondents or objects. There are several algorithms for discriminant analysis, each yielding similar results.

disproportionate sampling   *see* optimal sampling.

dummy variable   a variable that uses a number to represent a qualitative condition. Dummy variables are typically zero-or-one variables. For example, purchase behavior might be represented by a dummy where 1 = buy and 0 = do-not-buy. Such two-level variables are also called "dichotomous variables."

Durbin-Watson test   a test used for the detection of autocorrelation.

element   a member of a population.

equal distribution of ignorance rule   *see* Bayes' postulate.

equal interval method   *see* systematic sampling.

error-choice test   a structured test confronting the respondent with a series of values above and below the correct answer. Error-choice tests are disigned to reveal the existence, direction, and magnitude of the respondent's bias.

exogenous variable   a variable not explicitly included in the analysis, but which influences the value of the dependent variable(s).

expected monetary value   expected value expressed in dollars.

expected value   a criterion value that reflects both payoff and risk. Expected value is computed by summing the products of the payoff times the probability of each possible event associated with a particular decision alternative.

experimental error   the variation in the dependent variable not caused by the experimental treatment or by extraneous forces whose total effect has been isolated and measured. Experimental error is induced by chance.

experimental treatment   the manipulation of the independent variable(s) being tested in an experiment. Examples are a price change, a variation in product design, or a new television commercial.

experimental unit   a test unit which is subjected to the experimental treatment(s).

explanatory data   data used mainly to explain, instead of to merely describe, market (or other) phenomena.

exploratory research   research designed to more clearly define a research problem, as opposed to research that is designed to solve a problem.

exponential model   an equation in which the dependent variable is geometrically related to the independent variable(s). An example is $Y = \alpha + \beta^X$. Exponential models are also called "semilogarithmic models."

extraneous forces   variables, exclusive of the experimental treatment variables, which influence the dependent variable in an experiment. The term is often used outside of experimentation to refer to exogenous variables.

factor   an independent variable which is manipulated, or simply observed, during an experiment (experimentation). A synthetic variable, an index, summarizing two or more other variables (factor analysis).

factor analysis   a set of statistical tools for redefining a large set of variables into a smaller set of synthetic variables called "factors." (*Note:* Do not confuse factor analysis with factorial designs or factorial experiments.)

factorial design   the design of a factorial experiment, usually in the form of a matrix.

factorial experiment   an experiment designed to reveal the simultaneous effects of two or more variables.

factor loading   a coefficient indicating the importance of a factor in determining the value of a variable (factor analysis).

factor-score coefficient   a parameter specifying the

relationship between a factor and a variable (factor analysis).

F-distribution   a frequency distribution showing the probability of getting different *F*-ratios in a random sample.

field house   a research supplier specializing in the collection of survey data.

floppy disk   a small magnetic disk used to store data. Floppy disks serve as direct access storage devices for computers.

flow chart   a schematic diagram of a sequence of events.

focus group   a small panel of respondents, led by a moderator, gathered to discuss a particular subject.

forecast   the estimation of the future value of a variable. Usually "prediction" and "forecast" are used interchangeably, although there is a difference with respect to time; *see* prediction.

F-ratio   the ratio between the explained variance and the unexplained variance; also called the "F-statistic."

frequency distribution   a table showing a set of characteristics in one column and the number of objects having each characteristic in an adjoining column. Frequency distributions are sometimes presented on graphs.

frequency polygon   a curve on a two-dimensional graph obtained by connecting the points of a frequency distribution. A frequency polygon is similar to a histogram, except it replaces the bars with a curve.

Freudian psychoanalytical model   a model of behavior which

Freudian psychoanalytical model
(*continued*)
describes the consumer as a
creature controlled solely by
subconscious, sex-oriented
drives.

Friedman-analysis-of-variance-by-rank test   a test used to
determine if three or more
ordinal-data samples came
from the same population.

***F*-statistic**   *see F*-ratio.

***F*-test**   a test of statistical
significance using the *F*-ratio
and the *F*-distribution. The
F-test is used mainly to
determine if there is a statistical
significant relationship between
two sides of an equation.

futurology   the art of long-range
forecasting.

galvanic skin response (GSR)   a
measurement of the electrical
conductivity of skin. GSR is
used to measure a person's
response to external stimuli
such as advertising messages.

galvanometer   a device for
measuring galvanic skin
response.

gaussian curve   *see* normal
distribution.

generic concept of marketing   the
idea that art and science of
marketing is applicable in both
the commercial and nonprofit
sectors of society.

Gestalt psychology   that branch
of psychology concerned
mainly with the perception of
form and the organization of
the mental process.

GNP   gross national product;
the sum of all goods and
services produced by the
nation.

Goffman model   a behavioral
model which conceives the
buyer as an actor, performing
roles prescribed by reference
groups or by his or her own
self image.

goodness of fit   *see* tightness of fit.

Greco-Latin square   *see* Latin
square.

growth model   *see* time-series
model.

Guttman attitude scale   a metric
attitude scale that measures
both content (value) and
intensity of attitudes.

halo effect   the carry-over from
one judgment to the next. With
halo effect a respondent tends
to judge all attributes on the
basis of his or her reaction to
one particular attribute.

heuristic program   a model of a
decision process in which each
step of the process is governed
by a rule. The rules are based
on observation of the real-life
decision makers or on intuition.

histogram   a two-dimensional
chart in which a frequency
distribution is represented by
bars. Each interval of the
frequency distribution has a
bar whose height represents the
number of occurrences of
values within that interval.

historical data   *see* prerecorded
data.

Hobbesian model   a behavioral
model describing the consumer
as a political creature, concerned
mainly with his or her own
welfare, but willing to make
concessions to others to avoid
a "war of every man against
every man." The Hobbesian
model is mainly applicable to

purchasing agents. The model is sometimes called the "Hobbesian organizational factors model."

Hobbesian organizational factors model *see* Hobbesian model.

homograph a word that is spelled exactly like another word but which has a much different meaning. An example is "base" meaning "foundation" as opposed to "base" meaning "wicked."

homographic free association test a variation of the word association test which uses homographs. The respondent is asked to reply to each homograph with a synonym or short phrase. The method is sometimes used to identify personality traits or define stereotypes.

homoscedastic the property of having a constant standard deviation.

Howard Sheth model a model of consumer behavior describing the purchase process, and the forces influencing it, in analog form.

hypothesis a tentative assumption made for argument or for testing.

iconic model a model that is an exact replica (larger or smaller) of the object being modeled, at least with respect to the feature being studied. An example is a model airplane used in wind tunnel tests.

image the personality of a person, product, or institution as perceived by others.

image factoring one of several algorithms for factor analysis.

in-depth interview an extensive personal interview, typically exceeding 30 minutes and often involving unstructured questions and probing.

index of predictive association a statistic used to measure the association between two nominal variables.

item analysis a method of comparing questions to see if they measure the same dimension.

item nonresponse nonresponse error caused by a respondent's failure to answer a question.

itemized scale a scale that offers a limited number of categories for use in evaluating an object or attribute.

interval scale a scale of measurement in which the intervals are all equal (3 to 4 is equivalent to the interval 8 to 9, etc.), but zero is not absolute. Temperature in Fahrenheit is illustrative.

interviewer errors errors in survey data caused by interviewers through interaction with respondents, mistakes in interpretation and transcription of answers, and fraud.

joint correlation *see* multicollinearity.

joint probability the probability that two or more events will all occur.

Judgment forecast a forecast based on intuition or on a subjective evaluation.

judgment probabilities *see* subjective probabilities.

judgment sample a sample in which every element of the population does not have a

judgment sample (*continued*)
known probability of being
selected.

Kendall's tau   a statistic used to
determine the degree of
association between two ordinal
variables.

Kolmogorov-Smirnov test   a test
used to determine the statistical
significance between two
frequency distributions when
ordinal data have been used.

***K*-statistic**   *see* Von Neumann
ratio.

lagged relationship   a relationship
in which the value of one
variable is determined by the
value of another variable at an
earlier point in time.

Latin square   a special case of
factorial design in which the
matrix is always square ($n \times n$,
$n \times n \times n$, etc.) and which
assumes there is no interaction
between factors; also called a
"Greco-Latin square."

least squares   *see* method of least
squares.

life style   a person's activities,
interests, and opinions. The
term is sometimes used to mean
"psychographics" and may
include other attributes such as
occupation and family status.
There is no concensus on its
exact meaning.

Likert Attitude Scale   an ordinal
scale for measuring attitude;
also called the "Likert
Summated Scale."

Likert Summated Scale   *see*
Likert Attitude Scale.

linear   the property of linearity:
A linear function is an equation
of the first order. That is, it is
an equation in which no term
has an exponent greater than 1.
For example: $Y = 5 + 2X - 9Z$,
as opposed to $Y = 5 + 2X^2 - 9Z^3$.

**linear discriminant analysis
(LDA)**   a statistical method
for specifying a linear
relationship between a
nonmetric dependent variable
and one or more independent
variables. *See* discriminant
analysis.

linear regression analysis   a
statistical method for specifying
a linear relationship between a
metric dependent variable and
one or more independent
variables. *See* regression
analysis.

list broker   a firm that brokers
mailing lists; also called a "list
house."

list house   *see* list broker.

longitudinal study   a study based
on a set of elements measured
repeatedly over time.

McClelland model   a behavioral
model stressing achievement
motivation.

macrodata   data that pertain to
an industry, market, or the
nation. Examples are total
industry sales, population,
employment, and GNP.

**magnitude of possible random
error**   the degree to which the
true value may vary from the
estimated value at a given
confidence level.

Mann-Whitney test   *see* ranked
sums test.

MANOVA   *see* multivariate
analysis of variance.

market research   a term generally
used as a synonym for

"marketing research." "Market research" is, however, sometimes used to mean research which describes the marketplace while "marketing research" is applied to studies of the marketing process and marketing phenomena.

market-research forecast *see* poll forecast.

market segmentation the grouping of members of a market population into homogeneous sets (segments).

market test an experiment conducted in the marketplace.

marketing audit a comprehensive review of the firm's marketing program.

marketing concept the idea that every element of the firm should concentrate on the identification and satisfaction of customer needs.

marketing information system (MIS) an ongoing program which collects and disseminates market data.

marketing mix the combination of resources which make up the firm's marketing program.

marketing research the gathering, reducing, and analyzing of marketing data to assist management in making decisions (business). The gathering, reducing, and analyzing of data to explain market phenomena or to develop and test marketing theory (academic). The term is often abbreviated "MR." "Marketing research" is often referred to as "market research" although there is sometimes a distinction (*see* market research).

Markov chain a series of iterations in which each successive state is determined by the probabilities in the previous state.

Marshallian model a behavior model depicting the consumer as a purely rational and economic person set on utility maximization.

matrix a rectangular array of numbers. A matrix typically consist of a set of rows imposed on a set of columns.

matrix algebra that branch of mathematics concerned with the manipulation of matrices.

maximum likelihood criterion a criterion which assigns an object to the classification for which the object has the greatest probability of membership. (The object's true classification is uncertain.)

median test a test used to determine if two samples of ordinal data came from the same universe.

method of equal appearing intervals *see* Thurstone Attitude Scale.

method of least squares fitting a line to a scatter of points so that the sum of the squared differences between the estimated (line) values and the points is minimum. The least squares criterion can be applied to the fitting of a line in a two-dimensional space, a plane in a three-dimensional space, or a hyperplane in an n-dimensional space.

metric data data for which the units of measurement are interchangeable. Metric data, as opposed to nonmetric data,

metric data (*continued*)
can be directly subjected to
mathematical and statistical
manipulation. Examples are
population counts,
measurements, and weights.
Metric data are drawn from
ratio scales or interval scales.

microdata   data that pertain
directly to the individual, the
household, or the firm, such as
revenue, sales, costs, and
market share.

MIS   a common abbreviation for
both "marketing information
system" and "management
information system."

monadic test   an attitude-scaling
test which asks respondents to
position themselves on a scale
between two extremes, such as
"dislike" and "like."

Monte Carlo methods   a set of
techniques for simulating
stochastic processes.

mother-in-law research   research
done by consulting one's
family or friends (jargon).

motivation analysis   *see*
motivation research.

motivation research   the
application of clinical
psychology to the study of
consumer behavior; also called
"motivation analysis."

MR   *see* marketing research.

multicollinearity   a linear
correlation between two
independent variables; also
called "joint correlation" or
"collinearity."

multidimensional scaling   a set of
techniques for measuring
objects in a multidimensional
space. The hallmark of
multidimensional scaling is
that it takes a single piece of

information, such as the
ranking or matching of objects,
and generates multiple
measurements.

multiple-stage sampling   sampling
in two or more stages. First, the
population list is broken into
parts. A number of parts are
then selected. These parts are
the source for the sample. (They
in turn may be broken into
parts prior to drawing the
sample elements.)

multivariate analysis   data
analysis aimed at unscrambling
the simultaneous effects of
multiple variables. Multivariate
analysis seeks to specify the
dependency between multiple
variables or the groupings of
multiple variables.

**multivariate analysis of variance
(MANOVA)**   a method of
testing hypotheses concerning
responses to different
combinations of variables or to
different levels of the same
experimental treatment.
MANOVA admits multiple
dependent variables.

mutually exclusive   the condition
in which only one of two or
more events can occur.

naive experiment   an experiment
based on the assumption that
the net effect of the extraneous
forces will remain unchanged
during the experiment.

noise   disturbances in the
observed values of a variable,
caused by exogenous variables;
also called "irregular variation,"
"erratic fluctuation," and
"residual variation."

nominal value   a number used to
identify, not to count or

measure. An example is a social security number.

nonlinear the property of not being linear: A nonlinear function is one in which one or more exponents is not equal to one. An example is $Y = 3 + 2X^2$. Either a parameter(s) or a variable(s) can be nonlinear, e.g., $Y = \alpha + \beta^3 X$ or $Y = \alpha + \beta X^2$. The second case is often called "curvilinear."

nonmetric data data for which the units of measurement are not interchangeable. Nonmetric data cannot be directly subjected to mathematical or statistical manipulation. Examples are rankings and numbers used for identification. Nonmetric data are drawn from nominal or ordinal scales.

nonparametric data data which are not sufficiently similar to metric data to be treated like metric data.

nonparametric statistics that branch of statistics dealing with nonparametric (ordinal and nominal) data.

nonprobability sample *see* judgment sample.

nonrandom sample *see* judgment sample.

nonsampling errors errors unrelated to the sampling process. Examples are respondent error, interviewer error, typographical and posting mistakes, and computational errors.

normal distribution a bell-shaped frequency distribution in which the values are symmetrically distributed about their mean; also called a "Gaussian curve."

null none.

null hypothesis (H_0) the tentative assumption that there is no real difference between two variables.

objective techniques data collection methods which confront the respondents with direct questions and assume they are both able and willing to reveal their behavior and explain their actions.

open-end test an unstructured test consisting of incomplete statements which the respondent must complete.

ophthalmograph a device for studying eye movement. Opthalmographs are sometimes used to study how people read a particular advertisement.

optimal sampling a form of stratified random sampling designed to yield the smallest random error possible with a given sample size.

ordinal scale a nonmetric scale which measures objects in order of rank, i.e., 1st, 2nd, 3rd, etc.

original data data collected expressly for the study at hand.

paired comparison test an attitude scaling test requiring the respondent to choose between two objects.

parabolic model a second degree polynomial equation, such as $Y = \alpha + \beta_1 X + \beta_2 X^2$. Such models inscribe a parabolic curve when plotted on arithmetic graph paper.

parameter a value specifying the relationship between two variables (mathematics). The term is also used to mean a

parameter (*continued*)
value, such as a mean, based on population data rather than sample data (statistics).

parametric data   data similar enough to metric data to be treated like metric data. *See* metric data.

parametric statistics   statistics dealing with parametric (ratio and interval) data.

parsimony   economy in the use of resources. The principle of parsimony holds that a model should be simpler than the data upon which it is based.

Pavlovian learning model   a model of behavior depicting the consumer as being conditioned with repetitive stimuli associated with need-satisfying rewards; also called the "stimulus response model."

Pearson product moment correlation coefficient   a common measurement of simple correlation; also called the "Pearson *r*."

Pearson *r*   *see* Pearson product moment correlation coefficient.

percentage-of-moving-average method   *see* ratio-to-moving-average method.

personal probabilities   *see* subjective probabilities.

pictogram   a graph in which pictures are used to represent the size of the objects represented.

picture-frustration test   a projective-technique test which confronts respondents with a cartoon of people and (usually) speech balloons. One balloon contains a provocative statement and the other is empty. The respondent is asked to fill the empty balloon, thus revealing his or her attitude toward the subject of the picture.

pie chart   a graph in the form of a circle in which the segments of the circle are drawn like pieces of a pie. The size of each segment represents the relative size of the subset it represents.

PIMS   an acronym for Profit Impact of Marketing Strategies. PIMS is a system for estimating the effect of a change in marketing variables on profit.

planning horizon   the time period covered by the plan, projection, forecast, etc.

poll forecast   a forecast based on the expressed intentions of the market population; also called a "market research forecast."

population   the complete set of elements (objects, people, etc.) having one or more attributes in common; also called a "universe." An example would be all the residents of New York City.

population survey   *see* census.

posting   *see* tabulating.

precision   the degree of possible error associated with a statistic. Precision is usually measured by a confidence interval.

prediction   the estimate of the present value of a variable. Usually "prediction" and "forecast" are used interchangeably, although there is a difference with respect to time; *see* forecast.

predictive research   research that seeks to predict (forecast) values.

prerecorded data   data collected for some purpose other than the study at hand; also called "historical data." Prerecorded data can be primary or secondary data.

pretest a small survey conducted to test a questionnaire.

primary data data collected by, or expressly for, the firm.

principal components analysis a method of factor analysis. *Note:* principal components analysis has the same goals and produces results similar to other (classical) methods of factor analysis. However, since it works a bit differently, some researchers do not consider it as one of the factor-analysis algorithms.

prior probabilities *see* subjective probabilities.

probability sample *see* random sample.

problem study *see* ad hoc research.

profile analysis *see* cluster analysis.

program a set of instructions, written in a computer language, telling a computer what to do with the data (data processing); also called "algorithm" or "code," although these terms or code have meaning outside of data processing.

project design the plan-of-action for the research project. It typically contains the objective, method, resource requirements, and timetable; also called the "research design."

project manager a person assigned the responsibility for the administration and completion of a project, such as a market study.

projective techniques data collection methods which allow respondents to transfer their attitudes to a third party or inanimate object, thus relieving the respondents of embarassment or of tarnishing their self-image.

proportional sampling allocating sample elements to strata so that the size of each sample stratum is proportional to the size of the corresponding population stratum.

proximity clustering a method of cluster analysis which uses the interpoint distances of objects in an attribute space to group the objects into clusters.

psychodrama an elaboration of role playing in which several respondents act out a scene together.

psychogenic needs *see* psychological needs.

psychographics the elements in a person's life style which relate to his or her behavior as a consumer.

psychological needs learned needs acquired by observation and interaction with one's environment; also called "psychogenic needs."

Q-analysis the use of factor analysis to produce combinations (groups) of respondents: The factors are linear combinations of the respondents.

Q-sort a method for categorizing respondents on the basis of similarity in attitudes.

qualitative research research done without benefit of mathematics or statistics.

quota sampling a special case of stratified sampling in which

quota sampling (*continued*)
elements are drawn from the
population as a whole and then
assigned to strata. The drawing
continues until the quota
assigned each stratum has been
filled. Responses in excess of
the quota are discarded

***R*-analysis**   the use of factor
analysis to produce
combinations (groups) of
observed variables: The factors
are linear combinations of the
observed variables.

random error   error in sample
data caused by chance; also
called "statistical random
error." Chance causes the
sample to be a less-than-perfect
representation of the population
from which it is drawn.

random sample   a sample in
which every element of the
population has a known
probability of being selected;
also called a "probability
sample." (Every element having
an equal probability is a special
case of random sample.)

random variation   variation due to
chance.

rank correlation coefficient   a
method of specifying the degree
of correlation between two
variables; also called
"Spearman's coefficient."

ranked-sums test   a nonparametric
test of statistical significance.
The method is compatible with
both metric and nonmetric data.
It is also called the "Mann-
Whitney test," and the "*U*-test."
The test is useful for comparing
samples and for testing for the

existence of a trend line in a
time-series variable.

Rao's canonical factoring   one of
several algorithms for factor
analysis.

ratio scale   a scale of
measurement in which the
intervals are all the same (3 to
4 is equivalent to the interval
8 to 9, etc.) and zero is absolute.
Age, income, and population
scales are illustrative.

ratio-to-moving-average method   a
technique for computing a
seasonal index; also called the
"percentage-of-moving-average
method."

raw data   data in their original
form. An example is the data
recorded on questionnaires.

regression analysis   a statistical
method for estimating the
relationship between one
dependent variable and one or
more independent variables.
The dependent variable must
be metric. The independent
variables may be metric or
nonmetric, although
transgeneration of the
nonmetric variables is necessary
prior to specification of the
regression equation.

regressive forecast   *see* causal
forecast.

Reisman model   a behavioral
model which stereotypes
consumers as tradition-
directed, inner-directed, or
outer-directed.

reliability   the consistency with
which the same test,
questionnaire, or study
produces the same results when
applied under similar
conditions.

replication the repetition of an experiment, duplicating the original conditions as closely as possible.

research design *see* project design.

research supplier a firm which provides marketing research services for client organizations.

residual the difference between an estimated value and the true value (statistics).

residual variation *see* noise.

respondent errors errors in survey data caused by respondents' nonresponse, self-selection, misunderstanding, conscious or unconscious misrepresentation, ignorance, or poor prediction.

response rate the ratio of completed interviews to contacts, usually expressed as a percentage. (The contacts may be personal contacts, telephone calls, or mail questionnaires.)

restricted random sample a probability sample in which the elements are drawn only from selected segments of the population.

return on investment (ROI) profit expressed as a percentage of the capital invested. For example, an ROI of 10 percent would mean an annual return of $10 for each $100 invested.

reverse directory a telephone book in which subscribers are listed by their street address instead of by their last name; also called a "street address directory."

role playing a projective technique in which the respondent becomes an actor.

The actor then plays out a scene described by the interviewer. The method is commonly used with children.

rostering *see* tabulating.

Rule of Bayes *see* Bayes' theorem.

rule of ignorance *see* Bayes' postulate.

sample a set of elements drawn from a population, but not including every member of the population.

sampling error *see* statistical error.

scatter diagram a two-variable data set plotted as points in a two-dimensional space. For example, a set of sales/ advertising values might be plotted where the vertical scale represents sales and the horizontal scale represents advertising expenditures.

seasonal index a relative measure of seasonal variation.

seasonal variation variation associated with the time of the year.

secondary data data collected by an outsider not expressly for the firm.

secular trend *see* trend.

self-concept a person's idealized view of himself or herself; also called "self-image." Self-concept may have little to do with reality.

self-image *see* self-concept.

semantic differential test a structured test designed to determine the connotative meanings of a word and the intensity of those meanings as perceived by the respondent.

semantic differential test (*continued*)
Semantic differential tests are also used to measure attitudes.

semilogarithmic model *see* exponential model.

sentence completion test an open-end test consisting of an incomplete declarative sentence(s).

sequential sampling a sampling method in which a sequence of samples are drawn, thus increasing sample size by steps. until a predetermined criterion (or criteria) is met.

serial correlation *see* autocorrelation.

service bureau a firm offering computer services (data processing term).

significance level the probability that an answer is wrong or is outside the range of estimated values. For example, a significance level (s. 1.) of .05 would indicate a 5 percent chance of having the wrong answer.

sign test a nonparametric test of statistical significance. The sign test is used to determine if there is a statistically significant difference between two sets of metric or nonmetric responses.

simple correlation analysis correlation analysis involving only two variables.

simulation the manipulation of a model to determine the changes in one or more independent variables induced by changes in one or more independent variables.

simulation forecast a forecast made by simulating behavior or other phenomena over time.

SMSA *see* standard metropolitan statistical area.

social marketing marketing in the pursuit of nonprofit objectives, e.g., marketing in the promotion of traffic safety.

sociobiology a discipline which attempts to explain behavior biologically.

sociogram *see* sociometric diagram.

sociometric diagram a diagram of the leader-follower-colleague relationships and the flow of information between members of a group; also called a "sociogram."

sociometry that portion of sociology dealing with the relationships between members of a group.

Spearman's coefficient *see* rank correlation coefficient.

split-half analysis a method of checking on test reliability: The test is split into two parts, each with a comparable set of questions. The two sets of results are then compared. If similar, the test is considered statistically reliable.

split-run comparison a method of checking on validity. This is a variation of cross-validation in which the original sample is divided into two parts. The analysis is made using the first sample. The results are then compared with the second sample. The method is commonly used in the validation of regression and discriminant models.

SPSS *see* Statistical Package for the Social Sciences.

stability the consistency with which a measurement technique produces the same values when an object is measured again.

standard deviation a measure of variation. Standard deviation equals the square root of the variance. It is probably the most common and most useful measure of variation.

standard error of the sample mean an estimate of how much a sample mean may vary from the population mean because of random error.

standard error or the sample proportion an estimate of how much the sample proportion may vary from the population proportion due to random error.

standardized value a number derived by converting a value to its Z-statistic.

standard metropolitan statistical area (SMSA) an area consisting of one or more important cities and usually coinciding with the boundaries of a county.

stapel scale a scale in which respondents indicate how accurately each of a number of statements describes an object.

statistic an estimate of a parameter. A statistic is computed from sample data. A parameter is computed from population data. (This is a rigorous, yet narrow, definition.) The term is also used, not quite correctly, to refer to any statistical value.

statistical bias the unintentional favoring of one group of elements over another when both are from the same population. This error is caused by improper sampling

techniques or small samples; also called "systematic error."

statistical efficiency the relative precision of a sampling method for a given sample size. It is measured by comparing the standard error of an unrestricted random sample of the same sample size to the standard error produced by the selected method. Or, it is measured by comparing the sample sizes of the two methods when equal standard errors are produced.

statistical error error in sample data caused by the sample not being perfectly representative of the population from which it was drawn. There are two categories of statistical error: statistical bias and random error.

Statistical Package for the Social Sciences (SPSS) a package of computer programs for statistically analyzing data. SPSS is maintained by, and available through, the University of Chicago Computational Center.

stimulus research research that seeks to determine the effect of marketing variables on consumers.

stimulus response model *see* Pavlovian learning model.

stochastic having the property of chance. For example, a stochastic process, such as flipping a coin, is one whose outcome is not wholly controllable or predictable.

story completion test a projective-technique test in which the respondent is given the beginning of a story then asked to complete it.

stratified random sampling sampling in which the population is broken into strata and then a predetermined number of elements are drawn from each stratum.(The number usually varies between strata.)

stratum a subset of a population, whose elements have some characteristic in common setting them apart from members of other subsets. An example is a stratum which includes all members of the population between ages 19 and 24, inclusive.

street address directory *see* reverse directory.

structure the degree of standardization of a test (data acquisition). The underlying relationship between variables (interdependence methods of multivariate analysis).

structured test a test asking the respondent for specific answers, often limiting him or her to a list of specified replies.

subjective probabilities probabilities estimated without benefit of sample data; also called "judgment," "personal," "a priori," and "prior" probabilities.

survey instrument an esoteric term for "questionnaire."

survey supervisor a small independent operator who maintains a staff of interviewers to gather survey data. The interviewers are typically part-time workers.

symbolic model a model which uses numbers and other symbols to represent the process or object being simulated.

syndicated research research that is sponsored, or ultimately paid for, by two or more clients.

syndication the joint sponsorship of a project such as a market research study.

systematic error *see* statistical bias.

systematic sampling the selecting of every ith member of a population after starting with a randomly chosen member. The method produces a systematic sample which is a probability sample. Systematic sampling is also called the "equal interval method."

tabulating the transferring of raw data onto work sheets, punch cards, or other collection media; also called "posting" or "rostering."

tachtistoscope a projector that flashes an image on a screen for a very short and metered period of time. It is used to test the impact of words and symbols.

taxonomy the science of classification. The term is also used to denote a classification system.

t-distribution a bell-shaped frequency distribution whose size is dependent upon degrees of freedom, hence sample size; also called the "student t-distribution."

Technology-Dissemination Center a facility funded by the National Aeronautics and Space Administration for the dissemination of government sponsored technology. The centers (there are nine) also disseminate new product and marketing information.

test a set of one or more questions. Tests are designed to reveal the respondent's true behavior, belief, attitude, motive, psychological need, or other attribute relative to the study.

test control unit *see* control unit.

test market a special case of a test unit, usually a city or SMSA.

test units the individuals, firms, or markets observed during an experiment. There are two types: experimental units and control units.

thematic-apperception test (TAT) an extension of the picture-frustration test, but without the speech balloons. The respondent is asked to explain the scene, tell what is happening, and describe the characters.

Thurstone attitude scale an interval scale for measuring attitudes; also called the "method of equal appearing intervals" and the "Thurstone Differential Scale."

Thurstone differential scale *see* Thurstone attitude scale.

tightness of fit the degree to which a set of estimated values matches the set of true values (statistics); also called "goodness of fit."

time-series data data collected through observations made at different points in time.

time-series model a special case of the causal model in which time is the independent

variable; also called "growth model."

tracking study a study which monitors a product's acceptance or people's behavior over time.

transgeneration the conversion of data from one form to another. An example is the conversion of data in normal form to logarithmic form.

tree diagram a flow chart of a process, showing the alternate ways the process may go as branches of a tree. The process starts at the trunk, then branches two or more times, ultimately reaching each of the multiple (possible) outcomes.

trend a long-run tendency to change with time; also called "secular trend."

triangular comparison test an attitude scaling test which requires the respondent to choose between three objects.

trip to Delphi a visit with the experts. *See* Delphi method.

t-**statistic** a standardized unit of measurement similar to the Z-statistic, but reflecting sample size; also called the "student-t statistic." The t-statistic is especially relevant to variables measured in a small sample.

t-**test** a test of statistical significance used with metric data and especially appropriate to small samples.

two-way classification table *see* contingency table.

Type I error the rejection of a true hypothesis; also called an "alpha error."

Type II error the acceptance of a false hypothesis; also called a "beta error."

unique factor   a factor upon which only one variable loads; the converse of a common factor (factor analysis).

univariate analysis   data analysis involving only one variable.

universe   *see* population.

unrestricted random sample   a probability sample drawn from the population as a whole. Hence each element of the population has a chance of being chosen.

unstructured test   a test that gives the respondent great latitude in his or her reply. An unstructured test offers no prespecified replies.

U-**test**   *see* "ranked sums test."

validity   the extent to which a test, questionnaire, scale, or study measures what it is supposed to measure.

variance   a measure of variation. Variance equals the average (mean) of the deviations squared.

variation   the dispersion of observations about their mean.

veblian model   a behavioral model showing the consumer as a child of the environment, with society dictating behavior and consumption patterns.

Von Neumann ratio   a statistic used to check for autocorrelation; also called the "*K*-statistic."

VOPAN   an acronym for voice pitch analysis, a technique for measuring a respondent's response to stimulus such as an advertisement or new product.

word association test   a test which confronts the respondent with a series of words, then asks him or her to match each one with a word of his or her choosing. The purpose is to reveal attitudes.

Z-**statistic**   the standard unit of measurement for a normal distribution.

Name Index

Subject Index

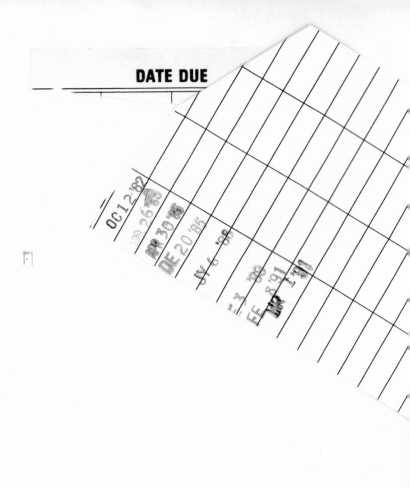